This is the first cross-cultural study of Chekhov's plays in production. Many now consider Chekhov a playwright equal to Shakespeare, and this book studies how the reputation evolved, and how the presentation of his plays varied and altered from their initial productions in Russia to the most recent postmodern deconstructions. In the process, Laurence Senelick analyzes how the reception of Chekhov's plays reflects social, political and aesthetic attitudes in specific countries. Particular attention is given to the staging of Chekhov in Russia before and after the Revolution and under different regimes; in the English-speaking world and in France, Italy, and Germany. There is also coverage of Chekhov in Eastern Europe and Japan. An examination of Chekhov's influence on the work of great directors from Stanislavsky, Meyerhold, and Tairov to Strehler, Brook, and Stein, and a discussion of important émigré artists, such as Komisarjevsky, Sharoff, and Pitoëff, are other major features of Senelick's discussion. The book provides valuable and informative illustrations of key productions.

THE CHEKHOV THEATRE

THE CHEKHOV THEATRE

A century of the plays in performance

LAURENCE SENELICK

Fletcher Professor of Drama and Oratory, Tufts University

CAMBRIDGE
UNIVERSITY PRESS

PUBLISHED BY THE PRESS SYNDICATE OF THE UNIVERSITY OF CAMBRIDGE
The Pitt Building, Trumpington Street, Cambridge CB2 1RP, United Kingdom

CAMBRIDGE UNIVERSITY PRESS
The Edinburgh Building, Cambridge CB2 2RU, United Kingdom
40 West 20th Street, New York, NY 10011-4211, USA
10 Stamford Road, Oakleigh, Melbourne 3166, Australia

First published 1997
First paperback edition 1999

Printed in the United Kingdom at the University Press, Cambridge

Typeset in 11/12.5 Monophoto Baskerville

A catalogue record for this book is available from the British Library

Library of Congress cataloguing in publication data

Senelick, Laurence.
The Chekhov theatre: a century of the plays in performance / by
Laurence Senelick.
p.   cm.
Includes bibliographical references and indexes.
ISBN 0 521 44075 0 (hc)
1. Chekhov, Anton Pavlovich, 1860–1904 – Stage history.
2. Chekhov, Anton Pavlovich, 1860–1904 – Dramatic production.
I. Title.
PG3458.Z9S877   1997
792.9′5–dc20   96–31555   CIP

ISBN 0 521 44075 0 hardback
ISBN 0 521 78395 X paperback

SE

This book is for Inna, Mila, Raya,
Tolya, Alesha, Arkasha and Serezha

Contents

Illustrations

Play list

(in chronological order)

Безотцовщина	*Without Patrimony* [thought to be the same play as the following]
Пьеса без названия	*Untitled Play* [usually known as *Platonov*]
На большой дороге	*On the High Road*
О вреде табака	*The Evils of Tobacco*
Лебединая песня	*Swan Song*
Иванов	*Ivanov*
Леший	*The Wood Demon*
Медведь	*The Bear*
Предложение	*The Proposal*
Татьяна Репина	*Tatyana Repina*
Трагик поневоле	*A Tragedian in Spite of Himself*
Свадьба	*The Wedding*
Юбилей	*The Jubilee*
Чайка	*The Seagull*
Дядя Ваня	*Uncle Vanya*
Три сестры	*Three Sisters*
Вишневый сад	*The Cherry Orchard*

Introduction

A funny thing has happened. Anton Chekhov, who was judged in his own time to be a playwright narrowly culture-bound, over-refined and obscure, whose drama was persistently characterized at home and abroad as "depressing" and "pessimistic," has become second only to Shakespeare in reputation and in frequency of production. Andrzej Wajda's remark – "Theatre in our European tradition derives from the word, from literature, the Greeks, Shakespeare, Chekhov,"[1] – is typical of the regard in which Chekhov is held. He is a synecdoche for all modern drama, indeed, in Wajda's debatable overview, for all drama from the Elizabethans to ourselves. Other contenders for the title are disqualified for being, like Ibsen, more rooted in time or, like Beckett, more constricted in vision.

Shakespeare's plays are multiplex and manifold, encompassing a universe of epochs, peoples, actions and emotions. Three centuries have had no difficulty in reading their own preoccupations into them. Chekhov's world, contained in some half a dozen major plays and a like number of one-acts, seems to revolve around one historically, nationally determined social class, one narrow spectrum of concerns, feelings and ideas. For all that we know about Shakespeare, there is still a sense that the expansive cosmos of his drama has not been circumscribed by his authorial intentions. When it comes to staging, there is little talk, except among dinosaurs in the English Department lounge, of "what Shakespeare intended." For Chekhov, on the other hand, one has to take into account a large corpus of prose, drafts, notebooks, twelve volumes of correspondence, a library of memoirs, sheaves of reviews of original productions. Even his notoriously ambiguous comments to actors of his characters merit serious attention. The scope for the appropriation of Chekhov by alien cultures and sensibilities looks at first to be quite limited.

And yet, of all playwrights, Chekhov provokes the strongest sense of proprietorship. "That's not Chekhovian" is a common cry of critics and spectators, precisely because a consensus of what is Chekhovian has congealed over the last century. What is or is not admissible has been made more prescriptive than in any approach to Shakespeare or Ibsen. Stage tradition, which once allowed Shakespearian actors to gain a reputation if they merely introduced a new piece of business or a new line reading, has in the twentieth century similarly restricted the presentation of Chekhov. Actors are often recalcitrant to a directorial interpretation or a fresh translation if it runs counter to their accepted ideas of a character's sympathy quotient (actresses, for example, have been known to cut lines in Arkadina's part to make her seem less selfish). Audiences, expecting to be sucked into a plausible and *gemütlich* world of bygone gentility, react angrily to productions that are more abstract, more physical or more surrealistic than what they expected. Quite unlike Ibsen and Beckett, the traditional Chekhov generated an affection in the playgoing public, which in turn bred a sentimentality he would be the first to deplore.

This is largely because Chekhov's plays first won popularity in the highly finished and seductive stagings of the Moscow Art Theatre, or in less expert imitations of them. They perpetrated a plethora of conventions of characterization, atmosphere and even placement of furniture that were difficult to supercede or supplant. The result was that, for a long time, Chekhov was seen in his own land as the irrelevant recorder of an obsolete way of life, and outside it as the quaint memorialist of a peculiarly Russian state of mind. The diaspora of Russian *émigrés* after the Revolution broadcast the maudlin nostalgia that had begun to cling to his plays.

Temporal distance was required before the characters and situations could take on a more figurative meaning. The Czech dramaturge Karel Kraus, speaking to a post-World War II, post-Holocaust, Communist-dominated Europe, explained that

a production of Chekhov can engage our interest in two ways. One is connected with the feelings and attitudes of the Russian intelligentsia in the gelid climate of reaction and repression which followed the attempt on the life of Alexander II; the other is the complex destinies of characters unable to attain their ideal life and fulfilment because they are locked into a system of illusions in order to protect themselves not only from others but from themselves: the collapse of this system of illusions, which discloses too cruel a reality, demands that ongoing existence be made tolerable, bearable – a new scaffolding of self-mystification.[2]

This was a seminal redefinition of Chekhov for the age of existentialism. It enabled him to become "Chekhov our contemporary." Even in its heyday, the Art Theatre's idealizing and ennobling of Chekhov had been called into question. The theatre's leading supporter in the critical camp, Nikolay Éfros, had noted that although "Chekhov the writer is very mild mannered, he is essentially cruel."[3] During the Cold War era, that cruelty became the dominant element in Central and Eastern European stage productions.

This strain rarely was heard in English-language theatrical treatment of Chekhov, where his icon as the bard of twilight Russia was replaced by a new effigy: the wry, indulgent observer of human vagaries. From *frater dolorosus*, he became a Son of Man whose view from the cross prompted him to ironic laughter. The comedy in his plays, once overlooked or deleted, now rose to the surface, often coarsened to buffoonery. The periodic rediscovery that Chekhov was a comic dramatist was a necessary antidote to the clichés of lyricism and melancholy; but this in turn became a cliché. Now, in the all-too-knowing "postmodern" phase, Chekhov is familiar enough to enter the stockpile of cultural tokens and totems; this allows him to be theatrically deconstructed; traditions, recognized as such, are deformed, discarded or reconstituted. He has the resilience of a real classic and is capable of withstanding hard treatment.

For better or worse, Chekhov's plays were written at a time when the stage director was becoming a paramount factor in the theatre. In the wake of Ibsen, the dramatist's message took precedence over the actor's virtuosity; in the wake of Wagner, the unified "vision" of a single maker took precedence over the individual contributions of performer, musician and designer. The technical innovations of the modern stage, including electric lighting and *mises-en-scène* intent on reproducing "real life," required expert handling to blend and harmonize the various elements. Chekhov's development as a playwright from 1888 to 1904 coincides with this move from a stage governed by histrionic and spectacular display to one in which ensemble effect and the creation of "mood" reigned supreme. Ibsen's works can still be seen as permutations of the nineteenth-century star vehicle; Hedda, Ellida, Borkman and Rubek are larger than life, surging up in the foreground and eclipsing the other characters. Their fates are what matters. This remains true of Chekhov's first performed full-length drama *Ivanov*: its effect stands or falls by the leading man's interpretation. But Chekhov's "Big Four" can succeed on stage only with strong and coordinated ensemble playing, best achieved under the baton of a single "conductor." Much of what occurs happens beneath and between the lines; much of the meaning is conveyed by the spatial configuration of the characters, by oeillades and tentative gestures that pass between them; so that individual performances, no matter how extraordinary, are insufficient to achieve the desired result. Consequently, the stage history of Chekhov's drama is a chronicle less of great performers in starring roles than of the success and failure of directors and acting companies in realizing his plays and communicating them to a given audience at a particular moment in history.

This book is a survey of the ways in which Chekhov's plays have been interpreted on stage in something over a hundred years' time: in the process, it comments on the interests and tastes of certain societies as well as on the usual theatre-historical concerns. The danger of such an approach lies in ignoring Dr. Johnson's injunction about enumerating the stripes of the tulip. I have tried to treat in selective detail those productions whose contributions were either highly symptomatic of a cultural climate or added something new and important to our understanding of Chekhov. Admittedly, even in a bad production, a single line reading or a telling piece of business may shed light, but it would be tedious to accumulate all such instances. Perhaps someday someone will apply Marvin Rosenberg's coverage of Shakespearian tragedy to Chekhov, and go line by line through the plays, listing every recorded rendition of a given moment. I am not that someone and cheerfully relinquish the task of a "variorum" Chekhov to others.

The greatest space in this survey has been meted out to the Russians, because Chekhov has meant the most within the cataclysmic changes undergone by Russian society over the past century. Separate chapters are devoted to British and American productions, because they have the greatest interest to the English-speaking reader, although it is demonstrable that they have had less resonance elsewhere. Great European directors have been more influential in disseminating new concepts. I have also been somewhat synoptic in treating Chekhov in Great Britain because two good books by Patrick Miles have already covered much of that ground; but I have tried to cite observers and practitioners he has not. Spatial limitations have prevented me from dealing with Chekhov in the Scandinavian, Hispanic and Dutch cultures as well as in the British Commonwealth;[4] in most of these cases, the usual model applies: epigones of the Moscow Art Theatre prevailed until very recently, when more idiosyncratic or parochial approaches obtained. Similar constraints have also forced me to omit any discussion of Chekhov in film, dance and opera.

This is not an objective account. It is full of prejudices, many of them my own. Over the course of forty-some years of playgoing, I have seen a flock of seagulls, met a dynasty of uncles and sisters, and travelled through a wilderness of cherry orchards. I learned to approach Chekhov as an actor under Alvina Krause and as a scholar under Nils Åke Nilsson. I have sat through rehearsals of and performed in my translations and those of others, attended innumerable Chekhov conferences and celebrations all over the world, and spoken on the subject to all kinds of audiences. Not surprisingly, I have not sought to conceal the opinions that have formed, particularly when evaluating those productions of which I have personal experience. The theatre historian often has to rely on the record of journalistic criticism, a dubious source at best; it is salutary to be able to match one's own reactions against those of the press and to convey impressions obtained on the spot.

It is current practice in writing about opera to cite the title in the language in which a given performance was sung: so we get Wagner's *I maestri cantori* at La Scala, Verdi's *Le trouvère* at the Paris Opéra, and Offenbach's *Orpheus in the underworld* at the London Coliseum. I had originally intended to follow this practice, referring to Sharoff's *Il gabbiano*, Barrault's *La cerisaie* and Stein's *Drei Schwestern*, not to mention Stanislavsky's *Chaika* and *Vishnevy sad*. But I soon realized that this would hopelessly confuse the reader, particularly if I carried accuracy to distinguishing *The Sea Gull* from *The Seagull*, and *The Three Sisters* from *Three Sisters*. So a compromise is in place: I have adopted a consistent translation and spelling of the plays' titles, and on an earlier page they are keyed to the original Russian names. The foreign-language title is provided the first time a play is mentioned in a given linguistic context. Characters' names are also standardized, and are listed in a separate index. The Moscow Art Theatre is abbreviated as MAT. Unless otherwise indicated, all translations from foreign languages are mine.

I have used a method of transliteration from the Cyrillic alphabet which is intended to be user-friendly to the English-language reader with no Russian. Within the text, such familiar spellings as Meyerhold, Eisenstein and Chaliapin are used, although more technically accurate versions are given in the transliteration of Russian titles in notes and bibliography. Soft and hard signs are deleted. Я is given as *ya*; ю as *yu*; й within a word as *i*; ы, terminal й, ий and ый as *y*. Э appears as *é*; but no distinction is made between е and ё, which are both rendered as *e*.

A book that covers as much ground as this one owes many debts to the migrants picking in the orchards before me. Here I must recognize not only scholars but also the many theatre people I have encountered along the way; for it is truism, still not sufficiently endorsed in the academic study of drama, that directors and actors can be as insightful as any critic and a production can be as illuminating as any piece of writing, if not more so.

The scholars and critics from whom I have learned, both from the printed page and in conversation and correspondence, include J. L. Anderson, Jean-Pierre Barricelli, Aleksey Bartoshevich, Jean Benedetti, Robert Brustein, Sharon Carnicke, Ellen Chances, David H. Cheshire, J. Douglas Clayton, Toby Clyman, Donald Fanger, Erika Fischer-Lichte, Daniel Gerould, Christine Hamon-Siréjols, Benjamin Harshav, Michael Henry Heim, Vladislav Ivanov, Robert Louis Jackson, Julius Kagarlitsky, Simon Karlinsky, Vladimir Kataev, Rolf-Dieter Kluge, Alma Law, the late Harry Levin, Felicia Londré, David Maxwell, Aya Mihara, Nils Åke Nilsson, Richard Peace, Harvey Pitcher, Herta Schmid, Paul Schmidt, Virginia Scott, Savely Senderovich, Anatoly Smeliansky, Inna Soloveva, Jurij Striedter, Ieva Vitins, and Andrzej Wirth.

Actors and directors with whom I have worked and spoken, to my inestimable advantage, include George W. Angell, Claire Bloom, the late Jacques Chwat, Ron Daniels, Robertson Dean, Oleg Efremov, John Emigh, Zelda Fichhandler, Gerald Freedman, the late Minnie Galatzer, Jeremy Geidt, Spencer Golub, André Gregory, Giles Havergal, John Hellweg, Jon Jory, David Kaplan, the late Alvina Krause, Robert David Macdonald, Jeffrey Martin, Vinnie Murphy, Natacha Parry, the late Raymond Pentzell, Edward Petherbridge, Marilyn Plotkins, Philip Prowse, John Pym, the late Michael Quinn, Marilyn Redfield, Harry Ritchie, Richard Schechner, Lloyd Schwartz, Nicholas Scott, Kenneth Tigar, Richard Trousdell, Yutaka Wada, Douglas Wager, Kathryn Walker, Irene Worth, the members of the Manhattan Project and all the casts who have appeared in my translations.

I also owe thanks to playwrights, dramaturges and literary advisers who have shared their perceptions and appreciations of Chekhov with me: Robert Anderson, the late Philip Blackwell, Robert Chapman, the late Paddy Chayefsky, Michael Bigelow Dixon, David Feiner, Cynthia Jenner, Margaret Lynch, Laurence Maslon, Arthur Miller, Bob Scanlan, Irwin Shaw, Barry Stavis, Megan Terry, Jean-Claude Van Itallie, and Susan Weinacht.

In selecting illustrations within budget constraints, I looked for images that would be both representative and unfamiliar; I have often chosen moments from the play-within-a-play of *The Seagull*, the last act of *Three*

Sisters, and the scene on the road in *The Cherry Orchard* to present striking contrasts. Appeals for illustrations were met generously by Christine Autant-Mathieu; Richard Buck and the staff of the Billy Rose Theatre Collection, New York Public Library; Jarka Burian; Paula Court; Scott T. Cummings, former editor of *Theatre Three*; Rob Orchard of the American Repertory Theatre; Paul Schmidt; and Josef Svoboda. In every case, I have tried to locate the copyright owners of the illustrations, not always with success.

As ever, Dr. Jeanne Newlin, former curator, and the staff of the Harvard Theatre Collection have made my work much easier. Other librarians who smoothed my path were Vyacheslav Nechaev of the Central Theatre Library in Moscow; and Louis Rachow of the International Theatre Institute in New York. My graduate research assistants Thomas Connolly, Randy Kapelke, Sergei Ostrovsky and Michael Zampelli showed outstanding resourcefulness in following up even the most tenuous leads. Michael McDowell was characteristically diligent in processing my words, and Sarah Stanton of Cambridge University Press was a supportive editor from the inception. Her successor in guiding the project, Victoria L. Cooper, has been unfailingly responsive and enthusiastic. Whenever I, like Epikhodov, would indulge in histrionic despair, she, like Vershinin, would respond with a rosy prospect of the future.

CHAPTER I

Compromising with the theatre (Russia 1880–1896)

> [*The Wood Demon*] had been painstakingly staged, but those set-
> pieces wings, canvas walls, swinging doors, offstage thunder never
> for a minute reminded me of the nature I knew. It was all from *a
> stage I knew*, but I wanted it to be from *the life I knew*.
>
> Vladimir Nemirovich-Danchenko[1]

THE PRE-CHEKHOVIAN STAGE

Chekhov's relation to the theatre can be tracked along a curve bounded
by poles of attraction and repulsion. The earliest phase of his playgoing,
when he was a gymnasium student in Taganrog, was uncritically enthusiastic. Throughout the 1880s and nineties, this enthusiasm was pro-
gressively tarnished by first hand experience of theatre in the Russian
capitals; he was impelled to promote reforms. In the period from 1898 to
his death in 1904, when he was closely associated with the Moscow Art
Theatre, Chekhov's impulsion between admiration and disgust became
more feverish and more extreme.

The schoolboy Chekhov took part in domestic theatricals, and, after
his bankrupt family moved to Moscow, leaving him alone in Taganrog to
finish his courses, he became an inveterate spectator at the Civic Theatre
there.[2] "In those days we were all gripped by a theatrical fever," recalled
a classmate. "All our savings and pocket money went for gallery seats."[3]
The Taganrog management had refurbished the repertory to suit a new
playhouse constructed in 1865. Whereas the local company had formerly played an outworn stock of Kotzebue, vaudevilles and grandilo-
quent patriotic pieces, the new management sought to introduce "the
latest thing" to this thriving trade centre on the Black Sea. The repertory
lists of the theatre from 1868 to 1879, when Chekhov was still a resident,
show that he had the chance to see operas by Rossini, Donizetti and
Verdi, as well as an ever-increasing number of good Russian plays and

foreign imports. Gogol appeared with some frequency, and gradually the staples of the repertory came to consist of the "new drama" of Potekhin, Ostrovsky and Dyachenko, in addition to the well-made melodramas of Sardou and Dennery.[4] Newness does not imply depth – Dyachenko's society dramas are one step away from *Lady Audley's Secret* – and these problem plays, dramas and comedies of *byt* or "everyday life" were imbibed indiscriminately by the impressionable adolescent along with romantic melodrama: Dumas' *Kean*, Burdin's *The Mail Robbery*, Barbusse and Crisafully's *The Murder of Coverley* whose villain ends up run over by a locomotive. The actors in these plays comprised a generation of flamboyant personalities who held an audience rapt by the virtuosity of their playing, little subordinated to the script.

A medical student in Moscow, Chekhov embarked on a sideline of comic journalism and through his brother Nikolay, a painter and part-time scene designer, came into contact with the city's bohemia. This phase coincided with the Moscow theatre's imminent awakening from a decade of torpor. The years 1882 to 1898 are marked by both administrative and scenic reforms which rapidly transformed the Russian stage.

Increasing pressure from amateur groups, "people's" theatres and influential playwrights had led emperor Alexander III to sign a decree (24 March 1882) abolishing the monopoly of the Imperial theatres in the capitals. The Imperial dramatic theatres, the Maly in Moscow and the Alexandra in St. Petersburg, retained their peculiar subsidized status, as the administration reaffirmed old principles, particularly the *emploi* system by which actors were assigned a specific "line of business." The presence of the administration could be felt at every level, most painfully through punishments, fines and various stoppages of pay for artists who did not learn twenty-five lines of text a day, displayed insolence to their hierarchic superiors or failed to show up at rehearsals. The possibility of arrest was still on the books, though rarely put into practice. With the aim of improving the artistic management, the administration invited the dramatists Aleksey Potekhin and Aleksandr Ostrovsky to be directors of the troupes. The results were disappointing: the former soon turned into a dictator and the latter dismissed anything that wasn't his own work.

The chief opportunity provided by the 1882 reform was the opening of private theatres in the capitals. An onslaught of provincial entrepreneurs was expected, but failed to materialize. The endemic problem of Russian theatre was the limited size of its audiences. Moscow with its

700,000 inhabitants could barely support three legitimate theatres, even though the Maly received state subvention. Only two new theatres were founded in Moscow between 1882 and 1889, and only one serious enterprise opened in St. Petersburg. These were essentially commercial ventures, although their impresarios proclaimed ideals of art and creativity, in line with the Russian belief that drama assisted the enlightenment and spiritual development of the nation. In practice, these managers based their calculations on the box-office and the untutored taste of the "esteemed public."

The private dramatic theatres in Moscow were run by the "wizards and warlocks" Mikhail Lentovsky and Fedor Korsh. Lentovsky's initial expensive ventures foundered in bankruptcy, but the merchant class, to whose taste he catered, enabled him to make a fresh start. In 1886 he opened the Skomorokh (Merry Andrew) Theatre with the highest hopes of a reputable repertory of legitimate drama to be offered to a working-class audience. He even wrote to Tolstoy, offering to mount *The Power of Darkness*; this provoked the ire of Pobedonostsev, Procurator of the Holy Synod and tutor to the heir apparent, who urged a decree instituting a double censorship for all "people's" theatres. Lentovsky had perforce to address the middle classes whose simple tastes were reflected in his bills. Plays of Gogol and Ostrovsky and even *Hamlet* could be found there, but increasingly the bulk of the repertory was composed of translated farces, melodramas and particularly *féeries*, Lentovsky's speciality. His productions abounded in pyrotechnical display, explosions, fires, collapsing bridges, and all the impedimenta of sensationalism, which Chekhov called "bitter-sweet, German Liebergothic rubbish . . . gun-powdery balderdash."[5] His chief complaint about Lentovsky's extravaganzas was that they were merely heightened realism tarted up with special effects rather than a true stimulus to the imagination.

While Lentovsky robustly catered to the popular craving for spectacle and sensation, Korsh slapped a veneer of culture on his commercialism. When he took over Anna Brenko's Pushkin Theatre in 1882, its actors and public alike assumed that he would carry on its policy of serious literary drama by the best Russian authors. Instead, Korsh maintained a stable of hacks to churn out translations of European bedroom farce and well-carpentered dramas of adultery; this practice, abetted by clever publicity, greatly enlarged his audience and reached ranks of society new to the theatre. To Korsh's credit, he encouraged Russian writers to turn their talents to the stage, soliciting Chekhov to write a comedy in the spirit of his humorous tales. He instituted an unheard-of policy of

Friday matinees at reduced prices for students; every week would bring a production of a classic or an intriguing new piece. Important works such as *The Power of Darkness*, *A Doll's House* and *An Enemy of the People*, along with plays by Becque, Rostand and Sudermann, were first seen in Moscow at Korsh matinees, much frequented by a youthful and vociferous audience. The profits enabled Korsh's theatre to give two hundred and five performances a season, whereas the Maly offered only one hundred and eighty. A Korsh premiere normally drew the entire literary and artistic world of Moscow, and Stanislavsky would attribute to him the decade-long nurturance of a theatrically sophisticated public ready to accept the reforms of the Moscow Art Theatre.[6]

For a while, Chekhov wrote what amounted to a behind-the-scenes gossip column. This activity meant scraping up an acquaintance with actors and managers; his correspondence began to be laced with tidbits of greenroom scandal and pithy *aperçus* about the latest productions. Growing familiarity bred contempt but could not uproot his perennial fascination with the stage. Significantly, his first collection of stories is entitled *Fairy Tales of Melpomene*, and his early works teem with vignettes of backstage life, usually presented as caricature or sardonic social commentary. There is nothing idealized in Chekhov's gallery of thespians, who are depicted as vain and petty; but he often found them more attractive than the solid citizenry, with its demands that theatre have a redeeming social purpose. As for playwrights, he was amused by their pretensions and exasperated by their undeserved successes.

A special *bête noire* was *Fumes of Life* (1884), a dramatization by the fashionable Bolesław Markiewicz of his novel *The Abyss*; in *The Seagull*, Arkadina's bad taste is indicated by the inclusion of that play in her repertory. Chekhov had always disliked Markiewicz's practice of putting his closest friends recognizably into his fiction (an aversion overlooked by literary critics sniffing out the "originals" of Chekhov's characters). In 1883 Chekhov had taken *The Abyss*, "that long, fat, boring ink-blot," to task in his column, but, instead of writing a parody of the play as he first announced, he penned a review noteworthy for its tone of personal animosity:

We have seen and smelled *The Fumes of Life* – a drama by the famous Moscow dandy and man-about-salons B. Markiewicz, the very drama that sank with such a crash through the floor of the Theatrical–Literary Committee. It sank without the slightest crash at Lentovsky's theatre, although it treats of persons and places dear to the heart of Moscow. [. . .] On the whole, the play is written with a lavatory brush and smells foul.[7]

The play that provoked such abuse is a five-act society melodrama whose heroine, Olga Rantseva, betrays her adoring husband, is taken up and then repudiated by a noble old Count, becomes a pariah in Petersburg society, weds a scoundrel who robs and abandons her, and at last dies in an odour of sanctity, repentant and contrite, declaring that her life has been nothing but delusive "fumes."[8] A role that involves five costume changes, the opportunity to run the gamut from lubricity to piety, and an almost continual presence on stage would have immediate appeals to the prima donnas of the day.

Yet Chekhov's animosity towards this play may have been generated more by his dislike of Markiewicz than by the genre itself, for he was often complimentary to friends whose high-society dramas were all but indistinguishable from *Fumes of Life*. Prince Sumbatov-Yuzhin, a popular leading man at Moscow's Maly Theatre, wrote a similar play, *Ties That Bind* (*Tsepi*), about an erring wife who connives to steal their daughter away from her self-sacrificing husband. Chekhov not only thought it good[9] but appears to have imitated in the last act of *Uncle Vanya* a scene in which characters do household accounts during an emotional crisis.

Attending rehearsals, hearing of dramatists' clashes with managers and performers, Chekhov's observations grew more caustic and rebarbative. "Actors are capricious and conceited," he wrote, "half-educated and presumptuous," and "actresses are cows who fancy themselves goddesses."[10]

Actors never observe ordinary people. They do not know landowners or merchants or village priests or bureaucrats. On the other hand they can give distinguished impersonations of billiard markers, kept women, distressed cardsharps, in short all those individuals whom they observe in their rambles through pothouses and bachelor parties. Horribly ignorant.[11]

To some degree, Chekhov could keep his critical faculties divorced from his personal feelings. Two of his former schoolmates, Aleksandr Vishnevsky and Nikolay Solovtsov, who had become actors, remained among his intimates, and he later kept up a close relationship with several prominent stars. He boosted Lidiya Yavorskaya, a popular leading lady who excelled in such plays as *La Dame aux camélias* and *Fumes of Life*. Chekhov's younger brother Mikhail, no fan of her talent, "especially disliked her voice, screechy and cracked as if she had a chronic sore throat. But she was an intelligent woman, progressive, and for her benefit would stage plays that seemed racy at the time."[12] The critic Kugel characterized her as "somewhat mannered, with a dash of

Europeanism, she acted on stage and off, and was vain of and drunk on her success."[13] Chekhov was not unaware of her shrill affectations, but they had a protracted affair, a forecast of his eventual marriage to another actress, Olga Knipper.

By the late 1880s, as he grew better acquainted with the travails of playwrights, Chekhov's "avowed disgust for our theatre" was aggravated by its poorly disguised opportunism and lack of artistic purpose. "One must try with all one's might to transfer the theatre from the grocer's hands to those of literature, or else the theatre will decline." "The salvation of the theatre is in the hands of literary people."[14] At the same time, he distrusted pretentiousness and was to disapprove of Ibsen because "There's no vulgarity (*poshlost*) in him. You can't write a play that way."[15] Chekhov was particularly irritated by the theatre's claims of social relevance and truth to life, of being a school for the people. To a literary friend about to write a play, he pleaded, "I implore you, please fall out of love with the theatre."

True there is a lot of good in it. The good is overstated to the skies, and the vileness is masked . . . The modern theatre is a rash, an urban disease. The disease must be eradicated, and loving it is unhealthy. You will argue with me, repeating the old phrase, the theatre is a school, it educates and so on [. . .] But I am telling you what I see; the modern theatre is not superior to the crowd; on the contrary, the life of the crowd is more elevated and intelligent than the theatre . . . [16]

When his friend the millionaire publisher Suvorin proposed to invest in a theatre in St. Petersburg, Chekhov tried in vain to dissuade him. However, once Suvorin's theatre was a *fait accompli*, Chekhov showered his friend with advice, recommendations and suggestions for casting.

In letters to would-be dramatists, Chekhov continually came back to the need to see and understand how plays worked in the theatre. He was reluctantly compelled to reject Bjørnstjerne Bjørnson's metaphysical drama *Beyond Human Power* which he found moving and intelligent because "it won't do for the stage, because it can't be played, there's no action, no living characters, no dramatic interest,"[17] the very argument Nina advances against Treplev's play in *The Seagull*. His critiques always concerned craftsmanship, not aesthetics: "avoid clichés," "be compact," "use realistic dialogue," "vary the characters," "put your climax in the third act but be sure the fourth is not anticlimactic . . . " His eminently practical comments on Gorky's plays had to do with their effects on an audience and how "points" were to be made. Even his references to his own plays were meant to clarify particulars for the performers or react to specific circumstances. As early as 1887, Chekhov was insisting that the author must control his play, select the cast and issue instructions for its performance.[18]

The evolution of Chekhov's drama reflects a gradual liberation from the playhouse traditions to an idiosyncratic and original vision that puts new demands on the theatre. When Chekhov set to write plays for production, he was torn between creating pieces that would succeed because of their conformity to accepted norms, and pieces that went beyond the clichés and conventions of the popular stage. He also had to face the fact that audiences were expecting the dramatic equivalents of his prose fiction, either hilarious anecdotes or thoughtful sketches of modern life. Ever present in his consciousness were the physiques and voices of prominent actors, the furniture and configuration of the average stage-set, and the standard responses of the Moscow public.

IVANOV IN MOSCOW

For all his familiarity with greenrooms and pleasure gardens, Chekhov was not instantly recognizable in the theatre world. When the twenty-eight year-old author shyly introduced himself to F. Mukhtorov in an intermission before his farce *The Bear* came on, Mukhtorov, Russia's leading publisher of plays, found "the name 'Chekhov' all but unknown to me."[19] In this closed world of professionals, Chekhov had to conform to conventional usages if he was to earn a place on the stage.

His first plays to be produced were written hastily with specific performers in mind. They followed no artistic agenda, but aimed to cash in on current trends. Throughout the 1880s, curtain-raisers and display material for benefits were among the most lucrative and frequently performed plays on the Russian stage. As a well-known comic author, Chekhov was frequently asked by friends in the profession to provide one-act farces (*shutki*) for their bespeaks. The monologue "The Evils of Tobacco" (1886) was written for the talented but alcoholic comedian Gradov-Sokolov, and *Swan Song (Calchas*, 1886/7) designed as a twenty-minute show-piece for the great Davydov. When Davydov performed it at Korsh's on 19 February 1888, he larded it with so many ad-libs about great actors of the past that Chekhov could barely recognize his text. *The Tragedian in spite of himself* (1889) was dashed off in a day at the request of the comic actor Varlamov.

The Bear, devised as a vehicle for Chekhov's friend Solovtsov, had been inspired by his performance as a sailor wooing a debutante in *Winner Take All*, an adaptation of Pierre Berton's *Les jurons de Cadillac*, at Korsh's

Theatre. As he worked out the role of Smirnov, Chekhov had in mind Solovtsov's ruddy face, stentorian voice and abrupt manner.[20] The playwright Nemirovich-Danchenko, a shrewd appraiser of theatrical values, saw the one-act on a benefit program in 1888 and immediately sniffed out the distinction of this "most interesting," "well crafted little piece."

It's a farce but full of life. It was played *very rambunctiously, but not inartistically* [. . .] The play exudes fresh talent and theatrical originality. Mr. Solovtsov played warmly and sincerely, but he didn't have enough of the kind-hearted, hot-tempered "bear." And he didn't come across as a landowner of the steppes. As if worried about the fate of the play, for stage reasons, the actor sacrificed the originality of the character.[21]

This evaluation is of interest, given the crucial role Nemirovich had in the success of Chekhov's later plays; it also indicates how the idiosyncrasies of Chekhov's characters were already being flattened out to suit stage convention.

The Bear and its successor *The Proposal*, which were soon played all over Russia, earning bounteous royalties, derive much of their absurdity from the erratic characters' avowed "convictions" and "principles." The one-act "joke" traditionally parodied the clichés of dramatic tradition. In V. Bilibin's wildly popular one-act *I'm Fed Up with Living!* (*Zhit nadoelo!*, 1889), the hero, like so many lugubrious heroes of the time, decides to shoot himself. "I'm fed up with living! . . . Living is boring! . . . Today is the same as yesterday, tomorrow is the same as today . . . Women, wine, cards . . . cards, wine, women. Nowadays all respectable people shoot themselves. It is simply indecent for a respectable person to live in this world."[22] Chekhov's farces similarly restate as high-spirited comedy his own distrust of philosophic systems and rigid credos which fail to take human behaviour into account. He had already mocked the "I'll shoot myself" attitude in his story "Man. (A Bit of Philosophy)" (1886), "How hard and boring it is to be a human being! . . . A human being is a slave not only of passions but of his nearest and dearest. Yes, a slave! I am a slave to this motley, merry-making throng which . . . ignores me."[23] At the end these turn out to be musings not of a Russian Schopenhauer but of a footman tired of waiting at a ball.

The theme of world-weariness and spleen runs through *Ivanov*, Chekhov's first full-length play to be staged. Given its proximity to his early farces, it very well may be that he set out to write a satire, and only gradually discovered that he was drifting into the realm of high drama. This may explain not only the play's unevenness of tone but Chekhov's own reference to it as a "miscarriage."[24]

Ivanov was hastily composed for Korsh in two weeks, almost on a bet, and was staged as hastily, opening on 19 November 1887 for the benefit of Nikolay Svetlov, who played Borkin. As a letter to his brother Aleksandr indicates, Chekhov saw the play as a collocation of roles, and felt dependent on the actors to remedy his deficiencies as a playwright; he ended, "However bad the play may be, I have created a type which has some literary significance, I have provided a role which no less a talent than Davydov has undertaken to play, in which an actor can show himself off and display his talent."[25]

Vladimir Davydov, a star of the Alexandra Theatre in St. Petersburg, had been one of the first actors to include Chekhov's stories in reading recitals of the mid-1880s. He had temporarily moved to Korsh's private enterprise in Moscow to punish his home theatre for not acceding to salary demands. Stout, easy-going and avuncular, he was primarily a comedian, outstanding in Gogol and Ostrovsky, with a special line in corrupt bureaucrats. Chekhov evidently touched up the identification of the actor with the character, for in the first version of *Ivanov* Borkin refers to the protagonist as "Nicolas-voilà," a tag from a vaudeville refrain popularized by Davydov.[26] The whole cast was strong, including Glama-Meshcherskaya (who, in Chekhov's words, excelled as "sick pussies") as Anna. Only Davydov praised the play's novelty; the rest of the actors regarded it as merely another premiere off the repertorial assembly line. Four rehearsals were all *Ivanov* got, but this was not exceptional. (When the Moscow Art Theatre revived *Ivanov* in 1904, it devoted seventy-four rehearsals to it.)

Audiences were not preconditioned to this drama of a "superfluous man."

Some expected to see a merry farce in the style of Chekhov's stories of the time . . . others expected something new and more original from him – and were not disappointed. The success looked to be uneven, some hissed, others, the majority, applauded loudly and called for the author, but, by and large, *Ivanov* was not understood, and for a long time the newspapers went on explicating the personality and character of its main hero.[27]

As would become his wont, the dramatist was reluctant to take a curtain call and had to be dragged on stage by Davydov, who led the applause.[28] Chekhov wrote to his brother Aleksandr, "Theatre buffs say that they have never seen in a theatre such a ferment, such general applause and hissing, and never at any other time have they heard so many arguments as they saw and heard at my play."[29] Whatever the response of the first-nighters, the reviews were mostly negative: the play was deemed by the *Moscow Leaflet* (*Moskovsky listok*) "deeply immoral," "a disgusting mess," "cynical piffle"; the *Russian Courier* (*Russky Kurer*) was disturbed by the "buffoonery," "*double entendre* jokes," "shopkeeper wit." M. A. Protopopov characterized Ivanov as a "buffoon and phrasemonger," and Dr. Lvov as a man confected "out of papier-mâché." Chekhov was chided for neglecting genre boundaries and imbedding a domestic tragedy within a society comedy. The last act, in which Ivanov dies of a heart-attack on his wedding-day, was especially excoriated. Even the few favourable reviews found the ending "relatively cold." The shrewd essayist Nikolay Éfros, present at the premiere, said that "the finale is sharply out of keeping with the rest of the play and even provoked a kind of scandal."[30]

The next morning Chekhov ran into the fashionable playwright Viktor Krylov, who patronized him as a neophyte and offered to correct the play's *gaucheries*. Chekhov remembered, "He was very surprised when I turned him down."[31] The author was less dismissive of the written notices which burned into his brain, for he kept quoting them in his letters.[32] A good deal of the critical carnage could be attributed to Ivanov's character, when set in the context of Russian thought in the 1880s. Not long before the play appeared, "Suckling Pigs Made into Hamlets," an article by the populist pamphleteer Nikolay Mikhailovsky sarcastically mocked latter-day "Hamletists" with their tendency to brood and to rationalize their inaction and depression. The novelist Gleb Uspensky in his story "A Responsive Heart" put into his hero's mouth a speech which condemned Ivanov for his moral deadness in not vilifying society.[33] Most politically engaged *littérateurs* assumed that in *Ivanov* Chekhov was "idealizing the absence of ideals,"[34] and endorsing his protagonist's passivity. Yet Chekhov himself was a regular scoffer at Hamletism: "I'm a Moscow Hamlet. Yes. In Moscow I move through homes and theatres, restaurants and editorial offices and wherever I go all I say is: 'God, what boredom! What aggravating boredom!'"[35] In the first version of *Ivanov*, unfortunately, he had not managed to clarify his own attitude towards his protagonist: was Ivanov a parody or a type of the "superfluous man"?

The general public came to see *Ivanov* simply because it was a conversation piece, and it was a conversation piece chiefly because an incomparable actor was playing the lead.[36] That Chekhov had written a play was not a preponderating factor and *Ivanov* was withdrawn after three performances. Chekhov himself disliked the vulgar playing of the comic scenes, the actors in the last act trying to "clown around and kick

up their heels": they turned it into "a showbooth and a pothouse, horri-
fying me." Noting the "protracted, tiresome interval" between the two
scenes of the last act and the audience's bewilderment at the hero's
unexpected death,[37] he determined to rewrite the play before its publication and in case it were ever revived – which seemed unlikely.

A year later, Chekhov informed Suvorin, "I've been reading my
Ivanov. I think if I wrote another Act IV, and got rid of some stuff, and put
in a monologue which is already lodged in my brain, the play will turn
out to be legitimate and extremely effective."[38] By legitimate [*zakonny*],
he meant a serious drama which would conform to standard stage practice and answer the accusations that his "originality" and "novelty"
derived from ignorance of the laws of the drama.

To understand *Ivanov*'s divergence from the common notion of a play,
we note that the biggest hit in Moscow at the time was Petr Nevezhin's
"staggering" drama *Second Youth*. Purporting to treat the burning issue of
divorce, it tells of an honourable man who seduces his children's governess, cannot get his wife to consent to a divorce and grows desperate.
Matters degenerate as the two women become enemies. The eldest son,
a university student, kills the governess, and, while in prison, tries to reconcile his parents, to no avail. Acted by such polished technicians of the
Maly as the *grande dame* Glikeriya Fedotova and the swarthy romantic
lead Sumbatov-Yuzhin, "the theatre rang with hysterical sobs, especially
when Yuzhin who played the young son, after shooting dead his father's
mistress, comes on stage in fetters to beg forgiveness of his mother,
played by Fedotova. The play made a fortune." While both their plays
were running, Chekhov and Nevezhin met in the lobby of the Maly.
"What are you writing now?" Chekhov politely asked the veteran hack.
Nevezhin answered proudly, "What is there left to write after *Second
Youth?*"[39]

To make *Ivanov* conform to this model of a "block-buster," Chekhov
concentrated on the unsatisfactory last act: he shortened the comic
scenes with the best man, combined two separate tableaux into one and
reworked the finale. Amusing episodes of the wedding supper, its toasts,
and Ivanov's tipsiness were replaced by more emotional, even hysterical
passages. Entertaining details from everyday life – Borkin's attempt to
organize a dance (Act II), Lebedev's story about gastronomic treats and
the lackey with the hot pies (Act III) and the farcical matchmaking of
Borkin and Babakina (Act IV) – were relegated to the background. A
minor character with the silly name Dudkin (Bagpiper) was dropped.
Anna Petrovna's earthiness disappeared, along with Ivanov's nickname

for her, "my tiny rebbitzin" and a host of other Jewish jokes. Her inner drama was indicated in the new version by her song about a siskin. Dr. Lvov's priggishness was toned down. To keep Ivanov from seeming the mere victim of scandalmongers, Chekhov added Sasha to the attackers in Act IV and provided Ivanov with a long speech in his own defence. His shady financial dealings with Lebedev were cut out, and the on-stage heart attack was altered to an offstage suicide by pistol. Such a suicide had been a cliché of the Russian stage since the 1873 denouement of Luka Antropov's comedy-melodrama *Will o' the Wisps*. The astute critic Aleksandr Kugel summed up Chekhov's reliance on a climactic *felo de se* as a "sacrifice made . . . to the god of theatrical gimmickry," literally ending the play with a bang.[40]

These and other changes made Ivanov seem less the "deliberate cad" or "out-and-out scoundrel" the Moscow reviewers had called him. But in the process Chekhov turned out to have written two different plays: a four-act, five-scene *comedy* for Korsh which quickly vanished from the bills, and a four-act, four-scene *drama* which was to enjoy great success. The comedy concerned a weak, vacillating, ordinary man, who gave up on life and died suddenly, almost by chance, whereas the drama was about a would-be "hero" riven by a deep psychic laceration, who chose to end his life by suicide.[41] If in the first version Chekhov coarsened Ivanov for the sake of clarity, in the second he amplified the contradictory features. But like Cibber's version of *Richard III*, the "Korsh" *Ivanov* occasionally had more appeal for actors than the more polished version.[42]

IVANOV IN ST. PETERSBURG

While Moscow was weeping at Nevezhin's fustian, literary circles in St. Petersburg were reading the text of *Ivanov* with considerable interest. F. A. Fedorov-Yurkovsky, the broad-minded director-in-chief of the Alexandra Theatre, alert to the spirit of the times, chose it for his benefit. His choice was out of keeping with the Alexandra's routine. For all its pleiad of fine actors, the bulk of its repertory was made up of original works and adaptations by the play-doctor Viktor Krylov. One intelligent member of the troupe, Pavel Svobodin, confided, " . . . what a horrible thought that one must go to the theatre again and ponder the lines of a role written by Viktor Krylov."[43] A two-year boycott of Krylov had been attempted, but abandoned, for the leaders of his faction were too powerful. They included Nikolay Sazonov, who would create Trigorin in *The*

Seagull, and Mariya Savina, at whose behest Markiewicz had written the detested *Fumes of Life*. Savina, an actress of great technical polish, shone in roles of elegant society matrons; befriended and admired by Turgenev (she had created Verochka in his *Month in the Country* before moving on to play Nataliya Petrovna), she thought herself an arbiter of literature and had considerable clout in the theatre's affairs. She was no friend of innovation, and Chekhov, after getting to know her, was to jot in his note-book, "Savina is to actresses what Krylov is to writers."[44]

No one at the Alexandra leapt forward to take the lead in *Ivanov*, and Chekhov wondered if Davydov would swallow his pride and return to St. Petersburg to play it; more important, "Can Davydov manage to be wishy-washy at times, frantic at other times?"[45] Davydov agreed instead to play Lebedev, expecting that Sazonov would be cast as Ivanov; Chekhov submitted, gracefully. But Sazonov turned down the lead, and the director sent Chekhov a telegram on 13 January 1889: "In your absence impossible to cast play. I can't cope with casting. You must come Petersburg no later than 18th. First rehearsal must take place 20th."[46] Chekhov did not come. In the meantime the role was offered again to Davydov, as an inducement to return to the theatre's ranks.

Davydov was dubious, for as, he lamented to Chekhov, he was so depressed by the cut-and-dried approach to theatre at the Alexandra that he contemplated early retirement.[47] His depression turned to alarm when he read the revised *Ivanov*, and insisted that he failed to understand it.

As a friend, as a man who respects your talent and wishes you well in all things, finally, as an actor who has served art for 21 years, I heartily beg you to leave me Ivanov as you created him in the first version, otherwise I do not understand him and I fear I shall fail. I give you my word this is no whim, but a candid explanation and desire to do both of us good. If for some reason you cannot comply with my request, then I am ready to play Kosykh with more satisfaction than Ivanov.[48]

To students of Russian theatre, Davydov's complaint sounds familiar. When Gogol attempted to interpret his comedy *The Inspector* as a ponder-ous Christian morality, the great actor Shchepkin begged him to leave his characters alone. Davydov was a careful player who worked out each characterization in great detail and left no room for improvisation; once his delineation took shape, it was set in stone. Gradually, however, he was talked into accepting the new recension of *Ivanov*.

Chekhov was less familiar with theatre in Petersburg than in Moscow, but, having heard good things about Savina, wanted her for Anna. She

1 Mariya Savina as Sasha in the first St. Petersburg production of *Ivanov*,
Alexandra Theatre, 1889.

in turn asked that the part be given to someone else, as she preferred the younger, more attractive role of Sasha. When he learned this, Chekhov declared himself ashamed that there was nothing in the play worth her acting. "If I had known she was going to play Sasha and Davydov Ivanov, I would have entitled my play *Sasha* and built everything around that role and turned Ivanov into a secondary part, but who knew?"[49] So he "decided to give this role a radical reshaping . . . so far as the framework of the play allows."[50] He reworked and enlarged it with Savina in mind, adding the scene of Ivanov joking with the happy girl. Savina recalled that Chekhov attended all the rehearsals, but modestly kept out of the way and rarely came backstage.[51]

The rest of the cast was impressive, because the occasion celebrated Fedorov-Yurkovsky's twenty-five years of service and the Alexandra actors could not refuse to appear in his honour; still, the company complained at an early rehearsal (one of eight) that they had no punchy exit-lines or strong curtains.[52] They approached *Ivanov* as a run-of-the-mill drama, and sought no new techniques or artistic nuances; rather, they latched on to any moment fraught with stage effect, and by the usual means created superficially well-rounded characters. Strepetova, the Anna Petrovna, was a first-rate character actress with a penchant for realism. The popular comedian Varlamov used his slippery humour to make Lebedev the most sympathetic figure in the play. Even in minor roles, the performances were excellent, with the refined tragedian Vasily Dalmatov as Borkin and the intelligent Svobodin as Shabelsky. Although Chekhov fully expected the play to fail when it opened on 31 January 1889, it was greeted enthusiastically from the start and met with an ovation after the Act III confrontation between Ivanov and Anna. The author and director were called out for a bow. At the cast party, toasts compared the play with Griboedov's classic comedy *Woe from Wit*.[53]

It bears remembering that the scene so enthusiastically received was the most melodramatic, with Davydov shouting "Shut up, Yid bitch! . . . The doctor told me you're going to die soon"; on realizing what he had said, he grabbed his head in horror and, hiding his face in his hands, broke into hysterical sobs. When Strepetova heard his death-dealing words, she gave the graphic impression that they had struck her a fatal blow, and suddenly shrank into herself. "Only a stone, I think, would fail to weep at the distinctive voice with which she uttered the words, 'When, when did he say that?'" one spectator declared. Even in the Korsh production this moment had inspired an observer to write to Chekhov that "such a scene must shake the spectator more powerfully than 'the super-effective' melodrama *Second Youth* . . . " It seemed as if Davydov's acting, monotonous when the play began, "was alive and romantic in the 3rd and 4th acts."[54]

The critics were ecstatic over the Alexandra *Ivanov*. *Russian News* [*Russkie vedomosti*] carolled, "Chekhov's play is a living work, unhack-neyed, containing the stamp of originality and talent."[55] For all this alleged freshness, what they were extolling was Chekhov's seeming mastery of conventional stagecraft. The minority report came from humourists on the sidelines, who aimed their sights at the play's ostensible vulgarity. "I. Grek" [i.e., Y] of *Splinters* [*Oskolki*], who summed it up as "drama of four acts about a Jewess, a concertina, a count, virtue, an organ-grinder and a pistol," was bemused by the fact that each act opened with a trivial occurrence:

Act I (The Ivanov garden)
Ivanov feels a head-ache coming on . . .
Act II (The Lebedev home)
Lebedev is showing his guests a way he has invented of washing down vodka with water . . .
Act III (The Ivanov home)
The curtain rises prematurely and the spectator is unexpectedly presented a picture of Dalmatov, Varlamov and Davydov drinking vodka on stage. The actors retain their presence of mind and go on drinking vodka as if this were part of the play and talk about pickles and other hors d'oeuvre.[56]

This last joke is particularly revealing. The scene that opens Act III is one of Chekhov's characteristic experiments. He shows Ivanov's study invaded by the banality of everyday life and submerges the hero's private anguish in a flood of apparently irrelevant chatter. As the literary theorist Chudakov later noted, what puzzled the satirist was the seemingly "extraneous" elements "which many assumed to be Chekhov's attempt to reproduce real life."[57] An ironic layering effect was mistaken as failed naturalism or even anti-theatricality.

Chekhov sneaked away again on opening night, fearing that the ovations were a binge that would later give him a severe hangover. When the excitement died down, his dissatisfaction returned: he wished to see a more energetic player take on Ivanov, and he approved only of Strepetova's Anna because she seemed to suffer and live on stage. Complaining of the time he had wasted on actors, he belly-ached, "I should give up theatres of all sorts and devote myself to my business – literary fiction. These actors are convinced they're your benefactors. A play, you see, is worthless until they create its success."[58] Like many playwrights, he resented the actors' share in his brain-children's upbringing, especially as he became increasingly aware that his plays required a new conscientiousness in the actors, a willingness to drop "ham" from their diets.

While Korsh's Theatre put on the revised *Ivanov* with an excellent cast in September, Chekhov kept tinkering with the script, publishing a third version with more explanations between Lvov and Anna, and the removal of Ivanov's dream monologue in the last act. He was still touching it up in 1901. The reason behind this compulsive dissatisfaction was that the play remained an uneasy compromise between the mannerisms of boulevard drama and the subtleties of Chekhov's conception. The emotional histrionics that so pleased the Petersburg public were at odds with the innovative use of atmospherics, eloquent environment and ironic juxtaposition.

By September 1889, Chekhov had three plays running simultaneously: in Moscow, *The Proposal* at Goreva's Theatre and *The Bear* at Abramova's; and in St. Petersburg, *Ivanov* at the Alexandra. He had been established as a prominent dramatist in record time. Still, the success of *Ivanov* did little to efface the image of Chekhov as a humourist from the mind of the average playgoer. After *The Proposal* was played for Tsar Alexander III at the Krasnoe Selo Theatre, the sovereign inquired what else this Chekhov had written. "*Ivanov*" came the reply. When the Tsar looked blank at this common name, the Inspector of the Imperial Repertory added, "The comedy *Ivanov*, Your Majesty, and *The Bear*." "Ah, yes! *Ivanov, The Bear* – I never got to see them – pity!"[59]

THE WOOD DEMON

Meanwhile, Chekhov had begun work on another play even before the *Ivanov* revisions were completed, a collaborative comedy to be written with Suvorin. When his colleague dropped out, Chekhov reworked it into what became *The Wood Demon*. A visitor to Yalta in summer 1889 found that Chekhov had been composing the play out of sequence: the first two acts and the end of the fourth were finished, but of Act III only the episode of the slap was done, to provide an opportunity for Solovtsov: "He's a specialist at such scenes."[60] Chekhov boasted to Suvorin that "nowhere in the whole play is there a single lackey or peripheral comic character or little widow."[61] Recent experience led him to eliminate supernumerary roles and make sure that each actor had enough to do: "It's unconscionable of authors to bring on stage postilions, police inspectors, constables. Why make the poor actor get in costume and make-up and while away whole hours in a piercing draft backstage?"[62]

Although he intended to offer the play to the Maly in Moscow, Chekhov also hoped that Svobodin, the well-read actor who had played Shabelsky at the Alexandra, would sponsor the play for a Petersburg benefit performance. When Chekhov expressed anxiety that the play might not be "theatrical" enough, Svobodin reassured him,

Yes, my friend, even Shakespeare has plenty of untheatrical passages! Set aside this needless care and do *your own* work, [. . .] Be true to yourself despite all the rules and remember that the plays of Viktor Krylov and the late Dyachenko are theatrical to the nth degree. Give us your beautiful material, and we shall build on it without prejudice to your intentions, I assure you on my twenty years' experience that this is a trivial matter.[63]

It is unlikely that Chekhov's fears were allayed by the suggestion that actors would flesh out his barebones material; as things turned out, theatricality was the rock on which the Petersburg project foundered.

The Wood Demon had first to be passed by the Repertory Committee for the Petersburg State theatres, made up of Grigorovich, the critic who had persuaded Chekhov to be a serious writer, the playwright Potekhin, the actor Sazonov who had turned down the role of Ivanov, and Vsevolozhsky, director of the Imperial theatres. Svobodin agreed to read it aloud to them: after Act I, "the remarks about living characters, real personalities, the author's talent were mixed up with criticism about the absence of action, *longueurs* etc." No criticism was levelled at the second act.

The third act, with its storm and stress, the monologues of the professor, the Wood Demon, and Voinitsky one after another, and the finale itself plunged my listeners into a certain confusion . . . "It's a novella, a beautiful novella, but not a comedy . . . " Grigorovich exclaimed, "It's strange, it can't possibly be put on stage in this form, I love him like my own son, this is how Dostoevsky used to write . . . it's something halfway between *The Devils* and *Karamazov*, powerful, lucid, but not a comedy."[64]

The meeting dragged on for twelve hours, and finally Vsevolozhsky took Svobodin aside, to explain that a play so inimical to the tastes of the Imperial Court would have a deleterious effect on the promotion of Russian drama in the State theatre system.

Persuading me not to stage the play, with great concern and sympathy he told me that, as the first in line to have a benefit, I could harm myself and my fellow benéficiaires by putting on *Wood Demon*: Grand Dukes would come to it, he knows their views and tastes, this play would very much dampen their eagerness to come to Russian plays. Dear Antoine, if we were Frenchmen, you and I, and we knew an Antoine who had a Théâtre Libre, we would stop and ask what we are to do with something on which so much labour, talent, heart and mind have been expended! Now more than ever I am convinced that *Wood Demon* will do splendidly in Moscow and earn what it deserves; Grand Dukes don't go to the Maly Theatre.[65]

Chekhov's response was bitterly self-deprecating: "There's nothing strange in the fact that a young writer of fiction should write a play unsuited for the stage."[66]

The Moscow theatre world was of the same opinion. There Chekhov had promised the title role to Aleksandr Lensky, leading light of the Maly, and the other roles, Chekhov assured him, had been conceived with specific Maly actors in mind, as if it were a standard repertory piece.[67] After reading *The Wood Demon*, Lensky, an actor reputed to have great taste, advised Chekhov to "write fiction. You have too cavalier an attitude toward the stage and dramatic form, you respect them too little to write a drama. This is a more difficult form than that of the short story, and, forgive me, you are too spoiled by success to start learning the elementary, so to speak, ABCs of dramatic form and loving them."[68] Chekhov may have remembered such supercilious and proprietary attitudes when, in *The Seagull*, he has Treplev attack the second-raters who hog the arts. But even Nemirovich-Danchenko, who admired *The Wood Demon*'s living characters and neat plot development, alerted Chekhov to the play's deviation from theatrical norms. He pedantically explained that audiences must grasp the core of the plot if a play is to be a success.[69] As for Suvorin, the original collaborator, he disliked the end of Act III, all of Act IV, and recommended throwing out the characters of Ivan Ivanovich and Fedor Ivanovich.

Bowing to this "expert" advice, Chekhov made some revisions and then offered the play to his friend Solovtsov, who had co-founded a private theatre in Moscow with Mariya Abramova, a romantic actress who had invested a small inheritance in it. The offer was purely a commercial transaction: "Abramova is buying the play from me at a good rate. Well and good, so I'll sell it."[70] Unfortunately, the production that opened at Abramova's on 27 December 1889 did nothing to confute the experts. The holiday-making audience expected to see a "real" wood demon on stage, as in a fairy pantomime, and actors from Korsh's Theatre who filled the boxes whistled and hooted at their competitors. The lines could not be heard. The slap scene, so intentionally "theatrical," failed to come off in performance. The role of *la belle* Elena was taken by the obese Mariya Glebova; as Chekhov's younger brother remembered, "to see the *jeune premier*, the actor Roshchin-Insarov, making a declaration of love to her was positively incongruous; he called her beautiful, yet could not get both his arms round her to embrace her. Then the glow of the forest fire was such that it provoked laughter."[71] If the theatricality was inept, untheatricality remained the chief charge against the play. Pseudonymous "Ivan Ivanov," critic for *The Performer* [*Artist*], yawned, "Such everyday conversations over vodka and hors d'oeuvre have already bored everyone both at home and at friends', and there's no need to go to the theatre and sit through four acts of a 'comedy' to hear people inquire after some stranger's health and squabble ten times over."[72]

Chekhov withdrew the play, which had been at best received with indifference. It fell into almost instant oblivion and neither critics nor theatrical practitioners gave it a thought for decades. (The only exception was the urbane critic Prince Urusov, who tried unsuccessfully to persuade Chekhov to publish it, and who always considered it superior to its revision *Uncle Vanya*.) Chekhov's reputation as a viable dramatist had suffered badly, and, in the circles of Russian art, the notion of such a thing as a "Chekhovian" play would have seemed absurd.

CHAPTER 2

A brace of gulls (Russia 1896–1898)

I have read and reread *Seagull* several times over and find I am
simply in despair; I feel that it is almost unbelievably splendid, but
what it's about, where the splendour lies, I cannot figure out at all.

Chekhov's German translator Czumikow, 29 January
1899[1]

The first production of *The Seagull* at the Alexandra Theatre in St.
Petersburg in 1896 was an unqualified disaster. The revival at the
Moscow Art Theatre two years later was an unqualified success. Such is
the theatrical legend adhering to these events which gets repeated in
biographies of Chekhov and histories of modern theatre. Like most
legends, it is an accretion of half-truths and exaggerations around a
kernel of truth.

This accretion began in Chekhov's lifetime, when partisans of the
Moscow Art Theatre used *The Seagull*'s success there to bolster its artistic
programme, while participants in the Petersburg debacle sought excuses
for their failure. In Soviet criticism, this evolved into an exemplary fable
of how progressive ideas triumphed over retrograde, tsarist hackwork. In
fact, the differing fates of the two productions help to explain why
Chekhov is not the last playwright of the nineteenth century, but the first
playwright of the twentieth.

ALEXANDRA 1896

Although he was in good odour at the Alexandra Theatre on account of
Ivanov's success, Chekhov originally intended *The Seagull* to be staged
elsewhere, probably at Korsh's in Moscow, for the entrepreneur
regarded Chekhov as "his author." But when Chekhov read it to Korsh
in the blue drawing-room of the actress Lidiya Yavorskaya, who had
long solicited a play from his hands, the pros were non-plussed. "Darling,
it just isn't stageworthy," Yavorskaya is reported to have remarked. "You

have a man shoot himself offstage and don't even let him talk before he dies."[2] Identifying mutual friends as the originals of characters, they protested their embarrassment that Chekhov should publicize private love affairs. Korsh renounced any claim on the play and Yavorskaya did the same on behalf of Suvorin's St. Petersburg Theatre of the Literary-Artistic Society. She did not find Nina an effective showpiece, and hardly saw herself as Arkadina, although the role was in some measure based on her.[3]

Chekhov resolved to give the play to the Maly, but at the last it was the Alexandra which accepted *The Seagull* without reservation. The unsuitability of this most subjective of plays should have been patent, however. For years, the Petersburg intelligentsia had refrained from attending the Alexandra. Although it was the State theatre for Russian drama in the administrative capital of the empire, it discounted the classic native repertory in favour of translations and adaptations, in deference to the Court's disdain for things Russian. Its reputation was as a comedy house, featuring outstanding performers in flimsy vehicles. The hits of the 1895/6 season were three farces: Velichko's *The First Fly*; *Vava*, an adaptation of Maupassant's *Yvette*; and *Matrena the General's Lady* co-authored by Viktor Krylov with Savina dazzling in the comic lead.[4] *The Seagull*'s immediate precursor, *Pashenka*, was *Fumes of Life* with a Dostoevskyan heroine, a temperamental girl who runs away from home to become an operetta singer and shoots the nobleman who seduced her. Nina Zarechnaya would strike Alexandra personnel and audiences as a pale shadow of Pashenka.

Krylov had just relinquished his post as stage director to Evtikhy Karpov, who was ambitious to stage new plays by renowned writers.[5] *The Seagull* was Chekhov's first produced full-length play not to have the name of a male protagonist emblazoned in the title. Whether or not "The Seagull" stands for Nina or some more abstruse idea is arguable. But Karpov, the director self-selected to bring the play to life, immediately seized on Nina as a heroine "wounded to the heart," and regarded the rest of the characters as "petty, egotistical little people, involved in their own vulgar and puny little feelings and ideas."[6] With this emotional configuration in mind, he could hardly realize "those hidden dramas and tragedies in every figure of the play" later indicated by Nemirovich-Danchenko.[7]

The play had been scheduled for mid-November, but was put forward to October because the much-loved actress Elizaveta Levkeeva requested it for her benefit. Chekhov joked that "the role of the heroine of seventeen, a slender young lady, will be played by the beneficiary herself."[8] In fact, Levkeeva, a fat, moustachioed comedienne who specialized in outspoken old maids and dowagers, had no intention of appearing in it. She simply wanted a new piece by a popular author to swell her takings.

The author himself was eager for Savina to play Nina, while the director, more astutely, saw her as Arkadina. In the event, Savina was cast as Nina but failed to show up at the first rehearsal, 8 October 1896, sending a note to explain her withdrawal: "Reading the play again tonight, having glanced over the role of Nina a few times, I have decided I cannot play this role. I don't like disobliging the author and the beneficiary by my refusal, and, if necessary, I am ready to play Masha."[9] In a letter to Suvorin she explained her refusal by saying that Nina needed to be blond and wigs did not suit her. More pointedly, she realized that the emphasis on Nina's age and freshness would put her more mature looks at a disadvantage.[10]

As it happened, she did not play Masha either and probably never expected to, this role being too secondary for her star status (besides, the actress cast as Masha refused to step down). Arkadina was not offered to Savina, perhaps because it was too sharp a satire of aging divas. That role was given to Dyuzhikova, a good actress in pathetic melodrama, specializing in frigid *grandes dames*, but arid and devoid of humour. Her lack of charm and coquettry had nothing in common with Arkadina's *cabotinage*.[11]

Chekhov wanted Davydov for Dr. Dorn, particularly because Dorn has the last lines and a strong tag could make or break a play. Davydov himself chose the part of Sorin.[12]

Of the eight rehearsals held on the stage of the Grand Duke Michael Theatre, a sumptuous house used for French drama, the first two took place without most of the leads, and only Sazonov, as Trigorin, had his lines by heart. At the third, by which time Vera Komissarzhevskaya had been cast as Nina and Chekhov had arrived, half the actors were still on book and only faintly acquainted with the blocking, as they wandered about, scripts in hand.[13] They relied heavily on the prompter for their cues. As Petr Gnedich, a Maly stage director, reported, most of them saw *The Seagull* as nothing special: "They looked to see how many sides of lines they had; they saw that there was little action, lots of dialogue; they glued on moustaches, beards and whiskers, put on the chance costumes brought from the costume-shop at the last minute, memorized the part and came on stage."[14] The routine of these experienced players was not to build up a character gradually, but to grasp an inner essence and portray it in broad strokes. That was all very well for the standard repertory farce but not for *The Seagull*.

Gnedich believed that the actors, given no scope for their usual techniques, were bored by the play's "wearisome, nervous, tremulous, morbid lassitude." Their interest could be piqued only if they could halt the quiet conversations and "seize each other by the throat, begin to choke one another or pour poison in a glass, drink it and start to die in convulsions, in short, whenever they got to repeat an age-old trite effect."[15] They construed the "plot" of Chekhov's play to be that of popular gypsy romances sung in music-halls and restaurants or, indeed, of *Pashenka*: the ruination of an innocent girl, seduced and abandoned. The Alexandra zeroed in on that gratifying intrigue.

The obtuseness of the actors in regard to the play's innovative features is exemplified by Roman Apollonsky, the handsome *jeune premier* cast as Treplev. Chekhov's innovation lay in depicting the psychology of a modern decadent; the part may even have been based on a youthful poet, Viktor Bibikov, who had died of tuberculosis in 1892.[16] By 1900 Treplev would be regarded as a plum for young actors who specialized in "neurasthenics" like Tsar Fedor and Raskolnikov. Uninterested in literary trends, Apollonsky knew nothing of this. In 1904, long after the Moscow Art Theatre had rehabilitated *The Seagull* as a moving and stageworthy work, Apollonsky wrote in a memorial article that Chekhov

the playwright is undoubtedly inferior to Chekhov the man of letters, and therefore some of his things are not entirely suitable for the stage . . . sketching this or that image or situation, he indulges in artistic subtleties which are inexpressible on stage and yet are so tightly interwoven into the general background that they cannot always be separated. That is the reason for his work's failure.[17]

The office of the Imperial theatre ordered no new scenery. The Act I park was a composite of "routine" forest pieces, the interiors an assortment of old box-sets which were several sizes larger than any actual dining-room or parlour. The only new scenery to be painted by the nominal designer Aleksandr Yanov was a flat with a view of the lake for the first act and the manor-house in the second. Chekhov found them too operatically "luxurious" and "gorgeous," at odds with the modest tone of the play.[18]

Most playwrights undergo a shock of non-recognition when they attend rehearsals, and Chekhov was no exception. He complained that the actors "act a lot, there should be less acting," "the main thing . . . is to be simple, without theatricality . . . They're all simple, ordinary people."[19] To Suvorin he wrote that the "disgusting acting" made the play "quite invisible." Chekhov particularly objected to Dyuzhikova: "Arkadina is a deceitful, unintelligent woman, quickly shifting from one mood to another, conceited and egotistic, but Dyuzhikova shows us a clever, good, truthful woman . . . Not a bit like my actress Arkadina." Apollonsky delineated Treplev in rough, choppy strokes. As Trigorin, Sazonov, essentially an adept of farce and operetta, was insincere in his suffering and lacked any trace of the intellectual; even Karpov had to admit that his lack of a sense of the character could not be recompensed by technique.[20] "Look at how Apollonsky walks," Chekhov grieved. "Treplev doesn't walk like that . . . He should have a nervous walk . . . and Sazonov isn't like a writer. Was Trigorin really like that? He's a stage star, not a writer . . . and Chitau . . . she overacts . . . In my Masha everything is simple . . . she's simplicity itself."[21]

The exception to these complaints was Komissarzhevskaya. Although Chekhov had never seen her before, he rapidly realized how well she was incarnating his country girl, and predicted an enormous success with a thunderous ovation after her first act soliloquy.[22] "With her miming and voice, Komissarzhevskaya almost moved me to tears. I felt that my throat was torn out."[23]

The critics were to complain of Karpov's awkward blocking and generally careless direction, but he did attempt one original touch. Fearing that the appearance of carpenters swathed in sheets during the play within-a-play would raise a laugh and spoil Nina's soliloquy, he brought on a couple of actresses to portray shadows. Chekhov was exasperated: "Why? . . . Why these wenches? Don't you understand, look . . . the two carpenters who built the stage simply wrap themselves in sheets and stand at the side . . . That's all! . . . And you give us shadows!"[24] Still, he grudgingly assented.

In later years, Karpov, trying to exonerate himself from the debacle, claimed that, from his first reading of *The Seagull*, he was alert to its Turgenevian "pastel tones, penetrated with sorrow, alive in its slightest details, truthful and subtle in its characters."[25] He and many of the participants in the Alexandra fiasco preferred to put the blame on the audience.

In choosing a play by Chekhov for her benefit, Levkeeva had been governed purely by financial motives. With her comic catchphrases and grimaces, she was a byword for belly laughs to the general public, which also knew Chekhov primarily as the author of funny stories in *The Petersburg Gazette*.[26] Her aficionados were known as "Gostinodvorians,"

2   Vera Komissarzhevskaya as Nina in Act I of the first production of *The Seagull*,
Alexandra Theatre, St. Petersburg, 1896.

from the tradesmen and counter-jumpers of the commercial district the
Gostiny Dvor: "tired businessmen" would not be an inaccurate translation. They came expecting a farce like *The First Fly*, and when they failed
to get one, they made one.

On 17 October 1896, when the curtain went up on *The Seagull*, there
were only about ten literary figures and a dozen Chekhov fans in the
house.[27] The first laugh was not slow in coming. It was a titter at Masha's
taking snuff. Confused by the opening scenes, the Gostinodvorians
began to look for pretexts for laughter, and coughed in the meantime. An
epidemic of yawning broke out. "How long is this going to go on?"
raised both laughs and outraged cries of "Ssh! Silence!" Sorin's remark
about his unpleasant voice, Shamraev's reminiscences and the shadows
that Chekhov had so distrusted in rehearsal provoked giggles, but the cue
for general derision was Nina's soliloquy, which was drowned out by
guffaws. Raising her voice and sharpening her focus, Komissarzhevskaya managed to reclaim attention, but the laughs broke out again
at Arkadina's "It smells of sulphur." When the sun went down at the end
of Act I, shouts of "Why is it so dark?" were heard. The actors were hes-
itant to come out for a curtain call, and Chekhov left the auditorium to
wait out the play in Karpov's office.

In Act II, when Treplev brings in the downed gull, one wag asked
"Why does Apollonsky keep carrying around that dead duck?," while a
theatre administrator was heard to pontificate, "This is no play, it's utter
nonsense." Another source of merriment was Sorin's wheelchair, which
Chekhov had insisted on; the raked stage kept it sliding towards the footlights. The low-keyed ending of the second act confused and disappointed spectators accustomed to "strong curtains." Thrown by their
reception, the actors began to ad-lib dialogue, a fresh inspiration for the
mockers. Treplev's bandage renewed the amusement in Act III, the
trading of insults between himself and his mother proved to be hilarious,
and by the last act, the least little thing caused an uproar. Every move of
Sorin, still wheelchair-bound, was met with hilarity; and when Nina
draped herself in a white tablecloth to repeat her first-act soliloquy, all
restraints were off. The line "A phial of ether exploded" caused such an
Homeric outburst (partly because the actor substituted the word
"bottle," evocative of hard drinking, instead) that the curtain came down
to it. There was no applause at the end, nothing but whistling, hisses and
more laughter.[28]

The wits of the press had a field-day. For weeks, the *Petersburg Leaflet*
(*Peterburgsky listok*) ran pasquinades identifying Chekhov with Treplev,

such as one beginning, "He's no champion of routine, he's a defender of new forms."[29] Another humourist calling himself "Poor Jonathan" summed up *The Seagull* as "fantastical-lunatical scenes with a prologue, an epilogue, tomfoolery and a flop. (The plot borrowed from a mental hospital)."[30] Yet another described the last act as "Apollonsky's study. Ten or so performers, with nothing to do, have played a game of lotto and exited."[31] For them, the overall impression left by the play was one of dementia.

Not all the mockers were philistines. Even so experienced a theatrical commentator as Aleksandr Kugel asserted that *The Seagull* was "not a play at all, but a series of dialogues without a definite point."[32] Suvorin himself, although he had composed in advance a press notice announcing the play's success, confided the play's flaws to his diary: "little action, few dramatically interesting developments in the scenes and a great deal of space given to the trivia of life, sketches of unimportant, uninteresting characters . . . it's all disorganized . . . All the important things are narrated."[33]

Without predicating a conspiracy theory, one may safely assert that there were hidden agendas behind much of the adverse reaction to the play. Analyzing the 1896 reaction two years later, Prince Urusov, a sophisticated and open-minded critic, recalled that *The Seagull* had "exasperated old men of letters by its innovations," particularly the abrupt beginnings and endings to the acts, the "poetic but relentless pessimism of the author," eccentric characters like Masha, and the suspicion that Chekhov sympathized with Treplev and his "decadent" playlet. Now in his thirties, Chekhov was drawn into a new circle of acquaintances and interests which often irritated his old friends. "Modernism" was a positive term for Chekhov; he had grown close to the actors Davydov and Svobodin because they "are very, very interesting. Both are talented, clever, sensitive and both, undoubtedly, are modern."[34] He liked Hauptmann, had a taste for Maeterlinck and Strindberg, and showed an interest in the symbolists. This could only annoy reactionaries, who already disapproved of his friendship with Tolstoy.

Yet, Urusov pointed out, young writers too were irritated because Chekhov's "symbolism" was not programmatic and he portrayed Treplev as a failure; they objected to the absence of tendentiousness in the characters. Liberals associated Chekhov with Suvorin and *New Times*, and unreasoningly sought to sink a play "of that camp." But finally, Urusov opined, the failure was a combination of adventitious factors (the casting, audience hostility) and essentials: "the complicated psychology of the characters, the boldness with which the author reveals shameful secrets of life, like the cloacae on which palaces are built."[35]

In Chekhov's own description, the first night was "lacklustre, grey, low-spirited, wooden . . . the depression was complete." The Petersburg correspondent for *The Fan (Teatral)* noted that "the complete absence of ensemble feeling and general tone in the performance," along with the clumsy staging, made it seem an amateur recital taking place on a professional stage.[36] But even here, there was dissent, for many of the actors were singled out for praise. Pavel Gaideburov, a freshman at Moscow University, estimated that the Alexandra actors played as well as they did in other plays, some of them wonderfully. He cited Modest Pisarev as an incomparable Doctor Dorn, a creature of "frank cynicism" and "irresistible charm," "childishly simple"; "it was hard not to forgive him the naive cruelty with which he refused to reciprocate the love of others."[37] Davydov made Sorin an unforgettably living character, "compelling you to forget that you are in a theatre."[38]

On the other hand, Varlamov, an elemental comic genius afflicted with elephantiasis, manoeuvred his unwieldy bulk along the stage, trying to get a laugh on every one of Shamraev's lines. According to Gaideburov, this was the result of baldfaced confusion: what was such an actor doing in such a play? "I think that, in playing *Seagull*, each of the interpreters must have experienced more or less Varlamov's lack of comprehension; the deep outward rift between the traditional form of stage art and what were then the new demands made by Chekhov's drama gaped too unexpectedly."[39]

Except for Vera Komissarzhevskaya, who came across as a thoroughly modern Nina. Chekhov's good friend, the writer Ivan Leontev, lavished praise:

a dream, like a phantom, a slender, fair-haired girl with a pale, drawn face, large stricken eyes, depressed and jerky movements . . . Nervous, rapid speech, plucked from her heart by her deep sincerity . . . And in the sounds of her mournful nervous voice, the spectator felt the profound spiritual drama, inner disquiet, dissatisfaction, passionate protest against the vulgarity of the life around her, the agonizing search for a new one.[40]

Her exquisite voice resounded as the call "of the muse of the new drama," "the strung chime" of the whole performance.[41] The actress's own demand for creative experimentation coincided with the emotional and intellectual demands of Chekhov's drama; but it would be a mistake to assume that for her contemporaries her performance consciously revealed a new school of playwriting. When they proclaimed her luminosity, they were characterizing her personal brilliance, and, although some identified her with Nina uttering "a passionate call for a deep, heartfelt, humane dialogue of soul to soul,"[42] no one declared that a new style of acting was required to play Chekhov.

When Suvorin suggested to Chekhov that he carry out some revisions, the author touchily left town the next day and did not answer Suvorin's telegram requesting that he re-rehearse *The Seagull*.[43] When Karpov in turn resisted Suvorin's insistence for a touch-up rehearsal, the two of them simply cut a few discordant elements, including Sorin's wheelchair, the living shadows in Treplev's play, and the repetition of Nina's soliloquy in Act IV.

News of the scandal spread, but the second night audience, which came expecting the worst, was attentive and well behaved. The applause after Act I was sparse and uncertain, for the spectators were confused, charmed by the play while trying to figure out what had so offended the first-nighters. As their interest wafted across the footlights, the actors improved, and by the end of Act III, calls for "author" were heard. The following day there appeared Suvorin's long critical article summing up the play's virtues and scolding the first-nighters for their rude behaviour. On 21 October, Komissarzhevskaya could write to Chekhov announcing "a complete, unanimous success."[44]

Each succeeding performance evoked a more sensitive reaction from the audience and more assured acting from the players,[45] and before the limited run of eight performances ended, Karpov requested a reprise of another three. But the box-office returns prior to the fourth performance had amounted to a mere eight hundred rubles, so the theatre's administrator struck the play from the repertory.[46] *The Seagull* was then successfully revived in Kiev, Taganrog and other provincial towns, providing Chekhov with handsome royalties, but stirring in him no desire to see the play resuscitated in the capitals.

MOSCOW ART THEATRE, 1898

The Moscow Art Theatre had been founded as an alternative to such theatres as the Alexandra. At an epic luncheon at the Slav Bazaar restaurant on 22 June 1897, the wealthy amateur actor and director Konstantin Alekseev alias Stanislavsky and the prize-winning playwright Vladimir Nemirovich-Danchenko posited a roster of plays with serious artistic or social merit, an ensemble company devoid of stars, and a staging practice that would be sedulous in preparation and execution. Almost from the first, Chekhov was included in their plans. In a program and budget presented to prospective share-holders in May 1898, Nemirovich listed "realistic plays," *The Seagull* and *Ivanov*, as the only two contemporary Russian dramas in the projected repertory.[47]

Nemirovich's close acquaintance with Chekhov and his sympathy with the author's artistic goals made such inclusions imperative. For him, *The Seagull* beat with "the pulse of modern Russian life."[48] The little personal contact Stanislavsky had had with Chekhov, on the other hand, was fortuitous or formal. "It is hard for me to confess that at that time, I was not very attracted to Anton Pavlovich. He struck me as arrogant, aloof and not devoid of malice."[49] Twenty years after the premiere, Stanislavsky was to insist that "everyone realized that the fate of the theatre hung on the outcome of this production,"[50] but at the time the fate was more financial than artistic. The legends surrounding this premiere have built on the picturesque account Stanislavsky later provided in his autobiography *My Life in Art*. His own initial dislike of the play and reluctance to help stage it, based on its earlier failure; Chekhov's equal reluctance to have it revived (it took two strongly worded letters from Nemirovich to persuade him); the dependence of the theatre's future on the success of this, the first season's final offering; and the actors' jittery nerves on opening night, all capped by what a press agent would call a "smash hit" – these have become familiar stories. But here again, the vividness of the anecdotes mask the more profound meaning this production had both for the future presentation of Chekhov and for the development of the Art Theatre's style.

Despite Stanislavsky's initial resistance to the play, there was no real disagreement between him and Nemirovich as to its quality. As the former wrote to the latter three months prior to the play's opening, "I understand only that the play is talented, interesting, but I don't know what approach to take to it."[51] This attitude, by no means hostile, reflects the prevalent feeling that *The Seagull*, though significant, was enigmatic. Both directors took it for granted that the play was too cryptic for the general public: it had to be not only performed, but interpreted. "I keep re-reading *Seagull*," Nemirovich wrote to Chekhov, "looking for those little bridges that the director must make the audience cross without becoming mechanical. The public is not yet able (and perhaps never will be) to yield to the mood of the play . . . "[52] The word "mood" – *nastroenie* – had already been spoken in relation to *Ivanov* and the Alexandra *Seagull*, and would later be commonplace, but at this time it was still a neologism.

Mood would become the Art Theatre's all-important tool of transmission. Meyerhold would later say that the MAT's treatment of Chekhov had identified it as a "Theatre of Mood," and much ink would be spilt over whether the Art Theatre's atmospheric approach abetted or hampered the emotional appeal, hypnotic effects and special rhythms of Chekhov's plays.[53]

"Art" ("Khudozhestvenny") in the theatre's name was another buzzword which some of its contemporaries found pretentious. (And it is especially unfortunate that in Great Britain it is now known as the Moscow *Arts* Theatre, as if it were a follower of William Morris or some fringe group in Hampstead. In its English-language publicity, it always called itself the Moscow Art Theatre.) As Prince Mirsky has pointed out, the word *khudozhestvenny* had a special meaning for the Russian intelligentsia of the 1880s and nineties:

it conveyed . . . a certain mellowness and lack of crudeness, an absence of too apparent "purpose," and also an absence of intellectual elements – of logic and "reflection". It was also colored by Belinsky's doctrine that the essence of "art" was "thinking in images," not in concepts.[54]

To be "artistic" in this sense involved a deliberate reorganization and restatement of reality, devoid of didacticism. Stanislavsky's imagistic approach, rather than Nemirovich-Danchenko's more analytic methods, were to define the Art Theatre's style.

This aesthetic program surfaces when Stanislavsky calls his plan for *The Seagull* not a *Regiebuch* or *rezhissersky eksemplyar*, but a *partitura* or score. The play is read as an orchestral symphony, in which every element contributes not to exact meaning, but to atmosphere and affect. Up to that date the Art Theatre's sole success had been its opening production, A. K. Tolstoy's blank-verse chronicle of sixteenth-century Muscovy, *Tsar Fedor Ioannovich*: a success due chiefly to a careful recreation of the period through stage groupings and antique artefacts. At a loss to understand what Chekhov was getting at in *The Seagull*, Stanislavsky fell back on this Meiningen-like approach and sought in the contemporary life of educated Russians the same striking tableaux, the same telling mannerisms, the same pregnant pauses, and the same picturesque lighting that had enthralled audiences at *Tsar Fedor*. "We begin where [the Meiningers] leave off," Nemirovich was to declare, suggesting that the MAT was applying the Germans' antiquarian methods to modern plays.[55]

Stanislavsky understood *The Seagull* to be a romantic melodrama:

Nina was a pure creature ruined by that "scoundrelly Lovelace" Trigorin, and Treplev was a misunderstood Byronic genius. There was no attempt to elicit these interpretations organically from the actors. The Art Theatre troupe, composed of recent graduates from the Moscow Philharmonic and amateurs from Stanislavsky's Circle of Art and Literature, were not proficient enough to evolve rich characterizations in the short time at their disposal; but they were pliable in the hands of the two directors.

That *The Seagull* was to be less an actors' play than a director's piece was confessed by Nemirovich in a letter to Chekhov during the rehearsal period. He had encountered the Maly Theatre's Sumbatov-Yuzhin:

Sumbatov expressed the opinion (which I think he conveyed to you as well) that it is one of those plays which especially requires strong, experienced actors and cannot be saved by the directing.

An odd opinion! I argued with him very forcefully. Here are my arguments . . .

First of all, the play has been in the hands of strong actors . . . and what did they do, did they make a success of it? In other words, precedent is not on the side of Sumbatov's opinion.

Second, in the leading roles – Nina and Treplev – I always prefer *youth* and the performer's artistic naïveté to their experience and outworn routine.

Third, an experienced actor in his sense is bound to be an actor of a certain hamminess [*shablon*], however lucid – it may be harder for him to present the audience a new image than it is for an actor who is still a neophyte at theatrical banality.

Fourth, Sumbatov obviously understands directing to mean only blocking with a prompter, whereas we enter into the very depths of tone for each character in detail and – even more important – the ensemble, the general mood, which is the most important thing of all in *The Seagull*.[56]

Stanislavsky's score was, in Nemirovich's words, a "striking example of [his] *creative intuition* as a director. While remaining indifferent to Chekhov, he sent me such a rich, interesting, completely original and profound set of materials for staging *Seagull* that it was impossible not to wonder at this ardent, brilliant *imagination*."[57] Unlike Karpov who simply moved the actors around like counters, Stanislavsky "through-composed" the text, setting it to details of mood. As he completed each act at his estate, he posted it to Nemirovich in Moscow, who then rehearsed the actors to it, as if they were instruments in an orchestra. His only corrections were to tone down Stanislavsky's burgeoning fancy, but he never altered the way the characterizations or conflicts were handled. "*The Seagull*," Nemirovich explained to his partner, "is written with a very fine pencil and in my opinion requires extreme prudence in its realization.

Sometimes, one cannot dissipate the spectator's attention with details from everyday life. The spectator is always stupid. He must be treated like a child."[58]

Virtually none of Stanislavsky's directions in the score concern issues of style, except in the scene between Treplev and Arkadina in Act III. "In order to make the play more alive and understandable for the audience, I very much recommend you not to be afraid of the *keenest* realism in this scene."[59] Since it is a scene of emotional violence, full of insult, recrimination and remorse, by "realism" he seems to have meant a Zolaesque brutality, a visceral rawness unpolished by acting technique. And in the final production, this scene, like the equally strident Ivanov–Anna episode, was indeed cited as a highpoint of the evening.

But such crude "realism" was at odds with the general tone of the play set forth in the Stanislavskian score. The attention to detail, with the actors' every move, pause and intonation prescribed in advance of rehearsal and with all the detritus of real life in evidence, constituted a kind of pointillism. Another painterly analogy was offered by Vsevolod Meyerhold, who had been cast as Treplev, a role he had wanted to prepare for his graduate piece at the Philharmonic: in 1906, he referred to Stanislavsky's work on *The Seagull* as "scenic impressionism." In Act I, the audience could not glimpse where the characters went when they left the stage. "Crossing a little bridge, they disappeared into a black patch of thicket, *somewhere*." Later in the play, with the landscape invisible through the windows, characters entered "in galoshes, shaking off hats, laprugs, shawls – a sketch of autumn, a freezing shower, puddles in the courtyard and slender planks laid over them."[60]

Unlike naturalism, in which the reproduction of observed reality constantly called attention to itself, Stanislavsky's individual strokes, when seen from the auditorium, blended together to create a layering effect. Marianna Stroeva has compared this to the coating of white primer shining through the top layer of an oil painting: every stroke was unified and illuminated by the underlying luminosity.[61] No detail had significance in itself, but stood out for a moment and then was reincorporated into the whole. Each signifier only pointed the way back to the integral significance.

There were twenty-six rehearsals, sixteen run by Nemirovich, ten by Stanislavsky. This may seem a great improvement over Karpov's eight, but compared with the year-long rehearsals the MAT would later indulge in, it represents the rush to build a success.[62] They took place in the Hermitage, a small derelict music-hall in a Moscow pleasure garden

3 Act II of the Moscow Art Theatre *Seagull*, with Simov's setting for Act I reused. L.–r.,
Masha (Lilina), Arkadina (Knipper), Nina (Roksanova), Dorn (Vishnevsky),
Sorin (Luzhsky) and Medvedenko (Tikhomirov). The prompter's box indicates
that the troupe is still at the Hermitage Theatre.

with a shallow stage which did not allow for Stanislavsky's panoramic
ambitions.[63]

Many of his more daring and subtle ideas were necessarily compromised in production. To begin with, it was necessary to alter the conventional stage space, to prevent the actors from drifting down centre or on
to the apron, thus divorcing themselves from their surroundings.
Stanislavsky had envisaged the set-pieces as a blockade, to interrupt and
intervene in the movement. The designer, Viktor Simov, went for a
somewhat more naturalistic approach, turning the sets into living spaces,
albeit infused with a certain romanticism. Stanislavsky in his score had
tried to keep action moving on several planes at once; but owing to the
Hermitage's cramped stage and Simov's inexpertise at painting outdoors scenery, the director's three planes were reduced to two, upstage
and downstage. The same setting was used for Acts I and II, which was
convenient and economical, but played hob with Chekhov's symbolic
distinction between Treplev's turf, the overgrown park, and Arkadina's
domain, the manicured croquet lawn.

The lighting was similarly compromised. In Act I, the lunar disc shone through a canvas slit as if the moon were rising higher and higher, filtering through clouds.[64] Stanislavsky had wanted a lantern as well, but, having to plant the park downstage, Simov realized that such a light would show up the two-dimensionality of his plywood trees, and so he diffused his light in a traditional manner.[65] The glare of the footlights also vitiated Stanislavsky's intention of having the moonlight turn characters seated downstage into silhouettes. Prince Urusov would later complain that the red lighting at the start of Acts I and IV were "completely phoney," "dim and sinister," and prevented both visibility and audibility.[66]

The brighter lighting of Act II did in fact expose the crude daubs of Simov's landscape. (When Chekhov was asked if Simov had managed to create a good lake, he replied, "Well, it's wet."[67]) A similar schism between Stanislavsky's conception and Simov's realization gaped in Act III. The director had planned the set on a bias sloping away from the audience, the stage-floor littered with trunks and suitcases. The designer planted his scenery frontally and limited the clutter to a couple of travelling bags. (Stanislavsky would later get his obstacle course of valises in *The Cherry Orchard*.) For all that, the setting seemed so lived-in that it extracted a gasp from the spectators. Unlike the anonymous and elegant stage furniture at the Alexandra Theatre, organized for maximum symmetry and presentational value, these furnishings were tasteless in style and homely in configuration.

Recalling the play's reception at the Alexandra, the MAT directors knew that the play-within-a-play was a stumbling block to the audience's acceptance. "Here," Nemirovich emphasized, "the nervous tension of Treplev and Nina must dominate the pleasant mood of the others."[68] So from the very rise of the curtain, Stanislavsky's score emphasizes neurosis, and the word *nervously* recurs in regard to Treplev. His anxiety over the reception of his playlet was to serve as a lightning-rod for the Art Theatre's own jitters and the audience's uncertainty as well. I suspect that Stanislavsky may have shared a fellow-feeling with Treplev. In 1905, in his program for the Studio on Povarskaya Street, he expanded Treplev's line, "One must portray life as it is, and not as it ought to be, but as it appears in dreams" by writing "One must portray not life itself, as it flows in reality, but as we vaguely sense it in reveries, visions, moments of sublime uplift."[69] In 1905 this was a fashionable motto of the symbolists; but its sense was already apparent in Stanislavsky's work on *The Seagull* in 1898. The misprision that he is a "realist" is contradicted by his preference of *nastroenie* (what is intuited) over *byt* (quotidian trivia), or, more precisely, by his manipulation of *byt* to create *nastroenie*.

The critical moment was Nina's address to the World Soul, which had evoked such hilarity in Petersburg. Stanislavsky decided to prepare the spectators for it by displaying "Chinese shadows" of Nina through the stage curtain, and by scoring it to the everyday life of the estate: it was recited "to the accompaniment of croaking frogs – and shrieking land-rails."[70] Nemirovich preferred silence with the possible exception of a tolling bell, an amendment which Stanislavsky adopted. But he also justified his sound effects: "Bear in mind that I added frogs during the play within the play just to achieve complete silence. Theatrical silence is expressed not by soundlessness but by sounds. If the silence is not peopled by sounds, you cannot achieve the illusion."[71]

It was at this point too that he had the other actors turn their backs to the spectators, a directorial trick which had hitherto been associated with André Antoine's "slices of life." Stanislavsky had already employed this *mise-en-scène* in *Tsar Fedor*, but there it acted as a compositional element in the reproduction of a banquet scene from a famous painting. Here it was to serve a dual purpose in uniting both on-stage and off-stage spectators, to usurp the audience's initiative by monitoring its response through the planned reactions of Treplev's family and friends. Unfortunately, in production, the impression was ruined by the tableau having to be lit by the footlights; and even so enthusiastic an admirer as Prince Urusov objected to the daring innovation. "The actors hunch together in embarrassment, compelled to speak to one another askance, twisting themselves into profiles – otherwise, they can't be heard, – while their silhouettes, illuminated by the footlights, present no particularly attractive sight."[72] Stanislavsky would persist in future in turning his actors' backs to audience, to emphasize that the characters were living their own lives, divorced from the public's.

To live on stage, to be not actors but human beings, required a seamlessness in the usual relations between persons and objects. Stanislavsky, according to Nemirovich, "had a remarkable grasp of the boredom of the country-house day, the half-hysteric irritation of the characters, the tableaux of departure, arrival, an autumn evening, he knew how to fill the course of the act with appropriate objects and characteristic details."[73]

The operative phrase is "the course of the act": earlier playwrights, even Ostrovsky, had broken their acts into *yavleniya* or "French scenes," marked by the entrance or exit of major characters. Chekhov discarded this convention in *Seagull* and Stanislavsky sensed that the audience's attention must be rivetted at all points. The uninterrupted action was abetted by the close relationship between character and environment. The stage-set was not a backdrop for demonstrations of acting skill, but a correspondence, in the Baudelairean sense, with the characters' emotional states. Years later, the playwright Leonid Andreev would point out that the distinguishing feature of the MAT productions of Chekhov was what he called *panpsychism*: the imbuing of everything on stage, from a leading character to a cricket to a stove, with a soul.[74]

As Meyerhold explained it, the gist of Stanislavsky's treatment of Chekhov was

the poetic nervous system, the hidden poetry of Chekhov's prose. Before Stanislavsky, all they ever played in Chekhov was the plot, but they forgot that in his plays the sound of rain on the window-pane, the clatter of a bucket dropping, dawn peeping through the shutters, mist over the lake are indissolubly (as hitherto only in prose) connected with human behaviour, cooperate with people's actions. This was a real discovery at the time. [75]

Meyerhold believed that the MAT achieved this only in *The Seagull* and *Uncle Vanya*, and that their later Chekhov productions got shunted on to a siding of excessive naturalism.

Traditionally, curtains parted to reveal a fully lit stage, so that the audience could spectate without hindrance. Stanislavsky's score opened *The Seagull* in darkness,[76] set in relief throughout the act by the striking of matches by Medvedenko, Sorin, Treplev and Arkadina. At this period, unsmoked prop cigars were conventional tokens of a character's urbanity. Actual matches and cigarettes, whose smoke would waft across the footlights, went beyond realism to connect the audience sensually with the world on stage.

Originally, Stanislavsky had planned a continuous coming-and-going throughout Act III; but in rehearsal, he discovered this to be distracting and concentrated on three central *tête-à-têtes*: Arkadina and Sorin, Arkadina and Treplev, Arkadina and Trigorin. It was in this act that he began to compromise most between theatrical effectiveness and psychological truth. His note on Sorin's stroke was "Do this scene as realistically as possible to fool the audience. Play it so that they think Sorin has died. This will wring the audience's nerves and focus its interest on the goings-on on stage."[77] As Stanislavsky had hoped, the "realistic" conflict between the actress and her son was the first scene to be broken by applause. The departure at the end was organized as a Meiningen-style crowd scene, and some critics found that the slamming doors reminded them of a bedroom farce.

4 Simov's dismal and asymmetrical setting for Act IV of the Moscow Art Theatre
Seagull,. Compare this with the more traditional set-up at the Alexandra
Theatre, figure 8. L.–r., Dorn (Vishnevsky), Treplev (Meyerhold), Sorin (Luzhsky),
Polina (Raevskaya), and Masha (Lilina).

Act IV went all out in atmospherics of rain and wind, with
Stanislavsky adding pauses to make the sound effects more conspicuous.
Throughout his score, he had amplified pauses and silences, timing them
from five to fifteen seconds: this enabled the auditors to sense that there
was something behind the seemingly banal dialogue and enabled the
actors to find for themselves an inner justification. Every act curtain rose
and fell to a pause of ten to fifteen seconds to give a feeling that life goes
on. Nina's parting speech was scored to the whistling of the wind after
she has opened the French doors, and once she was gone, "Treplev
remains immobile 15 seconds, then drops the glass from his hands."[78] His
decision to commit suicide was taken during the lengthy pause, and the
director left it to the actor to work this out.

Simov's setting for the last act came closest to the score's requirements: the kind of room in which, Olga Knipper recalled, "you wanted
to wrap yourself in a shawl."[79] In this cold and empty space, the only
note of cosiness was Treplev's workroom down left. The correspondence
of characters and objects was apprehended by many of the reviewers.
The censorious *Moscow Leaflet* (*Moskovsky listok*) recognized with distaste
that "one could feel in the characters' deportment, their movements,
their words, every sound of their voices a forlornness and morbidity that

bordered on madness. The wind whistling in the flues, the slow measured tolling of a church-bell, the semi-darkness that prevailed on stage,
the sound of a gunshot with which the play's hero ends his stage life
harmonized with this in tone."[80] The critic Sergey Glagol recorded more
enthusiastically: "Evening. Outside an autumn wind is blustering and
howling at the windows . . . A little fire flickers in the fireplace. They play
lotto and the calling out of the numbers is audible . . . According to theatrical cliché the characters ought to rant and rave, but here their function is carried out by the elements: wind and fire." The protracted
pauses, since they were filled by these elements, did not interrupt the
action but moved it on, interweaving the dialogue with the voice of
nature. "In some scenes . . . the characters are silent for a few minutes,
whch may seem almost a non-dramatic heresy, shattering the most elementary technique of works meant for the stage . . . In life sometimes
people are silent for hours on end, and this silence often has a most profound meaning."[81] The usual theatrical "let's get on with it" had been
replaced by real time.

One of the Art Theatre's greatest admirers, Nikolay Éfros, described
the conveyance of meaning beyond dialogue:

Once you'd seen it, you never forgot the deep grief, the eerie, almost horrible
feeling that echoed in your soul from those wordless, almost automatic waltz
turns that Masha made, and indeed all its hopelessness, accompanied by
Kostya's music drifting in from the next room. She simply went and spun round
a few times at a waltz tempo. That's all . . . And never had her maimed life been
so painful as in those seconds of no dialogue.[82]

Stanislavsky, for all his adherence to "truth," was still a fond adherent
of stage effect. Four times in his score Nina's narrative of her tragic fate
was broken by loud laughter from the next room. "This is a very crude
effect," he admitted, "but it works on the audience. Of course I don't
insist on it." The tolling bell from Act I was repeated when she recited
the soliloquy: "This effect is not high quality either!!!" Treplev's dropping a glass from his hand is characterized as "Just a little stage effect!!!"
And at the very end, Stanislavsky marked a slight pause to precede
Dorn's revelation of Treplev's suicide, "in order to put the audience on
edge."[83] Suspense was stretched to the utmost at the moment when
Chekhov wanted the curtain to be already on its way down.

Although the first-nighters were still somewhat confused during Act I
and *The Seagull's* success was still in doubt following the play-within-the-
play, the more sensitive spectators grasped from the onset "a special,
mournfully poetic something which gripped the heart . . . an undefin-

able, extra-verbal, possibly musical, but definite *power* issued from the stage," according to Boris Zaitsev.[84] Another writer, Tatyana Shchepkina-Kupernik, forgot from the first moments that she was in a theatre, as if it were "living life – and we were all watching it by chance."[85] For the first time, the audience of intellectuals and profession-als were seeing the "way we live now" subjected to the same careful reproduction that had hitherto been lavished only on the past. "Every scene was a genre painting, full of splendour and beauty," wrote the lawyer Konovitser.[86] During the intermissions, as expectation became more and more heightened, the audience walked about with "the strange face of birthday boys and girls, and at the end (for heaven's sakes, I'm not joking) it would have been entirely possible to go up to some lady you didn't know at all and say, 'So? How do you like the play, eh?'"[87]

After Dr. Dorn's last line, another lawyer wrote, "I was beside myself. I had never experienced such a daring ending! And for a long time I remained alone in my seat half-oblivious when the lights went out . . ."[88] At the fall of the final curtain, there was a long pause and then a tumultuous ovation. Even the ordinarily buttoned-up Éfros leapt on to his seat and shouted that a telegram of congratulations be sent to Chekhov. The success of both the play and the theatre was confirmed, and by the next day ticket-scalpers were at work. Chekhov's friends inun-dated him with descriptions of the performances. Nemirovich-Danchenko was rapturous:

Not a word, not a sound was lost. The audience was touched not only by the general atmosphere, not only by the story [. . .] but by each thought, by every-thing which is you, you the artist, you the thinker, everything, in short, every psychological movement, – the audience was got at and seized by the throat. [. . .] The general tone is staid and extremely *literary*. They listened to the play in an astonishing fashion, as never a play has been listened to before.[89]

A less partial witness, Prince Urusov, asserted, "People will write about *The Seagull* when we are long gone . . . At times it seemed as if life itself spoke from the boards – and a theatre can give nothing greater than that!"[90]

The consensus was that the acting honours were borne off by Mariya Lilina (Stanislavsky's wife) as Masha, Iosofat Tikhomirov as Medvedenko and Olga Knipper as Arkadina. Although too young for the part, Knipper's simpering and histrionic Arkadina constituted a cri-tique of the professional stage. Meyerhold's Treplev, which Nemirovich had shaped to be "tender, touching, an obvious degenerate,"[91] was praised for his fire, though some believed he rather overdid the sulphurous element. Most conservatives felt, indeed, that the entire production smacked of "morbidity," for the directors meant to aggravate the pain of living and turned "all the characters into abnormal, psychologically deviant individuals," and the stage "into a consulting room for mental patients. One feels in the movements of the characters in action, in their deportment, in each of their words, in each of the sounds emitted, how lost they are; their abnormality touches on madness . . . The actors obey the intent indicated by the directors, which is why their personalities were totally effaced."[92] In other words, characters rather than star turns had filled the stage.

The Dorn of Chekhov's boyhood acquaintance Vishnevsky was thought to be too much the traditional *raisonneur*, full of "fake-art . . . an absence of that hypnotic sincerity, which is all that can reconcile a spectator with the basic phoniness of stage productions."[93] He could not efface the memory of Pisarev in the role at the Alexandra. Nemirovich had originally wanted Stanislavsky, "a wonderful technical actor," for Dr. Dorn, the "one character who demands more experience and control";[94] it was the provincial tragedian Darsky, who had played Shylock with a Yiddish accent for the Art Theatre, who was first cast as Trigorin. Darsky's professional habits proved inimical to the MAT, and he left the company. When Stanislavsky had to assume Trigorin, Vishnevsky was assigned Dorn. The reviewers and Chekhov's friends alike agreed that Stanislavsky failed to understand his role: he presented a smooth operator, a confident seducer, with none of the self-effacing irresolution Chekhov had intended. He displayed no writer's temperament although in places he seemed to be imitating Chekhov. One correspondent described him as "slapdash" (*tyamty-lyampty*), and went on to describe Mariya Roksanova's Nina as too angular, devoid of "that sinuous line which constitutes the splendour of art."[95]

The inexperienced Roksanova, a student of Nemirovich who dubbed her "a little Duse," was artificial and mannered, and would leave the troupe in 1902. For all of Stanislavsky's care, and Simov's providing a small stone pedestal for Nina's monologue to suggest a sculptural aspect, laughs were still heard at that point on the Art Theatre's opening night, because Roksanova whined and sobbed and made even the most well-intentioned spectator hard put to control himself.[96]

Preconditioned by these opinions, Chekhov was to share them when he eventually beheld a performance privately got up for him at the International Theatre. In addition to being too elegant and formal, he complained that Stanislavsky's Trigorin "dragged along the stage like a paralytic,"[97] and prescribed an injection of sperm to cure his impotence. With memories of Komissarzhevskaya still fresh, he had nothing good to say about Roksanova; her interpretation was not helped by the fact that Stanislavsky had cut her line "I am a seagull. No, that's not it. I'm an actress. Yes, that's it." Appalled by the pacing, Chekhov insisted that they end the play with Act III. "I refuse to let you to do Act IV."[98]

The author's carping was the only sour note in a chorus of hosannas. The painter Levitan, who saw a later performance on a scalped ticket bought at twice the official price, wrote to Chekhov:

Only now did I understand [the play]. In the reading it made no especially pro-found impression on me. But here, remarkably, carefully rehearsed, lovingly staged, organized down to the slightest detail, it makes a great impression. How am I to tell you, I've not yet recovered – all I'll say is, I experienced the most sublime artistic moments when watching *Seagull*. That same sorrow emanates from it as emanates from life when you scrutinize it closely. Very, very fine. Even the audience, our audience – the audience at Aumont's and Korsh's, – grasped that, and finds itself in the grip of a real work of art. As for the director's finesse one can only offer heaps of thanks. The few rough spots are insignificant. It wouldn't have been staged like this at the Maly. Your play evokes the liveliest interest, that's clear . . . [99]

Levitan's remark about the nature of the audience is telling. The public at Aumont's and Korsh's were well-intentioned, middle-class and educated, but not necessarily the *intelligentsia*, those with serious, pro-gressive interests in social and artistic concerns. If the general public responded to Chekhov, clearly a breakthrough had been made. But the Art Theatre actors considered themselves members of the *intelligentsia*; unlike the average professional, who had been narrowly devoted to career after leaving elementary school, they had been to gymnasia and conservatories and came from respectable family backgrounds. Their lack of technique was compensated for in *The Seagull* by a *sovuchnost* or re-ciprocity of feeling with its characters.[100] They and the author spoke the same language, as Nemirovich was to recall four decades later: "When we first played Chekhov, we were all 'Chekhovians'; we carried Chekhov within us, breathed with him the same enthusiasms, cares, thoughts."[101]

In turn, the MAT productions of Chekhov, beginning with *The Seagull*, nurtured the audience its founders had hoped for: teachers, doctors, university students and land reformers. The day of *The Seagull*'s premiere, there were merely six hundred rubles in the box-office; the next summer, Shchepkina-Kupernik saw the square in front of the Hermitage Theatre jammed with

people, chiefly young people, students, coeds, who had spent all night there –
some in comfort on folding chairs, others with a book and a lantern, some gath-
ered in groups, dancing, some warming themselves – life seethed in the square –
so that in the early morning they could get tickets and then run off to work,
undisturbed by a sleepless night [102]

This response was what Chekhov had in mind when he wrote to Olga
Knipper, "I'm of the opinion that your theatre ought to stage nothing
but modern plays, exclusively! You should deal with contemporary life,
the same life the intelligentsia lives and which goes untreated in other
theatres in the fullness of their non-intelligence and partially their lack of
talent."[103]

The Seagull was, in Vishnevsky's words, the "to be or not to be of the
Art Theatre."[104] Its success diverted the Art Theatre from its aim of
staging spectacular versions of the classics and led it to examine modern
life. Stanislavsky always regarded *The Seagull* as the most integral and
poetic of his Chekhov productions.[105] As Gnedich predicted in *New
Times*, the rehabilitation of *The Seagull* was "a pledge of a bright future
not only for one particular theatre but for the Russian theatre in general.
Work in the theatre has entered a new phase . . . – the first step has been
taken."[106]

CHAPTER 3

Moscow nights (The Moscow Art Theatre 1898–1905)

> So long as the pre-Chekhovian theatre tried to produce
> Chekhovian drama by its methods, Chekhov remained on the
> periphery of theatrical practice. Only when the Chekhovian actor
> or, more accurately, the Chekhovian *ensemble* came on stage could
> the problems of revealing Chekhov in the theatre be solved.
>
> Pavel Gaideburov[1]

UNCLE VANYA

However indebted the Moscow Art Theatre may have felt towards
Chekhov, the gratitude was not wholly reciprocal. Although the success
of *The Seagull* had restored his faith in his playwriting abilities, Chekhov's
wariness about commitment and his dissatisfaction with the playing of
Stanislavsky and Roksanova kept him from naming the theatre his
official interpreter. He had been regularly solicited by the Moscow Maly
Theatre to provide plays for actresses' benefits, and in February 1899 its
newly appointed chief stage director A. M. Kondratev asked him "most
humbly" to be allowed, the following season, to stage *Uncle Vanya*,
Chekhov's recension of *The Wood Demon*. All the actors of the Maly,
Kondratev asserted, appended their pleas as well.[2]

Chekhov complied, and the play was entrusted to Sumbatov-Yuzhin,
a believer in Chekhov's talent who nevertheless felt that his internalized
style demanded "a different kind of acting." The MAT considered
Sumbatov its enemy because he constantly condemned "fads" in art and
championed the independence of the actor's individuality over the
director's demands.[3]

Since the Maly was a State theatre, all repertorial decisions were
entrusted to an official committee, whose decisions had to be unanimous
if a play were to be accepted for performance. In 1899 the committee
was made up of four members: two professors from Moscow University,
Sumbatov, and Nemirovich-Danchenko, who, from the time of the

MAT's founding, served without pay. The committee's president vetoed *Uncle Vanya*, because he found the gun fired at Professor Serebryakov offensive. So Sumbatov, who had privately rejoiced over the way Chekhov had nailed "the academic philistines,"[4] proposed that the Administrator of the Moscow Imperial Theatres, who had the right to produce a work whatever the committee's decision, sponsor *Uncle Vanya*. The Administrator agreed but Chekhov himself, exasperated by what he considered niggling criticisms, protested at the cuts he was still required to make in Vanya's denigration of Professor Serebryakov.

The Administrator then appointed Sumbatov president of the committee, charged with investigating the matter. At a new session, Sumbatov voted for and both professors voted against *Vanya*; the absent Nemirovich turned in his resignation two days later. Nemirovich's resignation helped him avoid charges of conflict of interest, for in a week *Uncle Vanya* was in rehearsal at the Art Theatre.

Unchastened by his failure with *The Seagull*, Evtikhy Karpov also entered the scrimmage and tried to solicit *Vanya* for the Alexandra, particularly because Komissarzhevskaya was eager to play Sonya.[5] Agreeing to this, Chekhov also suggested Ge or Samoilov for Astrov (a part Samoilov had already played in the provinces), the romantic tragedian Gorev as Vanya, Sazonov who had been so bad as Trigorin as the Professor (a sardonic suggestion) and Davydov as Waffles (an inspired piece of casting).[6] In reply, Karpov explained that Gorev and Ge were hopeless. "A lot of thought will have to be given to those roles . . . What do you think about Davydov for Uncle Vanya and Sazonov for Astrov? Write me very frankly."[7] Chekhov assented, but was less sanguine about the "insignificant cuts" Karpov requested. While this parley was going on, however, Petersburg audiences got to see their first *Vanya* on the amateur stage. On Davydov's initiative, the "Society for Artistic Reading and Music" staged an unadvertised *Uncle Vanya* on 8 January 1900 in a small auditorium. Its success led the Society to plan a revival.

Neither this revival nor the Alexandra production ever took place, for by then the Moscow Art Theatre's *Uncle Vanya* had opened to acclaim (26 October 1899). Nemirovich reported in detail to Chekhov that the production had "considerable importance to the existence of my theatre. [. . .] I viewed the performance less as a director than as the founder of a theatre mindful of its future."[8] As Nemirovich hoped, Chekhov came to acknowledge the difference between Karpov's hackwork and the Art Theatre's dedication; he gave the exclusive rights to *Vanya* to Nemirovich, who immediately informed the Administrator of the

Imperial Theatres of his monopoly. Karpov called Nemirovich a dog in the manger, for, like many in the theatrical establishment, he considered the MAT a passing fad.

Nemirovich's nimble moves had brought Chekhov the playwright one step closer to becoming the Art Theatre's house dramatist. Although textual scholars are reasonably sure that Chekhov wrote *Vanya* prior to *The Seagull*, in many ways the former is the more innovative play. The melodramatic entanglements of *The Wood Demon* have been transmuted into subtler inter-relationships, the external events into internal developments. The actress who shared the role of Sonya with Lilina recalled that when, in a rehearsal of Act III, she knelt at the words, "Papa, one must be merciful," and kissed Serebryakov's hand, Chekhov intervened.

You mustn't do that, this really isn't a drama. The whole meaning and the whole drama of a person is internal, and doesn't exist in external phenomena. There was drama in Sonya's life before this point, there will be drama after it, but this is a mere incident, an aftermath to the shooting. And even the shooting is not a drama but an incident.[9]

In these "scenes from country life," the focus has shifted from intrigues to a more evocative portrayal of a symbiotic group and to what Osip Mandelshtam was later to call the "propinquity" that binds them together.[10]

Chekhov felt comfortable in an advisory capacity during *Vanya*, and lavished advice on Olga Knipper on how to play Elena: the doctor is infatuated by her beauty, but he is not the love-sick lunatic Stanislavsky was enacting, and he knows in Act III that Elena is leaving forever. Meyerhold was not cast in *Vanya* (he later played Astrov in the provinces), but he assured Chekhov that the feeling prevailed among the actors that "playing a Chekhovian person is as important and interesting as playing Shakespeare's Hamlet."[11] Type-cast again in a neurotic part in Hauptmann's *Lonely Lives*, Meyerhold consulted Chekhov on his interpretation. Among his perceptive comments on how to convey anxiety on stage, Chekhov remarked, "nowadays almost every civilized person, even the most healthy, experiences such irritation nowhere so much as in his own home, his own family, for the discord between present and past is felt first and foremost in the family."[12] These comments could also apply to the domestic malaise of *Vanya*.

There is no indication that family jars were uppermost in Stanislavsky's mind as he created his stage-plan for *Vanya*. Rather, he attempted to reproduce, through naturalistic means, a general ambience of petty provincial futility. His epigraph for his score read: "Verily life *per se* is stupid, boring (a Chekhovian phrase – emphasize)." Unlike that for *The Seagull*, this score was packed with prop lists, for the characters were to be weighed down by the impedimenta of routine. Nemirovich had to prevent Stanislavsky from filling the first act with the continuous swatting of mosquitoes, meant as insect embodiments of life's niggling aggravations.

"Uncle Vanya is a sniveller; Astrov is a whistler" was Chekhov's typically laconic instruction. Originally, Vishnevsky was to play Astrov, and Stanislavsky Vanya; only after the roles were switched did Nemirovich find the forward gear for the play. Stanislavsky did not conceal a streak of cynicism in Astrov, but he also brought to the role a poetic sensitivity and chivalric restraint. With a couple of strokes, "he made one feel a secret element, dangerous forces of the will, dormant in the tipsy country doctor." Knipper later said she always felt sorry that Elena didn't run off with him.[13]

Vishnevsky's Vanya disappointed, but praise was lavished on the lyricism of Lilina's Sonya. Knipper's Elena was less successful; on opening night, overcome with stage-fright, she seemed to be reciting her lines. Many felt that Vasily Luzhsky caricatured the Professor, playing him with a Heidelberg accent, an affectation of certain faculty members of Moscow University.

Nikolay Éfros later adjudged *Uncle Vanya* to be the MAT production that best wed the poetry of Chekhov's text to its scenic expression. Certainly, most contemporaries found that *Vanya* presented a stronger illusion of real life than *Seagull* had. A letter to Chekhov from a doctor of medicine reveals the remarkable reverberations the production drew from the intelligentsia. Deeply impressed by the last scene, he attempted to analyze its charm.

The real point, in my opinion, is the tragic quality of these people, the tragic quality of these ordinary routines which now fall back into place, fall back forever and forever shackle these people. And the real point is also that the fire of talent can light up the life and soul of the simplest, most ordinary people. Every street teems with these simple people, and everyone contains a portion of such an existence. And so, when I saw that last scene, when everyone has left, when the most endless routines go on with crickets, ledgers, etc. I felt almost physically ill – and I personally took it very much to heart. I felt as if as if everyone were leaving me, as if I were sitting and doing accounts . . . [14]

Though the white-collar class discovered its own malaise reflected so authentically, Chekhov and the Art Theatre still remained caviare to the general. Another correspondent informed Chekhov: "The play is too

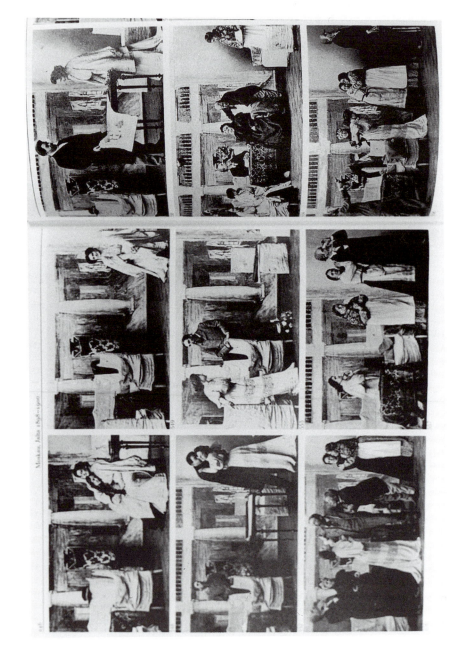

intellectual for the average audience, the masses, they can hardly come up to it."[15]

In fact, long before *Uncle Vanya* was played in the capitals, it had been produced in the provinces, and there, as Maksim Gorky testified, for all the play's power, audiences failed to respond. Gorky had seen *Vanya* at the Nizhny Novgorod Dramatic Theatre in 1898, when he

wept like a female, though I'm far from being a nervous type, I went home stupefied, shattered by your play, I wrote you a long letter and tore it up. One can't clearly express what this play calls up in one's soul, but I felt as I watched its characters as if I were being sawn in half by a dull saw. Its teeth go straight to the heart, and they make the heart clench, groan, cry out. I feel it to be something terrible. Your *Uncle Vanya* is an entirely new form of dramatic art, a hammer you use to beat on the empty pate of the public. And yet they remain unscathed in their obtuseness and fail to understand you either in *The Seagull* or *Uncle Vanya*. Will you go on writing plays? You do it wonderfully!

In the last act of *Vanya* when the doctor, after a long pause, mentions the heat in Africa, I started to tremble in admiration of your talent, and in fear of the people, of our colourless, beggarly life. How wholesomely you have struck at their soul and how accurately! You have an enormous talent. But, listen, what do you think you've achieved by such strokes? Will the people be cured by it? [. . .] I am far from being a virtuous person, but I howled as I watched Vanya and company, although it's very stupid to howl, and even stupider to mention it. You know, it struck me that in this play you are a cold devil to people. You are

---

5 *Uncle Vanya* at the Moscow Art Theatre, 1899. Like many theatres, the MAT issued postcards illustrating its productions: this sequence shows the course of Act III. In order of appearance: Olga Knipper as Elena, Mariya Lilina as Sonya, Stanislavsky as Astrov, Vishnevsky as Voinitsky, Luzhsky as Serebryakov, Raevskaya as Mariya Vasilievna, Artem as Telegin and Samarova as Marina. Note the painted drops and the rather shallow staging.

1. ELENA ANDREEVNA You have lovely hair.

2. ELENA ANDREEVNA (*alone*) . . . sometimes he comes here, not like the others, handsome, interesting, attractive, just like the moon shining through the dark . . .

3. ASTROV I don't suppose this interests you much.

4. ELENA ANDREEVNA (*not seeing Voinitsky*) Spare me... let go of me.

5. VOINITSKY I saw it all, Hélène, all...

6. SEREBRYAKOV I have invited you here, my friends, to inform you that we are about to be visited by an Inspector General...

7. VOINITSKY You ruined my life! I haven't lived, haven't lived! Thanks to you I wasted, destroyed the best years of my life! You're my worst enemy.

8. SONYA You must be forgiving, papa! Uncle Vanya and I are so unhappy!

9. VOINITSKY Where is he? Ah, there he is! (*Shoots at him.*) Bang!

(These are 9 images from a series of 11 covering Act III.)

indifferent to them as snow, as a blizzard. Forgive me, I am perhaps mistaken, in
any case I am voicing only my personal impression . . . [16]

After Gorky had had the chance to see *Vanya* staged at the Art
Theatre, his admiration shifted somewhat from the play itself to the
players. When he took up his pen again, he was less adulatory of the
author's work, more circumstantial about the production. Discounting
the misinterpretations of Vishnevsky and Stanislavsky, he praised
Knipper, Lilina and even Grigorev as the farmhand. "In general this
theatre produced on me the impression of a substantial, serious business,
a major concern."[17]

Uncle Vanya confirmed the Art Theatre in the path it had taken after
The Seagull. The gradual merging of Chekhov's achievement with
Stanislavsky's in the public mind, even its eventual effacement by the Art
Theatre's accomplishments, had begun. "From this point on,"
Stanislavsky was to assert, "our destiny was in the hands of Anton
Pavlovich: if he gave us a play, we had a season; if he did not, the theatre
lost its peculiar aroma."[18]

THREE SISTERS

Chekhov, anxious to finish some short stories, did give the MAT nothing
for the next season, a dearth the theatre regarded as a calamity. He did
have a drama in mind, but played cat-and-mouse, stringing the theatre
along as he worked out the play to his own satisfaction. Chekhov's
growing attachment to Olga Knipper and the Art Theatre's solicitation
of a play written "to order" eventuated in *Three Sisters*, whose large cast
and elaborated ensembles derive directly from Chekhov's awareness of
who would be playing what. "What a role there is for you in *Three Sisters*,"
he teased Knipper. "Ah, what a role! If you give me ten rubles, I'll let you
have it, otherwise somebody else gets it."[19] The very title indicates the
move away from a single protagonist to a drama of collocation with
opportunities for elaborate genre pictures.

Chekhov's technique had grown more complex since *Uncle Vanya*, an
increase in artistic sophistication that had not been matched by a similar
evolution of the Art Theatre's abilities. More accustomed now to theatrical practices, he was edgy at having to convey his desires at a distance
and decided to attend the rehearsals. "I cannot abandon four important
female roles, four young women of the intelligentsia, to [Stanislavsky] for
all his talent and his understanding."[20] His misgivings were well founded.

When, on 29 October 1900, he finally read *Three Sisters* to the assembled company, they were baffled. "Some called it a drama, others a tragedy, without noticing that these labels embarrassed Chekhov [. . .] The play-wright was convinced he had written a merry comedy, and in the reading everyone took the play to be a drama, wept as they listened."[21]

This version was never performed. From late October to early December 1900, Chekhov came to the theatre almost every night and took an active hand in correcting what he saw as errors. He rewrote the first two acts, spoke in more detail about the characters' traits and even insisted on the presence of an army colonel to make sure the actors would not caricature military deportment. He also enthusiastically orga-nized the sound effects for the town fire. He vetoed Stanislavsky's plan to have Natasha in Act II slam doors and peer under the furniture for bur-glars, believing that a straight nonstop cross from stage right to stage left was far more bloodcurdling.

Wintering in Nice, Chekhov revised the last two acts substantially and posted them back to Moscow. Only after Chekhov's departure from Russia did Stanislavsky write his directorial score. Knipper became an intermediary, conveying Chekhov's wishes to the directors, who often took issue with the author. However, by correspondence Chekhov could affect only matters of detail and not the overall vision, so, for all his tactful admission that the Art Theatre attained the essential in his plays, a gulf yawned between his intentions and the director's concept.

At first, the play in rehearsal, Stanislavsky recalled, "had no reso-nance, no life, seemed long and boring."[22] Not until he recognized the need to stress joy and laughter, the characters' velleities rather than their realities, did the play begin to work. Meyerhold, who was playing Tusenbach, jotted down in a notebook the basic motifs of Stanislavsky's concept:

Longing for life.
Call to work.
Tragic quality against laughable [background] comedy.
Happiness as future destiny.
Work. Loneliness.[23]

Still, for all his insistence on stiff upper lips, Stanislavsky could not help bedewing the play with tears and sobs, mournful faces and meaningful glances. He later confusedly tried to explain: "We understood one thing: the play needed sadness and affliction. We attain this sadness by means of laughter, since three quarters of the play rests on laughter. For the audience, however, there was no laughter, the play emanated an appalling sorrow."[24]

He organized the play on a rhythmic plan. "The first act, joyous and alert; the second, a Chekhovian atmosphere; the third, terribly nervous; to be played rapidly on the rhythm and the nerves; at the end, strength is broken and the rhythm subsides."[25] What he meant by a Chekhovian atmosphere was the contrast of chilly night and cosy room, a symphony of sound effects from snowflakes pattering on the windowpane to a distant accordion and a mouse squeaking under the sofa. The last act, like the first in *The Seagull*, was held together by nervous tension and anxiety. The final tableau of the three sisters was to be foreshadowed in each of the previous acts.

For the first time in a score for Chekhov, Stanislavsky felt free not merely to illustrate but to supplement the author; his copious stage directions swelled the play into a novel, with specifics both descriptive and psychological. If *The Seagull* and *Vanya* contained some details from everyday life that were more naturalistic than atmospheric, in *Three Sisters* these details, and in particular the scoring for sound effects, were meant to configure the spiritual life of the characters.[26] Stanislavsky still tended to confuse priorities, devoting as much attention to scenic trivia as to general atmosphere, in his belief that every detail had parity with every other. "How to do this mouse noise. Take a bunch of tooth-picks made from goose quills and run your hand over them."[27] He could not refrain from extraneous invention, and twice had Bobik's rubber ball bounce out of the house to be retrieved. At the same time, he prevented a misguided authorial intervention. Chekhov wanted Tusenbach's dead body to be carried by a crowd across the upstage area; Stanislavsky, more stage-wise, feared that a crowd of extras rumpling the backcloth would steal focus from the sisters downstage and vetoed this stage direction.

Nemirovich insisted on the need to bring ordinary life into the play, so Stanislavsky asked Simov to design a home not for a general's daughters but for a captain's. This reduction was symptomatic not only of his attempt to reach a wider audience, but of a desire to underline the ponderous pettiness of provincial life, to demonstrate how what Wordsworth calls "the dreary intercourse of daily life" could become hostile. An alien spirit of vulgarity incarnated in Natasha with her veneer of wholesomeness and her inner vacuity intruded into the sisters' living-space and gradually usurped it. By the last act, the sisters, evicted from their comfortable home, sat on the sidelines, as if in a bivouac, loitering among falling leaves.[28] Natasha was the indispensable norm:

Stanislavsky saw her as an unconscious predator, a force of nature, as amoral, gradual and inevitable in her depredations as life itself. His directorial score stressed that she must be always affectionate, eager to avoid misunderstanding. Lilina, who based her look on her children's governess, played Natasha with a honeyed drawl, a deliberately careless walk, a cloying sweetness that was more appalling than any common scold could be.

When Nemirovich returned from consulting with Chekhov in Nice, he was surprised to find that Knipper's role as Masha and Margarita Savitskaya's as Olga had been recast with other actresses. Stanislavsky alleged that the original players did not suit the parts, especially in Act III, where Knipper delivered her "confession" in a tragic tone. Calling a special rehearsal, Nemirovich filled in Knipper and Savitskaya on the proper psychological impulses, and their roles were restored.[29] Knipper then tentatively built up Masha, a process that can be followed step by step in her correspondence with Chekhov.

Stanislavsky says that I make the role too dramatic. You understand, the role still hasn't come to a second boil. The bone of contention with Nemirovich is the third act, Masha's confession. I want to do the whole act nervously, by fits and starts, which means the confession should be powerful, dramatic, the gloom of surrounding circumstances gains the upper hand over the joy of being in love. Nemirovich prefers this joy of being in love, so that Masha, despite it all, is filled with this love and makes her confession not as a criminal. Act II is full of this love. In Nemirovich's interpretation, act four is the climax, in mine it's act three.[30]

She was right in terms of her role; he was right in terms of the curve of the play. Masha was to become her most deeply felt part, noted for its avidity for life, a repudiation of resignation which liberals and conservatives alike read as a protest against their society.

To meet Stanislavsky's demands for ordinary life, Simov brought in the most commonplace objects – a damask tablecloth, provincial wallpaper, yellowed painted floors, a threadbare Turkoman carpet, a cuckoo clock that was slow to strike and then counted out the time hurriedly, as if embarrassed. He strove to make the Prozorov microcosm seem claustrophobic and ramshackle, although he was not allowed to construct a low ceiling for Olga's bedroom because it prevented the cheap seats from seeing the action.

Such realism proved appealing to audiences, but it was a means towards another end. "All *this* life," Nemirovich insisted, "the life shown in this production was filtered through the world-view, feelings, tempera-

6 Simov's setting for Act III of *Three Sisters* at the Moscow Art Theatre, 1901. L.–r.,
Stanislavsky as Vershinin, Vishnevsky as Kulygin, Litovstev as Irina, Kachalov as
Tusenbach, Knipper as Masha. Far left, the portrait of the sisters' parents (posed
for by the actors who played Andrey and Olga) has been moved from the Act I
drawing-room to Olga's bedroom.

ment of the author. It received a special tinge, which is called poetry."[31]
To find the poetry within the everyday became the Art Theatre formula
for Chekhov. Stanislavsky's score was intentionally musical, and Gorky
was to describe the performance as "music, not acting."[32] To underscore
this musicality and bring out the eloquence of the dialogue, Nemirovich
wanted fine speakers: hence his insistence that Olga be played by
Savitskaya, who had acted Antigone. When Meyerhold left the
company, angered at not being made a shareholder, Tusenbach was
assigned to Vasily Kachalov, whose mellifluous tones became legendary.
Some felt that Meyerhold's hatchet-faced Tusenbach with his rasping,
restless manner was preferable; others had found him overly tragic. But
the replacement by Kachalov suddenly made Tusenbach full of *joie de*

vivre, and lent his speeches a more optimistic tinge. Making no effort to reproduce the traits of a russified Baltic German as Meyerhold (a russified Baltic German) had done, Kachalov concentrated on Tusenbach's poetic inner world. The result was to ennoble the inept baron.[33]

The fullest instance of this ennobling process could be seen in Stanislavsky's Vershinin. The part had first been given to Ivan Sudbinin, a recruit from Korsh's Theatre, but when he failed to make sense of it, it was handed to Kachalov, who had just entered the company. He was appraised and approved by Chekhov but thought too untried. Only as a last resort did Stanislavsky take it on. Connoisseurs were right to complain that Stanislavsky's Vershinin had little in common with Chekhov's hen-pecked carpet knight; he imbued the character with a vagrant charm and a military fatalism. His complaints about his home life and his wooing of Masha were set to the strains of Andrey's offstage violin. His speeches about the future were heartfelt efforts to give meaning to his dreary life. His feelings for Masha were permeated with purity, and their "tram-tam-tam" was a jubilant love song. Here, as with Astrov and later Gaev, Stanislavsky "reworked the modest score of the Chekhovian roles in such a lofty, monumental style that at moments he even made one believe in Chekhov's *power* – something which is probably not in Chekhov."[34] By his playing as much as by his staging, Stanislavsky aggrandized and exalted the Chekhovian repertory, which explains why imitative productions, which copied the true-to-life details but lacked this poetic grandeur, seemed so dull.

Three Sisters opened at the Art Theatre on 31 January 1901, and the fashionable first-nighters failed to make it the noisy success expected; on the second night, a more responsive audience was composed exclusively of the intelligentsia: "school-mistresses, coeds, university students, minor officials. The same public which is shown in Chekhov's plays."[35] As soon as tickets went on sale for the six remaining performances in the season, they were sold out in three hours.[36] With each successive performance, enthusiasm grew and soon it became the favourite play in the theatre's repertory. Even so, Olga Knipper felt the need to assure Chekhov: "Despite the abuse in the press, it's a success with the public,"[37] for of all the MAT's Chekhov productions, it was the only one savaged by the critics.

By this time it was clear that the Moscow Art Theatre was not a nine days' wonder, but a serious artistic enterprise that challenged the theatrical establishment. Now that Chekhov was closely associated with it, his playwriting and Stanislavsky's bright ideas were confused in the critical mind: it was not always clear where one began and the other left off. Given that the arts in Russia were highly politicized, and that the MAT was regarded as left of centre, the conservative press had little good to say about it or Chekhov. As Nikolay Éfros summed it up, on the morning after the play opened "most of the public learned that it hadn't liked *3 Sisters*"; Chekhov was accused of pirating himself, regressing, and stuffing his play with improbabilities.[38]

Even Chekhov's old friend Suvorin confided to his diary that he found it all boring and monotonous, except for Act I. He was bemused by the stage effects, among them

A battle of clocks, music, alarm bells, fiddlers and a singing girl, whom the yardman chases off with a broom to the delight of the audience. I scrutinized the audience. Nobody even thinks of weeping. The three sisters on stage weep, but there's not a bit of it in the audience. Everything on stage is rather trashy. [. . .] You are glad to leave the theatre, freed from the nightmare, from stupid and vulgar people, from trivia, from drunkenness, from petty vanity and betrayal. What a difference between these arid scenes with all their pretensions and the scenes of Gogol and Ostrovsky which also sketch petty people and petty passions. There it was all humanized by humour, here it's the opposite – the aridity dehumanizes, stupefies.[39]

The Art Theatre was liberal but far from radical; its social conscience resided mainly in Nemirovich, for Stanislavsky was essentially apolitical. Consequently, the most vehement attacks came from Marxists. Nikolay Rusanov likened the intellectual level of the play's characters to that of coral polyps in a reef, devoid of any awareness and barely sentient of their environment. Anatoly Lunacharsky in an article "On the artist in general and on certain artists in particular" called *Three Sisters* a decadent, harmful play, written to please the "Chekhovians"; not simply Natasha but all the characters personified *poshlost* or crass vulgarity. He saw Irina's and Tusenbach's desire to work as taking bread out of mouths of those who needed to work. In his opinion, Masha should have left home and followed Vershinin, since real people ought to "sacrifice their souls for the great cause." What real people do was irrelevant, declared Mikhail Olminsky in turn, for the play was devoid of realism: "such a prolonged and poorly motivated crying jag doesn't happen in real life." "The meaning of life is not the return of a paradise lost, but service to an unknown but radiant future."[40]

Absurdly out of proportion as these criticisms seem, it must be allowed that the Art Theatre had its own *parti pris*. As director and actor,

Stanislavsky tended to side with specific characters. Just as *The Seagull* had been staged as an unequal competition between the *Wunderkind* Treplev and the hack Trigorin, so the MAT's *Three Sisters* identified with the longings of Masha, Olga and Irina, and consequently ignored the character flaws that vitiated them. As for Natasha, an article in the *Moscow News* (*Moskovskie vedomosti*) offered an alternative view of her not as a vulgar termagant but as a good wife struggling with her husband's addictions to drink and gambling.[41]

Russian News (*Russkie vedomosti*, a newspaper which Lenin was to call tedious and pedantic) condemned the play as a mere sequence of scenes coagulating to produce a cheerless impression; but it granted that the play's poverty was saved by beautiful staging and acting.[42] Other critics found a way to damn with faint praise, by questioning whether such a pointless play was worthy of the Art Theatre's production values. A certain V. G. in the *Moscow News* attacked its "pitiful mediocrity" and "wretched phoniness": "Do they never feel pangs of conscience for so often using their extraordinary god-given talents not to raise, but to lower the artistic taste of the public, by passing off paste diamonds for the genuine article?"[43]

The very aspect of homely familiarity was attacked by some as indicative of the play's triviality, and by none more than Viktor Burenin. Burenin, a columnist at Suvorin's *New Times*, was a well-established playwright whose historical dramas made up in technical expertise what they lacked in originality. He stood for the reactionary theatre buff who thought Chekhov a poor dramatist because he did not provide the standard peripeteias, *scènes à faire*, strong curtain-lines and messages of the well-made play. Burenin attributed *The Three Sisters's* "stupid success" to publicity which "hypnotized the public and especially the younger element while obfuscating any wholesome meaning". "Chekhov," he declared, "is the minstrel of hopelessness."[44]

In *New Times* Burenin published *Nine sisters and not a single fiancé or Talk about Bedlam! A symbolic drama in 3 acts with mood* (1901). The opening stage direction, a shaft aimed at Stanislavsky's sedulous verism, goes on for pages and constitutes Act I in its entirety. After a very convincing rainstorm, the nine sisters, no muses they, enter "in matutinal house-coats, tousled and dishevelled, in down-at-heel slippers, their 'kissers' all made up, and deliberately cast from the worst possible actresses, so that 'realism,' 'truth,' and 'nature' will be all the greater." Burenin portrayed the dialogue as inarticulate sounds or unison recitation of "Lord, how boring-making and puke-making! [*Skuchishcha i toshchishcha!*] This is what

modern life in Russia is like!" In his no-nonsense view, Chekhov's sisters
were merely suffering from terminal virginity: a vigorous love life would
instantly dispel the vapours that assail them.[45]

The root cause of all this critical abuse was identified by the writer
Leonid Andreev, who, as "James Lynch," penned a couple of perceptive
essays on the play. In one, he intuited that what seemed to be questions of
art or theatre or even stage-directions concealed a reveille from social
torpor. The play's opponents were not only objecting to the notion that a
man of the theatre might be a herald of the future; they feared, correctly,
that the Art Theatre had turned into a symbol, "a banner, a principle,
that enigmatic but indispensable thing, *not in whose name*, but *under whose
cover* people fight for their own dearest interests." The theatre and its
management were hardly revolutionary, but what the factions reacted to
was a kind of camouflaged protest in "the most real Chekhovian dramas
[which] acted as involuntary transmitters of gaiety."[46]

Andreev admitted that the play's reputation as a "weepy" had made
him reluctant to attend; spectators left moaning hysterically "ach,
Knipper" and overdosing on sedative valerian drops. Yet halfway
through the first act

we stopped being spectators and we ourselves with our playbills and opera-
glasses turned into the characters of the drama. Never had any theatre reached
the height of ceasing to be a theatre as this one did. At times it even stopped
being artistic, for even art has boundaries beyond which it is transmuted into life
and absorbed as one of life's basic elements. The story of the three sisters,
related by Chekhov through the lips of the Art Theatre actors, is not a fiction or
a fantasy, but a fact, an event, something just as real as stock options at a savings
bank.[47]

Andreev's initial reaction of commiseration for the sisters turned, during
the following week, into a desire to take advantage of the life available to
him. The tragic theme song of *Three Sisters*, as he heard it, was the almost
painful wish to live. It was not pessimistic, but "a bright, wholesome
play."[48]

This brightness was dimmed by the "lachrymosity" *[plaksivnost]* which
Chekhov complained Stanislavsky had added to his work[49] and which
intensified over time. In 1905, a year of political agitation and reaction,
the production seemed to condense the tension in the Russian atmosphere. Four years later, Aleksandr Blok, who had dedicated a poem to
the play, returned home from a performance "shaken to the core . . . The
last act was played to hysterical cries. When Tusenbach went off to the
duel, the hysterics reached their climax. When the shot rang out, some

ten persons immediately screamed lachrymosely [*plaksivno*], disgustingly and fearfully, from dreadful tension, as only people in Russia can, in fact, scream. When Andrey and Chebutykin weep, lots of them weep, and I almost did too."[50]

The opportunity *Three Sisters* offered for self-indulgent grief made it the "most favourite, most widely attended and most deeply felt Chekhov play." Shchepkina-Kupernik told the author, "looking at it, you forget you're sitting in a theatre, but feel you're watching other people's lives."[51] The sense of real life was so vivid that prospective playgoers would propose "paying a call on the Prozorovs," rather than going to the theatre. Nemirovich always considered it the best rendering of Chekhov the MAT ever did, a Tolstoyan achievement on Stanislavsky's part.

THE CHERRY ORCHARD

Of all Chekhov's plays *The Cherry Orchard* was the most embroiled in misunderstandings between the author and the director. Chekhov, a forty-one-year-old invalid, now married to Olga Knipper, had settled permanently in Yalta, and the epistolary interchange between him and the Art Theatre chronicles the myriad instructions and explanations the play required. Ill health obviously exacerbated Chekhov's irritability, but at the same time, it is clear that Stanislavsky and Nemirovich, inflated by their former successes, felt that they understood better than he how his plays were to be staged.

For two years after *Three Sisters* opened, Chekhov wrote nothing for the theatre. Often bedridden, racked by tuberculosis, he concentrated on fiction, but in early 1901 the seed of an idea for a play germinated. The earliest intimation of a schism in interpretation came even before it was written. On 7 September Stanislavsky informed his sister, "He is writing a farce, this is a great secret. I can just imagine. It will be something impossible about the freakishness and vulgarity of life. I am only afraid that instead of a farce an ultra-out-and-out-tragedy (*ras-pro-tragediya*) will result again. Even now he seems to think that *Three Sisters* is an hilarious little joke."[52] And indeed, when Chekhov completed *The Cherry Orchard*, he informed Lilina, "It turned out not a drama, but a comedy, in places even a farce."[53] As soon as he had read the play, Stanislavsky protested to Chekhov: "It's not a comedy, nor a farce, as you wrote – it's a tragedy; whatever outlet into a better life you revealed in the last act. I can hear you saying: 'Excuse me, it really is a farce' . . . No, for an ordinary person it's a tragedy."[54]

Nemirovich, as usual, was more perceptive of the play's virtues: "The most remarkable act in mood, dramatic effect and cruel audacity is the last one, in grace and lightness the first one. What's new in your work is the clear, sunny and simple dramatic quality. The predominant note used to be lyricism, now it's true drama . . . In this respect a great step forward."[55] He noted not just the dramatic tension but a streak of cruelty, an element Gorky had already spotted, but which would not come to the fore in a Russian production until the 1960s.

Cross-purposes affected the casting. From the very inception, Chekhov had strong opinions on this score. Ranevskaya was intended to embody a credo he had once expressed to a friend: "The main thing is to be cheerful, not look at life so abstrusely; it's probably and in fact a great deal simpler."[56] He had originally envisaged Ranevskaya as an old woman, and, knowing that the MAT had no one to play her, he suggested that they recruit Olga Sadovskaya of the Maly, who specialized in Ostrovskian crones. She was not available, and in any case it was clear that the Art Theatre had no interest in hiring an outsider whose technique was rigidly presentational. "For three years," Chekhov chided Nemirovich, "I've been planning to write *C.O.* and for three years I've been telling you to engage an actress for the role of Lyubov Andreevna. Now you've been dealt a hand of solitaire that won't work out."[57] He rewrote the role for a younger actress, but fearing that Knipper might transmit traits of Arkadina to Ranevskaya, he still envisaged his wife in other parts, "silly little" Varya or the governess Charlotta.

Charlotta Ivanovna was conceived as a role of considerable thematic importance, requiring a comedienne. "Charlotta is a question mark. Muratova might be good, but not funny, It's a role for Mme Knipper."[58] When other actresses were suggested for Charlotta, Chekhov balked: "How glad I am that Khalyutina has got pregnant, and how sorry that it cannot happen to other players, for instance Aleksandrov or Leonidov. And what a pity Muratova isn't married!"[59] But ultimately Muratova played Charlotta and Olga Knipper took on Ranevskaya, a role that would be identified with her for the rest of her career.

Another crucial difference of opinion occurred over Lopakhin, arguably the closest thing to a protagonist in the play. Chekhov stressed the businessman's delicacy of spirit beneath his boorish exterior: "Lopakhin is the central role. If he doesn't work, the whole play will fail. Lopakhin must not be played as a loudmouth, he must not be the standard stage merchant. He's a sensitive man."[60] From the first, he had in mind Stanislavsky, the millionaire scion of a mercantile family sprung from peasant stock, who was fond of saying, "Our whole business developed because my great-grandfather once sold two sacks of peas."[61] Perhaps too mindful of these facts, Stanislavsky cast himself as the feckless *barin* Gaev whom Chekhov had planned for the suave Vishnevsky. "To my mind," the director explained to Chekhov, "Gaev must be as frivolous as his sister. He says whatever comes into his head. He notices it only after everything's been said. I think I have found the proper tone for Gaev. I've even managed to make him an aristocrat, although something of 'an old crackpot.'"[62] In later years, Stanislavsky complicated the character, but at the start he overdid the "aristocratic" element; the writer Ivan Bunin was annoyed at the way Stanislavsky's Gaev exhibited his "repulsive refinement" by cleaning his nails with a batiste handkerchief.[63] Stanislavsky also took a sentimental view of Gaev, making him more sensitive, less resilient than the script warranted. At the end, after Ranevskaya made her exit, this Gaev stayed on stage for a star turn, stuffing his ever-present hanky into his mouth to keep from sobbing, as he turned to reveal his broad shoulders heaving convulsively. Since Stanislavsky's Gaev was, as one observer states, "the tuning-fork by which the whole ensemble of *The Cherry Orchard* was attuned,"[64] such emoting unbalanced the delicate equipoise of the comedy.

Lopakhin was finally entrusted to a less talented actor, Leonid Leonidov, who, as Nikolay Éfros later remarked, played as if he and the character were standing next to one another.[65] Encouraged by the directors, Leonidov fell into all the traps of coarseness and overstatement that Chekhov had feared, with no complexity or underlying thought.

Chekhov had insisted that anyone could play Anya, so long as she was young, and he feared that Lilina, whom he saw as Varya, would make Anya "an old-fashioned girl with a high-pitched voice and nothing more."[66] In the event, thirty-eight-year old Lilina insisted on playing sixteen-year-old Anya, but for all her bouncy stride and breathless behaviour she was reminiscent of Arkadina's method of playing a girl in her teens ("as if on tiptoe"). Her "farewell, old life, greetings, new life," which demanded an instinctual optimism, was uttered in a histrionic tremolo.

Chekhov had insisted that Ranevskaya was not a hard part to play: "You must come up with a smile and a way of laughing, you must know how to dress."[67] Knipper, however, tended to idealize her characters and ornament them with "filigree" and attractive grace notes. Years later Stanislavsky would note that the salient element in her acting was "Sentimentality . . . [she is] just afraid of genuine healthy feeling taken from the bowels of nature, [and] prefers lesser but genteel feelings. [. . .] Knipper . . . adds a dose of sugar. That's why [her] laughter begins as a smirk, tears turn to coquettish lamentation or anger, feminine caprice, etc."[68] Knipper stinted on Ranevskaya's frivolity, indolence, and effortless charm, and emphasized her irritability. Chekhov's Ranevskaya is incorrigible and indomitable; Knipper, however, played up her love of homeland and played down her attraction to her lover in Paris. Since the actress pitied her character, so did the public.[69] Nemirovich objected to this as a basic misinterpretation and tried to correct it in his later Italian staging.

In returning to the genre of farce, Chekhov had intended to create a lighter, more intimate and compact play than *Three Sisters*. His earlier characters had been drawn from specific social milieux: artists in *The Seagull*, rural intelligentsia in *Uncle Vanya* and officers in *Three Sisters*. *The Cherry Orchard*, like a *commedia dell'arte* scenario, featured masters and servants.[70] We are no longer dealing with the fates of bohemians or siblings rebounding off one another, but rather with a ludicrously distorted reflection of the masters' vagaries in the servants' pretensions. Therefore, the casting of the employees was as crucial as that of the employers.

A subtle problem arose with Firs, who had been written by Chekhov with the actor Artem in mind. Chekhov detested any form of slavery, and the juxtaposition of the superannuated valet with the upstart footman Yasha was meant to contrast servility with lackeyism. Artem, an elderly writing-master, had already played Shamraev, Waffles and Chebutykin, and was a darling of MAT audiences, with a tendency to stereotype. Originally, Chekhov ended the second act with an enigmatic scene of non-communication between Charlotta and the old retainer, in which he tells a story of participating in a murder years earlier. Such a tale would help undercut the image of Firs as an "old dear," as Ranevskaya calls him. Stanislavsky felt the scene was too downbeat to conclude the act; he got Chekhov's agreement to cut Firs's anecdote and transfer Charlotta's autobiographical monologue to the top of the act, ending instead with the more "romantic" scene between Trofimov and Anya. This dislocation, combined with Artem's penchant for investing his roles with warmth and tenderness, put Firs out of kilter. When Chekhov eventually saw the MAT production, he wrote to his wife: "Ah, if only Muratova and Leonidov and Artem weren't in Moscow! Artem plays really vilely, but I just keep mum about it."[71]

Such basic disagreements stand behind Olga Knipper's later remark that "Work on *Cherry Orchard* was difficult, agonizing, I should say. No one could understand anyone else at all, the directors argued with the author."[72] Chekhov was interested in examining how human beings behave when caught up in an historic process. For him, the passage of time was a natural occurrence, an unalterable law to be accepted, no crueller than the change of seasons. Stanislavsky, however, understood the play as a tragic tale of changing eras and generations in the life of Russian society. However necessary change might be, when it forced people to destroy one another it was invariably cruel.[73]

The directorial and casting choices had a serious effect on the play's reception and the transmission of its meaning. In its early years the MAT never excelled at comedy; by displacing or omitting the troupe's few comic talents from primary to secondary roles, it diminished the play's farcical element. Then, by casting the strongest, most attractive actors in the roles of the improvident landowners, and relegating Lopakhin to a second-rater, the theatre effectually took sides in the debate and shifted the emphasis to make the plight of the dispossessed gentry the focus of concern. The audience's sympathy was to be pegged to Ranevskaya and Gaev from the outset, sacrificing Chekhov's ironic objectivity. Knipper established Ranevskaya as the play's centre, positioned between two new trends in Russian life: Lopakhin's practical materialism and Trofimov's idealistic reforms.[74] Such directorial leanings, later enhanced by the nostalgic retrospection of post-revolutionary émigrés, turned *The Cherry Orchard* into an elegy for a nest of gentry demolished by coarse "progress."

After playing the uncongenial role of Brutus in *Julius Caesar* every night, a weary Stanislavsky set about writing his directorial score in record time, dashing off the first act in a day. Ignoring Chekhov's insistence on a sense of richness and luxury, he called for a house in which "the floors creak" and plaster falls. Its layout reproduced his own beloved estate Lyubimovka.

Chekhov, by now familiar with Stanislavsky's fondness for sound effects, tried to head him off: "Haymaking goes on about June 20 or 25, I think by then the thrush has stopped singing, the frogs more or less shut up. Only the oriole is left . . . If you could present the train without any noise, without a single sound, go to it."[75] The same day he wrote to Knipper, "Konst. Serg. wants to drive a train through the second act, but I think I have to stop him. He also wants frogs and corncrakes."[76] Exasperated by the director's attention to circumstantial trivia, Chekhov complained to Nemirovich: "I kept the spectacular side of the play to a

7 *The Cherry Orchard* at the Moscow Art Theatre, 1904.
(a) Act I, l.–r.: Gaev addressing the bookcase (Stanislavsky), Yasha (Aleksandrov), Varya
(Savitskaya), Firs (Artem), Lopakhin (Massalitinov), Simeonov-Pishchik (Gribunin),
Ranevskaya (Knipper).
(b) Act II, l.–r.: Trofimov (Kachalov) and Anya (Lilina) in the romantic ending preferred
by Stanislavsky

(c) Act III, l.–r.: Stationmaster (Bulgakov), Pishchik, Lopakhin, Ranevskaya.
(d) Act IV, l.–r.: Charlotta Ivanovna (Muratova), Gaev, Varya, Yasha, Ranevskaya.

minimum, no special sets are needed and gunpowder doesn't come into it."[77]

In like manner, Stanislavsky regularly amplified Chekhov's own stage directions. Throughout Act II the characters swat mosquitoes, a piece of business first conceived for *Uncle Vanya*. When Ranevskaya says: "Come, come . . . My darlings. (*Embracing Anya and Varya.*) If only you both knew how I love you. Sit right next to me, that's right," the director glossed this as: "A kissing scene. They do not smack but slobber. – They moo, wheeze, catch their breath, and laugh . . . It ends of course with tickling and fighting. – Ranevskaya begins to defend herself with hay and towards the end slings it at them. They almost overdo it. General roars of laughter and affection." After the scene with the passerby, Stanislavsky intended to bring in a bevy of peasant girls coming back from mowing. "We see a group of women coming from the fields. Particoloured sarafans, erect rakes and shining tresses take shape sketchily on the horizon which has moved into the distance." And during Trofimov's monologue "we hear . . . a sound like a cart crossing sand – and on it a male voice sings, unexpectedly stops singing and urges on the horse, talks to it, then starts singing again, the horse whinnies. In the distance a dog barks in the village and two voices swear at it."[78]

Stanislavsky's fondness for proliferating "corroborative detail meant to give verisimilitude to an otherwise bald and unconvincing narrative" was carried to extremes. It was as if by this time he regarded himself not as the playwright's interpreter but as a collaborator, filling in the unspoken with subtext and creating a novelistic context rather than a dramatic background. His opening instructions for Act III go on for pages, sketching elaborate dance movements and inventing a host of new characters as party guests, including "a shop-assistant in a jacket and red tie, a very young boy (old lady's son), dancing with a tall, skinny daughter of the priest's wife," "the priest's wife, an old military man with his wife, an old lady in black," "a neighbouring overseer – an old, kindhearted German with a goatee and a pipe," "a woman sitting in the doorway watching the crowd," and more daughters for the priest's wife.

In the scene between Ranevskaya and Trofimov, the director has her "run to Petya, as in a French melodrama. She kneels before him, holding him by the hand as if seeking help. She has put her head on the table (still on her knees)." It wasn't enough that Chekhov has Lopakhin almost knock over a candelabrum. "Anton Pavlovich fearing crudeness wants to tone things down, so the candelabrum almost falls over. I think this is a half-measure. It would be better if the candelabrum falls and breaks, not on stage, but back in the salon."[79] Stanislavsky proposed ending the act this way:

Trofimov and Anya lead Ranevskaya upstage pursued by Lopakhin. In the salon the polka has changed to a kamarinska. We can hear the powerful trampling – and the trivial remarks of the dancers – the glasses tinkle from the trampling. We hear the voice of Lopakhin on a spree. In the billiard room, lively play. From the trampling in the empty drawing-room a small piece of moulding has broken off and dropped on to the floor.[80]

Meyerhold noted, "The secret of Chekhovian mood was hidden in the *rhythm* of its language . . . Had the Art theatre not caught the rhythm of Chekhov's works, had it not known how to recreate this rhythm on stage, it never would have achieved that second face which created its reputation as a theatre of mood; this was *its own* face."[81] However, the doleful mood distilled for the three earlier plays was not right for *Orchard*, where the rhythmic overlapping (*perepady*) of the actors altered the meaning of Chekhovian "mood." In lieu of the atmospherics of *The Seagull*, Stanislavsky opted for an overall pace embodied in the lines. His elegiac interpretation of *Cherry Orchard* led to the performance being played at the same tempo and rhythm throughout, serenely and unhurriedly.

Even though the Art Theatre saw the comedy as a "heavy drama," other notes were allowed to creep in. Chekhov gave *carte blanche* to Ivan Moskvin to make the accident-prone Epikhodov an even greater figure of fun than he is in the script; Moskvin, whose only previous Chekhovian role was Rodé in *Three Sisters*, provided *ad libs.*, malapropisms and mispronunciations ("livolver" for revolver, "cli-MATE"), off-key reprises of his songs, and elaborate business, such as stealing an apple from the buffet in Act III and tossing the core at Trofimov. After Chekhov's death he accrued as much tasteless comic business around the character as any clown in Shakespeare ever did with Hamlet's gravedigger;[82] but even then the English novelist Hugh Walpole could see in Moskvin's interpretation a "spirit imprisoned" within the clownish exterior. Watching Moskvin at the beginning of Act II, Walpole linked him with Knipper and Stanislavsky in Act III of *Three Sisters* for putting the audience "in the presence of an art that is so supreme, so apart from the art of any other country or any other period, that you have no terms of comparison with which to estimate it."[83]

At the premiere, 17 January 1904, Nemirovich called from the stage, "This theatre, Anton, is your theatre!"[84] By now, the MAT had registered its proprietary claim on Chekhov, and to most onlookers, its interpretation was the definitive one. The directors themselves were dissatisfied with their results, Stanislavsky referring to the opening night as "only a mediocre success and we reproached ourselves that we had not managed to demonstrate to the highest degree the importance, beauty and worth of the play."[85] Immediately after the celebratory opening and acclaim, Chekhov querulously voiced his own disappointment: "It's not right, not right . . . None of it: neither the play nor the production. I didn't manage to express what I wanted. I didn't see it quite right and they couldn't understand what I wanted."[86] Once back in Yalta, he stopped sharing the blame and laid it squarely on the Art Theatre; petulantly, he made the unreasonable observation that the fourth act "which must last 12 minutes maximum, goes on for 40 minutes with you."[87] To his wife he wondered: "Why on the posters and in the newspaper adverts is my play so persistently called a drama? Nemirovich and [Stanislavsky] positively see in my play something I did not write, and I am ready to take whatever oath you like that not once has either of them read my play attentively."[88] The stage history of *The Cherry Orchard* will unfold along these lines of divergence of opinion.

The critics observed a new element in the Art Theatre's treatment, a sense that the transparent fourth wall which used to let them spy on scenes from everyday life was now crowded out by a real microcosm. The characters and properties seemed to be scattered through space by the winds of time, especially in the last act when the stage was strewn with luggage and portraits stood on the floor with their backs to the wall. Of all Chekhov's plays, *The Cherry Orchard* has the most of what Vladimir Nabokov would call "homunculi": characters mentioned but never seen, an offstage world making the orchard all the more remote and isolated. Stanislavsky brought these phantasms on stage: both the *dramatis personae* and those only mentioned were given equal life. The critic Yuly Aikhenvald admired the

> chance nameless passerby with a tree-limb in his hand; he appears to the specta-
> tors for only a moment with unsure steps, with verses of Nadson and Nekrasov
> on his drunken lips, – but his face flashed before us a complete drama, a whole
> life, wasted, bitter, pitiful.[89]

In his estimation, all the characters breathed life and ought to be in reality as they were on stage.

Not every cultivated spectator approved of the Art Theatre's omniclu-sive realism. The Ukrainian art critic Nikolaev came to Moscow as if "I were going to Mecca" to see the eighth performance, and was struck by the already famous scenery, especially the Act II landscape which resembled a painting by Levitan.[90] But, Nikolaev pointed out, perspective has to be observed in a work of art, and proportion meted out to the figures, so that attention not be dissipated. In Stanislavsky's work, there was no foreground, middle ground or background, or rather, no secondary and tertiary characters. The burgeoning details were overdrawn and diverted the spectator from the main points.

The whole third act of the play is portrayed so that you cannot for a second concentrate and investigate carefully the subject being unveiled before you by the stage picture. All those dances, card tricks, recitations, games, all this kaleidoscopically changing bustle of a ball improvised on a country estate grips you with its striking picturesqueness, its striking likeness to reality, and, becoming its involuntary participant, you, as in reality, lose the ability to follow the changes in the interactive characters of the play, i.e., you lose the most substantial thing, the reason you came to the theatre. I had to exert really incredible violence to tear myself away from the wonders of the director's talent to listen to the dialogue between Ranevskaya and Trofimov.[91]

The virtuosity of the acting, full of calculated effects, always straining for attention, also came in for reproof. Nikolaev feared that the emblematic nature of the play and its tragic essence had been overshadowed by the lush beauty of the staging.[92] Another parody by the hostile Burenin, *Cherry jam on a treacle base*, dealt almost exclusively with stage effects and reduced the actors to fowls conversing in birdsong.[93] Chekhov was becoming indistinguishable from the Art Theatre's pyrotechnics.

Nemirovich was keenly aware that they had been gilding the lily, and believed that in the first years of its run *The Cherry Orchard* was a "heavy, ponderous drama." Only over the course of time did it achieve "its lacey, graceful" quality. "Had the theatre tried to obtain this effect, it would have had to renounce the whole stream of environmental and psychological details which at the time was flooding into the foreground in all its overabundance and enormity, but which now only glistens like a spray, clear and bright."[94] By 1929, Nemirovich was citing the first act of *The Cherry Orchard* as the most perfect model of consistent style, by which he meant the harmonic combination of all parts of a performance in a single key.[95]

What helped them to move to a lighter, more water-colour tonality was criticism from the "decadent" camp. Meyerhold also singled out the ball scene as the chief indicator that the Art Theatre no longer understood Chekhov. He insisted to its author that "the play is abstract like a symphony by Chaikovsky . . . in [the ball scene] there is something

Maeterlinckian, terrifying," and he later referred to "this nightmarish dance of puppets in a farce" in "Chekhov's new mystical drama."[96] The poet Andrey Bely devoted an essay to a symbolist interpretation of *The Cherry Orchard*, in which the ball was "a crystallisation of Chekhov's devices":

In a room downstage a domestic drama is taking place; while, at the back, candle-lit, the masks of terror are dancing rapturously; there's the postal clerk waltzing with some girl – or is he a scarecrow? Perhaps he is a mask fastened to a walking-stick or a uniform hung on a clothes-tree. What about the stationmaster? Where do they come from, what are they there for? It is all an incarnation of fatal chaos. There they dance and simper as the domestic calamity comes to pass.[97]

All this was a far cry from Stanislavsky's cluttered facsimile of a dowdy provincial party.

Another element of *The Cherry Orchard* much elaborated in later criticism seems to have been absent in the reception to the first production: the play as portent of future political cataclysm. Much has since been made of the characters of Trofimov and Lopakhin as harbingers of the Russian Revolution; but at the time, no journalist or reviewer in either capital suggested such a reading. As we shall see, the situation was otherwise in the provinces; but these lessons were drawn chiefly in retrospect, often by foreigners. One of these was the English diplomat Maurice Baring, who had learned Russian to immerse himself in the culture, and attended the first production of what he called "the most symbolic play ever written." "It summed up the whole of pre-Revolutionary Russia . . . all of them dancing on the top of a volcano which is heaving and already rumbling with the faint noise of the coming convulsion."[98] But he wrote that in 1922, with all the prescience of hindsight.

Chekhov's death in 1904 seemed a crushing blow to the Art Theatre: it meant that the house author on whom it was so dependent, would provide no new plays. It was condemned to replay the old ones *ad infinitum*, cultivating Chekhov surrogates, or applying Chekhovian techniques to works of other authors and periods. But his death also had its benign aspect: the author was no longer around to quarrel with points of interpretation or challenge their authority as his mouthpiece.

As an act of homage, Nemirovich staged *Ivanov*. Although he valued the first act as "one of the best Chekhovian nocturnes," and Ivanov "as a man broken down by struggle. Dissatisfied and dissatisfying,"[99] he also had to admit, "nowadays you don't run into Ivanovs . . . or Sara Abramsons . . . or Lebedevs . . . Even such behaviour as Sasha's is not to be met with."[100] Consequently, the time was put back to the 1870s. Staged in the same season as A. K. Tolstoy's *The Death of Ivan the Terrible*, meant to show "life under oppression," Nemirovich presented Ivanov's world as deoxygenated by political torpor.

Ivanov followed an unsuccessful experiment of Stanislavsky's in mounting three one-act plays of Maeterlinck, and the actors seemed relieved to abandon the Belgian's nebulous vagaries for the more familiar territory of Chekhov's country-houses. The play was treated as an old-fashioned period piece with all the minor characters exquisitely elaborated. Knipper channelled her widow's grief into a tragic rendering of Anna, Stanislavsky contributed a skilful caricature of Count Shabelsky, and Kachalov, who had wanted to play the character role of Borkin, created an Ivanov who evoked sympathy and empathy. This was a refined and noble man wearied by himself and others, a man with "a worn-out conscience." His outbursts of temper and irritation were interpreted without crude effects and shouting – all was in harmony and fanned by a gentle grief. As the pastels of the MAT were brushed over the primary colours of a play devised for Korsh and Davydov, they all acted, "as if Chekhov's ghost were listening in."[101] The production met with little enthusiasm, and, despite a brief revival after the Revolution, the play itself fell into oblivion.

AFTERMATH

Chekhov's dissatisfactions with the Art Theatre have been well documented. He perversely refused to acknowledge Stanislavsky's achievements. At the end of his life, he named the most remarkable interpreters of his characters to have been Davydov as Ivanov, Komissarzhevskaya as Nina, and Svobodin as Count Shabelsky.[102] All three were professional actors working for Imperial or commercial managements. Players of the Moscow Art Theatre were conspicuous by their absence. In his correspondence, Chekhov regularly complained that Stanislavsky was over-weighting the emotional balance of the plays, but his tact prevented him from actively interfering in the stage direction. Once, when Lilina fell ill and her understudy Skarskaya stood in as Sonya, Chekhov asked her to be more muted in the argument scene of Act III, to shed tears "more lightly." She replied that she had wanted to cry silently, but Stanislavsky had asked her to cry harder, to which Chekhov merely replied, "Well, I'll mention it to him."[103] His remarks to the actors were usually cryptic and allusive. Muratova asked Chekhov if Charlotta should wear a green necktie. "She can, but she doesn't have to." He told Leonidov that Lopakhin should walk neither like a merchant nor like a professor of medicine: "Play him in yellow button-boots." "Listen, Lopakhin doesn't shout. He's rich, and rich men never shout."[104] Such hints were not enough to overrule the strong opinions emanating from the directors.

According to Karpov, Chekhov once lamented,

> even at the Art theatre, all those property details distracted the spectator, kept him from hearing . . . They push the author into the background . . . [. . .] You know, I would like to be played quite simply, primitively . . . Just as in the old days . . . A room . . . Downstage a sofa, chairs . . . And good acting by good actors . . . And that's all . . . Without birds and mood created by props. I'd very much like to see my play interpreted that way. [. . .] I write about life . . . It's a greyish, every-day sort of life . . . But it's not annoying, snivelling . . . Sometimes they turn me into a crybaby, sometimes into a bore . . . Yet I did write a few volumes of funny stories . . . [105]

One must consider the source, since Karpov begrudged the Art Theatre's successful co-optation of Chekhov. Nevertheless, this is every playwright's ideal, to have his lines preponderate over all the other elements in a stage production. Chekhov was not unaware that the Art Theatre, for all its missteps, had popularized his plays.

What struck the original spectators of the MAT's Chekhov productions most forcefully was that, like the Maly Theatre in the palmy days of its Ostrovsky premieres, company and author seemed to be totally and intimately amalgamated. It was as if the plays were written and staged by the same person, an impression all the more mysterious since, when read, the text of Chekhov's dialogue seemed trivial in the extreme. The Art Theatre unveiled the covert, repressed feelings underlying the bad jokes and banal conversation. What distinguished Chekhov's drama from all other plays at the time was what Stanislavsky called the "submarine" course of the through action, the "subtext" underlying the dialogue.

Stanislavsky deciphered Chekhov and made him stageworthy. Every scenic moment was carefully worked out in terms of the integrity of the entire production, with a hitherto unheard-of application of technical effects. Sleigh bells jingling, a swing creaking, crickets chirping were copies of reality, insinuated into the familiar tableaux. Quotidian materiality became the theatre's aim; it scorned artificial props and used ordinary domestic articles wherever possible. Simov's modest sets, suggestive of the Russian Itinerant school, were not self-sufficient displays of painterly technique, but strove to create a bland and inconspicuous background for the stage action.

These productions were enthusiastically greeted by the general public, especially the provincial intelligentsia, which was moved by the subtle and poetic reproduction of its own life, recognizing its own personal grief in the longing of Chekhov's heroes. This grounding in a specific everyday life constituted a theatrical extension of the masterworks of Russian literary realism. Writing in 1923, the poet Osip Mandelshtam described why the educated classes, steeped in Turgenev, Tolstoy and Dostoevsky, could find the MAT so congenial.

For the intelligentsia to go to the Moscow Art Theatre was almost equal to taking communion or going to church . . . *Literature*, not theatre, characterized that entire generation . . . They understood theatre exclusively as an interpretation of literature..into another, more comprehensible and completely natural language. . . . The spirit of that generation and of the Moscow Art Theatre was the spirit of Doubting Thomas. They had Chekhov, but Thomas the intellectual did not trust him. He wanted to touch Chekhov, to feel him, to be convinced of his reality.[106]

Stanislavsky's spelling-out of the implicit was in keeping with this trend.

As to the famous "pauses" in the Chekhov productions, Mandelshtam read them as a "celebration of pure tactile sensations." In fact, over time they became self-indulgent trademarks produced mechanically. The actor Mgebrov who worked at the MAT in 1908/9 recalled that they "were held precisely by the numbers and the actors were recommended to count the seconds mentally during the duration of these pauses."[107] Such a professional deformation indicates how the Chekhovian repertory came to inhibit the Art Theatre. Since *The Seagull* saved the MAT 's fortunes in its very first season, Stanislavsky felt an obligation laid on him by society and culture and he carried it out masterfully; the Chekhov productions became the theatre's great triumph. These successes enclosed the theatre in a narrow circle, not easy to escape. When the Art Theatre actors played Chekhov, their interpretations were related to a specific reality; this required incomparably more observation and sensitivity than did the creation of imaginary characters. If they could not, to use Stanislavsky's later term, "re-experience," then they had to imitate subtly a familiar, almost daily experience. The method elaborated in the Chekhov productions was hard to apply to Ibsen or Maeterlinck and totally inimical to Shakespearian tragedy.[108]

Stanislavsky's own penchants ran counter to naturalism. Although, as he was to teach, he preceded along an inner line of emotional logic, he infused all his roles with a genuine theatricality.[109] Imbued with romantic idealism, fond of stirring stage effects, he found himself wedded to

Chekhov, the most intimate and most static of Russian dramatists. Trained in Shakespeare, Molière, Pushkin and comic opera, he was tasked to realize texts devoid of theatrical flamboyance. He did not understand Chekhov, with whom he had very little in common. The paradox was that the theatre's spiritual leader, endowed with an inquiring mind and a vivid imagination, had to find ways to bring to stage-life not legendary or historic heroes but country doctors concerned with ecology and provincial misses yearning for Moscow. It took the intermediacy of Nemirovich to clarify Chekhov for Stanislavsky; but once Stanislavsky was bitten by the Chekhov bug, he brought to the plays a bold scenic conception and his own magnificent acting talent. Trying to strike traditional sparks of theatrical pathos from the soggy longings of Chekhov's characters, Stanislavsky idealized them.[110]

CHAPTER 4

Competitors and imitators (Russian Empire 1898–1917)

> Your *Uncle Vanya* plays here [Novocherkassk] all season, makes a
> profit. [. . .] Suffice it to say that at the final . . . performance, the
> actors at the end of the last act cried real tears. It's a fact . . . A
> cheerless life is no stranger to the heart of a hardworking actor.
>
> Ivan Rostovstev to Chekhov[1]

IN THE CAPITALS

No longer could the established companies scoff away the Art Theatre
as a passing fancy, a dilettante's hobby. With the success of *The Seagull* in
1898, it was established as a serious rival, not only vying for ticket-buyers
but challenging the policies and practices of the State theatres. The
Moscow Maly's reaction was characterized by one observer as "the
Gospel's foolish virgin with no oil for her lamp suddenly hit by the beam
of an electric floodlight."[2] The Maly survived on the virtuosity of its
stars in sloppily staged classics, and was ill prepared to face comparison
with a more up-to-date competitor. Although its leading actress Mariya
Ermolova detested what she called Chekhov's "pessimism,"[3] many
Maly actors, led by Sumbatov-Yuzhin, were eager to bring him into the
repertory. The Maly might even have stolen a march on the Art Theatre
by being the first to revive *The Seagull*. When the actress Nikulina
expressed a wish to stage it for her benefit, Sumbatov had contacted
Nemirovich to see if this would conflict with the newly founded Art
Theatre's plans:

I don't know [Nemirovich's] troupe, [Sumbatov wrote to Chekhov] but for your
play it is very important to have a staff of excellent directors. As to our staging it,
Nemirovich worried me greatly with his opinion that Nikulina is too old for the
role of the actress and . . . how can I put it, is unsubtle, sharp-edged and far too
set in her stage techniques. Moreover, I really don't know whom we've got for a
Seagull. The male roles, I think, we'll manage very well.[4]

83

The Art Theatre's triumph rendered a Maly *Seagull* an endangered species, and its acting collective was sorely disappointed when *Uncle Vanya* then slipped through its fingers.

Over the next six years a kind of mutual boycott operated between the "Chekhovian whisperers and marionettes of Carriage Row" (as the Maly actors called their MAT adversaries) and "the tenants of the Little (Maly) place," as Stanislavsky's actors referred to their counterparts. At Maly rehearsals, a typical instruction was "Just don't do it the way it's done at the Art Theatre," and similar snideness was bandied about at the MAT. Only Chekhov's vaudevilles – *The Proposal* (1891), *The Bear* (1898) and *The Jubilee* (1904) – appeared at the Maly; none of his full-length plays would be staged there until 1960.[5]

Similar animosities prevailed at the Alexandra Theatre in St. Petersburg, which felt it had a prior claim on Chekhov; but when the Art Theatre launched its tours to the northern capital, their productions came as epiphanies to the open-minded. Vasily Toporkov, a student at the Alexandra's acting school, had heard his instructors Davydov and Stepan Yakovlev complain about how naturalism, the MAT approach and over-rehearsing were destroying the Shchepkin tradition of generic emotional realism and the living talent of the actor. Then he saw *The Cherry Orchard:* the room in the old manor house struck him as vaguely familiar, not a stage set but a recognizable room.

Toporkov's sense of being in a theatre was also shaken when the actors began to talk. "These weren't actors! Living people were conversing in sleepy voices. Whether it was good or bad – I had no time to understand." Stanislavsky's performance sparked another revelation.

Everything Gaev did was done with shocking aloofness from the audience, he was wholly there amidst the denizens of the cherry orchard . . . Stanislavsky made no impression on me as an actor. Of the usual arsenal of acting techniques he used none – no effective intonations, no *coups* of any kind, no deft "gimmicks" to evoke applause. None of it. I could not even tell if it was any good from our actors' point of view. I simply couldn't take my eyes off him, he seemed to have bewitched me.[6]

Toporkov, who would later become a luminary of the MAT troupe in the 1930s and forties, continued to think that the stars of the Alexandra were, individually, the better actors. "The Alexandrines were remarkable performers, some of their talents bordered on genius. But, once on stage, each was concerned only with his role. [. . .] Yet even the most talented performers, not knit together by a common ideal, could not direct the attention of the spectator to the general profound concept underlying the play."[7] This was to be a stumbling-block when Chekhov, so needful of a well-knit ensemble, would be staged in Petersburg.

In 1902, Telyakovsky, administrator of the Imperial theatres, decided to proclaim the entrance of Alexandra into the twentieth century by rehabilitating its staging of *The Seagull.* Conditions seemed favourable. Petr Gnedich who had replaced Karpov as director of the repertory had a better sense of what the Art Theatre was getting at, and solicited Chekhov directly for both *Three Sisters* and a revived *Seagull*: " . . . of course, I would be grieved not to have you. Believe me, the history of your *Seagull* would not be repeated . . . Unless your plays can be introduced in the repertory, there is no way to create a foundation for a project which is only just begining to take shape."[8] These words indicate how Chekhov's stock as a dramatist had risen under the MAT's skilful management, and how even the Alexandra had to go with the flow. The author's preliminary refusal seemed absolute: "Now I hate that theatre, I can't stand your actors, because they don't learn their roles and they play their own words . . . For its creator's sake don't stage *Seagull* . . . "[9]

To allay Chekhov's fears, a serious effort was made to redress the errors of the past. Instead of the eight rehearsals *The Seagull* had had in 1896 ("as many as I could get," Karpov apologized), the revival was meted out eighteen. The provincial tragedian Mikhail Darsky, who had briefly played Shylock in the MAT's first season, was chosen as director. Darsky's most difficult task was to get the actors to avoid overexplicitness, since their standard procedure was to use their talent and technique to fill out the sketchy outlines provided by the average dramatist. He established a fourth wall, turned the actors' backs to the audience, and filled the evening with pauses and "mood *à la* Stanislavsky . . . with real grass in the garden."[10]

Varlamov, who was now entrusted with Davydov's role of Uncle Sorin, wanted to know whether the man he was playing was good or bad and came up with dozens of "adjustments," using every trick at his disposal to raise a laugh. Ivan Shuvalov brought out Trigorin's irresolution, but, like Stanislavsky and Sazonov before him, neglected the character's intelligence. If *The Seagull* can be said to exhibit variations on the theme of apathy, then Trigorin is the theorist of vegetative indifference, a shrewd intellect that elaborates a justification for its infirmity of purpose. Instead, Shuvalov presented merely a spoiled and self-satisfied observer from the sidelines.[11]

Gnedich had wanted Komissarzhevskaya for Nina to play in tandem with Nikolay Khodotov as Treplev, but she had left the company before rehearsals began. Nina was given to the Maly actress L. V. Selivanova, who did a worthy job, but couldn't sustain comparisons with her predecessor. Khodotov, a temperamental foe of routine usually cast as "neurasthenics," made Treplev the hero of the production. But all eyes were turned to Arkadina, which was now at last assumed by Mariya Savina.

Savina had enthusiastically admired the Art Theatre *Uncle Vanya*, but, a diva of the old school, she was unable to leap the hurdles of the "new drama." Showing little interest, she rehearsed casually, unable to see any profit in the play for herself or her public. To a friend she wrote, "We're all chewing on *The Seagull*, and nothing good, nowt but bad do I expect of it."[12] In performance, Kugel reported, "Savina created a splendid comic type of Arkadina, which was, save the mark, to the play's advantage, although I think the author had in mind a more psychologically complicated, i.e. tragi-comic type."[13]

New scenery was provided, with the third and fourth acts copied from Art Theatre designs: the last act, in particular, was composed of complicated flats arranged at sharp angles and diagonals, offering glimpses of other rooms beyond an enormous salon, much as in Simov's plan. But the vast Alexandra stage magnified the proportions, so that the human beings were lost in space. The sense of everyday routine and lived-in environment evaporated amid the long stage crosses, the expensive furniture and the distances between the actors. The intimate bond between objects and performers, so crucial to the Art Theatre's success, was absent in the conventional theatrical appurtenances and the coolness of presentation.

Yury Belyaev concisely summed up the production values, indicating the rather one-dimensional interpretations:

There was a charming and moving Nina (Selivanova), a bewitching actress Arkadina (Savina), a wishywashy and weakwilled Trigorin (Shuvalov), a typical old man Sorin (Varlamov), a nervous, sensitive Treplev (Khodotov), a cute and sweet Masha (Panova): there was a house of the most intricate architecture with rooms in all directions . . . In short, everything was in place. Only one thing was missing. There was nothing of Chekhov literally and figuratively.[14]

Mediocre was the adjective that sprang to the lips of the connoisseurs, but the play appealed to the general public, did good business and was kept on the program.[15] Telyakovsky was satisfied with the "extremely decent" performance and noted in his diary the most important omen for the theatre's future: the director Darsky received a curtain call, only

8 The spacious set for Act IV of *Seagull* at the Alexandra Theatre revival, 1904.
Contrast this with figure 4.

the second time that had ever happened. "Until now there was no stage
director at the Alexandra and it was not even considered necessary to
have one. They would call out and applaud only actor-performers and
sometimes authors."[16] Significantly, it was a Chekhov drama that con-
ferred prestige on the director's function.

Chekhov was reinstated as an official part of the Alexandra repertory,
which continued to follow in Stanislavsky's footsteps. By this time, the
notion of what was "Chekhovian" had taken hold and when an hilari-
ously funny production of *Jubilee* was revived at an Alexandra benefit in
1903, the audience was outraged: "How can such a fairground show be
produced on a cultured stage?"[17] They had forgotten Antosha
Chekhonte the author of comic anecdotes.

Savina realized the necessity of renovating her stock of leading roles,
and when she toured to Odessa in 1904, opened as Ranevskaya in *The
Cherry Orchard*, staged by her colleague Anatoly Dolinov, who tried as far
as possible to copy the Art Theatre. She was simply trying to cash in on
the play's popularity, and had no faith in it:

This "orchard" is worse than any fairy-tale pantomime: such a mass of things and such a lot of noise . . . One must be true to life, Dolinov [. . .] is awfully stuck on the play, its "ideas" etc., but yesterday I pointed out that "nothing will come of nothing." [. . .] Be as hypocritical as you like, audiences are still audiences and boredom is still boredom. Mine is no sort of role and, of course, this cools my enthusiasm.[18]

N. Vulf who played Anya believed that Savina was looking for a "general state which would correspond with Ranevskaya's image."[19] and, during rehearsals, she made some wonderful discoveries about Ranevskaya's instantaneous transitions from tears to laughter and the presentiment of disaster when she swept through the ballroom and blindly groped for the tables and chairs. The image never gelled in performance however: in Act II, Savina was impervious to the lyricism of the "sins" monologue, in Act III she mixed up the lines and blocking. She only played the role twice and on tour. "The failure," she explained, "came from the fact that everyone expected something special from me, even the author according to Knipper, but there was no material."[20]

Chekhov's death provoked a spate of "memorial" productions, to trade on the news value. His former favourite Yavorskaya put on an *Ivanov* at Petersburg's Novy Teatr that would have set him spinning in his grave, reviewers reported. Komissarzhevskaya, for her part, was intent on opening her new theatre with a fresh revelation of Chekhov. N. A. Popov, who directed *Uncle Vanya* for her in October 1904, repudiated the Art Theatre model, but his reforms seem to have been chiefly external; the interior settings were portentously symbolic, the Act III drawing-room a massive museum, full of the detritus of high art – a grand piano, paintings, a Madonna and child – all swathed in ghostly dust-covers. The acting did not come up to Moscow Art standards, except in the case of Komissarzhevskaya's Sonya, her glorious contralto voice suffused with humiliation, yet summoning hopes for the future on the eve of Revolution; she transformed the country mouse into a figure of intense human suffering.[21]

For the most part, St. Petersburg was content to apply Art Theatre camouflage to its Chekhovian tributes. In the 1904/5 season, the Alexandra actor Molchanov scheduled an MAT-style *Seagull* for his benefit, for which Savina refused categorically to act Arkadina to Komissarzhevskaya's Nina: "To play second fiddle, and in such a role at that – *merci*! Find a play with equal roles – and I'll act it with pleasure. The playing-field is not even." She rejected Ranevskaya too: "This role is deeply repugnant to me . . . I shall be a flop in it, because I cannot violate my self."

"I don't see any 'new forms' in Chekhov," Savina was quoted in an interview. "All the power, all the tragic effect of Chekhovian plays lies in their simplicity. And to act Chekhov one must not philosophize cunningly, but be simple."[22] Such a statement is unobjectionable and even echoes Chekhov himself, but it begs the question. Savina and the whole school of acting from which she came could see in plays only the opportunity afforded by a role, and a role was evaluated by the number of lines. Nothing went unspoken. What Savina called a role was not to be found in Chekhov: there were too many minor touches and details, not enough overt action or "points" to be made. Consequently, the only Chekhovian part in which she succeeded was *Ivanov*'s Anna, a "sensational" character whose drama is expressed in duets with the hero, not in interplay with the other characters.

The Alexandra nevertheless kept at Chekhov. In 1905 at the height of the popular uprisings, it decided to stage *Cherry Orchard*; it seemed timely, and "the speeches of Petya Trofimov about future life were taken by the youth to be revolutionary."[23] Its other productions were a *Vanya* in 1909 and a *Three Sisters* in 1910. A decade earlier, when Komissarzhevskaya had been eager to play in *Three Sisters* for her benefit, its author had tried to dissuade her by libelling his own work: "The play has proven to be boring, draggy, awkward; I say 'awkward' because it includes four heroines and the atmosphere is, as they say, 'inauspicious.'"[24] In 1910 his fears were borne out, for the Alexandra's old habits persisted. Each character remained an isolated demonstration of thespian ability, and when dancing began at the Shrovetide party in Act II, Davydov who played Dr. Chebutykin came downstage centre and performed a Cossack dance as a music-hall turn, which was met by an ovation.[25] Chekhov's plays required not the creation of individual images, no matter how "modern," but the reproduction of an incessant flow of life.

SCENES FROM COUNTRY LIFE

In some ways, the provinces were better off than the capital in their opportunities to see Chekhov. His farces and *Ivanov* were regularly played, and *Uncle Vanya* had its pre-MAT premiere in Nizhny Novgorod. Touring stars like Komissarzhevskaya frequently included Chekhov in their programs.[26] The downside to this abundance was the crude state of most theatrical enterprises. In Elets, for instance, the amateur circle far outshone the professional troupe; when Chekhov sent Nina to Elets at the end of *The Seagull*, he and his audiences were aware that he was dooming her to work with half-drunken barnstormers before a raw, unrefined public.[27]

On leaving the Art Theatre, Meyerhold planned to launch his own acting company in Kherson, a move which alarmed Chekhov, who, for all his misgivings about the MAT, had not approved of the young actor's quitting it. The dramatist felt Meyerhold needed bucking up, for "he won't have an easy time in the Kherson theatre! There is no audience for plays there, they still demand the fairground booth. After all, Kherson is neither Russia nor Europe."[28] Meyerhold planned his season in imitation of the Art Theatre's repertory, including *Three Sisters, Uncle Vanya* and *The Seagull*, in that order. With an enthusiastic cast of coevals from the Philharmonic and the MAT, he mounted each in a few days' time with minimal props for a run of no more than three days.

Kherson, with a population of 35,000, could provide only two thousand playgoers and among them only three hundred real fans; but it turned out, thanks to Meyerhold, to be the first provincial town in Russia to see productions modelled on the Moscow Art Theatre. Meyerhold himself admitted that his first directorial work was "in slavish imitation of Stanislavsky" even though he no longer agreed with all the aspects of that approach,[29] and his example was copied by numerous actors who sat in the MAT auditorium filling their notebooks with all the production details they could observe.

Three Sisters, which opened Meyerhold's first season on 22 September 1902, had already been played in Kherson by another troupe; but it was unrecognizable in the new staging, "done with the sensitivity of a concert."[30] "A fresh breeze through the birches" was audible in the first act, "nasty autumn weather whistled at the window" in the second, and "a nagging general nervousness" pervaded the third.[31] An article in a local newspaper indicates what caught the audience's attention in *Uncle Vanya*:

> Two ladies: Did you notice, darling, how the flower pot was knocked over?
> And how the clocks ticked?
> And the little curtain?
> And the cricket?
> And the thunder!
> And the rain!
> And how the gig went over the bridge?
> And how the harness bells jingled?

And the professor's wife's outfit?
And the sleeves on her mantle?
With lace!
And ruching!³²

Meyerhold repeated his roles of Tusenbach and Treplev, and added Ivanov and Astrov to his resumé. His Astrov was more fiery and high-strung than Stanislavsky's: "distraught, tormented, unable to forget the patient who died under chloroform, angry at the fate that marries professors to girls like Elena,"³³ an interpretation which the Art Theatre had intentionally foregone.

Meyerhold's success enabled him to open a second season in Kherson as "The New Drama Association," a name emblazoning the fact that his repertory embodied modern principles of the theatre, but he soon exhausted the town's possibilities and had to keep on the move. In 1904/5 his company played in Tiflis (now Tbilisi), the capital of Georgia. The outposts of the Empire usually suffered Russian cultural colonization, although a process of assimilation had taken place in the first Georgian-language productions of Chekhov. In Grigory Volsky's version of *The Bear* (1889), not only were character names changed but the duel was altered from pistols to sabres, to correspond with Caucasian custom. To bring across the paradigmatic nature of *Ivanov* (1890), M. Nasidze rebaptized Nikolay Ivanov Niko Dzhimbarashvili (the play itself was retitled *A Victim of Lack of Character*) and Jewish Anna became an Armenian. Even with these adjustments, the critics found the play schematic and boring.³⁴

The *Uncle Vanya* which had so affected Gorky came to Tiflis in 1899. What struck the reviewer for *Caucasus (Kavkaz)* was that everyone in provincial society could identify with the subtly drawn characters since everyone had encountered talented people who frittered away their talents.³⁵ But often, Georgian intellectuals saw something alien in the Chekhovian personality. Discussing a Georgian translation of *Cherry Orchard* in 1904, a reviewer referred to "the general character of Russian life, the natural temperament of those sons of the North, typical Russian traits,"³⁶ as if the torpid dreaminess of Chekhov's heroes had nothing in common with Caucasian impetuosity. Meyerhold's Chekhov productions in Tiflis were much admired, despite some complaints of over-much realism: *Three Sisters* was cited for its audacious placement of characters who "sat down, took their places on stage not always facing the audience, but with their backs to it, i.e., to the wall supposed to be removed to allow the audience to see what's going in the room."³⁷

As for *The Cherry Orchard*, the success of its Moscow opening led to a great demand for the performance rights. Komissarzhevskaya hoped to open her new theatre in St. Petersburg with "this insanely difficult work."[38] A group of Petersburg actors, as well as troupes in Taganrog and Nikolaev, the Kiev Literary Society Theatre, an impresario in Voronezh and many others inundated Chekhov with requests.

Meyerhold was, however, first in the field, putting on his *Cherry Orchard* in Kherson almost immediately after the Art Theatre opening, so that he could not have seen Stanislavsky's production or the script licensed for it. Despite Meyerhold's later remarks about the comedy's mystical overtones, one reviewer characterized his production of *Orchard* as "an ordinary sort of play with farcical lackeys, chambermaid and governess." The character of Trofimov was played by the director so comically that his "Hail to new life" speech got a laugh.[39] Later Meyerhold would move to the role of Gaev.

The overgrowth of *Orchards* meant that many were stunted and badly pruned. Evtikhy Karpov saw the play in 1904 in a Yalta playhouse produced by a troupe from Sebastopol. Although large letters on the posters announced that it was staged in conformity with the Art Theatre *mise-en-scène* under the supervision of the author himself, the results belied the advertising. After an hour's wait, the curtain went up on "Tacky, torn scenery. Wretched stage dressing. A few bentwood chairs. A bargain-price, obviously rented, newish 'wardrobe' cupboard. In the window a splayed branch crudely cut out of paper, tasked to stand in for the cherry orchard all by itself," the hackneyed staging one would expect of a backwoods "the-ayter." Art Theatre influence was evident primarily in the assistant director posted backstage who,

while the play went on, never stopped whistling, cawing, cuckooing, chirping, croaking, tweeting, muffling the actors' lines with the voices of birds and frogs. He could not, however much he tried, drown out the prompter who literally crawled out of his box to give the actors the text of the play. The prompter's hoarse bass drowned out the voices of the actors and the birdsong and the frogs' croaking. The result was something incredibly crazy. The actors, unable to hear the prompter, flung themselves around the stage in dismay, deafened by the sounds of 'wakening nature.' Not knowing their lines, they mercilessly garbled the text, went astray, made absurd pauses, allegedly 'to feel the mood.'

The packed house was unable to understand the dialogue, and the irritated back rows shouted out, "Louder! What? Can't hear you! Prompter, don't shout! Birds, shut up!" Embarrassed on Chekhov's behalf, overcome by a migraine, Karpov crept out after the third act.[40]

Such fiascos and falsely advertised epigones of Stanislavsky could not dampen the enthusiasm of the provincial public for Chekhov's plays. The crowding in Yalta testified to that. "All one needs is your name on the poster – and there's a full house," the provincial director Ivan Rostovtsev had written to Chekhov in 1900 from Novocherkassk; contrary to Karpov's anecdote, he insisted that "the actors pull themselves together: they treat each of your phrases, every word, with real reverence and don't allow themselves a single omission."[41] From the first, audiences were gripped by the masterful depiction of a readily identifiable accidie in *Uncle Vanya*, and empathized with Treplev's shattered nerves and inferiority complex.

The Cherry Orchard had a particularly strong effect on university students who identified with Trofimov. While writing the play, Chekhov had kept informed of the student uprisings which began in Petersburg in 1899 and culminated in a mass demonstration in March 1902, brutally repressed by the authorities. He had worried over how to imply Trofimov's political involvement without provoking the interference of the censors; a number of Trofimov's second-act lines about past injustice and present inequity were replaced for performance by more anodyne statements. Despite these excisions, Kachalov had infused the role with memories of his own student days in Petersburg, when he attended left-wing demonstrations and carried a volume of Plekhanov in his pocket.[42]

Outside of Moscow, alert spectators were reading between the lines in a way that would later become an innate skill of Soviet audiences. A student in Kazan, V. N. Baranovsky, reported to Chekhov his pleasure, his "inexplicable, inexhaustible bliss" at hearing Trofimov's "passionate, bold, vigorous and truthful appeal to . . . to that vivid new life, . . . to active, energetic and seething work, to courageously intrepid struggle."

The theatre was packed to bursting, the lift of spirit was enormous, incredible!! I don't know how to thank you, how to express my heartfelt and most profound gratitude for that happiness you gave me, him, them, all humanity![43]

Baranovsky was so worked up by the experience that he followed up this perfervid praise the next day, relating the play directly to burning political issues of the moment:

What a fool our censor is to allow such a thing to be performed and printed! All the salt is in Lopakhin and the student Trofimov. [. . .] "The perennial student" is a collective character, he's all students. Lopakhin and the student are friends, they march hand in hand "to that bright star, blazing there . . . in the distance."

All the characters in the play are allegorical . . . The *Cherry Orchard* is all Russia.[44]

The value of the provincial stage to the reception of Chekhov and Chekhov's reciprocal value to its development are clearly epitomized by the career of Pavel Pavlovich Gaideburov. When the twenty-one-year old actor-manager organized his first provincial season in autumn 1899, the poster for *The Seagull* informed the world that it would be staged "according to the *mise-en-scène* of the Moscow Art Theatre." But, since Gaideburov had no clue as to the principles underlying Stanislavsky's physical production, a mechanical simulacrum of externals did not get far. Moreover, his company was composed not of like-minded experimenters but of actors who cared simply for personal success; many were cocaine addicts or libertines who initiated affairs with fans to ensure the theatre's popularity.[45]

Gaideburov's knowledge was somewhat improved when his wife and lead actress, Skarskaya, a sister of Komissarzhevskaya, spent the 1899/1900 season in the Art Theatre company; neither of them subscribed to Stanislavsky's aesthetic, however, and they polemicized against the "dictatorship of the directors." After her season at the MAT, Skarskaya entered Nezlobin's company in Nizhny Novgorod and asked to have *The Seagull* put on for her benefit. This, the most prestigious, best managed of provincial theatres, mounted it in two rehearsals, the director leaving the actors to block it themselves because he wanted to go for a steambath. "It tells us," Gaideburov later recalled, "not only how Chekhov's plays were rated by the theatre, but what was the general public's attitude to Chekhov, for it was the general public which determined the attitude of the box office: working on *The Seagull*, the theatre, evidently, was convinced that the play would not be repeated . . . but the benefit was a success."[46]

Despite ignorance of the new dramatic technique, when he opened his season in Novgorod with *Uncle Vanya* on 20 September 1901, Gaideburov had evidently achieved some of the desiderata. Advance publicity insisted that the company was inspired solely by "a sincere desire to serve art," and no farces would be staged. "The entrepreneur pursues no purely commercial aims."[47]

Chekhov's very name on the company's playbill constituted a manifesto of ideological and artistic principles, aimed at bringing the progressive-minded part of the populace to the theatre. Not that Chekhov's name was a literary standard around which political insurgents might rally; on the contrary, he was best known to the public at large as a comic writer. His longstanding association with Suvorin, his avoidance of factions, Mikhailovsky's well-known criticism that Chekhov was a writer indifferent to the contradictions of life were tokens of his uninterest in politics. The supposed apathy was abetted by the "atmospherics" of Chekhovian productions, an idiosyncracy generally accepted as "Chekhovianism."

Gaideburov's decision to open his eclectic repertory with *Uncle Vanya* was planned as a first step in the direction of creating a movement that would enhance life through art. The choice of *Vanya* to inaugurate his Nizhny Novgorod season reverberated like a scandal in society, since everything about the play ran counter to the theatrical traditions of the paying customers. The set designer of Nezlobin's company (which had failed the previous season) had been asked to provide the scenery, but he refused to build a box-set with side doors and windows, considering such realism to be a betrayal of "theatricality." In his opinion, everything on stage had to bear the seal of convention, and therefore even doors had to be traditionally theatrical.[48] An interview with the chief of police to obtain the necessary permits turned into a lecture on popular provincial taste:

What? . . . You've decided to open the season with *Uncle Vanya*? Never heard of the play, no . . . Or, excuse me, – it's Chekhov, isn't it? I remember, I remember, he wrote some funny anecdotes, so I've heard . . . Right, right . . . At the moment there's a whiff of sulphur about this *Uncle Vanya* . . . Trouble, your affairs are in real trouble. You don't know our public, obviously . . . You see, our folks are very demanding when it comes to theatre . . . Spoiled . . . Are your actresses pretty? What do they look like? I say, what about their looks? Our public won't put up with ugly little kissers.[49]

In the face of this obtuseness and his own inexperience, Gaideburov was bowled over by the warm reception awarded the play and the eight thousand rubles he made by featuring "intellectual" plays, including *Three Sisters*, throughout the season.

The rest of Gaideburov's pre-Revolutionary career was that of a missionary, proselytizing for Chekhov and the new drama. He founded the Itinerant Theatre and then the Palæstra Theatre, which, unlike ordinary provincial touring companies, would seek out the most remote communities and reveal to them the gospel of modern literature. There was barely a corner of Russia where the Itinerants did not act Chekhov. Pogroms and uprisings often interrupted the tours, but *Uncle Vanya* was played to full houses in even obscure backwaters. As a youth, Evgeny Vakhtangov applauded Gaideburov's first *Cherry Orchard* in remote Vladikavkaz. Shortly before World War I, the newspaper *The Day* (*Den*) could report, "Strange as it may seem, there is absolutely no classical

theatre in Petersburg. To see Shakespeare, Tolstoy or Chekhov, you have
to go to the ends of the earth, to the outskirts of the city, where
Gaideburov's theatre shelters amid factories and plants."[50]

One of the adventitious discoveries of this high-minded migration
was that staging Chekhov did not require the trappings of the Moscow
Art Theatre. "Ariel," a reviewer of Gaideburov's *Cherry Orchard* in 1918,
compared the experiment of "denaturalizing" the staging "with the now
classical production of the Muscovites." The decorative aspects were
kept to a minimum: the first act took place against a background of
white walls, a burning stove at one side and a small drapery at the other;
the second against a broad sky cloth, with the setting sun blazing brightly
and then gradually dimming. The third had a sketchily painted drawing
room, the music kept offstage and shadows of dancers seen moving
through an open door. Unconsciously answering Nikolaev's objections
to the MAT *Orchard*, "Ariel" found that keeping the scenic elements
simple in a play of profound psychological content "condenses the
power of experience, economizes and sharpens the spectator's attention,
focussing it on the essentials . . . *The Cherry Orchard* can be (and should be)
freed from that tiresome and essentially useless (and at its worst injurious)
emphasis on detail, which Stanislavsky's theatre brought to the play." At
the same time, the reviewer felt called-upon to note that by freeing the
play from details of time and space, Gaideburov "also deprived it of that
invisible but indispensable character – the aroma of the ancient, moribund, sweet-smelling 'cherry orchard.'"[51] The difficulty of balancing
universality and nostalgia would remain a crucial issue in later stagings
of the comedy.

CHAPTER 5

Chekhov goes West (Europe 1888–1938)

> *The Cherry Orchard* is already being translated for Berlin and Vienna, but it will have no success there, since they have no billiards, Lopakhins or Trofimov-style students.
>
> Chekhov to Olga Knipper[1]

The pattern of Chekhov's acceptance on the stages of Northern and Eastern Europe rarely varied. He would first be known as the author of theatrically adept vaudevilles. As his full-length plays were published in inadequate translations, they evoked little interest or were buried in equally inadequate productions, welcomed by a handful of connoisseurs. Only after the Moscow Art Theatre had shown the way, either on tour or to visitors from abroad, was Chekhov performed in anything like appropriate conditions; and only after World War I did he become a standard feature in repertories, usually when his cause was championed by talented refugees from the Russian Revolution.

CULTURAL COLONIALISM

In countries where the Tsarist hegemony acted to russify the native culture, Chekhov was not much appreciated. When, after its triumphs in Germany, Bohemia and Austria, the Moscow Art Theatre toured to Warsaw in May 1906, the Poles boycotted it. Despite the respect of the well-informed for Stanislavsky and his efforts, attendance at a Russian performance was classed as a betrayal of patriotism. The few Polish literati to pay a call on *Uncle Vanya* did so "in order to criticize one more time . . . the most boring work in literature."[2] To their surprise, the production struck a note of longing in them, so the reception of the MAT's *Cherry Orchard* in 1912 was warmer. By then, *Vanya* had become a fixture on Polish stages in Warsaw and Cracow: its "nightmarish" atmosphere of empty lives and taciturn suffering made more of an impression than the details of the story. Władysław Prokesz staged *The Seagull*, renamed

The Lapwing, in Cracow (1907) as an "autobiographical" play, with Trigorin as Chekhov. There was still the sense that Chekhov's psyche was so specifically Russian that he could not possibly have any meaning for Poles.

Finland, another victim of cultural colonialism, would accept Chekhov primarily through one of its own directors, Eino Kalima. He had studied in Moscow and Petersburg on a scholarship, and was deeply impressed by the MAT's principles, especially the call for spiritual truth, the primacy of the director, the restrained acting and the use of the natural stage voice. Without any preconceived notions, he saw *Vanya*, *Three Sisters* and *Cherry Orchard* there, and was won over by their richness. In 1914 Kalima joined the National Theatre in Helsinki, which was famous for its productions' intimacy, powerful emotional content and brisk tempi. His essay "Thoughts on the Art of Drama" (1915) offered ideas on Chekhov that quoted Stanislavskian concepts and terminology, but also adopted a Tolstoyan viewpoint, stressing ethical themes and the brotherhood of man. Kalima's Chekhov was an agnostic student of life, who struck a divine chord and achieved a note of eternity.

Kalima's productions respected the original stage directions, and insisted that the actors live their parts completely, but through instinct rather than intellect. But at this point in his career the successes were partial. His *Uncle Vanya* (*Vanja-eno*, 1914) had no cohesive ensemble and the most prominent roles were played by the youngest actors. The settings by Karl Fager were based on photos of Simov's scenery. In Kalima's elegiac *Cherry Orchard* (*Kirsikkapuisto*, 1916), the restrained staging emphasized the tragic disappearance of the old life rather than hope for the future.[3]

The independence of Poland and Finland immediately expelled Chekhov from the national repertories, along with Gogol, Ostrovsky and Tolstoy, and anti-Russian feeling obstructed their return. After Poland gained recognition as an independent state in 1919, it sought to isolate itself in every way from Russia. Theatres adopted the organization of the MAT as a useful structure, but deliberately rejected its aesthetics, particularly its fondness for psychological realism. Its house author was neglected as well. *The Cherry Orchard*, when toured to Warsaw in 1928 by the Prague group of Art Theatre defectors, could be appreciated, in the sarcastic words of the critic A. Słonimski, as a warm-hearted satire along the lines of French impressionism or *The Pickwick Papers*. Ten years later, reacting to a Polish production in Warsaw, the same critic now found the characters Dostoevskian and too subversive to be laughed

at. With fascists next door, Chekhovian despair was a dangerous sentiment to adopt.

CZECH CHEKHOV

Chekhov was first seen on a Bohemian stage in two inconsequential performances of *The Bear* in Brno in October 1889. *The Proposal* directed by
František Kolár at the Prague National Theatre in 1890 got a better
reception, and both plays were soon regularly revived throughout the
country.

The foremost translator of Chekhov into Czech, Bořivoj Prusík, held
the field from 1896 to 1904. Unfortunately he cut and clipped for no clear
reason: in *Uncle Vanya* he left out Astrov's speech about trees in Act I and
in *Three Sisters* abridged Vershinin's philosophical vagaries. He was also
cavalier about accuracy; for example, "I've never had enough flowers
like these in my life" became "I've never had money for flowers in my
life," and Olga's "You're not in a merry mood today, Masha" turned into
"You're in a merry mood today, Masha."[4] Prusík's inability to place his
translations had less to do with his ineptitude than with the Prague
theatre's westward perspective. It was reluctant to accept innovation
from Russia, particularly from Chekhov who seemed to lack "technique," and preferred tried-and-true hits from Paris and Berlin. Sending
his *Seagull* to the literary manager of the Prague National Theatre,
Prusík wrote to a friend:

You don't know the trouble we have with dramaturges; the last one didn't know
any author but Sardou, translated him himself, and *Madame Sans-Gêne* triumphed for almost two whole years. He keeps dragging on stage old French
farces, which made not only our fathers but our grandfathers laugh. If anything
from the Slavonic stage gets on, it's usually only the sort of thing you read in the
Illustrierte Zeitung was played in Berlin or Munich. But I'll try all the same.[5]

After sitting on the play for two and a half years, the dramaturge turned
it down, probably having heard of its fate in St. Petersburg. Finally it
opened at Švanda's theatre in Smichov outside Prague on 26 December
1898, and failed; the critic for *Thalie* opined, "the play is not stageworthy," though he granted it contained food for thought for high-
brows.[6] Chekhov was rebuked for his "inaccurate view" of life.

Uncle Vanya, better appreciated by the press, was widely performed
from 1900, despite the audience's obvious boredom and the players' perplexity. Even a brilliant performance in 1901 at the National Theatre
could not prevent the observation that Chekhov was out of step with the

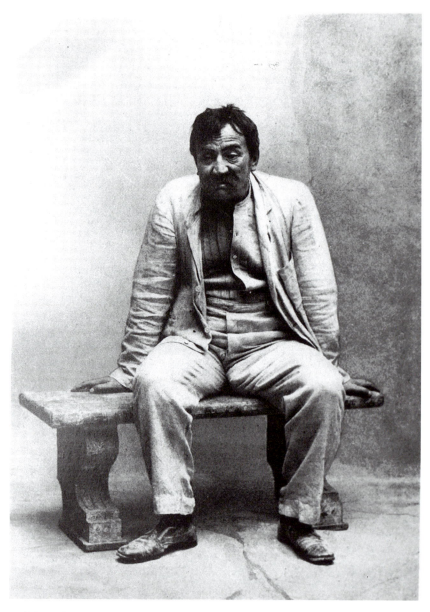

9 Eduard Vojan as Astrov in *Strýček Váňá* (*Uncle Vanya*), Prague National Theatre, 1901.
Contrast this unflatteringly naturalistic depiction with the more *soigné* Astrov of
Stanislavsky in figure 5.

ordinary Czech play. Švanda staged Prusík's translation of *The Cherry Orchard* in November 1904, amid scenery from a Czech play performed the same evening; nevertheless it had a favourable reception. When it was put on at the National Theatre in January 1905, the critics oddly noted similarities to *Midsummer Night's Dream*, and applauded the management for staging works of literary quality rather than mere commercial ventures.

The Moscow Art tour in 1906 had an enduring effect. After reading about Russia for so long, Czech intellectuals finally came face to face with the real thing. Under this spell, the Prague National Theatre decided to stage *Three Sisters*. In its desire to emulate the MAT, it turned to Stanislavsky for help, appealing for incidental music, set designs and costume sketches, especially of uniforms with the addresses of the firms that might provide them. Stanislavsky enthusiastically ordered a special rehearsal for photographs to be taken. He pointed out that uniforms made to order were expensive, and advised against having them built in Russia, recommending German tailors in Prague.[7] The result was splendid. The farewell scene between Masha and Vershinin (Hana Kvapilová and Eduard Vojan) was considered a model of modern acting. The management, proud of its ensemble effect, planned to tour it to Vienna on a double-bill with *Hamlet*, but the Austrian authorities barred this visitation of Slavonic culture.

Under the Czech Republic (1918–39), Chekhov's work received less attention. New productions in 1919 of *Seagull* (Vinohrady Theatre) and *Cherry Orchard* (National Theatre) were received coolly, even hostilely: no one had time in the postwar world for the "singer of mournful grey atmosphere," the exponent of Russian passivity and melancholy. The theatrical vanguard of futurism and constructivism was already installed, and naturalism seemed *démodé*. Not until the Kachalov group (see chapter 8) appeared in Prague in 1921 and the original MAT returned there the following year was Chekhov somewhat restored to favour. The aesthetic debate was complicated by politics, since the attitude to these troupes varied depending upon whether critics and spectators were reactionary or progressive, White Russian émigrés or enthusiasts for the Soviet experiment. "It is quite impossible for us to welcome *The Cherry Orchard* as we once did," wrote one of the latter.

When we now see the flaccid and frivolous landowners, capable only of pining but not of action, squandering their estate on Parisian diversions, [. . .] we cannot avoid rebuking the author for being too kind and indulgent to them, he should have judged them more sternly and angrily. Why should we get involved with them, pay them attention? [. . .] It would be far more important [. . .] to show nascent, penetrating trends which are striving for new forms of life, to show something more than the ungraduated student Trofimov and delicate, pretty young Anya.[8]

Amid the general neglect, a version of Chekhov's untitled novice play was staged in German at the Vinohrady Theatre on 28 January 1929, and then revived in Czech. The manuscript of this bulky early work had been discovered in a safe-deposit box in Moscow in 1920 and published three years later. Produced in a realistic manner with well-rounded characterizations, *Der Mensch Platonoff* nevertheless failed, for the director had no idea whether to treat it as an intimate, lyrical drama or an ironic comedy. This question would continue to bedevil later attempts to shape Chekhov's juvenilia into a cohesive play.

The only major production of Chekhov in Czechoslovakia before Hitler's invasion was Vojta Novak's *Three Sisters* at the Prague National Theatre (1932). The theatre hoped to reveal the play's up-to-date appeal by showing how the characters' dreams of future liberation had been realized under present conditions. What takes place within in the play is a "feverish striving of the human soul to be filled with something positive in life"; its actions constitute a seismograph of the darkness and decadence of a bygone era. According to one socialist critic,[9] in these passages about the future Novak had changed the "grinding sound of history's wheel" into "piano music"; he suggested that all eyes should be turned to Soviet Russia, where the hopes of the three sisters were becoming reality.

NASTROENIE = STIMMUNG

By the time of Chekhov's death, *The Bear* (*Der Bär*) and *The Proposal* (*Der Heiratsantrag*) had been seen on eleven German stages, but *The Seagull* (*Die Möwe*) was not produced until 1909. Chekhov failed to catch on in the German-speaking theatre at first, despite the fact that several important directors, including Jürgen Fehling and Heinz Hilpert, were very fond of his work. Siegfried Melchinger has suggested that a partial explanation is the difficulty of translating Chekhov into German.[10]

Had the poet Rainer Maria Rilke carried out his plan to translate Chekhov this problem might not have existed. After his first trip to Russia, he and Sofija Šill prepared a translation of *The Seagull* for publication. Dubious though he was of the play's stageworthiness, fearing that the mixture of comedy and drama might dilute its effectiveness, he hoped it would be staged. Rilke was so attracted by Chekhov's plays that he also intended to translate *Uncle Vanya* and wrote to the author for a corrected copy. Unfortunately, his *Seagull* went unpublished and *Vanya* went untranslated.[11]

Instead, Chekhov fell into the hands of hacks. Traditionally, German translators tended to use their versions as commentary or advance interpretation of a text, to make explicit what was implicit in the author's intentions. Chekhov's reticence, the clarity and special rhythm of his dialogue, his colloquialisms and careful pruning of superfluities were resistant to this sort of treatment.[12]

The first German rendering of a major play was issued in Chekhov's lifetime: *Three Sisters* (*Die Drei Schwestern*) by Wladimir Czumikow, published in Leipzig in 1902 as "the only authorised translation." Czumikow had been in correspondence with the author and may have seen the MAT productions, so his work had a spontaneity and authenticity lacking in later versions. His German was fluent, natural and correct; but, like Constance Garnett in English, he tended to be less colourful than the original, which reduced the impact of certain passages. There were also unfortunate omissions, such as the stage directions about Soleny's use of perfume and Andrey's pushing the pram, Kulygin's joke about "hokum" being read as Latin and Chebutykin's farewell to Irina. Still, for almost fifty years it was the only version available to the German reader, and so "exercised a major influence on Chekhov's reception in Germany before World War II."[13]

Another factor in preventing Chekhov's popularity with German playgoers was that, from the start, gloom and doom were the keynotes of interpretation. Chekhov's reception was part and parcel of a genuine intercultural interest, but the primary features of his writing to be stressed were its foreignness and its pessimism. Exalted dejection exemplified by Hauptmann's plays and the style of the tragedian Josef Kainz permeated the German stage. However, the dying falls and neurasthenia that were attractive in native German drama, when projected on to Chekhov, lacked appeal.

Even Heinrich Stümcke, an enthusiast and editor of *Bühne und Welt*, who had published his own translations of Chekhov, admitted that the playwright would have to contend with a "certain opposition from the public and the critics." Granting that the author was a master of atmosphere, he deplored the lack of plot and absence of effects.[14] The initial German *Seagull* in Stümcke's translation at the Breslau Lobe-Theater

(1 November 1902) was a complete failure: the audience "was occasionally irritated to the point of anger."[15] *Uncle Vanya* (*Onkel Wanja*) was first shown privately to guests of the Akademische Dramatische Verein at the Munich Schauspielhaus in March 1903. An anonymous reviewer, remarking that "The usual idea of a stage play is not *Uncle Vanya*," doubted whether it could be successfully transferred to a public theatre and concluded that Chekhov's plays attained "neither Tolstoy's power of dramatic expression nor Gorky's originality."[16]

Two years later, the Berlin public did get to see *Vanya*; the director E. Welitsch tried to recreate the atmosphere of a Russian estate, but was thwarted by the Teutonic mannerisms of his actors.[17] Even Stümcke predicted a short life for the play by noting that, though excellent in concept, it suffered from a serious blunder. The painstakingly gradual depiction of psyches, stroke by stroke, was "suddenly violently interrupted by an unbelievably explosive stage effect," i.e., the gunshot. "On stage a short scene should be enough [. . .] to enlist us against the Professor and for Vanya."[18] It had four performances.

Then came the Moscow Art tour of 1906. Nemirovich-Danchenko expected the Germans to understand Chekhov since Germany was the birthplace of *Weltschmerz*. As usual, his predictions came to pass. Hauptmann wept during *Uncle Vanya*, and pronounced it played by "gods of art."[19] The actors Kainz and Sonnenthal attended every performance, the latter cancelling a long planned tour to do so.[20] Alfred Kerr, Berlin's leading critic, became a vehement proponent and propagandist, fascinated by the difference between traditional German directorial style and the Moscow art of ensemble: as he saw it, the interaction of the cast created something "unspeakably human" on the stage: life not in its actions but in its hiatuses and twilight zones. However, because he knew barely a word of Russian and imbibed the plays in their stage form and not as texts, he deemed Stanislavsky's creativity superior to Chekhov's. As dramatic literature, *Uncle Vanya* and *Three Sisters* were adjudged more narrow and limited than *The Wild Duck* or *Michael Kramer*.[21]

On the other hand, Stümcke, who knew the texts thoroughly, objected to what he called Stanislavsky's "environmental staging" (*Umwelt-Regie*) as deflecting from their main point. But his term failed to gain the popularity of Kerr's coinage "*Stimmungstheater*" or "atmospheric theatre" to describe this phenomenon; it long reverberated in Germany as a useful tag. The *Berlin Daily* (*Berliner Tageblatt*) went so far as to prescribe the Art Theatre as a course in stagecraft:

90 percent of German directors should learn from the Russians how a stage image can be thoroughly penetrated with truth without superfluous emphases. Look how truthful it all is! Learn to act simply but so that your acting pierces to the heart's core. Learn to serve the author's concept, forgetting yourself, coming on stage as a different person, and not simply disguised in another costume . . .[22]

This advice was heeded: Friedrich Baisl, star and the director of *Uncle Vanya* at the Monaco Hoftheater in 1913, went so far as to rent the sets and costumes from the MAT. Unfortunately, the many copy-cat productions that followed in the wake of the Art Theatre tour put so much emphasis on *Stimmung* that absolutely nothing transpired on stage. When Stümcke's *Seagull* was revived at Berlin's Hebbeltheater in 1909, Siegfried Jacobson found it "unbearably boring."[23] A Viennese audience considered it "rather tepid" and incomprehensible, owing to its "select painting of atmosphere."[24] It had more success at the Munich Lustspieltheater in 1911/12 when it ran for twenty-five performances, despite the fact that, in the words of a theatre journalist, "the unique work, whose effect consisted entirely of atmosphere, offered no small difficulties for the director and performers."[25]

Perhaps in reaction to the brutalities and privations of war, a brief Chekhov fad ran through the German-speaking theatre in 1916–19, with *The Cherry Orchard* (*Der Kirschgarten*) in Vienna, Munich and Berlin; *The Seagull* in Berlin (twice) and Leipzig; and *Ivanov* in Berlin. The Viennese *Orchard* was directed by Emil Geyer at the Neue Wiener Bühne as a "tragicomedy": one reviewer found it "literary drama in the truest sense of the word,"[26] and the audience waited with impatience for Lopakhin's axe to fall. The 1918 Berlin version directed by Friedrich Kayssler was, on the other hand, a huge success, but the play then disappeared from the German stage for twenty years. *Three Sisters* was first produced at Berlin's Schillertheater in 1926 by Jürgen Fehling. Critics who compared it with the MAT original found it lacked resonance, but its feminism seemed timelier than ever: "Women's fate nowadays is reflected in it: death, loss of prospects, hopelessness, which the world holds out to millions of girls today."[27]

It is noteworthy that the greatest director of the German-speaking world, Max Reinhardt, failed to rise to the challenge of Chekhov. He staged only *The Bear* (Kleines Theater, Berlin, 1905). The missed opportunity is puzzling. His strengths as a director included the assemblage of strong ensembles and the evocation of atmosphere by potent sensual means. He had in fact projected an *Uncle Vanya* in November 1902 just before he launched the productions of *Salome*, *Earth Spirit* and *The Lower*

Depths that established him as a major director. Throughout his career, similar unrealized Chekhovian projects crop up, often preceding a spate of creativity in other directions: he planned a *Three Sisters* in October 1918, shortly after his rehearsals of Wedekind's *Spring Awakening*. In 1927, a *Cherry Orchard* was in the works for Vienna's Theater in der Josefstadt. In fact, the only full-length Chekhov play to appear on a Reinhardt stage was Felix Holländer's *Ivanov* of 1920, at the Kammerspiele of the Deutsches Theater, Berlin, with Alexander Moissi in the lead and Werner Krauss as Lebedev. When Hitler came to power in 1933, Reinhardt left Germany and planned to protest the subjection of the arts with a touring company including Helene Thimig, Paula Wessely, Max Pallenberg and Vladimir Sokolov, in a repertory of four plays, including *Three Sisters*. That too failed to materialize. In 1942, Reinhardt, a refugee in Hollywood, was still plotting out a *Three Sisters*, but death supervened.[28] One can only assume that the impression made on him by the Art Theatre was so strong that he was unable to devise an approach resistant to the charge of scenic plagiarism.

The most surprising of Reinhardt's unfinished projects was a *Platonov* in 1928. Although Reinhardt lost interest, it received its first German adaptation as *Der unnützige Mensch Platonoff* (*That worthless fellow Platonov*) at the Preussiches Theater, in Gera, Thuringia, in 1928, translated by René Fülöp-Miller and directed by Helmut Ebbs as a domestic tragedy. Despite the success of Friedrich Domin in the lead, it remained a conversation piece, rather than a viable addition to the repertory.[29]

Hardly had the German-speaking stage and its public grown used to Chekhov when this familiarity was proscribed by the Third Reich. The National–Socialist interpretation of art as an expression and exhortation of the *Volk* robbed the drama of autonomy and turned it into political propaganda. Literature was expected to serve the State's educational aims of discarding the sick and clearing the way for the healthy; if a work of art failed to fulfill this obligation, it was judged otiose or guilty of "spiritual high treason."

Chekhov was among the offenders. Friedrich Bethe, chief dramaturge of the Frankfurt am Main State Theatre and Cultural Custodian (*Kulturwart*) for Hesse-Nassau, made this clear in his appraisal of Bergner's drama *A Soul in Danger* (*Eine Seele in Not*, 1933):

We are dealing with a hypersensitive psychic drama, a bit in the mood [. . .] of Ibsen, Chekhov or Hauptmann's *Lonely Lives*, hence an expression of artistic human relations, whose existence, like that of all overly delicate patients, we must reject. [. . .] These are the decadent problematic sexes of the not-too-distant past, whose mere existence in our memory has a ghostly effect and makes us shudder. All these sick people were swept away by the war and afterwards by our Führer.[30]

Hypersensitive, overly delicate, sick, lonely, decadent – on the lexical scale of Nazi literary criticism these, along with degenerate, were applied as "*coup de grâce* words," pronounced to destroy. *Weltschmerz, mal du siècle*, ennui and boredom, all expressions covering the malaise that afflicts Chekhov's characters, were stricken from the Nazi vocabulary. They were replaced by life-creating vitality, the will to construct. The writer's task was to set forth the exceptional, not the ordinary, the champion, not the average man.

The Hitler–Stalin pact temporarily exempted Russian literature from the quarantine. Three of Chekhov's plays did get produced under the Third Reich: *The Cherry Orchard* in Berlin (1938); *The Seagull* in Gera (1941); and *Three Sisters* in Berlin and Vienna (1941) as a star vehicle. But the tenor of the times (and Stümcke's inadequate translation) led to the critical consensus that *Three Sisters* "was tolerable only due to the first-rate performances."[31] In September 1944 the Deutsches Theater was ordered closed and the run ended.

CHEKHOV NOT À LA MODE

To paraphrase a description of Henry James's mind, French culture at the turn of the nineteenth century was so fine that no idea from abroad could penetrate it. The attempts made to introduce the French to Russian literature were careful to distinguish between those authors who might and those who might not be easily assimilated. To make sense of Chekhov, he was called a naturalist of the Zola school. K. Waliszewski's monumental *La littérature russe*, published in 1900, described Chekhov's plays as "completely devoid of action and psychological differentiation of characters."[32] Melchior de Vogüé, whose book on the Russian novel championed Dostoevsky's cause, compared Chekhov's one-acts to amateur snapshots obeying the sacrosanct call, "Don't move." As to the full-length plays, they were packed with tiresome people and evoked inescapable boredom. Too pessimistic for the French, Chekhov was a creator of passive and impotent heroes, animated by "enigmatic Slavic souls."[33] (This may mark the debut of this undying phrase.) Such opinions were abetted by the French translation of Lev Shestov's essay "Creation *ex nihilo*" which characterized Chekhov as the minstrel of hopelessness.

Despite the bad press, André Antoine decided to introduce Parisian playgoers to Chekhov and in 1900 commissioned and began work on a translation of *Uncle Vanya*, which came to naught.[34] In 1902 he brought Lidiya Yavorskaya to the Théâtre Antoine, where, along with *La Dame aux caméllias* and plays by her princeling husband, she acted in excerpts from *The Seagull* and Gorky's *Petty Bourgeoisie*. Even the well-disposed and well-informed condescended that "the Chekhovs and Gorkys, up-to-date though they may be (excellent story-tellers but mediocre dramatists) . . . are nowhere near making us forget that mover of ideas and marvelous architect, our own Dumas, or Shakespeare the ancestor of us all."[35]

On 11 May 1908 a complete play by Chekhov was first presented in French: *The Proposal* (*La demande en mariage*) at Jules Berny's Théâtre des arts, a group devoted to the latest in drama, such as Wilde and Shaw. No photographs survive, but the illustrations to the published text of 1922 show a Ukrainian hut with high windows, an icon corner and characters in Little Russian folk costume, braids, peasant shirts and shiny boots. This was generic Russian dressing. Heavy investors in tsarist bonds, the French had entered a Russophile period, and there was a sympathetic audience for Slavic art.[36] This taste was to be satisfied more through the stage than the page: between the world wars, only forty-two per cent. of the French population read books and only an insignificant percentage of the nine thousand titles published every year was devoted to translations, of which Chekhov's works made up little more than one per cent of the entire press-run.[37] Diaghilev's Russian seasons of opera and ballet promoted a idea of Russia that was primitive, garish and "Oriental." Chekhov failed to match that image, and when Antoine, in 1914, mooted a *Cherry Orchard* for the Odéon, there was no follow-up.

ITALY BRINGS UP THE REAR

Italy came late to Chekhov with an *Uncle Vanya* (*Zio Giovanni*) played by the Palmarini-Campa-Capodaglio Company in Milan on 22 August 1922. The *Corriere della sera* spoke of a grey atmosphere in which the characters trembled like painful shadows. Chekhov might be a clever creator of characters, but he was no dramatist, at least not for gross palates. Only the finest tastes could be expected to appreciate him.[38] In a land where theatre was a popular entertainment, this was indeed damning with faint praise. Despite Pirandello, the heavy hand of melodrama still lay on the Italian stage, and pride of place was given to movement and action.

Milan in April and May 1924 saw both a *Seagull* (*Il gabbiano*) with the Capodaglio-Calò-Olivieri-Campa company and Marta Abba as Nina; and a *Cherry Orchard* (*Il giardino dei ciliegi*) with the Maria Melato company. Audiences appreciated the former but were confused by the latter. Sarcastically, the critics complained of too much of a good thing. "In our theatre, which goes from romantic lushness to at times flat, raw *verismo*, his spiritual realism provides a characteristic note which is all his own . . . Let's not overdo it."[39]

These and other occasional productions in the 1920s lacked the coordinating work of a director, a function that only gradually took hold in the Italian theatre. The importance of an integrated *mise-en-scène* was not affirmed until the foundation of the Accademia nazionale d'arte drammatica in 1934; Italy's first *Three Sisters* (*Tri sorelle*) was cast from its second company, by the young female director Vanda Fabro in 1941. By that time, the skeleton key to Stanislavsky and the Chekhovian mysteries had been forged by émigrés.

CHAPTER 6

Comes the Revolution (Russia 1917–1935)

> In fact, "a huge stormwrack" did advance on us, a violent tempest
> did pass over our society, "washing away the indolence, the indiffer-
> ence to work, the wallowing in boredom" . . . although it was by no
> means the tempest wished by the generous soul of Chekhov, whose
> heart would have been painfully broken by so much oppression of
> people and their spirits, for he cruelly felt the slightest coarseness
> even in everyday life.
>
> Olga Knipper paraphasing *Three Sisters*[1]

WHO NEEDS CHEKHOV?

Chekhov had rapidly become a Russian classic. By the time of his jubilee
in 1910, he was firmly ensconced in the pantheon of great writers and a
popular conception of his form and substance had congealed. When the
Petersburg cabaret The Crooked Mirror offered Boris Geier's skit *The
Evolution of the Theatre*, in which a simple love triangle is performed in the
styles of Gogol, Ostrovsky, Chekhov and Leonid Andreev, enough com-
monplaces existed to support a clever parody. The Chekhovian pastiche
"Petrov," an ingenious splicing of lines, situations and attitudes, painted
an hilarious portrait of woolly-minded bathos. Geier included the
offstage gunshots, the watchman tapping, the grand piano playing in the
distance, and the rhetorical leitmotifs.

All last night the old lindens were rustling in the garden . . . the old lindens . . .
that have seen so many tears and sorrow . . . When we moved here, it seemed to
me that we had been buried in a grave . . . a grave . . . Moscow . . . Oh, if only I
might see Moscow again . . . (*Sits, burying her head in her hands.*) *Moskva* . . . *Moskve*
. . . *Moskvoy.*[2]

Reducing Chekhovian longing to the recitation of grammatical declen-
sions of Moscow was a brilliant stroke of comedy. Intentionally ignoring
Chekhov's ironic awareness of his characters' shortcomings, Geier's

"Petrov" formulated once and for all the standard platitudes about Chekhovian drama.

Although Chekhov's jubilee was largely a chorus of praise, dissenting voices were audible. At a meeting of the Petersburg Literary Society, Russia's leading feminist Olga A. Shapir described Chekhov as the poet of grey, workaday depressives and complained that his female characters lacked any clear outlines or strong emotions, despite the fact that since the 1880s women had been in the forefront of political reform movements. His works, she opined, tend to mock both female emancipationists and mothers.[3] These accusations were met with applause, an indication that Chekhov's apoliticism was increasingly out of step with the turbulent factions and upheavals that preceded and accompanied wartime preoccupations.

Chekhov's lack of popularity immediately before and after the Revolution resulted in part from the belief that he wrote only about gentrified despondency. The Moscow Art Theatre's own productions of Chekhov, the cornerstone of its renown, were growing stale. An evening of Chekhov sketches and farces played by the Art Theatre Studio was berated for its "naturalistic" tempo, an imitation of the parent house which turned brisk comedies into draggy dramas.[4] As Nemirovich-Danchenko himself admitted, their acting of Chekhov was suddenly emitting "notes of sentimentality and preachiness."[5] Noting that *Uncle Vanya* "after ten long years is now starting to sprout clichés," the theatre retired it on 23 February 1913, hoping to renovate it after a few seasons. Nemirovich, who had long disliked the mawkish aspects of Stanislavsky's staging, recognized that part of the problem lay in the MAT's proprietory attitude towards Chekhov. The author's sister Mariya and his widow, he observed, "even take Chekhov to be a kind of privilege of the Chekhov family and the Art Theatre, as it used to be. [. . .] And a new generation does not want to have to deal with our domestic sentimentality. It will be on my side!"[6]

Nemirovich's critical finesse was matched by his alertness to currents of political change; thanks to him, the Art Theatre was not caught entirely unawares by the October Revolution. Two weeks before it broke out, the MAT, for the very first time, offered performances for workers in such locales as the Theatre of the Soviet of Workers' Deputies: the show chosen to indoctrinate the proletariat into High Culture was *The Cherry Orchard* with most of the original cast. Ironically, the MAT had first been conceived in 1898 as a "publicly accessible" theatre at popular prices, but economic necessity and municipal licensing had prevented that, and helped turn it into a theatre of the intelligentsia. In 1917, by government decree, its audiences were made up exclusively of workers given free tickets at their factories and unions. Such untried playgoers had to be trained in what Stanislavsky considered proper behaviour in a temple of art, so the program read: "The performers of the Art Theatre accept applause with deep gratitude, but will not come before the curtain, considering this harmful to the artistic integrity of the performance."[7]

Too depleted financially and morally to develop new productions, the Art Theatre had perforce to rely on Chekhov. In its first "Revolutionary" season, its revivals of *The Cherry Orchard* and *Three Sisters* made up ten per cent of the repertory. The actors were alert to the changed mood wafting in from the audience, and began to hearken to the prophetic notes in the plays. It suddenly dawned on Olga Knipper that they used to perform *Three Sisters* "without giving meaning to the ideas and experiences and chiefly the dreams that underlie it. And now the whole play sounded different. It was not simply dreams, but a premonition of the storm."[8]

In the 1918/19 season, *Ivanov* was added (and just as quickly dropped). *Izvestiya*, a mouthpiece of Bolshevik policy, was bemused: "Why did the Art Theatre need to revive the depressing, and if I may, even annoying *Ivanov*?" Revivals of intimate dramas about helpless Russian intellectuals offered no answers to the questions of the labouring masses; consequently *Ivanov* was a nuisance, and "the friends of the theatre, who overflowed the auditorium on opening day, did not reward the performers with a single round of applause." Judging by the crowd of several thousand that besieged the House of Unions to hear Art Theatre actors recite excerpts from *Hamlet* and *Julius Caesar*, *Izvestiya* diagnosed "a craving for the monumental [as] the distinguishing feature of the times."[9]

The Art Theatre was out of step in the march towards the monumental. Maksim Gorky was calling for a Communist theatre that in a time of heroic catastrophe had to be epic and romantic. Art was to train the people to feel the "spirit of the struggle." "Which is more useful to the socio-aesthetic education of the masses," he asked, "Chekhov's *Uncle Vanya* or Rostand's *Cyrano de Bergerac*, Dickens' *Cricket on the Hearth* or any of Ostrovsky's plays? I am on the side of Rostand, Dickens, Shakespeare . . ."[10]

In this uncongenial atmosphere, *Uncle Vanya*, which had been in mothballs since 1913, was dusted off: the premiere took place on 4 December 1918 in Great Auditorium of the Polytechnic Museum. Stanislavsky, far from excited at tutoring the great unwashed, jotted down in his copy of the program, "First day labour for hire (!!!?)," explaining what he meant in a letter to the actor Vasily Luzhsky: "You know that *under no circumstances will I* take part in a performance that smacks of day labour. Now more than ever, because day labour is becoming our chief activity . . . It is important for all of us that the performance on the 21st be not merely good, but staggering."[11] To his close friend, the critic Lyubov Gurevich, he confided more wryly,

My life has changed completely. I have become a proletarian and yet am not needy, because I perform day labour (meaning, – I act on the side) almost every day when I'm not needed at our theatre. Not that I have stooped so low as to give up art. So I act in whatever can be decently staged outside our theatre. I'm ashamed to say our old friend *Uncle Vanya* comes to my aid. We are acting it at the Polytechnic Museum with new business, no curtain, new sets and costumes. The result is a highly original performance, incomparably more intimate than at our theatre. Sometimes we play *Uncle Vanya* in the First Studio. This too is very pleasant.[12]

The elitist Petrograd journal *Theatre and Art* (*Teatr i iskusstvo*), always sceptical of the Muscovites, was unimpressed by the Art Theatre's belated stab at community outreach. It noted that theatre in general had become so "crude, sluggish, deadly dull" that it was hardly worth devoting space to it. "Everything that was artistic and idealistic in the Russian theatre has been swamped by a wave of vulgarity. [. . .] But, after all, what can you put on in the theatre now except art for the general public? A sailor stands up, a cabbie stretches out in the theatre. – 'You bore me, Uncle Vanya!'"[13] Nor could Stanislavsky accustom himself to spectators who did not behave as a congregation and keep reverent silence; once, following a noisy first act, he came out in full costume and makeup as Astrov, and firmly demanded that the audience "respect the actor's work," keep silent and refrain from cracking nuts.[14]

Uncle Vanya and some Chekhov one-acts and stories dramatized for touring purposes proved to be more durable than *Ivanov*. Chekhov's works eventually made up a quarter of all MAT productions in 1919. By the third season, *Vanya*, which had been performed only 192 times between 1899 and 1913, was put on ninety-five times, and by itself constituted twenty-five per cent of the repertory.[15]

An English visitor, the writer Arthur Ransome, reporting on the effects of the Revolution, saw one of these performances in the First Studio, a house that sat barely two hundred (21 February 1919), and was struck by the "new smartness of the boy officers of the Red Army, of whom a fair number were present . . . " To his mind, *Uncle Vanya* was of purely historical interest, since the life and characters it depicted had been swept away and "it will be a hundred years at least before anyone in Russia will be able to be unhappy in that particular way again." Even so, Ransome had to recognize the power of the drama as the Art Theatre played it.

> The subject of *Uncle Vanya* was a great deal more remote from the Russian audience of to-day than was the opera of *Samson and Delilah* which I heard last week. And, if I realized that the revolution had come to stay, if I realized that Chekhov's play had become a play of historical interest, I realized also that Chekhov was a great master in that his work carried across the gulf between the old life and the new, and affected a revolutionary audience of to-day as strongly as it affected that very different audience of a few years ago. Indeed, the play seemed almost to have gained by the revolution, which had lent it, perhaps, more irony than was in Chekhov's mind as he wrote. Was this the old life? I thought, as I stepped out into the snow. If so, then thank God it has gone![16]

Luzhsky, who had played Professor Serebryakov since the opening night in 1898, was well placed to identify the differences between pre- and post-Revolutionary audiences. The old MAT crowd had held the high calling of professor in veneration and used to be shocked by Vanya's disrespect until they came to understand Serebryakov's hollowness. The new spectators shared Vanya's opinion from the outset, seeing the Professor simply as an outrageous, heartless no-talent. They didn't get Luzhsky's academic in-jokes of the Heidelberg accent or his sawing the air in a platform manner, but, inured to street fighting, they roared with laughter when the pistol shot frightened him. The proletarian public was also more demonstratively sympathetic to the plight of Vanya and Sonya and wept loudly during the last scene. In the famine winter of 1918, one of the playgoers brought Vishnevsky some game he had shot, saying "Take it, it's yours for *Uncle Vanya*, you suffered a lot in that."[17]

This untutored sympathy and Ransome's generous assessment of the play's newly ironic significance were not shared by the ideologues of the brave new world. A mere month after the Englishman had seen *Vanya*, a left-wing periodical protested,

> You have to be phenomenally obtuse to dredge *Ivanov* and *Seagull* out of the bin and endlessly stage *Cherry Orchard* and *Three Sisters*. That's what our best theatre –

the Art Theatre – is doing. What are we to expect of the rest in that case? [. . .] It's time to abandon to their own eras down-in-the-mouth, grief-stricken Chekhov, bourgeois Ostrovsky, smugly virtuous Dickens etc. Each fruit has own season . . . The theatre must now present bright, gripping spectacles, joyful and powerful experiences, and not staged funerals.[18]

The drumbeats for a Bolshevik art that reflected Bolshevik experience were growing deafening. The LEF movement and many other program-matic experimenters condemned all pre-Revolutionary art as obsolete. Meyerhold, the first important theatre worker to join the Bolsheviks, could settle old scores with the MAT by proclaiming an October Revolution in the theatre. Chekhov was to go into the garbage along with Meyerhold's former colleagues, his plays dismissed as irrelevant to a time when to be pessimistic was at best *démodé*, at worst subversive. Meyerhold staged the second version of Vladimir Mayakovsky's agit-prop play, *Mystery Bouffe* at the bluntly named Theatre of the RSFSR-1. In its prologue, the futurist poet snidely commented that most theatres present mere "keyhole peeping."

> You look and see–
> flopping on sofas
> Auntie Manyas
> and Uncle Vanyas,
> But uncles and aunties
> Don't interest us,
> Uncles and aunties we can get at home.[19]

Petr Kerzhentsev, who would become a literary Robespierre in his cam-paign for a theatre of the future, asked rhetorically, "What else can you call a theatre but a museum where the performers seriously act and the audience seriously watches plays by Chekhov about gloomy people, who don't know how to struggle with life, who weep over their vanishing past and are powerless to do anything to hold on to it?" Even more lethal was Trotsky's characterization of the Art Theatre as "Insulars," the opposite of Fellow Travellers, "who do not know what to do with their high tech-nique or with themselves. The things going on around them strike them as hostile or at least alien. Imagine people living today in the spirit of Chekhov's plays. *Three Sisters* and *Uncle Vanya* in 1922!"[20]

Luckily for the Art Theatre, it had supporters in high places. The People's Commissar for Enlightenment Anatoly Lunacharsky insisted on the value of traditional culture as a background for new forms; his mandate was to preserve the best of the "bourgeois heritage," and so to prevent "artistic nihilism." To maintain the classics he rescued the former Imperial troupes and the MAT by qualifying them as "academic theatres" under his direct administration, which kept them carefully sheltered from the uninhibited innovation that characterized Russian theatre in the early twenties. Even Lunacharsky, however, qualified Chekhov as a "subdued writer" who might seem "out of keeping."[21]

A more unlikely admirer is alleged to be Lenin, who also attended *Uncle Vanya* at the MAT Second Studio. His wife Krupskaya laconically recalled, "He liked it."[22] Nikolay Podgorny, in the auditorium that night, was at first "a bit embarrassed and lost my head at the realization that Vladimir Ilich had come to our theatre to see *Uncle Vanya*, a show which might be thought superfluous to a Soviet spectator." During the second intermission, the young actor ventured the question, "'Vladimir Ilich, are you bored watching this show?' 'Bored?' he replied. 'No, how can you ask! A remarkable author, remarkable words, remarkable players!' . . . "[23]

Such is the account of an award-winning Soviet actor writing in 1940, a time when both Chekhov and Lenin had been stamped into icons of Stalinist culture. During the 1920s, however, a variant version made the rounds of the émigré community:

"Lenin was at the Studio, he saw *Uncle Vanya*." "Well, what happened?" – "Nothing. He arrived without warning. He just happened to take a seat." – "And was the Okhrana there?" – "There were three men of some sort, but basically it was modest, no pomp. He watched the whole performance, didn't say a word. In the intermission he squinted and didn't say a word." – "And then?" – "Well, after the show, somebody from the powers-that-be came up to him and Lenin said, 'What wonderful actors and what a wonderful theatre, but why do they perform plays of this sort? Is it really necessary to stir up such feelings? One needs a call to cheerfulness, work, joy. There's Ostrovsky, Gogol and Pushkin, there's Goethe, Schiller and Shakespeare.' And, with an ironical smile, he added: 'All of it is what is now called "bourgeois," but that kind of bourgeois stuff should be given to the people.'"[24]

This Lenin is more closely aligned to the doctrine that Lunacharsky was promoting at the time, a shrewd judge of how middle-class taste could be turned to the advancement of the Party.

A FEAST IN PLAGUETIME

Typically, the two greatest directors of the Bolshevik era, Vakhtangov and Meyerhold, never staged Chekhov's major plays. Predilections and events sent them to the farces.

In 1919, Vakhtangov was made head of the Directing Section of the Department of Theatre of the Commissariat of Enlightenment. He proposed a House of Theatre that would be a prototype for the popular stage, where the best plays of each Moscow company would be shown: the first day would be devoted to the MAT's Chekhov productions.[25] Despite this nod in the direction of his teacher Stanislavsky, Vakhtangov had his own artistic agenda. If Stanislavsky was proud that people came to the MAT not to see productions but to visit the Voinitskys and Prozorovs, Vakhtangov aspired to bring them into a circle of actors who plied their trade with skill and panache. The spectator was never to forget for a moment that he was in the theatre or that the actor he was watching was the master of a craft.

Criticizing a student production of *Jubilee* directed by Boris Zakhava, Vakhtangov pointed out that the actors were playing the mature comic Chekhov, not the young, effervescent farcical Antosha Chekhonte. To achieve the proper effect, Vakhtangov piled up the furniture in the set, forcing the actors to readjust to exigent circumstances, creating eccentric behaviour that arose naturally from their encounter with impossible spatial conditions. In addition, he insisted on "a farce rhythm, three times quicker than before, but without omitting any of the inner motivations or psychological justifications"; he used a bell to establish the pace. Barricaded, crushed, flat on their stomachs, harried by the bell, the young actors improvised hilarious business.[26]

In September 1920 Vakhtangov prepared his own evening of Chekhov one-acts: *The Wedding*, *The Jubilee* and a dramatization of the short story "Horse-thieves" at the Chaliapin Studio. Boris Shchukin as Merik the horse-thief stopped the show with his speech describing how the villagers had punished him by pulling him on a rope through ice-floes in a river. Vakhtangov interrupted this "perfect" interpretation by complaining of its petty naturalistic simplicity and insisted that Shchukin "give the whole substance of the thoughts and feelings that each phrase contains, to sculpt them as a sculptor shapes plastic forms, every intonation and expression."[27] Shchukin succeeded by using the whole gamut of his voice without sacrificing truth and naturalness. He had gained "power of expression."

So successful were these one-acts that they were revived at studios, concerts, military hospitals and army camps well into World War II, setting an accepted style for Chekhov's farces. "The Chekhov evening" also marked an important stage in Vakhtangov's development as director by opening out the naturalistic acting of the Art Theatre. But he was moving well beyond their exuberant merriment, for another pillar of Vakhtangov's faith was the grotesque. "The theatre of everyday life must die," he proclaimed. "Actors of 'characters' are no longer necessary. Anyone capable of playing characters must feel the tragic quality (even comic actors) of any characteristic of the role and must learn to manifest it grotesquely. The grotesque is tragic and comic."[28] On 26 March 1921, he jotted down:

I want to stage *The Seagull*.
Theatrically. As it is in Chekhov . . . I want to stage [Pushkin's] *A Feast in Plaguetime* and Chekhov's *The Wedding* in the same performance. *A Feast in Plaguetime* is inside *The Wedding*.
These are plague victims who don't yet know the plague is here, that mankind has been set free, that you don't need generals at weddings.
In Chekhov there is no lyricism, but tragedy. When a man shoots himself, it is not lyrical. It is either Banality [*Poshlost*] or Bravado [*Podvig*]. Neither Banality nor Bravado was ever lyrical. And both Banality and Bravado have their tragic masks.[29]

When he wrote these words, his new production of *The Wedding* was already playing at the fifty-seat Mansurov studio. His first version had been benign, smiling blandly at a society which had not undergone a "paroxysm." It lacked the eccentric theatricality and formal acuity that was to characterize the second version. To raise *The Wedding* to the level of *Vanya* by turning it into a tragi-farce and using a procedure he had applied in the past, Vakhtangov treated the characters as marionettes. Instead of creating animated toys (as he had done in the Chauve-Souris cabaret's "March of the Wooden Soldiers" in 1910), he followed the precepts of the symbolist poet Fedor Sologub in seeking to reveal the dead or inanimate element in a living being. What Vakhtangov hoped was that the spectator would start to laugh, but as he was gradually overcome by horror, the laughter would die on his lips. Once the clockwork mechanism and the necrotic strain at the heart of humanity were revealed, amusement would turn to terror.

Vakhtangov began his new work on *The Wedding* with the question, "How are we to portray Chekhov's characters, are we to approve them or condemn them?" In effect, he used music to accomplish both aims. The play opened with a manic quadrille, accompanied by a tinkling piano, when suddenly the puny, worn-out ballroom pianist, a character invented by the director, banged his head on the keys and wept bitter drunkard's tears. From the start it was made clear that this was not everyday life, but reality converted into "a phantasmagoric panopticon."

10 Isaak Rabinovich's design for Vakhtangov's *The Wedding*, Moscow, 1921.

When the pianist bumped his head, each of the dancing chimeras stopped and stared round as to ask, "Everything I see – people, objects, room, and even myself – do they really exist or do they only seem so?"[30] Then came a waltz, which set the tempo for the opening dialogue.

If the only reality of the performance was, as Nikolay Volkov called it, "sticky stupefaction,"[31] then the quadrille was a desperate attempt to break out of it, but unsuccessfully and mechanically. Each guest had his own passion or ambition, and was eager to prevail over the others. The pretentiousness of tasteless gowns, cheap fans and elaborate hairdos, eloquent of these vulgar claims to fulfilment, all clashed. The actors singled out the most squamous features of their characters: the father-in-law was an opportunistic Babbitt, hiding behind a mask of bonhomie; the bridegroom a tedious malcontent, whose monotonous voice, like Chinese water torture, drove people crazy; the telegrapher Yat was a pygmy Don Juan; the bride showed more interest in food than in her new husband.

But behind their sordid exteriors they cherished a dream of "the sublime" that was as intense as the three sisters' desire for Moscow: "Once a general gets here this will be a real wedding."

It may be vague, but it is a dream, it may be illusory, it may be rotten, never to be fulfilled, but it *lives*! Vakhtangov reveals what is pitiful and human in these people at the same time, striving to show not only fragments of their life, but in particular the fantastic gaucherie of this life, the idiocy, the social cynicism which doomed people to such a vile and absurd existence.[32]

Only the "General," played by O. N. Basov with a rolling nautical gait, contributed warmth and charm. His arrival brought the dead to life. Deafening them with his naval commands, he accidentally pushed the right corner of the table towards the audience. Hidden beneath a white tablecloth, it suddenly looked like a ship's prow aimed at the footlights, with a story-book captain at the helm. The banquet table, actually composed of several small tables covered with a common cloth, turned into a ship, its sails the napkins waved by the guests trying to shout down the "General."

When he discovered that he had been invited to the wedding under false pretences, the "General" began to wail dolefully "Chelove-e-ek! Chelove-e-ek," – which means both "Waiter" and "Human Being" – and this hopeless cry of a humiliated old man reverberated off the spectators. He seemed to be calling on society for redress. A long pause ensued. The "General" stumbled past the table to exit upstage. Another painful pause. To the sounds of a slow waltz, the characters stood, backs to the audience watching him depart as their dream evaporated, the waltz died out, the party was over. Reality burst in. Then the music struck up the same quadrille that started the play but this time at a mournfully slow tempo. When, at the very end, with tears in her voice and a feeling of anguish, the midwife Zmyeukina begged, "I need atmospherics! . . . I need atmospherics! . . . ," the sense of a puppet-show had vanished.

As the curtain fell slowly, the public sat petrified, prey to a deep emotion, before breaking into thunderous applause. Michael Chekhov, the author's nephew and one of the finest actors of his day, was at a performance. He roared with laughter during *Jubilee*, but when the curtain fell after *The Wedding* and Vakhtangov's students asked him for his impressions, he was bathed in tears, murmuring "What a horror! What a horror!" "Zhenya," he gasped to Vakhtangov, "what's you've done is ghastly . . . "[33]

This was not a fashionable try at modernizing a classic to "revolutionary taste." Vakhtangov believed that contemporaneity could be found only when a theatre artist strove to create something eternal. The result of the production was that Chekhov the satirist acquired a power no one had previously imagined. True, the satire's target was bourgeois vulgarity, this time viewed not as an Aunt Sally for Marxist denunciation, but rather *sub specie aeternitatis*. Steeped in the satiric tradition of Gogol, Shchedrin and Sukhovo-Kobylin, Vakhtangov had tried to wring mordant laughter, sardonic outrage and bilious mockery from Chekhov. *The Wedding* was made to be as trenchant as Dostoevsky's tale of social humiliation "A Nasty Anecdote." But the treatment went beyond its specifically Russian character to link up with the savage caricatures of Goya and Daumier. This, as well as banality's tragic aspect, is what Vakhtangov showed to be hiding behind Chekhov's seemingly insouciant humour.

As usual, it was the old guard that clung to its proprietary notion of Chekhovianism. The Berlin émigré paper *The Rudder (Rul)* was deeply offended by this interpretation. It labelled Vakhtangov an "aesthete," an evil destroyer of Chekhov's intent. "The accumulated pigs' snouts" with their heavy makeup and posing nauseated this critic. But snouts were topical in Soviet Russia. In March 1921, Lenin's New Economic Policy of limited capitalism was passed, *The Wedding*'s candelabra and potted palms decorated new private restaurants, and the acrid stench of the feast in plaguetime would waft through the comedies of Mayakovsky, Mikhail Bulgakov, Nikolay Érdman, and others.

Vakhtangov died too soon to apply these concepts to *The Seagull*, nor was the minor mode of *The Wedding* sufficient to establish a real confrontation with the Art Theatre style. Nevertheless, the grotesque approach had a great influence on the later work of Vakhtangov's students. It also pointed to a way of making *The Cherry Orchard* work.

LAUGHING IN THE ORCHARD

By October 1920 Lunacharsky, disturbed by increasing factionalism in the arts, issued a policy statement whose guidelines were to remain in force until the dissolution of the Soviet Union. Intended to direct energies towards a common goal, it reiterated that new art had to build on the achievements of the bourgeois past, but they in turn had to be purified of vestiges of decay and depravity. If workers in the arts were sufficiently propagandized, a critical treatment of the classics would insure a high level of revolutionary ideology in production.

Nemirovich-Danchenko had to take cognizance of this. Planning for the MAT's return from its American tour in 1924, he pointed out the impossibility of returning to the old repertory in the old style. The Art

Theatre might never recover from the critical lambasting such a tactic would receive.

> Let's not even mention *Uncle Vanya*.
> It's absurd to start work on *Three Sisters* – both the subject and the age of the cast make it absurd.
> *The Cherry Orchard* will not be permitted. That is, lamenting gentlefolks' estates will not be permitted. But the play can't be staged from any other angle (such as the "Hail, new life!" angle).
> *Ivanov* is impossibly out of tune with the "wide-awake era."[34]

But in default of suitable new plays and new angles, Chekhov continued to preponderate at the Art Theatre, a preponderance which led an English observer, Huntly Carter, to declare it "out of the main current of contemporary affairs" in Russia. The new Communist audience wanted "its mind drawn inwards upon its own problems and then reflected outwards to the wider and practical process of solving them." It hadn't the patience to watch an atmosphere being condensed, particularly when it is "rather an atmosphere of moonshine than sunrise, a moonlit seagull haunted space, and not the vigorous dawn of a new life."[35]

Nemirovich had misjudged the suitability of *The Cherry Orchard* to the "wide-awake era." Of Chekhov's full-length plays, it was the only one considered adaptable to Soviet circumstances, precisely because of its "Hail, new life!" angle. As early as 1922, Gaideburov offered a bright and joyous *Cherry Orchard* when his Itinerant Theatre toured civil-war-torn Samara; a soldier of the White forces watched it from a pre-Revolutionary standpoint, and at the words, "We shall plant a new orchard," he burst out, "Don't do it."[36] But for the Reds, the gardeners were Trofimov and Lopakhin, regarded without irony as architects of a utopia. Lopakhin in particular was to be interpreted not as one of the *kulaks* liquidated during the collectivization of the farms but a man of vigour and vision, a proto-Stakhanovite. Stanislavsky himself suggested,

> Give even Lopakhin in *Cherry Orchard* the wide-ranging scope of a Chaliapin, and young Anya the temperament of a Ermolova, and let him chop down with all his might whatever has outlived itself, and let the girl, who with Petya Trofimov forecasts the advent of a new era, shout to the whole world: 'Greetings, new life!' – and you will understand that *The Cherry Orchard* is alive for us, a close, contemporary play, that Chekhov's voice resounds in it cheerfully, provocatively, for it looks not backward but forward.[37]

To realize this progressive vision, a refurbished *Cherry Orchard* opened at the Art Theatre in 1928 (following a similarly renovated *Vanya* the previous year), with a cast half veterans, half newcomers. The opening night was less than perfect: when Knipper entered in Act I, she was given an ovation, forcing actors to stop the action, something unheard of in that sacred grove. And when the curtain rose on the curtain-call, Stanislavsky was caught shaking his fist at the actress who played Varya for some fault of hers.[38] For all the lip service to relevance, the producers were attacked, by Gorky among others, for continuing to play it as a drama and not a comedy.

In 1925, the literary manager of the Second Moscow Art Theatre, Yury Sobolev, had laid out a theoretical basis for such an interpretation in the trade journal *New Spectator* (*Novy Zritel*); and by 1932, Nemirovich's own protégé, Ivan Bersenev, was addressing the company on the incomprehensibility of *The Cherry Orchard* to contemporary society. He too recommended that, to bring out its relevance, it be staged as a comedy.[39] The common bond between comedy and communism was pointed out by the critic Bachelis: "Chekhov wanted the break with the past to be cheerful and merry . . . He almost literally followed Marx's precept – a precept everybody knows! – that laughter allows people to break easily with their pasts. The Art Theatre lagged behind Chekhov. *It didn't want to laugh . . .* "[40]

The first attempt to stage *The Cherry Orchard* as "almost a farce" (as its author had called it) was made by the Leningrad Comedy Theatre in 1926, under the direction of Konstantin Khokhlov, who extended sympathy only to Lopakhin and Anya, for, in his words, "They are the ones who chop down the old, unnecessary cherry orchard, which lets no sunlight penetrate the window of the cold and arid house."[41] Gaideburov, restaging *Orchard* at the Bolshoy Dramatic Theatre in Leningrad, refitted it along the lines of Marxist sociology: at the moment when Trofimov apostrophized Anya with his lofty sentiments, the designer Tatyana Bruni provided an "industrial landscape [which] began to glow with kindled fires," an effect which even the reviewers of the day found ham-fisted.[42]

However, it was Andrey Lobanov's *Cherry Orchard* of 1934, played at Ruben Simonov's theatre-studio in Moscow, that proved the most effective salvo in the assault on the Art Theatre's "monopoly" of Chekhov. Lobanov wanted to show up the decadence and degradation of the gentry; he and his designers Boris Matrunin and N. V. Kuzmin went to extremes in their definition of a social comedy. Following Vakhtangov, Lobanov claimed that it was a mixture of genres, with the vaudeville ingredients as powerful as comedy, drama and tragedy; but in excising lyricism, he removed its heart.

11 N. Kuzmin's costume sketches for Charlotta and Lopakhin in Lobanov's production
of *The Cherry Orchard*, Moscow, 1934.

Simov's old Art Theatre sets had always demonstrated "a fondness for that life"; Matrunin's scenery aborted any nostalgia by denuding the estate of warmth and beauty. The rooms were angular, filled with period furniture that bore the stamp of neglect and obsolescence. Doubt was thus cast on the owners' affection for their home; Ranevskaya and Gaev were shown to be bound to it by force of habit. Because the characters were alienated from nature, there was no orchard, not even a landscape in Act II. This was set in a claustrophobic cheap eatery, from which a drunken Petya Trofimov was ejected by waiters, and then in a stuffy, darkened bathhouse where he conspiratorially addressed his harangue to a bunch of gymnasium students.

With the grotesque to the fore, the throughline was located in Dunyasha, Charlotta and Epikhodov. Ranevskaya's tenderer moments merely threw into contrast her epicurean egocentrism; svelte in an elegant kimono or making up at a dressing table, she was played by A. I. Delektorskaya as essentially impure. So Yasha's relationship with her was thrust into the foreground, and made unequivocal. He was the witness of her Parisian past, she needed him, and he became all the more boorish, which she disdained to notice.

More decadence lay behind Gaev's puerility. Lobanov's notes to the actor who played the role reveal the brutality of his attack.

3. Doesn't like to wash.
   [. . .]
8. Clings to life, which he sees as lying on the sofa, playing billiards, borrowing and spending money.
   [. . .]
10. A layabout, a parasite, takes money even from the maid-servants. Annoyed by people who ignore him. He's an "misunderstood hero," hangs around people who pay him no attention.
    [. . .]
12. Suddenly seems knocked for a loop: can't mooch around the house any more or loll on the sofa, there won't be his favourite junk, the bookcase with its spiders, those old walls. With the sale of the estate the ground's shot from under his feet and it's obvious his game is up. His house is tumbling down to the last rafter and him along with it. He goes to the job at the bank in town like a captive bear, taken from his native forest to a zoo, where he will soon drop dead. [. . .] [43]

Since Lobanov despised the characters, they were to be ruthlessly mocked and their orchard sentenced to be liquidated. Indeed, the actors sympathized more with their characters than the director did and tried to tone down some of his more garish colours.

Ruben Simonov spoke for the audience: "No tears did we shed when the cherry orchard was chopped down. Ranevskaya's helplessness did not stir our pity."[44] Yet, for all of its eccentricity and desire to shock, Lobanov's production epitomized attitudes which had been expressed at the time of the play's premiere in 1904. It accorded with Gorky's condemnation of Ranevskaya and her family as egotistic, simultaneously infantile and decrepit.[45] Controversial though it was, the production stayed in the studio's repertory for many years.

Lobanov's production and its imitators came towards the end of the trend to challenge traditional interpretations of the classics. His audacity was an anachronistic and politically retrograde leftover from the theatrical eccentrism of the 1920s. In 1932, Stalin had for the first time named writers "engineers of souls" and spoken of "socialist realism," which two years later was legislated as the "fundamental method" for all the arts. The classics were to be the pillars of the repertory, and the MAT's methods and style the model for all theatres in the USSR. Any manifestation of "formalism" was under attack and anyone who dabbled in experimentation and initiative was hounded literally to death by the press and the Committee for Artistic Affairs.

FAINTING SPELLS

Meyerhold was one of the first to topple before the winds of change. After a decade of bold experimentation, from 1933 on he staged nothing but classics and in a more respectful and ornamental manner than he had in the twenties. Although the very first play he ever directed had been *Three Sisters*, Meyerhold avoided Chekhov in his pro-active Bolshevik phase, and did not return to him until 1935, the seventy-fifth anniversary of the writer's birth, a time when Meyerhold admitted "The Chekhov of *The Cherry Orchard* and *Three Sisters* is not at all close to us today."[46] Nor was he himself as close to Soviet life as he had once been; although his brilliant re-thinking of the opera *Queen of Spades* had been well received, Meyerhold was kept busy fending off accusations of "formalism" and irrelevance. Awaiting the construction of his new playhouse, he was rehearsing *Boris Godunov* and planning a *Hamlet*, so his work on Chekhov can be seen as expedient pot-boiling.

Still, although much of his energy was directed elsewhere, although his eagerness to provoke was dampened by the repressive climate, and although the project corresponded with none of his current tasks, Meyerhold's choice of three farces as his contribution to the Chekhov celebration had an element of defiance to it. Conceived as a "musical melodrama-bouffe," *The Jubilee*, *The Bear* and *The Proposal* were retitled *33 Swoons*, computed by Meyerhold to be the number of fainting-fits that occur in the plays (fourteen in *Jubilee*, eight in *Bear*, eleven in *Proposal*). "But we will have more," he announced to the actors, to serve as idiosyncratic *jeux du théâtre*, the pivot of the production" . . . The actors must live from swoon to swoon."[47] He also mooted a screen with super-titles to tote up the swoon count. Each swoon was to be accompanied by music composed by Shostakovich, with the orchestra as a separate character in the plays. Percussion, wind and brass instruments on the left underscored the male swoons, strings on the right did the same for the female swoons, with a grand piano centre stage for "philosophically abstract moments."[48] In practice, the swoons only fixed the tempo of traditional readings of the plays.

"First, we must find the thought of the author; then we must reveal the thought in a theatrical form . . . I am going to use the technique of the traditional vaudeville as the *jeu* . . . Everything will contribute to this *jeu*."[49] These instructions to the actors stressed technique and theatrical tradition. To the world at large, Meyerhold proclaimed more

pretentiously and less candidly that the swoons exemplified the neuras-
thenic legacy, the weak-willed, socially conditioned passivity of the intelligentsia of the 1880s and nineties.[50] Little of this could be demonstrated
in Chekhov's scripts, but such cant was now standard among artists
under Stalin. While some of the critics enthusiastically picked up the
"social" motif, they still wondered whether the actors had to be quite so
spasmodic in depicting a neurotic bourgeoisie.

In the early phases of rehearsal, Meyerhold insisted on care and delicacy towards the text to bring out everything in it, and went in great
detail over the kernel of each character. "Chekhov's vaudevilles cannot
be seen as independent of Chekhov's whole system of drama."[51]
Working on the servant Luka in *The Bear*, one must keep Firs in mind. He
called Shipuchin, the harried secretary in *The Jubilee*, the toughest role in
the Russian repertory. Although he lingered over such realistic features
as the hot summer day in *The Proposal*, with everyone pouring sweat,
Meyerhold wanted to avoid "*bytovizm*" (kitchen-sink naturalism) and preferred to take a musical approach. Sweat should be not merely a picturesque token of reality, but should bring out the absurdity of Lomov's
arriving in a tailcoat, top hat and gloves.

The unit setting by Viktor Shestakov was framed by galleries running
from the side portals and culminated upstage in symmetrical stairways.
Forecasting the architectural design of the future Meyerhold Theatre, its
spatial relationships were to serve as a constructivist model in which all
sorts of plays might be staged: bright, antiseptic stage dressing – panels
both permanent and moving, curtains, covers on furniture – and a
neutral white light evenly illuminating the stage. The scenery had both
an emblematic and a functional character: some details (door, window,
cupboard, table, sofa) defined the place of action and were used as set-
pieces. The cupboard in *Jubilee* became a hiding-place, and the grand
piano in *Bear* stood in for a horse when Smirnov sat astride it. Meyerhold
insisted that the period props be appropriately tasteless.

In spite of elements that suggested a carefree concert recital, participants and observers leave no doubt that Meyerhold directed the farces
by the show-and-tell method, giving specific line readings and
demonstrations of stage business to the actors, brilliantly dissecting the
words, sounds, characterization and style.

You, Ivan Vasilevich, will be having a hat that is slightly too large, although it
will not appear so at first to the audience. You are a country bumpkin, and you
have borrowed your father's best hat to pay this call in; his head is a bit bigger

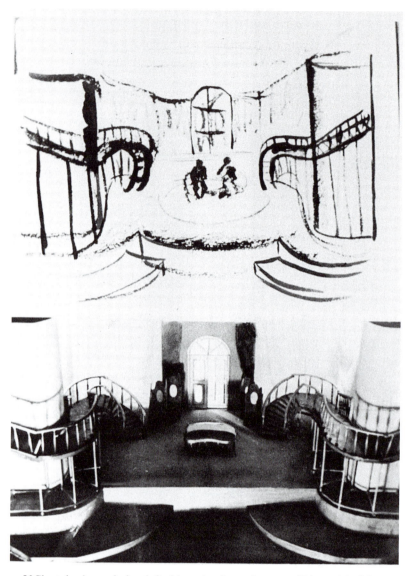

12 V. Shestakov's rough sketch for his setting for *33 Swoons* and his model of the set, Meyerhold Theatre, Moscow, 1935.

than yours. Then when Chubukov claps, you will allow the hat to slip down and cover your ear as though it were involuntarily coming to the assistance of your weak heart. That is why the audience must see a little more of your ear under the hat than it did the first time just now.[52]

The weak heart was another invention of Meyerhold's which required Igor Ilinsky to have constant recourse to a water carafe, until, at a climactic moment, he pours it over his head.

The carafe was just one of innumerable hand-props Meyerhold injected into the farces to stimulate "the circulation of their vaudeville blood." In *The Proposal*, Lomov and Natasha fought over a napkin and tray while disputing ownership of fields. In *The Jubilee*, the deputation of shareholders presented Shipuchin with a stuffed bear. The symbolic value of the props and set-pieces tended to diminish the characters, whose genuine concerns were displaced to objects, which were then manipulated in clown acts. On occasion the physical gags these props inspired proved genuinely funny, but for the most part they clogged the action and lumbered the plays with directorial ingenuity. Like Vakhtangov, Meyerhold was reducing Chekhov's people to puppets, but, unlike Vakhtangov, he was unable to infuse them with deeper meaning.

Although Meyerhold had asked for simplicity, lightness, humour, the performers came across as "life-like but heavy," forced and stilted. Ilinsky felt that he failed to take on a life independent of the director's scenario, and was too scrupulous in polishing and relishing the details.[53] *The Bear* was perhaps the most successful, certainly the most distinctive of the three, less grotesque since Meyerhold's wife Zinaida Raikh and Nikolay Bogolyubov were different from the other actors: a matched couple who looked good together.

The press was largely favourable, but to the actors the first couple of performances felt like flops, for the audience barely laughed. The lashings of stage business and fainting fits robbed the production of pace, and even Meyerhold said

We tried to be too clever and consequently lost sight of the humour. We must face the truth: the audience at any amateur production of *The Proposal* would laugh more loudly than ours did, even though Ilinsky was acting and Meyerhold directing. Chekhov's light transparent humour was crushed beneath the weight of our theories and the result was a disaster.[54]

Despite Meyerhold's own awareness of failure, he hoped to show the production to Stanislavsky at his home. This confrontation of the master of Chekhovian mood with a jumped-up puppet-show never took place, owing to Meyerhold's arrest and subsequent judicial murder. *33 Swoons* would be the last new work ever seen by the public at Meyerhold's theatre.

CHAPTER 7

Chekhov learns English (United Kingdom and Ireland 1900–1940)

When I first tangled with a play of [Chekhov] it was as an actor in a stock company at Oxford, England. We were all very young, all reveled in the gloomiest emotions. With sobs and tears we sorted out those of the largest size. The undergraduate audience received our efforts with hilarity such I have never heard in any theatre. Looking back, I blush for us and bow to them. Their attitude was entirely healthy and [Chekhov] would have approved it completely.

Margaret Webster[1]

LUNATICS AND LOVERS

Misapprehensions of Chekhov had an early start in the anglophone world. A year before the author died, a reference work by Professor Leo Weiner warned its readers: "A pessimistic view runs through all his productions, and all his characters seem to be fit subjects for the psychiatrist."[2] That same year, the allusion to mental illness recurred in Alfred Bates's anthology *The Drama*: "Everywhere we behold the same strange assemblage of neurotics, lunatic and semi-lunatic . . . The society thus brought before us is like a nightmare. All its members are bent on one thing only – the solution of the problem of life."[3] Implicit was the assumption that the problem of life was not an urgent concern of the English, who might be thought to have solved it.

Luckily, the official introduction of Chekhov to the British stage was affected by someone who was both sympathetic and knowledgeable. George Calderon had spent two years (1895–7) in Russia learning the language, immersing himself in the literature and "absorbing a profound and thorough expertise of Russian ways and thought, supporting himself by writing articles and giving lessons in English."[4] Calderon's own plays were produced by the Independent Stage Society between 1909 and 1912, and, although they never attracted much public favour, were worthy *pièces à thèse*, technically modelled on Scribe but filled with contemporary types and vivid dialogue.[5] Calderon was eager to introduce Russian drama to the English public, and sought the opinion of no less an expert than Meyerhold on what was most exciting on the current scene. Meyerhold's ensuing essay on the Russian dramatic tradition prompted Calderon to write for *The Quarterly Review* (July 1912) the best informed article on the subject in any Western language.

The first British production of Chekhov, *The Seagull* at the Glasgow Repertory Theatre (2 Nov. 1909), though nominally directed by Alfred Wareing, was translated and guided by Calderon. The Repertory Company's "programme was mainly drawn from Ibsen and the Court Theatre's seasons in Sloane Square, London . . . the staple diet for the four years of the Rep's existence . . . was Shaw and Granville Barker, St. John Hankin, John Masefield and Pinero."[6] Evidently this constellation of modern dramatists was dimly aware of Chekhov's kinship to them, for in a 1905 letter to Laurence Irving, Shaw had remarked: "I hear that there are several dramas extant by Whatshisname (Tchekoff, or something like that) – the late Russian novelist who wrote The Black Monk &c. Have you any of them translated for the Stage Society, or anything of your own that would suit us?"[7]

Calderon took pains in a preliminary lecture to explain that "a play of Tchekhof is a reverie, not a concatenation of events," and was at variance with crude naturalism.[8] In a surprisingly enlightened reaction, the Scottish reviewers, no doubt echoing Calderon's precepts, were quick to pick up on what they called the play's "Ibsenite" or "odd and elusive" symbolism. The staging strove for transitions from group moods to individual reactions, to achieve something close to Stanislavsky's "through-line" or "super-objective" *avant le lettre*, despite the inability of British actors to maintain an inner life when not speaking lines. "The impression of overwhelming humanity owed much to the fine all round acting . . . for the ensemble was so perfect that it would almost seem invidious to select individual names," reported one critic.[9]

London was more backward. There, the progenitrix of a Chekhov production was the Princess Bariatinska, alias Lidiya Yavorskaya, who had settled in England in 1909. She produced *The Bear* in May 1911 as part of a week's triple bill at the Kingsway Theatre. Shaw's germinal interest in Chekhov as fodder for the Stage Society came to fruition that same month, when it produced *The Cherry Orchard* at the Aldwych Theatre; he characterized it as "the most important [production] in England since that of *A Doll's House*."[10] The under-rehearsed cast included such luminaries-to-be as Mary Jerrold (Varya), Harcourt Williams (Trofimov) and Nigel Playfair (Pishchik), but they could not compensate for Kenelm Foss's sluggish direction and the miscasting of an inexperienced young amateur as Ranevskaya. Accustomed to the format of the traditional problem play, the public took Lopakhin to be a brutish villain, the Gaev family to be charming victims, and, in one case, Epikhodov to be the "raisonneur."[11] Epikhodov (Ivan Berlyn) proved in particular to be a stumbling-block, since his knockabout antics made no sense. "What he was doing in the household of an apparently sane woman like Madame Ranevsky was only one of the many hopeless puzzles with which the Stage Society presented us," recalled the novelist Hugh Walpole.[12] Primed for social issues and drama of reform, the Stage Society could not come to grips with the characters' self-involvement; its audiences, who arrived expecting a debate on questions of the day, walked out before the final curtain.

A. B. Walkley's notice in *The Times* laid the blame squarely at the Stage Society's door: "Russians are foreigners, but, even so, it is highly improbable that they are such fools as they seem in the English version of Chekhov's comedy." Still, it joined the consensus that this was a play decipherable only by Russians: it "cannot but strike an English audience as something queer, outlandish, even silly." The *Daily Telegraph* similarly conflated the norms of British life with conventional playmaking: "an atmosphere, a social life, a set of characters, so different from those which we habitually meet, was, and must be, a shock to a well-regulated and conventional English mind." Putting a sociologist's face on his confusion, its critic decided that " . . . the play was written to set before our eyes how certain conditions weigh so heavily upon Russian society and upon the Russian character, as to make them in a large measure sterile and unproductive."[13] As usual, the journalists lagged in comprehension behind the intelligent playgoer. While agreeing that *The Cherry Orchard* "presents an average picture of Russian society," Arnold Bennett added the proviso that it "presents the picture with such exact, uncompromising truthfulness that the members of the Stage Society mistook nearly all the portraits for caricatures, and tedious caricatures . . . His truthfulness frightens, and causes resentment."[14]

When Calderon's two translations were published in 1912 with his Glasgow lecture as a preface, the *Times Literary Supplement* opined, "Russian melancholy we know; this futility may be another side to it – a tragic helplessness; which has been observed by Sir Hubert Parry in some Russian music. But it is not a feeling which we share in Western

Europe, and the difference of temperament may well keep Chekhov from our affection." The *TLS* predicted that the English would grow impatient with Chekhov's "flabby people" and fail to greet him with "love and admiration."[15] This was borne out when the Adelphi Play Society offered a single Sunday night performance of Calderon's *Seagull* in the accurately named Little Theatre (31 March 1912), with the manageress Gertrude Kingston as Arkadina. The translator's lecture on Chekhov's method was abandoned on this occasion, owing no doubt to the fact that there was almost no one present at the advertised time for the performance to begin.

The animating impetus behind this venture had again been Princess Bariatinska; although in her forties, she assumed the role of Nina, adorning it with a heavy Russian accent. One critic thought "she played certain scenes with a restraint in speaking and acting without which Chekhov's delicate analyses cannot be achieved"; but another complained that both leading ladies failed to realize that "her individual part was important only in correlation with the rest." This exercise in prima-donnery met with a singular lack of enthusiasm.[16]

It was *Uncle Vanya*, a more compact and accessible play, which first established a reputation for Chekhov as second only to Shakespeare. In May 1914, the Incorporated Stage Society offered two performances in Mrs R. S. Townsend's translation at the Aldwych Theatre. Walkley, who had condemned *Orchard* so roundly, was impressed by *Vanya* as "a world of talkers without listeners" whose characters blended "the good and bad, weakness and strength." Desmond MacCarthy found it "an unforgettably good play," the more tragic for the sheer ordinariness of Chekhov's victims, suffocating in their "sighs and yawns and self-reproaches, vodka, endless tea and endless discussion."[17]

On the first night of *Vanya*, Shaw is reported to have said to a colleague, "When I hear Chekhov, I want to tear my own plays up."[18] While others were puzzling over the fecklessness and apparent meaninglessness of Chekhov's characters, Shaw perceived serious political and social implications in these evocations of melancholy and futility. Just as he had heralded Ibsen's attack on the life-lie, he promoted the fundamental realism and sanity of Chekhov's vision and purpose. However, his essays had turned Ibsen into a Nordic GBS, and he similarly recast Chekhov in his own image, interpreting him as a fatalist unsympathetic to the characters in *The Cherry Orchard*. "He had no faith in those charming people extricating themselves. They would, he thought, be sold up and set adrift by the bailiffs; therefore he had no scruple in exploiting and even flattering their charm."[19] This style of exploitation was closer to Shaw's usual *modus operandi* than to Chekhov's.

When he came to subtitle *Heartbreak House* (1913–16) a "Fantasia in the Russian Manner on English Themes," Shaw was indulging in self delusion. His preface alluded to Tolstoy's "ferociously contemptuous manner" as well as to Chekhov; for ultimately Shaw has more in common with Tolstoy's moralizing shock tactics than with Chekhov's distanced *laissez-aller*.[20] What Shaw chiefly failed to learn from Chekhov was reticence and the use of the pause: his people never shut up. When Vershinin or Trofimov starts speechifying, he is always undercut by his own behaviour or the inappropriateness of the moment; whereas Shaw's characters too often comprise a debating society intent on scoring points. Nothing in Chekhov is inconsequential except speech; nothing in Shavian speech is ever inconsequential. The American critic Stark Young was to point out the absurdity of Shaw's pronouncements on the subject:

Chekhov sees his people as rooted in something, which means that he begins with what they are, their quality, and from this he derives what they will express. Mr. Shaw, for all his prattle about their class, clichés, bogies, culture and complacent, urgent or ironic circumstances, sees his people in the light of their opinions.[21]

WILD GULLS AT COOLE

But Shaw, after all, was not English. He was Irish, and percipient Irishmen, instead of alienating Chekhov by remarking "How Russian," immediately spotted similarities. One commentator noted that "the essential *futility* of Tchekov's characters is precisely that of which Larry Doyle complained in *John Bull's Other Island*, a play written half a dozen years before Tchekov was heard of in these longitudes."[22] Another writer considered that the Irish mentality and environment were so akin to those of Russia that one might merely change the names in Chekhov's plays and easily pass off characters and locales as Irish. "There is much of Ireland in the atmosphere and the people of *The Cherry Orchard*: the fatalism, the kindliness and the little irritations . . . "[23]

Chekhov was wielded as a weapon in Irish cultural skirmishes. Yeats had wanted to stage continental drama at the Abbey Theatre, but he had been overruled by Lady Gregory and Synge, who preferred a native school of *lumpen*-naturalism and poetic peasant drama. Their rival, the Irish Theatre Company, staged both Anglo-Irish and European plays,

many for the first time in Ireland, and to the taste of its managers
Edward Martyn and Thomas MacDonagh (who thought Chekhov the
best foreign playwright), and of their supporter George Moore.[24] In
January 1915 Martyn put on Marian Fell's translation of *Swan Song* on a
triple bill with Villiers de l'Isle Adams's *The Revolt* and an Irish-language
play. *Swan Song* had been announced as a "prelude to a longer work [by
Chekhov]," and indeed the Irish Theatre bravely ended its 1914–15
season with *Uncle Vanya*.

It was a risky choice given the company's amateur standing, but
MacDonagh believed *Vanya* was easy to rehearse. To precondition the
public, the management announced rather daringly that it was a play
impossible to understand unless read ahead of time. Moore proved this
assertion with a leader in *The Irish Times* (24 June 1915); having never read
Vanya himself, he rambled on about *The Cherry Orchard*: "No one ever had
a more beautiful touch than Tchekoff, and in the last analysis, art is
touch: in painting, in sculpture – yes, and in literature – and that is why
women do not produce as beautiful works of art as men."

This muddled prelude had its effect on the press, which found the play
"incomprehensible" and the male characters "eccentric cranks, who
give vent to some extraordinary philosophic views about things in
general. The ladies, being vastly more human, are interesting in their
way."[25] *Freeman's Journal* attacked it for being "like one of those post
impressionist pictures which would look just as well if turned upside
down . . . we are informed that 'woods to the right of the spectator' are
indicated by 'green curtains,' which on an occasion like this is a great
strain on the most powerful imagination."

If *Freeman's* was put off by green, *New Ireland*, which granted that a
"subtle   atmosphere   was   conveyed,"   objected   to   monotones.
Characterizing Chekhov as a photographic realist, the reviewer
explained that "the tone of his work is uniformly grey." " His characters,
varied and crowded as they are, all seem to have that tired feeling, that
feeling of boredom and ennui which is a distinctive note in Russian literature." Worse, for an Irish public, "there is not a laugh . . . in his four acts
. . . " except for those uncalled-for. Joseph Holloway, the Pepys of the
Dublin theatre, agreed: "they all moved about awkwardly – spoke list-
lessly and were mightily depressive – one could imagine people wanting
to shoot each other in Russia." Chekhov was like Synge "ever harping on
age and beauty – only the sickly dwell on such themes."[26]

The production gave rise to a parody in Percy French's variety show
How Dublin Does it (Little Theatre 19–22 Jan 1916): "*Gloom* as done at the

Irish Theatre," "A Russian Hair and Curtain Raiser." This proved to be a big hit, featuring wolves howling in the forest, moon- and candle-light, a peasant woman, Orfulkoff, an "asthmatic subject," and his fiancée Little Tileoff (= "to have a slate missing, to be cracked").

ORFULKOFF. Tileoff and I are happy since the doctor diagnosed us.
ZOGITOFF. What was the doctor's diagnosis, Orfulkoff?
ORFULKOFF. We are to die to-night. (*Coughs.*)
TILEOFF. How I love that cough!
LITTLE MOTHER. There can be no funeral! There is no vodka!
ORFULKOFF. Tileoff and I will wander away into the forest – the snow will be our winding sheet.

(*Wolves howl.*)[27]

Yet, when *Vanya* was revived on 12–17 February 1917, familiarity appears to have brought about a revised verdict. *Freeman's Journal* now called it "peculiarly interesting for the comparisons it offers between Irish and Russian character," and *The Irishman* "a masterpiece." "There is a marvelous atmosphere, to use the trite phrase, about the play. It shows little action, and gains from the failure, for the mission of the author was to show wasted lives, capable of great effort, but choked by a system which restrains mental activity as effectively as it hampers civil liberty." The shock of recognition shines through these reconsiderations.

The Jubilee on another triple bill (3 December 1917–5 January 1918) confused the critics who were expecting introspection rather than farce. But this was merely a diversion preliminary to the Irish Theatre's mounting of *The Cherry Orchard* in Calderon's translation. Martyn again attempted to prime his public with a long essay in *New Ireland* (21 June 1917): " . . . if ever the mirrour of social life in its especial inanity has been held up to us with the sure hand of genius, it is in this curious drama." He compared the dialogue with what might be heard at parties or clubs.

If then, as I have suggested, Tchekoff is the delineator of incoherence, on the other hand it must be granted that his method, if carefully examined, will be found remarkably coherent. In fact he seems to have reduced the incoherence and absurdity of average humanity to a system . . .

This advance publicity did not prevent the *Orchard* from being chivvied by the press. This "picture of peasant life" disappointed *The Irish Times* with its stilted, inconsequential dialogue, devoid of passion or conflict. *The Leader* accused Martyn of Bolshevism and wanted to know why an Irish theatre was presenting an English version of a Russian

play.[28] Many of the complaints were directed at the production's inade-
quacies; there was no elbow room on the tiny stage, so that characters
had to stand and stare, or wander about aimlessly. The acting also left
much to be desired: the reviewer for the *Irish Program* could imagine the
Lopakhin of Paul Farrell (the "Irish Elocutionist") "shouting for a
Shellilah and Donnybrook." And Holloway complained that Oliver
Clonabraney as Pishchik "looked, acted and walked about almost like a
miniature pantomime giant and spoke in a mechanised spasmodic way
as unreal as his appearance almost."[29] The one real discovery in the cast
was the Firs of Jimmy O'Dea, later to win fame as a comic dame.

"If *The Cherry Orchard* was not cuffed about as badly as *Vanya* was, a
possible explanation is that, as many critics pointed out, what Chekhov
implicitly prophesied for imperial Russia could be construed in terms of
the Irish situation."[30] In this particular case, the *Orchard* held topical
significance, for Irish manor-houses were undergoing a like desuetude.
The trees on Lady Gregory's estate at Coole had been chopped down for
fuel during the Troubles, and in 1927 she would sell the land to the
Forestry Department. Martyn's own ancestral home at Tulira was
derelict because his tenants wouldn't pay their rent. When the play was
revived on January 26, 1920, the notices improved. Holloway commented ironically, "One night *The Cherry Orchard* was loudly applauded
and Mr. Martyn said, 'That must not be, it will never do for us to play
down to the level of public taste!' As if the public were ever to be found
at the Irish Theatre."[31]

By the end of the World War, the leading lights of the Irish literary
theatre movement were burning low: Martyn was ill, Moore had left the
country, and Yeats "had ceased to be interested in people."[32] Even the
Abbey Theatre turned to foreigners to stock its repertory, staging works
of Evreinov, Martinez Sierra and indeed minor Chekhov (*The Proposal*
on 28 April 1925). The Drama League put on *Three Sisters*; but at the
more up-to-date Gate, its artistic directors Hilton Edwards and Micheál
MacLiammóir found Evreinov and Gogol more appealing Russians.
They didn't get around to Chekhov until their sixth season of 1932/33,
when they offered their public a double serving of *The Cherry Orchard* in
August and *The Seagull* in November. The experience must not have been
sufficiently encouraging, for they did not return to him for another forty-
five years.[33]

In 1933, in a comment on these developments, the Abbey Theatre presented Lennox Robinson's comedy *Is Life Worth Living? or Drama at Inish*, a
blandly satirical look at the influence the "new drama" was having on

provincial stages. In the course of this self-styled "exaggeration," an acting troupe comes to a small Irish seaside resort with a repertory of Ibsen, Strindberg, Tolstoy and, of course, "Tchekov." "I now confine myself entirely . . . to psychological and introspective drama," explains the actor-manager, "because . . . they may revolutionize some person's soul." A pall falls on the town and rain is incessant. The populace becomes addicted to this regimen of morbidity and is transformed from a pleasant community of mediocrities to a hagridden coven of depressives. They make suicide pacts, buy weed-killer to dispose of old relations, leap off the pier. As one sensible nay-sayer to the new drama remarks, "Sure you couldn't wear nice clothes going to that class of play; the best you could do would be a sort of half-mourning."[34] Only with the forcible closure of the theatre and the arrival of a circus does the town return to normal. For Robinson's satiric purposes, Chekhov was lumped together with the rest of modernist European theatre as a propagandist for an unwholesome world view, long on introverted negativity and short on common sense. Like many of the reviewers, what Robinson thought was missing in Chekhov was the Irish love of a joke. Although Irish fiction began to display the effects of Chekhov's influence, he would not have a similar effect on native drama until the late 1940s.

ANGLO-SAXON ATTITUDES

The image of Chekhov as *il penseroso* was perpetuated by postwar London productions, which continued to confuse the author with the lameness of the staging. In reaction to *The Seagull*, produced in 1919 at the Haymarket by the Art Theatre co-founded by émigrée Vera Donnet, the reviewer for the *Sunday Times* again deposed the now formal testimony that, "Chekhov's earth is always without form and void, and darkness is always upon the face of his lake . . . Here is a coterie of Neuropaths, all adepts in the art of making themselves eternally unhappy."[35] At the play Michael Lykiardopoulo, former secretary of the Moscow Art Theatre and now a refugee from his homeland, overheard two women beside him remark, "These Russians, you know, they drink all day long and all night; men and women. And then they all go Bolshevist."[36] Lykiardopoulo was impelled to put the blame squarely on the playwright's English admirers.

For many years I have been under the impression that Chekhov was the pet victim invariably chosen by all London stage societies for their histrionic and murderous experiments in 'Russian' drama, with the result that to mention today in England merely the title of any Russian play means evoking nightmares of morbidity, sordidness and infinite tediousness . . . [37]

Misplaced enthusiasm was not dispelled but rather fortified throughout the 1920s: the English continued to label Chekhov the spokesman of bewhiskered melancholia but they also began to appreciate something more in him. The mood of embittered disillusion that permeated English society in the wake of the Great War's futile devastation suddenly made the yearnings and futility of Chekhov's people seem more apposite. While J. Middleton Murry, Katherine Mansfield, S. S. Koteliansky and others proselytized for Chekhov the short-story writer; his plays were seized on as expressions of a familiar malaise. Russian émigrés such as Prince Mirsky were bemused by this new fascination, which struck them as morbid and misguided. Constantine Nabokoff, writing in 1924 in *The Contemporary Review*, warned that "One has to be thoroughly acquainted with Russian life in order to understand the delicate and sure touch with which Chekhov introduces us to that gloomy world." To provide a social context for understanding the plays, Nabokoff drew a parallel between the Russian and Galsworthy.[38]

A spate of translations made Chekhov's writings more widely available, but not necessarily more lucid. The 1904 censored script of *The Cherry Orchard* was used as copy-text for Julius West's 1915 version, reprinted three times over the next decade, and for Constance Garnett's translation, first published in 1923, regularly reissued and still in print. Garnett's prestige as the translator who made Dostoevsky, Gogol, Tolstoy, Turgenev and other Russian masters accessible to English speakers lent a *cachet* to her Chekhov as well, especially when her translations fell out of copyright; but they were suffused with a literary gentility which turned his characters into proper Edwardians.[39] In the meantime, reports of Stanislavsky's handling of the plays were drifting back to London. Granville-Barker saw *Cherry Orchard* at the MAT in 1922 and was impressed by "the personal magnetism" of actors like Olga Knipper and "a close rapport between the actors that was evident even when they were not actively doing anything on stage."[40] But until the English acting profession and the habit of rehearsing a play from "sides" could be reformed, little headway could be made in production.[41]

Three Sisters was finally staged in March 1920 by Mme Donnet's Art Theatre at the Royal Court in Harold Bowen's translation, with Harcourt Williams as Vershinin; despite the evident inability to make sense of the play's dense texture, she followed it up with *The Cherry*

Orchard in 1920 at St. Martin's Theatre (Edith Evans's Charlotta walked away with the reviews). Solemn though the production was, the play was appreciated and there were calls for a commercial management to venture into these waters; it would take five years for this call to be heeded.

In the dog-days of 1925, Nigel Playfair, the enterprising manager of the modish Lyric Hammersmith, invited to his theatre a youthful company from the Oxford Playhouse. Their play was *The Cherry Orchard* directed by J. B. Fagan; Fagan had already staged an *Uncle Vanya* which was perfunctory and under-rehearsed, funereally paced and saturated with the blues.[42] *Orchard* was similarly misconceived, and only two of its actors – Fred O'Donovan (Lopakhin) and O. B. Clarence (Firs) – had established reputations. The rest of the young cast, including John Gielgud as "Trophimof," Mary Grey as "Madame Ranevsky," James Whale (later Frankenstein's film-director) as Epikhodov, Alan Napier (later Batman's butler) as Gaev and Glen Byam Shaw (later an outstanding director) as Yasha, would quickly make names for themselves. Gielgud, who had up to then played effete roles, wore a bald-pate, scruffy beard and eyeglasses to impersonate the perennial student, and declared "it was the first time I ever went on the stage and felt that perhaps I could really act."[43] Audiences were bewildered: "Is this a picture of a Russian lunatic asylum, or a skit on the futility of Russian folk, or a piece of ultra-realism or ultra-symbolism or dadaism, or what?"[44] But by the middle of the second act, they had fallen under the play's spell.

The transfer to the Lyric had been strongly backed by Arnold Bennett, an avid admirer of Chekhov's fiction, who had been arguing with managers for years that audiences were now ready for such a venture. The attempt was in the nature of a selfless experiment; no one was really convinced that it would take off.

The first performance was splendidly received. But we did not believe in it. On the Thursday after the first performance (Monday) none of us believed in it, and Fagan met the directors and agreed without argument that the thing was a failure. But a few days later he was believing in it (by reason of the enthusiasm of small audiences), but the returns were still awful, and the loss heavy. Then the returns enormously improved.[45]

The turning-point came when Lady Cunard wrote a letter to the *Daily Express*, deploring their unfavourable review and urging the play's merits. This testimonial from a social celebrity doubled the audiences. Despite the torrid nights, the theatre was packed from floor to ceiling, making this *Cherry Orchard* the first real Chekhovian success in the London theatre. Chekhov's refusal to preach and his lack of tendentiousness were highly attractive to the new generation of "bright young things." Margaret Webster found the production "had a touching laughter and tears quality, though it was probably more Irish than Russian."[46]

The critics remained sharply divided: James Agate extolled the play in the *Sunday Times* as an "imperishable masterpiece," and was seconded by Herbert Farjeon in the *Sunday Pictorial*; Basil M. Hastings' anathema in the *Daily Express* had hailed Lenin for wiping out the characters' way of life. For him, the play was "fatuous drivel," and he animadverted on people who are always "ready to be bemused by a name ending on 'ov' or 'ovsky.'"[47] The vehemence of the negative attitudes can be explained only in part by xenophobia or Little Englandism. Rather, Chekhov was dimly felt to be the spearhead of a concerted attack on the dramatic establishment.

One of the last surviving masters of Victorian playwriting, Henry Arthur Jones, was made apoplectic by this incursion of modernism into his professional world (even if Hammersmith was off the beaten track). According to his daughter, "My father did not like Ibsen, but he hated Tchekov and other Russian dramatists." He attended the first night of *The Cherry Orchard* and, as he noted in his diary, resolved not to enjoy himself, despite the audience's "pretense" to do so. Rendered virtually incoherent by the experience, "he said that the whole play gave him the impression of someone who had visited a lunatic asylum and taken down everything the inmates said." He penned a "very mischievous letter" to Nigel Playfair, beginning and ending "Oh, my God! Nigel Playfair, oh, my God!," and rebuking the manager for taking "several hours of the short life which remains to me." Jones's formula for play-writing, which he jotted down for Playfair, was: "(1) The plot is the first thing. (2) The end (*dénouement*) is the *chief* thing."[48] With such a credo, he could hardly abide Chekhov's submerged *fabula* and open endings.

Jones's opinions got into the papers and helped foment a controversy which raised interest in the play: even the production's over-earnestness and deadly pace were accepted as tokens of its voguish Russianness. Loss turned into profit, and after a month "this most disconcerting and original play" was transferred to the Royalty Theatre in the West End. For Bennett, the transfer marked "a definite turn in public taste toward true plays."[49]

Taking a tip from Playfair's gamble, Philip Ridgeway decided to launch a full Chekhov season at the Little Theatre. The first production,

13 Philip Ridgeway's *Seagull*, Little Theatre, London, 1925, with, l.–r., Randolph McLeod, Miriam Lewes, Valerie Taylor, John Gielgud, Margaret Swallow and James Whale.

The Seagull (1925), largely directed by John Gielgud (the nominal director was the Birmingham Rep's A. E. Filmer) who also played Treplev, failed to achieve a blend of comedy and sentiment; but by that time the public's desire to see a Chekhov play overruled the critics. The gamble paid off, and soon Ridgeway's pleasure at full houses was enhanced by laudations of his conscientiousness.

To see all five of Anton Tchekov's plays within six months, and in the London public theatres, is an experience which even a year ago the most optimistic of us hardly anticipated . . . to produce uncommercial masterpieces is the whole business of the Sunday societies; but it is not the business of the Fagans and Ridgeways to risk ruining themselves in the cause of idealism; and the fact that their risk has turned into success does not decrease our debt to them.[50]

Ridgeway soon realized that staging Chekhov required special qualifications and perhaps a touch of exoticism; his chief coup was to hire Theodore Komisarjevsky to take over the directorial tasks. As an émigré, Komisarjevsky and his tailoring of Chekhov to English tastes are dealt with in chapter 8. By the time he had finished, Chekhov was as firm a fixture in the English cultural décor as Dickens, and, just as Dickensian implied bonhomous eccentricity and roast goose, so Chekhovian, as popularized by Komisarjevsky, came to mean moon-drenched land-scapes, broken love affairs and exquisite plangency.

The adjective Chekhovian began to be applied as a compliment to English playwrights. Ronald Mackenzie's *Musical Chairs* (1932), directed by Komisarjevsky and starring Gielgud, dealt with a generational conflict between Polish oil factors and Americans, and was deemed an *Orchard*-like play, possibly because its staging required careful orchestra-tion. This requirement was more obviously native to the varied moods of *Strange Orchestra* (1931) by Rodney Ackland, set in a Bloomsbury boarding house. It was the first modern play Gielgud had directed, and he care-fully copied Komisarjevsky's methods.[51] Gielgud was also a prime factor in the later success of the plays of N. C. Hunter, which sought to trans-plant the ostensible fragility of Chekhov to a familiar landscape of Dorset manors and wind-swept shingles.

The earlier commonplace that the plays of "cheery Tchehov" were plotless, an assemblage of melancholy characters chewing over "a few grievances," to which the author merely adds "a suicide or two and leaves them to worry the thing out to the bitter end,"[52] was not obliter-ated by Komisarjevsky. Rather, it was overlaid with a pastel wash. Peter Ustinov parodied the average bathos in *The Love of Four Colonels* (1951), with army officers knitting in swings and *non sequitur* conversations stalling over unpronounceable names. The self-pity and slow motion brought to the mind of restive playgoers a line from *Measure for Measure*: "This will last out a night in Russia when nights are longest there." Ivor Brown took Komisarjevsky's *Three Sisters* as an occasion to complain,

these ladies [. . .] reminded me of those sororal duos and trios who croon their heart-break into microphones. Was not Chekhov, after all, a kind of sublime crooner, continually cultivating his Muscovite Blues? And may not that be the reason why, neglected in England for a quarter of a century, he recently became 'box-office'? He spoke for the defeated, for the self-pitying, for the parlour philosophers whose babbling of -isms and -ologies is only a veil for inertia. The mood of our English nineteen-twenties was doleful enough.[53]

One of the few English productions before World War II that broke out of this mold was Tyrone Guthrie's *Cherry Orchard* at the Old Vic (1933), part of a season which also included *Henry VIII* and *The Tempest*. A year earlier, in his book *Theatre Prospect*, Guthrie had hailed Komisarjevsky's Chekhov as "the future of naturalism in the theatre; in a poetic purpose not content merely to imitate the outward forms of commonplace things and reason about them, but which attempts the glorification of the commonplace by currying it to form a logical,

14 Elsa Lanchester as Charlotta and Charles Laughton as Lopakhin in Tyrone
Guthrie's *Cherry Orchard*, Old Vic, London, 1933.

musical and pictorial pattern of abstract significance."[54] His brother-in-
law Hubert Butler prepared a new version intended to make the inhabitants of the *Orchard* "far more human and normal" and the play itself "a
comedy rather than a prose poem." "It presented Chekhov not as the
exponent of Russian gloom but as a charming and easily intelligible

humourist."[55] In this Guthrie, known for his lack of sentimentality, was aided by the Ranevskaya of Athene Seyler, an actress more adept at comedy of manners than poetic feeling.

Ignoring Fagan's success, Guthrie claimed that this was the "first time that an English version of the play met with a large popular audience."[56] This owed much to the presence of Charles Laughton as Lopakhin and his wife Elsa Lanchester as Charlotta. During the run, the film *The Private Life of Henry VIII*, in which they both enjoyed a *succès fou*, was previewed. Contrary to audience expectations, however, Laughton did not tear a cat (or gnaw a fowl) as half-literate Ermolay, a part he rendered with extraordinary sensitivity in a Yorkshire dialect. Misconceptions still prevailed: when Flora Robson as Varya accidentally tripped and fell one night, the audience remained solemn, thinking "How very Russian."[57]

Just as Guthrie had sandwiched a Chekhov play into a Shakespeare season at a Shakespeare house, thus upping the reputation stakes, so John Gielgud in planning a repertory season at the Queen's Theatre in 1938, followed *Richard II* and *The School for Scandal* with *Three Sisters*, which borrowed lustre by its association. Gielgud first asked Komisarjevsky to stage the Chekhov, but when the Russian proved to be unavailable, he chose Michel Saint-Denis, a nephew of Jacques Copeau and founder of the Compagnie des Quinze; Gielgud had already worked with Saint-Denis in André Obey's *Noah*, and admired his work with student actors as much he distrusted his authoritarianism in rehearsals. Recollected by many as one of the best examples of teamwork ever seen on the London stage, *Three Sisters* revelled in a superb ensemble that ranged from Michael Redgrave as Tusenbach to Alec Guinness as Fedotik, with Gielgud as Vershinin, Peggy Ashcroft as Irina, Gwen Ffrangcon-Davies as Olga, Leon Quartermain as Kulygin, and Carol Goodner as Masha. Given eight weeks to rehearse instead of the usual three, the cast was able to grow into their roles to a remarkable degree. For the first time, English audiences were seeing an indigenous company approximate the MAT.

The production was also noteworthy as the first real attempt to apply Stanislavskian principles to a professional English production of a classic. Rehearsals began just after Saint-Denis had completed an exhaustive study of *An Actor Prepares*, the partial English version of Stanislavsky's text on acting which had been published the previous year. He had already used some of its exercises at his studio, and now applied other sections in rehearsals. Saint-Denis' approach was peremptory; he arrived at the first rehearsal laden with detailed notes on blocking and stage business and completely overrode Gielgud's attempts to co-direct. Nevertheless, Peggy Ashcroft, who had already experienced Komisarjevsky and thought him a "rather destructive director," was delighted to find Saint-Denis "incredibly creative and positive."[58] Redgrave, in his eagerness to impress the director, had tried to base his role on his reading of Stanislavsky, but was cautioned by Saint-Denis to throw away certain lines: "You speak as if the lines were important. You speak as if you wanted to make it all intelligible, as if it all made sense." When Redgrave started spouting the "Cranes and birds of passage" speech, he was interrupted: "No, no, no – this man is a bore, and he has no personality. You are playing this as if you had personality and were trying to make sense of this speech." Redgrave recalled, "From that moment on my performance started to grow, I had something to work on, the fact that I was playing a bore . . ."[59]

A martinet when it came to the text, Saint-Denis also sought out meanings in the kinetic and spatial relations of the characters. Unlike Komisarjevsky, who pruned his Chekhov to suit the trim proprieties of English taste, Saint-Denis allowed life to burgeon as messily as it liked, and then shrewdly concealed the art with which he had encouraged it. The choral soup-eating in Act I, Soleny's magnetic attraction to mirrors, Kulygin's fixation with a broken water-pipe in the last act were typical moments of eccentricity in a fluid, unstaunchable progression.

The realistic sets were designed by Motley and the impressionistic lighting by George Devine. As a Swedish observer reported, "from the moment the curtain goes up, the atmosphere is completely Russian, as Russian as any production of the Moscow Art Theatre. And yet how sympathetic and understandable these people are!"[60] Ivor Brown, most xenophobic of the London critics, noted that this was no mere imitation of the Russian model, but "a restatement of an exquisite play made not only with exquisite sensibility but also with technical power."[61] Its financial success led to West End backing for a company at the Phoenix Theatre to be directed by Saint-Denis in *Uncle Vanya* and *The Cherry Orchard*, along with works by Ibsen and Shakespeare; *Orchard* was to be star-studded with Edith Evans, Peggy Ashcroft, Gwen Ffrangcon-Davies, Ralph Richardson, Cyril Cusack and Alec Guinness, under-studied by Peter Ustinov. But the outbreak of war and the subsequent closure of the theatres cancelled it in rehearsal.[62]

During the Battle of Britain, the performing arts were meant to provide distraction, light entertainment and patriotic uplift: Chekhov could hardly contribute to the war effort. Only as the war was ending did

15 Act III of *Three Sisters* directed by Michel St. Denis, Queen's Theatre, London, 1937.
L.–r., Michael Redgrave as Tusenbach, Frederick Lloyd as Chebutykin, Peggy Ashcroft
as Irina, John Gielgud as Vershinin and Leon Quartermaine as Kulygin.

he re-emerge. At the New Theatre in 1945, John Burrell directed a slow-
motion *Uncle Vanya* that carried on the tradition of Chekhov as a poet of
regret and frustration. The production's distinction resided in the cast:
Laurence Olivier played Astrov and Ralph Richardson Voinitsky, with
Margaret Leighton as Elena and Harcourt Williams as Serebryakov.
Richardson's Vanya was "all 'fuddled clumsiness and gauche petulance,'
'lubberly and earth-bound, dreaming of the heavens he never
stormed.'" Olivier's Astrov was generally thought too sophisticated and
confident for a country doctor, too close in fact to Stanislavsky's smooth
seducer.[63] Ultimately, the significance of this *Vanya* lay less in individual

performances than in its affinity to its public. "The play made complete sense in wartime London," Ariadne Nicolaeff has recalled. "His characters were extravagantly alive through our awareness of death shared with Chekhov. They were trapped but lived dangerously because the central conflict took them over the edge."[64] The era of living dangerously could not be perpetuated, however, and the playing of Chekhov returned to a familiar and consoling mode.

CHAPTER 8

At home abroad (Europe and England 1917–1938)

This *Uncle Vanya* has the rare merit of describing for us in four acts
an almost morbid boredom of people who never bore us.
Edmond Sée on Georges Pitoëff's production[1]

The Moscow Art Theatre tours to Poland and Germany and later to
France and the United States introduced Chekhov's plays in so polished
and persuasive a guise that non-Russian directors were content to create
facsimiles of these originals. This led to a certain flatness and standardization in the staging of Chekhov, characterizing him as the subfusc bard
of "twilight Russia." The sluggish rhythms, deliberate underplaying,
and mournful cadences in these epigonic productions were not counter-
balanced, as they were at the MAT, by consummate acting, comic
touches and intimacy with the subject matter.

When fugitives from Russia settled in the West, they tended to capital-
ize on their association, however fleeting, with the Art Theatre, even
when their own theatrical backgrounds were more variegated and
experimental. These émigrés acted as dragomans who successfully
mediated between their past culture and their host culture. These
mediations were not without misunderstanding, cross-purposes and
occasionally wilful distortion; but, like a happy mistake in cooking or
chemistry, were frequently productive of a successful compound, unfore-
seen by its originator.

THE PRAGUE GROUP

In 1919, when plans for a major Art Theatre tour fell through, a group of
its actors went ahead with an independent summer sojourn in Southern
Russia and the Ukraine, as a temporary escape from the hardships and
food shortages of Moscow and as a short-term commercial venture.
Their repertory included *The Cherry Orchard* and *Uncle Vanya*, along with a
concert program of Shakespeare and Dostoevsky. The most illustrious

actors in this troupe were Vasily Kachalov, Olga Knipper-Chekhova and Maria Germanova, and it was managed by close associates of Nemirovich-Danchenko. After playing the university town of Kharkov, in late June they found themselves in territory controlled by the White Army. General Denikin's troops managed to occupy Kharkov without a battle, and from that day forth the Kachalov group was involuntarily separated from Moscow and the parent company.

With the eventual defeat of Denikin's forces, there was a mad scramble to get out of the path of the Red Army. After many vicissitudes, the Kachalov group managed to reach Georgia, which at that time was an independent state. It stayed in Tiflis for five months in 1920 while the Mensheviks held power there and the English and Germans occupied the rest of Georgia. Without sets, costumes or other theatrical accessories, all of which had been lost at the time of Denikin's defeat, the group put on a recital, which included Chekhov's sketch "The Surgery," and was warmly received. The first fully staged production was *The Cherry Orchard* on 15 April. To some Georgians it was a revelation; at last they understood what Chekhov was all about. "On reading the play, you feel that something is missing, it isn't quite realized in flesh and blood, and it takes the stage to flesh it out fully . . . it's like an opera libretto, which demands musical expression."[2] This reviewer for *Community* (*Ertova*) held up the Moscow artists as models on which to rebuild the ruined Tiflis theatre.

But other journalists sounded like Bolsheviks in finding Chekhov out of date and beside the point. Life provided more powerful stimuli.

Down came the curtain, and, on my way out, I wonder: do I feel yearning or grief? The answer was no. *The Cherry Orchard* made no impression on me of any sort. Too much time has passed since the play was written . . . The soul of anyone who has been through the dreadful upheavals and experiences of those times froze when confronted by the grief and depression that this work of Chekhov's pursues so assiduously, and nothing echoed in the depths of his soul. Indeed *The Cherry Orchard* seems to be an historical memory.[3]

When *Uncle Vanya* was put on in Tiflis, the complaints that Chekhov was pallid and his heroes ineffectual became louder. It was time for the Kachalov group to seek more sympathetic hosts. In fall 1920 it shilly-shallied over whether or not to return to Moscow, where the MAT had already planned its season without it. For reasons of safety, and to find a new market, it moved westward, playing Vienna, Prague, Bratislava and Berlin. In 1922, the troupe split: Kachalov, Knipper and some others returned to Moscow, while the rest settled in Prague where the government allowed them a small allowance and a playhouse, the Vinohrady Theatre. As the Prague Group they continued to tour, appearing in Paris and London in the late 1920s and early thirties. Of Chekhov's works, they added *Three Sisters* to their repertory, along with an evening of one-act plays and sketches.

Despite a huge Russian colony in Paris which supported a number of theatre groups, amateur and semi-professional, Chekhov was rarely seen save when the Prague Group paid a visit. Except for his farces, the usual Parisian fare was classics by Gogol and Ostrovsky or boulevard comedies. Perhaps the difficulty posed by mature Chekhov for amateurs was too great, or possibly the note of yearning was too poignant.[4]

Because the Kachalov/Prague Group preserved many of the MAT productions in amber, they were influential in introducing them and their principles to a public unfamiliar with the originals. Defending his protégée Germanova from attacks by the Soviet press, Nemirovich insisted that the Prague Group was conserving and perfecting authentic Art Theatre traditions. The technique underlying their lyrical impressionism was impeccable; the Italian critic Silvio d'Amico noted "a secret rhythm, as of dance, regulates every gesture and expression."[5] But their status as exiles enshrined their appearances with an aura of bereavement and nostalgia.

CHEKHOV ITALIAN-STYLE

One of the members of the Prague Group broke off to become a director in his own right. Petr Sharov had supplemented his MAT training with heavy doses of stylization, working with Meyerhold at his failed Studio, Komissarzhevskaya's Theatre and Interlude House (1905–7), where he acted in Maeterlinck, Blok, and Wedekind. After stints at the Crooked Mirror cabaret and Suvorin's theatre in St. Petersburg, in 1914 Sharov was named co-director with Vakhtangov of the Art Theatre's First Studio, while playing in *Lower Depths* and *Cherry Orchard* on the main stage. With the Prague Group from its inception, Peter Sharoff, as he now called himself, left in 1927 to become Oberregisseur at the Düsseldorf Theatre, where Luise Rainer was among his students.

Tatiana Pavlowa (actually Tatyana Pavlovna Zeitman) had no connection with the Art Theatre. As a young actress in Russia, she was associated with the touring companies of Orlenev and Sanin. After emigrating to Italy in 1921, she took two years to learn the language and formed her own troupe. Pavlowa infused Russian culture into her productions by hiring such directors as Sharoff and Nikolay Evreinov and such designers as Aleksandra Ekster and Sergey Sudeikin; she introduced her own version of Stanislavsky's ideas, stressing the consonance between the characters' inner and outer lives and their scenic expression. But she had no particular brief to plead for Chekhov: her own favorite Russian authors were Gorky and Ostrovsky.

In 1929 Pavlowa invited Sharoff to Milan to direct Ostrovsky's *Storm*, whose success led to the idea of staging a Chekhov play. Steeped in Stanislavsky's methods, he now had to apply them to the tempestuous and flamboyant dynasties that dominated the Italian theatre. At the start, this led to overdoing the surface realism. His first Chekhov production, *Uncle Vanya* (*Zio Vanja*), opened in Milan on 3 June 1932 with the Kiki Palmer company and was reasonably successful. However, as Silvio D'Amico pointed out, it was not enough to depict plain gestures and poor, monotonous intonations realistically; there was a need to feel and reveal what underlay the gestures and words.[6]

Between 1933 and 1943, Sharoff, who became an Italian citizen in 1938, was the foremost director of Chekhov in Mussolini's Italy, tempering Art Theatre naturalism with his own penchant for fantasy and inventiveness. His productions brought a keen attention to detail and atmospheric ensemble to the Italian stage along with an exact and punctilious rhythm. After the war, he was widely in demand in Holland, Germany and Austria as a guardian of the true grail of Art Theatre traditions.

Capitalizing on Sharoff's success, Pavlowa asked Nemirovich-Danchenko to direct an Italian-language *Cherry Orchard* (*Il Giardino dei ciliegi*) in Milan with what he called her "big-nosed and black-eyed troupe." Despite his advanced age (72) and without an assistant, Nemirovich rehearsed the company for five weeks from one in the afternoon to eight at night, personally demonstrating Pishchik's dance moves and Charlotta's card tricks. His interpretation of several characters differed from Stanislavsky's, as he wrote to a colleague in America:

I decided to try and achieve what I always thought about this play and the way Chekhov thought of it. I always found that Olga Knipper, for all her charm, simplicity and affecting qualities, does not play it right, but quite wrongly in fact. She overloads it, as it were, with high drama. Chekhov told me "Ranevskaya has a wasp-waist," which was his laconic way of defining her unusual flippancy and inordinate frivolity. Which led me, with my director's flair, to think such a change of form would lend the whole performance great lightness, grace, a tone of comedy ... From her first line, the audience took Pavlowa to be a fascinating, tender, moving but impossibly frivolous person. And, without exaggeration, each of her lines drew forth a sympathetic laugh. The whole play began to glow with a comic quality, but when Ranevskaya wept, the audience wept with her.[7]

This lightness of tone also chimed in with the swifter style of Italian acting and speaking. To clarify the play's social meaning, Trofimov's ideological aspect was brought into focus, without eliminating his absurdities. When *The Cherry Orchard* opened on 19 January 1933, the Milan papers praised the harmony of the production, the unusual simplicity of the acting and the director's "iron hand." Now, Nemirovich-Danchenko decided, the play should be made into a Hollywood film directed by Lewis Milestone.

THE MASK OF KOMIS

The chief agent in popularizing Chekhov in England was another émigré director, Fedor Komissarzhevsky, better known there as Theodore Komisarjevsky or, to his co-workers, Komis (and to the irreverent, Come and seduce me). The series of Chekhovian productions he launched were far better integrated and skilfully mounted than anything that had been seen before. But this did not happen overnight, and his earliest efforts were slow to efface the caricature of Chekhov uppermost in the English mind.

Komis began with two performances of *Uncle Vanya* at the Court Theatre in November 1921. What the critics liked about it was that he seemed to have imposed order on Chekhov's chaos, and tamed the savage Russians into *salonfähig* Englishmen.[8] Still, little attention was paid to his work until an *Ivanov* at the Duke of York's (6 and 7 December 1925) for the Incorporated Stage Society. Circumstances were not propitious: rehearsals were sporadic, and the scenery was unavailable until opening night, when it had to be rebuilt during the intervals. Komis claimed to have chosen the play in hopes of working his way through the canon chronologically; but its association with *Hamlet* also made a canny appeal to English tastes. The *Hamlet* strain certainly struck John Gielgud, fresh from playing Trofimov for Fagan, when he saw it.[9]

Komis interpreted Ivanov as an heroic failure, an unsuccessful rebel against the inertia that surrounds him. J. T. Grein, that veteran of lost causes in English progressive theatre, evidently felt an affinity when he declared that Ivanov's "protest and his struggle against the fate that overwhelms him, *commands our sympathy.*"[10] The bulk of the reviewers saw him strictly as a Russian suitable case for treatment and were irritated by what they took to be his helplessness and vacillation. *The Times* weighed in, "All this might have been prevented, if only his case had received proper medical attention," and Desmond MacCarthy in the *New Statesman* explained how hard it was for an actor to draw a tragic quality out of seemingly pathological traits, though Robert Farquharson achieved some refinement in the role.[11]

Whatever the displeasure with the play, there was nothing but praise for Komis' directorial mastery. He extended the opening of Act I to produce "a pool of silence," "of beauty and apprehension; and the entrances and exits of the second act party were beautifully managed." Komis imported to England the continental notion of a director's theatre, orchestrated and harmonized to the rhythm of emotional content. Comparing *Ivanov* with Granville-Barker's staging of *The Madras House*, one enthusiast pointed out that, "As a producer Mr. Komisarjevsky has a power no English one has: he is a master of *tempo*, of *piano* and *forte*, especially of *piano*."[12]

Ivanov convinced Philip Ridgeway that Komis was the director to nurse the Chekhov fad to full flowering, and it was the four plays staged in 1925–6 in the miniscule Barnes Theatre remodeled from a London cinema, that brought Komis renown and Chekhov a permanent place in the English repertory. Produced on a shoestring with little-known actors, they became a kind of epiphany for many English literati who found that Chekhov reflected their own tragic confusion in the cynical twenties. The explosion of the myth of English civility and stability encapsulated in country house life had begun during the Great War, and "the cherry orchard," as Shaw had pointed out, seemed to mirror that collapse. When the Russian novelist Ilya Érenburg attended Komis' *Three Sisters* at the Barnes, the "English intellectuals" who packed the house reminded him of "Russian intellectuals at the turn of the century."[13]

Arnold Bennett, more sensitive to the gradations of English society, recognized that this kind of spectator was not an *intelligent* in the Russian sense but *l'homme moyen sensuel*. At the same play, Bennett's feeling of weariness was at first shared by "a decent Philistine man, sitting just behind us, [who] said at the end of the second act that he had been disappointed and bored. But he liked Act III better, and Act IV still better. On the whole Chekhov had succeeded with him."[14] Komis had woven his spell so as to convert the philistines.

The paradox is that Komis had been the least Chekhovian director on the Russian stage, and Chekhov was totally alien to him. Although he was the half-brother of Vera Komissarzhevskaya and the son of one of

Stanislavsky's mentors, his application for work at the Art Theatre had been rejected in 1910 and again in 1914, for they sensed he was "not one of our sort." Working for Nezlobin, a rival entrepreneur, in Moscow and at his sister's theatre in Petersburg, Komis developed a reputation as an eclectic director, who sought out the characteristic style for each playwright he staged. His work was highly coloured and advanced in its use of unit sets and cubist forms. Unfortunately, in 1917 he thoroughly offended Stanislavsky by publishing a book purporting to elucidate the master's theories. "The margins of Stanislavsky's copy of Komisarjevsky's book are filled with the former's splenetic commentary 'Lie!', 'How vile!', 'I said exactly the opposite!', 'He should be sued for this!'"[15] Komis' own work rarely showed any signs of Art Theatre atmospherics, but was noted for its airy effervescence.

But in 1925 Komis was taken by the English to be the exclusive representative of Chekhov, Stanislavsky & Co., a charade he upheld with panache. Unlike the Prague Group, he made no effort to replicate the Art Theatre, but staged the plays in the spirit of his own aesthetics, full of romantic contrasts. Form first, then emotion was his formula. Uninterested in subtext or three-dimensional characterizations, he compelled the actors' speech and movements to follow a musical principle. Everything was bent on creating the image of a world that was mysterious, enchanting and gone forever. This should not be considered a betrayal of Chekhov's intentions. Rather, it corresponded with what the English theatre had come to expect of a Russian dramatist and what Komis considered one of the aims of his art. As Aleksey Bartoshevich explains, "his productions show how one culture draws from another what it needs and how it uses the émigré as a middleman without paying much mind to his own preferences. He acts as an interpreter explaining the content of his own culture in his own personal language."[16] The result of this artificial symbiosis was to elevate Chekhov on the English stage to the position of a perennial favourite.

Komis' Barnes series opened on 17 January 1926 with *Uncle Vanya*, its run extended for three weeks at the Duke of York's; it played in a simplified setting, with the first three acts roughly the same locale. Komis recognized that the characters' "Russianness" was a stumbling-block for the English, and so he stressed universality of character. He also began his somewhat deplorable custom of heightening the love interest, in this case by eliminating Astrov's "silly moustache" and other eccentricities.[17] Sentimentality was reduced by omitting some lines and transposing others: Elena's exit in Act II was delayed and Vanya's "She's gone" cut, so that she could overhear his soliloquy and interject, "This is really hateful." Sonya's reference to the angels in her final monologue also disappeared. Finally, Komis attempted to play up the comedy, although he was aware that "It is easy to turn Chekhov's plays into skits by accentuating certain points, and thus make the most tragic 'inner' situation humorous."[18]

The Barnes *Three Sisters*, which opened on 16 February 1926 and ran twice daily for eight weeks (revived 25 October and 23 October 1929) could be described, like Saint-Denis' later staging, as "the most legendary of all English Chekhov productions."[19] Komis attributed its success "to the fact that I evolved the way to convey Chekhov's inner meaning and make the rhythm of the 'music' of the play blend with the rhythm of the actors, giving the necessary accents with the lighting and the various outer 'effects'."[20] The synæsthesia was a contagion caught by James Agate, whose review evoked Manet, Vuillard and Utrillo, along with the work of composers, conductors and poets.[21]

While trying to free English acting from social restraint, Komis had no qualms about cutting and reorganizing the play to eliminate ambiguities and to underscore the more mawkish aspects of the relationships. John Gielgud, who was cast as Tusenbach, relates of the 1926 *Three Sisters*: "Tusenbach, shorn of the lines about his ugliness, was played (by Komisarjevsky's express direction) as a romantic juvenile . . . When I questioned him about the 'ugly' lines being cut, he shrugged his expressive shoulders and said, 'My dear boy, the English public always demand a love interest.'"[22] A decade later, watching Michael Redgrave play Tusenbach in Saint-Denis's production, with pimples, steel-rimmed spectacles and a funny straw boater, Gielgud wondered "why Komisarjevsky, who was a Russian, should have deliberately misled me in the reading of the part . . . because I would have been very happy to have played it ugly."[23] Gielgud's lovesick baron led one critic to describe the relation between him and Irina as the maudlin romance between a neurotic Adonis and a Christina Rossetti maiden in a drawing by Arthur Hughes.[24] Still, for the actors, Gielgud recalled, "playing Chekhov in the twenties and thirties was to us like discovering a new form."[25]

The cosmetic surgery Komis used to make Chekhov attractive to suburbanites is revealed in Victor Emeljanow's study of the promptbook.[26] He employed Constance Garnett's translation, which, lexically if not tonally accurate, reeks of gentility. For decorative reasons, the action began in May 1870, which made hash of Tusenbach's "approaching storm-wrack" and anachronisms of Rodé's Kodak and the playing of a

Sousa march. The tiny shadow-box stage with its thrusting apron was divided for Act I into a kind of veranda with French doors opening into the dining-room, a straightforward way of segregating the groupings and clarifying the action. Light was used to convey the seasons or to hint expressionistically at the presence of invisible characters.

Komis extirpated ambiguities (the sisters' edgy reactions to one another), reduced verbiage (the dinner table dialogue was pruned since the diners could not be seen) and increased physical action (Olga helped the maid set the table, which was out of keeping with her social standing). Any fence at which an English spectator might balk was torn down: all patronymics were deleted, Irina's nameday became a birthday, Dobrolyubov turned into Balzac, Protopopov rebaptized Petrov. All references to ages and physical attributes vanished, and rhetorical statements of social problems and visions of the future ruthlessly pared down. The act ended with the two junior officers taking a photo of the cast, a piece of business which has since become traditional. "Overall, the effect of these changes was to make the act become much more conventionally dramatic."[27]

Act II was moved up to January 1871, a mere eight months after the first (suggesting an urgent reason for Andrey's marriage), and was played rapidly, with no pauses or moments of inaction. The main source of illumination was a table lamp, with other lights emanating from doors as they opened. The duo between Masha and Vershinin was truncated to leave only the self-consciously romantic speeches, and Soleny's character was softened. At the end of the act, to keep the focus on Irina's breakdown, Vershinin and Kulygin were not allowed to enter with Olga: the curtain fell as she burst into tears and dropped to her knees.

Rather than the two years' interval Chekhov implies, Komis compressed the time before Act III to seven months, with the fire taking place in October 1871. Chekhov's carefully orchestrated series of comings and goings and recurrent bursts of hysteria were rearranged to heighten the act's cumulative effect. Irina's initial outbursts were deleted, Olga's confession watered down and Irina given a new line in reply: "What you say sounds so sensible – so horribly sensible – but what's the use of it, what's the use . . . (*sobs*)."[28] Natasha's intrusion was omitted, Kulygin was allowed only one entrance, and Andrey's outburst was made more matter-of-fact. This pruning concentrated the climax in the latter dialogue between Olga and Irina, and all the critics mentioned the flickering shadows cast by candlelight that blotted out the sisters.

Act IV was the most drastically altered. Instead of ejecting the sisters out of doors, Komis returned to the Act I setting and hung a line of washing across a corner of forestage. Since the time was now August 1872, there was no autumnal melancholy or symbolic change of seasons, and the shadow of a maple branch stood in for the fir trees. All the moments of farewell took place within the frame of the French windows. Andrey and his perambulator disappeared, perhaps because with Natasha present at the upstage piano throughout the act next to a flesh-and-blood Protopopov, he could hardly describe her aloud as a fuzzy animal. The valedictory of Irina and Tusenbach lost its awkwardness to become conventional English understatement; he was given a new exit line, "Don't! Please don't," to prevent Irina from accompanying him. With the deletion of the Andrey–Ferapont exchange and the strolling musicians, the farewells of Vershinin and Masha were more direct. Kulygin was not permitted to intrude into the sisters' emotions, and new lines enabled Chebutykin to make the unspoken obvious:

CHEBUTYKIN. Well, Nicholas insulted Solyony again and had to apologize . . .
    but refused . . . He did it rather rudely, I'm afraid, and the crank . . . well . . .
    damn it all . . . the crank shot him dead.
IRINA. Oh!
CHEBUTYKIN. On the spot . . . the Military Police took him away . . .
IRINA (crying). I knew . . . I knew something terrible was going to happen to
    him . . .
CHEBUTYKIN. Nicholas was a fine chap. .. But one lieutenant more, one less in
    the world – what does it matter . . . nothing matters . . . nothing (he hums.)[29]

By trimming away Olga's last lines, Komis concluded the play with her statement "peace will be established on earth, and happy people will remember kindly and bless those who have lived before," as the band played Sousa's jaunty *Double Headed Eagle March*. Confidence and optimism sprang from stiff upper lips.

Komis' alterations may not have been as radical as those Nahum Tate and John Dryden inflicted on *King Lear* and *The Tempest* during the Restoration, but the aim was identical: to adapt a work to the taste of a specific public by removing anything out of keeping with current dramatic norms, and, in so doing, to popularize an author. Komis did his work almost too well, for when *The Cherry Orchard* opened at the Barnes on 28 September 1926, critics expected the action-packed emotionalism of *Sisters*; they complained of a "uniform slowness" and thought the farcical moments, entrusted to Charles Laughton as Epikhodov and Martita Hunt as Charlotta, to be inappropriate and trivializing. Their familiarity with this play was greater, owing to the production at St.

Martin's in 1920 and J. B. Fagan's much-liked version five years later; they wanted to savour the tragedy in the plight of Gaev and Ranevskaya. The comic elements in Tyrone Guthrie's production would later be attacked for the same reason. But Komis was eager to understate the pathos.

A revival of *Three Sisters* at the Fortune Theatre in 1929 was as acclaimed as the original; by this time, Chekhov's status as a major dramatist was so intact that dissenters had to be more outspoken in their attacks. The rabble rousing columnist Hannen Swaffer harrumphed:

> Lenin was right . . .
> There was not one original idea. There was scarcely one original phrase. It was all just drabness and misery.
> Chekhov is all shadows, all despair. I never saw a moral in it, nor any ennobling thought.
> It is merely the ineffectiveness of the effete, put down for analysis.[30]

There was a germ of truth to Swaffer's carping: just as West End theatre as a whole tended to depict the life of the leisured classes with the working classes as comic relief, so Komis' elegant recensions attributed to Chekhov's characters an essentially middle-class veneer of reticence and fastidiousness.

These features were conspicuous in Komis' last English Chekhov, *The Seagull* at the New Theatre (1936) with Gielgud as Trigorin, Edith Evans as Arkadina and Peggy Ashcroft as Nina. Instantly filling a large London playhouse, it established Chekhov as "the most popular of international dramatists. For a play written about 1900, this is a decided achievement."[31] The playgoers might have no notion of his historical placement, but appreciated a recognizably realistic modern drama, set in conventional scenery and period costumes.

Although Komis' reputation was firmly assured by this time, the critics had seen the Prague Group's *Seagull* in London in 1928 and 1931, and were now capable of drawing comparisons, not necessarily to his advantage. This time Komis' penchant for romanticism came under attack, especially his treatment of Treplev's Oedipal attitudes and Trigorin's demeanour. Gielgud, on the verge of his New York *Hamlet*, was now recognized as the finest Shakespearian actor in the English-speaking world; his characteristic throbbing vocalism could be heard in the Russian novelist, tricked out in impeccable evening dress and a Borsalino hat. But Stanislavsky's *My Life in Art* was available in English translation to help raise questions about the natty, self-conscious lady's man Gielgud enacted. Komis himself was displeased with the Treplev of

16 The moon rises over Act I in Theodore Komisarjevsky's *Seagull*, New Theatre, London, 1936. L.–r., Frederick Lloyd as Sorin, Ivor Bernard as Medvedenko, John Gielgud as Trigorin, Edith Evans as Arkadina, Peggy Ashcroft as Nina, George Devine as Shamraev, Leon Quartermaine as Dorn and Claire Harris as Polina.

Stephen Haggard, considered the finest young actor of sensitive types; he made the poet "a moaning neurotic."[32]

Komis' self-indulgent pacing and muffling of emotional tension also incurred negative comment. The *New English Weekly* announced that "no producer who still interprets Chekhov yearningly and in slow-motion is going to get any praise from me. That phase has lasted long enough. The production at the New Theatre is beyond description soulful and an invisible hassock for the reverential is supplied to every seat . . . to play *The Seagull* as though it were the Bible and at the tempo of a funeral march is ironically to underline" the fact that Chekhov is a *petit-maître*.[33]

What this comment illustrates is that Chekhov was now part of the canon, and the English theatregoer was sufficiently familiar with him to apply a connoisseur's discrimination to the niceties of interpretation. To this end, Komis had been indispensable: his productions were, in Margaret Webster's words, "a revelation – tender, compassionate, aware." What he revealed was that Chekhov's plays were "gay, constantly erupting into firework 'happenings,' not just grey all over."

Moreover, Chekhov gave Komis the opportunity to demonstrate a new style of *mise-en-scène* in which the actors played as a team, the sounds and silences were exquisitely orchestrated, and the lighting "was modulated with a fine eye for the dramatic use of shadow, really deep shadow, varied only by a single pool or shaft of light," to "unbearably moving" effect. The Barnes Chekhov productions were the best work Komisarjevsky ever did,[34] and he remained supremely confident of their rightness. Referring to the "three truly English productions" – the *Cherry Orchards* of Fagan and Guthrie and Ridgeway's *Seagull* – and the "French" *Three Sisters* of Saint-Denis, he insisted that they failed to "feel" Chekhov. "I am sure that personally they are much happier misunderstanding him, but as artists they are doing him a rather poor service."[35]

PITOËFF AND THE SUFFERING ARTIST

Georges Pitoëff was to Chekhov in France what Komisarjevsky was to Chekhov in England; but, whereas Komis had no real affinity to Chekhov and devised an assimilative method from without, Pitoëff believed he shared Chekhov's vision of Russia and tried to convey it in a method both international and timeless. However, Pitoëff's interpretation was just as partial as anyone else's; having been infected by Chekhov in his 'teens, he always viewed him sentimentally as filled with a tender love of humanity, and turned a blind eye to Chekhov's irony and cruelty.

This vision was determined by Pitoeff's training and background. Half Armenian, half Russian, Georgy Ivanovich Pitoev was a scion of a rich mercantile family; his father ran the theatre in Tiflis for a while. Unconstrained in his choice of career, Pitoev studied mathematics and jurisprudence in Moscow and engineering in Petersburg, but a passion for theatre was ignited by the MAT's Chekhov productions and by Vera Komissarzhevskaya who befriended him. While studying law in Paris between 1904 and 1908, he frequented the Comédie française, but was drawn to the work of Antoine, Firmin Gémier, Lugné-Poë, and Romain Rolland's concept of *théâtre populaire*. He also directed some Chekhov one-acts at the Cercle des artistes russes in Montparnasse, founded by his father (1905–8).

On his return to Petersburg, Pitoëff got involved in Komissarzhevskaya's new company which Meyerhold was turning into a laboratory for his experiments in "stylized theatre." Later Pitoëff travelled across Russia with Gaideburov's Itinerant Theatre, playing in *Ivanov*, *The Cherry Orchard*, and directing *Three Sisters* and the farces. In 1912 he organized "Our Theatre" in Petersburg, putting on *Ivanov* and *Three Sisters*, among other classics. It was planned as a democratic conveyance of culture to the audiences of peasants and proletarians. At a time when the MAT was playing *Sisters* with all the apparatus of ultrarealism, Pitoëff, a true disciple of Gaideburov, staged it with four velvet curtains, two screens, a few chairs and two light sources.[36] "After Act Three one of my friends asked me to provide him with all the details of this scenery so he could recreate a similar room. I answered: 'Take a good look, we have no sets or rooms. A few daubs were enough to suggest the whole picture . . .' This room was not so much the three sisters' room in Chekhov as the image of all rooms of all Russian three sisters, immortalized by the author."[37] This attempt at universality was typical of an era when the best Russian theatres were trying to reproduce the crisis of Russian life; with variations it would inform all Pitoëff's later Chekhov settings.[38]

In winter 1914, he went back to Paris where he met Ludmilla Smanova, the daughter of a minor Russian official. They married in 1915 and moved to Geneva, where he was to stage seventy-four plays by forty-six authors. On behalf of Russian charities, he played Astrov and Ludmilla Sonya in Russian in private homes, charitable institutions, and émigré hotels, first in Lausanne, then in Geneva.[39] Jacques Copeau, the reformer of the French stage, dropped in on an improvised reading of a partial translation of *Vanya*. "Had I heard [Pitoëff] only that evening, I would never have forgotten the sound of that voice nor the movement of those eyes."[40] At Copeau's behest, Georges and Ludmilla began work on a French translation of Chekhov's major plays, while playing *The Proposal*, *Swan Song* and a revival of *Uncle Vanya* at various halls in Geneva. Of the latter, a newspaper attested that

their incomparable attractiveness, which immediately won over a hall full of sceptics and jaded playgoers, comes from their not restraining, as most actors do [. . .], the exotic intimacy of their personalities. [. . .] And the plethora of silences was listened to as if they were sentences and words pronounced by the hands Madame Pitoëff knows how to use as no actress has ever done before.[41]

Copeau invited Pitoëff to play *Vanya* (*Oncle Vania*) at Le Vieux-Colombier in Paris, where it opened on 15 April 1921. Under this impressive aegis, the semi-professional, modern dress production of an obscure Russian play was paid a great deal of attention by the critics, who ranged from the tentative to the enthusiastic. For some, like Marcel Achard, it was merely "a curious, literary document and a dramatic snippet to serve the history of the Russian people."[42] Jean Schlumberger, founder of the *Nouvelle revue française*, close associate of Gide, spoke for French traditions of symmetry and balance in complaining that "this art [. . .] disdains that emphasis on action without which our taste for architecture goes unsatisfied."[43] In contrast, the reporter for the important theatrical journal *Comœdia illustré* was led to attest that "*beautiful, truthful theatre demands minimal action. Uncle Vanya would have enraptured Flaubert.*"[44]

Copeau retained his objectivity as a practical man of the theatre; in a long letter to Pitoëff, he frankly broached the problem of the tyro troupe's ineptitude and exhorted him to demand more of his actors or hire better ones. "Unconsciously and involuntarily you take everything on yourself, and [. . .] the whole structure of the play was deformed, all the interest displaced, by the fact that you and Ludmilla become the centre of interest of the drama."[45] Nevertheless, eager to launch Chekhov in advance of his competitors, Copeau continued to parley with Pitoëff over future productions, in particular a *Cherry Orchard*.[46] These negotiations broke down because Olga Knipper's rights were protected by the Czech government, and Copeau feared litigation if he went ahead without authorization.

Legal niceties proved no hindrance to Pitoëff who then moved definitively to Paris to restage his Lausanne *Seagull* (*La Mouette*) and *Uncle Vanya* at the Théâtre des Champs-Élysées. This elegant little home of opera and ballet had just been taken over by Jacques Hébertot, who meant to change it into a showcase for the latest developments in drama and production techniques. *Vanya*, which opened on 4 April 1922, had the same minimal production values as in Genevan lecture-halls. A palisade of birch trees was sketched against a blue velvet sky, their trunks vanishing into the sky-borders. A table with a samovar, four benches and two garden chairs constituted the furniture; the summer heat was suggested by the lighting.

The script had been heavily cut. Vanya's monologue in Act II was replaced by a brief silence; Pitoëff's son Sacha later stated that this was to strengthen the *coup de théâtre* in Act III, hardly a Chekhovian consideration. A more ineffable factor was the thick Russian pronunication of the French dialogue by the Pitoëffs and a few of their colleagues. For some, "The Russian accent helps to understand plays translated from Russian. Without the accent, they would be almost unintelligible."[47] In other words, indulgence could be extended to so clearly unFrench a phenomenon. The exoticism of the enterprise was encapsulated in Marcel Achard's remark, "everything is Russian in this play, irresistibly . . .

17 Act I of George Pitoëff's *La Mouette* (*The Seagull*), Studio des Champs-Élysées, Paris 1921. Ludmilla Pitoëff on the small stage as Nina.

inexorably. The atmosphere is Russian. And the characters Russian. . . . And Russian the silence and the snow which play great roles. And Russian too the scenery."[48] In a Paris newly peopled by refugees from the Revolution, there was both charm and discomfort in this Slavic excess, and a tinge of xenophobia could be traced in the distance maintained between French tradition and Russian innovation.

The Seagull, which followed on April 23, made no effort to bathe the play in anything like its original atmosphere. Without the money, manpower or will to copy the Moscow Art Theatre, it offered to a handful of loyal spectators a theatre of poetic essence. Few realistic elements persisted in the scenery: some gnarled tree trunks framed Nina's platform and a bright and luminous painted flat by Birel-Rosset showed the lake hemmed in by hills. Acts II and III were played in the same interior setting, so mention of the croquet lawn was suppressed.[49] Gaunt, lantern-jawed Georges played Trigorin, Ludmilla Nina, and the remarkable character actor Michel Simon Sorin. Rather than translating *Seagull*, Pitoëff adapted it audaciously, a common practice to avoid disorienting Parisian playgoers (Benjamin Crémieux was doing the same thing with Pirandello).[50] Vodka was distilled into "eau-de-vie"; the characters' names were reduced to sobriquets or generics, Pushkin substituted for Nekrasov, the tunes hummed by Dorn, titles of plays, novels and characters replaced by those known to the French public.

These efforts at assimilation were evidently necessary, since, even with them, Pitoëff's *Seagull* struck most observers as outlandish, "a Russian, very Russian play," unconnected with anything in French life. *Le Temps* underlined the alien quality of this shapeless drama: "The pleasure we derive from this play cannot be compared to the impression it might make on a Russian spectator. [. . .] we compare [the characters] with ourselves, we contrast their uncertainty with our conviction, their confusion with our clarity, their apathy with our activity . . . "[51] In that light, some critics applied hindsight to see the play as kind of guide to current Russian affairs: "All previous and maybe present Russia is included in this four-act play. You find the weariness and grieving of the Slavic soul, a certain insecurity, passion and disorder, dreaminess and apathy. There is something prophetic in this play: it presages a tempest and explains it."[52] These references to the Slavic soul, encouraged by Pitoëff himself, would become endemic.

Pitoëff's view was that, for all their insignificance, Chekhov's characters were less hyperbolic siblings of Dostoevsky's, consumed by an inner fire. In his opinion, *The Seagull* was not a drama of real life but an allegory of the artist's fate. It was similar to Pirandello's *Six Characters in Search of an Author* in posing "the problem of artistic creation"; however, Chekhov practiced

not Latin analysis, but the intuition and ever so pathetic subconscious of the Slavic soul. In the realm of artistic creativity, the human being is eternal, free; in his daily life, he is limited and doomed to perish. [. . .] Can the artist, whose work isolates him from others, endure their company? Art is a cross imposed by God, a mission with which He charges certain chosen ones. The heroine declares that art sustains her, uplifts her up to inaccessible regions where she escapes the blows of fate.[53]

Pitoëff obviously identified with Nina in this high-flown conception of the artist's isolation and transcendence. For most Parisians, the play's dramatic interest resided in Ludmilla, for "she brought what was necessary to sustain and develop these mirages: a confident sympathy, an absence of effort"; but few of them cared for this "desperate romanticism." [54]

When the Moscow Art Theatre visited Paris in December 1922 and played *The Cherry Orchard* at the Champs-Elysées, Pitoëff told Hébertot, "We are all sons of Stanislavsky, often prodigal and rebellious sons, but always proud to love him."[55] Still, recalling that in 1904 he had regarded the original production as an "example of the perfect realism" he now found himself "overwhelmed with astonishment at [the *mise-en-scène's*] pointlessness."[56] This, along with commercial considerations, seems to have convinced him to refrain from directing his beloved Chekhov for several years.

It was not until 1929, after a series of failures, that Pitoëff abruptly decided to mount *Three Sisters* (*Les Trois soeurs*) in a fortnight with a company that for the most part had never played Chekhov. The first readthroughs of Rodolphe Darzan's lively translation conveyed desperate monotony, which led to even more cuts than usual, from a phrase to half a page. The first things to go were all the long speeches about the future. Perhaps Pitoëff wanted to diminish the "hope deferred" aspect or, given the time constraints, was simply making life easier for Jean d'Yd who played Vershinin, the role most drastically abridged. The hasty rehearsals took place in a climate of tension, as the director proliferated explanations and added to the confusion by insisting "Don't play sad, don't play drama."[57] The actors feared another flop, so worked with exceptional zeal and concentration. "After all," Pitoëff's daughter pointed out, "one had to be able to present the characteristic grief of such a blighted, ruined existence as that of Chekhov's three sisters, whose life had no point but to prepare the future for coming generations."[58]

The opening on the snowy night of 26 January 1929 at the Théâtre des Arts constituted one of Pitoëff's most striking achievements. "I still remember the profound impression of *Three Sisters* on the spectators . . . I confess that such an ensemble, such an interpretation will never be seen again in France."[59] That aged veteran of the naturalistic avant-garde, André Antoine, praised it in his diary as a "profound production, one of the most significant in the modern French theatre . . . In this performance I saw what I never have seen in France up to now: movement of actors, a *mise-en-scène* that takes advantage of the full stage space and allows such freedom – all this is wonderfully vivid and new."[60]

There was the usual critical paltering, for Chekhov's technique still seemed esoteric. "All the characters . . . divagate and natter and talk incoherently for three hours by the clock" (Lucien Descaves). "Chekhov's play is an accumulation of mere observations, without structure, without the author's reaction: it's an excellent photograph, but not a work of art" (Gaston de Pawlowski). "All these people stricken with collective neurasthenia seem to us a proper bedlam. How can one have a Slavic soul?" (Lucien Dubech).[61]

It was the constellation of the three sisters – Marie Kalff as Masha, Maria Germanova as Olga and Ludmilla Pitoëff as Irina – who made it work. Not only did their sensibilities neatly intermesh, but the Russian accents of the last two contributed to the atmosphere. For Pitoëff, there was a secret explanation for the sisters' defeat: they lacked vitality owing to a physiological deficiency inherited from their mother who could breed none but imperfect, fragmentary creatures, disarmed in advance in the struggle with reality. The tragedy of the sisters' "larval" nature was supposed to enrich and complement the comedy of manners, although nothing in the acting revealed this hereditary taint.[62]

The little socio-historic mulch in which Pitoëff's earlier Chekhov productions had been vestigially rooted was gone entirely; the new reality was abstract, a generalized image of a world where humanity is not allowed to achieve its hopes and aspirations. The staging made a virtue of necessity by employing only blue draperies, a few sticks of furniture, and the orchestration of beautiful voices to produce its effects. In this spartan environment, the three sisters, almost silently, solely by the inner concentration, disengaged an emotion far superior to that of cheap tears or artificial histrionics. The critics, distrustful of emotional abandonment, welcomed this restraint. *Le Figaro* called Germanova "a Nordic Duse of profound and concentrated power," Ludmilla "dramatically, childishly delightful," and Kalff "astonishing in her naturalness, savagery and secret strength."[63] Irina's "pale face, frenzied glance, fragile, bright silhouette and pathetic voice," Masha's "mournful, consuming inner fire" and Olga's "immutable nobility"[64] were matched by the mixture of lucidity and scepticism in Georges' Tusenbach and the dissonant buzzing of Paulette Pax's Natasha. Pitoëff was expert at revealing the emotional drama through significant detail and surface incidents, without "*explications ou tirades.*" Playwrights in the audience were struck by the masterful way in which minor events in Act III led up to the siblings' confessions; forty years old though the play was, it still seemed technically audacious in the land of the *pièce bien faite*.

The effect on an impressionable mind can be gauged from the recollections of Jean Nepveu-Degas, a lycée student who had never heard of Chekhov. The light in the opening scene, filtered through the gauze window onto a table being set behind curtains which suggested a back room, said it all.

We felt introduced not into some set design, but into the real home of the Prozorovs; we still knew absolutely nothing about them, but henceforth we could not imagine them as other than they would appear in this frame. All the poetry of everyday life, all that dense flow of time, hour upon hour, intertwined with habits, cares and joys was presented to us from the outset. And a young reader of Proust could already sense that secret bonds were going to be established between this 'quest for lost time' – whose meandering paths he was beginning to wander on his own by means of books – and the revelation of this surprising dramatic universe.[65]

But it remained a *succès d'estime*. The critic for *Candide* summed up the problem by asking: "Does the French audience like the play? I don't know. In any case, its production is a success allowing *amateurs* to rummage in an alien soul."[66] Put off by the paucity of action and "production values," the general public stayed away. It would be ten years before Pitoëff produced a Chekhov play which was an undisputed success with both the cognoscenti and the crowd.

This can be accounted for by a change in mood over the course of that decade. *Les années folles* had preferred its Russians to be gypsy singers in nightclubs or amusing entertainers like Balieff, master of ceremonies of the Chauve-Souris cabaret. By the mid-1930s, with the consolidation of fascism and the worldwide depression, Parisian high spirits had sunk; the prevalent sense of despair and anguish was coupled with political protest leading to the rise of the Popular Front. In the artistic realm, the calls of Romain Rolland and Firmin Gémier for a people's theatre were enjoying a resurgence. The Cartel of innovative directors, Pitoëff among them, had moved from the fringe to the centre of theatrical life. Clipped and devalued, once arcane expressionistic techniques of the 1920s had become the common currency of theatre of the 30s.[67]

Pitoëff's only full-fledged commercial success with Chekhov occurred in the year of his death, on the eve of apocalypse in Europe. *The Seagull* (*La Mouette*) which opened on 17 January 1939 at the Théâtre des Mathurins was imbued with tragic feeling even as it affirmed a faith in mankind's essential creativity and moral strength. The set was starker than in 1921: Treplev's platform stage was framed by the same dark blue velvet curtains, but the park had dwindled into two symbolic tree trunks that soared into the flies. In Act II the croquet lawn was again an interior, a veranda drenched in summer sunlight, filtered by long white curtains. This radical simplification also suppressed Stanislavskian sound effects; as with *Three Sisters*, recordings of Russian music were played, and Dr. Dorn's romantic ballads replaced with popular tunes known to habitués of Russian restaurants.

The heart and soul of the interpretation was again Ludmilla's Nina, whose "spiritual originality and faith filled the performance with the

light of hope."[68] Although Pitoëff admitted that there are no heroes in
Chekhov, he identified his wife with this "young apostle" and staged
everything around her. "It is one of the roles she interprets with the
greatest grace, emotion and conviction," he explained. "Indeed it
awakens resonances which, I believe, marvellously identify the artist with
the character acted."[69] She and Georges' Trigorin were set in opposition, for the writer was shown to be sterile, devoid of creative afflatus.
Hence his bitter thirst for self-assertion in his relations with Arkadina,
played by Germanova and later Marcelle Génia in a similar key. For all
her external splendour, she too was insubstantial and hated anything
that showed real feeling or spiritual purity. The cross on her bosom
testified not so much to her piety as her deep hypocrisy and inner deceit.
Jean-Richard Bloch wrote "Never since Molière has simplicity and
merriment served to camouflage such cruelty."[70]

On this occasion, the critical choir hymned a paean of unbroken
praise. By now the ultra-Russian Chekhov had become a "classic" and a
"masterpiece." Benjamin Crémieux bestowed French literary citizenship on him: "Truly, one gets the same feeling of perfection from *The
Seagull* as from *Antigone* or *Bérénice*." Bloch moved beyond French borders
to declare his universal status: "Chekhov is probably, far and away above
Pirandello and Bernard Shaw, the great writer for the theatre of this
half-century."[71]

"Every moment snatches from the spectators gasps of surprise and
astonishment" at the truth revealed.[72]

Chekhov's voice is [the Pitoëffs'] voice: we will not have artists who can play *The
Seagull* as they can, with those smiles close to tears, those pianissimo songs, those
melopeias which echo Mussorgsky. The signs of lassitude and physical age
which, most regrettably, one must note in them, have disappeared. They have
recovered their freshness, their innocence. They act like angels.[73]

Seagull ran for months to sold-out houses whose audiences, poised on
the brink of war, made earnest efforts to appreciate the meaning of
Chekhov's characters. "There was something unusual in the excitement
that gripped the Parisian public, as if it had lost all sense of moderation,
balance, critical flair."[74]

In going for "symbolic abstraction," Pitoëff, in Giorgio Strehler's
judgement, lost the "earthbound weight" and "plastic reality" of
Chekhov.[75] But, for its time and place, it was precisely this abstraction
which led to his success. Despite the initial diffidence of the critics,
Pitoëff communicated the profound and concentrated potency of

Chekhov's dramatic tension with an affectionate deference and a spontaneous, persuasive gentleness. Edmond Sée spoke of the "nudge" given the spectator by the sense of deep sorrow.[76] Lugné-Poë pointed out how new this theatre was to a public used to declamatory stars and celebrities, and how it answered Antoine's call for new scenic methods.[77] In stark contrast with the French theatre, the seeming naturalness and colorlessness of the intonations made the point. Subtlety would be the common ground where French and Russian sensibilities would meet.

CHAPTER 9

America discovers Chekhov (USA 1900–1944)

I hate a play with a dead bird sitting on the mantelpiece shrieking,
"I'm the title, I'm the title, I'm the title."

Noël Coward on the Lunts's *Seagull*[1]

By the early 'twenties, "show business" had become a synonym for professional theatre in the United States. The star system was firmly in
place, and commercial Broadway theatre, ruled by a sodality of powerful managers, was flourishing. This was unhospitable soil for trans-
planting Chekhov.

The student magazine *Yale Courant* published the first American translation of a Chekhov play, *The Cherry Garden*, in 1908: as the title shows, a
very literal rendering, made by Max Mandell, a Russian instructor. *The
Bear* appeared within the year, then in 1912 came the first collection of
plays, including *Uncle Vanya, Ivanov, Seagull* and *Swan Song*, Englished with
dozens of blunders and misreadings by Marian Fell. From that point on,
new translations of individual plays appeared almost annually, but their
woodenness perpetuated resistance to staging Chekhov. *The Nation*[2] pronounced his drama tedious and pointless, full of unmotivated actions.
Reviewing a rendering of *The Cherry Orchard, The Dramatist*, a trade
journal for aspiring playwrights which evaluated the commercial potential of new plays, reported,

In place of plot development there is a mere portrayal of inept circumstance.
And in place of story there is nothing but the disconnected interests of several
pairs of puppets . . . the whole reflects more the infirmities of the author than
any other code or fad in contemporary drama . . . the antithesis of dramatic
method. Surely the rankest American amateur would be suspected of softening
of the cerebrum should he seriously submit such a soufflé to the producing
manager.[3]

As a matter of fact, many American amateurs were spearheading a
progressive movement for a modern theatre and the "artistic drama" of

Ibsen, Chekhov and Shaw which "had been given scant houseroom."[4] Born shortly before the outbreak of World War I, the "Little Theatre" Movement and its chief organ *Theatre Arts Magazine* insisted on a new program: the elimination of the star system and the substitution of the ideal of the ensemble; a simplified, appropriate and decorative staging, the development of a new body of poetic drama; and a sharp cleavage between commercial theatre and a new professional art theatre. To realize these goals and to introduce New Yorkers to the best works of European dramatists, the Washington Square Players and its off-shoot the Theatre Guild were founded.

Chekhov remained a stranger to the American stage, except for *The Bear* (1915) and a dim *Seagull* (May 1916) in the Fell (in both senses) translation, both put on by the Washington Square Players at the Bandbox Theatre, New York. The programs of new drama, including Eugene O'Neill, offered by the Players had so far been received enthusiastically; but when they took a chance on Chekhov, the result was disastrous, because, as Lawrence Langner recalled, "like most amateurs, we played it in semidarkness."[5] The review in the New York *Tribune* struck the usual notes of exasperation, with the rider that the Russian state of mind had nothing in common with Americans: "One loses patience with its people, and feels that the exercising of just a little common sense would wipe out all the complications . . . After the first act the play seems constantly to be wearing black lest the audience forget that utter wretchedness is the perennial state of mind in Russia . . . [The characters] take a purely Russian delight in being miserable."[6]

There was, in fact, a great deal in a Chekhov play which Americans could recognize: the sense of an unconfined land mass with vast spaces between habitations, and of unlimited resources placed by nature at the disposal of humanity, with the proviso that it free itself from slavery, both material and psychological; provincial doldrums and the myth of the alluring big city; psychic atmosphere read as mood swings. These and other affinities had an essential though indefinable influence of Chekhov on American theatre practitioners from the mid-1920s through the 1950s.

The editor of *Theatre Arts*, Sheldon Cheney, deplored the provincialism and lack of broad appeal in the Little Theatres, with their emphasis on community roots and local subject matter. He looked to European-style art theatres, controlled by an Artist-Director, to be the solution.[7] Only gradually did American journalists suggest that the Moscow Art Theatre might serve as a model for scenic reforms. In 1913, a writer in

The Drama cited "the Seagull Theatre of Moscow" as an "ideal sub-sidized theatre," although she considered it post-impressionist in style, and was most post-impressed by its adaptations of great novels.[8] Another commentator, a Russian, insisted that "your little theatres can learn more from the Moscow Art Theatre than any other in the world."[9] When it was announced in 1923 that the MAT was about to visit the United States, the news was welcomed by the Little Theatre movement as the advent of a saviour-guru whose precepts and object lessons would redeem the American stage from its crassness and catch-penny formulas.

The MAT had no intention of proselytizing. The tours had been pro-jected by Stanislavsky to improve the theatre's finances and his own per-sonal exchequer, to consolidate the young company with older actors who had returned from voluntary exile in Prague, and, incidentally, to avoid the turmoil caused in the Moscow theatre world by Soviet admin-istrative reforms. When the MAT toured the US, its repertory included *Three Sisters*, *The Cherry Orchard* (which constituted one-third of all per-formances in the first season), and, in the second season, *Uncle Vanya* and *Ivanov*, in many cases with the actors who had originally created the roles. (Stanislavsky agreed to appear on stage only to swell the box-office receipts.) These revivals of decades-old productions in no way repre-sented the theatre's latest researches; they were treated as family heir-looms, carefully preserved and burnished for display to strangers, masterpieces of psychological naturalism that Stanislavsky had per-fected but had long outstripped. Writing to Nemirovich from Berlin on the first leg of their marathon, Stanislavsky had lamented the inappropriateness of this outdated repertory: "When I perform the scene of parting from Masha in *Three Sisters*, I get embarrassed. After all we've been through, there's nothing to cry about in an officer leaving and a lady staying. Chekhov delights me not."[10]

Nevertheless, the Chekhov plays were precisely those most likely to appeal to American taste. The American theatre had its own traditions of understated realistic acting (Joseph Jefferson, Mrs Fiske, William Gillette) and highly naturalistic stage effects implemented by an advanced technology as practiced by Belasco. Where American audi-ences might have rejected the MAT productions of Andreev or Hamsun as too remote from their interests, they immediately responded to the subdued lyricism of the Chekhov plays. Even the finale of *Orchard* was found to parallel the post-bellum topos of leaving the old homestead.

Who were the first American audiences for the Art Theatre?

According to L. A. Leonidov, the MAT's business manager, they consisted of:

First, our little Slavic brothers and Russian Jews, earlier refugees to America to escape all sorts of Russian oppression.

Second, American snobs – the most fickle and insincere element.

Third, the spectators most especially devoted to us were American actors and directors.

They came to us as to a university.[11]

Although neither the theatre people nor the sensation-seekers knew Russian, they were struck by the masterful acting and the extra dimension that Chekhov took on when transferred from page to stage so thoroughly. Alexander Woollcott, the waspish reviewer for the New York *Herald*, asserted "that this inertia of all Chekhov's puppets puzzles and irritates the blunt American mind";[12] but it was a shibboleth of sensibility among the literati to be affected by the Slavic mood. "In those dear dead days of the twenties," a reporter retrospected a generation later, "how we hugged to our hearts the delicious pessimism of the Russians who were already becoming very old hat in Russia!"[13] John Dos Passos "'wept buckets' over *The Cherry Orchard*." This sensitivity intersected with the American conviction that "all foreigners are *Art*."[14]

The perceived pessimism of Russian literature was in marked contrast with the buoyant optimism of jazz-age America, and, combined with the sheer outlandishness of the names, was prone to evoke hilarity among the uninitiated. Philistines laughing at Chekhov or high-brows weeping at him both found it difficult to recognize that he himself had a comic outlook. The Theatre Guild was surprised to discover his comic facet.

Where all American productions of these plays had been done in gloomy darkness, the Russians turned on the lights and actually let the audience see what was happening. This was so revolutionary in American art theatre circles that some of our foremost scenic artists began to show suicidal tendencies.[15]

Stanislavsky's desire to keep actors' faces brightly illuminated always won over atmospheric lighting.

Since Americans had no long-established take on Chekhov, they adopted wholeheartedly the Art Theatre's. Analyzing the MAT's effect, Stark Young observed that,

Some of the players were manifestly past their prime, but it mattered very little; what they did seemed forever right and fine. I saw there on the stage Chekhov's characterizations, so whimsical, pitiful, keen, exact; I saw Chekhov's art come true, all the strange, incessant flux of it, its quivering and exposed humanity, its pathetic confusion of tragic, comic, inane and grotesque. I saw more than ever the likeness between Chekhov's method and Shakespeare . . . And out of this modern and realistic art I got something of the same thing that comes off from Shakespeare: the tragic excitement, the vivacity and pathetic beauty, the baffling logic of emotion, the thrill that comes from a sense of beauty.[16]

Young pointed out that America had actors as outstanding as any the Russians could show; what was remarkable was the ensemble effect, and he cited it to Americans as the paragon of a troupe working together for years under the same leader and possessed of a "racial or popular life from which they can draw their belief and idea." (He was not privy to the internal dissensions that were fracturing a company composed half of old stagers and half of young Turks.) For him the Art Theatre's Chekhov became the benchmark of theatrical excellence: if one reads Young's reviews over the next decade and a half, one finds the MAT the invariable standard of comparison. In 1929, he wonders "how anyone who could understand the values in . . . a play of Chekhov's, could fail to see that the last act in *Street Scene* . . . is empty and made up."[17] Habima's *Dybbuk* is cited as the best thing since the MAT *Cherry Orchard*, Mei Lan-Fang as the highest point of excellence since the MAT Chekhov. The Old Vic is rebuked for having no artistic message like the MAT's.

Even before the Russians had arrived, the Neighborhood Playhouse, an outgrowth of the Henry Street Settlement in an immigrant quarter, had arranged in 1923 for its actors to study with Richard Boleslavski, a former member of the MAT and its First Studio. Boleslavski not only introduced elements of Stanislavsky's system to America but directed two of the three plays the Neighborhood Playhouse presented in 1923. Several of the actors in the MAT company decided to remain in the US, including Leo and Barbara Bulgakov (who staged a *Seagull* in New York in 1929), Akim Tamiroff, Vera Soloviova and Maria Ouspenskaya; Michael Chekhov and Andrius Jilinsky would arrive a few years later. They were eager to make a living, but unappreciated by the commercial theatre, they did so by teaching.[18] Even though they may have been exposed to Stanislavsky in limited doses and at discrete moments in the development of his ideas on acting, this exposure became their stock-in-trade. Voluntarily or not, their pedagogic value was enhanced by an intimation of proximity to the godhead, an expertise at imparting the magic gospel. And the gospel which Stanislavsky had so suavely interpreted was the plays of Anton Chekhov. To stage them was to borrow lustre from the MAT.

The earliest results of the confrontation with the Moscow Art Theatre could be seen at Eva Le Gallienne's Civic Repertory Theatre: her first season (1926) offered the first American *Three Sisters* and Goldoni's *Mistress of the Inn* (both plays the MAT had presented), followed by *The Cherry Orchard* (1928 and 1933, with the émigrée star Alla Nazimova as Ranevskaya) and *The Seagull* (1929). Le Gallienne was an actress of considerable culture and taste, capable of reading Russian and translating the plays herself; she worshipped Duse and Komissarzhevskaya as her patron saints. Her comments on the plays, stressing the need for ensemble acting and the human dimension, were lit by sharp insights. For example, Le Gallienne noted that Chekhov's two Mashas and Varya were all in black.

Just as in painting there is a note of black somewhere on the canvas, so Tchekov in his plays has nearly always that note of black in one of his female characters. It seems to bring the other figures into relief in a curious way; from a director's angle it is immensely intriguing; of course it is true, too, that the wearing of black is an outward manifestation of an inner state of mind, especially when worn by young women . . .[19]

Unfortunately, Le Gallienne's ambitions as a producer and director often outstripped her capabilities; although she tried to emulate the MAT's stage pictures and deliberate rhythms, her casts were uneven, and her achievements admirable more for good intentions than for consummate artistry. She offered readings rather than interpretations. Even so, those critics who judged her results to be second-rate praised her endeavours, and her Chekhov exercised a potent effect on artistically immature audiences. Irwin Shaw had read *The Cherry Orchard* and was left cold by it; but when, at the age of sixteen, he saw Le Gallienne's production, "I was dazzled by what was revealed on the stage and became a convert to the theatre then and there."[20] The standing-room queues which wound in double lines outside the Civic Rep were made up not of those "one sees in upper-Broadway houses. Young people by the dozens with fine keen faces and with books under their arms . . . the people who cannot afford $5.50 for a theatre seat and who must choose wisely how to spend a dollar." (They also included a large contingent of gay men and lesbians, who patronized Le Gallienne because of her own reputation for sexual unorthodoxy.)[21] This enthusiastic special interest exuded an odour of uplift and high seriousness that would cling to Chekhov

Le Gallienne's devotion to a true repertory schedule prevented her productions from being seen by more than devotees, and her greatest hits, playing three or four times a week at the outset, never accumulated runs to rival those of commercial theatres. *The Cherry Orchard*, which had started with sixty-four sold-out performances in the Civic Rep's first season, was given only twice in its second, and played 108 times in all over the course of four seasons.[22]

Academic theatre provided a more adventurous venue for exploring Chekhovian variations. In 1928, Hallie Flanagan staged *The Marriage Proposal* at the Vassar Experimental Theatre in three styles: realistic, expressionistic, constructivist. Her notion of realism was perhaps satiric, since the setting for the Russian farmhouse looked like a Persian chamber with a view of St. Basil's Cathedral through the mullioned window. Expressionism was taken to mean a vivid clash of colours, a rhythmic pulse of voices and sharply patterned movement, with a masked Lomov doomed to fall before Natalya, symbol of pursuit and dominance. Meyerhold was the inspiration for the constructivist version, with curtain and box-sets whisked away to reveal an undecorated stage spilling into the audience, and covered with see-saws, swings and ladders for the antics of super-acrobats. As Flanagan reported, tongue firmly in cheek, "The audience accepts realism, grows restless under expressionism, but comes completely, and uproariously into constructivism, which in experiment proves to be much in the rhythm of our time."[23]

Flanagan, who was later named head of the Federal Theatre Project, hearkened to the *dernier cri* in the European theatre, and in a college setting, had the freedom to broadcast it. In the professional theatre, Chekhov remained a high-brow vehicle for ambitious players. What the critics often took away from Le Gallienne's productions tended to be impressions of individual performances. For Brooks Atkinson, the triumph of her *Cherry Orchard* was "Nazimova as pliant and gracious as a lily in the leading part."[24] The Trigorin of the great Yiddish actor Jacob Ben-Ami made *The Seagull* beat "with the same faint pulse of pensive doom."[25] Such praise led the shrewd Jed Harris to consider that Chekhov could serve as a showcase for stars; in January 1930 he mounted a well-received *Uncle Vanya* at the Cort Theatre.

The choice was peculiar. Harris, who had made his name as the producer of such fast-moving, wise-cracking shows as *Broadway*, *The Front Page* and *The Royal Family*, had just announced his imminent retirement. Since the critical establishment viewed Chekhov as full of passive melancholy, it wondered what kinship existed between the American showman and the Russian author, but it was precisely Harris' box-office acumen that distinguished this *Vanya* from the Chekhovs of Le Gallienne, Bulgakov and other disciples of the Art Theatre. It displayed a "variety

18 Hallie Flanagan's experiment in styles: *The Marriage Proposal*, at Vassar College, 1928. At top, the "realistic" version; center, the expressionist version, and, bottom, the constructivist version.

19   Eva Le Gallienne's *Cherry Orchard* with Alla Nazimova as Ranevskaya and Harold
Moulton as Trofimov in Act III; sets and costumes by Aline Bernstein;
Civic Repertory Theatre, NY 1928.

and [. . .] greater vitality [which Harris] induced from an endless
succession of hints and subtleties."[26] He avoided the relaxed monotone
that had so far characterized Russian plays in New York (twelve years
later, Stark Young could still have reason to complain that "Chekhov in
performance in English nearly always suffers from what seems to be
some sort of notion we have that thinking is slow, that when you are, as it
were, philosophizing you must go slow.")[27] Harris instead strove for
flashes of comedy to counteract the despair.

The cast was diverse, to put it mildly: Astrov was played by the dapper
leading man Osgood Perkins who specialized in fast-talking rogues and
elegant romancers; Lillian Gish, whose fragile mimicry was no longer at
a premium in a Hollywood gone sound-crazy, played Elena. Walter
Connolly, a stalwart of the Theatre Guild, concentrated the hatred of
Vanya, while Eugene Powers caricatured the professor. The Italian actor
Eduardo Ciannelli, a specialist in sinister gangsters, was oddly miscast as
Telegin. At the time, however, Harris was praised for harmonizing these
disparate elements and achieving a personal style.

That Chekhov on Broadway was regarded primarily as an opportunity for the display of individual talents is clear from a recollection of Lillian Gish: George Jean Nathan told her to get out of *Vanya* because her role would be overshadowed by Sonya's final monologue. "She'll wipe the floor with you."[28] Evidently, Nathan, the most cynical of American critics, had never read the play before; and in print he was to declare his impatience with "Russian drama with a stage inscrutably occupied by Mishka Vaselenavitch Klooglosvetloff, a retired professor . . . and a heterogeneous and very puzzling assortment of Pishkins, Boropatkins, Sergius Vodkaroffs, Abrezkoffvichs and Olthidors, all of them in whiskers."[29]

"Chekhov will always remain, to the boob *Art*, and, to the enlightened entertainment" countered the program note, throwing down the gauntlet to those who would put up resistance to Harris' experiment. This essay, supplied by Russian-born Rose Caylor, Ben Hecht's wife, who translated and adapted the play, meant to interpret Chekhov to the still benighted: phrases such as "Beautiful, fragmentary, elliptical" and "the little gray moth-like theme of man's pursuit of the unattainable" made up a mosaic portrait of Chekhov as admirable but ethereal. Caylor trimmed and tuned the play to prevent audiences from taking umbrage at enigmatic behaviour; she pointed up Astrov's "dandyism" by making him more reticent, played down Vanya's importuning Elena, and kept her from protesting overmuch at Astrov's suit. Bothered by the characters' awkward pauses, she filled them in. Even Sonya's ambiguous last words, "We shall rest" were edulcorated into sentimental gush:

We shall be happy because we shall have everything . . . The wheat fields will be there, and the blue cornflowers – And the woods in the spring! And Mother, and those we loved . . . and who loved us in return . . . And those who, in this existence, didn't love us. *She sobs suddenly.* They'll love us . . . They'll want us . . . *She weeps passionately, agonizedly. This is the suffering about which, in that future, she will speak to God. This, and not the other, is the truth. And so she weeps.*[30]

Apparently these maudlin emendations made the play acceptable to the average ticket-buyer, for this "panorama of evanescent shades," as Brooks Atkinson called it, ran for twelve weeks in New York, and then toured Boston, Baltimore, Philadelphia, Pittsburgh and Chicago, returning to New York in November, proving that Chekhov could be financially viable if titivated with celebrities.[31] When Boleslavski's American Laboratory Theatre opened *Three Sisters* in 1930 with no less illustrious an MAT veteran than Maria Germanova as Olga, it was condemned as "amateurish." No better sign of Chekhov's appropriation by the professional theatre could be wished.

With Le Gallienne's *Three Sisters* and *Cherry Orchard*, Harris' *Uncle Vanya*, and matinees of the Bulgakov *Seagull* at the Comedy Theatre, the New York stage saw four Chekhov productions in one season, a fact which Brooks Atkinson considered "incredible." "Only fifteen years or so ago this best-loved of Russian dramatists was, as far as the English-speaking nations were concerned, the demigod of the professionals alone . . . General indifference has now warmed into something verging upon idolatry in New York." He granted that the interest might still be largely limited to the theatrical profession, but for all that "How does it happen that plays once avoided as lugubrious and shapeless now appear to be etched in light?" Atkinson attributed it to a similarity between the stagnation in American artistic life and that of Russia in Chekhov's life-time.

After a period in which the vitality of the country has been dissipated in speculation and the inflation of business and industry, and in which the spirit of adventure has trickled out of art, after a period of general emotional flattening . . . Chekhov is writing the things we understand . . . With us it is a bastard intellectualization of the normal artistic impulses, and a cheerful surrender of art to business. There is no fire, no aspiration, no conviction, no direction in the arts. [. . .] it is a period completely lacking in the creative impulse.[32]

In 1930, however, in a less sanguine opinion piece, Atkinson felt compelled to grant that Chekhov "is the idol chiefly of the professionals . . . although playgoers with an intellectual cast of mind believe in his genius the large public is bored by him, finding his plays long and dull." For all its rapturous reviews and long run, *Uncle Vanya* could not achieve the popularity of *Street Scene* or *The Green Pastures*. Since Chekhov had been on the boards regularly for five years, the public's apathy could not be attributed to misunderstanding or insufficient time to acquire a taste for him. Rather, for Atkinson, the continued coolness towards Chekhov revealed a fundamental difference between the American need for certainty and Chekhov's avoidance of closure.

Most plays are designed to illuminate one aspect of life; proceeding from some concrete impulse or principle, they profess to arrive at a definite conclusion. In fact, the temper of our creed-ridden civilization leads us to expect from every writer a statement of dogmatic opinion.[33]

Atkinson's *aperçu* may explain the greatest lacuna in the history of American Chekhovian production: the absence of any staging by the

Group Theatre. Although the Group avowedly based its principles of organization and aesthetic dedication on the Art Theatre, although it avidly read and discussed the latest theatrical tidings from Moscow, the only Chekhov play it attempted was *The Bear* as part of an entertainment at Green Mansions, in Warrensby, New York. In part this was because of the Group's insistence on fostering new, socially relevant drama, and in part because the times seemed to demand the delivery of political messages to its audiences. As a functioning part of American society, the Group was duty-bound to put on American plays. Somewhat defensively, its leader Harold Clurman found the critics' comparisons of Chekhov's plays with the Group's discoveries, especially Paul Green's *The House of Connelly* and Clifford Odet's *Paradise Lost*, "academic, empty and useless." But Odets had himself described his protagonist "the entire American middle class of liberal tendency" as being in the same state of disarray as Chekhov's intelligentsia.[34]

It was not until the summer of 1939, without a new script at hand, that the dispirited Clurman embarked on his first classic and began to rehearse *Three Sisters*, despite his belief that the production of a classic would attract no financing. Of all Chekhov's plays, he found *Three Sisters* "the most American," "because it deals with young people" and their talk of getting away from an old life; Le Gallienne's production had reminded him of a small American town in 1925. He was eager to escape the clichés of languid sophisticates and promoted the characters as "just guys," "wonderful, healthy people whose health and fullness is not given an opportunity to expand in the world in which they live . . . The spine of the play might be to find a full life in a world that has no opportunity."[35] This interpretation had great appeal for the Group actors, who, using a text prepared by Odets, sought an idiomatic style that would point up connections with contemporary America. Unfortunately, owing to lack of interest on the part of backers, and to an incompatibility between Stella Adler's florid Masha and Morris Carnovsky's muted Vershinin, the effort was soon abandoned. Chekhov was supplanted by Robert Ardrey's *Thunder Rock*. "Clurman found some truth in the Broadway maxim that it was impossible to raise money for a classic without stars."[36]

The star system remained the vehicle which gained Chekhov entrée on the New York stage. The Theatre Guild sponsored a glamorous *Seagull* in 1938, with Alfred Lunt and Lynn Fontanne as Trigorin and Arkadina in Stark Young's no-frills translation. The most scintillating adepts of high comedy in North America, they surrounded themselves with a remarkable, if ill-assorted group of players, including Sydney

Greenstreet as Sorin, Uta Hagen as Nina, and Margaret Webster as Masha. The Lunts were embarking on a national tour, and their "primary motivation" in attempting *The Seagull* "was to add a very different kind of play to their repertoire." The New York appearance was in essence a try-out.[37] Russian-born Robert Milton, nominally the director, dealt only with movement and gestures, while the Lunts, who usually worked from externals, took charge of characterization and motivation. (Later, they requested Eva Le Gallienne to restage the play.) Realism was served by having a genuine dinner eaten offstage in Act IV, but atmosphere had to be sacrificed to the needs of the matinee-goers. So Robert Edmond Jones's dim lighting was heightened to a brighter general illumination.

This led to the critical complaint that the production was too elegant and glossy; it told the story neatly enough, but sophisticated playgoers missed the half-tones and plangency they had come to expect of the Chekhovian ethos. Nathan joked that, owing to their predilections, the Lunts confused Chekhov with Molnár. Outside New York, reviewers showed their ignorance of Chekhov by expecting a diverting sex comedy. In fact, the Lunts had deliberately pointed up the comic elements, leading Richard Watts in the *Herald-Tribune* to admit, "there is a strange, sly humor about it . . . due to the curious suggestions of whimsical laughter that the Lunts manage to put into it upon occasion . . . Only the Irish can equal the Russians in leaping back and forth with speed and abandon, between bitterness and gaiety . . . "[38] The Lunts had benefitted from Stark Young's percipient remarks on the play. He alerted them to "an elusive but wholly robust wit proceeding from within a gentle nature and therefore not inhuman or cruel; pervading all; and giving a vibrant proportion to the whole."[39] *The Seagull* garnered "the best set of reviews that ever greeted the Chekhov play in this city" and *Stage* magazine pointedly contrasted its "exciting theatre" with Komisarjevsky's "moody tableau." It presented the Lunts an award for performances "which overrode the brooding, introverted Chekhov legend: set two human and plausible people in the middle of a brilliantly played, brilliantly adapted revival of a moss-grown masterpiece."[40]

The next stellar Chekhovian production on Broadway was *Three Sisters* staged by Guthrie McClintic in 1942, with a cast composed of luminaries of the American stage and screen: Katharine Cornell (Masha), Judith Anderson (Olga), Ruth Gordon (Natasha), Dennis King (Vershinin) and Edmund Gwenn (Chebutykin), a mixture of Americans, Canadians, Englishmen and Australians, of diverse schools and differing styles. The idea for the revival had come from Gordon, essentially a comic actress, who wanted to play Masha; Cornell, a leading lady of romantic intensity, was willing to assume Olga,[41] but McClintic, her husband, promoted her to Masha and demoted Gordon to Natasha. He tried to get Lunt and Fontanne for Vershinin and Olga, but failed. Had the trio of Gordon and the Lunts occupied centre stage, *Three Sisters* might have taken on the brittle wit of a society comedy. As it was, McClintic seemed to subscribe to the view that Chekhov's play is a tragedy peopled by three wonderful women and a she-monster.

Clifford Odets was asked to adapt the text, but the new translation was eventually made by Alexander Koiransky, a former Art Theatre designer who had helped ghost-write Stanislavsky's *My Life in Art*.[42] (He and McClintic also composed additional dialogue to be spoken by characters upstage and on the sidelines.) Although McClintic claimed that he was not trying to recreate a Russian ambience, Koiransky's background was supposed to guarantee authenticity; his interpretation held that "Not circumstances but character defeats" the Prozorovs and their circle. But Cornell refused to believe that Masha had had a physical affair with Vershinin, interpreted by Koiransky as "a dashing officer"; the sexual frustration increased her looking for "my man" in Act IV to a frantic pitch. Any ensemble spirit was also foiled by McClintic's finding ways of thrusting Masha into the foreground; in Act III, he gave her a white pillow to clutch against her black dress, a singularly eye-catching device.[43]

Before the play settled into the Ethel Barrymore Theatre, the premiere was held in Fort Meade where the soldiers were reported to be responsive.[44] McClintic had cannily gauged the taste of his wartime audience: in 1942, the analogy of women bearing up bravely as their men marched away was best treated heroically, not ironically, even if Chekhov's officers are only removing to another cushy billet. All the newspaper critics but one were enthusiastic, and *Three Sisters* ran one hundred and twenty-two performances in New York, with thirty-nine weeks on tour: "the longest run any Chekhov play has ever enjoyed in this country . . . and the longest run *The Three Sisters* ever had anywhere," McClintic proudly recorded.[45]

Life magazine, which was the rectal thermometer of American cultural temperature, ran a picture spread on the production which summed up its appeal: "this drama of somber moods was rich fulfilment for playgoers tired of cream-puff comedies and loud musicals . . . As a play it is a talky vehicle," but offered the chance to see leading ladies

20 Stiff upper lips in the last act of Guthrie McClintic's *Three Sisters. Life*'s caption to this
picture was: "Saying goodbye are Masha and her lover (Dennis King). With Irina's
baron killed and Olga *(right)* made school headmistress, the sisters are condemned to a
life of boredom." Katherine Cornell as Masha and Judith Anderson as Olga.

swanning around in period costumes. The emphatic gerunds of captions
flattened out the characters: "scheming to control the house," "raving
drunk and moaning miserably," "professing love for Irina," "saying
goodbye." The final tableau was summed up thus: "With Irina's baron
killed and Olga made school headmistress, the sisters are condemned to
a life of boredom."[46] There was nothing enigmatic or obscure about
Life's Chekhov, who might easily have been serialized on daytime radio.
    Two years later *Life* devoted a spread to Eva Le Gallienne's revival of
The Cherry Orchard, which ran for ninety-six performances on Broadway

before launching a five-month tour. By this time, the experts had decided that the director's task was "to create the atmosphere – crystalline, spring-like, yet with autumnal overtones – in which the play is steeped," an impression which may have been a lingering remnant of the Art Theatre's visit. The co-director in this case was Margaret Webster, Le Gallienne having succeeded to the role of Ranevskaya, and she seems to have gone for pace and comedy, especially in Joseph Schildkraut's Gaev and Leona Roberts' Charlotta. Consequently, she was judged to have missed the play's peculiar fragrance. Le Gallienne would later insist Chekhov was inimical to "the slow, solemn approach" so commonly applied.[47] However, the notion of Chekhov as a delicate blossom, easily crushed, was too ingrained in American minds for a brisker, less reverent approach to be accepted, especially during war-time when the ubiquitous sense of bereavement and separation called for respectful handling.

CHAPTER 10

Under duress (Russia 1938–1945)

When I think of what our actors need, what our audiences live by,
what the art of the MAT requires, it seems to me that a production
of *Three Sisters* is an absolute necessity for our creativity.
Pavel Markov, dramaturge of the MAT[1]

THREE SISTERS MADE OVER

Deft as he was at dealing with the Soviet authorities, Nemirovich-
Danchenko vacillated over whether to stay in the USSR. In 1925, he took
his Musical Studio to America and capitalized on its success to extract a
contract from Paramount Pictures as a scenarist and adviser. Two years
of fruitless busy work in Hollywood sent him back to Europe. Successful
stints directing in Italy and Germany were not enough to convince him
to resettle at his advanced age, and so he returned to Moscow.
Stanislavsky, sequestered at home pleading ill health, had virtually abdi-
cated responsibility in running the MAT, and died in 1938, canonized by
the Stalinist establishment. By this time, the theatre had become a veritable waxworks of socialist realism, performing propaganda plays about
recent history and adaptations of nineteenth-century novels.

Nemirovich's decision to direct Chekhov came slowly at the age of
eighty-three; he deliberately retarded his preparations, wavering
between *The Seagull* and *Three Sisters*, without wholly rejecting *Uncle
Vanya. Cherry Orchard* was still in the repertory, but stank of the museum,
inviolably preserving the old stage pictures and Simov's sets (Vladimir
Dmitriev had renovated the second act so that clouds could scud across a
cyclorama). All that kept it going were Knipper's lyricism and the hoary
traditions of the other "old-timers." Nemirovich's dreams of revising
this production from top to bottom had been tried out in Milan, but he
felt it was not the proper time to carry on such work in Moscow.

As his mind veered more and more towards *Three Sisters*, he broached
his choice to an ever widening circle of actors and directors, who greeted

it with no special enthusiasm. There was a general desire to include Chekhov in the rota of socialist authors, but this particular play failed to capture their imagination. Nikolay Khmelev sniffed at the prospect of Tusenbach, for he dreamed of playing Astrov. Klavdiya Elanskaya, who was later acclaimed as Olga, at first considered her "no sort of role," and Aleksey Gribov condescended to take on Dr. Chebutykin as "just another of his true-to-life old duffers." Only Alla Tarasova caught fire when offered the part of Masha.[2]

Nemirovich viewed his task as one of revitalization, a curious responsibility for an octogenarian. At the opening rehearsal, he indicated the distance between the MAT's original production and the current state of affairs: " . . . life has not only changed completely, but it has filled us – as artists – with new matter, guided us along a path where one must and can look at Chekhov in a new and different way, and feel Chekhov afresh . . . "[3] In 1901, Leonid Andreev had declared the play's theme-song to be "To want to live, excruciatingly, agonizingly, painfully to want to live!"[4] But Stanislavsky had notated this tune so as to be sung, "It's impossible to live." Nemirovich, in line with Stakhanovite optimism, chose to sing two different tunes: longing for a better life (not a plangent, whiny longing to escape life, but something active though devoid of the element of struggle), and deep faith in the future, in Tusenbach's storm about to break over the land and sweep away deceit, money-grubbing and antipathy to work. The characters were seen not as futile and trivial, but as fine minds in magnificent and handsome bodies. They were to be interpreted in a style of "virile strength."[5]

"My concept keeps roaming around a particular realm," the aged director told his actors.

One thing is obvious in the sisters – a desire to tear themselves away from the life which now surrounds them, a profound and agonizing dissatisfaction with the reality which supports the most clear-cut vulgarity [*poshlost*] – vulgarity not in the sense of baseness [*podlost*] (one must go deeper), but in the sense of being earthbound, in the absence of dreams . . . So all of that, dreams and reality, dreamers in the middle of lacklustre reality and vulgarity – that, in my opinion, is the core of the production.[6]

Nemirovich's preliminary eloquence caused ears to prick up, even though he admitted he had no pre-conceived plan of staging, which was taken as another sign of his "dotage." In part, this was due to his refusal to stake out innovations. His early comments suggest that the look of the old Art Theatre production might reappear in a new and improved version; but since he had already stressed the inability of modern actors to treat Chekhov as Chekhov's contemporaries understood him, this was taken to refer only to externals. In fact, Nemirovich was consulting with the designer Dmitriev about the look of the Prozorov home, but his seeming uncertainty was a tactic to convince the actors that all the important decisions depended on them and would be made in rehearsal. Accustomed to protracted development, he had even been reluctant to offer "longing for a better life" as the connective tissue of the production. What he did insist on was that the actors read *Three Sisters* with clear eyes and feel completely free in dealing with it, with one proviso: they must preserve "absolute artistic honour," so that everything really would be "reborn." He also suggested that if they were not successful in retrieving the play's core, then it would not be revived, and a future "collective of enthusiasts" would have to take on the mission. To this end, he regularly attacked the actors in rehearsal for relying on tried-and-true techniques, to stir up panic and prevent them from lapsing into easy choices.

Nemirovich's hesitations and his refusal to predict success had many causes. For one thing, he was an unqualified admirer of the 1901 production, which he attributed wholly to Stanislavsky. He renounced any attempt to vie with it, but instead chose the path of most resistance, clearing away the underbrush of clichés which were clogging the Art Theatre's development: the leaden weight of circumstantial naturalism, the flaccid rhythms and turgid speech patterns, the "half-tones" of synthetic "Chekhovianism." Hence the emphasis on a bright, courageous Chekhov and the clash of lofty dreams with oppressive reality.

The strongest lever in prying away this debris was the concept that Chekhov's characters "must be more poetical, artistic."[7] The original production had sought to depict stifling provinciality; Simov's last act set had presented a small glade of saplings, with piles of bricks near a fence, and a plain bench before a tiny veranda hidden by two ordinary striped awnings. Nemirovich let in fresh air and flowers. Dmitriev's designs supplied huge, graceful windows and shimmering birch-trees. The sisters were moved from a remote backwoods town to a suburban Moscow villa and a comfortable way of life.[8] Everything from uniforms to dressing-gowns was made beautiful; everything debasing or cold was eliminated.

The whole production was replete with everyday life, its routines, its details, mingled with moving rituals, a multiplicity of things, sounds and rustlings, weather, the time of day or night, genuine tokens of the period and milieu. And all this was alive, not "theatrical," but flowing and mingled with life itself. But even the nooks and armchairs and window-blinds and clock chimes and the pie for the party and Shrovetide with its mummers, and the glowing lamps on the

21 V. Dmitriev's last act birches for *Three Sisters*, directed by Nemirovich-Danchenko, Moscow Art Theatre, 1940.

table, and the humming in the stove, with all its supportive significance for the texture of a Chekhov production remained only indispensable auxiliaries, as if they were serving a more important task. We rejoiced in it not because it corresponded with something familiar, but because it intimated that mysterious significance hidden in real everyday life and spoke of the realities of spiritual life, which had an even greater existence.[9]

This was spring water to thirsty minds in a society in which materialism and positivism were enforced from above. Soviet editors of Stanislavsky were busy cutting the words "spirit" and "soul" from his posthumous editions. Nemirovich's almost symbolist correspondence between the humdrum world and a more meaningful spiritual sphere was a bold rehabilitation of values officially debased and negated.

Although neither Nemirovich nor Dmitriev ever said as much, they seemed to have decided to merge the stage picture with the auditorium. The ornament on the scene curtain was extended to the side wings, and the emblem of the seagull to the borders, while the geometrically straight, symmetrical silhouettes of the bare trees and the huge windows led the eye upward. This displacement and extension provoked a sense of spaciousness, a subtle effraction of the fourth wall.[10]

Since Nemirovich's production was kept in the repertory well into the

1960s, a whole generation attended it with deep respect, but it was the spectator of 1940 who fully experienced the shock of the new. Then "it was full of air and light, pellucid and harmonious" from the first "vernal" act of Irina's nameday party to the autumnal valediction among old trees shedding their leaves. The buoyancy and brightness were maintained even in the crepuscular aura of the Prozorov parlour, the night of alarums and excursions, the compression produced by Natasha's obtrusive and constrictive furniture. Although abetted by the lighting plot, this radiance seemed to be spiritual, proceeding from the actors' seamless and palpitant togetherness, conveyed to the spectator from the very first moments. "The spectator seemed imperceptibly drawn into the course of someone else's life, which immediately initiated a mysterious relationship with his own and remained there long after the show was over."[11]

In the course of rehearsals, Nemirovich discovered a musical princi- ple as the secret of Chekhovian drama: scenes were written in musical tempi, one in 4/4 time, another in 6/8 and so on. Likening the play to a Chaikovsky opera, he achieved a remarkable rhythmic pattern, which made audible the beating of the Chekhovian heart.[12] The sisters consti- tuted a musical trio: Elanskaya's Olga conveyed an image of great spiri- tual purity, never depressed, always facing up to problems courageously. Tarasova as Masha despised the life she lived and strove for whatever would do away with the hated *status quo*; she was forceful rather than morbid. Angelina Stepanova's Irina emitted a feeling of soulful reverie: even if life clipped her wings, she could not and would not be reconciled with it, but kept aspiring to something more. All the characters, exclud- ing Natasha, affirmed life through their inner restlessness and dissatisfac- tion.

The power of the impression was sustained by the perfection of the ensemble: naturally, old timers compared this cast with the originals to the formers' disadvantage, but this cut no ice with a new generation. They thrilled to Mikhail Bolduman's stern and restrained Vershinin, Gribov's sage Chebutykin. Boris Livanov's Soleny was such a swash- buckling bully that he set the pattern for the role for decades. As for Khmelev's intrepid Tusenbach, he deeply believed in the future; his monologue about the storm-wrack was the high point of the sunny first act, full of joyous hope in Masha's meeting with Vershinin and Andrey's sincere love of Natasha.

This atmosphere was sharply distinguished from the gloomy aliena- tion and slow tempo of the second act. The same rooms became unrecognizable: no light, no flowers, no air. Instead of the sickly sweet hausfrau created by Lilina, the Natasha of Anastasiya Georgievskaya was a monster of crassness, a petty bourgeoise eager to flout the sisters' hopes and dreams. After the nadir of Act II, the power of optimism began to gain the upper hand once more. Irina's bedtime speech about going to Moscow was a hopeful prayer, uttered boldly and urgently. In the last act, the house was surrounded by the beauty of nature: a wide expanse of land, a graceful lane of white birches, with golden leaves drifting on to the stage. The sympathetic fallacy bespoke the possibility of another, beautiful life, rich in meaning. Just when it seemed that all the dreams had perished, the military band struck up jauntily. In Stanislavsky's original production, Olga's final monologue had resounded with pellucid grief; now Elanskaya pronounced "Peace and happiness will come to the earth" with conviction and passionate fervour. In Chekhov, Chebutykin remains seated on the bench, reading the paper and quietly murmuring, "Makes no difference, makes no difference . . . ," a sardonic Greek chorus undercutting the sisters' expectations. Nemirovich banned Chebutykin from the finale, to prevent him disrupting the triumphant hymn to the future with his "Ta-ra-ra-boom-de-ay." His sisters stood clutching one another, as the music died away. "Olga's words about the future, which reveal the secret of life and the meaning of human suffering, reverberate in the bright stillness of an autumn day."[13]

What struck the younger spectators was that the staging was evolving before their very eyes, for Nemirovich had decreed a transparent "*mise-en-scène* without *mise-en-scène*." All the movements seemed entirely natural, uncontrived and unillustrative: even the occasional immobility was not tedious. Crosses from one stage area to another were accompanied by lighting changes. They provided a wide-angle view of the actors, as well as close-ups that occasionally segregated from the circumambient reality Irina and Tusenbach or Masha and Vershinin or Vershinin debating Tusenbach or Irina running down the garden path, arms outstretched, moaning "I knew it, I knew it." Without calling attention to themselves, these moves heightened the emotion and focussed the mind.

Newness was conveyed not only visually, but aurally. There was no declamation, which was the common mode of discourse in the Stalinist theatre; the dialogue came across as simple conversation, but there were moments, as in the Act I exchange of Tusenbach and Irina, or the scene between Irina and Olga behind screens in their bedroom when only their voices could be heard, which might have been musically notated.

For the first time we heard from the stage a kind of new language, new speech, which sounded unusual (in no other show had anyone talked *like that*), but seemed natural to a Chekhov play. Its pure and strict musicality had a simplicity of a higher order. The voices seemed to merge in an harmonious polyphony of performance, inchoate from the very start . . . Its cantilena corresponded with the interrupted life on stage.[14]

Another, more profound effect of the production went unmentioned by the critics of the time. Two months before Nemirovich began his rehearsals, Stalin had received a Seagull badge, both a token of his "service" to the theatre and a recognition of the theatre's servitude to him. Highly privileged and exempt from the closures and censorship visited on lesser companies, the MAT was, in return, obliged to serve as the theatrical mouthpiece not only for Stalinist esthetics but for politics, endorsing Party decisions in its newsletters and bulletins. As a subtle resistance to this co-optation, Nemirovich's theme of "longing for a better life" referred not to the future desired by the pre-revolutionary intelligentsia, a future which had turned out to be the dreadful present. Rather, it alluded to the past, and stood for an ethical vision and a tragic meaning of individual lives that had been lost among the brutalities and humiliations of the 1930s. "If only we knew" was a generation's plaint for the meaningless violence that had been visited upon it.

The premiere of Nemirovich's *Three Sisters* took place on 20 April 1940. Three weeks later, he began formal work on *Hamlet*, but, when he died shortly thereafter, the production was aborted: Stalin found *Hamlet* unnecessary in a time of action. *Three Sisters* was Nemirovich's swan song, and may well have been the greatest staging of a Chekhov play in the history of the Art Theatre. Its effect in Russia was profound, but the outbreak of the war prevented it from having a greater influence on the refurbishing of other classical plays.

When the West got to view this *Three Sisters* after the war, it was less impressed. Of course, much of the newness had worn off, and the actors had settled into their roles in a more routine manner; nor could Europeans share the Soviet spectator's feelings of release and moral nostalgia that it evoked. However, the antipathy it aroused was due less to the production itself than to the international political climate.

Michel Saint-Denis, who had seen the original MAT *Sisters* on tour in Paris, had his doubts about the renovated version: granting its high quality and welcoming the simplification of the outdoors setting, he was distressed that a "fresh coat of paint" had been applied. Noting a lack of unity in the fourth act set, he was bothered by the contradiction between wings daringly made of unpainted hessian and a backcloth painstakingly painted in a realistic manner. More important, the simplification had damaged the style and meaning.

The play had been speeded up in tempo . . The poetic values had been damaged in favour of a more optimistic, more clearly constructive meaning. Nostalgic melancholy, even despair, had given way to positive declarations.[15]

Saint-Denis was distressed that the actresses were all middle-aged, twenty to thirty years older than their roles, and he particularly mourned the loss of "poetry." He preferred Stanislavsky's version.

It was less clean, especially in the open-air scenes, always so difficult to do in a naturalistic style. The stage was loaded with too many bushes and trees and ponds and bridges which never succeed in giving more than a bad imitation of nature. But for the rest, and also for the acting as a whole, it had much more melancholy; it was much more Chekhovian than the recent *Three Sisters*.[16]

Damage has been done to Saint-Denis' roseate memories of a theatregoing past; since he had determined that Chekhov is melancholy, he could not accept the heartiness of Nemirovich's vision.

Saint-Denis' opinion was echoed at various decibel levels by Russianborn Englishmen when the MAT brought *Three Sisters* to London in 1958. Nicholas Nabokov complained of its "strained optimism," and William Gerhardie wrote an indignant letter to the *Times* protesting "vandalism" and "injury."[17] The harm inflicted on their memories of the play was abetted by their hostility to communism; in the Cold War, any reinterpretation of a pre-Revolutionary masterpiece could be seen only as barbarity.

FLYING BLIND

The Great Patriotic War froze the Russian theatre world in place. Innovation and reformation were subjugated to the needs of propaganda and morale. The next experiment in new forms for Chekhov came in 1944 with a *Seagull* directed by Aleksandr Tairov, leader of the Kamerny (Chamber) Theatre. Tairov, long a proponent for theatrical theatre, had created a highly eclectic repertory, offering stylized and musical interpretations of Racine, Shakespeare, Shaw, Ostrovsky, O'Neill, Bulgakov, Lecocq, Chesterton and Brecht; his designers had included leading futurists, cubists and suprematists. Like Meyerhold, he had come under increasing attack for his "formalism," but managed to survive owing to a success with Vishnevsky's paean to the Soviet navy and commissariat, *An Optimistic Tragedy*, in 1933. The authorities deeply distrusted Tairov as the last representative of "bourgeois aestheticism," however; and, although the Kamerny Theatre managed to hold on to its government patronage, its days were numbered.

Moscow had just been liberated from Nazi siege in 1943, and the actors were allowed to return home; the Kamerny Theatre had been badly bombed, but it reopened on Christmas day. After a few revivals, Tairov decided to rehearse *The Seagull* and Ostrovsky's *Guilty Though Innocent* simultaneously, perhaps because they were both plays about nineteenth-century actors and could provide an escape from current events. He had long been pondering Chekhov's comedy and now chose it to celebrate the fortieth anniversary of the author's death. The company was enchanted by the choice, for it sidestepped Tairov's difficulties with the Committee for Theatrical Affairs, the incoherence of their own lives and the hopeless situation of the theatre. He managed to mount it in under a month.

In his youth, Tairov had once been entrusted by Gaideburov with a Chekhov production but had drowned it in a chaotic musical accompaniment. It never opened and he never returned to Chekhov. Now he sought to reveal "Chekhov the poet, akin to Pushkin and Shakespeare"[18] in what was first and foremost a director's interpretation; the actors' performances, though serious and thoughtful, were subservient to the overall concept.

To allay any suspicions of the censor, Tairov announced that he was adopting an optimistic outlook that attested to man's capability to overcome all obstacles through belief in his own potential. To keep the focus on the words, the physical production was that of a "concert performance," intended to put Chekhov "face to face with the public." "How people eat, drink, wear their jackets" was not at issue here. Black and grey velvet drapes, a device learned from Gaideburov's Itinerant Theatre, were supplemented by a low platform, a few flimsy draperies disposed differently in each act, some armchairs, a grand piano and a desk in Treplev's room, a little table, and a stuffed seagull on the piano. Light played over the backdrop to suggest locales or create a patch of moonlight during Nina's monologue. "Picked out by the spotlight filtering through the delicate layer of fabric, the illuminated contours of a window, narrow birches, water were barely seen against a grey background and give the impression of a room, a estate or lake – a spare, light and expressive background."[19]

In the absence of makeup, costumes or props, Tairov cautioned the actors against emphatic delivery and external theatricality. A spectator who didn't know them would just assume their real faces were made up and a form of alienation would be achieved. His wife, the great actress Alisa Koonen, had known the role of Nina by heart since her apprenticeship at the Art Theatre; Nemirovich had even jokingly nicknamed her "the Nina of Patriarch Pond." But at the age of forty-five and without recourse to cosmetics, she was nervous about assuming the part. Tairov explained that youth is an inner feeling, and an actor who can evoke it will be convincing without makeup. It was to be her last role.

The modesty of the production plan disguised Tairov's real aesthetic manifesto, his debate with the authorities over the audience's heads about the basic responsibilities of art:

The author in this play is carrying on a serious, very sincere, often contradictory dialogue with himself. So I don't want to see people in wigs and glued-on moustaches; I'd even like to abstain from all sorts of "magical" theatrical devices. One must try in a pure form to convey to the spectator Chekhov's musings on real human beings, new art, to influence them through Chekhov's words and poetry. In atmospherics, in its very form of production we must try to present what Chekhov lived by, what he dreamed of, what made him suffer and what he loved.[20]

A third of the script was cut, dropping all lines and stage directions that contributed to what Tairov saw as inessential secondary characters and episodes and the fabric of day-to-day reality. As an exponent of lyrical theatre, he expunged such homespun moments as Arkadina's argument with Shamraev, her dispute with Sorin over money, and the lotto game. In abridging the text, he tried to bring out what he saw as Chekhov's philosophy and the play's central theme: the struggle through new artistic forms to attain the highest truth. To this end, by discarding a recreation of reality, he turned *The Seagull* into a Platonic dialogue on art, a discourse between Treplev and Trigorin. Sergey Durylin, one of the production's few admirers on the critical bench, said it was staged as "Treplev dreamed of seeing a play in his new theatre,"[21] and the Italian theatre historian Ettore Lo Gatto adjudged it an unexpected resurgence of pre-Revolutionary symbolism. Tairov considered Nina's soliloquy of prime importance in this scheme, Chekhov's own earnest and undisguised musing on human existence, in which he was revealed as poet and thinker. Excising Arkadina's sneering comment about decadence, Tairov set it to Chaikovsky's music; indeed, Chaikovsky filled all the pauses, turning the play into a symphonic melodeclamation. This style of performance, the recital of poetry to piano accompaniment, had been an invention of the actor Nikolay Khodotov before the Revolution. By reviving it, Tairov seemed to be rehabilitating Treplev's legacy.

Tairov's other theme was that of a selfless love enduring through profound suffering. All the characters are in love, but all are unrequited, "This lack of fulfilment," Tairov remarked, "creates an unbroken tremulousness throughout the play, a sensation of covert anxiety."[22] Nina's ruined life was to knit together both themes: that of the struggle for great and original art, and that of tremulous love. At the end of Act III, in her goodbyes to Trigorin, Koonen was wearing a scarlet shawl over her plain grey dress, and as she ran offstage, waving the shawl, the light fringe blew upwards. She felt as if she were flying into a beautiful future – the seagull taking wing from her native lake. This feeling was conveyed to spectators, since, as Kachalov told her, the fringe gave the impression of the bird's pinions.

The whole fourth act was constructed as Nina's monologue, occasionally interrupted by Treplev's lines and again recited to Chaikovsky accompaniment. After he voiced his doubts about his abilities, she appeared wrapped in a white shawl. In her abandonment and humiliation, she confessed her love for Trigorin, but this confession resounded with a passionate, consoling, steadfast faith in her calling as an actress. "I strove to make those words 'Now I am an actress' a joyful triumph over spiritual grief and pain, because such is the path of a real artist ready to reach his goal through any experiences."[23] Nina's words, delivered with striking simplicity, became Koonen's testimony of patience and faith. The finale, played pianissimo, was starkly graphic in underlining the play's symbolic meaning: a bright spotlight pinpointed the stuffed gull on the piano, its wings outspread as if ready for great exploits and self-sacrifice.

For all of Tairov's past distinction, few reviewers found it necessary to cover his latest effort, given wartime concerns and his own peripheral status in an era of cultural standardization. They dismissed his *Seagull* as a variation on a Chekhovian theme, complaining of Koonen's age, bad acting, and "Meyerholditis." Playgoers used to the opulence that, consonant with Stalin's taste, was the norm in revivals of the classics, were shocked by the production's "poor theatre" aspect. On the other hand, this *Seagull* had a strong appeal to musicians and artists like Svyatoslav Richter and Nina Dorliac. Tairov's old master Gaideburov was delighted by the way the narrow focus had highlighted the play's lyricism. "The idea itself, like the white Seagull with its outspread wings, overshadowed the production concept, and the image of the performance as a creative revelation of the play's internal movement arose on stage with logical consecution."[24] One young student, moved to tears, couldn't wait to take up the theatre as a profession, so impressed was she by this "young, subtle, new production."[25] But general lack of interest conspired to keep this preliminary sketch from maturing into a full-scale rendering; it soon closed. Four years later, the theatre, famed for its "own personality" and lack of academic routine, was also closed.

At the same time, the critics had no intention of rubber-stamping the same old thing. Yury Zavadsky's *Seagull* at the Mossovet Theatre was meant as a riposte to Tairov, yet was unanimously damned for being antiquated, devoid of ideas and unconcerned with any principles aesthetic or social. Its Treplev was passive and static, more like Ibsen's Oswald, lacking any fervour in the struggle for the new. By pausing after every word, this *Seagull* took four and a half hours to waddle to its conclusion. Instead of a contemporary restatement of problems, it was an archaic restoration of the hackneyed devices of the Chekhov theatre. New forms were definitely needed.

CHAPTER II

Breaking with tradition (Russia 1950–1970)

A general Chekhovian tone is a good thing, of course, but a tone is
not a meaning. And each of Chekhov's plays has, in addition to a
general tone, its own inimitable meaning.

Anatoly Éfros[1]

REPRIMING THE CANON

Even before the Great Patriotic War, the ukases of Party congresses had
decreed positive qualities and epic heroism for literary treatment.
Chekhov was tightly ensconced in the pantheon of literary classics, but it
took some intellectual contortion to bring him in line with the program,
a task which was first laid on the Moscow Art Theatre. Privileged stars
like Vasily Kachalov were expected to mouth the party line in payment
for their privileges. Speaking of Chekhov's characters in January 1939,
he described them as "confused, unaware, they live for the future . . . Just
as our finest communist intelligentsia lives by its faith in building communism, so they believe that out of their bones, corpses, sacrifices, a
beautiful life will grow."[2] When the young actor Viktor Gromov was cast
as Trofimov, Olga Knipper insisted that he respect the perennial student
for his potential to carry out the task he had set himself, since Trofimov
was filled with "a potent faith and truth of his own." And when Gromov
next moved up to the part of Uncle Vanya, Knipper explained that
Voinitsky was a fighter who would not yield his ground.[3]

But altering the ethos of the Chekhovian world had to go beyond individual characterizations. The plays continued to resist socio-political
tampering, which made ideologues distrustful of the author. Aleksandr
Fadeev, who ran the Writers' Union, complained that the plays contained "no outstanding peasant, worker or intellectual"; and a critic
reviewing *Uncle Vanya* in Tambov uttered the familiar observation, "My
God, what a boring world! . . . A ghastly gallery of people who have
touched bottom socially."[4]

Nemirovich managed to incorporate the Soviet homilies into *Three Sisters* without compromising his own vision or insistence on quality, but the rest of the canon remained recalcitrant. Between 1898 and 1959, the Art Theatre had presented *The Seagull* only 110 times, a mere two per cent of all its Chekhov performances during the period. It remained, in the words of the theatre's literary manager Pavel Markov, "one of the main problems for the Soviet stage."[5] The solution, in his opinion, was to come up with a correct interpretation of Nina without oversimplifying the other characters.

After the war, the MAT was able to translate tragic passion into heroic terms in an *Uncle Vanya* (1947), directed by Mikhail Kedrov; for the first time a virile Voinitsky, played by Boris Dobronravov, eclipsed the scene-stealing magnetism of Astrov. Markov spelled out the social significance of this approach:

Before the Revolution, Uncle Vanya's rebellion lacked initiative and was only half-hearted. The new interpreters have brought out the bitter tragedy of this intelligent, talented man, engulfed in the depressing atmosphere of humdrum daily existence . . . Treated this way, Vanya's character has been given its true meaning. As for Sonya's character, this has received an extra philosophical dimension: her closing monologue, which no longer conveys sentimental solace, expresses an unshakeable faith in the future.[6]

Some went farther down this road. In 1950 Lobanov rehearsed an *Uncle Vanya* at the Ermolova Theatre, based on the premise that Voinitsky's house was the centre of the district's political activity. The first two acts represented the repressive regime of Alexander III (after all, the Professor's name was Aleksandr), and Serebryakov was played from the start so as to deserve assassination. The gunshot in Act III was to break a porcelain pot as the signal for a rebellion ("A gunshot means revolt!" pronounced the director). And the last act was performed to the smell of gunpowder. "We must evoke not compassion and pity but respect for the image of the heroes' action. We hymn courage, ardour, labour!"[7] This production never opened.

A *Cherry Orchard* at the Mayakovsky Theatre in 1956 incarnated the theme of retribution in Mariya Babanova's Ranevskaya.[8] More judgmental than Knipper had been, Babanova stripped her heroine of illusions. Babanova, an actress who had worked closely with Meyerhold in his constructivist period, approached the character with the "maximalist" eyes of the 1920s and thirties: to lose an ideal and part with illusions spells doom. This Ranevskaya was refined, intelligent, proud, with a clear-sighted idea of her fate; she cautiously but covertly distanced herself from the vulgarity around her: Gaev's chatter, Yasha's coarseness, Lopakhin's solicitations. For all her indulgence to others, she passed a stern and pitiless sentence on herself. Once she lost the orchard, her life was over, for, with the world of happy innocence gone, she lacked a foundation on which to build a new life. At the end, she staunched the tears, donned a mask by carefully putting down her veil, and left without a backward glance.

Most of the Chekhov performances staged for his jubilee year 1960 were programmatic and dutiful responses to a government edict. Their perfunctory conservatism seemed to echo the dire statement of the Art Theatre actor Viktor Stanitsyn: "There is no need for a re-staging of the Chekhov plays. The present production is still in an unbroken tradition of original business and interpretations."[9] It was to crawl out from under this dead weight of tradition and speak to the times that many directors turned to the neglected works, *Platonov*, *The Wood Demon* and, especially, *Ivanov*.

Vilar's *Ce Fou de Platonov* (1956) seems to have inspired the first Soviet production of *Untitled* in Pskov the following year, when it was condemned as a pointless experiment with a worthless work. V. Istomin-Kastorsky's staging was attacked for de-emphasizing the social background, concentrating on the Don Juanism and playing up the farce. Another production at the Vakhtangov in Moscow in 1960 was even more harshly assailed: the play was deemed an unstageworthy disservice to Chekhov's reputation.[10]

Yury Zavadsky, a former pupil of Vakhtangov, was responsible for the first revival of *The Wood Demon* (Mossovet Theatre, 1960). The title character (Nikolay Mordvinov) was meant to be heroic, but his distance from the others, who ate continuously throughout the play, rendered him ludicrous.

Ivanov had virtually been forgotten. In 1955 Stanislavsky's last pupil Mariya Knebel staged it at Moscow's Pushkin Theatre; intrigued by the general animus to the play, she used it to revise the accepted concept of what was Chekhovian. B. Smirnov's Ivanov was no whiner or sufferer, but, building on Kachalov's interpretation, flung himself heroically into the mob of philistines; his suicide came like a death on the barricades.[11]

The Maly Theatre, which had never staged a full-length Chekhov play, was also under compulsion to do so in 1960. Boris Babochkin, chosen to direct it, was reluctant to begin with *The Seagull*, and so he too turned to *Ivanov*. Babochkin's was the first Russian production of Chekhov since Vakhtangov to be described as "cruel," a word that would be heard more and more frequently over the next decade. The motto for this period might be called "thoroughpaced objectivity." Identification with the heroes, which had provided the pathos of the original productions, and an open defence of them, a socialist-realist tactic, were both replaced by allegedly objective inquiry.[12]

According to the critic Kugel, when Chekhov revised *Ivanov*, he had wanted Davydov to be replaced in the title role by Sazonov or Dalmatov, dynamic and flamboyant actors who could make the central dilemma engrossing. The Ivanov played by Babochkin himself was the opposite: inhibited, sober, arid, devoid of poetry and romance. Yet for all his vacillation, he was treated as a tragic figure, whose central problem was a marital one. With neither goals nor a will to live, he still possessed the courage of his ideas. Fists clenched in his pockets, he dissected the causes of his malaise with surgical rigour; his condition was seen as dangerous to Soviet society which sought to dissuade youth from joining in his passive revolt. This was a programmatic expression of similar trends in other Chekhovian performances of 1960. But neither Babochkin's nor Knebel's approach to *Ivanov* rehabilitated the play, because they were essentially polemical solutions to certain directorial problems; they lacked ambivalence or a conveyance of the depressive longing that defined the hero's nature.[13]

The central difficulty was that, in the Khrushchev era of mild thaw, most of the old certainties were discarded without being replaced by well-defined alternatives. A respected remnant of the past, Chekhov was produced only when directors found ways of making him vital; but his continual presence was evident in the various motifs, moods, and forms of the era's drama and staging.[14] Even Nemirovich's revision of *Three Sisters* at the Art Theatre underwent a change in interpretation as younger players replaced the original cast. Its optimism sounded naive: a Vershinin who genuinely believed in his lucky stars could hardly outlive the horrors of the Great Patriotic War and its Cold War aftermath. Bolduman's Vershinin had carried out a moral duty sweeter than his love for Masha, just as many Soviet citizens in the late 1940s believed labouring for communism was superior to any personal ambition. But now, private life rather than public service began to be openly permissible as a citizen's concern. Actors of a new generation brought to their roles different, more intimate values, sensibilities of the sixties when the happiness Chekhov's characters had foretold for the future had not been made flesh. A. V. Myagkov now acted Tusenbach as a hero out of a Volodin play, "ashamed to be happy," quiet, peaceable, but gregarious and eager to understand others. The Masha of I. P. Miroshnichenko was a real "bird of passage," allowing nothing to stand in the way of her freedom: Tarasova's spiritual energy and gushing heart were replaced by personal integrity, so Miroshnichenko could be cruel to her husband and indifferent to Irina's hysterics. She was deaf to the music of the finale. Made up to look like a perverse Chekhov, Evgeny Evstigneev played Chebutykin as a grotesque buffoon, not so much a doctor as a man of letters turned quack, bitter, sneering, gimlet-eyed. Artem's Chebutykin had been pitiful and Gribov's moving in his naive simplicity; Evstigneev craved no pity or sympathy, but emphasized irony and cynicism.[15]

TOVSTONOGOV'S *THREE SISTERS*

Again it was a rethinking of *Three Sisters* that made the first bold move towards serious reinterpretation, this one directed by Georgy Tovstonogov at the Bolshoy Dramatic Theatre (BDT) in Leningrad in 1965, just as the "Thaw" was coming to an end. Apart from Nemirovich, Tovstonogov was the only director who had both the political *savoir-faire* and the professional skill to head a Soviet theatrical Olympus for three decades. After important revisionist productions of Dostoevsky's *The Idiot*, Gorky's *Barbarians* and Griboedov's *Woe from Wit*, his encounter with Chekhov was inevitable. *Three Sisters* was his favourite Chekhov play, but he rejected "traditions established by both critical literature and stage interpretations."[16] To some degree, the production served as testing ground to determine what relevance Chekhov's plays had to contemporary life. Tovstonogov wanted to find a present-day meaning in the tragedy of heroes who all, except for Natasha, were dear to him yet provoked "contradictory feelings." As usual, Tovstonogov followed standard Art Theatre techniques in preparation and rehearsal, since he did not intend to dispute the greatness of Nemirovich's 1940 production or quarrel with its method. His *Sisters* was more theatrical and imagistic than Nemirovich's naturalistic approach, but lacked the inner harmony or poeticization of life of the earlier staging.[17]

Defining the central idea, Tovstonogov considered that the director must first pose the question: "is it only the times and surrounding activity that keep people from living intelligently, beautifully, positively?"[18] A modern Soviet conscience had to attribute much of the fault to the characters themselves and their weak wills. Their indifference and cruelty had to be faced up to, not justified. "No one can reconcile Chekhov's sympathy for his characters with his mercilessness to their frailties,"

Tovstonogov insisted.[19] Exploring the dialectic of "sympathy" and "ruthlessness," he came to the conclusion that a special brand of feeling was needed for a Chekhov production. Brechtian alienation was suitable: one must stand aside from the characters and distance oneself, in order to create a "ruthlessness" towards them. In the actual production, however, the tragic intimacy of the characters eclipsed the director's tendency to be a prosecutor.[20]

Tovstonogov thus eschewed blatant optimism for an understanding of "the destructive power of inaction and Chekhov's protest against it."[21] He was drawn to the theme of "collective murder," a phrase he used to describe the characters' failure to so much as lift a finger to avert catastrophe, although they were well aware of the impending duel between Soleny and Tusenbach. "The theme of the intelligentsia, their relation to life is one of the most important in modern art . . . In our theatre the theme of the intelligentsia is embodied in a series of productions. Chekhov's *Three Sisters* is the natural continuation of a major discourse . . . "[22] Therein lay the contemporaneity of the production: Tovstonogov cast a cold and fishy eye on the now unravelling freedom of the early sixties. In his view this superficial license had contaminated a generation which shared the sisters' paralysis of the will in voluntarily surrendering their home to Natasha's "fuzzy animal." The intelligentsia, by failing to establish a new ethical standard, had yielded its domicile to exploiters. Throughout the sixties, the fashionable tone of Russian theatre had been febrile, lyrical and protesting. Tovstonogov's puritanical objectivity swam against this current, and put off many of his contemporaries.[23]

Although Tovstonogov forgave his heroes neither their eloquence nor their inactivity, he treasured their spiritual worth and purity of intent. Without belittling their ideals or sneering at their ineptitude, he tried to impart meaning and poetry to their impoverished purposes. He arranged the conflicts so that every character except Natasha disclosed how painful it was to feel futile and how impossible were the chances of happiness. Eager for new experiences, Olga (Zinaida Sharko) suffered but refused to give in; Irina (Emiliya Popova) crippled herself by agreeing to marry the baron but on losing him seemed emptied; Masha (Tatyana Doronina) enjoyed an impossible happiness, but her life disappeared when Vershinin did.[24] Efim Kopelyan's Vershinin was wearily conscious of his burdensome responsibility, but kept going because it was disgraceful to be an idle philistine. Soleny (Konstantin Lavrov) was a man cruelly done out of his share of sympathy, who painfully hungered for a soul-mate. Against them all Lyudmila Makarova's sharply defined

22 Tovstonogov's production of *Three Sisters*, Gorky Dramatic Theatre, Leningrad, 1965. A "close-up" of Tusenbach (Sergey Yursky) and Irina (Emiliya Popova) set against the epic sweep of the setting in Act II; upstage Soleny (Konstantin Lavrov).

Natasha erected an uncompromising bridgehead of real life, because she refused to wage battle by the sisters' rules.

The epic tone of the production emphasized the wind of history blowing through the characters' lives. The designer Sofiya Yunovich provided an enormous stage space, airy and uncircumscribed. The realia of everyday life were present, but arranged in an expanse open to the winds, which evoked a moving image of Time and Russia. The black, white and grey palette drew an immediate response from a public raised on movies; similarly, stage-wagons, a device borrowed from Meyerhold's *Inspector*, provided "close-ups." Tovstonogov wanted the audience to look the characters straight in the eye, and so the duets were thrust into their midst. Up close to the dreamy ecstasy of Tusenbach's love for Irina, spectators were made uneasy. The "wide screen" could single out Masha and Vershinin when they were isolated in their happiness, highlight Soleny and Tusenbach during their crucial encounters, and at the end bring the three sisters face to face with the auditorium.[25]

The scale of the scenography had a more complex function, for it was an audacious attempt to depict the ominous pressure of time in a Chekhov play. As soon as Tovstonogov sought to make the insensible passage of days painfully sensible, all the parameters of Chekhovian production changed; mood and atmosphere were not put at issue, but rather confirmed in a new way. He slowed down the march of time, drew out the minutes, interrupted the dialogue with long sustained pauses. Defining the mood of the first act, Tovstonogov said that its most important foreshadowing was the father's death a year before. The whole act was penetrated with a sense that a year's moratorium had ended. Now "one must think of life in motion and receding."[26]

A striking clock initiated the action, and its incessant tick-tock took on a fateful meaning over the course of the performance. Time in its changes shredded dreams, oppressed hopes, and destroyed them all. The joyous, resonant intonations of Act I faded gradually into notes of sterile grief and mortal agony. The distance between the ideal and the real lengthened to infinity. As act followed act, it became harder to breathe, as expectations were dashed by the passage of time. Only Natasha was aided by time, which opened up perspectives to her: children, love affairs, new rooms. In the last act, Tovstonogov widened the borders of the stage to its full extent. The theme of nature, beautiful but indifferent, came in to embrace the characters. Faith in human potential, even when unconsummated, was unaffected by the march of time.[27]

The effect on audiences was profound. The playwright Leonid Zorin summed it up:

This deeply dramatic production is, if you like, a tragedy, but not an enervating tragedy; rather, it issues a call for action. This tragedy demands a decisive reckoning with the social inertia, whereby even goodness, decency and faith in a better life turn out to be forms of indifference to and toleration of evil.[28]

It was an important summons at a time when stagnation was becoming the order of the day.

Tovstonogov's ultimate faith in human potential was out of step with a growing mood of despair. As the Krushchev thaw recongealed under Brezhnev, the extinction of hope was reflected in an increasing recourse to Chekhov. Referring to these revivals of the late sixties and early seventies, the theatre historian Tatyana Shakh-Azizova noted,

The famous Chekhovian world looks strange on our stages now. The variegated everyday life, littered with characters, has become drier, poorer, scanty in details . . . 'Antidomesticity' is expressed not only by the fact that sometimes walls, the outer boundaries of homes, are missing and people live literally in drafts, open to the wind. More often there are houses and walls, and they are strong, but their strength is that of fortresses. The theme of life as a prison is beginning to become a leitmotif.[29]

In 1969, Leonid Kheifets staged an *Uncle Vanya* with the characters literally locked in their house. The stage was reminiscent of a narrow cage – a long grey fissure in which the heroes had difficulty standing upright, moving or breathing. This image was elaborated in the labyrinthine estate of Mikhalkov-Konchalovsky's 1971 film of the play, and picked up by Adolf Shapiro in a Tallinn *Three Sisters* (1973). There the Prozorovs lived in a small house with high walls and no doors or windows, in a dim, diffused light. In the last act, the director provided no garden; the characters could not move in nature or at will. At the end, apparently copying Stanislavsky's piece of business, Andrey ran on stage chasing a big rubber ball. The ball bounced off the walls but could not roll away. The cage remained a cage.

THE APOTHEOSIS OF IVANOV

In the 1950s and sixties, the conflict at the centre of new plays by Arbuzov, Rozov, and Volodin usually consisted of an opposition of the intelligentsia with the routine and mundane, a clash of a generation of positive idealists with one of negative cynics. Right and wrong were clearly apportioned. But in 1970 the publication of Vampilov's play *Duck Hunting* (not produced until 1976) complicated this Manichæism. His hero Zilov, Chekhovian in his messy mixture of aspirations and pettiness, gave rise to a series of similarly conflicted protagonists. In discussing Zilov, the actor and director Oleg Efremov compared him with Pechorin, Lermontov's fatalistic "hero of our times," while Anatoly Smeliansky alluded more pertinently to Ivanov.

The "lost hero," or Zilovian type, at odds with himself and out of synch with his surroundings, almost became an *emploi* of the 1970s. It was no coincidence that Efremov played Turgenev's superfluous man Rudin in the movies and Zilov in the theatre and directed *Ivanov* at Moscow Art Theatre within a period of three years (1976–8). Other actors also made a speciality of this type: Andrey Mironov enacted Rudin on television and O. Dal took on Pechorin and Zilov, as well as Von Koren in a film of Chekhov's *Duel* (1973), significantly renamed *A Bad Good Man*. The duel was reconfigured as a fight between the polarities in the hero's character.

In the seventies, with a dearth of good new plays, actors often had to channel their creativity into the classics and revitalize forgotten figures or provide new readings of roles already made famous. A transfer of the popular Zilovian type to the past is reflected in the ten major revivals of *Ivanov* that took place between 1970 and 1978;[30] this was a work that had been considered unplayable for nearly eighty years. Chekhov's early play was a perfect match for the period of stagnation. All the old miasma of the Russian intelligentsia bubbled up anew: social apathy, cynicism and an ailing conscience blighted by infidelity to ideals. As soon as each production opened, it entered into a debate with the others.

The *Ivanov* directed by Mark Zakharov and M. Shtein at the Lenin Komsomol Theatre in 1975 startled the public by its choice of lead. Evgeny Leonov, the Soviet Union's most popular comic actor, was short and plump with the face of Winnie the Pooh (he was in fact the voice of Pooh in Soviet animated cartoons). But this was merely a reversion to Davydov's portly wishywashy Ivanov which had preceded Kachalov's noble sufferer of 1904. The appeal lay in the actor's resemblance to everyone sitting in the audience, not a Russian Hamlet but the drabbest *intelligent* possible. Leonov presented a first-generation intellectual of peasant stock, hoarding his kopeks and disheartened by others' expectations of him.

Zakharov and Shtein made the characters embodiments of ideas: Lvov dreamt of a universal restructuring of life, Anna Petrovna and Sasha sought an all-consuming love, Borkin had his get-rich-quick schemes, Lebedev his generally meliorist attitude. Each was sharply focussed on an *idée fixe*, and only Ivanov was unfocussed. This was in line with Chekhov's insistence that Ivanov's tragedy lay in the want of a central idea. Everyone tried to mould Ivanov to his will, while he remained bereft and incomprehending, ready to weep under the pressure of all the demands on him.[31]

The prevalence of drunkenness and bottles revealed the mud beneath the elegy from the very first scene with Borkin. The distance between Ivanov and his environment was indicated not by his spiritual effusions, as in earlier productions, but by his sobriety. The tragic elements were invested in a maternal Anna, sensitive to Ivanov's malaise and aware of his better side. As played by the slender Inna Churikova, she still saw him as the hero of her youth who was capable of the extraordinary feat of marrying a Jewess; she would embrace him ritually, as if blessing him. Even when he shouted at her, "Shut up, kike bitch," her face dissolved into a radiant smile. When she had her fit on the floor, Ivanov sat dully staring into space: blind to his past and future, he killed himself because he could not be absorbed into the Lebedev's healthy but vulgar household.

Zakharov refuted the heroic tradition as well in a new conception of Chekhovian space. The stage, designed by O. Tvardovsky and M. Makushenko, was wide open, bordered by trees left and right, giving the sense of a dark corridor, in which Ivanov stood as in a prisoner's dock. The upstage area, Lebedev's estate, duplicated the downstage area, Ivanov's estate, in every detail. The gaping doorways, empty window-frames and total bareness of the stage floor emphasized an equality of vacuity. Ivanov might complete his progress upstage or downstage, but it would make no difference; he would never escape himself. Recurrence and repetition, monotony and inertia underlined the lack of action. The duplication was extended to lines, moves and gesticulation. Ivanov's hands repeatedly made the same gesture of shooing away flies. Two gun-shots were heard at the end: a double suicide, one for the characters who didn't understand him, and another for the audience who did.[32]

The *Ivanov* debate was engaged by Oleg Efremov, seven years into his tenure as artistic director of the Moscow Art Theatre, when he mounted his production immediately after Zakharov's. (He would later deem it the favourite of his Chekhov stagings.) Chekhov himself once called the want of faith and ideals and an empty heart a "disease worse than syphilis and sexual paralysis." For Efremov, this was a diagnosis of his own era, but he eschewed "modernizing" Chekhov – "dressing Baron Tusenbach in a denim suit," as he called it.

Sometimes in the fight against clichés, undertones, pauses, multivalent innuen-dos underlined by spare gestures, contemporary directors fall into anti-cliché, and replace quiet speech with desperate screams, pauses with feverish tempi, restraint with sweeping gestures; Chekhov's heroes, deprived of their intellect, appear to the spectator as coarse and affected "Struwwelpeters."[33]

David Borovsky created an unusual set for a Russian production: an empty stage encircled by the colonnaded façade of an aristocratic home. It had the classic attributes of MAT scenery by Simov or Dmitriev, but the "Caucasian Empire" façade with its pillars and annexes and dimly lit windows conveyed not warmth, but the awkward abandonment of a ruin. Like veins visible through the skin of an emaciated body, the leafless branches of autumn trees peered through the walls causing an odd interaction between interior and exterior. Ivanov wandered about, unable to find a place for himself in a *nature morte* so devastated as to appear plundered. As he sadly repeats, "My land gazes at me as at an orphan."

This sense of being orphaned was consummate in the lead per-formance of Innokenty Smoktunovsky. Smoktunovsky had been a pris-oner of war and brought to his renditions a haunted quality, abetted by his pale, gaunt looks and unearthly voice. His reputation had been made as Prince Myshkin in Tovstonogov's *The Idiot*. In conformity, this Ivanov was a refined, agile, high-strung hero, whose morbidity was the reaction of a hypertense conscience demanding more of the world than others did. A total antithesis to Leonov, he was a true prince of Denmark in the Kachalov mould, a prophet or messiah, devoured by shame at his inability to pay debts or meet obligations.

Afflicted with spiritual paralysis, Smoktunovsky's Ivanov walked through the play like a somnambulist; he froze in place, crumpled his elegant jacket, never knew what to do with his long, slender hands. Other persons' talk was tiresome for it prevented him from remembering; his voice, barely audible, "tired of its own sound,"[34] broke his monologues down into lexical *disjecta membra*. This Ivanov greeted death as a happy release. The shot was never heard; the tittering guests in the Lebedev home, waiting for hors d'oeuvre and a wedding, parted to reveal a man hunched over in the middle of the floor.[35]

To enliven the old-fashioned exposition, Efremov opened the play with a segment of Act II, the party guests discussing Ivanov, before returning to Act I. Unlike the usual MAT ensemble tradition, with every character three-dimensional, Ivanov was singled out. As in Meyerhold's production of Andreev's symbolist play, *The Life of Man*, two grey old ladies quietly sat with their knitting at the left side in the first half, at the right in the second, the Parcae or Macbeth's bubbles of the earth. Although Efremov admired Sasha and presented her without irony, he downplayed the role of women in Ivanov's fate, putting special emphasis on Chekhov's comment that his ruling principle in this play was "not to let women obscure the centre of gravity that exists outside them." The "centre of gravity" of Efremov's staging was the coalescence of one man's morbid depression with the depression of his own times.

The *Ivanov* at the Leningrad Pushkin Theatre (1978) directed by A. Sagalchik had the last word, and took a middle-of-the-road position. Igor Gorbachev's Ivanov was an hereditary intellectual and master of a once cultivated estate, who hesitated in the face of life's demands. Everything was deferred, nothing brought to a conclusion. This Ivanov was akin to Uncle Vanya: too much within his world to stand outside it and fight.

M. Kitaev's design suggested an ancient garden; wildly hypertrophied bindweed had reached the proportions of gigantic tropical lianas. Amid this pallid verdure stood Anna's piano and Ivanov's desk, overgrown with dark foliage like tree trunks. The garden was a graveyard, the vegetative characters on the brink of catastrophe. This was "antidomesticity" with a vengeance. When Ivanov shot himself, the overgrowth vanished, leaving an empty stage flooded by spotlights, like an open square now available for future construction.[36]

The line from *Wood Demon*, "A war of all against all" defines the atmosphere of these productions, marked by lack of contact between characters indifferent to one another and heroes with morbid sensibilities and trenchant expressions. In their early forties, Leonov, Smoktunovsky and Gorbachev were all actors of a generation whose dramatic protagonists did not shoot themselves. In each production, Ivanov was made to stand for a a certain moral principle: Leonov's decency, Smoktunovsky's refinement, Gorbachev's refusal to use one's strength and power to poison someone else. The theatres "rectified" Chekhov by giving Ivanov sharply defined characteristics, but, for all that, the productions seemed partial, incomplete, built more on calculated contention and a need for refutation than on synthesis.[37]

Marianna Stroeva perceived of the 1960s that once the traditional abundance of sentiment and pregnant pauses had been eliminated,

the subtext immediately entered the text. And the Chekhovian word, full of grief and bile, spoke with sober harshness in the productions of Babochkin, Tovstonogov, Éfros, of the tragic meaninglessness of life, devoid of idealism. Between these two extremes – the cruel Chekhov and the sentimental Chekhov – Chekhov was imperceptibly lost, the Chekhov who despite it all continued steadfastly to believe in man – such as he is.[38]

ÉFROS THE TERRIBLE

Of the three directors mentioned by Stroeva, Anatoly Éfros stirred up the greatest controversy. His *Seagull* at Moscow's Lenin-Komsomol Theatre in 1966 and *Three Sisters* at the Malaya Bronnaya the following year were noted for their sharpness, wit and stridency; some deemed them brilliant, others crude and vulgar.

Something of an adult *terrible*, Éfros began his work on *The Seagull* with the statement: "Let's pretend we are the first to stage *Seagull* for the very first time. Without the usual clichés of lyrical performance with pauses. Without all sorts of stratifications of 'Chekhovianism.' Actively. Dynamically."[39] This was not so difficult, since Éfros tended to turn any play into seething self-expression and to endow his own personal feelings with universal dimensions. His productions led audiences in the mid-sixties to regard the theatre as a confessional, where *mea culpas*, spiritual disrobing and absolution could take place. During the era of stagnation, his stage assumed the function, but not the air, of a church.

Consequently, since *The Seagull* is a play about the artist's torment, Éfros broke down its action into stations of the cross. The spell-binding lake was effaced by the image of a scaffold on which Treplev was to be executed. Once again, the cage image returned: this gibbet-stage was an unpainted platform of newly sawn planks surrounded by a high, unadorned fence that hemmed in living space, and could be penetrated by neither landscape nor light. When the fence turned into the walls of a room, there was no lived-in cosiness: home was a prison too.

"It's curious that Chekhov did not write the play from Trigorin's standpoint," Éfros remarked. "He sympathized with Nina and Treplev . . . Not that Treplev's standpoint is our theatre's, of course, but I must say he's superior to Trigorin."[40] In fact, Treplev became the be-all and end-all of the drama, and every character in it was defined in relation to the youthful rebel, in whom Éfros saw a potential Aleksandr Blok. Valentin Smirnitsky played him as restless, childish, and hyperactive.

Éfros eliminated the Russian conventions of Chekhov: the tepid conversations, the interrelationships, the "objectivistic" intonations and even the famous pauses and "mood," in short, the poetic smoke and mirrors which were considered an integral part of Chekhov's drama from the early days of the Art Theatre. Aggressively antilyrical, he stripped the play of romanticism and turned the "cosmic" collision of lonely people in a hostile world into a prosaic but compact tragedy. Driven into direct confrontation, the characters were fatally unable to make contact.[41]

The critic Rudnitsky remarked that cries, shouts, groans and hysterics issued from every corner of the stage, as if, like the spectators, Chekhov had grown up in a communal apartment with one kitchen, one bathroom and forty residents. The actors were not afraid to embrace contemporaneity or to bring Chekhov closer to a familiar site of experience. To this end, Éfros imbued the play with themes and tones from his favourite postwar dramatists Viktor Rozov and Edvard Radzinsky. The themes of uncompromising youth on a collision course with a world of hypocrites and talent's incompatibility with fakery were derived from Rozov; Radzinsky supplied the acrid, ironic intonation.

The characters were hostile to one another in a nasty, unambiguous way. Olga Yakovleva as Nina was a direct antithesis to Treplev: pragmatic, single-mindedly aggressive and ambitious. Éfros unmasked her insurmountable desire for fame and career that made her the most dangerous traitor to Treplev. Her finely chiseled figure appeared in black at the beginning of the play within a play; kneeling at the edge of the platform, she used her soliloquy to flirt, aiming it not so much at the excited author as at the celebrities from the capital. When Treplev ran off, humiliated by his fiasco, Nina lost interest in the complex-ridden young genius and became one with her "public."

In her scene with Trigorin, barely listening to the writer's problems as Aleksandr Shirvindt recited them, she baited her traps for his captivation. At the act's end, she grabbed a thin, flexible fishing rod and began cutting swaths through the air with it in a wild fury that hinted at a submerged sensuality. Trigorin, as flabbergasted as the Moscow audience, saw a predator awakening in this provincial miss. Éfros inflicted poetic justice on Nina: her irredeemable crime against Treplev was rewarded by illness and having to work in a theatre in Elets, just deserts for betraying an artist.

The response to *The Seagull* was indignation and outrage. People rushed to Chekhov's defense with all the usual bromides, but Éfros did not protest. Somewhat later, he admitted that he had stripped the play of its indispensable poetic pollen; he thought he was in a Brechtian way laying bare the play's profound significance, but eventually realized he had regarded the characters without much affection. He explained that modern actors have difficulty performing Chekhov because their inner experience is so shallow: hence the kitchen-sink stridency and noisy arguments. A few years later he attributed the anxiety of the actors in his first Chekhov to their weak and impressionable natures, a caustic diagnosis of both his staging and the whole theatrical generation.[42]

A Western critic has observed that Treplev's art is that of an exile for he had to live as one: this situation is reflected not only in his stubborn opposition to establishment art but also in his work. Éfros' productions shared this attribute: aggressive but unstable, impermanent; they perpetually questioned their own methods.[43] This element was to the fore when Éfros first considered directing *Three Sisters* (1967). While wintering in a deserted Yalta, he acutely sensed what he imagined Chekhov had felt in his "tepid Siberia." It was an image of exile, of being cut-off from life, of the inaccessibility and impossibility of Moscow. The metaphysical principle of the play emerged from the problem of transport.[44] (Ivy Litvinov once questioned why the sisters didn't simply buy tickets and go.) Moscow was seen through the exile's transparent memory as a remote Isle of the Blest, where life was rich and real. *Three Sisters* therefore became a play about a lost spiritual homeland.

Viktor Durgin and A. Chernova designed an empty space, its back wall painted with black trees holding barren birds' nests. Another coatrack-like tree with gilt iron leaves stood oppressively centre stage, like the legendary oak in the Pushkin poem Masha keeps reciting. Other set-pieces – the enormous ottoman that took up a quarter of the floor, a gramophone with its morning-glory horn, a grand piano and a clock with no hands that jutted out onto the proscenium were both things and metaphors, like a props room ill met by moonlight. The dominant colour was green, as if the stage were wearing a tsarist military uniform.

The motif of exile was exfoliated gradually. At the start everything was expectant and hopeful, a background for the torment to come. A lilting waltz, lifted from the Czech film *The Shop on Main Street*, played impetuously and seductively throughout the act. This anachronism immediately destroyed all sense of historical distance and created a familiar bond with the audience. It also hearkened back to Vakhtangov's *Wedding*, the tragi-grotesque played to dance music.

The descent towards despondency was charted by the sisters' elegant gowns, whose colour changed from act to act: green to ash-grey to black stripes. Their men were incapable of anything but complaints and endlessly philosophizing. For the future was only for breeders like Natasha and Protopopov: the sisters were barren.

Instead of the usual opposition of civilized Prozorovs vs crass philistines, Natasha (L. Bogdanova) was the most polite of them all, while Soleny (S. Sokolovsky) was the best educated and the best-behaved. The struggle was not for selfhood or the house, but for the ownership of culture. Over-educated Irina worked at the post-office, while the super-subtle Tusenbach ended up in a brick factory: the intelligentsia was edged out of the culture business. Masters and servants all lived in fear of being expelled. "Don't throw me out!" was the theme song.

Éfros staged the play as Treplev might have done; it was performed tempestuously without half-tones or nuances: every petty grievance exploded into a noisy brawl. For the first time in a Russian Chekhov production, sexual motivation was uppermost: Natasha had needs which frigid Andrey could not meet, so she was justified in taking a lover; Irina was a capricious *demi-vierge*, Masha a coarse predator, and Olga repressed and repressive. In the farewell scene, "not only does Vershinin not dream for an instant of the possibility of staying, but he even rejects the idea of being late." Nikolay Volkov glanced at the clock over Masha's shoulder and signaled to Olga that he had to hurry.[45]

The critic Vadim Gaevsky noted that Chebutykin's offstage drunken laughter in Act III preceded his entrance the way a groan might announce an ancient Greek tragedian.[46] Diminutive, dishevelled Lev

Durov, scion of a long line of clowns, rushed on stage, wound up the gramophone and hysterically danced "a macabre dance of despair" to jazz tunes. Jerking and writhing like a marionette plugged into an electric socket, he expressed the *intelligent*'s despair and self-contempt at being unable to improve anything or break through the circle of lies.

But the most radical reinterpretation was Lev Krugly's Tusenbach, drenched in irony, waltzing his way through the play. His first monologue about "longing for hard work" was an oafish rhapsody, as he squirmed towards the climactic words, "The time has come." The audience was devastated in recognizing the sharp contrast between Chekhov's prognostication and the forced labour of the previous fifty years. In Smeliansky's image, Éfros created a short circuit between two different eras, and when the audience was properly electrified, Tusenbach hammered out the final words of the monologue with a deadly sarcasm: "I w-i-ill w-o-o-rk, and in some twenty-five or thirty years, ev-v-e-ery o-o-one w-iill w-o-oork. E-v-very o-one!"

This mask of irony dropped in the last act, when the Baron exchanged his uniform for a two-piece civilian suit and derby to go to work. A Chaplinesque note crept in as he circled the stage in balletic steps. Moving towards the spectators and Olga Yakovleva's Irina, he said "Tell me something" despairingly, longing for love. And her response, "What? What? What?" sounded harsh, calculating, forlorn. Up to this point, her character had been a series of beautiful silence-filled poses, as if she were performing in Treplev's symbolist playlet. Tusenbach danced off with his original gesture of invitation to the waltz, shouting "No, no, no," each time softer but more decisive. He was the only one to desire change, to move beyond a state of resignation, and he was on his way to be killed, producing a profoundly pessimistic ending.

Tovstonogov's *Three Sisters* in Leningrad had been more restrained, harmonious, attentive to the play's intellectual meaning, but it was far less emotionally powerful and certainly not as scandalous. Éfros had put an end to "academic" Chekhov and the ideology of optimism; he suggested that only a revival of moral law would alter circumstances. The box-office was stormed for tickets; spectators fainted during the performance. The audience read into Chebutykin's dance its own awareness of the century's ghastliness. Dreams of a better life had been blotted out by nightmares of terrors past and to come.

The triumph was short-lived. The production immediately came under attack, reproached for "mocking work," for having "decided to engage in a polemic against the MAT production, by counteracting its essentially positive concept with a negative vision, a resignation to banal, paltry, empty life." Angelina Stepanova who had played Irina in Nemirovich's *Three Sisters* put her signature to a condemnatory article in *Pravda*. Éfros replied,

In interrogating myself, I was convinced that I had staged the production out of love of Chekhov, out of a desire to make him necessary. But not by that love which is above reality, suffering, compassion and sorrow. No, my love wanted to absorb all that. Not blind love which knows not the distance that separates us from the author, but love capable of accepting this distance. A distance full of changes in life and in art.[47]

The production was banned in early 1968, a few months before Soviet tanks put a premature end to the Prague Spring.

HATCHING NEW GULLS

The use of Chekhov as a pretext for aesthetic debate continued through-out this period. Boris Livanov probed the Hamlet parallel in *The Seagull* at the MAT in 1968. The theatricality of life was brought out by Enar Stenberg's *art nouveau* setting which located not just Treplev's play but Chekhov's on a trestle stage. What for Stanislavsky would have been a house, a drawing-room, a lake, became obvious stage sets for a house, a drawing-room, a lake. Picturesque plywood gratings were let down from the flies to make Denmark a prison. Each actor played the role the direc-tor had selected for the character's stage life: in a white blouse and black cloak reminiscent of the melancholy Dane, O. Strizhenov tragically declaimed Treplev's monologues; his symbolist drama was taken seri-ously. (Later, when Sergey Desnitsky took over the role, he was told to play Romeo.) Arkadina (Angelina Stepanova) was a chic millionairess, costumed as gorgeously as the Queen of Denmark; her particular mono-drama was tinged with Dürrenmatt grotesquerie. Nina and Masha were transmuted into emblems of heavenly love and earthly love respectively, with Masha the betrayed Ophelia. Useful as this may have been in ana-lyzing Treplev, it turned the play into a melo-monodrama, not unlike his own playlet.[48]

Oleg Efremov's *Seagull* at the Sovremennik in summer 1970 was seen as a counterblast to Livanov's, with everyday life heightened to a symbol and variants from Chekhov's drafts inserted to show the characters living or wishing to live by art alone. In fact, all the petty intramural intrigues, rancor and disillusion that had built up in the Sovremennik over the years were grafted on to Chekhov's text. Ill-disposed to these well-bred characters, Efremov tried to turn Chekhov into a caricaturist, and infused the play with disarray characteristic of the sixties. "No one can

23 Enar Stenberg's design for Act IV of *The Seagull*, directed by Boris Livanov,
Moscow Art Theatre, 1969.

break into another person's being," Efremov explained. "Each one withdraws into himself."[49] While grating on each other's nerves, the characters remained isolated. Their intimate avowals could be uninhibited, because no one listened and nothing resonated off anything else. The most sensational piece of business came during Trigorin's exposition of his literary life to Nina: the two of them spent it digging up the flowerbeds centre stage for worms to use as bait. At the end of Act II, the director brought all the characters on stage: drinking, squabbling, hating one another, they talked and acted all at once, paying no heed to their surroundings. When Treplev shot himself with a hunting rifle before their eyes, the shot sounded like a direct reproach to persons so self-involved.[50]

This *Seagull* was the last production of the Sovremennik, a theatre which had been founded to embody the ideals of the sixties generation; its closure signalled the miscarriage of those principles of personal integrity. Efremov was then named director of the moribund Moscow Art Theatre, but, emblematically, his company refused to join him there.

CHAPTER 12

Ferment in an age of stagnation
(Russia 1970–1990)

Fifteen years ago, not to see the productions of Lyubimov and Éfros was the equivalent of not reading *Novy Mir*.

A. Minkin[1]

THE ORCHARDS ARE DYING

Elegy had been the accepted tone for *The Cherry Orchard* throughout the 1950s. The Art Theatre's Yury Zavadsky declared its subject to be "the scheme of time passing . . . The desire to hold onto time – to stop it – is the inner rhythm of the play."[2] But for the post-Thaw Soviet theatre the time of the cherry orchard had passed irrevocably; no one wanted to turn back time in its flight, or share the tears of characters who dwelt in the ashes. The MAT theme of a stable world to which the heroes bade farewell for ever and aye had been exhausted by the sixties, along with a monogeneric reading of the play. But there was still resistance to the replacement of the traditional *mise-en-scène*.

Restaging the play at the Soviet Army Theatre in 1965, Mariya Knebel evaded calls for novelty and the new tendency to cruelty, and continued to offer a moral experience. Starting with the question "Are Chekhov's characters capable of shaking off the dust of old life and turning to the future?" she eschewed sociological explanations and focussed on "changes of formation." "The time is long gone for *The Cherry Orchard* to show us a departing gentry and an advancing merchantry." What mattered to Knebel was human steadfastness in the face of loss.

It seems to me that in this last of his plays Chekhov understood very well what it means to *lose* something infinitely beloved . . . Each of us has lost and will lose our own 'cherry orchard.' Each of us is trying to hold on to it. The moment when you lose 'the cherry orchard' you think you lose everything. But ahead lies life, a thousand times richer than any loss.[3]

In keeping with this optimism, Dobrzhanskaya's Ranevskaya evoked admiration, not pity, for the way she dealt with her grief.

To conduce to allegory and metaphor, Knebel and her designer Yury Pimenov stylized the bygone life. The airborne curtains created not the image but the memorabilia of an orchard and the life associated with it; like them, life fluttered in and out, beautifully devoid of any practical function. To stage this play without a real orchard was for a director trained at the MAT an innovation no less radical than Tovstonogov's magnification of actions and passions. This innovation was not, however, appreciated in full measure, since, as at the Art Theatre, the world on display was stable and integral.[4]

Any new interpretation that broke with the MAT tradition had to begin by rethinking the orchard itself. In 1904, despite the urgings of Bely and Meyerhold, its stage embodiment could not be fully symbolic, for the story had too much contemporary relevance. In the 1970s, however, questions arose, Why don't the characters defend the orchard? What does it mean to them? Russian theatre had either to pitch its lyricism and elegy higher or else repudiate them. It chose the latter course, showing the downfall and the vacuity but not the beauty doomed to destruction. At the Tallinn Youth Theatre in 1971 there were no white blossoming branches on stage; rather, the faint outlines of leaves and flowers almost imperceptibly began to seep through the wall of the dilapidated house, its furniture swathed in dirty dust covers. In the past Ranevskaya's drama had been in the foreground, but here she stood in the middle distance, both because the director Adolf Shapiro refrained from taking sides, and because the decrepit look of the orchard contradicted remarks about its erstwhile beauty. Here the theme was the contrast between the orchard's reality and its inhabitants' delusions of it.

For some years, the Taganka Theatre under Yury Lyubimov had been the hub of licensed artistic dissent: preferring collages of literary and poetic material to plays, Lyubimov applied a Brechtian technique that conveyed between and beneath the lines anti-establishment messages to his avid audiences. His methods were at odds with those of his counterpart Éfros; but in 1975 he invited Éfros to stage *The Cherry Orchard* at the Taganka with its company. Éfros temporarily retired the harsh ambivalences of his usual approach and adopted the style of his host: frank and clear cut, perhaps more aggressive than was called for in Chekhov. To loosen the grip of a heavily symbolic interpretation loaded with meaning, he went for graphic simplicity and a swaggering, breezy acting

24 Valery Levental's design for *The Cherry Orchard*, directed by Anatoly Efros, Taganka, Moscow, 1975: an embodiment of nostalgia.

style. *The Cherry Orchard* became a play about doomed people who cannot hear the footfall of fate or will not face reality.

Éfros' *Cherry Orchard* was framed by the characters mournfully singing Epikhodov's ballad:

> What care I for the noisy world,
> What are friends and foes to me,
> Were but my heart afire
> With the flame of requited love.

(This bleak device must have had appeal, for Galina Volchek imitated it when she staged the same play at the Sovremennik the following year.) This haunting refrain was intoned at times almost automatically, for none of the characters did anything deliberately.

Lyubimov and his house designer Borovsky had long extolled "anti-scenery," a functional space uncluttered by set-pieces and furniture; Éfros, more cautiously, invited Valery Levental (formerly of the lavish Bolshoy Theatre) to design a visually gorgeous and evocative set. Picking up a hint from Giorgio Strehler's *Orchard*, both stage and actors were clad in white. White curtains billowed in the breeze, family portraits were strewn about, and a white cemetery filled with flowers stood centre stage, heaped with all the remnants of the Chekhovian home. As usual with Éfros, the scenery set forth an "exoteric" metaphor that spelled out the production's meaning.

Given the blatancy of its emblemata, the production should have failed, but was saved by powerful performances by Alla Demidova, an actress of intense poetic allure, and Vladimir Vysotsky, the wiry, husky-voiced chansonnier who was the Taganka's *alter ego*. Éfros' tendency to focus on single themes, with little concern for secondary or tertiary characters, singled out Ranevskaya and Lopakhin, divorcing them from their usual sociological context.[5] Demidova's Ranevskaya tried to repress her agonizing memories of Paris and her lover, but her past exploded in the violent hysterics of a broken wanton, making her inscrutable to those around her. She had an "itch" (Demidova's words) for Paris. "Yes, the smoke of the fatherland is sweet, but her husband died there, her seven-year-old child drowned there."[6] Hence her weathercock mind: it's hard to part with the orchard but it's impossible to stay and die there. With a nervous severity, Demidova projected both the degenerescence of her culture and the incandescence of decay. Taganka audiences were alert to clandestine messages, so fugitive phrases became percussive with significance: "I'll drink some coffee" sounded like "I'll drink some poison"; and "the sun's gone down" came across like the onset of the apocalypse. Smiling calmly at the return of Gaev and Lopakhin from the auction, she asked casually, "Who bought it?" This complicitous, antemortem smile may have been the most incisively Éfrosian moment in the production.

Mariya Knebel had been the first to suggest, cautiously, a love between the enriched peasant and his former mistress. Vysotsky's Lopakhin loved Ranevskaya tenderly and painfully, and understood the futility of his feelings. Quiet and concentrated in his snow-white suit and shoulder-length hair, he even penned his minstrel's voice within strict bounds. This Lopakhin was one of the few to live up to Trofimov's characterization: "You have the refined, delicate fingers of an artist and a refined, delicate soul." The manly nobility of his feelings for Ranevskaya led to his premonition that his own role at the end of the story would be that of the "ax in the hands of fate."

When Ranevskaya heard of the sale, she screamed and collapsed as if shot in the belly. Then, his voice no longer held in check, Lopakhin crowned the festivities with a boorish bacchanal, deafening himself to humane feeling. The dance of the "new master" was another metaphor, this time for Russia's future. As Ranevskaya broke into convulsive sobs, Anya strode around the stage decisively and spoke excitedly of building a new orchard, oblivious to her mother's pain.

By the play's end, brittle Ranevskaya had lost everything. As a black mourner's cloak was laid upon her shoulders, she strained to clutch the single branch of cherry thrust halfway into the auditorium; but she failed and was left sobbing in despair. While the farewell procession, set to a metronome, circled around her in a melancholy spiral, she was allowed to break away and orate to the house, "My life, my youth, my happiness, farewell!" The others took her by the arm and dragged her back to the cemetery. Lopakhin in a plum-colored suit, elegant, intelligent, was the only spiritual aristocrat among them, and the sale of the orchard looked to be his tragedy, not hers.[7] Éfros did not stop there in his anatomy of the play's nervous system: Firs (G. Roninson) did not "quietly lie down" but, in perplexity, hunted for a way out and died on the floor with a groan. The mercilessness of the performance and its morbid tension converted the longing for "the ineradicable beauty of the cherry orchard" into a longing for the ordinary.[8] This tragic principle was shown to be not one of Chekhov's ideas, but a result of the historical context: pragmatism was levelling spiritual values in Soviet society. "The sound of the snapped string" was a warning more to the audience than to the characters.

The orchard failed to blossom again in Petr Kirillov's design for the 1976 version staged by Galina Volchek at the Sovremennik's new house; it marked an unfamiliar direction for that theatre, coldness rather than warmth, "stylization" rather than style. Dark, gnarled, skeletal trees surrounded the raked drafting-table of a stage; no house, only a high double door at the back glistening like the promise of a way out. Downstage was a well, its seeming bottomlessness drawing people to it. Every word cast into the well sent back a fearful echo, cold and dead. "In general the theme of the well – an image of time – is taken to be the most important in the production."[9] The theme of passing time recurred in the finale when the characters moved across the twilit stage carrying lighted candles, like the fate figure, Someone in Grey, from Andreev's *The Life of Man*. But here the flickering candles were held by the mortals themselves, while "the wax wanes, devoured by the flame," and shadow-like, they slunk towards nothingness.

In Volchek's feminine (though hardly feminist) reading, the women of the play were its heroes, the central motifs were the women's restlessness and uselessness. Wearing ballgowns "from a Zaitsev novel," the actresses were impeded by the gauze overdrapes and long trains meant to attract male attention to their grace. "All the heroines dream of love," noted one critic.[10] Varya was a virgin aggressively desperate to be wed, Dunyasha a giggling nymphomaniac incapable of looking at a man without wanting him. At the outset, she woke the dozing Lopakhin with a sloppy kiss; he thrust her away in horror. Tatyana Lavrova invested her Ranevskaya with infantile intonations and angularity; a jittery neuropath, she could not sit still for a moment. The blocking kept her on the margins, alien to her own estate, which she might have described in Nina's words as "empty, empty, empty, cold, cold, cold."[11]

In contrast to decadent Demidova and fragile Lavrova, the Ranevskaya of Alisa Freindlikh at the Leningrad Lensovet Theatre in 1979 was made the culprit responsible for the orchard's demise. Behaving with mannered Parisian chic, Freindlikh was vulgar even in her way of using a long cigarette holder. She dwelt in her private world, excited by the orchard, curious about the bookcase, but oblivious to other people. She greeted Varya coldly and ceremoniously as if she had parted from her only yesterday, barely recognized Trofimov and then forgot about him almost at once. What mattered to her was the past (money, sex) and the future (Paris). Only once did she react to the present, in response to Trofimov's "He robbed you blind . . . "

Deprived of its usual rivet, the play broke into two halves, the first dominated by a comic hero – Gaev (Igor Vladimirov who also directed); the second by a tragic hero – Lopakhin (L. Dyachkov). The production began comically, as if adopting the critic Batyushkov's idea that *The Cherry Orchard* was a collection of *"nedotepas"* (Firs's earthy insult, roughly, "half-baked blockheads"), all variants of Epikhodov. Gaev almost skipped from topic to topic, and in Act II danced a freylekh to the accompaniment of the Jewish orchestra.

But by the end of Act III all eyes were focussed on Lopakhin. Glumly in love with Ranevskaya, he never noticed her vulgarity. His purchase was a greater tragedy than her loss, for with it he lost her forever. As the final curtain came down, he crossed the forestage, mournfully swinging his key-ring; it fell from his hand and noisily hit the floor. He burst into sobs. So the play ended as a tragedy, with Lopakhin its sympathetic hero, belonging neither to past nor future, and shattered by the present.

At the Maly Theatre in 1982, Firs became the hero. When Meyerhold's theatre had been dissolved in 1935, his company was absorbed into other troupes. The great buffoon Igor Ilinsky wound up at the starchy Maly and after some readjustment became one of its luminaries. Now, at the age of eighty-one, he staged *The Cherry Orchard* in a gaudy, noisy *mise-en-scène*, with enormous flowering trees that grew shorter in each act. The costumes were sumptuous, the sound of the snapped string a low-pitched roll of thunder, and a veritable symphony orchestra played at the ball. A similar grandiosity affected the performances: Tatyana Eremeeva enacted Ranevskaya as the heroine of a romantic melodrama, waiting impatiently to tear herself away from the boring estate, overcome with relief when it was sold. The only character moved by the fate of the orchard was Ilinsky's Firs, because he, the guardian of integrity, felt responsible for it and symbiotic with it. He longed for moral harmony and a caring household filled with loving kindness. On discovering that the doors were locked, he was thunderstruck and suddenly lost his strength, his knees buckling under him. At the end a branch bent down to canopy the supine Firs. This dollop of sentimentality flavoured the whole production, so that pity for the old retainer was the residual audience reaction.

In each of these productions, the ball in Act III had been made the concentrated essence of whatever *leitmotif* the director had chosen. At the Leningrad Pushkin Theatre in 1972, the cynosure of the ball was an unending round dance, inescapably circling like a siege manoeuvre. At the Sovremennik, Ranevskaya was the centre of attention, edgy, lonely and quite superfluous. The only one to have a clear understanding of what was going on was Firs, sarcastically watching the ghastly merriment of the tipsy crowd and openly despising them all. At Éfros' ball, Ranevskaya's tragic deterioration clashed with Lopakhin's frantic victory – the whole scene was permeated with a mad phantasmagoria of closure. At the Lensovet, the ball was subdued and ironic, the guests kept in the background; Lopakhin's climactic appearance dominated when, instead of dancing the traditional solo of the "new landowner," he pitilessly forced Ranevskaya to dance with him till she dropped. At the Maly, since Firs could not occupy a central position in it, the ball was disjunct, a train of box-cars devoid of couplings. Adopting a more or less metaphoric approach, none of the directors attempted to realize the symbolist "ghost supper" prescribed by *fin-de-siècle* writers; but they had parted definitively from Stanislavsky's busy microcosm.

BIVOUAC AT THE TAGANKA

Although he had hosted it, Lyubimov did not care for Éfros' *Cherry Orchard*. When he staged his first Chekhovian venture, *Three Sisters*, in

1981, he laid his own ax to the Taganka, challenging the authorities by a deliberate act of provocation.

The program listed, along with the Taganka cast, players from past productions at the MAT: over the course of the evening, tape recordings broadcast Kachalov's velvety, intellectual Tusenbach from the twenties, along with Sergey Yursky's tortured baron and Emiliya Popova's brittle Irina from the sixties. They were quoted not to demonstrate the archaism of earlier styles, but to convey a whiff of delicate nostalgia. This device underlined Lyubimov's controlling idea for *Three Sisters*: the action was seen as protracted in time over the more than eighty years of the play's existence, as a comment on the devolution of Russian culture, and, in particular, on the militarization of Soviet society from the invasion of Prague in 1968 to the Afghan War of the eighties.

The usual Chekhovian props were stacked in a corner stage left: a bed's headboard, an old white cottage piano, lights, paper flowers, ambrotypes in carved frames. But this Prozorovian islet was tiny. Over it rose the dusty iconic frescoes of an ancient monastery, which had evidently been turned into a barracks. Stage right stood iron bunks, covered with dirty uniforms, and upstage hung the most primitive metal washbasins. In Yury Kononenko's design the garrison aggressively invaded the three sisters' little world just as E. Denisov's musical score used bold military marches to drown out Chaikovsky, Vivaldi and even the speeches of Vershinin and Tusenbach. Amid this contradictory mingling of past and present, a plain deal platform was placed centre, half trestle stage, half unfinished shed. Before it stood rows of ordinary bentwood chairs, where the characters sat, their backs to the house when they weren't performing. At times they would turn and stare at the audience scornfully or quizzically. The film maker Grigory Kozintsev had some years earlier proposed that Chekhov could be played "quickly, energetically, in an unattractive prosaic milieu."[12] This radical dismantling of the Chekhovian stereotype seemed to take up his challenge.

Orderlies infiltrated the Prozorovs' life. When Irina (L. Selyutina) brutally battered the back of her head against the wall, shouting "Throw me out, throw me out!" an orderly took her unceremoniously by the shoulders and held her firmly in his grasp, as Olga (M. Politseimako) crossed to her and slapped her hard across the face. A bouquet was thrown in the waste-basket. There was no room for elegies or rhapsodies here; personal outbursts were not allowed. Long before the duel, Chebutykin (F. Antipov) twice mimed it and Tusenbach (V. Matyukhin) rehearsed his own death, falling on the platform in convulsions. And after the duel,

Soleny (M. Lebedev) held up hands as bloody as if he had not shot a baron, but slaughtered a pig. In his boorishness, Soleny was a pivotal character, who embodied the naked aggression at the root of the production.[13]

Another key to the interpretation was Alla Demidova's Masha. An officer's greatcoat casually thrown over her shoulders, she brought an atmosphere of *fin de siècle* elegance to the stage; her bold frankness, intensity of speech and gesture provided a touch of tragedy. Only she could stop the flow of history by interrupting her rapid movements with a long, formal pause. Mistress of time and space, she began the performance by calmly, pensively remarking, "I think a human being ought to believe in something . . . Either you know what you're living for or else it's all nonsense, drivel." Works of art or masterpieces of nature are not enough, when the moral traditions of the Russian intelligentsia have been so lethally eroded.[14]

To the right of the stalls was an enormous reflective metal wall that mirrored the spectators, so that the drama unfolded not just in their presence but with their participation. As Masha pronounced her line, the true epigraph of the production, the wall slowly opened to the sounds of a regimental band. Since *Three Sisters* inaugurated the Taganka's new building which lacked the homey, studio-like ambience of the old, the audience, unfamiliar with the theatre's physical properties, was startled by this sudden aperture. Noise and air from the streets around Sadovoe Circus, Moscow's historical hub, breezed into the house. A nocturnal cityscape, typical of Moscow – trams, autos, neon and electric lights, the old bell-towers of the Church of St. Martin the Confessor – impinged on the theatrical frame. A dying regime was boldly and unceremoniously merged with Chekhov's world. The implication was, You want to go "to Moscow"? Well, here's Moscow. You want to know "what will come after us?" Here it is.[15]

This opening statement more than hinted that the sisters' plight was a contemporary one with existential overtones. The voices rang in various registers but their remarks were addressed mainly to the audience, illuminated by the same light that lit up the stage. If Masha was kept at a distance, Natasha (N. Saiko) was observed in close-up. Elegant in a grey décolletage that admirably matched the notorious green belt, this was a fresh, energetic woman, past mistress of *savoir vivre*; her tone was gentle and coaxing, but dry and harsh when necessary. Natasha's pretensions of "tomorrow the world" were more attractive and more audacious variations on the sisters' aspirations. When she appeared in a white nightdress

25 Lyubimov's *Three Sisters* at the Taganka, Moscow, 1981. L.–r., L. Selyutina as Irina, Alla Demidova as Masha, M. Politseimako as Olga. At back, A. Serenko as Ferapont.

with a military greatcoat slung over her shoulders, it was clear that she wanted her affair with Protopopov to resemble Masha's with Vershinin. When she made advances to Soleny, it was because she had to outdo Irina.

At the end, old nanny Anfisa (G. Vlasova) stepped jauntily to the military march, celebrating the fact that she was living "all on the government money," a sardonic allusion to the socialist system that supported all the spectators. As Olga, Politseimako had begun her role in low-keyed, intimate tones, tinged with good humour. She concluded it with

lordly cruelty and spoke her final speech as a class dictation for sopho-
mores, indicating punctuation marks and powerfully impressing the
obligatory Marxist–Leninist optimism on the text. Implying a sarcastic
subtext, she boldly stated, "A time will come," took a pause, came down
to the apron and almost sneered, "when sufferings will turn to joy for
those who will live after us (?), universal happiness will come to the earth
(?), and they will recall with kind words and bless those who live now (?)."
What had often been uttered as a mendacious consolation was twisted
into the enduring rhetorical questions of Russian life. As she spoke, the
metallic wall opened again to an even darker night. The audience's
reflection was replaced by the brash military band.

Lyubimov's *Three Sisters* was flung out as an act of defiance; instead of
the customary elliptical, unemphatic acting for which his troupe was
known, the actors were peremptory and schematic. The liberal press was
friendly and drowned out the minority complaints, but the muffling of
controversy robbed the production of its true significance. Replacing
vigorous protest with sarcasm, Lyubimov seemed to be repudiating his
own artistic ideals. It was his last work shown to the public for some time.
Two years later he would be stripped of citizenship while out of the
country, and the Taganka turned over to Anatoly Éfros.[16]

VANYA AT A LOSS

Lyubimov's attempt to make Chekhov reverberate with the problems of
Soviet life was an extreme case; some of his illustrious colleagues tried to
come to terms with current conditions by offering meliorist compro-
mises in their stagings of Chekhov. The same year that Lyubimov
opened *Three Sisters*, Tovstonogov returned to Chekhov, with *Uncle Vanya*.
"Why do Chekhov's heroes interest us, why do they evoke sympathy?" he
asked. His answer could be read as another appeal to contemporary relevance: "Their lives contain a vast urge towards spirituality, a feeling that
the reality surrounding them is not the way things are supposed to be."[17]
He had been considering *The Wood Demon*, and wondered why the
suicide was missing from its revision, *Uncle Vanya*: he decided it was
because, by the last act, Vanya had come to realize that he was responsible for his own happiness. The realization dawns in the interim between
Astrov's "Our situation is hopeless" and Vanya's next line fifteen minutes
later. For three acts, the characters look outside themselves for the cause
of their suffering; in Act IV, Serebryakov, the alleged culprit, leaves, but
everything gets worse. "It is precisely in Act IV that Astrov says the line

about the hopelessness of his and Uncle Vanya's lives, and after this Ivan Petrovich has an intense zone of silence." How and why this zone of silence exists became the starting-point for the production.[18]

Eduard Kochergin designed a house façade of natural wood overlaid with crackling varnish. Its see-through wall also served as a curtain: the middle section went up to reveal the tea-table with its samovar. When the actors were first shown the set-models, they objected to it, complaining of its lack of logic. The ensuing dialogue, recorded in the rehearsal protocols, reveals the recalcitrance and resistance of Stanislavsky-trained stage personnel to the vast symbolic sets that had by now become standard for Chekhov.

TOVSTONOGOV Well, I like the inhospitable quality [. . .] And it has to be inhospitable. Like a crypt.

EVGENY LEBEDEV (SEREBRYAKOV) Enormous windows – that's no crypt.

KOCHERGIN But it's a country house.

LEBEDEV Tolstoy's country house has lots of windows – and it's cramped.

TOVSTONOGOV I think there ought to be a sense of desolation.

LEBEDEV The windows are twice the height of a human being. Openings like that smack of the theatre, not a house.

KOCHERGIN Over the last decade everyone's made Chekhov into a modernist. There are no windows on stage, nothing. For me Chekhov is a classic, like Racine, and I am expressing his classicism. Even within a stage with wings, within a naturalistic country house.

OLEG BASILASHVILI (VANYA) But the MAT has just made news by renovating its scenery . . .

TOVSTONOGOV The need for something new was suggested by the play. Obligatory novelty, fashion, losing the artistic concept, is boring. And unnecessary. What's needed is the image of an inhospitable country house.

KOCHERGIN It shouldn't just be inhospitable, but gloomy and inhospitable.

LEBEDEV What happens in the play is that a former ideal has collapsed. The relationship to the house has changed, it used to be their world. So the house itself should be hospitable [. . .]

TOVSTONOGOV The scenery has the most important thing – a sense of poetry. And there doesn't have be unity between the actors and the scenery. We can't just go back to Simov, counterpoint is necessary.[19]

These cross-purposes persisted, so that when *Uncle Vanya* opened at the Leningrad BDT in April 1983, one reviewer entitled his essay "Unclear Innovation." In opposition to the stately novelistic tempo of his 1965 *Three Sisters*, Tovstonogov speeded everything up and changed the polyphonic structure of the piece to provide solo scores for the characters. Perhaps taking a tip from Lyubimov, he made the actors look at the audience, even during general conversations: every line became a public confession. All earlier Voinitskys had been imbued with romantic overtones, but the Vanya of Oleg Basilashvili was devoid of external significance; from his first entrance his aggressive irritability and squeaky voice conveyed weakness. His movements were quick but unsure, belying his natty suit, and his handsome face was distorted by grimaces.

Earlier interpretations had situated Vanya's *anagnorisis* in Acts II or III: when Dmitry Orlov's Vanya realized that Elena didn't love him, he stood leaning in the doorway and lowered his head as if trying to cry out in pain. But Basilashvili's Vanya had surmised long before the curtain had gone up that he has been "stupidly cheated." His hopeless love for Elena was a straw for a drowning man to clutch at.[20] By the play's end, all the characters had to repudiate a spurious faith and start life from square one. Discarding false ideals and plans, no longer expecting joy out of life, still they did not surrender. "Their eyes may be full of tears, but they need no comforting."[21] This was the unflinching moral Tovstonogov offered to his compatriots, but to them it sounded hollow.

COMING TO TERMS WITH THE MAT

When the Sovremennik languished, and Oleg Efremov left his own actors to become the artistic director of the Moscow Art Theatre, ructions were expected. The putrid Lazarus that the MAT had become was not quick to revive at the command of a chain-smoking messiah. Some recalcitrant actors were retired, others bribed. But eventually Efremov prevailed. When he came to restage *The Seagull* in 1980 and *Uncle Vanya* in 1985, the tone was one of reconciliation and forgiveness.[22]

Almost as if to placate the spectre of Stanislavsky with sound effects, *The Seagull* opened with an electronically produced overture of the cries of gulls, alternating throughout with the quiet pealing of bells: these sounds were quotations, not just to create atmosphere but to evoke the Art Theatre of the past and signal that the production was moving into a realm of memory. The MAT tradition was to avoid distances between foreground and background. Efremov placed a sixty to seventy foot expanse between the proscenium arch and the upstage area. Two or three characters would be isolated on the forestage in "closeup" and sheltered from their environment, before flowing back upstage into the general chatter as another couple came into focus. The star of the show was a neo-classical gazebo, which designer Valery Levental gave the status of a living character. Always in sight, it moved up and down several times: there the play-within-a-play was staged and there Trigorin

26 The omnipresent gazebo of Valery Levental's *Seagull*, directed by Oleg Efremov, Moscow Art Theatre, 1980.

explained his life to Nina. Chekhov's characters were mere figures in a landscape, dissolving and vanishing within a world of natural beauty.

The production added many of the lines Chekhov had cut and shuffled speeches and scenes, so that Act I began with Treplev and Sorin, Act II with Trigorin and Nina. Employing long pauses and serene rhythms, Efremov organized the Chekhovian polyphony into a seamless flow from one episode to another. This was in opposition to the "montage of attractions" beginning to take over the Russian stage. The running stream of upstage life acted as an accompaniment to the duets and trios. In the lead quartet, the younger generation was not given preference, because Efremov was not looking for culprits. The lack of value judgements did weaken the tension, especially in Act III; but it benefited Anastasiya Vertinskaya as Nina. In the first three acts (which preceded the only intermission), it was her audacious youth and vigour which, rather than talent, attracted the men. In the last act, her voice awakened old Sorin as if her mere presence were life-giving. But the modern twist was to reveal the darkness within the brilliance, so that her courage and agony might be appreciated. The seagull theme – I am slain, I am enslaved – vied with the actress theme – I am alive, I am free. It was not so much a scene played with Treplev but a dialogue continued with Trigorin. The lesson was Chekhovian: when people are on the edge of an abyss, one step can be fatal, but they can go on living, though it's not a choice for the faint-hearted.

Unlike his staging of *The Seagull* at the Sovremennik, Efremov strained to hear every single character, despite their garrulity (they were so talky that they didn't even notice the on-stage death of Sorin). Where other Treplevs stormed, Andrey Myagkov moped in a minor key; prematurely aged, he could barely ignite the embers of his love for Nina. Tatyana Lavrova's Arkadina was comic in her egotism, panicked by the encroachment of age. Instead of the usual ironic portrayal of Dorn as a superannuated fop, Innokenty Smoktunovsky drew a portrait of the epicure as Greek chorus, Proust's Swann adrift on a Russian estate.[23]

The Strehlerian "white theatre" darkened in Act II to a murky space with the characters in sombre clothing. At the end, Treplev's gazebo-stage loomed like a ruin, the wind whistling through its crannies. But the theme of faith amid the ruins emerged triumphant despite all the disillusionment. Everyone faded and died, except Nina who rose like a phoenix. Treplev perished because he could not escape from the past and Trigorin because he could not remember the past. The upstage area with its lotto players was engulfed in darkness, into the past; the white columns stood out, the ragged curtains blew behind her back and, after Treplev's suicide, Nina, standing alone in a black, rain-sodden dress, repeated her monologue in tragic tones. The last words were "Horror, horror, horror." For once it didn't sound like a parody, since Treplev's death revealed the true meaning of her abstractions.[24] This time around she was not a provincial miss, but an *Actress* who had experienced suffering and grasped the meaning of symbolic visions. The unity of spirit and matter, the oneness of the eternal life cycle acquired a truly human intonation.[25]

In an interview, Efremov expressed the opinion that Chekhov himself had gone through something like Nina's experiences. "[He] was dealing with the important problem for him of a creative state in which art and duty combine."[26] The sense of collective catastrophe, of the alienation of one's nearest and dearest was also an autobiographical reflection upon Efremov's own transition from the Sovremennik to the MAT, and the birth pangs of creating a new ensemble. But only the earliest performances conserved the subtle correspondences that gave substance to the play's overall shape. Later, it all fell apart, leaving nothing but bare form, hollow acting and the shrieks of seagulls lamenting a defunct theatre.[27] When Anatoly Éfros saw it, he was unimpressed, finding that a requiem or dying fall, no matter how powerful, could not make up for the perfunctory acting that preceded it. *The Seagull*, he insisted, is so imperfect a play that it needs special treatment to avoid looking like an old-fashioned melodrama. In Efremov's interpetation, the sense of life and the conflict between Trigorin and Treplev was lost in a "general Chekhovian tone."[28]

"If I am honest, I take responsibility" was the founding motto of the Sovremennik. Thirty years later, the motif of constructive patience and responsibility surfaced once again in Efremov's Art Theatre *Uncle Vanya*, which premiered in February 1985, on the eve of an historic upheaval. Low-keyed and elegiac, it returned to the theme of the responsibility of decent people to their society. In Andrey Myagkov's interpretation, Uncle Vanya's "wasted life" was neither celebrated nor mourned, because life as such could not be wasted. Dr. Astrov, as Borisov and later Efremov played him, was enslaved to the daily grind but struggled to break free of it.

Far upstage the house designed by Levental seemed to emanate from an autumn landscape by Isaak Levitan. A benign nature infused it, so that even Vanya's room was piled with apples. When darkness fell, a faint ember slowly flickered up from the arid land and glowed dimly, beckoning the way along a path. As one critic insisted, this was more than picturesque; it was a call to prolong the "long quotidian work of the conscientious Russian *intelligent*."[29]

Mikhail Gorbachev attended a performance on April 30, the eve of the traditional May Day parade, which he would review from atop Lenin's tomb. He was the first General Secretary to take the liberty of attending a Chekhov play the night before the proletarian festival. A week later Gorbachev phoned Efremov to report his impressions: Astrov had delighted him, and Smoktunovsky's Voinitsky had broken his heart. But he was a busy man and hoped that he could find the time some day to chat about theatrical affairs in general.[30] Lenin's dismissal of *Uncle Vanya* at the Art Theatre had been avenged.

CHAPTER 13

Out of the rubble (Central and Eastern Europe 1945–1985)

> How are we to enter [Chekhov's] world without breaking in? How
> are we conscientiously to convey his message, as he does it, without
> intervention or commentary? Is the most modest, most self-effacing
> eavesdropping an interpretation in itself? And if we believe our
> reading is in line with his artistic views, how are we to put this on
> stage?
>
> Otomar Krejča[1]

A COMMUNIST WORLD-VIEW

Floundering in the wake of the war, the nations of Central and Eastern
Europe, soon to be known collectively as the Eastern bloc, found themselves occupied not only by Soviet troops but by Soviet culture. Newly
installed Communist apparatuses promoted Russian art over indigenous
products as the "basis for a democratic and aesthetic tradition."[2] So, as
early as October 1945, Vienna reopened its Komödie Theater with the
Uncle Vanya (*Onkel Vanja*) directed by Leon Epps that had been aborted
five years earlier; it turned out to be the first truly successful interpretation of the play on the German-speaking stage.

That same month Leipzig offered *The Seagull* (*Die Möwe*) in the context
of a Russian Music and Theatre Week, and at year's end the Deutsches
Theater in the Russian sector of Berlin offered an important staging of
Vanya by Ernst Legal. In his critique of this *Vanya*, Paul Rilla, in typically
turgid prose, laid the cornerstone for the socio-historical reinterpretation
of Chekhov that would become endemic in the German Democratic
Republic:

In past decades Chekhov was esteemed as the dramatist who affirmed the
insignificance and desolation of human existence in pictures of melancholically
delicate, melancholically turbid realism and charm. This was certainly not
incorrect. But it would be a mistake to signify this art as "timeless," to identify it

235

with "life" instead of understanding it as the reflex of a quite specific historical and social situation.

Now is just the time to stress the social signature of the Chekhovian play even at the cost of any atmospheric values. [. . .]. Once one knows the historical determinism in Russia that put a full-stop to the decaying bourgeois world, one will also grasp the great instinct and awareness of the future set in motion by Chekhov.[3]

This transformation of Chekhov from a pessimistic, passive observer into an intuitive herald of revolution was heavily influenced by the Soviet critic V. Ermilov. Measured on a Marxist scale, characters were labelled as positive (Sonya, Marina) or Dostoevskian (Vanya, Astrov, Serebryakov and Elena).

The most rigorous imposition of Soviet cultural hegemony took place in East Germany, in order to extirpate any surviving vestiges of Nazism. Even when it was merely a Russian zone, the occupying authorities stimulated interest in Soviet culture by making available large editions of their classics in German translation. These included Hilde Angarowa's rendering of Chekhov's plays, illustrated with photographs of the original Moscow Art Theatre productions (1947). Soon the standard versions, Angarowa's translations were "prone to linguistic swagger," unnecessarily elaborate and flowery; in line with the Marxist reading, they also maximized class tension, especially in *Uncle Vanya*. Typical of the GDR's political paternalism were the later translations of Gudrun Düwel (1964), couched in a genteel idiom with speeches amplified to guide the reader to a proper understanding of the dialectic process.[4]

As the repertory became swollen with Russian classics, the need to convey the right message and, incidentally, to effect the injection of Russian spirit into German soul became a duty of the *mise-en-scène* as well. A much-publicized anecdote tells of a *Cherry Orchard* in Dresden when Soviet citizens clambered onto the stage to demonstrate how Chekhov was to be played.[5] Not only theatres, but theatre schools found considerable difficulty in promoting national approaches that might be seen as inimical to communism. The approved acting curriculum, the Stalinist recension of Stanislavsky, interpreted his wish that the life of the human spirit be made manifest to mean "Serving one's nation." This Red Stanislavsky was proselytized for by Maxim Vallentin, who opened an acting school in East Berlin in 1945, and two years later a Theater-Institut in Weimar. This missionary work was also pursued at the Maxim Gorki Theatre in East Berlin from 1952. For communist actors and director, the simple-minded idealism of Stalinist Stanislavsky clashed with a more dynamic alternative, Brecht's epic theatre which was establishing its own aesthetic canon. Brecht's style of confrontational truth seemed to cancel out what was derogated as Stanislavsky's "art of facile truth." But as the government of the GDR grew more sclerotic, the mummified Stanislavsky was officially preferred to the more mercurial, less predictable Brecht. The Russian effacement of epic theatre as the official academic style culminated in 1953 at a Stanislavsky Conference in Berlin, which, like a church synod, established an orthodoxy for dramatic training and performance. 1954, a Chekhov anniversary year, spawned innumerable and often half-hearted clones of the MAT, including the East Berlin productions of Wolfgang Heinz, who Gorkified Chekhov. Ironically, the most genuinely Stanislavskian production in German in those years was Peter Sharoff's 1956 *Drei Schwestern* at the Vienna Volkstheater with sets inspired by Simov's original scenery and Martha Wallner as a grandiose and impassioned Masha.

Historically, resistance to Russian culture had been a tenet of Polish patriotism, but with the new alignment of powers, this became impossible. Avid for theatre, Poles flocked to hastily renovated playhouses, in quest of "stage truth." Polish artists and critics were eager to update the pre-war formulas for rehearsal and repertory, but in the meantime Poland's classics were banned and Russian drama abounded. The MAT was promoted as the theatre most fully reflecting the principles of Communist Party's cultural policy: lip-service was paid to this credo by theatre artists even though they regarded Stanislavsky as an old-fashioned liberal. While politicians announced that his System was a means of achieving "socialist realism," theatre practitioners read it as "real-life truth in the staging of Chekhov's dramas."[6]

In October 1949, a festival of Russian plays was held in Warsaw as a token of "Polish-Soviet friendship"; none of the works of the Russian satiric or fantastic tradition were produced, except for Griboedov, put on by amateurs. Of the pre-revolutionary dramatists, only Chekhov and Gorky were presented in quantity; Chekhov was touted as a sagacious, kindly secular saint, whose plays were repositories of wisdom for the reconstruction of the world. A prize was given to Bronisław Dąbrowski's *Three Sisters* (*Trzy siostry*) at Cracow's Słowacki Theatre, one of the few productions to satisfy the critics' new call for socialist realism. Dąbrowski's Chekhov was infused with a sense of renascent hope, the actors' work steeped in "an atmosphere of warmth and tenderness." The director recalled "how after the scene between Tusenbach and Irina all you could hear was a quiet breathing from the house, and a storm of applause broke out" at the line "If I die, all the same I shall participate in life this way or some other."[7] The rest of the Chekhov productions in the competition were faulted for spurious romantic and formalist tendencies.

For want of a Polish repertory to meet the new criteria, Chekhov remained a staple until the mid-1950s. By then professional journals were complaining of the *cul de sac* into which Stanislavsky's increasingly formulaic curriculum was leading the actor, compelling him to play Chekhov and Shaw, Molière and Shakespeare in the same manner. After Stalin's death, as control on artistic matters slackened, Poles, bored with party-line Stanislavsky, took a strong interest in the early revolutionary theatre of Meyerhold and Mayakovsky. The debate was catalyzed by an article published in 1958 by N. Modzelewska.[8] She did not entirely abandon Marxism-Leninism, for she characterized the weak-willed Chekhovian intellectual as a "product of his epoch," content with remaining an outside observer, solacing himself with a chimera of the future. However, while calling Chekhov's heroes "knights of eternal discontent," she attacked the MAT's interpretation and its epigones, and, pointing out the grotesque and absurd elements in the plays, recommended an ironically satiric approach.

A Moscow Art Theatre tour to Poland summoned a last-ditch defence by the conservative critics, who argued that to make Chekhov contemporary was a gimmick rather than a "deepening of thematics."[9] But the fight for modernism was led by Zenobiusz Strzelecki, designer and director, who observed that naturalism was all right for the MAT, because "there each performance is a museum piece," but not the proper style if Chekhov were to remain relevant. Pictorially, at least, impressionism, with perhaps dashes of expressionism and surrealism, was more appropriate to "convey the loneliness and distress . . . while Buffet's realism would certainly be suited to [the characters'] resignation."[10] In Strzelecki's 1959 production at the Polski Theatre, Warsaw, of *The Seagull*, a play which had rarely been professionally staged in Poland, the action took place on rounded fabric-covered platforms against silhouettes of leafless black trees and a canvas sky cloth with a moon sketched in for Act I and clouds for Act II. The interiors were sparsely furnished in white for the third act and black for the fourth.

Another move away from Soviet influence was Zamkov-Słomczyńska's *Lower Depths* at Cracow's Teatr Stary in 1960; it stunned the spectators by removing all specific Russian references and locale, and substituting sarcasm and mockery for socialist heroics. Its success inspired Adam Hanuszkiewicz to try the same thing two years later at

Warsaw's Teatr Dramatyczny with *Platonov*.[11] This, the first Polish version of *Untitled Play*, was an obvious contribution to the literary debates about new interpretations of Chekhov. For Hanuszkiewicz, the way to bring Chekhov closer to contemporary audiences was to extract him from his Russian milieu by removing all social context. The scenography was not by an experienced set-designer, but by Krzystof Pankiewicz, an abstract painter of lush colour, who provided an empty stage furnished with loose hanging tatters and a haphazard arrangement of actors.

Hanuszkiewicz's *Platonov* was savaged by the establishment critics, even those who wanted to see a modern Chekhov. It was too "polonized" for their tastes. They hated the design and the incidental music which they found excessive, alarming and inappropriate. Andrzej Wirth couldn't decide if the director was going for farce, psychological drama, contemporary grotesque or something else. Roman Szydlowski objected to the cuts, the slow tempi, the long pauses; to his mind, all that was left was the love interest and that made it seem like a melodrama. Melodrama, rather than grotesquerie, was also suggested by the lack of a uniform acting style.[12] Despite the carping, both Gustav Holoubek as Platonov and the production won awards at the Annual Festival of Russian and Soviet Art in Katowice. Fifteen years later, when Hanuszkiewicz restaged *Platonov* at the National Theatre, the critics reversed themselves and called it a complete success, for now they found this style of Chekhov more meaningful than the traditionally lachrymose one.[13] But by then Stanislavsky's System had been overthrown and the critical establishment released from the dead hand of socialist realism.

A THEATRE OF CRUELTY

The Seagull, Cherry Orchard, Three Sisters, the one-acts and dramatized stories inundated the Czech stage as early as the 1946/7 season. On the initiative of the government and the Party, between 1948 and 1953 twenty-three editions of Chekhov's works were issued, and nineteen productions of his plays opened, most of them replicas of the Moscow Art Theatre. The fiftieth anniversary of his death saw even more.

In those post-war years questions of faith were uppermost. Ignoring the fact that it was uttered by an unreliable character in *The Lower Depths*, Soviet ideology promoted the line "Mankind, the word sounds proud" as a slogan. The betterment of humanity was to guarantee a radiant future under Communism. The significance of the proliferation of Chekhovian productions to this ideology was all the greater since, as the critic M. Smetana pointed out,

on our stage there are very few plays about contemporary life, in which the theme of people's spiritual reeducation might be worked out purposefully and profoundly, and important problems of morality and emotion might be established . . . One must infect the spectator with Chekhov's dreams of beauty . . . teach the younger generation to reflect on life, deeply and honourably to face all its important questions. In short, our theatre does not have the right not to perform Chekhov's plays, not to acquaint our spectators with the heritage of a great writer and thinker. Ours is the very generation to realize everything Chekhov could only dream of and long for.[14]

During this time, Otomar Krejča was teaching dramatic art at Prague's National Theatre (Národní Divadlo), a mouldy colossus whose intellectual windows were sealed shut. His students saw Chekhov only as an obligatory item in the curriculum. Beyond the Party homilies, no one was looking for a key to "Chekhov our contemporary": no one except Krejča. In discreet ways, he experimented in escaping Marxist dialectic and Cartesian logic to raise existential questions in Chekhov. Playing Tusenbach, Krejča copied Kachalov, with his pimples and his myopic bespectacled gaze; but on his final exit he tried to reveal a Chekhovian pitilessness, an "ontologically sick" world, by implying that nothing will ever change on the ahistoric plane of human existence.

In the sombre political climate of the late 1950s, Krejča laid plans for a *Seagull*, an unpropitious idea since the authorities declared the play too pessimistic. To meet this objection, he had the bright idea of omitting the last line announcing Konstantin's suicide, but it proved to be unworkable. As Krejča later insisted, nothing can be deleted from Chekhov, for his plays are constructed as intradependently as Gothic cathedrals.

In 1960 Krejča's former director at the Vinohrady Theatre, Jiří Frejka, committed suicide, driven to despair by the bleak outlook of events. Only then did Krejča with a small group of like-minded friends embark on a new staging of *The Seagull*. The newness derived in part from the abolition of the box set. Josef Svoboda, an admirer of Piscator and Gropius, called himself not a scene designer but a scenographer; he dismissed standard settings and manipulated the stage space so as to remind the audience of the studios and workshops that generated the work. While granting that a traditional *mise-en-scène* might be "instructive," he preferred an approach which managed to realize Treplev's dream of a stage of unusual depth. His *Seagull* was practically bare, with a lane leading upstage through pools of light. Branches unattached to trees hung overhead, and a couple of garden chairs and a table summed up the furniture. Impressionistic images were projected on the cyclorama.[15]

Since the choice of play had been dictated by current problems both in the theatre and throughout Czech society,[16] the production was gorged with the kind of sentimental psychology and direct political statement that Krejča would later disown. He entrusted his message to Nina whose return in Act IV was a mission to convey the author's bitter "envoi." Most audience members took this message to be "We are responsible for our own lives." Later Krejča confessed this had been a serious mistake, since no character in Chekhov should have the last word. "There is no monologue in which the author declared his ultimate opinion. No character has the right to the biggest spotlight."[17]

In 1965, Krejča, along with his close associates, the dramaturge Karel Kraus and the playwright Josef Topol, took a leave of absence from the National Theatre. They then proceeded to found the Divadlo Za Branou or Theatre Beyond the Gates, whose main task was to seek fresh means of expression and visualization to convey the classics or modern drama to their contemporaries. "Our aim being pleasure in the theatre, we chose as our second production *Three Sisters*."[18] It was to be decisive for Krejča's scenic experiments and his views on the actor's central place in the evolution of a work. "I found 'my' Chekhov in collaboration with the actors in an almost suicidal confidence in the possibilities of the actors' art," he later explained.[19] This was the natural result of his belief that plays exist only when they are performed by living human beings. Once the first choice is made in a rehearsal, an unforeseeable series of possibilities arises. Nevertheless, the single choice that must be made from the myriad of possibilities is as obligatory for a given staging as the completed form of a line of dialogue had been for the author.

Krejča also recognized that the director necessarily brings to a playwright's world his own experiences, which are in turn illuminated by it. Based on his personal past, therefore, he could declare that for all their farcical elements, Chekhov's plays were not comedies but "segments of the human comedy." He chose to emphasize a feature which Gorky had noticed, "coldness and cruelty."

May one state the only slightly off-kilter opinion that Chekhov is stern, cruel, merciless to his characters? Does he really like them? Does he love anything except his truth about them? [. . .] And is such ultra-righteousness, like many other absolute values, more than a little inhuman? [. . .][20]

27 Josef Svoboda's scenography for Otomar Krejča's *Tri sestry* (*Three Sisters*), Prague,
1965, with Krejča as Dr. Chebutykin seated by the swing, l.

Like Ibsen, Chekhov was concerned with exposing the escape into life-
lies, a tactic which is independent of period and milieu. So, Krejča
believed, Chekhov's plays could easily set up a mirror for the present.

Three Sisters established Krejča's reputation as the greatest textual
scholar of Chekhov working in the theatre, and turned out be the most
successful revisionist exegesis of its time. Krejča decided that there was
no unity amongst the sisters, but rather "a concrete relation made of
comprehensible human disharmony." This determined the first "stage
direction": Irina, pensive, sure of herself as if she had just discovered
something very important, steps forward gaily, looks out the windows.
Masha measures her with a glance and goes to sit on the sofa behind the
table. She reads, motionless. Irina reaches the chair, leans on its back
and makes slow head movements. "Today the weather is really very
fine." Olga, her eyes half-closed, has watched her and rebukes her
thoughtless pleasure: "A year ago Father died, the same day as your
nameday, May 5." The rest of the play followed from this essential lack
of accord among the characters; but the directing created a profound
harmony capable of embracing the greatest dissonances. It corresponded to the definition of dramatic action offered by Krejča's colleague Jindrich Honzl: "Action – the very essence of dramatic art – fuses
word, actor, costume, scenery and music so that that we recognize them

as conductors of a single current which traverses them by passing from one to another or several at once."[21] The strange polyphony was duplicated in the blocking, the *mise-en-scène* a sort of sublimated realism with impressionist touches and abstract blotches. Contradictions were exposed, even accentuated, but consolidated rather than isolated. At one of the last open rehearsals, alarmed colleagues complained that, instead of the clarity they expected of Chekhov, they saw the chaos of a zoo with wild animals attacking one another. Krejča would often be reproached for eliminating the nostalgia and emotional charisma: but he never humiliated the characters.[22]

Again Josef Svoboda created the scenography: on a wide, deep stage, grey compartmented wing-pieces led in diminishing perspective to a grey back wall sunk in darkness (Svoboda believed grey to be the Chekhovian colour *par excellence*). The furniture was selected from fine antiques: in the first two acts a crystal chandelier above a large round dining-table up right, in Act III parallel screens. In the last act, two branches hung down over a denuded stage, with a swing on ropes down right. "Thus is realism dismantled, without the locales losing their specificity. Colours emerge from memory, lots of green in Act I, the officers' uniforms a bright green: Irina, the youngest, brown and brownish in the last act."[23]

Sound was used not for atmosphere, but to "underscore and overscore the tension." In the last act, a fiddle tune, a harp song, the distant gunshot and the martial music blended into a *danse macabre*. "Now the figures track across the stage. Death is amongst them. In the withdrawing noise we see the marching men, waving to the stay-at-homes. The fascination here is wholly identical with Chekhov's intended effect."[24] At the very end, Chebutykin, played by Krejča himself, sailed over the spectators' heads on the swing. On an empty, blankly lit stage Irina and Masha whirled like wounded birds, flying to opposite sides, deaf to Olga's speeches. It was a cruel and tragic ending, the inevitable culmination of a gradual build-up of details. By divesting Chekhov of sentimental cliché, by denying his status as the portraitist of *fin de siècle* decadence, Krejča brought out what was hard, sharp and glaring in him.

Krejča's *Three Sisters* remained in the repertory of the Divadlo Za Branou for six years, until the theatre was liquidated; it was also shown abroad in twelve different countries, exercising a profound influence on rethinking Chekhovian production. In 1970, he produced *Ivanov*. Returning to the earliest, Korsh-Theatre text, Krejča promoted a minor character, Egorushka, into an idiotic master of ceremonies. The play

28 The bark-covered fence and plush-covered interior of Svoboda's scenography for
Krejča's *Ivanov* of 1970, dominated by the pendulous chandeliers.

opened with Egorushka's giving two heavy chandeliers a push that set
them swaying like a metronome. His animal howls, uttered at various
moments, made him a gutteral chorus, compared by one critic to Benjy
in Faulkner's *Light in August*.[25] These howls were orchestrated with piano
and dance tunes, the funeral march of a rural orchestra and the watchman's clacker to create a unifying score. Svoboda's space was enclosed
by a palisade of rough-hewn unpainted wood, furnished with green
plush upholstery; Ivanov dwelt on the audience side, while society lived
on the other side of the fence. All the characters remained on stage
throughout, a device Krejča first employed in his *Lorenzaccio* the previous
year. White light was directed on the stage for line readings, green light
for moments of subtext, producing an effect reminiscent of *The Ghost
Sonata*. The extraordinary dimension given by juxtaposition, super-
imposition or opposition of several levels or themes kept the drama from
progressing in a linear fashion; rather, it seemed to increase in volume.[26]

Krejča had been invited to Brussels to restage *The Seagull* in 1966, and he reworked it at the Divadlo Za Branou in 1972, carrying on the radical restructuring of the text already begun in *Ivanov*. He adopted Sergey Eisenstein's concept of montage as a way of bringing the audience into the work. The actors performed Act IV from beginning to end, with excerpts from earlier acts inserted and interpolated to compose a montage of twenty unequal parts. Each of the first nineteen excerpts was divided into two confrontational moments: first, a portion of Act IV, and then a corresponding scene removed from a preceding act and played in its entirety.[27] Bricolage was superimposed on montage: Svoboda brought together a mass of disparate objects, birches, furniture, mirrors, the junkpile of Chekhovian memory.

When the authorities closed the Divadlo Za Branou, Krejča was assigned to an uninteresting municipal theatre in Liben on the outskirts of Prague, the Divadlo S. K. Neumann. After a period of administration and no directing, he broke his silence in 1974 with *Platonov*. The play was chosen for obvious reasons: it dealt with the demise of the ideal in a morass of deceptive relationships and pervasive baseness. With only two actors from his former troupe and without his usual six-months' rehearsal period, Krejča applied to *Platonov* the same configuration he had used in *Ivanov*. All actors were on stage at all times, surrounded by a tall wooden fence, and Platonov's room was suggested by a floor, bed and wardrobe. The characters were introduced gradually as if strolling along a promenade, and then separated into groups according to affinities or plot requirements. The action was dissected into discrete sequences set off against one another.

Everything is flooded with unrealistic green light. Only as people appear does white light, that is, reality, replace it. Over and over experiences and memories are evoked and punctuated by light. The harsh light of Dr. Chekhov makes humanity tangible, but collectively, not as individuals, stripped of illusion, i.e., cruelly.[28]

In 1976 Krejča was able to escape his enforced obscurity by being appointed Schauspielleiter at Düsseldorf for two years. His first season was initiated by *The Cherry Orchard*, in a setting he co-designed with Theodor Richter-Forgach. It opened the vast proscenium and extended the already huge stage to the back wall until it was thirty-six metres deep. A wide road on the ground cloth led the eye to the rear perspective, then went vertical and returned to the audience, suggesting arrival, sojourn and departure. It created an image of life both as global habitat and as railway station with passengers caught between stops. A veil of luminous whiteness, in exquisite bad taste, hung over all, standing in for the orchard and the conventional drapery of an operetta set. There were no walls; each room was defined by its contents, heaps of hideous if luxurious furniture, but only the action or movement of the characters allowed the audience to determine their function. Sitting or lying amid beds and sofas (for they rarely stood up), the characters were engulfed in things.[29] Between Acts I and II, the veil fell covering the furniture, to become a shroud over oddly shaped tombs, so that Trofimov orated in a graveyard. When Ranevskaya said she expects the roof to cave in, it already had, taking her with it. At the play's end when the tables, billiards, bureaux, and chairs were shoved aside and put away, the stage became the lumber-room of the past.

Krejča was bombarding the actors with reifications of Chekhov's "concentrated everydayness: his quotidian situations are seen in their strangeness, their oddness, their uniqueness." Chekhov's was an "unstable, almost inflammable world." "He writes with a scalpel."

One must X-ray the text . . . each phrase is only a key to something else, and that something else goes far beyond the characters even when they are "doing nothing but" chatting. A single word or exclamation repeated can have an immense radiation . . . The Chekhovian pause is [not fly-catching melancholia, but] a collision, an accident, a confusion – especially in the daily activity of characters, in their desires and interests.[30]

Extending the technique he experimented with in *The Seagull*, he displaced or echoed dialogue; fugitive lines on given themes (the desire to leave, death, Varya's marriage) were concentrated in a single knot, as if the play were a critical essay on itself. Krejča dislocated elements better to underline the ensemble structure, reinforce and concentrate themes, and prolong their resonance. In Act II, the duet between Anya and Trofimov was intercut with the Gaev/Ranevskaya/Lopakhin scene; the pauses in the speeches of the first two were filled with the reverberant actions of the others. In the first pause, Anya was rapt in thought, astonished to discover the expression "fall in love"; in the next, she tried to understand Trofimov's question, "What is the point of our lives?" The pauses became swollen with meaning but were played naturally as moments of reflection.

In Ingeborg Engelmann's rendition, Ranevskaya was flesh-and-blood, prone to migraines (she put on a cold compress in Act III) and erotic frissons: she embraced Trofimov tightly, had her thighs kneaded by Yasha, wanted to be desired by Lopakhin (Werner Snitzer), whose sensuality was blocked by class conflict. When they did kiss in Act II, they quickly drew apart, terrified by this revealed truth. Krejča was one of the first directors after Vakhtangov to master the comic grotesquerie of the Chekhovian world: his guests danced with chairs on their heads, Epikhodov climbed the bookcase to escape muscular Varya, a diminutive Gaev sat on an ashtray. At the close Firs was almost hidden behind the furniture: a dusty insect, he stretched out on a bench so small that his legs dangled over the edge. The past that ended with him was equally ridiculous – an invention of the masters, which, like them, collapsed without dignity.[31]

Until the Velvet Revolution liberated Czech theatre, Krejča would continue to reinvent Chekhov outside his homeland. He restaged *Platonov* in Düsseldorf in 1977, and in 1980 created a striking *Three Sisters* (*Les trois soeurs*) for the Atelier théâtral de Louvain-la-Neuve. Here he took a different tack, attempting to create a dialectical synthesis between psychological naturalism *à la* Stanislavsky and the rhythmic, lyrical theatre of psychic states Meyerhold had envisaged. Béatrice Picon-Vallin has made enormous claims for Krejča's achievement, including

aleatory perception (not everything can be seen, and the director knows it), globalizing (capable of pulling together the threads of a dispersed narrative), ultimately transversal, conscious or unconscious (invoking the spectator's capacity for *associations*, both internal, getting inside the performance, and "private," putting the spectator on stage) which allows the audience to penetrate to the very heart of the creative process, theatre in the making.[32]

The scenography evoked a fairground carousel with its wooden horses, and the acting, divested of emotion, accentuated the absurdity and inhumanity omnipresent in everyday life. Rapid and staccato, it seemed a profanation of the traditional nuanced emotional atmosphere. Audiences in Belgium, where *The Seagull* and *The Cherry Orchard* had first been produced in Brussels in the 1920s, reeled from the revelation and rejected it. Although some critics referred to Krejča's as "de echte Tsjechov," Flemish and Walloon directors went on staging the plays as "weepies" and rambles through the print cabinet.[33]

All in all, Krejča mounted five Chekhov plays seventeen times: six in Czechoslovakia, eleven in his provisory exile. When he returned to the international scene with a *Cherry Orchard* in 1991 (see chapter 17), he had nothing new to say. The lessons had been learned too well. But those lessons were ineffaceable. Combined with Svoboda's scenography, Krejča's conception had been more violent than anything since

Vakhtangov. Instead of muted pastels, hysteria; instead of elegance, vulgarity and aggression; instead of sadness, desperation. His vision, revealed to the West at the World Theatre season in 1968, inaugurated a radical reinterpretation of Chekhov both there and in the Soviet Union.

CHEKHOV BALKANIZED

After Romania's so-called "liberation," productions of Chekhov were undistinguished and indistinguishable from the usual Art Theatre simulacra. The National Theatre of Bucharest *Three Sisters* (*Trei surori*, 1950), directed by Mony Ghelerter, brought together the most resplendent names in the Romanian theatre: both actors and director won a State Prize, and the production was revived and toured regularly to 1956. It set the style for Romanian Chekhov,[34] until Lucian Pintilie challenged it with *The Cherry Orchard* (*Livada cu vişini*) at the Lucia Sturza Bulandra Theatre in Bucharest in 1965.

Pintilie admitted that his forte was comedy, so, not surprisingly, he found the play to be full of "a very special, strange, magical comedy: its reality hides an unusual universe, essential reality surges out from apparent reality." He was among the first to spot the connection with Beckett, and suggested that such a play about "our unconsciousness and all its consequences" be re-titled *Oh! les beaux jours*. "It's the story of an agony devoid of atrocity, an idyllic agony, unconscious and irresponsible," a tale of death by drug addiction, "Lyubov engulfed in sand, smiling, her eyes aglow with morphine, as we hear the music of the spheres." All the characters were delirious fanatics, with Trofimov an unopposed Robespierre. "He, like Anya and Ranevskaya, floats between two equally imaginary realms, past and future. [. . .] he doesn't really stand for anything new."[35] This interpretation was also startling for its time and place in breaking away from the walls and windows of naturalism and flooding the open space with light. It had a powerful influence on the young directing student Andrei Serban.

Pintilie could not pursue his non-sociological approach during the reign of Ceausescu; his later experiments took place outside Romania, and he eventually settled in the United States. A production of *The Seagull* in Berlin in 1969 signalled to the German critics an elaborate withdrawal from the Stanislavsky tradition and a recourse to Meyerhold. All atmosphere and human space were leached from the nearly empty stage, covered by a sand-coloured platform like a sounding-board. The figures acting on such a flat surface were reduced to beings no longer capable of suffering the strain of their own nature. Pintilie also inquired more minutely into the characters' passions, concentrating on the withered sexuality of Nina.[36] In a post-Freudian *Three Sisters* staged in Paris in 1978–9, sexuality was again at the core. Pintilie saw the sisters as three faces of one woman, mythological mother, child and erotic female, so he grouped them closely throughout. Irina seemed never to get beyond puberty, while Masha savagely flaunted her repressed libido in the last two acts.[37]

By the late 1970s, the deliberate effort to renovate Chekhov was apparent on most of the stages of Slavic Europe. The impress of Ionesco, Beckett, and all the Poles from Wyspianski to Mrożek could be felt. The Stanislavskian model was particularly under attack in Yugoslavia, a country which had long resisted the Soviet Union's dominance in the Communist world. As early as 1960, the director Milenko Serban was insisting that whether one went back to the post-impressionism of Vuillard or to a symbolic décor, "one must above all abandon the painted set."[38]

Perhaps the most successful because the most extreme of these revisitations was *Three Sisters* at the Hungarian Theatre in Subotica (1977). The audience entered to a scene of calculated serenity: Olga and Masha lay side by side, the latter, in a long black gown and devilish coiffure, reading and whistling. Irina played with a white parasol with childish abandon. Tusenbach dozed in a swing, Chebutykin snored over his newspaper, Ferapont snoozed under a bush next to the nameday cake, Soleny, his pants rolled up, fussed over a fishing rod among reeds and rushes. A nervous vibration ran through this all-too-peaceful setting for destructive ordeals of loneliness.

The reed-bordered space designed by Zsoltan Kölönte evoked a sense of both breadth and enclosure, through which the audience had to stumble amid actors to get to its seats. What made it all the more difficult for them and for the characters was the peculiar flooring: two or three layers of foam rubber in uneven thicknesses. The marshy mud puddle of a floor betokened a loss of internal equilibrium. The director György Harag intended the impossibility of walking and standing to represent suffering on several levels. The sisters were on home ground and knew their way about; but in time lost their spiritual footing. Tusenbach stumbled clumsily, Natasha made vigorous entrances and exits, always accompanied by a retinue of servants; the naturally inert Chebutykin walked only when drunk and then crept away. Kulygin did gymnastics, but fell down. Soleny remained immobile. There was no final tableau of wistfulness, for the sisters spoke simultaneously in a welter of voices which grew louder as the military music reached a crescendo.[39]

THE WEST AWAKES

In contrast with the forced feeding of Russian drama in the East, West German theatre gorged itself on everything but Chekhov. Between 1947 and 1975, only sixteen productions of his plays took place in the Federal Republic;[40] when one considers the large number of richly supported municipal theatres, this paucity is all the more remarkable. An increase became perceptible in the sixties during a debate over approaches to staging. By the mid-seventies, reinventing Chekhov had become a growth industry.

In 1949, for the first time in three decades, a German *Seagull* took flight: Gustaf Gründgens' production at the Düsseldorf State Theatre, with himself as Trigorin, opened the aviary for other versions in Berlin and Vienna. However, audiences preoccupied by economic recovery and anxious for stability and security took little interest in the *Weltschmerz* and lethargy that continued to typify these interpretations. Atmospherics, decadence and symbolism were dismissed as outmoded attributes of an idyllic past. "We laugh at the problems of this bygone world although we appreciate the poetry" was the gist of the criticism. Most West German analyses of Chekhov continued to speak of his pessimism and indifference. In his *Theorie des modernen Dramas* (1956) Peter Szöndi articulated this "epic" view of Chekhov, which, curiously, he ascribed to Slavic origins:

Its origins probably lie in Russian expansiveness and in the immanent lyric quality of the language itself. Loneliness is not the same thing as torpor here. What the Occidental most probably experiences only while intoxicated – participation in the loneliness of the others, the inclusion of individual loneliness in a growing collective loneliness – seems to be a possibility inherent in the Russian: the person and the language.[41]

Such an idea could not help to naturalize Chekhov within German culture.

What also slowed down directors was the wretched level of available translations, which were either "literary" and theatrically inadequate or insufficiently canonical to be published. The most widely circulated version of Chekhov's plays in the immediate post-war period was that of Sigismund von Radecki, a cheap paperback published in Stuttgart in

1960: it abounds with inaccuracies and Russicisms, clumsy constructions and incomprehensible phrases. The Chekhov boom on the German stage was retarded until new improved translations appeared.[42]

While German directors were still ventilating the old psychosomatic sighs, new inspiration arrived from Milan, Prague, London, and Stockholm. Another important stimulus was the so-called Theatre of the Absurd: between 1953 and 1957 *Waiting for Godot, Endgame* and the plays of Ionesco had their first German productions. Chekhov was quickly identified as a precursor. The osmotic line between comedy and tragedy, the characters' inability to act, their escape into dreams and illusions and their "failure to communicate," the isolation and lack of contact, the decay of a narrow-minded bourgeois society, language reduced to empty formulas and clichés, waiting as a symptom of mortality – all these elements suddenly made Chekhov seem in the swim. West-German doubts about the relevance of Stanislavsky's psychological realism hardened into the conclusion that his methods were directly opposed to Chekhov. "Half a century lies between *The Seagull* and Beckett's *Godot*, but a straight line leads from this Slavic nihilism to the wait for *Godot*," proclaimed a journalist.[43]

Gaining steam, the attack on illusionistic, atmospheric traditions came to a head in 1965 with *Three Sisters* (*Drei Schwestern*) directed by Rudolf Noelte at Stuttgart's Hebbel Theater. Noelte assumed that the play was radically and schematically constructed of blocks, dominated by monologues. He cut emotional moments, including Masha's ta-ram-tam-tam and the usual Act III hysteria, and located the play on a spacious unit set, obliterating intimacy along with scene changes. The familiar affects of scepticism, melancholy and vague sentiment were replaced by a dry, inexorable tragic nihilism, difficult to endure. This was Chekhov pared down to Beckett, with little opportunity for displays of temperament. Most significantly, Noelte created a true dialectic among the characters, revealing hitherto overlooked traits and attitudes.

The effects of Noelte's recension were most obvious in the last act: after Tusenbach went off to his duel, Irina walked into the house. The vast set remained totally empty for a few seconds, alone in its sterile beauty. A harsh white light broke over the scene and a clock struck abruptly. Irina met the news of the Baron's death in silence, in a chair facing the audience. She turned her head slightly from left to right, her mouth agape like a tragic mask; only then did she bow her head and sob "I knew it." Olga's last line chimed in immediately, "The music is so gay . . . time will pass and we shall leave for ever, we shall be forgotten . . . but

for those who live after us, our suffering will be transformed into joy."
This was spoken ponderously, in a tone bereft of hope. The sisters sat at a
distance from one another, while upstage Chebutykin read and the
leaves rustled. Forty lines were reduced to four, to avoid any summing-up
of the play's themes. "But," proclaimed Henning Rischbieter, the
influential arbiter of the journal *Theater Heute*, "this Chekhov born of the
present is more decisive, more provocative than anything we have seen
up to now on the German stage . . . a new phase in our understanding of
Chekhov's drama."[44]

In no time at all a full-fledged controversy had been engaged. Its
pretext was a production of *The Seagull* (*Die Möwe*), directed and designed
by Willi Schmidt for the Munich Kammerspiele in 1966, and set in a stylized, bright green grove with transparent interiors reminiscent of an
aquarium. In an article in *Theater Heute*[45] Schmidt, not unlike Krejča,
demanded a neutral attitude to the complex psychic structure of the
characters, equivalent to Chekhov's cold, analytic gaze. He argued that
Chekhov be played in a major key, the material kept cool, his heroes not
judged; the pauses were to be mere highlights, not triggers for mood.
These alterations would make Chekhov modern and easier to play than
he had been in 1900. This Chekhov was a sceptic *par excellence*, no aggressive prognosticator of revolutions.

The Munich public's response was to find Schmidt's subdued
Chekhov boring, dusty, old hat; they giggled at Treplev's last, silent scene
because it was held for much longer than usual. The critic Siegfried
Melchinger explained that even if ennui was Chekhov's theme,
Germans had no patience with it. "In no other land with a theatre has
the tradition of realism as a performance technique been so destroyed as
it has in Germany," Melchinger lamented.

In Germany the theatre has become a game of shocks. It's like that elsewhere,
but not exclusively. Elsewhere they learn, apply and accept techniques other
than shock: nuance, sensitivity, unspoken language, concentration.[46]

Shock tactics continued to be the standard method for bringing
Chekhov up-to-date, most obviously in Peter Zadek's *Cherry Orchard* (*Der
Kirschgarten*) at the Stuttgart Staatstheater in 1968. Throughout the late
sixties and seventies Zadek was deemed "der Verderber," "The
Corrupter," in Ivan Nagel's words a mocker at anything society held
sacred and a celebrant of anything public opinion judged immoral.
Anarchic and erotic in butchering sacred cows, Zadek's methods were
summed up by rival director Peter Stein as "Shakespeare with his
trousers down."

The Cherry Orchard had been the most popular of Chekhov's plays in Germany and Austria after the war; the high-water mark being Peter Sharoff's 1965 Vienna production, the first in the German-speaking world to bring out the comic elements. Zadek's *Orchard* was a revision of an earlier televised performance of 1966, designed by Wilfried Minks: the main elements of the set were a wall on a low platform parallel to the footlights and two porches right and left. Entrances and exits were stressed to the point of mania, with long, accentuated sliding movements. The estate was shown to be shabby and tawdry, far into its decline. Behind a long table, the masters and servants huddled together to share common soup spoons and casually arrayed bottles of bubbly. Zadek played up the proponents of the coming revolution: Trofimov (Peter Roggisch) came across as a career agitator-to-be, unkempt, crude, in a trenchcoat rather than a student uniform; Anya (Rita Leska), who at the start observed the grownups with a teen-ager's cold curiosity, adopted his radical slogans with enthusiasm. The sole token of resistance to this belief in the future came from Ranevskaya (Edith Heerdegen) in her accusation that Trofimov knew nothing about emotional suffering. The only fully drawn character was the Firs of Hans Mahnke, mechanically shuffling, always about to topple over; at the end, the director could risk concealing the old man almost entirely, supine on a bench behind the table, his white-begloved finger in the air.

The intentionally spare realism of Zadek's production was meant as a riposte to Noelte's "rich" attack on Chekhov's characters; but, because it almost totally eschewed any creative contribution from the actors, for Henning Rischbieter it failed to go beyond Noelte's *Three Sisters* in exploring the text.[47] Volker Canaris disagreed; for him, Zadek's approach was a step forward in the rejection of sentimentality and preciosity, and a step closer to Chekhov's poetic diagnoses. Siegfried Melchinger disapproved of what he saw as Zadek's distortion of the Meyerhold tradition; but when he came to report on Otomar Krejča's *Three Sisters*, where the "old text" was an incentive for the director's reinvigorating vision, Melchinger had to grant that the notion of a production being "true" to a work was a myth. Krejča's manifesto of the director's freedom and Melchinger's acceptance of it provided the theoretical grounding for a whole series of wildly eccentric stagings, with Chekhov's sceptical humanism as the rationale.[48]

This was abetted by Peter Urban's translations of all of Chekhov's prose, plays and letters in fifteen volumes (1973–81). Urban's project was equivalent to Ronald Hingley's Oxford Chekhov, but with a serious difference. Eager to make Chekhov sound like an Englishman, Hingley was not overscrupulous in his attention to rhetorical repetitions, sentence structure and such stylistic devices. Urban eschewed facile coinages, retaining the idiosyncratic phrases and unusual lexical and structural choices of the original. Highly restrained in his rendering, he erred on the side of exactitude, which provided dramaturges and directors the abundant raw material for their own alterations.

Among the new "manipulative" stagings was Zadek's next exercise in Chekhov, a *Seagull* at Bochum in 1973, wherein any historical, political, philosophical, or intellectual concerns were discarded in favour of an exclusive concentration on the "psycho-physical presence of the actor and the elemental event wherein 'people behave in front of people the way they are.'"[49] His first season at Bochum had been a spectacular series of assaults on his audience with violent deconstructions of *Little Man, What Now?* and *The Merchant of Venice*. The choice of *The Seagull* seemed sedate in contrast, and although it was performed half as often *Little Man*, it won for Zadek the highest accolades from the same critics who had sneered at the "slapdash" experiments of the previous season.[50]

The designer Götz Loepelmann laid a surface of overlapping thick planks separated by a scaffolding of steel pipes over the greater part of the orchestra pit and the forestage; much of the down left rake was covered with brown sailcloth. A sort of life-guard's stand of steel piping stood in the first rows of the auditorium, relocating Treplev's amateur stage among the spectators. The lake, which Chekhov had envisaged as a background, was sited behind the audience.

Spectators were also seated upstage, in front of a crumpled aluminium foil drop. The other scenic features were two non-reflective mirrors, and two wagons of spectators facing one another, with the stage floor the focal point between them. The lighting was kept very bright throughout, only occasionally dimmed or yellowed. The tables and chairs needed for the action were rearranged unostentiously. Zadek's point was that such a material construct, negligent of any aesthetic properties, was the correct arena for the development of physical and mental reality. Its immediacy and clarity were reminders that human beings were performing for human beings. This might seem to be a platitudinous truism about live theatre, but it revealed straightway that Zadek's *mise-en-scène* had nothing to do with the Russian intelligentsia at the turn-of-the-century or a debate on art vs reality.

Zadek was interested in the interlocking and unrequited loves. The intense desire to live and love was obvious even in the Sorin of Hans Mahnke; after each of his near-fatal apoplectic strokes, he strained with irritated discipline to pull himself together and live again. Hermann Lause, puny, high-shouldered, with incipient baldness and thick lenses refracting his large, sorrowful eyes, overloaded Treplev with inhibitions: he moved with a rapid, wooden gait, stuttered his words and sputtered his gestures. After Nina's Act IV visit, he flung his writings into the orchestra pit, and with unwonted serenity, walked off to meet his death.

In the first three acts, the Nina of Rosel Zech played against convention as a prim, short-haired young lady, boyishly angular in movement. This paid off in the last act, when, drenched with rain, she came to pay her adieux to Treplev and her youth. Then she was neither a poetic, fragile victim (the favourite interpretation in the West) nor a sober believer in the future (the favourite interpretation in the East), but, in her slippage between dementia and nostalgia, suggested a provisional existence, open to anything – including the possibility of turning into the Arkadina of Lola Müthel: a totally selfish histrion, a composite of artful effects.[51]

The style of German Chekhov initiated by Noelte's 1964 *Three Sisters* had been characterized by Rischbieter as "the highly sensitive aesthetic reduction of the play to a social condition *in extremis.*" The Zadek approach successfully supplanted it with an intensification of the characters' grotesque aspects and the situations viewed from without. The most extreme exercise in grotesquerie was carried out by Manfred Karge and Matthias Langhoff in their Bochum staging of *The Cherry Orchard* in 1981. They had learnt their materialism from Brecht and had already practiced it in their East Berlin production of *The Wild Duck*. Artists between two worlds, exiles from the GDR not yet at home in the GFR, they turned an alien gaze to the bourgeois world of their new environment.

The characters comprised a social group viewed from such a remote angle as to seem ridiculous. Keenly aware of the satires of Mayakovsky and Érdman, Karge and Langhoff updated the costumes to the 1920s, so that turn-of-the-century landowners were conflated with the venal practitioners of Lenin's New Economic Policy. The play opened in semi-darkness as a blonde marcelled Dunyasha came out the centre door to do up Lopakhin in his collar and tie. Firs used an electric coffee-machine. Gaev was nothing but a clothes-horse played by an actor decades too young for the part. Barefoot in sandals, Trofimov sprang across the stage, swinging his arms (*à la* Lopakhin), smiling constantly. None of the characters wallowed in mood: the lines were merely effusions of a social type and the gestures failed to illustrate the lines. The

29 Ranevskaya (Anneliese Römer), Lopakhin (Branko Samarovski) and Gaev (Michael Rastl) in the empty landscape of Act II of *Der Kirschgarten* (*The Cherry Orchard*), directed by Manfred Karge and Matthias Langhoff, Bochum, 1980. At right, Firs arrives on a bicycle with sunshade and lap-rugs.

danger of this farce approach was that feelings, even Varya's shrill reaction to abandonment, ceased to mean anything.

In Act II, all the characters were laid out in deck chairs in front of four doors cut in a white wall revealing a photographic landscape cloth with a railway track. Firs swathed them in plaid laprugs like mummies. The passerby, a kind of Gorkian tramp, surged out of the landscape, as if to suggest that there were no better men in prospect, no bright future, no compensatory hope. The directors restored Chekhov's original ending to the act, with Firs and Charlotta (who bicycled on stage) a brief interlude set outside the petty bourgeois world. It was an aggressive reduction of the GDR's ideological attitude to the West.

The most fully rounded of these inept figures was Anneliese Römer's Ranevskaya, a chain-smoking *mondaine* in high-button boots and a fur coat, with a raucous voice, a blend of self-pity and world-weariness: life in Paris has gone to hell, so what? Too bad. Life was to be lived. Act III was played as a masked ball in a salon behind glass doors, where one mask vomited on the stairs and Firs spat in the champagne, already diluted with water from a flower vase. Ranevskaya stalked the stage, a ringmistress in white breeches, high boots, black tailcoat, top hat, and whip. Her desperate search to replace her lost lover and her lax, indifferent lasciviousness were shown by seating Trofimov on her lap and kissing him (why not seduce her daughter's admirer?). She held her mask before her face until the end, refusing to display her grief.

The fourth act was trampled under in the hectic pace of departure: padded Epikhodov was clownishly trapped under an immense armchair, Varya clattered around with her keyring, Lopakhin's chainsaws whirred outside. The farewell of Gaev and Ranevskaya occurred in a single mute moment, leaving only Firs. As played realistically by Gert Voss, an actor barely forty, with a hairnet over his bald head, the old retainer could have been Krapp, a middle-aged man whose life has long been over.[52]

As might be expected, the critical camp was divided in its reaction. Heinz Klunker appreciated the staging as a sideswipe at "a whole tradition of production" that went back far beyond Noelte to Stanislavsky. Some of his colleagues found it refreshing in its irreverence and vivacity, no more off-putting than outlandish photos in a family album. But the headline in *Die Zeit* spoke for the adherents of tradition: "Karge/Langhoff chop down *The Cherry Orchard*." Characterizing this *Orchard* as a violent farce peopled by parasites out of George Grosz, animated only by cupidity and brute sexuality, they felt personally affronted that "We theatergoers" should be identified with "these extinct types, these people who no longer matter."[53]

The *reductio ad absurdum* of these "manipulative" productions, with their satirical unmasking of gargoyle characters, was reached in Roberto Ciulli's *The Seagull* in Mülheim (Theater an der Ruhr, 1984). Stanislavsky had proclaimed the stage's function to be mimetic; Ciulli, like so many of his German coadjutors, redefined the function as metaphoric. By cutting half the text, he contracted the play to a few graphically symbolic lines; the characters were reduced to a common denominator and then schematized.[54]

The show opened with a blind Sorin feeling his way with a cane to a red theatre curtain, an action in keeping with the surreal images and not always legible psychic crises of the production. They stood for Treplev's plans for a new theatre as well as his nightmare: Johannes Hellmann, tense and wide-eyed, sat in a framework of steel pipes like a bird on a twig, while the blasé Trigorin (Volker Roos) pursued Nina, and croaked like a mortally wounded gull in the pauses. Nina (Veronika Bauer) costumed as an ageless, whitefaced Pierrot with tinkling bells on a parasol was tied to a stake during the play-within-a-play, perhaps a wish fulfillment of Treplev's.

Life's arbitrariness was configured by the fortuity of games. The second act was a bizarre picnic, with a bout of musical chairs, and in Act III Sorin lay in an iron bedstead, waging a pillow fight with the others. In Act IV, snow fell over a black background, as the characters sat on a

30 Veronika Bauer as Nina at the stake in Treplev's play-within-a-play; *Die Möwe* (*The Seagull*) directed by Roberto Ciulli, Theater an der Ruhr, Mülheim, 1984.

mountain of suitcases around the empty bedstead – barely moving, still and dreamlike as a painting by Edvard Munch. An image of unseeing Fate, Sorin tossed the lotto pieces into a box and snapped the lid shut. At the end, with blood streaming from his temple, Treplev fell outside the curtain, and Arkadina was allowed to speak the last line: "It reminded me of the time . . . "

Not surprisingly, these directorial vagaries pushed the pendulum in the opposite direction, and throughout the 1980s, the German stage was also filled with lavishly illustrative productions, such as *The Seagull* of Augusto Fernandes in Hamburg (Deutsches Schauspielhaus,1982). It reeked *verismo*: the panoramic stage pictures crammed with three-dimensional trees, curtains that billowed in the breeze, asides and soliloquies delivered as voice-overs. As if to flesh out Ciulli's skeletal metaphors, overabundance was the keynote: all of Chekhov's discarded lines were replaced and all talk of love accompanied by groping, nuzzling, slobbering kisses. The quarrel between Treplev and his mother was protracted to include smashing dishes, tearing a dress, breaking a fishing-rod. In the last act, it took him forever to burn his manuscripts as he made endless trips to the stove like a wind-up Hedda Gabler. Such overexplicitness might have proved the bankruptcy of the Stanislavskian heritage, had it not been given new currency by Peter Stein.

OLD AND NEW AT THE SCHAUBÜHNE

At first Stein's *Three Sisters* at the Berlin Schaubühne would seem another effort to out-Moscow Moscow; but here the deployment of light and space evoked a more existential meaning. Karl Ernst Herrmann's scenery did call to mind a series of paintings: the first two acts took place in a spacious interior, a large, empty drawing-room lit from a windowed veranda. In the first act it was flooded with light, in the second enveloped in darkness, pointing the shift from radiant hope to inspissated gloom. The third act, up under the eaves, also used a very wide, almost dioramic space, but the stage grew shallower and the ceiling lowered. The oppression of the sisters and the confinement of their lives became palpable. Finally, for the Act IV exterior, Hermann gave in to his notorious taste for gigantism: the stage opened out to its fullest depth (45 metres) and height, with more three-dimensional trees (no birches, however) and a vista that seemed to stretch to the vanishing point. All these trappings of naturalism contributed to the symbolic message, for Stein added to the tableau of the sisters and Chebuytkin, Andrey far up-centre, pointing

31 The receding expanse of Act IV of Peter Stein's *Die Drei Schwestern* (*Three Sisters*), Schaubühne, Berlin, 1984.

out to his little son – what? the departing soldiers? the coming Revolution? the empty future?

Stein's only obtrusive directorial device was the occasional piece of music played beneath moments of musing and despair, which was never as effective as his exploitation of sounds and images provided by Chekhov. In the first act, when the party guests froze enrapt, listening to the humming top Fedotik set in action, it was as if grown-up children were arrested in eternity, hearkening to the music of the spheres. When the Shrovetide maskers in Act II came up the stairs into the darkened house and cast exaggerated shadows on the walls, they resembled Maurice Sendak's "wild things" – suppressed desires and passions clamouring to erupt into a household inhibited by Natasha's domestic tyranny and the sisters' own malaise.

As Olga, Edith Clever limited herself to a constant tone of complaint and grievance. Corinna Kirchhoff avoided playing Irina as an ingenue by having her, from the start, a bit hard, aggressive and prone to sulk. Masha, portrayed by the sharp-edged Jutta Lampe, made it clear that this was a woman totally at a loss, wholly unaware of what to do with her life. In each act there was a moment when the three came together in a monumental grouping. After Vershinin departed with his regiment,

Masha kept wandering around in ever-narrowing circles like a trapped animal, unable to come to rest. These circlets were miniature parodies of the sweeping loops in which the characters had drifted earlier in the play.

Most of the reviews waxed rapturous over the production's beauty; in Friedrich Luft's words "Chekhov's great elegy was sensually imprinted on our eyes." But Rischbieter thought it a step backward to a position halfway between Noelte's sensitive reduction of the play to a social impasse and a grotesque production seen from outside, like the Karge/Langhoff *Orchard*. Rischbieter was annoyed by Stein's indulgence in sentimental superflux and technical slickness, which seemed to cast no new light on the work. He summed it up as Peter Brook's "Dead Theatre," a museum piece, full of errant supernumeraries.[55]

His disappointment may have derived in part from *Three Sisters'* divergence from the Schaubühne program. The theatre had been founded as an alternative voice, a creative collective with a strong leftist and activist bent. After moving from its original space in the squalid bohemia of Kreuzberg to its superbly well-equipped house on Lehninerplatz, it was examined regularly for signs of *embourgeoisement*. In fact, Stein's *Three Sisters* could be seen as an extension of his earlier critiques of West German society. Erika Fischer-Lichte has described it as a confrontation of pyschological realism with historical and aesthetic factors that permitted its audience to enjoy a "socio-psychological discharge." The burghers of the Bundesrepublik were allowed to identify with figures in an obsolescent society; their own "bad and boring life" was illuminated by an artistic facsimile, and they were led to wallow in pleasurable sympathy with their own fecklessness. The production was not so much a prolongation of Stanislavsky as an interrogatory, stretching the naturalistic décor to its outer limits. The punctilious realism of costumes, props and gestures was scanned closely to reveal the black holes in the characters. Stein's *Three Sisters* became a moral autopsy of a neurotic family imprisoned in a house, whose only horizon was an empty sky painted on a cyclorama. Ultimately, the desire for solitude was greater than that for love.[56]

Nor had the Schaubühne abandoned its concerns with the dregs of society. That same season it performed Chekhov's early one-act melodrama *On the High Road* (*An der grossen Strasse*) in its old Werkstatt space near the Berlin wall. A huge warehouse room had been whitewashed and then artfully distressed with holes, patches of missing plaster, specks of black. At one end was a narrow ledge that served as the stage, with benches along the back wall. This was the roadside dosshouse, where pil-

32 The white-on-white setting of *An der grossen Strasse* (*On the High Road*), designed by
Gilles Aillaud and directed by Klaus Michael Grüber, Schaubühne Werkstatt, Berlin,
1984. L.–r.: Martina Krauel as Efimovna, Nina Will as a vagrant, Willem Menne as
Bortsov, Mathias Gnädiger as Tikhon Evstigneev and Urs Bihler as Savva.

grims and derelicts holed up in a proto-*Lower Depths*. As everyone knew,
the wall concealed The Wall, the river Spree with warning placards, and
on the opposite shore grey buildings, the East.[57]

As the audience slowly filtered in, the innkeeper Tikhon and a couple
of pilgrims were already on stage. Some of the sleeping forms were
dummies, others human. Gradually more entered so that there was
almost no floor space to move about in; they seemed glued to the wall or
fallen off it. At intervals Tikhon would renew the burning spill that provided the illumination (and was a crucial device for measuring time, suggesting the infinitude of night). The costumes were bleached in grey,
beige and off-white, except for the red shirt of the robber Merik. Most of
the makeup was pallid, but anyone connected with the gentry or alcoholism was painted in the style of the old Habima with great blotches of
cobalt blue and bright red, a Chagallian effect.

Karl Michael Grüber the director stretched the "dramatic sketch" to
two hours without a break. The play was taken very slowly with enormous gaps between lines: most readings were subdued, weary, almost

subliminal. Certain dramatic highlights – the handing-over of the locket, Merik's attack on Bortsov's former wife – were presented as frozen tableaux. The cumulative impression was erosive, but could not prevent this "dark and stormy night" with its contrived coincidences and overwrought violence from prompting laughter. The high road was meant to lead to despair, but the melodramatics of the plot were too much at odds with the presentational sophistication of the production, and with an audience schooled over the past decades to respond to direc-torial ingenuity.

CHAPTER 14

Ut pictura poesis *(Italy and France 1945–1985)*

For me Chekhov personifies theatre just as Mozart personifies music . . . Chekhov's theatre serves as the best of all answers to Rousseau's question. No, man is not good by nature, he is avaricious, hard, vain, peevish, selfish and vulgar. But in Chekhov's plays, despite the infirmity of human nature, deep bonds of affection and suffering connect all people.

François Mauriac[1]

THE ORCHARD TRANSCENDENT

In post-war Italy, directors of Chekhov either trudged in the footsteps of Sharoff (who had moved to the Netherlands, to remain faithful to "the lyric realization of the dream")[2] or dabbled in tentative experiment. Orazio Costa Giovangigli's *The Cherry Orchard* (*Il giardino dei ciliegi*, Teatro Quirino, Rome, 1946) acknowledged the Russian tradition while trying to bring out the play's universality through the décor. First planned in 1943, it was influenced by the atmosphere distilled by "the most valid and authentic Chekhovian memories" of Nemirovich's 1933 production. But Giovangigli wanted to go beyond environmentally determined characterizations to examine

traces of experience seen from a landscape as a psychic state, to achieve a staging of lyric character, open to a triple series of co-existent and inseparable interpretations: the forecasting of events, the event itself, and its anagogic projection: an aspect that derived from my researches into the interpretation that Chekhov had worked hardest to repress.[3]

What this meant in practice was a foregrounding of extravagant inconsequentiality, with maximal importance given to Firs and Charlotta as abstract dimensions of a surreality. Firs was so far outside the times that his nearly inaudible responses emerged from the distant past; he troubled the others like a mummified but obsessive conscience.

33 The Chirico-esque setting for Act II of *Il giardino dei ciliegi* (*The Cherry Orchard*)
designed by Tullio Costa Giovangigli for his brother Orazio,
Teatro Quirino, Rome, 1946.

"Like a ghost, he renders acceptable the invisible presence of the other surreal essences . . . " Charlotta, on the other hand, was presented by Giovangigli as a quasi-diabolical creature, the fantastical in naturalistic camouflage. A ventriloquist in contact with the spirit world, her voice was mediumistic. "If there is a cry to utter, Charlotta utters it; if there is an echo to resound, Charlotta sounds the echo; if the hearts of all the characters are to open to confession, who can begin the dangerous game? Charlotta." This impressed Giovangigli as Chekhov's most brilliant stroke, a renewal of the function of the Shakespearian clown.[4]

To project a universal significance, the settings by the director's brother Tullio were reminiscent of the surrealistic canvasses of Giorgio di Chirico and Salvador Dalí – ghostly, poignant, and packed with vatic symbols. The symbolism got out of hand in Act II, where Giovangigli tried to draw a likeness between rows of poplars and the telegraph poles which *fin de siècle* poets represented as "a wind-plucked harp." "With its long copper wires, the picture assumed a poignant reality when the young lovers pressed their ears against one of the poles – as all those of my generation did – to get drunk on this strange music descending, as it were, from heaven."[5]

By 1955, Giovangigli realized that his stylistic concept had become dated and would have to be superceded; he speculated that in future he would dispense with realism altogether, to bring the play closer to electronic music. His later productions never matched his hyperbole, however (he saw Vershinin with his two daughters as a "Chekhovian Oedipus").[6] Both he and Italy in general settled down to more staid versions, such as the elegant and seductive *verismo* of Luchino Visconti's *Three Sisters* (*Tre sorelli*) designed by Franco Zeffirelli (Teatro Eliseo, Rome, 1952). Zeffirelli set out to create "a dream Russia, one correct in its details with a remote, ethereal air." Visconti's penchant for Chekhov in the grand manner of Puccini persisted in his *Uncle Vanya* (*Zio Vanya*, 1955) and *Cherry Orchard* (1965), which displayed "a row of authentic – and therefore all the more fake and unconvincing cherry trees."[7]

The director who was to make *The Cherry Orchard* flower for all Europe was Giorgio Strehler. When he co-founded the Piccolo Teatro di Milano, his leftist politics drew him to a naturalism tempered by Brechtian alienation effects. The Soviet icon of Stanislavsky was a crucial point of reference, but Strehler encouraged what he called *immedesimazione* – identification with the character, but with an amalgam of Brechtian *Gestus* and Italian exuberance. Unlike Visconti who preserved a strict fourth wall, Strehler perpetuated the native tradition of playing to the house, so that local audiences continued to give standing ovations to bravado scenes. When he first turned to Chekhov, his concerns were sociological, but gradually his imagination unfolded to new aesthetic considerations.[8]

Strehler's 1948 *Seagull* exhibited a concatenation of three impotent systems: Treplev's "new world," feeble, immature and doomed to fail; Trigorin's world of outworn charm and convention; and the women's "weak world." A similar cosmic confrontation also structured Strehler's first *Cherry Orchard* of 1955, planted with the usual blooming trees.

Despite a warm reception from audiences, this *Cherry Orchard* dissatisfied Strehler; he later called it unrealized, in a state of suspension. He had begun to stage it, while exhausted, a few days after the creative explosion of his production of Goldoni's *Villegiatura* trilogy. Rushed, inexperienced and rehearsing on the *Villegiatura* set, Strehler let the same sense of *morbidezza* and the "end of a society" which had permeated Goldoni seep into Chekhov. This *Cherry Orchard* was simply a variation on the presentiment of cataclysm.[9] The style was naturalistic, the setting bourgeois, and the focus on "the day-to-day lives of individuals tragically trapped in antagonistic social and historical circumstances."[10] The old world was judged harshly, and even Trofimov, the "most extreme wing of the opposition," was made a part of the world he criticized. He would probably not remain alien in the "new world," Lopakhin's concrete and hostile reality. Such a polarization smacked more of Gorky's *Mother* than of Chekhov.[11]

Platonov e gli altri (1958/9), in a translation by the historian of Russian theatre Ettore Lo Gatto, also followed a major burst of creativity, Strehler's important productions of Brecht's *Threepenny Opera* and *Good Person of Setzuan*; and their ethos coloured the heavy-handed vaudeville of his treatment. All the characters were handled with acrid humour as contemporaries and yet "alienated," tragic and pathetic, alarming and ludicrous. The doctor's last line, "Now one must deal with the living" was a warning to look to the future, not through Chekhov, but through Strehler. Although it ran till two in the morning, even with cuts, the critical acclaim was overwhelming.[12]

When, after his great success in exploring lyrical space in Goldoni's *Servant of Two Masters* and *Il Campiello*, Strehler returned to *The Cherry Orchard* in 1974, he decided that, like *Platonov*, it was a mirror of his own times and its relevance had to be made manifest. Chekhov was a poet not of renunciation and despair, but of the pain of living and doing what needs to be done, to the bitter end.

A masterpiece on the scale of *King Lear*, *The Tempest* and *The Magic Flute*, like them *The Cherry Orchard* existed outside any historic period. To bring out this element, Chekhov had to be disengaged from literary, naturalistic and folkloric accretions. Stanislavsky had to be discarded in favor of a more universal, symbolic and fantastical perspective, but without falling into abstraction and a loss of reality.[13] Here Strehler offered his famous image of the play as a nest of Chinese boxes: the first is that of the "real," with its human interest narrative, *coups de théâtre*, events, atmosphere, characters, and family background. The second, which encloses and amplifies it, is the history box: the dialectical relations of social classes, with objects, gestures, and costumes alienated as part of the historical discourse. And the third, all-encompassing, is the box of life, a timeless parable about mortality, played out in a metaphysical dimension. The House, its Rooms, the Generations, the Master–Servant relations take on capital letters, and the play becomes a poetic paraphrase of human destiny.

Each box contained dangers to be avoided. The first invited pedantic key-hole peeping and a taste for reconstruction, *à la* Visconti; the second might isolate the characters as historic symbols, drain them of common humanity and petrify them as thematic figures (the Marxist approach). Strehler considered that Krejča had fallen into that trap, setting up Gaev and Ranevskaya as spokesmen of a vicious, deliquescent class. The risk of the third box was to place the characters outside time as neutral, universal ciphers. The director's task was to juggle all three boxes in a production "capable of vibrating like a light flickering to this threefold stimulation."[14]

The essential question of the orchard had to be solved first, for it was the hero of the play. Strehler believed that no one had previously realized it in all its plenitude. The symbolic abstractions of Svoboda and his followers, though interesting and poetically dense, evaded the problem. It had to be seen but not shown, foregrounded but not made too explicit. The design solution of his scenographer Luciano Damiani was brilliantly simple: the orchard was a "big top" of transparent gauze which, manipulated by stage hands, could palpitate to the feelings of the characters, float over the orchestra into the audience like an ideal ceiling, and rustle to produce a "transposed" sound. This living membrane was strewn with dead leaves, which fell on the stage in the last act.

This combination of sky and orchard which one minute undulates, seeming to murmur something gentle and tender, then hovers so as to perfect the characters before gliding down to caress them, is the basic symbol of the production. This imaginary orchard includes the audience too as we watch life going by, absorbed in the people who take part in it, well aware of our inability to change anything.[15]

Referring to Chekhov's letter to Stanislavsky about ladies in white summer dresses in a white garden (5 February 1903), Strehler was convinced that the play had taken shape in the author's mind as "a shooting white light."[16] His setting became an achromatic space, at once summer and winter. Whiteness guaranteed the assimilation of the protagonists into their environment, realizing Andrey Bely's remark in his 1907 essay that the "the characters are as transpicuous as shadows." White dominated the costumes, which evolved over the course of rehearsals as the actors pulled random pieces out of four wardrobe baskets. For Strehler, this improvisation was a metaphor for work on Chekhov: guided by the thread of a central critical idea, poetic intuition would correct the semantic study of a text in which "everything is written down."[17]

With the spatial puzzle solved, Strehler considered time. Real time in *The Cherry Orchard* does not correspond to theatrical time. The five years before the curtain goes up had been enough to change the world; hence the nervousness and tension in Act I. In actual performance, he renounced a slow "Russian-style" pace. Act I ran forty minutes, Act II thirty, Act III thirty-five, and Act IV the twenty minutes Chekhov had called for.

34 The shimmering leaf-spattered gauze hovering over the world of Giorgio Strehler's
Il giardino dei ciliegi (*The Cherry Orchard*), Piccolo Teatro di Milano, 1974.

Strehler was the first director to inquire minutely into the nursery aspect of the first act. At the Moscow Art Theatre, it had been the non-descript passageway mentioned in the stage directions, and other productions had followed that lead. Believing that "the space embalms childhood," Strehler filled it with remnants of the youth of Lyuba and Lyonya: two tiny desks painted white, a lacquered dwarf table, diminutive chairs, a magic lantern, toys. There they relived their childhood, weighing sugar in the miniature scales, drinking tea from doll's teacups. Gaev pulled a little wooden train and blew a whistle. The only "grown-up" pieces of furniture were a sofa and the centenarian cupboard, an intermediary between the *dramatis personae* and the real or imagined or symbolic orchard that dates from time immemorial. The creaking of its drawer suggested, as in a futurist play by Marinetti, that even objects felt pain.

When Gaev accidentally bumped the cupboard, it opened and a plethora of playthings poured out in a gentle avalanche, ending with a doll's perambulator that rolled along the stage like Grisha's coffin and jostled Ranevskaya, making her cry. The room then became a kind of cemetery of their youth: the siblings and Varya tried to put it back in order but could not, and wound up sitting on the floor amid old clothes and furs. They came down to the forestage to look at the orchard while a music box played, and behind a desk as she recalled her son's death, Ranevskaya sat at the crossroads of two childhoods. Also at a desk, dipping his finger in the ink-well, Gaev offered his solutions. Anya fell asleep on a school bench.

Act II had, for Strehler, the aspect of an interlude or polyphonic cantata. It was the only act in which nothing happens; the characters simply wait for sundown. The stage floor, steeply raked towards the audience, undulated into mounds; and the big grey carpet of the nursery was pulled up to become the sky. Against this starkly lit white rhomboid the pale costumes faded; the characters became geometric shapes in an abstract painting.[18] The toy train from Act I now ran from one end of the stage to the other, into the wings and back along the footlights, being simultaneously plaything, memory and hallucination. Downstage was the mystery of the non-existent orchard which stretched towards the orchestra, a curtain of light between stage and house.

The picnic atmosphere, with real wine and bread, evoked a *déjeuner sur l'herbe* painted by Renoir rather than Manet. Physicality erupted brutally at the start of Act II, as Yasha and Dunyasha all but made love, rolling in an embrace down the rake; while she rested, he speechified between her legs. This violent animal sexuality clashed with the sterility which seemed to control the others. Desire was absent although their physicality was conspicuous. The principal task of Firs and Yasha was to tend to their masters' bodies. Ranevskaya's body was that of a fragile plant or a porcelain doll; Gaev's that of a giant sleepy toddler, the baby Pantagruel. In contrast, in a radical departure from the usual casting, the Lopakhin of Franco Graziosi was slim and elegant, assimilated into the aristocratic world he was already supplanting.

As for the snapped string, Strehler decided to suppress it, since only the characters hear it. "Until anyone proves the contrary, today I believe that this famous sound is a literary hoax, a writer's sediment . . . created deliberately to give a rhythmic resonance to the last act finale."[19] After the characters hearkened to it within themselves, another pause ensued: a freeze-frame in which they watched in horror as the toy train crossed the stage, bearing with it the realization that they had trivialized the world.

What intrigued Strehler about Act III was the recurring image of billiards: balls bouncing, clicking, rebounding, a symbol of life as a gamble, not pure chance so much as criss-cross, conflict, collision, the Gaev family's ruinous reliance on luck. He decided ultimately not to put the billiard table centre, but did orchestrate the offstage sound effects, and littered the stage with chairs in a grouping that was constantly broken and reassembled. Without mentioning Ionesco, Strehler spoke of empty chairs as a symbol of waiting. Firs and Varya rearranged them, Ranevskaya scattered them, Lopakhin knocked them over, as he did the toys in Act I. Valentina Cortese's Ranevskaya achieved a comic note here, staging her life like a diva, tossing the torn telegram in the air like confetti, drinking champagne and breaking the glass, sobbing theatrically. Her powdered face made her look like a circus clown or disarticulated puppet, playing a doubles-act with Charlotta. She took Trofimov on her lap, not in lust but in imitation of a strange Pietà.

In the last act, the ancient cupboard remained, both reality and symbol, prolonging the age of the room. Before leaving, Anya played with the toys once more, suggesting that her dream of a future was only another puerile game. Then all the characters at the same moment donned black overcoats and shawls, as if angels of death had flung their black wings over the living. This group portrait of the entire cast, including Charlotta's black poodle, was shown in profile or from the back, heads bowed, as each of them moved upstage right into the wings. This valedictory image impressed on the audience's memory an etching of departure, which was theatrical, historical, existential, and true to life, all at the same time. Strehler calculated his *mise-en-scène* to the millimetre as an artistic epiphany arriving right on cue.[20]

At that moment, Ranevskaya, in her fur hat and coat, almost swooned, while the chivalrous Gaev, his coat flung casually over his shoulders, upheld her as if they were facing a firing squad. The pose was quite natural and yet sculptural. Their embrace, held for a few moments, pulled the action out of the inconsequential flow of life, to present the eternal plasticity of a monument. Ranevskaya was the only character oblivious to time: she was one to tell others they had aged, but never said it of herself. "This regret for a lost childhood," wrote Strehler, "makes her the symbol of our mysterious incursions into the ancestral world, up to that warm and silent maternal uterus which once protected us and for which we always feel profound nostalgia."[21]

In the role, Valentina Cortese was the beacon of Strehler's intent: mercurial, trembling, riffling her hair, incapable of standing still, registering sensations like the needle on an electrocardiograph.[22] Before leaving, Cortese caressed the furniture and then disappeared under the immense veil that came down to cover it all. Time swallowed her up. Firs lay down slowly on the sofa-cover, a catafalque of embalmed time, to flow away with the phantom past.[23]

This *Cherry Orchard* was arguably Strehler's greatest achievement to date, and certainly the most beautiful production of Chekhov of its era. The beauty arose not from ostentation, but from the white on white of a Malevich painting.[24] This dazzling blankness was its most influential legacy: the white orchard in bloom, the white cloud-capped background, the white appliqué on the white dresses of the women, the white suits of the men, the luminous harmony of etiolation between humans and heaven. By moving beyond the true-to-life, Strehler could play with objects, time and space as if they were the toys in the nursery.[25] As Georges Banu explained,

The stage stops being an inhabitable space and becomes a page for an *écriture* whose every term is symbolic, for it is filled only with objects extracted from the daily routine and whose only task is to focus anxiety and memory . . . The spectacle evacuates every possibility of even a fleeting confusion with reality.[26]

FORMAL ORCHARDS AND TRAINED GULLS

When the Moscow Art Theatre paid its last pre-war visit to Paris in 1937, there was no Chekhov in its repertory. The Soviet authorities were eager to promote a socialist–realist line, and so included only contemporary propaganda pieces. He also remained off the boards during the German Occupation. Yet, no sooner had the Allies reoccupied the city in autumn 1944, when *The Proposal* (*La demande au mariage*) was staged at the Théâtre Pigalle, rapidly followed by a *Cherry Orchard* (*La cerisaie*) and a *Bear* (*L'Ours*) at the Odéon and *Swan Song* (*Le chant de cygne*) at the Comédie Française. This resurgence connoted more than a desire for cultural "normalcy." After the Occupation, a "striving for the best, for faith and hope" was current. Although it was seldom stated in so many words, the post-war years, ideologically dominated by existentialism and communism, welcomed Russian authors. Communist writers tended, however, to characterize Chekhov with the usual bromides: "a great master of critical realism, a patriot of his people, a divulger and lover of life."[27]

Despite the ideological *imprimatur*, in the late 1940s and early fifties Chekhov's plays were relegated to studio theatres, because boulevard managements and state-supported houses thought them uncommercial, unperformable and boring. When Antoine Vitez began work in the theatre in 1948, Chekhov was taken to be very mysterious, the texts evanescent in meaning, obscured by Northern mist and Russian vapours, and definitely too long for so little action.[28]

This was perhaps the downside of the Pitoëff tradition, hardly dispelled by the series of revivals which Georges's son Sacha staged with his three sisters (beginning with *Oncle Vania*, Studio des Champs-Elysées, 1950). Sacha Pitoëff usually worked from his father's notes, but added new touches of his own; he perpetuated a certain stereotype of Chekhov as the recorder of the absurdity of everyday life, whose dialogue either meant nothing or was deliberately banal. The lines were delivered like "little dead or detachable leaves from 'life.'"[29]

The turning-point came with the fiftieth anniversary of Chekhov's death in 1954. Memorial productions burgeoned: Jean-Louis Barrault's *The Cherry Orchard*; a montage of novellas entitled *La matinée d'un homme de lettres* conceived by Tania Balachova at the Théâtre de la Huchette; *The Seagull* (*La Mouette*) adapted and directed by Suria Magito of the Centre dramatique de l'Est at the Théâtre Hébertot (supervised by Michel Saint-Denis); and Sacha Pitoëff's *Three Sisters* (*Trois Soeurs*) at the Théâtre de l'Oeuvre. Over the next few years, all the major plays would be restaged frequently, turning Chekhov into the most popular playwright in France. "One might think that an idiosyncratic process of crystallization had occurred and Chekhov, who for all his seeming simplicity is a complicated writer, was finally understood in France. The symphonic structure of his plays, their multiple levels hidden behind monologues and, in particular, dumbshows, had now become obvious."[30]

Georges Pitoëff had never tackled *The Cherry Orchard*, so that Barrault had the opportunity to discover the play for the French, who had hitherto seen it only in Russian as staged by the Moscow Art Theatre and the Prague Group. The Compagnie Renault-Barrault first played it in South America in the summer of 1954, and opened in Paris at the Théâtre Marigny the following October. Barrault considered it the manifesto of one of the most important periods of his artistic development, whose motto was

> Of man.
> By man.
> For man.

His *Cherry Orchard* not only initiated a new reading of Chekhov in France, but came as a reversal of Barrault's own creative self-awareness.

In an essay, "Why *The Cherry Orchard*?," Barrault rated the play as Chekhov's masterpiece because it was the most universal. Drawing on his experience as a mime, he described the play as a vast pantomime unrolling over the course of two hours' silence, and occasionally ornamented by a speech or a poem. Like all theatre, it was uniquely about the present moment and just as hard to grasp. For all its seeming slowness and stasis, the play was packed with action, whose catalyst was the sale of the estate.

> Act I The Cherry Orchard is in danger of being sold.
> Act II The Cherry Orchard is about to be sold.
> Act III The Cherry Orchard is sold.
> Act IV The Cherry Orchard has been sold.

The rest is life. Barrault aligned the characters along a scheme of time, with Gaev as the past, Lopakhin the present and Trofimov the future.[31]

Barrault held the play to be a parable, capable of projecting everyday life on the broadest metaphysical canvas. Without being sociologically realistic, it was imbued with lyric realism, so that everything on stage had to be real but not naturalistic: one could dispense with ceilings, trees, distant views which did not intervene physically in the action. He also avoided stylization which he equated with dehumanization.[32] The first and last act set accorded with Chekhov's stage directions, but the second act kept only a garden bench, crudely hammered together from rough boughs. In Act III, the ballroom was composed of arches and luxurious mahogany furniture. The light-plot for each setting was meant to correspond to the inner movement of the plot. The rising sun through the many windows suggested hope; the dark orchard of the second act conveyed bitter sorrow; the brightly burning sconces and brilliant chandelier in the third provided artificial light in a windowless space, where the orchard was invisible; Act IV seemed as if a hurricane had blown through.

The translator, Georges Neveux, was a well-known poet, the author of the lyrical drama *Juliette, ou la Clef des songes* (known abroad chiefly through Marcel Carné's weak film adaptation). Neveux, who had rendered Shakespeare, Lope da Vega, Shaw and *The Diary of Anne Frank* into French, scorned adaptation, although he claimed to translate the "soul" of the play, thus rationalizing his alterations to the text. "Why do you talk about the seventies," was updated to "the eighties" to bring the play closer to a time of revolution, and Buckle turned into Spinoza. Lopakhin's joke that Trofimov will soon be fifty was changed to seventy, since Barrault who played the perennial student was approaching fifty. In his eagerness to make the language as natural as possible, Neveux stripped away many of Chekhov's repetitions and added embroidery of his own. Eager to please an audience fond of Anouilh's whimsy, he had Charlotta say of her dog "He's not trained, but that'll come in time" and Ranevskaya reminisce, "My grandfather wrote a song about cherry-picking. If I had my guitar . . . " To strengthen the difference between Trofimov and Lopakhin, the latter was regularly coarsened; "You are needed to transform the world, the way a pike is for the cleansing of ponds. Wherever you have passed, nothing remains," he was told in Act II.[33]

The Prague group, the Pitoëffs and other émigrés had conveyed the idea that Russian plays in France had to be staged by Russians or with their assistance. Barrault made no attempt to lay on Slavic colour; the sets and characters kept referring back to a purely French reality. He recognized that the brisk French actor, accustomed to delivering speeches, had to slow down if he were to realize the action between the lines. "Therefore, *The Cherry Orchard, in French*, unfolds *for Frenchmen*, with a French slowness and not with a Russian slowness that would be meaningful only for Russians."[34] In Act I, the characters hummed "Le temps des cerises," a love-song redolent of *la belle époque*. Trimming the sails to suit a French craft may have pleased Parisian audiences, but it disturbed foreign observers: Kenneth Tynan found that Chekhov's genius shrivelled "under the searchlight of the French language" and that, with the mists dispelled, Chekhov's "vague evocative outlines" sharpened into "razor-edge silhouettes."[35] Which merely indicates that Tynan shared the English preference for a fogbound Chekhov.

Barrault's consort Madeleine Renaud had been alternating Marivaux's *Les Fausses confidences* with Feydeau's *Occupe-toi d'Amélie!*; those heroines' coquettry and frivolity were transferred to Ranevskaya. Short, ultra-feminine in lacy blouses, her doll-like eyes agog, her smile soft and alluring, her voice high-pitched, her dainty hands gesticulating vividly, Renaud suggested refined feelings, human frailty, and irresponsibility.[36] Similarly, Pierre Bertin's Gaev had a kind of careless elegance that smacked less of bygone Russia than of the early Romantics. Just as Renaud suggested the tradition of the charming Parisienne, Bertin was, in Robert Kemp's words, an "overblown Lamartine."[37] Nor was there much of the Russian merchant in Jean Desailly's Lopakhin, almost as dandified as Gaev, with a Velasquez beard and beautifully tailored suits with silk lapels. Nothing of half-literate Ermolay was left in his graceful movements and expressive gestures. Barrault accentuated Lopakhin's deep inner attraction to Ranevskaya: not love but a yearning for the past she represents. In the end, he could not conceal his own inner defeat, so his last look round was steeped in pain and sorrow.

Barrault as Trofimov and Nicole Bergier as Anya stood for a new era. Soulmates, elective affinities, alien to their surroundings, they danced together at the ball with a gaiety that was the only one to seem genuine; even while waltzing with others, they stole glances at one another from across a crowded room. Such complicity and an awareness of what was transpiring connected them throughout. At first, Barrault's Trofimov seemed unspectacular: cleanshaven, colourless, in eyeglasses that made him look like a budding anarchist. But Barrault endowed him with a mind, a sincerity and a beauty of feeling, free from all illusions.

The lightness of the acting dispelled the persistent idea of the play as a tragedy, and the high comedy was heightened even more by a message of historical progress. The critics all spoke of the pleasant mood in which people left the play. Marcel Capron entitled his review of the 1960 revival, "Joie . . . Joie . . . "[38] In fact, the revival deepened the performance, so that Lopakhin and Ranevskaya seemed to become more Russian with time, more in tune with the music of Chekhov's work.

Music was commonly evoked in discussions of Chekhov. Gabriel Marcel mentioned Debussy and Chopin, François Mauriac Mozart. Jean-Jacques Gautier exclaimed, "You listen to the play like music [for] it is also a work of music."[39] He was referring to André Barsacq's 1955

35 The passerby intrudes in Jean-Louis Barrault's *La Cerisaie* (*The Cherry Orchard*),
Théâtre Marigny, Paris, 1954. Jean Desailly as Lopakhin, Barrault as Trofimov,
Madeleine Renaud as Ranevskaya, Pierre Bertin as Gaev and Simone Valère as Varya.

Seagull at the Atelier, in Georges Pitoëff's translation. The simultaneous runs of Barrault's *Orchard*, Barsacq's *Seagull* and Sacha Pitoëff's *Three Sisters* provoked a great deal of re-evaluation. Barrault had omitted everything Russian to bring out the universally human subject of the play, and chose a French rhythm and tempo in which to perform it. Sacha Pitoëff went for a specifically Russian atmosphere, and Barsacq worked for a synthesis.[40] By providing alternatives the three directorial approaches freed Chekhov from the heavy hand of a single tradition.

This naturalization of Chekhov to the French stage was consummated the following year when France's state theatre, the Théâtre National Populaire, hauled *Untitled Play* out of the archives and, in Pol Quentin's adaptation *Ce fou de Platonov*, enthroned it in a repertory of masterworks by Shakespeare, Molière, Hugo and Musset. Although a version of *Untitled* had already been staged at the Theatre Royal, Stockholm, the press stressed the "discovery" aspect (though they tended to confuse it with *Ivanov*), and the play was discovered in truth for Europe and America, which saw more than twenty versions over the next three years, from Alma-Ata to Buenos Aires.

The thirty-two performances of the TNP, which had an influence far beyond their number, commenced on 17 May 1956; the brilliant cast included Jean Vilar as Platonov, Maria Casarès as Anna Petrovna, Daniel Sorano as Ivan Triletsky, Georges Wilson as Nikolay Triletsky, and Philippe Noiret as Osip. Before the first rehearsal, Vilar, who also directed, held twenty-three three-hour meetings with the adapter to revise, scene by scene and phrase by phrase, the "magma" of Chekhov's legacy, reducing a five-hundred-page script to about a hundred and fifty pages.[41] Vilar regarded the play as a rich repository of Chekhov's later themes, "loss of estate, pre-Revolutionary period, conflicts in which the women are all strong and decisive, the men weak and vacillating, role of usurers and the estate, tragic absurdity of provincial life, fear or scorn of religious subjects (Chekhov is agnostic)." Its great statement was

fate is formed by character. Which doesn't mean that all the heroes in our classics have character. Chekhov says somewhere about character: 'Why centre my heroes on a single feeling, when life is complex and the individual himself is alternately noble and vile, cowardly and courageous, etc . . .'[. . .]

The play ends tragically. Death of Platonov. And yet the tone of play is funny, lively, humorous.[42]

This led to critical confusion over whether the play was comedy or tragedy, citing a similar confusion in Vilar's performance. Dressed in a checked vest, cabbage green trousers, and yellow shoes, with waxed moustache and pomaded hair, he suggested a dandy out of Labiche or Offenbach.

Edouard Pignon's setting was unwontedly realistic and prismatic for the TNP, but that was part of Vilar's conception of the Russian spirit. The second act with its line of gradually diminishing and vanishing telegraph poles economically suggested the grey and boundless steppe. Vilar admitted that the dialogue indicated a quantum of realism, but it would be a mistake to let the enivronment dominate or constitute the central attraction. "I demand complete freedom. For a play by Chekhov as well as any other. Having established this principle, a director of any talent will nevertheless soon see that he is not free. The greater the play, the more the director is obliged to be an interpreter only and not a creator."[43] In response, the Russian director Boris Babochkin, voicing a certain Soviet proprietorship in Chekhov, objected to "the superficial knowledge of the epoch and the national character of the play."[44]

Hard on the heels of the discovery of *Platonov* came the reclamation of *Ivanov*, first seen on French television, then at the Théâtre d'Aujourd'hui in a production by Jacques Mauclair. René Allio's set opted for a selective realism, which used weighty, aged objects with an aura of ritual, such as the samovar, to indicate how far habit and banality had settled in.[45] The Chekhov biographer Sophie Laffitte considered it the best Parisian production of Chekhov, because of the deeply thought-out *mise-en-scène*, careful casting, and beautifully composed crowd scenes.

The Comédie Française itself bowed to Chekhov's new prestige, and in 1961 mounted *Uncle Vanya* in a translation by Elsa Triolet, with designs by Allio, who was rapidly becoming *the* Chekhov designer in France. As if to indicate its inexperience at this kind of material, the theatre appointed two directors, and studded it with stars. Over the next decade, Sacha Pitoëff spread the gospel of Chekhov through the provinces, André Barsacq provided a Barraultesque, comic reading of *Three Sisters* with Marina Vlady (1966),[46] and Marguerite Duras offered a bizarre adaptation of *The Seagull*. But in essence, there would be no reinterpretations of compelling interest until Antoine Vitez turned to Chekhov in the 1980s.

In 1972, a survey by Atac-Information noted that Chekhov was eighth among authors played in the state-supported theatres since 1945, with twenty-eight productions, just before Racine (26) and just after Labiche and Ionesco (30).[47] The citation of Ionesco is a reminder that over the course of the sixties a new repertory occupied the French stage. Beckett, Ionesco and Adamov were to prove not effacers of Chekhov, but guides to a fresh interpretation; Adamov even avowed that Chekhov provided the pattern for his own oblique dialogue. Barrault had already praised the "Russian soul" for "prolonging for us the path to the secret, subtlest acceptance of time passing," an absorbing concern of these playwrights. Ionesco would observe that Chekhov concentrates his attention first of all on the fact that "people die in company, of which they are a part."[48] Chekhov the absurdist was just around the corner.

FORBIDDEN GAMES

The absurdist interest in fortuity and mortality, which would later underlie Peter Brook's *Cherry Orchard*, was shared by Antoine Vitez, who had the benefit of knowing Russian and translating Chekhov for other directors. Vitez stressed Chekhov's "modernism," recalling that he was contemporary with Freud and Apollinaire's *Calligrammes*, another treatment of banality and blank spaces. Staging the vaudevilles at Jacques Lecoq's school and *The Seagull* (*La Mouette*) at the Conservatoire, Vitez came to the realization that everything in Chekhov made sense or had a sense, more sense than in life: "his style aims at giving the world and conversation or personal relations a theory. Nothing which is apparently 'by chance' escapes the intention of signifying or interpreting."[49] Claiming to have discovered Chekhov's cruelty in advance of Krejča, Vitez suggested that the malice and hardness of heart were self-directed and necessary accompaniments of this lack of gratuitousness. Unlike the classic

French stage which always shows *the* decisive day, Vitez explained, Chekhov shows us apparent vacuity or inaction in which a great many things, including crises, take place.

The next way to stage Chekhov, the only right one, which will of course be put down by the critics because the critics are always ten years behind the times, will perhaps be to do what he wanted: now that we have accumulated the signs, anyway now that I know the right way to do it, the interest will be in doing what I don't know exactly how to do, and thus to resume discussion or curiosity in that part of the collective memory or culture which is Chekhov. To play *The Cherry Orchard* as a vaudeville.[50]

And conversely to play the vaudevilles as if they were full-length Chekhov.

Vitez had a chance to try out his theories when he staged *The Seagull* at the Théâtre National de Chaillot in 1984, in a translation which deleted most Russian references. Indeed, Russian atmosphere was evoked only as an ironic quotation, by bringing in a samovar in Act III. Working from his own familiarity with his author, Vitez assumed a like familiarity in his public, and thus felt free to play with incoherence. There was no internal dramatic cohesion, but rather an emphasis on contradictions and divergent aims, the phoniness of acting, of situations and locales; the point was to convey an absence of centred integrality in Chekhov.

In this respect, Vitez was the director *par excellence* for Western European post-modernism: immensely learned, steeped in the latest literary theory, fascinated by semiotics and structuralism. His sober, cerebral experimental style, distrustful of sensuality, was antithetical to traditional Chekhovian atmosphere, and jeopardized it. Stanislavskian understated acting was replaced by overstatement, realistic representation was confounded by abstraction. According to Vitez,

We must acknowledge that everything in theatre is a convention, that everything is conventional in theatre. Using the same word to refer to a good and a bad convention is quite legitimate. The bad convention is the routine convention, which has become *normal* to the point that it is no longer noticed. Meyerhold tells us that we must reject that type of convention; instead, he promotes a conscious convention: the artist must create his own convention, i.e., his own system of signs, and have the public understand it.[51]

The sign system for *The Seagull* began with an expansive stage space, paralleled by high panels of rows of trees, backed by a vast sky with a setting sun and the frontage of the house. Treplev's low platform was level with the footlights, like a landing stage in the lake, located, as Zadek had done, in the audience. When the curtain of the little theatre was

36 Nina (Dominique Raymond) performs the play-within-a-play in Act I of Antoine
Vitez's *La Mouette* (*The Seagull*), Théâtre National de Chaillot, Paris, 1984.

lowered, inverting perspective, it became a wall preventing communication between Nina and Treplev on its opposite sides. Nina could thus be
seen dressing "backstage," and her stage audience's reactions perceived
(and mirrored) by the spectators in the auditorium. Meyerhold had
called such spatial inversion "paradoxical composition," turning the
audience into a double voyeur.

The scenography made no attempt to suggest that reality continued
offstage, since even on-stage reality was represented as counterfeit and
histrionic. The pasteboard nature of the trees and house was always in
evidence, enhancing the "realness" of the actors and the occasional
prop. In Act II, the house moved forward; in Act III its façade and
terrace came quite close to the footlights. The house interior of Act IV
was seen from a reversed perspective, vast yet shallow; after the final
gunshot, a panel rose to reveal the lake upstage. Emotional coloration
was supplied by lighting: the Act I sunset was romantic, full of contrasts;
the Act II noonday sun was sensual; the Act III daylight humdrum and
bleak; the Act IV evening uncanny and morbid. Yannis Kokkos the
costume designer kept to clear, contrasted colors: white for Nina and
Dorn, black for Arkadina, with few period elements.[52]

Years before, Vitez had spoken of *The Seagull* as the Freudian diminuendo of *Hamlet*;[53] prior to this production of Chekhov, he had staged *Hamlet* with many of the same actors. The contrast created not diminuendo but reductionism. Nina was seen by one critic to play "*All about Eve in the kingdom of Denmark*."[54] Propelled by great ambition but possessed of little talent, during the symbolist playlet she manipulated her drapery like Loïe Fuller and distorted her voice into *Sprechgesang*. Treplev used his fingers and toes to manipulate luminous sticks, while lying on his back like a vulnerable baby. Vitez's production was also obsessed by aging and age differences: Arkadina was older than Trigorin who was older than Nina. Bodies, voices and the text were never meant to harmonize or synchronize. This might explain why Jean-Claude Jay and Bruno Sermonne seemed too young and vigorous for Sorin and Dorn, and why there was a physical complicity between Treplev and Sorin, who both were juvenile and clumsy. Love became a "*jeu interdit*," a series of abortive attempts to retain a partner headed somewhere else, of uncouplings of desire and routine anguish, condemning everyone to his own solitude.[55] The many silences that punctuated the dialogue helped create an atmosphere of anxiety and mystery. The result was a black comedy.

The rejection of plot as narrative organization and the rhetorical deconstruction were meant to lay bare the text's mechanism and underline its disturbing strangeness. Vitez's strategy in reassessing the premises of theatrical verisimilitude can stand for that of most contemporary European directors. Respectful of Chekhov yet burdened by the anxiety of influence, he sought to relocate the play within the specific consciousness of his own culture. One might call this intellectual self-consciousness, overly aware of past opinions and fashionable attitudes, fearful of seeming naïve or old-fashioned. Knowing audiences are often willing to puzzle out the ideograms, which has replaced the more traditional "identification with the characters" or "emotional response." The more familiar Chekhov's characters and situations have become, the freer the director is to manipulate them in experiments testing the limits of theatrical reality.

CHAPTER 15

All-American Chekhov (USA 1950–1995)

Chekhov has been ennobled by age . . . He is as soothing and reassuring as the useless valerian drops dispensed by the doctors in his plays . . . an article of faith, like all stereotypes . . . the Santa Claus of dramatic literature . . .

Spencer Golub[1]

GETTING TO KNOW YOU

Perhaps the first phase in English-speakers assimilating Chekhov came to an end when they stopped spelling his name Tchekoff or Tchehof. As the more technical *kh* became standard, the sense of filtration by French or German intermediaries lessened, though it did lead to sounding his name "Check-off," as if he were an instruction on a multiple choice quiz. Anglophone critics knew his works only in translation, so the level of their reappraisals remained simplistically "content-oriented." The few conversant with Russian language and literature tended to paraphrase Soviet critics: David Magarshack's *Chekhov the Dramatist* owed a great deal to Balukhaty and Ermilov. Most of these writers were academics who disregarded the plays as stage vehicles, and rarely took into account Chekhov's connection with twentieth-century drama and its innovations. They projected onto Chekhov a personal identification as the quintessential liberal, far-sighted and humane.

Chekhov's comic aspect was first retrieved by theatre practitioners. "It is forty years almost to the day, since . . . *Cherry Orchard* was first produced in Moscow, and here in New York in 1944 the shrinkage in space and time has brought us closer to [Chekhov] than we have probably ever been," Margaret Webster exulted. "In our country every one of the revivals on record has been greeted with cries of astonishment because it has emerged so clearly that [the] plays are *not* gray and gloomy . . . but volatile, and gay and even farcical . . . "[2] Somehow this discovery had to be remade every few years.

Discoverers often went overboard in their delight at the *trouvaille*, and to make Chekhov more palatable for audiences occasionally naturalized him. The Provincetown Playhouse transmogrified *Platonov* into *Fireworks on the James* in 1940, and, more memorably, Joshua Logan wrote and directed *The Wisteria Trees* (Martin Beck Theatre, New York, 1950) which moved the locale of *The Cherry Orchard* to a postbellum plantation, where the servants were former black slaves, Lopakhin an enriched sharecropper, and Lyubov Andreevna Ranevskaya (Lucy Andree Ransdell) a Southern belle played by Helen Hayes at her most dewy-eyed. Strangely, the single nursery set in which all four acts took place reproduced the lunettes and window placement of the Art Theatre scenery. Logan's greatest liberty with the "plot" was to make explicit Lopakhin's love for Ranevskaya: a *scène à faire* in the last act had her coldly turn down his offer of marriage even though it might save the wisteria trees.[3]

There was something supererogatory about these transferences, since Chekhov had already been absorbed into American drama. Most American playwrights were steeped in his work and wrote what they thought to be a kind of poetic realism akin to his. Before World War II, he had a direct influence on Paul Green, Clifford Odets and Irwin Shaw. "It was because of Chekhov that I decided that I wanted to write plays," Shaw stated. During the 1950s, Robert Anderson, William Inge, Tennessee Williams, Arthur Miller, Paddy Chayefsky and others gave evidence of the power of example. Williams later came to believe "that he holds too much in reserve," but towards the end of his life was adapting *The Seagull* as *The Notebook of Trigorin*. Miller "fairly worshipped Chekhov at an early time in my life . . . the depth of feeling in his work, its truthfulness and the rigor with which he hewed to the inner reality of his people are treasured qualities to me." There was an in-built peril to this hero-worship. As Anderson pointed out, "American playwrights have gone aground, trying to be the American Chekhov. We have all ended up with conversation pieces."[4]

Actors and directors who were capable of brilliantly interpreting the works of Chekhov's epigones found their technique and training inadequate to cope with the master himself. Then too, the commercialism and union rules of the American stage insisted on circumscribed rehearsal periods and casts assembled for the nonce, factors that mitigated against the density of texture required for Chekhov. The repertory concept was only beginning to take root in the regional theatres, so there were few troupes in which masters of their craft worked together long enough to be able to present Chekhov with finesse and subtlety. These were endemic problems. More specific was a subtle misconstruction of his technique: the absorption of the Stanislavskian model into an indigenous American penchant for sentimental domestic drama and plays of self-discovery.

CHEKHOV OFF-BROADWAY

The fiftieth anniversary of Chekhov's death saw a resurgence of interest, evinced by a mass of publications and a large number of off-Broadway revivals, which, in John Gassner's opinion,

confirmed a mounting reputation. During the last quarter of a century it seemed indeed that [Chekhov] rather than Ibsen, was the founder of our century's realistic art [. . .] Chekhov, more than any of the old masters of modern drama, showed, apparently, without strain, that our wishes are not unrealizable.[5]

The problem of tempering realism without surrendering it was faced by Norris Houghton, when he directed a *Seagull* at the Phoenix Theatre in 1954. Housed in a former Yiddish theatre on Second Avenue, the Phoenix was a newly founded company, devoted to presenting lively revivals of the classics and premieres of bijou musical comedies. Houghton, its co-founder, was a recognized authority on the Russian theatre, whose book *Moscow Rehearsals* had given a lively account of the work of Stanislavsky and Meyerhold just before their deaths. For all that, he found it hard to imagine Chekhov's plays "being presented in a stylized milieu" and recommended "selective realism." Scenographically, this meant gauze scrims with a few foregrounded tree-trunks, and no solid walls for the interiors. A hanging ceiling indicated the contours of a room and circumscribed the actions, with some solid doors and windows and a sampling of period furniture, carpets, and ornaments.[6]

Relying on Magarshack's interpretation of the play, Houghton attempted to blend tragedy and comedy. But his efforts were undermined by a mere twenty-six days of rehearsal and a miscellaneous cast of variegated backgrounds. The émigré Czech actor George Voskovec played Dorn, the émigrée Russian actress Mira Rostova Nina, and the English actress Judith Evelyn Arkadina, while the very American Maureen Stapleton and Montgomery Clift assumed Masha and Treplev. The mixture of accents and styles left both the press and the audience unpersuaded; when Rostova's Nina asked, "Do you think I ought to be an actress," some spectators shouted "No!" Clift's film experience left him incapable of projecting his feelings beyond the proscenium, but it was precisely the presence of a Hollywood celebrity (despite the Phoenix's programmatic opposition to a star system) that guaranteed five sold-out weeks. Only Stapleton, using a native emotional *verismo*, engaged the imagination. Her Masha was an edgy neurotic, who sputtered "I'm in mourning for my life" in exasperation, well aware that the clock was running on her dreams. For some, the most memorable scene came at the end of Act I, when she simply laid her head on Voskovec's chest and whispered "I don't know why I'm living."[7]

In 1955 David Ross initiated a Chekhov cycle in Stark Young's translations hoping to refute the American acceptance of Chekhov as a bittersweet purveyor of incomprehensible symbolism; *Three Sisters* was soon followed by *Cherry Orchard* with a different cast.. Even as he emphasized "movement and rhythm" as major components, Ross insisted on maintaining the "period." However, since he performed in the ellipsoidal arena of the Fourth St. Theatre with the audience facing itself on opposite sides, the physicality was purely contemporary. The personal and economic limitations of the company, at first productive of a welcome degree of quiet intensity, had diminishing returns with each new opening. Brooks Atkinson found that Ross freed "Chekhov from rhetoric," but Eric Bentley, who had been laudatory about *Sisters*, thought *Orchard* inaccurate and unsubtle, with much straining for a *faux*-poetic effect.

George Voskovec's Slavic background must have been seen as an asset to Chekhov, even though his Czech career had been as a satirical clown; he played the lead in the Fourth St. *Uncle Vanya* from January to July 1956, with the matinee idol Franchot Tone as Astrov; Tone's presence made this the best attended of the three. Stark Young observed approvingly that the "Chekhov myth" of melancholia was dispelled; however, the deliberate lightness of tone removed almost all poignancy. When the run was over *Vanya* was filmed in Long Island City,[8] marking the first time the American movie industry had exploited Chekhov. *Ivanov* made its first New York appearance in 1958 at another fringe house, the Renata Theatre. For habitués of off-Broadway at least, Chekhov was now a drawing-card; the columnist Gene Frankel noted in 1959 that the Fourth Street was resuming its Chekhov cycle "because it is a successful investment. One always needs to draw an audience." Bentley, on the other hand, thought it time that the classics deserved more than mere revival; they needed accurate interpretation.[9]

Although a three-hour *Don Juan in the Russian Manner*, a version of *Untitled Play*, minus its first act, had been played by Barnard College and

Columbia University students in 1954, *Platonov* received its first professional American production at the Greenwich Mews in 1960. It met with
universal praise.[10] Alex Szögyi's adaptation was a pastiche of published
Russian, French and Italian versions, drastically cut to reduce the melodramatic quantum and replace it with farce. It took great liberties: in a
reversal of Chekhov's revision of *Ivanov*, Platonov was not shot but died a
natural death off-stage of heart failure. The critics agreed that this suited
the comic tone, played up by Amnon Kabatchnik's direction. Walter
Kerr was bemused by the difference between this tone and "the hushed,
hestitant and often somberly oblique inflection we have come – in this
country, at least – to associate with the Chekhov of the later plays."

> The comic and farcical elements were always apparent in early Chekhov, but
> until now we have never been able to imagine what might have happened if this
> fondness for meaningful masquerade ... given the substance of patient psychol-
> ogy, had been applied to a full-length form and a broad social subject.

Kerr saw an affinity to Molière in this newly revealed Chekhov, and wondered whether this was the dominant strain or only one of many in his
mature plays.[11]

When a modern-dress *Seagull* was presented by the Association of
Producing Artists (APA) at the Folksbiene Theatre in 1962, it was
immediately attacked for updating the action. The pervasive anachronism made the anxieties of turn-of-the-century Russians seem out-of-
place in an unspecified locale. The director Ellis Rabb demoted comedy
to burlesque, and introduced such silent movie gimmicks as freeze-frame
tableaux and speeded-up action, even though Debussy's "La plus que
lente" was used as mood music.[12]

These tendencies were programmed into the genes of American
theatre. Action was the usual desideratum, and, now given the license to
treat Chekhov as comic, there was an irresistible urge to go for the gut
response. Moreover, the large Jewish component of New York audiences
with its complex ethos of sentimentality edged with sarcasm and pragmatism viewed tsarist Russian life through immigrants' eyes. In
Broadway and off-Broadway productions alike, Chekhov's country
estates were converted into *shtetls* and his lackadaisical intelligentsia into
nebbishes and *schlemiels*.

A METHODIST *THREE SISTERS*

The various problems faced by the New York theatre in realizing
Chekhov surfaced most obviously in the much-heralded *Three Sisters*,

directed in 1963 by Lee Strasberg for the Actor's Studio, the Mecca of Method. A school which chose not to mount productions, it dominated the American stage after World War II, for its faculty and alumni were those who performed and directed the plays of Miller, Williams and O'Neill. Throughout the 1950s, the Actor's Studio was a legendary forcing-house for such actors as Marlon Brando and Ben Gazzara, Rod Steiger and Eli Wallach; it was the titular heir of the Group Theatre and promulgated the creed of Method acting. This doctrine was allegedly founded on Stanislavsky's system, although it placed far greater emphasis on internalization and the recreation of the actor's personal feelings than on external expression and the creation of a role. Inbred and self-indulgent as they were, Method actors were capable of exciting displays of emotional intensity and unpredictable readings.

Lee Strasberg, the Galician-born guru of Method, was a well-informed scholar of the Russian theatre, but also a dogmatic who brooked no heresies. Georgy Tovstonogov, the most "Stanislavskian" director of his generation in Russia, sat in on some of Strasberg's classes and found his teaching "in complete opposition to Stanislavsky: . . . demanding an emotional state all the time. That's just what Stanislavsky fought against. Strasberg took all of Stanislavsky's terminology . . . but he didn't possess the essence of Stanislavsky at all."[13]

Strasberg, goaded by his exclusion from the leadership of the new Lincoln Center company, founded the Actors Studio Theatre to stage plays for the public. In 1962, it received $250,000 from the Ford Foundation, a sum matched by Roger L. Stevens.[14] With such a subsidy, the Company began working in regular Broadway houses. After Jose Quintero's *Strange Interlude* employing only a few Studio personnel, Strasberg undertook *Three Sisters*, which he dedicated to Marilyn Monroe, the most celebrated of his students. A great deal was at stake: Strasberg was challenging rumours that he was incapable of assembling a full-scale production; he had to "put up or shut up." Moreover, if Strasberg was Stanislavsky's American heir (a title vigorously disputed by Stella Adler), then his production of a Chekhov masterpiece was bound to be authoritative and definitive.

A translation was commissioned from Randall Jarrell, one of America's finest poets; Jarrell knew no Russian but, working closely with the Slavicist Paul Schmidt, produced the best English version of the play available. A galaxy of stars enthusiastically offered their services to their former mentor: Kim Stanley (Masha), Geraldine Page (Olga), Shirley Knight (Irina), Kevin McCarthy (Vershinin), as well as Luther Adler, veteran of the Group theatre (Chebutykin) and a former member of Balieff's Chauve Souris cabaret, Tamara Daykarhanova (the old nanny Anfisa). However brilliant an acting coach Strasberg may have been, he proved to be pedestrian in rehearsal, avoiding table discussions, improvisations or intensive discussion of roles; like any summer-stock director, he gave line-readings, summarily sketched in the blocking, and relied on run-throughs. At times, he seemed to be conflating all of Chekhov into one play, as when Olga flung her housekeeping keys at Natasha's feet, a piece of business pilfered from *The Cherry Orchard*. The consequent performances at the Morosco Theatre were uncoordinated, the cast's vernaculars ranging from Daykarhanova's Russian accent to the Bronx inflections of Gerald Hiken's Tusenbach. Too narrowly focussed on discrete emotional displays, the show was wanting in pace, detail and continuity, "a formless, uninflected evening by the samovar."[15]

Nevertheless, the celebrity of cast and directors cowed the newspaper critics, who lavished praise on it: "a masterpiece," "a stunning achievement"; the New York *Post* raved "It's difficult to believe that there has ever been a more organic and total production of *The Three Sisters* anywhere, whether in Russia or in the United States."[16] It had evidently not seen Nemirovich-Danchenko's work. Geraldine Page's Olga reminded one reviewer of King Lear,[17] possibly because, aggravated by Natasha's pettiness, she exhibited her frayed nerves by vomiting loudly into a basin, the Method equivalent of "fie! fie! fie! Pah! pah!" The literary critic F. W. Dupee found this Olga, staring over the top of a screen, hair on end, hands shaking, "a faintly sinister figure" and wished the actress had intimated this more consistently. He had a similar complaint about the company as a whole:

They all shrink a little from conveying the darker implications . . . It is as if Strasberg had heard of the new English production of *King Lear* [directed by Peter Brook], with its overtones of Beckett and its consequent distortions of the text, and had sought to avoid perpetrating a similar pastiche. As it is, he couldn't have focused more sharply on the text as given, and the traditions of its performance, if he were Stanislavsky himself – which, I understand, some people almost believe he is. [. . .] A faster, wilder, more 'Gothic' performance . . . would, perhaps, have helped the company get around these difficulties. [. . .][18]

As Dupee's comments indicate, Strasberg had not rethought the play in any meaningful manner, but had simply sought to recreate the soul-stirring superficies of an archaic Art Theatre. Elia Kazan, one of the Studio's founders, was among the unimpressed, disappointed that each actor seemed compartmentalized, constantly nudging the audience to observe how pitiful he was and how deep his pain: "I thought some of the actors were behaving as if they were still doing classroom exercises, competing with each other to give 'great performances' and win Lee's approval . . . I would prefer more humor . . . and less self-indulgence, self-pity, and self-awareness. I detest emotional stripteases." Jarrell reported to Robert Lowell, "It was a disaster. As crude and exaggerated as Chekhov always is in this country."[19]

Nevertheless, the enthusiasm of the daily reviewers and the general public not only confirmed the primacy of the Actor's Studio and Strasberg's teachings as the Only Way, but led to a not very satisfactory television film, which memorialized the production's worst mannerisms. When *Three Sisters* went to London as the US entry in the International Theatre Festival, it was expected that, given its pedigree, leftist intellectuals and anti-establishment theatre practitioners would receive it warmly. Instead, audiences booed throughout and English critics who had long regarded the Method as folly had a field day: "a death blow to the 'method' school . . . slow, sleepwalking . . . Kim Stanley played Masha as though she were acting to her own reflection in the bathroom mirror . . . [the director has] a genius for destruction." "[It] accomplishes the supposedly impossible task of making Chekhov a bore."[20] The emotional onanism of the Strasberg version was bound to conflict with the more genteel approach of the English school; but such commentary also testified to the fact that in England Chekhov was assumed to be theatrically effective *per se*.

The failure of the Actor's Studio *Three Sisters* outside Manhattan had a number of potent effects. Strasberg and his cohort closed ranks; never again would he attempt to direct a play, but *en revanche* he became the most famous acting teacher in the world. Many members of the Studio felt betrayed by his devotion to stars. To those less invested in the Method and more inquisitive about alternative techniques, one thing was clear: if America's leading disciples of what purported to be Stanislavsky were incapable of interpreting Chekhov, other approaches were admissible and, indeed, necessary.

But no strong reversals were forthcoming. When Eva Le Gallienne restaged *The Cherry Orchard* for the Phoenix Theatre in 1968, she railed against "this Method acting and Actors' Studio stuff," but simply returned to her pre-war practices. Uta Hagen as Ranevskaya was not allowed to be "true to myself," and was forced to follow the sounds and rhythms of Le Gallienne's 1944 translation. The result was a lack of ensemble and even polish.[21] The cycle of Chekhov plays staged by the

English director Tyrone Guthrie at the new Minneapolis Repertory Theatre between 1963 and 1967 was significant for only two reasons: it represented Guthrie's growing interest in "family plays" (in which he lumped the trilogy of the House of Atreus), and was the first professional Chekhov productions to be played in the round.[22] But his casts, though praised as permanent ensembles, were still the mixed bill of headliners and utility players customary in American companies.

The success of the Minneapolis experiment did, however, demonstrate the most common strategy of the resident theatres popping up across the US: those that snared the large foundation grants, long lists of subscribers and ready local support relied on a limited repertory "of respectable classics . . . varied occasionally by a not too difficult play of Brecht or Beckett."[23] By the mid-1960s, surveys showed that the most respectable and dependable classics were 400–year-old Shakespeare, 300-year-old Molière and that comparative youngster, sixty-year old Chekhov.

The maintenance of Chekhov's eminent respectability led to complaints that American actors in his plays were "the bland leading the bland."[24] He was too elevated on his pedestal, hedged round by the awesome Art Theatre tradition and the alleged complexities of his subtext and nuanced feelings. Intimidated actors did nothing but speak the words simply and naturally, fearful of infusing them with temperament, histrionics or so-called Russian excitability. The only readily available alternative was the English "tradition," which American actors believed was to play Chekhov trippingly and to focus on the boredom; the result was judged to be "Sterile, uptight . . . so cerebral, so heady . . . existential depression."[25]

One American director who promulgated this characterization in contrast to his own style was the Greek-born, Yale-educated Nikos Psacharopoulos. He was the only professional American director who staged Chekhov on a regular basis, benefiting from his tenure at the Williamstown Theatre in Massachusetts. This summer venue had been in place for seven seasons before he took what was then a daring decision to put on *The Seagull*, later named by a poll of viewers the season's best show. Over the next twenty-five years, Psacharopoulos staged fifteen Chekhov productions: *The Seagull* (1962, 1968, 1974), *The Cherry Orchard* (1963, 1969, 1980), *Three Sisters* (1965, 1970, 1976, 1987) and *Platonov* (1977). (Others directed *Uncle Vanya*, 1964, 1972, 1984, and *Ivanov*, 1983. It was explained that Psacharopoulos felt too close to their protagonists to want to tackle them himself.)

Psacharopoulos went for grand emotion and big gestures: "It is a matter of the scale of intensity of acting being in relation to the scale of your perception of your problem in the scene. If your preception of your problem is big, you can get away with murder up there."[26] His Mediterranean temperament, colleagues claimed, alienated him from the Method; when there was a danger of the work becoming too internalized or too small, he would reach for opera. This operatic attack was in complete defiance of accepted ideas of a languid, delicate Chekhov. Rehearsing *The Cherry Orchard* in 1980, Psacharopoulos wanted Ranevskaya to be a passionate woman who hurled herself at things with a tremendous appetite, but he fell afoul of Colleen Dewhurst who saw her role as "Chekhovian." In Psacharopoulos's Chekhov, there were no primary and secondary roles: "Everyone was the romantic lead . . . Everyone's passion was utterly acknowledged." And everyone was constantly on the edge. In crowd or family scenes, he didn't care if each line could be clearly heard, so long as there was a swirl of movement, the words overlapping to provide a sense of life and vitality. His directions to actors could occasionally be as laconic as Chekhov's ("the success of the scene between Arkadina and her son in Act III depends on the length of the bandage") and his choices deliberately outrageous. He rehearsed *Three Sisters* on the tacit assumption that Irina was Chebutykin's daughter by the late Mrs. General Prozorova, while Rosemary Harris developed Irina, assuming that she was Vershinin's daughter by the dead mother. During the final aria in a later production, Olga (Olympia Dukakis) dragged Irina (Laurie Kennedy) off her bench to dance, and then recruited Masha: the Terpsichorean trio became a symbol of courage and bravery in the face of disappointment. Another element which Psacharopoulos accentuated in his Chekhovian welter was sexuality: suddenly something was at stake on stage, and, infused with this libido-driven energy, the plays became irresistible to summer audiences.[27] Psacharopoulos' Williamstown productions patented a specifically red-blooded American style of playing Chekhov. Crude and uneven though it was, it had the benefit of vitality.

MAKE CHEKHOV, NOT WAR

By the late 1960s, the decadence of traditional modes of Chekhovian staging coincided with a creative upheaval in the American theatre. A cocktail was fermenting, brewed of Grotowski's spiritual exercises, the Living Theatre's collective creation, protest against the Vietnam war, the drug-inspired aesthetics of acid rock, and the camp sensibility of the gay sub-culture. For some of the vanguard, the very use of scripts was suspect except as a point of departure for spontaneous improvisation and group creativity. Chekhov ought to have seemed an irrelevant, not to say retrograde, part of the old cultural cargo to be jettisoned on the road to Nirvana.

Yet many in the theatrical anti-establishment fixed on Chekhov as their patron saint. Megan Terry declared that no male playwright had seriously written about the family before Chekhov, and was struck by his ability to create "*whole* and *multi-dimensional female characters*"; she readily admitted his influence on her early plays and even confessed to carrying a photo of him in her wallet, "prominent among my other loves."[28]

In 1975, two *Seagulls* were staged by three of the most prominent innovators and practitioners – André Gregory, Joseph Chaikin and Jean-Claude Van Itallie. Treplev's demand for new forms evidently had a strong appeal, for the play was also performed that year at New York's Cubiculo by a company directed by Philip Meister, while the Actor's Studio experimented on yet another version with the Russian director Sam Tsikhotsky as adviser. Simultaneously, Psacharopoulos' Williamstown production was broadcast on television as part of WNET's "Theater in America" series.

André Gregory, whose company The Manhattan Project had gained fame with a psychedelic *Alice in Wonderland* and a farcical revision of *Endgame*, considered *The Seagull* "a crystal ball into which the avant-garde is gazing, hoping for an answer – any answer."[29] Working from a literal translation by Laurence Senelick, Gregory's actors reformulated their dialogue, paraphrasing the speeches, replacing such things as Dorn's snatches of romantic ballads with quotations from pop hits. As a work-in-progress, Act I was first revealed at the Lenox Arts Festival in the Berkshire mountains of Massachusetts, played on the terrace of Edith Wharton's Italianate villa. Against a backdrop of mountains with a rising moon, Treplev's line "No scenery, just first border, second border, and then empty space" suddenly made perfect sense.

This slowly evolved *Seagull* was eventually transferred to the Public Theatre, New York; but what had seemed cleverly innovative *al fresco* looked jejune and inadequate indoors. Ming Cho Lee designed an environmental space spread over the Theatre's third storey; the audience was forced to find new seats in each interval and watch the action from different vantage points. Costumes were only vaguely of the period, with blue jeans, sweaters and brightly colored tights worn by some. The actors' rawness was more conspicuous when confined, but even so, the production kept raising questions about the play and opened avenues to a fresh consideration of Chekhov. "The reason for all that," said Gregory,

is that I wanted to show a confrontation between a contemporary company and a classic writer – between the present and the past – and to try, in some way, to get into the future. But more than that, I wanted to point up the fact that, basically, we've all come out of the conventional theater . . . . Actually, I think the moment has come when the dividing line between the avant-garde and the commercial theater is no longer as strong . . .[30]

The critics would have none of it, hostile to what they regarded as "desecration." For many, Chekhov was a sacred text, whose exegesis had been established once and for all during the Art Theatre's tour of 1923. Later in the season, Chaikin also decided it was time for innovators to return to their roots. His group The Open Theater had functioned for ten years, first as an experimental workshop, then as a showcase for collective creativity. Despite its great success with such productions as *America Hurrah* and *The Serpent*, it had reached a crisis. Chaikin disbanded it because he felt that its voice no longer had meaning, its moment had passed; but he could find no relevance and joy in the works of others either. "It seemed to me that the theater should be at least as intense as living is, that it should be charged, and contain the eventfulness of life.[31]

Consequently, he and Van Itallie, who knit the Open Theatre's improvisations into finished scripts, turned to Chekhov as the guide to lead them back to theatrical tradition.

I saw *The Seagull* as a prophetic play, one that is humanizing to work on – a play both timeless and rejuvenating . . . I'm sure we've all gone to *The Seagull* because there is something in that play that has to do with our concerns as artists. The play is about creative people, the kind of work they do, how they lead their lives, where one's personal life and professional life begin and end. All the ideas in *The Seagull* are applicable to us, certainly in the confrontation between the old and the new, the conventional and the experimental.[32]

Van Itallie, who admitted to knowing no Russian, cobbled together his translation from ten other English versions and one in French. "I tried to find Chekhov's intention and rhythm and express them clearly in English, working aloud at first, with the spoken rather than the written word, listening for Chekhov in my own voice."[33] Difficult phrases, obscurities or literary allusions were cut, until the play lost its bearings in the world of art and every character began to sound like every other. Chaikin's *Seagull*, produced at the Manhattan Theatre Club, turned out to be traditional, deferential and dull, shedding no new light on the play. But in this case, the critics, their preconceptions unruffled, were as laudatory to Chaikin as they had been disdainful of Gregory.

Less radical than it seemed at the time was the all-black *Cherry Orchard* at the Public (1973), directed by Michael Schultz, in response to complaints that African–American actors were barred from the classics. Expectations of a drastic reinterpretation were dashed. This production too was respectful, expressing neither protest nor iconoclasm. Tentative parallels were drawn between post-Emancipation Russia and post-Reconstruction America: the landowners' skins were a lighter shade than those of the servants, and the passerby in Act II addressed Firs in an African dialect, as if the lower orders shared a *patois*. Ed Bullins, an over-powering voice on the black theatrical scene, assigned a political meaning to the characters:

the Blacks had gotten their 40 acres, their mule and more. But the leaders of the movement, the Black Bourgeoisie, like Madame Ranevskaya, were morally, materially and spiritually bankrupt. In fact, the House Slaves had acquired the Big House. And they played the Masters with so much more flair, style and soul than the absentee landlords . . . [34]

Trofimov was played in deadly earnest as a revolutionary activist, and Bullins singled out the Lopakhin of James Earl Jones as "brash, almost niggerish in power . . . " But the white establishment critics dismissed the production as the MAT in blackface, verging on melodrama when Ranevskaya fainted dead away on hearing that the orchard has been sold. They refused to draw any unsettling parallels.

IN ANOTHER GALAXY

Broadway continued to manhandle Chekhov in its inimitable fashion. The immensely popular *farceur* Neil Simon concocted a patchwork called *The Good Doctor* (1973), stitched together from Chekhov's stories and plays. Intended as homage, it (to quote one facetious reviewer referring to a popular car-wax) "Simonized" the Russian and denatured both writers. Chekhov became caricatured and slapstick, Simon washed-out and uncertain, with sticky sentiment in place of pathos, and delicacies of perception sacrificed to surefire laugh-getters. The error of equating the life of pre-revolutionary Russian intellectuals with that of East European Jewish villagers was compounded here. *The Good Doctor* was more Sholem Aleichem's world than Chekhov's, even if its wandering *klezmer* band could be traced to *The Cherry Orchard*.[35]

Uncle Vanya, which had been neglected on the Broadway stage since Jed Harris' 1930 version, was twice revived, without distinction, in 1971. The play's sudden popularity may have had to do with the success of Olivier's Chichester production, and with economics, for the cast is relatively small and the action may be limited, if need be, to a single setting. Another *Vanya*, directed by Mike Nichols at the Circle in the Square in 1973, exploited those limitations, although the star-studded cast must have been expensive. A cluster of international media celebrities – George C. Scott as Astrov, Nicol Williamson as Vanya, Julie Christie as Elena, Lillian Gish as Marina, and Cathleen Nesbit as Mariya Vasilevna – were held loosely together in a colloidal suspension. Both Scott and Williamson were dynamic and virile, but the American took a Method approach, while the Englishman was extroverted and flamboyant. Elizabeth Wilson, the Sonya, was of an age more suited to a matron than a young spinster, and Gish was too porcelain-like for the earthy nanny. The directorial concept of Nichols, who had made his reputation staging contemporary comedies of manners, was to have the entire action revolve around Elena whom he described as "extremely sexy and beautiful."[36] As it turned out, Christie, who had no stage experience whatever, was too insipid to provide the cynosure the director intended.

From the commercial standpoint, the production worked: performances were sold out because the public wanted to see film stars in the flesh, whatever the vehicle; and the daily reviewers were predictably enthusiastic. But the more serious critics and playgoers found it shallow, far too shrill and lachrymose, and ultimately boring. The directing lacked an integrative principle. Scott had tremendous charisma as Astrov, which sent some hearts a-flutter; but it was difficult to distinguish between Vanya's melodramatic self-indulgence, and that of Nicol Williamson as an actor. As Walter Kerr complained in the *New York Times*, the director had "disassembled" the acting company, "leaving individual performers to grope their ways alone through garden fog and parlor fatigue, unmotivated, unrelated, characterless and crying."[37]

An interesting side-effect was an incisive post-mortem in *Theatre Quarterly* by Richard Gilman, who taught drama at Yale; it anatomized the critics to a fare-thee-well, condemning them as naïve, benighted and illiterate when it came to Chekhov.[38] Gilman's accusations pointed up a fundamental problem faced by any American director setting out to stage Chekhov. Not only were the critics, ignorant of theatre history and literary criticism, retailers of hoary clichés, but audiences were usually coming to Chekhov for the first time. No familiarity could be assumed, and so it was difficult to go beyond "telling the story." Professor Leo Hecht praised an Arena Stage production of *Three Sisters* (1984) for making up Soleny to resemble Lermontov, but he pointed out that the likeness would elude most Americans.[39] In fact, Soleny may be even more effectively presented if he doesn't look a thing like Lermontov, thereby underscoring his romantic illusions about himself; this was a device later exploited by Yury Lyubimov for a knowing Russian audience. Both the resemblance and the lack of resemblance can work only when the public has frequent opportunity to see Chekhov on stage.

A POSITIVE IMAGE

The most portentous and discussed Chekhov production in the United States in the seventies was the work of a Romanian director, Andrei Serban, who staged *The Cherry Orchard* at the Vivian Beaumont Theatre for Joseph Papp's New York Shakespeare Festival (1977). Van Itallie contributed a rather bland English text, and the music was by Liz Swados, an unconventional composer who had previously worked with Serban on his glossolalial versions of Greek tragedy. The impressionistic and romantic sets and costumes by Santo Loquasto were very much in the Strehler tradition: a beautiful blanching of a fairy tale Russia. Later Serban was to renounce such aestheticism.

Response was polarized by a metaphoric approach that was radically untraditional for America. The usual doors, windows and solid walls were gone, so that Serban could set his tableaux against a luminous cyclorama, to create a panoramic rather than intimate effect. When certain characters addressed the audience directly, the rest of the cast froze in the background. The play became a peopled landscape. Serban himself asserted that "the orchard itself is really there, but at the same time it is a ghostly presence," and he filled the stage with troubling images: a cage-like ballroom, a plough dragged across a field by peasants; at the end, a cherry branch placed by a child in front of an enormous factory, a symbol of change. "All this is meant to elicit emotion rather than give information," Serban explained.[40] But at least one reviewer feared that Serban was "trying to say too much . . . about the conscious and unconscious life of the characters."[41]

The acting was electric but eclectic, for the cast combined highly technical actors like Irene Worth (Ranevskaya) with raw young talent such as Raul Julia (Lopakhin) and Meryl Streep (Dunyasha). Worth's was the outstanding performance, remarkable for such moments as piecing the

37 Santo Loquasto's décor for Andrei Serban's *Cherry Orchard*, Vivian Beaumont
Theatre, NY, 1977, with Irene Worth (center) as Ranevskaya and Michael Christofer
(right) as Trofimov. The cupboard, toy train and white expanse are all direct quotations
from Strehler's production.

torn telegram together slowly and painfully. The news that the orchard
had been sold was conveyed almost negligently by Anya as mother and
daughter passed one another in a dance figure. But such blithe understatement was less common than athleticism: Dunyasha performed a
striptease and at one point tackled Yasha like a football player. Michael
Christofer played Trofimov straight, without any comic touches, taking
his fervour at face value. In fact, Serban seemed to be contradicting
himself by making a political statement while trying to reinvent imagistic
stagecraft in the shadow of Strehler, Peter Brook and Robert Wilson.
The visual images were striking, but the meaning was often perverse or
inappropriate, and the result unmoving. Still, it was the first American
production of Chekhov to have an idiosyncratic *optique* and to try and
convey the play's multiple levels of meaning and a symbology.[42]

Serban's subsequent productions were less impressive: *The Seagull*
(Public Theatre, 1980) was a step back toward tradition, a cool, formal

staging full of *verité* acting. *Three Sisters* (American Repertory Theatre, Cambridge, Mass., 1983) made a concerted effort to present the characters as a kindergarten of obnoxious and monotonous brats. In 1983, his *Uncle Vanya* at La MaMa, New York, was notable primarily for a cavernous set by Loquasto, fifty feet by twenty, which kept the characters continually isolated from one another. In a cast headed by Joseph Chaikin, the acting was motley and undistinguished, punctuated by such jarring moments as Vanya sitting on the professor's lap and the professor lecherously pawing Elena. The subtext had bobbed to the surface. The critical consensus that Serban had a stunning visual sense but was incapable of producing a coherent reading of Chekhov seemed confirmed.[43]

THE SAME ONLY DIFFERENT

The innovations of these and other European émigrés were widely imitated; the American stage was soon covered with shimmering, all-white Chekhov productions, more distinguished by their imagery than their insight. These co-existed with more conventional, psychological stagings which tended to lack any point of view. Evidence of the slipshod approach to Chekhov in the professional American theatre is available in Susan Letzler Cole's description of rehearsals of Elinor Renfield's *Cherry Orchard* in 1985 and Maria Irene Fornes' *Uncle Vanya* in 1987. In both cases, the directors chose the least reliable translations for their work: Jean Claude Van Itallie and Marian Fell, respectively. Renfield and her cast were experienced professionals putting together a performance in two weeks, despite the director's admission that "the text is written as if coded and needs time and care to crack the code." Although the actors wanted improvisation, there was none. Nor was there a clear directorial concept: ideas were incorporated as they occurred in rehearsal, and questions of relationship were resolved by physical placement. The director relied on hyperbolic phrases and simplistic formulations to jump-start the actors: "That's all the scene is about: moving from behind the fence to the tree to beside her ask if you can be alone with her"; "This is a scene about how much of a man Trofimov is." Ready subtext was provided for the asking; acting problems always had priority over textual interpretation; and the director's major task appeared to be editing the actors' choices. One of them she praised for achieving his "first Chekhovian moment." At the actors' request, the second of the two weeks was devoted to uninterrupted runthroughs in order to set the sequence of events.[44]

In 1988–9, four productions of *The Seagull* at four leading regional theatres summed up the state of the art in the United States. In each, emphases were dictated less by the director than by the strengths of the company, and in no case did an overriding idea come across. At the Great Lakes Theatre Festival in Cleveland, Gerald Freedman's production was content to tell the story to an audience which had never seen Chekhov before. His staging was characterized by a strong narrative line and presentational, highly emotive acting; oddly, the actors' willingness to play surface feelings, including incest, was matched by a fear of accosting the play's melodramatic moments. A flashy Arkadina, a lightweight Trigorin, a flimsy Treplev and a whirling, weepy Nina, along with Van Itallie's chatty adaptation, vitiated the theme of artists at work and play. A background of jute cords kept Treplev's trestles and the lake always in view, but they absorbed light, so that the characters seemed like fish floating through dark and gloomy algae.

Also handicapped by Van Itallie's vapid dialogue (the actors' choice, not the director's), *The Seagull* at the Arena Stage in Washington was another "traditional" staging which made a few ineffectual and ill-advised stabs at innovation. The monologues were broadcast as amplified voice-over while the actor was bathed in a spotlight; the sound effect of a gunshot forecast Treplev's suicide at various moments in the play. But such expressionism clashed with Art Theatre bird calls and real food. A more daring approach was taken by Jon Jory at the Actors' Theatre of Louisville: his original concept was to stage the first act in the style of the symbolist playlet, and the last act in the "true-to-life" style of the early MAT, to chart Treplev's dwindling into a blocked hack. So in Act I, the set was schematic with a huge moon, a curtain of red slats, and the platform set downstage; here Treplev was physically intimate with the other characters. By Act IV, he was outcast on the forestage, outside the ultra-naturalistic picture-frame interior. Unfortunately, this left Acts II and III rather undefined. However, because Michael Frayn's translation enabled the themes of art to be heard, Treplev and Trigorin came across more as thinkers than is common in an American staging.

The most radical rethinking was done by Ron Daniels at the American Repertory Theatre in Cambridge, Massachusetts. *The Seagull* was played alternately with *Hamlet*, the casts doubled in such a way as to highlight the parallels: Hamlet/Treplev, Gertrude/Arkadina, Claudius/Trigorin, Ophelia/Nina, and so on. Daniels deliberately ignored all traditions and treated the work as if it were a new play. Costumes were more or less contemporary and the frame cottage overlooking an

38 Summering at Martha's Vineyard in Act II of *The Seagull*, directed by Ron Daniels,
American Repertory Theatre, Cambridge, 1992. L.–r., Erin McMurtry as Masha,
Stephanie Roth as Nina, Steven Skybell as Dorn, Michael Rudko as Medvedenko,
Jeremy Geidt as Sorin and Christine Estabrook as Arkadina.

expanse of deep blue water could as easily have been a writer's retreat in
Martha's Vineyard or Finisterre as an estate in rural Russia. Indeed,
Antony McDonald's set design was the most striking feature of the production, the bright colours of the earlier acts reminiscent of Miró, the
last act a constricted black box to hem in Treplev and his ambition. This
stripping away of preconceived notions was refreshing, but again the
acting failed to add up. Although the actor playing Sorin supplied a
craftsmanlike demonstration of old-fashioned "character work," most of
the cast gave what might be called post-modern performances: arbitrary
line readings, occasional spasmodic bursts of action, a loose congeries of
traits amounting to no particular psychology. One audacious novelty
was to have Arkadina strip to her naked torso to display her girlish
attributes; it was not incongruous given the indeterminate context, but,
like most stage nudity, attracted more attention than it deserved.
Chekhovian reticence was violated for no clear reason.

   This lack of reason is the giveaway. Except to display their *bona fides* as professional purveyors of the classics (a necessary credential for getting grants) and to provide strong roles for a resident company, there was no urgency to any of these productions. They came across as proficient *passatempi* or idle luxuries, but never as meaningful experiences conveyed through Chekhov's words and images; for the directors had neither sought nor found resonances to echo in the lives of their audiences.

THE RITE OF PASSAGE

The earlier generation of American playwrights had been inspired by Chekhov to apply his techniques to indigenous material, but they had rarely been tempted to tamper with his plays. A later generation, largely university-bred, were more haunted by Chekhov's spectre, and needed to exorcise his influence by "translating" him. In most cases, like Van Itallie, they neglected what would seem to be the preliminary initiation in such a rite of passage: learning Russian. It was more as if each dramatist communed with the dead Russian on a spiritist level and then disgorged his speeches and stage directions as automatic writing. Lanford Wilson, David Mamet and Richard Nelson each felt called upon to utter his own reduction; although much of their phrasing would have been called unspeakable if committed by a professional translator, the critics, themselves monolingual, nodded solemn approval and took seriously productions tongue-tied by these opaque texts.

Wilson claimed that his idea of theatre was founded on Brendan Behan's *The Hostage* and protested that "that stuff that Chekhov and Ibsen do," "realistic theatre doesn't bother me a bit"; still, he had Chekhovianism thrust upon him by the directors of the Circle Repertory Company off Broadway. Marshall Mason who staged the premieres of most of Wilson's plays there made a fetish of Chekhov and Ibsen; he considered that the glancing style of playing Wilson invented by the Circle Rep the equivalent to the style the MAT had evolved for Chekhov. When the CRC chose to produce *Three Sisters* in 1984, its producer Mark Lamos had Wilson take a crash course in Russian at the Berlitz School in order to produce a translation.[45] (Imagine a Muscovite taking a score of English lessons to turn Tennessee Williams into playable Russian.) The result is an amazing mélange of translatorese and fustian: Olga reminds Irina that she had "fainted and lay there absolutely moribund," Tusenbach explains that Mrs. Colonel Vershinin attempts suicide "only to nettle Vershinin," and Andrey complains that there are no "zealots" in town.

Mamet's relation to Chekhov is both more thoughtful and more personal. Working from a literal translation on an adaptation of *The Cherry Orchard*, he concluded that "the play is a series of scenes about sexuality, and, particularly, frustrated sexuality"[46]; the same frustration is recycled throughout, repeated by the various couples, and so Mamet compared Chekhov's comedy with such "revue-plays" as *La Ronde*. This is ingenious but also reductive, and, devoid of nuance, Mamet's text is often downright inaccurate: for instance, Ranevskaya's statement "Giants are pleasing only in fairy tales. In real life they're frightening" is misrendered as "Giants in fairy tales only please" and loses its second phrase. Assuming a director's function, Mamet often indicates when lines are to be spoken simultaneously. The production of this *Orchard* which inaugurated the New Theatre company at Chicago's Goodman Theatre in 1985, was found by the critics to be mannered and arch, in look sub-Serban.[47]

When Mamet adapted *Uncle Vanya* in 1988 he felt even freer to cut and clip; his text is riddled with italics to indicate which words should be stressed, whereas in Chekhov the rhythm of the lines achieves this for the actors. Hints are invariably heightened, tints deepened to primary colours, the implicit made explicit. "Chekhov's plays are like soap operas," Mamet later stated to an interviewer, and the director of the television version reiterated Mamet's earlier views in saying the play was "very much about sex and desire."[48] A Mamet version of *Three Sisters* (Atlantic Theater, NY 1991) was more respectful of the original, though not devoid of anachronisms and peculiar phrases.[49]

In short, the American theatre is on easy terms with Chekhov, because it has chosen to see him as benign; he is so naturalized that his thorns and brambles are barely noticed, and both his life and works have become a grazing ground for the creativity of others.[50] His status as tutelary spirit of the American drama was made manifest when the Acting Company, a permanent touring ensemble specializing in the classics, sought a way to promote new plays. Rather than drawing on American sources, its dramaturge distributed a series of Chekhov's short stories to a number of eminent playwrights, including Mamet, Fornes, Wendy Wasserstein and John Guare. The resulting series of one-acts known as *Orchards* (1985), veered towards the over-explicit, the one-note and the parodic. Meant as an act of homage, "celebrating [Chekhov's] versatility and durability,"[51] these plays emblazoned his name as a totemic propitiation of a venerated but misunderstood ancestor. Not so much dramatizations as inventive "inspirations," they suggest that what the American stage finds most congenial and nourishing in Chekhov is his anecdotal aspect.

Despite the pressure of feminism, deconstruction and imagistic scenography, Chekhov proved less amenable to revolutionary reinterpretation than Shakespeare had. In the repertories, a modified verism remained the style of choice; when Gerald Freedman mounted *Uncle Vanya* in 1991, he utilized a scenic space filled with two thousand props on a turn-table with fourteen settings. "We were aiming at Stanislavsky's ideal, a fusion of the naturalistic detail with poetic atmosphere [as] an 'emotional envelope' for the characters."[52] This style was occasionally countered by an abstract rendering, such as Ron Daniels' 1994 *Cherry Orchard* (ART), with its Malevich-inspired sets and steadfast renunciation of interpretation.

Another approach is to accept Chekhov as raw ore mined from a cultural lode, a Jungian substratum of themes and types, only incidentally connected to the theatre. When André Gregory returned to Chekhov in 1991 to run a series of open rehearsals of *Uncle Vanya* (Victory Theatre, New York), with Wallace Shawn in the title role, the tentative nature of these workshop presentations suggested that the previous generation's movers and shakers had, in imitation of Grotowski, renounced theatre as such, to explore a dramatic text as potential therapy for all mankind. "This *Vanya*," Gregory insisted, "is definitely not theatre. It is a sort of spiritual community in which people search not only for the darkest in themselves but also for the lightest." For him, the domestic drama was merely an Hitchcockian McGuffin, where the attempts at communication enable us "to sense more and more closely what life actually feels like as it passes, and to see the unfolding of the human being in all its ambiguity."[53] Pretentious as it sounds, this at least attempts to get beyond the surface soap operatics of the usual American production.

CHAPTER 16

Chekhov without tears (United Kingdom 1950–1993)

We have remade Chekhov's last play in our image just as drastically
as the Germans have remade *Hamlet* in theirs. Our *Cherry Orchard* is
a pathetic symphony, to be played in a mood of elegy. We invest it
with a nostalgia for the past which, though it runs right through our
culture, is alien to Chekhov's. His people are country gentry; we
make them into decadent aristocrats.

Kenneth Tynan[1]

OUR MUTUAL FRIEND

Tynan's observation was just. A sea-change had occurred in the British
notion of the Russian character; the Red savages and Dostoevskian
maniacs of the early part of the century had been domesticated by the
efforts of Komisarjevsky, Saint-Denis and war-time alliance into a
mirror-image of the British themselves. Shortly before the Cold War
broke out, one could read an authority on ballet soothingly declaring
that:

A definite affinity between the English and the Russian temperament has often
been suggested by writers who know both countries well . . . In no other country
have the great Russian authors found so large, sympathetic and even enthusiastic a reading public as in England . . . Tolstoy in his preoccupation with moral
problems strikes a particularly English note, while the tolerant, unfanatical
Tchekhov seems more English than the English; and it is significant that he has
never attained either the popularity or the reputation in Germany that his work
has enjoyed in this country.[2]

Russian exuberance, candour, violence, moroseness and proneness to
introspection and procrastination, qualities which might be more readily
equated with the American, Scandinavian or Celtic characters, have
evaporated in this chimera of Tolstoy as a bearded George Eliot and
Chekhov as a Slavic Trollope.

This assumption of assimilation was due chiefly to ignorance of the

305

social and historical context of Chekhov's works: the plight of his intelligentsia was identified with the decline of the English aristocracy, and their very specific crotchets equated with English eccentricity. His allergy to philosophical and political factions appealed to the British distaste for metaphysics and messages in the theatre,[3] where productions of Chekhov well into the 1970s relied more on strong individual performances than on directorial concepts. The paucity of ideas was compensated by the glamour of the casting. In his youth, the critic Michael Billington recalled, "Chekhovian" suggested actors and actresses of a certain age strolling nonchalantly and languorously across the stage; and, as Caryl Brahms put it, even the Moscow Art Theatre seemed vulgar "without Dame Edith, and Miss Seyler, and Sir John,"[4] ultra-civilized actors whose presence linked Chekhov with Wilde and Maugham. Class attitudes were conveyed through linguistic nuances; when Chekhov's few peasants or workers spoke in London working-class accents or bluff Northern dialects, they connoted a familiar but misleading distinction to their hearers.

Vera Gottlieb notes perceptively that "Over the eighty years of Chekhov production in Britain a strange anomaly has arisen: the plays are *always* staged within a period setting, or, at least, with period costuming; but, with very few exceptions, the period itself or social context of the plays has been ignored," implying "a self-imposed narrowing of understanding and vision which compounds the normal difficulties of translating or transposing a play."[5] Not only were political, ontological or ecological questions ignored, but the philosophic concept of distance was hard to induct in a country whose boundaries could be traversed in a day's auto trip. Gottlieb also traces "the emphasis . . . on 'tragic character' to the virtual exclusion of 'social comedy'," to the Stanislavskian obsession with exploring psychologies rather than ideas. Peggy Ashcroft, speaking as a conscientious actor, supported this thesis, when she explained that the central problem in Chekhov was a "a tremendously detailed study of a character," with the spoken line subservient to mood and atmosphere.[6] It would be impossible, however, to demonstrate that Stanislavsky ever had as enduring an effect on Britons as on Americans or Eastern Europeans; personality, rather than multi-faceted characterization, predominated on the English stage through the 1980s.

The apogee of this performer-oriented approach was probably the Chichester Festival *Uncle Vanya* in 1962. In true actor–manager fashion, Laurence Olivier both staged it and played Astrov, to whom he brought a new coarseness and vulnerability. He and Vanya (Michael Redgrave) would share conspiratorial laughs at the professor (Max Adrian), and there was a special tenderness in his dealings with the cackling nurse (Sybil Thorndike).[7] The most original aspect of the production was its employment of a unit set by Sean Kenny: a stark open platform of bare planks and a timbered wall with a door and two windows created a sounding board for exquisitely rendered shades of meaning. This made sense economically and technically, but eliminated Chekhov's symbolic progress from exterior to interior. Although the shared sense of doom between a packed audience and the stage that had informed the wartime *Vanya* was necessarily missing, this production's minute sense of detail and mastery of form led Penelope Gilliatt to call it "probably the best *Uncle Vanya* in English that we shall ever see."[8] Chekhov was still chamber music played by a group of virtuosi, rather than an orchestral piece to be interpreted by a conductor.

An incipient change was provoked in 1958 by the visit of the Moscow Art Theatre, with its *The Cherry Orchard* and *Uncle Vanya*. Some took the occasion to bolster the traditional stand. Despite the archival nature of the stagings and the advanced age of the actors, John Fernald, director of RADA, concluded that it is "essential to produce Chekhov in the detailed and highly naturalistic style which the Moscow Art Theatre . . . discovered was necessary . . . The kind of liberty taken by Jouvet with Molière should never be taken with Chekhov."[9] Others read different lessons from the productions. For Leo Baker, they illustrated the use of multiple acting areas, triangulated sets and interrelationships between players, missing from British theatre in general.[10] For Kenneth Tynan, they blew the dust off *The Cherry Orchard* to reveal it as something other than the *symphonie pathétique* the English invariably played.

As if in response to this revelation, Michel Saint-Denis' *Cherry Orchard* for the Royal Shakespeare Company (1962) tried to appeal not to the spectator's sympathy but to his laughter. Saint-Denis set about to tone down "the romantic and charming qualities which cling to the personalities of [the] household in order to emphasize the frivolity, the ineffectualness, and indeed the immorality of these representatives of a disappearing society."[11] At the first readthrough, Saint-Denis announced that "the text is an important result of something else and [the actors'] job was to find what that something else was"[12] over the course of seven weeks, but his company was too heterogeneous to seek it together. John Gielgud felt totally at home as Gaev, but Peggy Ashcroft's eagerness to bring out Ranevskaya's shallow volatility resulted in the suburban charm the director wanted to discount. Mixing such veterans

with such tyros as Judi Dench (Anya) and Ian Holm (Trofimov) prevented the ensemble from gelling, especially because the younger performers were intractable to Saint-Denis' brand of discipline. Trained in
a more improvisational manner, they found his methods fussy and
repressive. Lack of cohesion in the cast prevented this production from
attaining the legendary status of the 1938 *Three Sisters*; its most moving
moment was Pishchik's farewell.

One way to lift the curse of Komis and the heavy hand of atmospheric staging was to select plays previously overlooked. George Devine
of the English Stage Company offered a drastically cut *Platonov* at the
Royal Court in 1960. Devine retained the first act, because he saw contemporary relevance in its commentary on young intellectuals who had
failed to meet their responsibilities in a changing political climate. To
play up the melodrama, Richard Pilbrow's lighting and Richard Negri's
scene design made the approaching train a red eye growing out of the
darkness, seemingly sending a ton of metal hurtling into the audience;
the comic aspects were invested in the acting. By casting Rex Harrison in
the lead, Devine turned Platonov into a figure of exquisitely timed farce,
a "bearded satyr, febrile and wild-eyed."[13]

Clinging to his old familiar gesture of bunching his fingertips on his forehead,
pivoting from fool to worshipper, he steered the play unfalteringly over shallows
of bathos and rapids of absurdity. Timing every phrase with a skill as exquisite
as it is rare, sometimes muttering, sometimes shouting, yet always audible,
flicking a comic aside on its way without the slightest fuss, bickering, brooding,
being seduced, being cruel, being kind and always slipping, slipping, he made of
this wretched man one of the finest comic performances of our time.[14]

Outraged conservatives cried sacrilege, but at least one foreigner took
the point. The Polish theatre critic Roman Szydlowski was struck by the
absence of Chekhovian "mistiness" or melancholy, psychologizing or
emotional depth. For him, this fast-paced, sharply defined presentation
was reminiscent of *Look Back in Anger*.[15]

Osborne's play was, of course, the standard-bearer of British theatrical reform, which had its effect on the classics as well. A new kind of
"realism," gritty, politically engaged, left-wing in sympathy, merged with
an anti-realistic stagecraft borrowed second- and third-hand from
Brecht and Svoboda. Smaller, unorthodox performance spaces and
especially arenas in the round confounded the atmospheric tricks
common to the picture-frame stage. Actors seen in three dimensions in
these denuded locales needed a new kind of clarity and precision; snapshot close-ups rather than full-length portraits. Emergent from varied

backgrounds, they had fewer interests in common with the average matinee-goer, the "Aunt Edna" who preferred a well-mannered Uncle Vanya.

As a catalyst from abroad, the MAT was less congenial to these changes than was Otomar Krejča's *Three Sisters* which visited the World Theatre season at the end of the decade. The production had so much passion and sense of movement, especially in the final tableau of the sisters whirling around the stage, that some in the English theatre developed an inferiority complex about the old-fashioned approaches to Chekhov perpetrated in the West End.[16] Under the Czech influence, abandoning period settings and conventional *mises-en-scène*, directors began to transfuse the sense of the plays.

One of the first was Jonathan Miller. As a physician, he understood Chekhov's clinical stance, which found expression in the well-observed and -reproduced symptoms of the characters. "I am concerned to reflect emotion *accurately* on stage," Miller announced,[17] and to that end kept furnishings to a minimum, forcing atmosphere to condense not from surroundings but from personalities. In his nosological *Seagull* (Chichester, 1973), Sorin (George Howe) exhibited the effects of his stroke in his thickened speech. Dialogue overlapped, and characters broke up their talk with umms and errs added by the director, for Miller, under the influence of the social psychologist Erving Goffman, was engrossed by psycho-linguistic concerns. This approach to language kept him bound to naturalism, even though he was aware of the artificiality buried within.[18] Treplev's (Peter Eyre) Oedipal complex was anatomized to a fare-thee-well, aided by Irene Worth's crooning a nursery song as she bandaged his head. He prepared for his suicide with the care of a Freudian compulsive, stuffing his pockets with papers, downing what was left in Nina's glass and removing all traces of her presence. Doctor Dorn then took his time to rummage through drawers and collate the evidence he found. The whole episode took seven minutes.

As Miller later explained, in seeking to avoid the stereotypes accumulated around Chekhov, his method was deliberately reductive, stressing "Russian" raucous vulgarity and eruptive gaiety. " . . . for years Trigorin has been played as a rather silvery, distinguished figure, reminiscent of a slightly disreputable English gynœcologist. Arkadina . . . is usually played in a very English-actressy way, whereas it would be rather interesting to show her as a rather pudgy little spitfire played by an actress like Prunella Scales."[19] He regretted the grandness that Irene Worth has bestowed on the role.

Miller returned to Chekhov with an austere *Three Sisters* (Cambridge Theatre, 1976) that undercut the usual sympathy for the threesome. One spectator's "heart sank" at the outset when he saw the platform stage, the plain, grey backcloth and the naked spotlights.[20] Ignoring the fact that the play had later been rewritten, Miller accepted Chekhov's pre-liminary statement that it was a comedy; he worked against the notion of the sisters as glamorous and sensitive "Grade-A girls . . . pathetically defeated by the mediocrity of provincial life." In his view, they are quite ordinary and their fate is not tragic. Janet Suzman made Masha affected and pretentious, full of contempt for others, and in love with a stout, elderly bore. The most eye-opening performance was Angela Down's Irina: stiff, starchy, abrasive. She had none of the appealing femininity of Beatrix Thompson in Komis's version or Peggy Ashcroft in Saint-Denis's, but the lines certainly support an emphasis on the self-absorp-tion of youth. When Tusenbach was shot, this Irina pounded her fist on the ground, spitting out "I knew it, I knew it," furious with him for being such a fool. Conversely, the customarily repellent characters won a meed of sympathy: Natasha came off as funny rather than malevolent and Soleny as an harrassed, lonely alcoholic.

Miller took Dickens as an analogue for detailed characterization, with minute behaviourist details as clues to personality: Vershinin's way of holding a cigarette, Masha's luxuriating in his smoke while detesting Soleny's cigar, Soleny's topping up his brandy: these were lightning cari-catures in contrast with Stanislavsky's slowly built-up oil paintings. Without a formal décor, the actors composed a clear visual contrast between foreground and background, so the attention was often directed to the response to a speech rather than the speech itself. Miller also focussed on the Proustian theme of time lost and retrieved: before Peter Stein, he made the spinning-top an epitome of human life, an organism set in motion by a form of energy which then topples to a standstill. He ended the first act with the cast turning to the audience and holding its pose as the photograph is taken, freezing them forever in a single moment.[21]

Farcical comedy overwhelmed Lindsay Anderson's *Seagull* (Lyric Theatre, 1975), which also claimed to be following Chekhov's intention. Each act was preceded by a recorded Russian folksong, which is like introducing a Beckett play with "When Irish eyes are smiling." The cast, headed by Joan Plowright as Arkadina, were more a group of actors come together to do a play than people in real situations. One was reminded of the comment of the Scottish director Robert David

Macdonald: "All Chekhov's plays seem to me to be about out-of-work actors, and certainly all of his characters behave like out-of-work actors."[22] The exception was Helen Mirren, whose Nina was no Ophelia-like wraith, but a hearty, ruddy country girl whose blind admiration seduced Trigorin more than he seduced her. A streak of amorality ran through this Nina's survival tactics.

Each of these productions revealed a conscious effort to work against *idées reçues* of Chekhov and to acclimatize him to our times by thwarting popular expectations. But, as Vera Gottlieb points out, Miller and Lindsay used comedy "only as an aspect of dramatic form – not as a method of raising the issues through ironic detachment or as a source of politic questioning through distancing and to counteract empathy."[23] Comedy was more critical to concept in the Royal Shakespeare Company *Ivanov*.

Ivanov had been revived with little acclaim in 1950 with Michael Hordern in the lead. John Gielgud's star turn in 1965 grew out of the Hamlet analogy, aging its hero to forty-five and emphasizing his spiritual weariness. Gielgud's romantic acting bestowed a nobility on the character and overdid the adust melancholy. Penelope Gilliatt lamented that "everything happens in isolation, surrounded by dead air, which has become the hallowed English way of playing Chekhov."[24] In 1972, Derek Jacobi gave Ivanov a fuller emotional range tinged with lyricism in Toby Robertson's version, retitled *A Crisis of Conscience*.

David Jones' *Ivanov* at the RSC in 1976 was the first to rethink the play along contemporary lines. Jones, a director devoted to Gorky, impressed by Mark Donskoy's films and Russian actors' ability to veer rapidly from one emotion to another, took Chekhov's intention to be satirical. He fleshed out the secondary roles with Gogolian detail, but the centrepiece was John Wood's St. Vitus of an Ivanov. He was a comic eye-of-the-cyclone, a would-be solipsist pulled in all directions, the cause of chaos and confusion. Garbed in a Byronic blouse that ironized his middle-age, Wood downplayed soul in favor of a ferocious intelligence and a jumping-jack body. The high jinks were so uproarious that the rare moments of seriousness came across as vivid mood swings. Predictably, the critics grumbled that the manic Wood was too strong an antidote to the depressive Gielgud and craved more pain and vulnerability in the role. But that was precisely Jones's point: Wood the thespian show-off was the ideal exponent of Ivanov's emotional exhibitionism. The *Times* astutely noted that the production' wed Chekhovian bleakness to the robust hilarity of Ben Travers's farces, then enjoying a revival; this was said to reflect "something of the end-of-Empire mood that seems to grip the country."[25]

With the establishment of the National Theatre, the RSC, and other more or less permanent reps, it became fashionable for British playwrights to re-adapt the classics (e.g., Edward Bond's *Three Sisters*, 1966), despite an ignorance of the original language. Arguing from "inner conviction" (as Michael Frayn puts it), they declared an affinity for a given dramatist and, usually consulting a trot, produced a version which had the reputation and, invariably, the personality of their own writing. In the age of such radical recensions as Charles Marowitz's experimental Shakespeare, Ibsen and Strindberg, mucking about with Chekhov was natural.

In 1977 Richard Eyre of the Nottingham Playhouse commissioned Trevor Griffiths, an anti-establishment playwright of vociferous socialism, to create his own English *Cherry Orchard*. Steeped in Raymond Williams and György Lukács, Griffiths was a master of Marxist dialectic. He presented the Chekhov ensemble as a stagnant group whose consciousness was turned inward. As Griffiths explained,

For half a century now, in England as elsewhere, Chekhov has been the almost exclusive property of theatrical class sectaries for whom the plays have been plangent and sorrowing evocations of an "ordered" past no longer with "us," its passing greatly to be mourned. For theatregoers . . . Chekhov's tough, bright-eyed complexity was dulced into swallowable sacs of sentimental morality [. . .] Translation followed translation, *that* idiom became "our" idiom, that class "our" class, until the play's specific historicity and precise sociological imagination had been bleached of all meanings beyond those required to convey the necessary "natural" sense that the fine will always be undermined by the crude and that the "human condition" can for all essential purposes be equated with "the plight of the middle classes."[26]

This now-prophetic comedy invested all its positive significance in Trofimov and Lopakhin (oddly rebaptized with the upper-class name Alexander) as it dwelt on the social inequities within the group. Aware that the character-drawing of the student had been vitiated by the tsarist censorship and that the British theatre adopted Ranevskaya's view of him as an immature darling, an uninhibited Griffiths rewrote the part. His Trofimov, as played by Mick Ford, an actor usually cast as scruffy proletarians, was an impassioned idealist and outspoken Marxist, tugging nervously on his goatee. "I'm a perennial student" became "I'm still a student, and if the authorities have their way, I suspect I'll always be one." The orchard he evoked for Anya had the former owners hanging from the cherry trees, and his apostrophes were sprinkled with such abusive terms as "rancid meat" and "shit."[27]

Expressionist devices were also employed: Act II began with Charlotta's speech in Russian played through a tannoy, and the passerby, significantly renamed a "Vagrant," appeared in a World War I uniform. The backdrop for Act II was Gainsborough's painting of "Mr. and Mrs. Andrews," placid Georgian gentry situated in their proprietorship of nature. In bailing out sentimental bilge, Griffiths fell overboard into rough waters, having Varya treat the servants as harshly as Natasha does. He felt the need to fill in the ellipses and reticences of the text, and his ignorance of Russian language and culture led to overstated incongruities such as Varya's falling to her knees, kissing a crucifix and saying "God is with you, Mama!" as a "translation" of the simple "*gospod s vami, mamochka!*" (what's come over you, mama dear!)[28] In his eagerness to enlist Chekhov to the cause, Griffiths produced a cartoon of the forces leading to the Revolution.

Michael Frayne, a dramatist who did know Russian, produced a translation of *Cherry Orchard* for the National Theatre in 1978, in which Trofimov called himself the "vagabond student," an image perhaps deliberately reminiscent of Rudolf Friml. Here the central figure was Lopakhin, a self-made man propelled by his love of Ranevskaya. Albert Finney gave him an accent of class triumph denuded of shame: after the auction, he knocked over a vase, caught it in mid-flight and then jigged around it joyfully, jubilating like a child getting a long-awaited gift. In his journal, the director Peter Hall wrote of Chekhov:

His characters are so self-absorbed they are almost indifferent to other people's troubles. They blame others for being sad; they very rarely sympathise with them. From this total absorbtion [*sic*] in self comes Chekhov's comedy, for it means that every character says something surprising. It's a quite harsh atmosphere but loaded with action.

This ruthless narcissism he found very Russian, unsentimental and un-English.[29] So Dorothy Tutin made Ranevskaya a woman who loved everyone vaguely but didn't care for anyone in particular, kissing Firs' hands, then letting him tremble as he placed a footstool for her. When Anya appeared from behind Charlotta's carpet, everyone applauded; when Varya did, no one showed any interest, she was so much wallpaper.[30]

The production achieved its set aims, but was underestimated by critics. Hall had predicted that his Krejča-like cruelty would be found unacceptable, when, a few months earlier, he had read the favourable critical reception of a *Cherry Orchard* Peter Gill staged at the Riverside Studio. Hall concluded that the English prefer a Chekhov full of gentle pathos to a comic or passionate one.

The set for the Riverside *Orchard* was nothing but floor and walls of the same dark-stained tongue-and-groove wooden planks; the actors had to enter and exit through empty space, which worked for the dancers of the *grande ronde* in Act III and set up a tragic finale: Firs shuffled across the immense floor in slippers, never reaching his goal. The intimacy of Gill's staging was an element increasingly evident in English Chekhov of this period and appealing to an audience raised on television. The closeness of spectator to actor helped corner the comedy and cloister the emotions. In such productions as the Bristol Old Vic *Uncle Vanya* (1974) and Trevor Nunn's *Three Sisters* at the RSC Warehouse (1978/9) the least gesture and look were immediately perceptible.

The latter had begun as a small-scale production at Stratford's Other Place, with a suggestive backcloth by John Napier of a flaking golden iconostasis, candle-lit in its murkier moments. More physical than previous English stagings, it indulged the passionate outbursts of Suzanne Bertish's volcanic Masha and the tantrums of Susan Tracy's termagant Natasha, showing up their emotional kinship; but it was most noteworthy for its conservational tone and piercing whispers, exemplified by the understated Vershinin of Edward Petherbridge. The audience, in one reviewer's phrase, became "flies on the wall," keenly aware of the characters' refusal to confront their fears. The spectator's gaze constantly panned from speaker to hearer's reactions and occasionally had to glance away, to avoid an embarrassing frontal engagement with the characters' evasions.[31]

SHARED EXPERIENCE

The Seagull continued to be the most elusive of the Big Four. To convey Chekhov's concerns into a more accessible medium, Thomas Kilroy transferred the play to Ireland of the Celtic twilight (Royal Court Theatre, 1981). For many British playgoers, it made the social and economic context more readily comprehensible and brought the characters more clearly into focus. Their isolation suddenly made sense when Russia was John Bull's Other Island. The cultural crossover also pointed up the jokes: when Anna Massey as Isobel Desmond (the Arkadina figure) responded to her son's play by exclaiming, "Good Lord, it's one of those Celtic things," it brought down the house. Unfortunately, with the

39 Act I of *Three Sisters*, directed by Trevor Nunn, Stratford-upon-Avon, 1979. Far l.,
Edward Petherbridge as Vershinin and Suzanne Bertish as Masha.

landed gentry teetering on the brink of bankruptcy, Medvedenko as an underprivileged malcontent and Trigorin as a summering Englishman, Anglo-Irish relations ultimately overshadowed Chekhov's concern with problems of art.

The Seagull that stirred up the most controversy was that of Mike Alfreds. Alfreds, who founded the Shared Experience company in 1975, was especially skilled at turning panoramic literary works such as the *Arabian Nights* and *Bleak House* into dramatic experiments in acting style, and at bringing the processes of collective creation to "fixed scripts." In working on Chekhov, he sought to break through British constipation to achieve emotional volatility and an extroverted "Slavic" release. Unafraid of having lines sound foreign and stilted, he tried to avoid anglicizing the plays, though he realized that his actors would never be Russian: the result was to be a synthetic world infused with the soul of the play.[32]

His 1981 *Seagull* was played with minimal props and furniture and in rehearsal clothes; but the behaviour was realistic or, rather, what Alfreds called "super-realism": physicalized performances of characters in the grip of intense passion. "Chekhov can take rough handling," approved one critic,[33] but the common reaction was that of John Elsom, who huffed:

Chekhov was a naturalistic writer and naturalism depends upon the imitation of life. You have got to believe that you are watching realistically conceived people walking around in acceptably convincing reproductions of the landscapes and interiors of Chekhov's chosen plays.[34]

Nothing daunted, Alfreds filled his *Cherry Orchard* (Oxford Playhouse, 1982) with childlike exuberance, and eye-popping, hand-wringing clownish performances. He admitted that the balance between farce and feeling was lacking because of insufficient rehearsal time, but he repudiated the idea that the action was routine everyday conduct: this plot was extraordinary. He protested against the idea that Chekhov must be staged moodily or flaccidly, in white or beige; and in translations that made the plays "comfortable," by evening out the texture and thought patterns of the original. He was one of the few directors to recognize Chekhov's careful technique of verbal leitmotifs.

The Oxford *Orchard* was badly received, the critics objecting to the hectic frenzy and what they saw as grotesque hysterics. This led Alfreds to discover the one constant about Chekhov's plays: "People seem very proprietary in their view of how Chekhov should be staged. Critics speak of a 'Chekhovian balance' as if Chekhov has to be balanced like the BBC."[35] It was not the BBC, but another establishment institution, the National Theatre, which invited him in 1985 to recreate the *Orchard* as the third production of a newly formed group run by Edward Petherbridge and Ian McKellen.

Alfreds regarded the play as more slippery and elliptical than the rest of the Chekhov canon, its surface erupting in such bubbles as Firs' outburst of autobiography, which he restored. Eschewing realism, he wanted a design based on Boris Kustodiev's colorful genre pictures and skyscapes. In response, Paul Dart conceived an abstract box hung with white muslin, "inside an outer skin of blue sky and green earth" which "provided a limpid space within which to contain and illuminate this exemplary restoration."[36] Obviously drawing on Strehler, the white curtains and canopied ceiling took on different shapes and at the end tensed, snapped free and floated to the ground revealing a bright sky.

Lopakhin dominated this *Orchard* in Ian McKellen's vivid and intelligent reading, the only performance to make full use of creative improvisation. When he announced his purchase of orchard, he tossed his keys in the air and kissed the deed of sale. There was no consensus, however, about the cast as an ensemble. Some judged them to be energized by McKellen's mysterious source of power and swept up in the action. Others sensed a lack of cohesion, with the characters isolated from their social context. Sheila Hancock as Ranevskaya was no *grande dame*, but an ordinary woman, gushing, confused and evasive, pacing the borderline between fairy tales and a frightening real world. "Too middle class," was Vera Gottlieb's verdict, whereas Martin Hoyle found her devoid of the usual middle-class gentility.[37] The strongest disapproval was reserved for Laurance Rudic's Trofimov; Gottlieb found that by interpreting "the only character who suggests that change may be positive" as a "cold, self-regarding humbug" the play delivered "a reactionary message."[38] In his defence, Rudic, used to the more *laissez-aller* methods of the Glasgow Citizens Theatre, complained that the extended rehearsal period "exhausted all the possibilities," leading "to a rigid, repetitive type of performance, squeezed of all juice and any sense of interpretive danger."[39]

Whatever the disagreements, they were salutary. Even if the critics' favorite issues were trivialized or neglected, Alfreds revealed that the play was "not a weepie about real estate, nor a prolonged sigh for the never-will-be or the never-was, but something more like a diagnosis with recommendations for surgery – dazzling, dispassionate and tough."[40]

Beyond the affinity to Dickens, Chekhov was located within a Russian tradition, not of social purpose and realism, but of fantasy and satire: for the first time, British reviewers alluded to Chekhov as a reserved, intimate variation on Gogol, Dostoevsky, Mayakovsky and Nabokov.

Alfreds himself believed his best experiment with Chekhov to be a *Three Sisters* put on in 1986 with the Shared Experience Company. He approached it as an ironic tragedy: "The active theme of the play is how people cope with failure by constructing fantasies of a future happiness, or withdrawing into cynicism, or by trying to pretend that all is well. Even Natasha could be said to be a failure, because she never wins the acceptance of the sisters."[41] Like Miller, Alfreds saw the sisters as emotional and moral cowards and evaders. Against an abstract expressionist backcloth, Paul Dart's set was composed of four off-white columns speckled in black, representing both a colonnade and the birch trees; this was harshly back-lit as the audience entered. Black furniture and dark green uniforms abetted a pervasive melancholy and sense of deracination. In Act I, the furniture was scattered about; in Act II Natasha had arranged it neatly. The Act III fire was suggested by a feverish glow on the backdrop. The last scene was empty, so that the characters seemed to drift about in limbo. Three and a half hours were devoted to imbricating the textural and emotional web and the scrupulous details. Predictably, the critics split, most of the dailies complaining of the slow pace (they had to meet deadlines), the intellectualizing and the narrow emotional range; the weeklies praised the layering of emotion over hysteria.

WILD HONEY AND *PLAYER PIANOS*

Alfreds' strong opinions of the Chekhovian canon's meaning and style caused disruption among the critics, but there was enough unanimity about *Wild Honey* to win it an award as the best play of 1984. This was Michael Frayn's adaptation of *Untitled* for the National Theatre: regarding the play as a rough draft, he decided

to reorganise the story and characters that are beginning to emerge, and to give them more definite dramatic form. To this end I have felt free to reorganise the chronology of the play; to shift material from one place to another and one character to another; to write new lines and rewrite old ones.[42]

Subplots were eliminated, characters reduced to sixteen (though some new ones were added), and the tone firmed up by reducing the melodrama, "moving from lighter comedy at the beginning, through farce, to the darker and more painful comedy of the final scenes." The title came from Anna Petrovna's description of the Voinitsevs' honeymoon and its aftermath.

As both a West End playwright and a translator of Chekhov who had actually bothered to learn Russian, Frayn's credentials were impeccable. His great service was to reveal to British audiences Chekhov's ideological evasiveness and his taste for self-parody. But both his translations and *Wild Honey* were, as Vera Gottlieb pointed out, full of "many of the assumptions underlying 'English Chekhov': the theatrical *and* philosophical nature of the farce; a context of 'absurdism'; comic determinism; and an inability to 'play' the dynamics of 'tragi-comedy.'"[43] In anglicizing his translation, Frayn manipulated his characters artificially to illustrate a theme. His view of *Three Sisters* is of a play about lives poisoned by hope; his Bergsonian view of Chekhov's one-act jokes is that the "characters are reduced by their passions to the level of blind and inflexible machines."[44] He distrusted emotion as ludicrous or embarrassing, never a means of gaining control or fomenting revolt.

In his introduction to *Wild Honey*, Frayn granted that he deprived Chekhov's characters of their ambiguity. In performance they were almost uniformly ludicrous, leading observers to allude often to Feydeau, who had become assimilated to the English stage in John Mortimer's translations from the mid-sixties.[45] More to the point would have been a reference to the sex farces of Brian Rix, for Frayn naturalized the characters into types familiar from comic postcards and Ealing films. Only the murder of Osip the horse-thief was taken seriously, as a bloody portent of incipient revolution. Platonov's grief over his lost ideals and his sensitivity to *poshlost* were excised, and his Don Juanism set squarely at centre, expurgated of any pathology (since the reference to his wife reading Sacher-Masoch has vanished). The suicide was theatrically heightened by having Platonov run over by a train emerging from a fog, but this too was made absurd by the deluded hero trying to wave it down in a sort of "inane greeting." Ian McKellen presented both a demagogue and a holy fool, loved and pitied as the embodiment of others' youthful aspirations and detested as the embodiment of their failed ideals.

Given the masterful production of a well-carpentered comedy, the critical reaction was immensely positive. Zinovy Zinik even compared it with *A Midsummer Night's Dream* "with the amorous agency of Puck played by boredom and political impotence."[46] Sheridan Morley suggested that the raw mass of material in Chekhov's unpublished work offered other dramatists the chance to carve their own plays out of it; he looked

40 Trevor Griffiths' Chekhovian fantasia *Piano*, in a décor by Ashley Martin-Davies, Cottesloe Theatre, London, 1990.

forward to a Tom Stoppard or John Osborne version. But *Wild Honey* had been tailored to the taste of the West End, which proved fatal to it outside of London. In New York, it folded almost immediately to disastrous reviews. The critic for *Neue Zürcher Zeitung*, reviewing a Stuttgart production, was disturbed by the "false clowning, which led to much being undifferentiated. Chekhov's awkward yet brilliant juvenilia with his inimitable atmosphere was trivialized in the hands of a veteran playwright."[47] What was rough and inchoate in the original had been polished into a neat piece of boulevard stagecraft, as if Viktor Krylov had indeed undertaken to revise the work of his younger colleague.

The unlicked mass of *Platonov* proved irresistible to Trevor Griffiths as well, and his "theatrical mediation" *Piano* (Cottesloe, 1990) again resembled Chekhov moulded into tendentious shape by Gorky. With a nod to Nikita Mikhalkov's film *Unfinished Piece for Player Piano* (1976), Griffiths assembled a pastiche of idlers and talkers on a decrepit country estate, furnished it with a central symbol of fake culture – a tinkling pianola – and initiated a series of didactic discourses over the course of a summer's day. Like Frayn, Griffiths did not shy away from pratfalls and people hiding in suitcases; but there was an armature of class warfare undergirding the farce. Arguing that censorship had prevented Chekhov from introducing peasants into his plays, Griffiths included some sardonically Brechtian servants who intone "Lies eat the soul . . .

Everything is possible"; while Shcherbuk was portrayed as a proto-fascist and social Darwinian who vitriolically condemns them as "Scum, rabble, degenerates." The distance from Gaev's reference to Lopakhin as a boor is palpable; but in essence this was a "state of England" play tricked out in pre-Revolutionary Russian drag. The sense of tension on the eve of cataclysm was historically informed, even as its political chic induced a timely atmosphere of "breakdown and deadlock."[48]

Another un-Russian Chekhov undertaken by a dramatist with a successful track record was the *Uncle Vanya* of Pam Gems, directed by Kenneth Branagh and Peter Egan for the Renaissance Theatre Company, which, after nine weeks on the road, brought it to the Lyric Hammersmith in 1991. Despite some absurd gypsy dancing, the play was not rooted in the minutiae of any particular world. Kenny Miller's serviceable setting of scorched pinewood towers and huge vertical panels marbled in brown evoked Central Europe rather than Russia. The perfunctory alternation between comedy and hysteria left native-born reviewers cold, because it did not allow them to soak in an emotional subtext, but a Russian-born observer perceived astutely that *Vanya* had been

translated into the language of European culture, with a clear Calvinist stress on the sense of doom and grim predestination that surrounds our sinful, futile existence. Here even the notion of a Protestant work ethic comes to the fore with a twist. Sonya's exhortations to work [. . .] which, in a Russian context, are invariably interpreted as a parody of Socialist ideals, are here presented with the masochistic tears of joy of one who is glad to be back in the dreary routine of eternal earthly damnation.[49]

Chekhov as George Gissing may not have been in the minds of the directors, but it is an indication of the inevitable *données* that subliminally govern the transference of a play from one culture to another.

This production prompted Michael Billington to call for a three-year moratorium on Chekhov, to re-examine the source of his greatness and regard him with fresh eyes.[50] The British theatre seemed to have an infinite capacity for neutralizing extraordinary or strong-minded reinterpretations, digesting their superficial traits, and converting the plays to showpieces for skilful acting. A new production of *The Seagull* by Mike Alfreds in 1991 evoked none of the outrage of his earlier work, because so much of his innovation had grown commonplace, without becoming standard practice. Too often close acquaintance with the canon was made an excuse for sideshow attractions. *Three Sisters* was especially vulnerable to this abuse: in 1990 the sororal trio at the Royal

Court was cast from the Cusack sisters, with their father Cyril as Chebutykin (thus underlining the hint that he *did* sire Irina); in Robert Sturua's production at the Queen's Theatre Vanessa and Lynn Redgrave and their niece Jemma took the title roles (see chapter 18). More creative were attempts to bring the overly familiar situations and characters closer to the audiences' experience. A *Trinidad Sisters* (Donmar Warehouse, 1988), in an adaptation by Mustapha Matura, directed by Nicholas Kent, sacrificed Chekhov's finer points to an activist message, but, in the process, introduced a minority public to a play which had become part of the English collective unconscious.

The tendency to embroider the subtext of the Chekhovian play received a feminist twist in Helen Cooper's *Mrs. Vershinin* (Riverside Studio, 1988): while the windbag Colonel returns home, first from the merry nameday luncheon, then from the aborted Shrovetide party at the Prozorovs, his suicidal lady reveals in a series of flashbacks what has brought her to this sorry pass. An unhappy childhood, an uneasy honeymoon, sapphic frolics on the conjugal bed with her friend Anna, are repeated in freeze-frame for an hour and a half. Overly dependent on the audience's intimacy with the parent play, this exercise in pop psychology failed to grow from a well-acted case study into a Chekhovian *Rosencrantz and Guildenstern are Dead.*[51]

From the mid-seventies to the present, the trait shared by most British productions of Chekhov was an arch knowingness, a self-conscious awareness of the plays' traditions and a troubled need to confront them. Usually this was manifested in an eagerness to exorcise the spirit of Komisarjevsky and poetic melancholy. A wide spectrum of comedy, from warm humour to bitter irony, is now on display in the artistic choices; sympathy lavished on the characters' failings is replaced by harsh judgements of their limitations. What began as a salutary redressing of the emotional balance can lead to playing for laughs and over-explicit business: in Charles Sturridge's *Seagull* (Queen's Theatre, 1985), Masha vomited on hearing of Treplev's suicide.[52]

The mature theatergoer has had the chance, over three decades, to attend and evaluate a critical mass of Chekhovian production, allowing reviewers to compare and contrast, whereas their predecessors had had to intuit where the work of Komis, Guthrie or Saint-Denis interlocked with their author. When the National Theatre opened its third production of *Uncle Vanya* in 1992, directed by Sean Mathias, critics had the advantage of a wide range of reference against which to assay the Voinitsky of Ian McKellen and the Astrov of Anthony Sher.

Michael Redgrave's 1963 Voinitsky had been an "ungainly, muscular figure, built for action but constantly at odds with his own body, flapping and bumbling, yet illuminated by the sense of a refined intelligence going to ruinous waste"; this was considered the definitive Uncle Vanya, a bench mark against which to measure all others. Paul Scofield had imbued him with a "sepulchral melancholy," Peter O'Toole with a "woozy, raddled desperation," Nigel Hawthorne "an incoherent, uncontrollable rage, Donald Sinden a childlike helplessness and Michael Bryant a chilling bitterness and contempt." The Vanya of Richard Briers was a court jester, "engaged in a perpetual civil war between spaniel-like adoration in the presence of Elena and simmering outrage at the thought of her husband," but unendowed with the intelligence that made Redgrave's futility so moving. As for Astrov, whose glamour often eclipsed the title role, Olivier was the lion in the path; in more recent memory, Dinsdale Landen had presented "a turbulent sensualist in conflict with a strong superego," Albert Finney "a great bull who was finding the social code of the china shop hard to observe," and Ian Holm a clinically detached observer of his own moral and physical decline.[53]

Although McKellen and Sher both had impressive backgrounds as leading men in the classical repertory, they were cited for their comic flair and exuberant character work. McKellen's Voinitsky was understated, "a shambling, affable buffer, not to be taken too seriously"; the fever chart of his emotional tarantella ranged from desperate yelling to a self-disarming resignation. His rage seemed all the more inappropriate since Eric Porter's professor was himself a desperate invalid in need of pity. Devoid of the magnetism of Stanislavsky and Olivier, Sher's Astrov was "seedy, sweaty . . . more cynical, a bit feral." In his praise, Benedict Nightingale cited the production as a landmark on the road to true British Chekhov.

Only recently has our theatre begun to rise to Chekhov's challenges. That is the virtue of this *Uncle Vanya*. It may be muted, but it is not solemn. There are pauses, but they have content. The main actors are strong, but the supporting ones feel no need tactfully to evaporate . . .

He concluded, "Chekhov has come of age in England."[54]

CHAPTER 17

Chekhov sans frontières *(The world 1900–1995)*

> I think the staging of these plays may be entering a third phase. The first phase was to play him sentimentally . . . The second, marked by Otomar Krejča, was to play him cruelly. After the event . . . I glimpse a third phase, which is to exhibit Chekhov as a great allegorical author who passes for a painter of daily life but who uses it to paraphrase the great classic concerns.
>
> Antoine Vitez[1]

As early as 1906 the Moscow Art Theatre tours had helped explicate Chekhov to other cultures, without effacing the notion that he was essentially a Russian author. Their mission continued irregularly into the 1980s, but with ever lessening effect. The efforts to naturalize Chekhov, such as those of Pitoëff and Komisarjevsky, remained local phenomena. Not until the proliferation of theatre festivals and state-sponsored tours after World War II was there a free exchange of theatrical visions of Chekhov. Reciprocal trade agreements in the arts brought the *Three Sisters* of Strasberg and Krejča, the *Cherry Orchards* of Strehler and Barrault to the attention of others than those to whom these stagings originally spoke. A new wave of emigration added the ideas of Eastern bloc directors such as Lucian Pintilie, Andrei Serban and Thomas Langhoff into the Western mix. The crossing of borders and smudging of national boundaries resulted in Chekhov's entering the public domain. His Russianness was downplayed and his similarity to the "universal genius" of Shakespeare emphasized. As with Shakespeare, the preoccupations of the *animateurs* were projected on to his works, sometimes to the occlusion of his own intentions.

THE ORCHARD AS EMPTY SPACE

Peter Brook came late to staging Chekhov. This is all the more surprising in view of his Russian parentage and the many opportunities he had had throughout the 1950s and sixties to work with the leading actors of the English-speaking world. His experiments with an Artaudian Theatre of Cruelty, if applied to Chekhov, might have produced the British equivalent of Krejča's glaucous vision. In *The Empty Space*, which summed up his experience to 1968, Brook rejected the notion of Chekhovian slices of life; he saw the dramatist as a cautious, scalpel-wielding surgeon, removing a myriad of life's epidermal layers.

These he cultured, and then arranged them in an exquisitely cunning, completely artificial and meaningless order in which part of the cunning lay in so disguising the artifice that the result looked like the keyhole view it had never been. Any page of *The Three Sisters* gives the impression of life unfolding as though a tape-recorder had been left running. If examined carefully it will be seen to be built of coincidence as great as in Feydeau – the vase of flowers that overturns, the fire-engine that passes at just the right moment . . . touch by touch, they create through the language of illusions an overall illusion of a slice of life. This series of impressions is equally a series of alienations, each rupture is a subtle provocation and a call to thought.[2]

In Brook's opinion, Chekhov's disappointment with Stanislavsky arose because the Russian director had imposed an almost Manichæan point of view that deprived the characters of independence. Chekhov knew that in the theatre the narrative voice of the novelist must diversify into a polyphony, and for this Brook ranked him with Shakespeare.

These remarks preceded by more than a decade Brook's coming to grips with Chekhov in rehearsal, by which time he was arguably the most influential and charismatic director on the international scene. Since his move to Paris to explore the intercultural essence of drama, and his installation in the derelict operetta theatre Les Bouffes du Nord, Brook's experiments had become endowed with a mystical aura. His "Theatre of Nations" deliberately enlisted performers from diverse backgrounds in its quest to excavate a Jungian substratum of myth and common belief in everything it undertook. This search for a universal language preferred epic and elemental narratives for its raw material; when he did exploit literary texts, Brook picked such a work as *Carmen* which was bulky with accretions of legend, and stripped it to a minimal core.

Characteristically, in choosing *The Cherry Orchard* for his Chekhovian debut in 1981, Brook described it as a "theatrical movement purely played."[3] In his declared intention to "avoid sentimentality, a false Chekhovian manner that is not in the text," he seemed to be ignoring the fact that many of his illustrious contemporaries had already done so. Rather, he claimed to be rejecting the outmoded Russo-English tradition of his youth: "gloomy, romantic, long and slow. It's a comic play about real life." For Brook, the crucial factor of Chekhov's life was that he knew he was doomed and, even so, carried on with incredible energy. A similar duality saturates the play: the imminent collapse of a way of life should stimulate not morbid passivity, but buoyant vivacity. (In this regard, he considered the best production of Chekhov to be the film *Unfinished Piece for Player Piano*, because the characters share a *joie de vivre*.) Jean-Claude Carrière's adaptation of *Orchard*, made from a literal translation by Brook's mother-in-law Lusia Lavrova,[4] was intended to be curt and colloquial, like the dialogue in Beckett, and yet as light and limpid as the Russian original. It was the first French translation of Chekhov to reproduce all his ellipses.

Naturally, when a director as distinguished as Brook produced *The Cherry Orchard*, comparisons with Strehler were inevitable. The Russian critic Gaevsky detected a polemic between two theatrical cousins german: having begun their careers in the post-war period, Strehler, the leftist and Brechtian, had gradually moved towards a theatre of splendour, while Brook, the Oxonian aesthete, called for spareness and simplicity. Strehler was centripetal, creating a theatre of stasis; Brook was centrifugal, always on the move. Strehler elevated life to the clouds, while Brook brought things down to earth, staging his later shows on sand.[5]

Like Strehler, Brook had to answer the central question: how is the orchard to be portrayed? Ought it to be shown at all? Isn't Lopakhin grappling with a childhood mirage? Strehler broke with tradition by encompassing both stage and audience in a blossom-laden veil, whose palpitations were the seismographic record of the characters' feelings. Andrei Serban planted a couple of stunted trees to create a schism between the imagined orchard and its reality. Anatoly Éfros interspersed budding branches between tombstones as a cruel absurdity. None of these solutions could be wholly satisfying since none captured simultaneously both the concrete reality and what it engendered. Brook showed nothing. Ranevskaya's gaze located the orchard at the end of the upper light-row, which was also the location of the garden and bygone happiness; the orchard could also be glimpsed in the enormous bouquet of cut flowers that Epikhodov hid behind and whose aroma drifted into the audience.

The reduction of stage pieces to carpets, cushions and a few high-backed chairs was to distil the play into a poem about "life and death and transition and change." Adventitious details and local colour would

41 The blue carpets in Act II of *La Cerisaie* (*The Cherry Orchard*), directed by Peter Brook,
Bouffes du Nord, Paris, 1983 revival. L.–r.: John Blatchley as Trofimov, Irina Brook as
Anya, Natacha Parry as Ranevskaya, Martine Chevalier as Varya, Niels Arestrup as
Gaev, Robert Murzeau as Lopakhin and Guy Tréjean as Firs.

simply distract from those eternal aspects. In opposition to Strehler's matched sets and costumes in a world bleached of colour, Chloë Obolensky's garments, including the smart black and white lace and sequined dresses for Ranevskaya, contrasted the necessary historic information with the timelessness of the other design elements. As a motif, the blue of Brook's carpets replaced Strehler's white: objects were rarefied to define not a milieu but a situation.

Unlike Strehler, Brook tried to submerge the action in the flow of life, with all its terrible fatality and fugacity; the inner rhythm allowed for no framed episodes or deliberately contrived "moments." The "dramatic" component was reduced by ignoring psychologies; his characters were set in a mobile public space, stressing the passing moment in a Bergsonian *durée*. The screens and chairs betokened an alien environment in which, as in Beckett, the actors had to keep moving lest the characters catch sight of their own predicament.

Revealing as such Plutarchian contrasts with other productions may be, Brook's *Cherry Orchard* can also be seen as a direct progression of his own experiments. "While playing the specifics," Brook stated, "we also try to play the myth – the secret play."[6] More venerable than Firs, the rugs and pillows of the first act were both the ground-cloth of the oriental story-teller and a magic carpet, recalling Brook's previous production *The Mahabharata* and his African experiment The *Conference of the Birds*. In the second act, the rugs were rolled up by stagehands to stand in for fallen trees on which Charlotta balanced like a tight-rope walker. In the last act, again rolled up, they disclosed an asphalt floor that revealed the estate's desolation.

The ramshackle Bouffes du Nord, in its unfashionable locale, became the decaying manorhouse, with the audience integrated into the action. Ranevskaya went to bed up the stairs to the first balcony; a red carpet covered the centre aisle to celebrate her return; at the ball, the Jewish orchestra played behind the audience, the dancers incessantly came and went through a vomitorium; and in Act IV Anya spoke from the gallery (or attic), Varya threw Trofimov his galoshes from the dress circle. When the doors finally closed, Firs was left alone – with the spectators. More than in Strehler or Serban, the audience was implicated in the story, conniving imaginatively with the production.[7]

At first sight, this circulation of free energy in a constant flux between spectators and actors would suggest a recrudescence of the loving, indulgent Chekhov. What prevented a descent into bathos was the *presto* tempo; everything happened quickly, rushing towards the abyss at an insouciant fever-pitch. "The absence of vitality," said Brook, "would be a betrayal." This feast in plaguetime was served up without intermissions, with no single line or image allowed to arrest the velocity of two and a quarter hours' brief traffic on the stage. As in Barrault, this was abetted by swiftly spoken French dialogue, even though the cast was international, with Brook's wife Natacha Parry as Ranevskaya, the Norwegian Niels Arestrup as Lopakhin, and the French Michel Piccoli as Gaev.

Ranevskaya, mistress of the domain, was treated like a queen, but her kingdom was a house of cards. Drawing on his parents' experience, Brook conceived of Ranevskaya as an émigrée, returning after a long absence to find neither homeland nor home. Another interest that Brook shared with Strehler was the sibling relationship of Gaev and Ranevskaya, orphaned in the present. Act IV came as a liberation for the other characters, but for them it was the nadir of helplessness. They burst into tears like Hänsel and Gretel discovering they had lost their trail of crumbs. Their farewell to the house was not a statuesque pose, but a snapshot taken by a candid camera.[8]

For all of Ranevskaya's seeming centrality, Brook followed Chekhov in making Lopakhin the pivotal figure: in Arestrup's interpretation a supremely intelligent and calmly arrogant individual, locked in a tense struggle for the house, his living revenge and long-awaited triumph. When he got it, he fell into startling convulsions, losing self-control at the realization that he had wasted talk, time, love, the past, even the orchard itself to obtain soulless real estate, a true "empty space." In his frenzy, he knocked over a screen and revealed the whole family huddled behind it.

Such moments showed Brook's *mise-en-scène* to be a kind of code, easily broken, or combinations of silhouettes and poses that seemed to be fortuitous but were artfully contrived, like Tarot cards dealt by a shrewd fortune-teller. (The theme of predicting fate, a powerful one in Russian literature, was as strong here as in Brook's *Carmen*.[9]) Any metaphors were concealed, especially in group scenes. Ranevskaya's first entrance with its casual composition, dark colours, costumes and poses was reminiscent of paintings by the Russian Itinerants; but a closer look showed that it was geometrically constructed of diagonals and crisscrosses; the ostensible unpretentiousness of the arrangement added to the dramatic irony. For some, the seeming fortuity of the staging and the refusal to take sides bespoke an "oriental" cast of mind, a Zen view of "vastitude."[10]

When Brook's *Cherry Orchard* toured, it inevitably lost the specificity it had when set in the Bouffes du Nord. Nevertheless, its arrival in Russia was an epiphany. Suddenly Russian theatre people felt freed from the bonds of not only Stanislavskian tradition but the Aesopic and metaphoric styles of Lyubimov and Éfros. They were confronted not with an alien vision, but a clarification of their own instincts. Lev Dodin, who had succeeded Tovstonogov as Leningrad's finest stage director, stated,

Were I to name a *mise-en-scène* that embodies a certain norm and even ideal, it would be Peter Brook's *Cherry Orchard*. There are no symbols and no large constructs. The most complex things – the movement of the soul, or spiritual substance, if you will, are expressed by the simplest possible means. At the same time, everything is sketched out exquisitely, as if with invisible strokes in the air.[11]

Yet when Brook brought his production to the Brooklyn Academy of Music in New York, union rules demanding recasting brought down the house of cards. Overawed by his potent reputation, the critical response was respectful but hardly ecstatic. Instead of a delicately balanced ensemble, there was a group of disparate actors working "loudly and busily to promote their own parts," the same complaint that Kazan had leveled at Strasberg's *Three Sisters*. Uncoordinated in actions and reactions, ranging from television soap opera through Strasbergian Method to Old Vic in their styles, they seemed to be competing with one another. With Brian Dennehy overdoing Lopakhin's vulgarity in a loud and blustery manner, centrality shifted to the Swedish actor Erland Josephson as Gaev. He was able to convey in a gentle voice, teary eyes and fumbling for fruit pastilles "a complicated and subtle combination of melancholy, childish impracticality, and intellectual curiosity."[12] He and Natacha Parry (the only carry-over from the original cast) seemed detached from the circus antics of the rest of the players.

Because of the imbalance, Brook's brisk and non-nostalgic approach looked crude. Otomar Krejča's harsh Chekhov had never been heard of in the US, so Brook was faulted for letting Chekhovian objectivity slip into unnecessary cruelty. Dennehy's Lopakhin, in particular, seemed sadistic in his drunken exulting over his purchase and his dragging out the proposal *manqué*. Brook's "moral aspiration for the theater to disturb us into experiencing an intensified perception of everyday life"[13] failed to make an impact on the American image of Chekhov.

THREE LITTLE MAIDS FROM RUSSIA

The abiding interest of Western directors in traditional Asian theatre, from Meyerhold to Brook, Ariane Mnouchkine, and Eugenio Barba, eventuated in calls for intercultural and multicultural performance. In basing empirical experiments on the "untainted" inspiration of the oriental, these *animateurs* were not always aware that the East had already reciprocated by borrowing from Western theatre. Chekhov had become popular in Japan early in the century and is currently among the top ten foreign authors there. The first performance of a direct translation (as opposed to a liberal adaptation to a Japanese setting) was *The Proposal* as *The Dog* (*Inu*, 1910), in which an *onnagata* or *kabuki* female impersonator took the part of "Nataria," daughter of the landowner "Sutepan." A few months later, a biological female appeared in *The Bear* (*Kumo*). These two plays were frequently revived over the next three years.[14]

Kaoru Osanai, a proponent of *Shingeki* or modern theatre, visited Moscow in 1912, paying close attention to the Art Theatre; on his return to Tokyo, he staged Chekhov at his Free Theatre (Jiyū Gekijō), sedulously reproducing the Western styles, especially in *The Cherry Orchard*. This movement became very active, and by 1920 all of the major plays and many vaudevilles by Chekhov had been produced, and a lecture about his work delivered at the Gaiety Theatre in Yokohama.[15] Chekhov's *toska* (grief, yearning) entered the language as *tosuka*. In 1924 Osanai established the Tsukiji Little Theatre (Tsukiji Shōgekijō) to promote *Shingeki*, with an exclusively Western repertory, heavy on Ibsen and Chekhov, and striving for a "European," even naturalistic depiction of life. During the progressive westernization that came with post-war Occupation, this style flourished until the late 1960s. Then fresher influences from the West, as well as a determination to exploit native styles, helped the Japanese to move away from the primitive Art Theatre model. Existentialism was a particularly congenial philosophy for situating the Chekhovian play in an ahistorical frame.

At the behest of the Shiki Theatre Company in Tokyo, Andrei Serban recreated his New York *Cherry Orchard* there in 1977, followed in 1980 by a *Seagull* which was located around the spell-binding lake The designer Kaoru Kanamuri set out a huge pool of water, two or three feet deep, with a large seagull-shaped platform in the middle. The area was surrounded with birch trees, their reflections multiplied on the back wall. The real water allowed Yakov to be seen swimming and converted Treplev's platform into a Noh stage, lit by a moon reflected off the lake; at the end, it became his study, and he literally "drowned his book," scattering the torn fragments on the surface. The actor playing Treplev, who took Yukio Mishima as his model, painted his face white prior to his *hara-kiri*: on shooting himself, he fell face forward into the pool.[16]

Many of these features were repeated, more cohesively, in the Tokyo Engeki ensemble *Seagull* of 1993, directed by Hirowatari Tsunetoshi and bravely toured to Moscow and Taganrog. Although it was played in the round, it seemed in many respects to be an old-fashioned and respectful period piece, with an odd combination of loyalty to Chekhov's stage directions and complete freedom within individual moments. The play within a play, for instance, was staged not as a monologue but as a dance drama with five nude young men moving exotically around Nina to symbolize cosmic forces or evil demons or fate as they held Nina in their outstretched arms and moved her in a circle.

The circle was repeated in Okajima Sigēo's scenography: a bare islet of a platform sat in the middle of the monochromatic space, surrounded by a moat of transparent water and reached by four bridges, whose cruciform gave the critics something to ponder. Throughout the play, the water purled and babbled, while large silver acorns floated by incessantly, creating a mood of contemplative harmony and pointing up the estate's isolation. Cherry branches extended from the light-grid were both the traditional Japanese symbol for fleeting life and an intertextual comment. Fog rolled in to enfold Nina and Trigorin's farewell and Nina's last act entrance, clearing in time for Treplev's suicide.

At first, the older characters wore traditional kimonos, and the "young Turks" were barefoot and in jeans. By the middle of the play, they had all changed to the usual Chekhovian dress, except for Arkadina who carried on in something like the farthingale of Good Queen Bess as portrayed in a provincial theatre. The acting was highly physical, with abrupt entrances and exits, as if each encounter concealed conspiracy and danger. A sturdy, vigorous Treplev leapt on to the stage, and, bird-like, hopped on one leg. Even so, emotions were hidden by masks of politeness, and the characters froze in place to conceal their true feelings from prying eyes. There were no hysterics until, in the last act, brittle, nervous Nina thumped the floor and tried to drown in the water. In this interpretation, Treplev shot himself because he realized that his love for Nina could never match hers for Trigorin. As silvery leaves drifted down on to the sleeping Sorin, the torn white pieces of his manuscript circled slowly on the black backdrop. The use of traditional *topoi* of Japanese art distanced the sense of everyday life, to create a semblance of eternity and reflections of reflections.[17]

Respectfully, the Tokyo Engeki sought to graft deeply rooted national images on to a venerated foreign author. But Chekhov was so familiar an icon that other versions radically rejected both Russian and Japanese cultural specificity. Such was the case with Tadashi Suzuki's Company of Toga (SCOT), a prominent force in adapting Western plays to Japanese styles based loosely on Noh, Kabuki and folksong. Eager to reinstate the actor's body as the theatrical instrument *par excellence*, Suzuki forcibly effected collisions between East and West, beginning with versions of Greek tragedy, whose mythic content could be enhanced by the heightened techniques of traditional Japanese theatre. Suzuki abandoned the Greeks to stage *King Lear* (1984); the natural progression from Shakespeare was to Chekhov, with *Three Sisters* (1984), *The Cherry Orchard* (1986), and *Uncle Vanya* (1988).

For Suzuki, what lies at the root of human misery is the inability to live without illusions; Chekhov's point is that his characters cannot confront reality and must escape into imagination and fallacies of vision. By deconstructing sequence, psychology, and dialogue, Suzuki was trying to lay bare the characters' essence in a style derived from the Theatre of the Absurd. *Three Sisters* was offered as an intentionally untraditional model for a new theatre, and a vehicle for social criticism.[18] Half the dialogue was cut, and the four acts reduced to ten episodes lasting no more than an hour. Soleny, Fedotik, Rodé and Ferapont disappeared; Kulygin was boiled down to a single line. Vershinin and Tusenbach were merged into Man 1 and Man 2, who shared each other's lines and those of Chebutykin; voicing attitudes without consistency, they made up a confused antiphony of memories and voices past. But Suzuki provided no signposts to explicit meaning.

The two men and the three sisters were on stage throughout the play. Man 1 and 2 hid in large wicker baskets; talking heads most of the time, they would pop up to deliver their lines and then sink back out of sight. Near the end they emerged from their baskets as the Horst Wessell song was played, but eventually returned. The sisters, described by Suzuki as "deluded fools," crouched on mats, peering toward a distant Moscow, moving first in unison in halting steps and only gradually achieving individual gestures. Olga, her lines barked out by Suzuki's star Kayoko Shiraishi, was constantly complaining; Masha went on about her marriage and her love affair, relieving her anxieties with explicit masturbation, while Olga fed her with chopsticks; Irina grumbled about work and her wretched life. They each held a carrier bag and an open umbrella, and, when erect, the basket men had their own parasols. Some saw the umbrellas as the dreams of Moscow or a Western way of life, but they could also be read as scanty protection from pelting reality.

The other characters, Andrey, Natasha and Anfisa, were distinguished by greater mobility and more traditional wear. Natasha was played by a bearded man in an apricot-coloured kimono, with a baby-doll strapped to his back; he threw a tantrum, picked up an (imaginary) fork from the floor, and flounced off. Squatting Anfisa darted in and out with trays of food. A soundtrack of violin and piano music, the greatest hits of European romanticism, underscored the dreams and illusions. Superficially, this version sounds like a sardonic critique of westernization in post-war Japan and it was received with hearty laughter by the Japanese audience; but it went beyond specific cases to deplore the dehumanization of life in general.[19]

Suzuki followed up this interpretation with a metonymic *Cherry Orchard*, filling the stage frame with a gigantic tree, both dream and reality. Its material presence stood for the figment of the orchard, the way mannequins in Tadeusz Kantor's productions encapsulate childhood.[20] In Suzuki's *Uncle Vanya* a young girl dreamed every night of a mesmerizingly happy life. In her imagination the Chekhovian characters came to life, as desperate persons with no way out, yet constantly battling each other. It was a rather transparent metaphor for the current global situation. The girl grew unable to tolerate them as they became more grotesque and deformed; eventually, they all turned into "basket-cases" because her innocence made her unable to view them as real human beings.

THE HOUSE OF ALL NATIONS

Frontiers meant nothing any more: directors circulated freely, grafting their own conceptions on to the native traditions of their hosts. Anatoly Éfros transplanted his *Cherry Orchard* to Japan, explaining to the actors that its basic problem was life as a whirlpool of time. He then restaged it at the Finnish National Theatre in 1983, with a set by Valery Levental: this disjointed, grotesque production had its characters moving in circles and snow covering the stage at the end.[21] In 1987 Princeton University invited Tovstonogov to direct *Uncle Vanya*. Peter Zadek enjoyed a triumphant success with an "objective" *Ivanov* at the Vienna Akademietheater in 1990.[22]

Oleg Efremov, increasingly frustrated by the intramural politics of the Moscow Art Theatre, went farther afield to trade on his experience: in 1991 he directed the mainland Chinese premiere of *The Seagull* (a Cantonese *Seagull* had been staged in Hong Kong by Tsai Chin in the 1980s). The cast of the Beijing People's Art Theatre had already rehearsed for a month under Ren Ming, listening to lectures and tapes, watching films and videos. Efremov started with the last act and moved backward to the first to enable the actors to read the climax into their characters' earlier frame of mind. From his MAT staging, he retained the conflation of the first three acts into one, and the gazebo as an objective correlative for Treplev's feelings.[23]

Given its context, the Beijing *Seagull* was more adventurous than Efremov's *Ivanov* at the Yale Drama School that same year. Since some in his homeland regarded him as a burnt-out case and the MAT as artistically defunct, Efremov's translation to New Haven must be seen mainly as a token of *détente* in the new world order. He claimed that he simply wanted to introduce *Ivanov* to American audiences, and use it as a learning experience for himself as well as the actors. David Borovsky's set, lit in golden autumnal hues (an effect borrowed from Efremov's MAT *Vanya*), reprised the standard-issue Soviet design of dead branches over weathered wooden panels. As he had done at the Art Theatre in 1975, Efremov reversed the opening scenes so that the party guests were heard discussing Ivanov prior to his first appearance, thus setting up society as judge and jury (a long-accepted Soviet interpretation) and Ivanov guilty until proven innocent. What prevented Efremov from fully reinventing his earlier *Ivanov* were the usual American constraints: there were four weeks rather than four months of rehearsal, language barriers complicated communication, and the actors were unfamiliar with both Chekhov and Russian life. Their performances were more unbridled than those of their Muscovite counterparts, but contained less emotional truth.[24] The most typical and damaging miscalculation was to cast a movie star in the lead to add lustre both to a "university" production and to his resumé. But William Hurt was no Smoktunovsky; this all but inaudible Ivanov tended to gravitate downstage centre to pick at his psychic scabs. In Chekhov, star casting invariably displaces the author's meaning and leads to incoherence.

The junkets of directors rehashing previous triumphs indicates the impasse that Chekhovian production had reached by the mid-eighties. Despite the increasing proliferation of productions, their *raison d'être* was less and less in evidence. A perfunctory naturalistic or celebrity treatment was still occasionally seen in regional reps, with a glancing concession to a specific audience: Michel Tremblay's "translation" of *Uncle Vanya* at the Théâtre du C.N.A. in 1983 turned Marina into a Québecoise who spoke a local dialect. As a result her function became totally anecdotal.[25] More often, directors sought to avoid earlier interpretations by offering deliberately eccentric or counter-cultural visions, as in a 1993 New York *Seagull*, adapted and directed by A. M. Raychel, set in 1940s Hollywood.[26] Rarely did such bright ideas present a complex and insightful reading of a text or expose a genuine contemporaneity in the situations.

Borovsky's Yale setting for *Ivanov* seemed almost as old-fashioned as Simov's because up-to-date Chekhovian scenography now deconstructed both dramatic and psychological space, to leave fragments or moments of existence devoid of cohesive significance. The experimental Dutch company De Appel, for instance, turned the Prozorov residence into an immense triangle, diagonally intersected by the house seats. Great distances made communication and intimacy extremely difficult, and kept the spectators removed from the action. A gaping, ostentatious hole in the wall mocked the yearning for Moscow.[27]

Taken to extremes, this self-conscious side-stepping of sentimentality or naturalism often led to over-schematization. As the audience entered the workshop theatre at the Université de Montréal in 1982 to see *Uncle*

Vanya (*Oncle Vania*), the actors in sandboxes on either side of the stage were slowly putting on their costumes. Stage right was the realm of the nanny with its samovar; stage left was the men's universe, a study occupied by each in turn. At the apex of the triangle, present throughout, sat Vanya's mother, dressed in white and veiled like a bride, barring all outlets, blocking even the passage to the red Exit sign that glowed above her head; holding a book, she was a symbol of mother Russia at the dawn of a new age. The actors constantly cast oblique glances and gestures at her, suggesting the impossibility of communication; they behaved in a neutered, blank manner. Original and risk-taking as this was, it turned every gesture and movement into a semiotic valise to be unpacked and its contents oohed and aahed over by the spectator. The director effaced the author, who, along with the audience, was buried beneath an avalanche of signs.[28]

BRACING FOR THE MILLENNIUM

The most egregious efforts at storming the Chekhovian Winter Palace took place in the United States. In 1986, Joel Gersmann's company at the Broome St. Theatre in the university town of Madison, Wisconsin, attacked *The Cherry Orchard* like Red Guards discovering the imperial wine cellar. As if Chekhov stood for everything fusty about the Western theatre and their own liberal educations, they turned the play into a glittering ninety-minute soap opera of sight gags set to punk rock. Spilling out of this cornucopia of Reagan-era pop culture was a Gaev obsessed by television rather than billiards, Anya and Varya played by men in drag, and Yasha and Firs their female counterparts. In the finale, Ranevskaya and her brother departed for the future carrying a giant American Express card, as Lopakhin entered with a buzzing chainsaw. The anarchic exuberance of iconoclasm provoked a good deal of laughter, but ultimately the effect was strangely reminiscent of *A Clockwork Orange*: yahoos were trashing a gallery for no reason other than to proclaim their independence from responsibility, both artistic and humanitarian.

With the Barthian eclipse of the author, Chekhov's plays could become appropriated and exploited as a ragbag of evocative scraps from which to sew a crazy quilt of cultural allusions. This is clearly seen in the strange exchange between the Irondale Ensemble Project of New York, a creative collective based on improvisation around classical texts, and the St. Petersburg Theatre Salon, a *glasnost*-bred fringe group, founded in

42 Montana Lattin as a Nanny and Nicole Potter and Viktor Labintsev as the two Professors in *The Uncle Vanya Show* produced by the Irondale Ensemble and the St. Petersburg Salon Theatre, New York.

1988 to explore pre-revolutionary styles of performance. The Irondale's *Uncle Vanya Show* (1985–90) was a work in progress, routines in English and Russian held together by eccentric dance; it concerned Johnny Voinitsky, a late-1940s radio host in Charlevoix, Michigan, who broadcasts Chekhov's play in the delusion that he is Vanya. Chekhov's text was followed consecutively, but with much improvised dialogue, to produce "a collection of mini-entertainments," a demented collage of vaudeville bits and lighting cues. When the Russian troupe staged a visually abstract and emotionally charged *Ivanov* reduced to seven characters, the Irondale troupe was shocked by their theatrically textured acting.[29]

Then, at the behest of the Dorset Theatre Festival in Vermont (1986), the Irondale proceeded to adapt *The Cherry Orchard* to mirror the situation of derelict property in that state. *The Orchard*, "a new play by John Nassivera, suggested by Anton Chekhov's *The Cherry Orchard*," differed from a transposition such as *The Wisteria Trees* in its social purpose:

Nassivera believed the US to be on the brink of its own social revolution
and was eager to show how the characters were victims of their class and
the economic climate.[30]

Social concerns were also dear to the heart of the Cornerstone Theatre
Co., run by William Rauch and a troupe of Harvard alumni, whose prac-
tice is to select a classic play and rewrite it to reflect local realities: a Wild
West *Hamlet* in North Dakota, a revivalist *Tartuffe* in Kansas, a Paiute
Oresteia in Nevada. In Montgomery, West Virginia, a depressed coal-
mining town of three thousand, they staged *Three Sisters*. The West
Virginians seemed "to have an affinity for Chekhov," in their longing for
meaningful work and love of home (which is to read Chekhov as John
Steinbeck). In a reversal of the urban and rural tropes (and in alignment
with a specifically American pastoral), the sisters were metamorphosed
into rural West Virginians whose family had relocated to a northern
industrial city; their habitat was a trailer interior imbedded in railway ties.
They want to "sell the trailer, break with everything here, and go back to
West Virginia." New character names were selected from the local phone
directory, so that Kulygin became Kinison, an annoying computer pro-
grammer, Vershinin Archie Valentine a union lawyer. The imagery was
refashioned into local allusions: "Birds fly on and on" became "assembly
lines run on and on"; instead of trees it was smokestacks Nick Turpin
(Tusenbach) saw "for the first time in my life" before being killed in a
game of chicken played with forklifts.[31] Over the course of three and a
half hours, the working-class audience became thoroughly involved,
exclaimed at local references, and talked back to characters.

Three Sisters, perhaps because it is Chekhov's most fugual piece, seems
to have been the play usually chosen to reveal new messages by shifts in
emphasis rather than wholesale dismantling. In New York in 1980, Squat
Theatre presented a thirty-minute version (first shown in Budapest four
years earlier), the cast reduced to the sisters performed by three male
actors, who smoke and sip vodka to a live violin and a recorded piano,
until prompted to speech by the voice of an actress in the prompter's
box. The intentionally induced boredom became as much an indictment
of Chekhov as of his characters.[32] Hartmut Wickert made the analogies
with Beckett prominent in *Moskau Kommen und Gehen* (*Moscow Come and Go*,
Tübinger Zimmertheater, 1988), in which incessant talk covered those
"dangerous zones" in which nothingness bobbed to the surface. The
characters, actor-like, strove to forge a missing reality from language.[33]
Adrian Noble's 1990 London production insisted on Irina being
Chebutykin's daughter, an identification aided by the fact that Cyril

Cusack was indeed the father of the actress playing Irina. Mathias Langhoff, in a Parisian production, highlighted a homoerotic relationship between Tusenbach and Soleny, with Irina merely a convenient surrogate for their feelings for one another. Emily Mann's sisters, at Princeton's University McCarter Theatre, began at a great remove from one another, both spatially and emotionally, and by the final curtain had fused into a pillar of mutual support.

The most idiosyncratic of these restatements was that by the Wooster Group, an experimental company that works out of the Performing Garage in New York; it is characterized by

emphasis of process over product; resistance to a univocal narrative through the creation of a nonlinear structure; employment of diverse styles of performing; the overlapping of intricate aural and visual elements, often mediated by sophisticated technology; and the recycling of scenery, props and costumes from earlier pieces.[34]

The Group seldom drew on classic material, but *Three Sisters* had been suggested by one of its actors, Ron Vawter, because the centrality of the female characters provided strong opportunities for the women in the company. At the time, the director, Elizabeth LeCompte, had been deeply impressed by a documentary film about the Geinin troupe, a group of Japanese strolling players. The original concept was to have these strollers performing Chekhov's drama. Although that idea soon withered away, Japanese films remained an important influence: *Godzilla* and *Kwaidan* were both played throughout the rehearsals.[35]

What worked to foreground Chekhov over Masaki Kobayashi was the participation of Paul Schmidt. Schmidt, a distinguished Russian translator as well as an actor, provided an English rendition which LeCompte treated as a score. She described it as "a beautiful soap opera – I don't mean it's melodramatic, but that the language is simple and malleable. It's an idealized version of soap opera – very conversational, it can have great depth and at the same time, be very shallow."[36] The result was the most accurate rendition of a text the company ever staged. Schmidt himself played Dr. Chebutykin, much of the time with his back to the audience. Imbedding him in the play provided a kind of totem of authenticity, a promise that, whatever the divagations, Chekhov was still at the heart of the matter.

The sisters themselves were cast from mature actresses, to create "a hospital vision," a feeling of aging and illness, of being dealt with as an object. Irina, played by silver-haired Beatrice Roth, oldest member of the Group, sat in a metal wheelchair covered in fake fur. LeCompte, who usually conceived her pieces as choreography, explained to the cast, "We have got to play this like music. The only way we get away with the low lights, the soft music, the languorous mood, the constant moaning of the wind, is if the dialog [*sic*] is constantly and invisibly fibrillating."[37] Mistakes and missed entrances during rehearsals were incorporated to create this sense of oscillation between acting and quoting the script. Besides the Translator who offered commentary, there was a fast-talking Narrator to serve as a "free agent between the audience, which is now Liz, and the play"[38]; based on the *ben-shi* or storyteller of the Japanese silent cinema, she recited stage directions, introduced the characters, cued lines, asked questions, and handed round a wireless mike. The script was far from integral: Olga's opening monologue was broken into questions and answers for a more casual feel, the three scenes that open Act II were summed up by the Translator, and only a few pages of Act IV were staged, replaced by Japanese material.[39]

Brace Up!, as this production was titled, was not, according to LeCompte "an adaptation of Chekhov." "I think of it as a double portrait of Chekhov and the Wooster Group. We're not interpreting him. We're putting him on. We're inhabiting him."[40] Naturalistic "acting" or re-enacting, the bread-and-butter of the American stage, was in opposition to the company's style of reportage, of splintering consecutive stage time into simultaneity or juxtapositions of present and future. When Andrey (Willem Dafoe) suddenly appeared in shorts clutching a white hanky, the video screens on five television monitors projected the lipsticked mouth of his wife-to-be Natasha calling for her children. Actors were seen both on the screens in close-up or glimpsed seated at the table behind the stage – in long shot, as it were – to interrupt the audience's identification of the performer with the character.

The sound track served as ironic counterpoint. As Vershinin (Ron Vawter), in skin-tight jodhpurs, spouted philosophy into a microphone in the voice of a cigarette-ad, soporific Muzak accompanied him. "In a soundscape of storms, bells and what sound like scissors snipping, stillnesses change into beautiful explosions of ensemble action, creating a collage of linked moments always informed by the intelligence of the actors – a serious, but absurd show."[41]

The achievement of *Brace Up!* was to yoke Chekhov together with a late twentieth-century sensibility: omnipresent noise, technological advances and their negative aspects, narcissism in lieu of thought, a fixation on mass media, the ability to experience many things at the same time or in rapid sequence, the juxtaposition of past, present and future.

43 The human and video blend of *Brace Up!*, Wooster Group, NY. From l.–r., Anna Kohler, Michael Stumm, Jeff Webster, Christopher Kondek, Beatrice Roth, Willem Dafoe, Joan Jonas, Ray Fauchee (over her shoulder), Kate Valk (downstage), Peyton Smith (upstage), Paul Schmidt.

The relation of a sequential narrative was constantly foiled, and the sisters' desire to move from the periphery to centrality was conflated with the actors' problem of projecting a presence onstage.[42] Under the circumstances, there was no sense to LeCompte's statement, "the Wooster Group is challenging the Stanislavski interpretation."[43] It was amazing that she should think they needed to. Given the intricacy of the Wooster Group's work, its ignorance of the long tradition of anti-Stanislavskianism is a reminder that in the American theatre, it is the common fate to be born yesterday.

One of those not attracted by the Wooster Group's demolition of the text was Richard Schechner, self-styled "rabbi" of the anthropological school of performance studies. Seeking a means of staging post-Ibsenite drama without recourse either to period piece or radical deconstruction, he proposed an historicized *Three Sisters*. His work-in-progress (La MaMa, New York, 1995–6) offered a synchronic comment on Russian history as the narrative unfolded. Act I was an homage to Stanislavsky, a reasonably recognizable presentation of behavior as social comedy. Act

II was a synthetic evocation of Bolshevik theatre, the actors posed according to still photographs of Meyerhold's biomechanics and rising to sing Red Army choruses. Solzhenitsyn's accounts of labor-camp life were the inspiration for Act III: relegated to a gulag, the Prozorovs' already tenuous relationships broke down as they heaved cinder-blocks from one end of the stage to the other, the alarum-bell of the fire transformed to the guard banging a metal sheet. The last act abandoned this continuum of Soviet history: as Andrey wheeled the pram back and forth downstage, the others delivered their dialogue into microphones, without looking at one another. Instead of bringing the play into the turmoil of *perestroika*, Schechner provided a facile comment on mass communication in the electronic age.

THE FIRST CHEKHOV FESTIVAL

As if to sum up the *status quo* in Chekhovian *mise-en-scène*, an International Chekhov Festival was held in Moscow in October 1992, featuring three different *Cherry Orchards*, directed by Peter Stein, Andrei Serban and Otomar Krejča. (Brook had been invited but declined.) With bloody conflicts flaring up on the fringes of the former Soviet empire, and political unrest at home, the festival's "feast in plaguetime" atmosphere lent a certain hysteria to the opening of Stein's *Orchard*. Despite its five-hour length with entr'actes lasting forty to fifty minutes, there was a fifteen-minute ovation from the "first-nighters." Their taste clashed with that of the connoisseurs, one of whom remarked that Stein was contributing German humanitarian aid unneeded by the Russians. Still, the thousands who sat through Stein's *Orchard* till midnight felt a kind of historical pride watching poetic naturalism taken to the nth degree while a political tempest raged without.

With true German thoroughness, Stein carried directorial versatility *ad absurdum*, realizing every stage direction to its fullest. Theatrical time was converted into real time, so that it took forty-five minutes for the sun to come up. The second act field was covered with hay for Ranevskaya to frolic in: its pungent aroma reached the tenth row. Russians carped about Stein's slavishness to outmoded Stanislavskian principles, but these meticulous details were camouflage for a philosophic statement. Stein explained stage tradition to be merely an impulse that presses the modern director to substantiate himself with ever greater audacity and urgency. He was not interested in the "problem of humanism": like tourists, Chekhov's characters are traversing time and eternal nature. If there is truth to Pasternak's remark that Chekhov writes his people as if they were a landscape, then sunrise and sunset must be as important as the sale of the estate. The real subject of Stein's production was the confrontation of "indifferent nature," the characters' circumambience, with the world of human passions.[44]

In competition with nature, the leading figures were necessarily dwarfed. The secondary characters came to the fore, chief among them Branco Zamarovsky's exquisitely real Firs, a man of dignity, honour and responsibility who has become invisible. The circusy Charlotta of Elke Petry stalked the stage, in John Freedman's words, like Mayakovsky's Phosphorescent Woman.[45] Simeonov-Pishchik came across as a merchant out of Ostrovsky, Yasha as a young mafioso. Of the major characters, only Jutta Lampe's Ranevskaya was riveting, a subdued, serious woman whose affectionate diminutives were devoid of sentimentality.

Stein arranged the play's rhythms on a symphonic principle. It began *lento*, then quickened with the arrival from the station. When Varya opened the windows and the sun slowly began to penetrate the room, everyone fell silent before the mystery of nature: a variation on the moment with the spinning top in Stein's *Three Sisters*. The second act was the slowest movement, with Debussy playing in the distance. Act III, the climax, inverted Christophe Shubiger's nursery set, looking through doors into a flaming red ballroom which Stein said was inspired by Meyerhold,[46] the dark powers symbolized by guests in masks. The fourth act indulged in an immeasurable pause before leave-taking; the old Russian custom of sitting for a moment before a journey was protracted so that it had a real effect on the spectator's nerves, not unlike the extended pause Peter Brook had inserted in *Love's Labours Lost* after the announcement of the king's death. The audience held its breath, in presentiment of a calamity, while Firs carefully inspected boarded-up windows and tugged at them with impotent hands. Then the ax blows came in on a jazz rhythm, and a huge branch of cherry suddenly crashed into the room, breaking shutters and shattering glass.[47]

The Russian consensus was that, for all this concerted effort, there was little inner life, nor was the Meyerholdian key used to open anything. The party scene held no real horror in its rhythm or action, no sense of teetering on the brink, no genuine grotesquerie. The attraction lay in the pyrotechnics. In Anatoly Smeliansky's words, "the flora was beautiful but there was no fauna."[48]

The festival reopened all the old debates: is *The Cherry Orchard* a tragedy or a comedy? Does Chekhov need all that real-life impedimenta? Stein rejected comedy for a *Trauerspiel* set against a cosmic background; Serban, on the other hand, stressed the comedy in his Bucharest production. Essentially he resuscitated his 1977 New York staging, with Mihai Maescu's set duplicating Santo Loquasto's. But, in the wake of political events in Romania, the pratfalls, belly laughs and breakneck speed took on a new meaning, as if this Chekhov were burning to ashes in a wild Moldavian dance of despair. Serban strove for temperament and feeling, but not complexity; this primitive clarity simplified Chekhov and consequently prompted mirthful amazement. The spectators burst into laughter when Trofimov, a lisping, fanatical Klaudiu Bleonc, measuring space with his fists, spouted fiery monologues about the future. Asked whether this blend of poseur and psychopath was a parody of Ceausescu, Serban assented but said he also satirized Lenin, Trotsky, and "our whole crowd." In Bucharest, he went on, they'd probably be accused of sympathy with communism.[49]

There was no sound of a snapped string, no pathos, no rhythms, no mood: the stress was laid on ways of accepting unhappiness, so Leopoldina Balanuta's Ranevskaya was a tough survivor. Nor was there a house in Serban's scenography (Firs had to die under a clock). Everything was set in the orchard: the divan, the armchair, spectres of Ranevskaya and her drowned son strolling across the backdrop of the polygon of the enormous (former Soviet) Army Theatre stage: the history of the twentieth century was transformed into a series of parodic emblems meant to resonate in the collective memory. Russian peasants with scythes and rakes crossed the stage to stand for the eternal question "Who can live well in Russia?"; silhouettes of factory chimneys (the new life?) smoked on the horizon. Russians saw it as a very Western approach. As one critic pointed out, "The metaphor, poetic or forced, is characteristic of Serban's technique, an evasive and annoying gimmick: you can't always figure out whether the director is parodying anthology clichés or whether he is acting in naïve earnestness, not realizing that his Russian cosmos is kitsch *à la russe*."[50]

If Stein and Serban provoked discussion, Krejča evoked disappointment, especially for those who had venerated his theatre as legendary, inaccessible, known only from photographs. Profiting by the Velvet Revolution, he had reopened the Divadlo Za Branou in 1990, without manifestos or agendas. His *Cherry Orchard* seemed a continuation of its 1972 avatar, but with nothing to prove, totally traditional, "lifeless, literary."[51] According to the program note,

I am trying to understand the drama from within and understand it as accurately as possible . . . Chekhov for me is the Theatrum Mundi, an allegory of theatre, its pride, its aristocratic coat of arms. And even today I have not learned to approach him calmly 'like a professional' . . . Chekhov is my Cyrano nose, my eccentricity, my comicality, my pride, weakness and strength, my solitude, literary idol, my theatrical fate . . . [52]

None of this could be discerned in a production devoid of an orchard, a party, the sound of a snapped string, affection. Its faceless tedium took place within a set of lit panels, the objects slightly rearranged for each act, and dust covers drawn over furniture in Act II to suggest hillocks. Maria Tomašová's Ranevskaya was like a remote, stern Ibsen heroine, dry-eyed and assertive; she played her scene with Trofimov as if it were a Greek tragedy. Thereafter, she turned a deaf ear and blind eye to what fate had in store. Krejča emptied the play of lyricism, music (except for a waltz in Act III), colour, and specificity of locale or period. [53]

What the Russians deduced from this blankness and lack of historicity was that these productions had a different genetic code from their own. They wondered how European directors, primarily intellectuals, managed to stage Chekhov with so much directness and penetration. Alluding to earlier, more achieved works, the *Orchards* of Brook and Strehler and Stein's *Three Sisters*, Gaevsky stated

A simple idea lies at the base of these three dissimilar productions: everything is devalued, except human relations. They alone are valuable, nothing else exists. The homes are not "heartbreak houses," for forgiveness and understanding, consolation and condolence are possible there. [54]

In a period of dissolution and uncertainty, the Russian theatre needed these models from abroad, however imperfect, to help it find its own new direction.

CHAPTER 18

The perestroika of Chekhov (Eastern Europe and Russian Federation 1989–1995)

> The more time goes by, the farther we get from these people, the livelier, the more interesting, more penetrating the play becomes . . . The dramatist's brisk pencil catches characters and themes with precision, but doesn't flesh them out, leaving room for a new age to fill them with its own breath and concerns.
>
> Sergey Zhenovach[1]

KICKING AGAINST THE PRICKS

For two decades, those capitals of the Warsaw Pact farthest from Moscow were freest to imbibe theatrical trends from the West, and to experiment with styles and conventions that divagated sharply from Marxist-Leninist prescriptions. In the mid-1970s, David Borovsky escaped the Sleeping Beauty bramble bush that was then the standard Soviet setting for Chekhov when doing a guest stint in Budapest. For a *Seagull* at the Vig Theatre, he turned the whole stage into a lake; Nina immersed herself in it and then emerged, streaming with silver droplets, to proclaim "I am the world soul." When the curtain rose on the last act, the audience gasped to see this lake frozen over, the world of ice the World Soul had enunciated, but also the glacial political structure that congealed the potential for change.[2]

Hungary, with its early move to "goulash capitalism," was the Eastern Bloc nation to benefit most from an interchange with the West. The Katona Jozsef Theatre of Budapest, founded in 1981, had toured Europe extensively from 1987; the following year it had taken its *Three Sisters*, directed by Tamás Ascher, to the Théâtre de l'Europe festival where it met unanimous acclaim. In 1990 it reappeared there with a *Platonov* reflective of a world stranded in the wake of Communism.

An older Hungarian director, István Horvai, who had begun his career with the usual monotonal Chekhov of socialist realism, had already staged a modern-dress workshop *Platonov* at the Vig Theatre in

1978, with the spectators scattered throughout a large room where the action took place. It spoke to twenty-year-olds who were impatiently looking for a common truth. Horvai followed it up with a full-scale production in 1981. With a cast of actors in their thirties he attempted to say that if someone of that age had not found himself by then he was lost and the whole generation had perished. He omitted the older characters, who were represented by mannequins seated around a card table in the vestibule of a school-house designed by Borovsky. "We watch our own life with a feeling of catharsis," reported one critic.[3]

Ascher's concept went farther down the road of political allegory: he declared that Hungary and the Eastern bloc had hibernated too long, as had Chekhov's works there; whenever the will to act arose, it was stifled. Platonov was therefore reminiscent of a worn-out intellectual of the 1980s. "For forty years a very significant amount of mental and spiritual capital was wasted in Hungary and many people today live in the awareness of their lost potential. For me, *Platonov* is like a monument to these people and to the potential bartered away." After Platonov's death, the actors pressed their noses against a glass wall and ogled the corpse, reflecting the playgoers' gaze, and prompting an Hungarian critic to write, "A certain ambivalent feeling overcame me (and perhaps others), a mixture of personal experience and alienation; we stare at the extension of our own fate and at great theatre simultaneously."[4]

Poland too managed to develop its own distinctive theatre from the 1960s on; although Grotowski, Wajda, Flaszen and Kantor showed no special interest in Chekhov, their example could not but serve to inspire directors who did restage him. Treating the text very freely, they went for the grotesque with a vengeance, as in *Ten Portraits of The Seagull based on Anton Chekhov*, staged by Jerzy Grzegorzewski (Cracow Stary Theatre, 1979). After *solidarnoś* and freedom, Grzegorzewski's *Uncle Vanya* (*Wujaszek Wania*) at the Warsaw Studio Theatre (Teatr Studio, 1993) carried on that tradition; although it stuck closer to the text, the staging was a panorama of concise, metaphoric images, with obvious parody of the Moscow Art Theatre. What aided the blend of contradictory elements was a musical score by Stanisław Radwan which provided counterpoint and foreshadowing. In what was becoming the norm, the young cast was headed by a Vanya and Astrov under thirty.

The vast stage was cluttered with Chekhovian detritus – garden furniture, a grand piano, a tripod camera, a bench, white trunks of birches – cheek by jowl with the bare skeleton of an airplane wing and a white canvas daubed in grey. The indispensable samovar existed in several variants of different sizes, and was regularly disassembled and reassembled. For all the space, crucial scenes took place in a narrow passage between the stage and the first row or in labyrinthine corridors or almost in the wings, shoved to the periphery. Nothing in the unvarying lighting suggested the passage of time: the lights would go out and come up again to reveal the same tableau. Whole lines and situations, such as Astrov's departure for the factory and his remark about Africa, were repeated. The general feeling was one of excruciating boredom, inescapable recurrence, and time heavy on one's hands.

In this existential dead end, ways had to be found to beguile the time. The play opened with Marina and Astrov in slow motion moving the samovar from one end of the table to another, endless pauses interrupting their "game." During Serebryakov's lecture, his auditors were seated back-to-back in straight chairs like a train to nowhere (or Kharkov); a martinet schoolmaster, he patrolled them with a ferule. The goodbyes of Act IV were the occasion for a photograph, but no one actually left. As they made a show of departing, they took up seats in the passage like an auxiliary audience.[5]

Similar *leitmotifs* could be found in the *Platonov* adapted and directed by Jerzy Jarocki (Teatr Polski, Wrocław, 1993). It began in the dark, with only a chessboard and chessmen lit, as the pool of light widened to reveal the General's widow playing against the Doctor. Although the stage space was big enough to contain the whole estate and a forest intersected with railway tracks, the action was often confined to a small cage-like room, its windows steamed with rain. The actors, playing universalized characters, were masks caught in intricate lies. All this was to provide yet another mirror for the audience to see itself as the same superficial, hypocritical and idle types. Jarocki was not so much interpreting Chekhov as using Chekhov to express his own concerns.[6]

The disintegration of the Soviet Union enabled the newly independent republics to reject Russian cultural hegemony with a will. Robert Sturua, Georgia's most distinguished director, had been slated to direct *Three Sisters*, but renounced it as too Russian, and turned to Shakespeare and indigenous classics. Ironically, his only Chekhov production was put on in London as a showcase for three Redgraves (Vanessa, Lynn and niece Jemma at the Queen's Theatre, 1990). Over the course of five weeks' rehearsals, Sturua's energetic and exuberant prodding unblocked the constipation of the English approach to Chekhov. Influenced intellectually by Bakhtin's work on Rabelais and pictorially by Tumanishvili and Toulouse-Lautrec, he offered a carnival ambience, presided over by an enormous grandfather clock. "Frantic, manic and vaguely paranoid" from the start, the sisters were prone to mood-swings and tantrums, gesticulating wildly, draping themselves on furniture and self-knowingly commenting on their own behaviour. The *kermesse*-like subversion of values was interrupted between Acts III and IV, when Irina was ritually dressed for sacrifice; and as the regiment marched away, the sisters joined hands to sing "Auprès de ma blonde.". For all the antics, the residual impression was low-keyed and morose, suggesting ruin rather than survival. The British reviewers, conditioned by expectations of psychological realism and emotional empathy, were confounded, torn between appreciation of a liberating vision and dis- taste for so ludic a Chekhov. The academic Gordon McVay went so far as to call it "cultural barbarism." Sturua himself, who had courted con- troversy, shrugged, "In general, I think that it's not only producers and actors who are trapped by their own clichés, but, even more so, the audi- ence!"[7]

Eimuntas Nekrošius and the State Theatre of Lithuania overthrew cultural colonialism with his *Uncle Vanya* by theatricalizing the inertia. Although Serebryakov's repressive domination of Vanya's life could be read as the stifling hold of the USSR over Lithuania, Nekrošius went beyond political allegory to a similar "circusization" of the text. Over the course of four hours, the intelligentsia was made to act out its impotence in ridiculous ways, often through pantomime. The play opened with an extended dumbshow of Astrov treating Waffles with folk remedies; he later subjected Vanya to cupping. This undercut both his scientific status (he seemed the quack the Professor claims he is) and his ecology. His maps were the size of postage-stamps, held up by tweezers, and he revealed his alcoholism by spilling a decanter of vodka over the stage; he and Vanya "pumped iron" in their competition for the affections of Elena. All this was in the ubiquitous presence of Waffles, a mute witness to Vanya's recurrent embarrassment.

The characters' physical attributes were also caricatured. Sonya's "lovely hair" consisted of long blonde braids in the style of Humperdinck's Goose Girl. The professor, played by a young actor, leaned on his cane at a 45-degree angle, as if going uphill against the wind. This *tour-de-farce* was compounded by three comic floor-polishers who glided around the stage in felt slippers, performing knockabout interludes. The implication was that they were down-to-earth Lithuanian peasants whose reactions condemned the silliness of their Russian masters. The slapstick came to a climax when Serebryakov

44 Nadezhda Gultyaeva's scenography for *Uncle Vanya* directed by Eimuntas Nekrošius,
Youth Theatre, Vilnius, 1986.

announced the sale of the estate and was answered by the chorus of
Hebrew slaves from Verdi's *Nabucco*. The ensuing chases, swoons and
smelling salts were scored to a polka. In the last act, Vanya struggled violently to retain the phial of morphine while Astrov and Waffles searched
him, finally trapping him under a chair on which Astrov sat; both a gag
and an obvious image of confinement.

For all the horseplay, the most striking moments were controlled and
subdued, especially in Act II when Astrov and Sonya played their scene
on either side of a wicker stand in a downstage corner, isolated by a
square of white light. The play ended in silence. The servants dismantled the set, taking down the backdrop, a huge Dufy-like painting of
promenaders in a wooded landscape, and stacking it against the wall, a
suggestion that imitation is as close as man can come to nature. Astrov
muffled himself in a bearskin (perhaps because his first name Mikhail is
the Russian nickname for a bear), crawled to the landscape, rubbed
against it like a dog, and pretended to depart. In fact, he stayed on stage
while Sonya shrieked out her aria on a sustained note of defiance; his
talk about leaving was just more talk.[8]

CHEKHOV UNDER *GLASNOST*

The first effect of *glasnost* on the Soviet Russian theatre in the late 1980s was to enlarge the repertory. Suddenly, plays which had banned for decades crowded the stage, and the earlier seepage of Western influences became a torrent. There was a good deal of catching up to do, but eventually glutted by productions of Bulgakov, Erdman, and the absurdists, the post-Communist Russian theatre turned back to its classics, and Chekhov in particular became "a touchstone for assessing today's theatre."

> He is, to a large degree, the symbol of theatre itself in Russia. Moreover, he is perceived today as a metaphor for past culture, for its language and soul, a culture impenetrable to us, gone forever, yet somehow a standard for measuring one's own life.[9]

Yearning for the classics was a yearning for stability and firm parameters on every plane. Through Chekhov one might be able to reach back to the sensitivity and refinement obliterated by eighty years of Communist lies, bloodshed and authoritarianism. To this end, the productions of Strehler, Brook and Stein were highly attractive models, because, for all their *distanciation* and abstraction, their fundamental humanism was untainted by decades of "socialist realism" and academic tradition. They enjoyed the prestige of things long hidden and inaccessible, while their styles still trailed recognizable clouds of original Art Theatre glory.

The Russian directors who had represented innovation in the 1960s and seventies were now dead (Tovstonogov, Éfros) or *hors de combat* by reason of obsolescence (Efremov, Lyubimov). Another veteran, Adolf Shapiro, Estonia's leading director of Chekhov, was invited to the Bolshoy Dramatic Theatre in St. Petersburg, formerly Tovstonogov's domain, to stage *The Cherry Orchard* (1992). Half-way through rehearsals, Svetlana Kryukova who had been cast as Ranevskaya published a letter in the press berating her colleagues for preventing her from creating a fully rounded character and for betraying thirty years of Tovstonogovian tradition. In the recent past, her letter would have been the signal for a crackdown by the authorities; now it stirred a ripple of scandalized amusement.

In the event, Shapiro's production seemed very much in line with current European *Orchards*. Eduard Kochergin's scenography provided a bare but spacious box of smooth-hewn planks, indiscriminately planted with trees and furniture; in the second half of the play, as in *Godot*, the leaves had fallen. Shapiro wanted this production to "tell about time lost, how time is to be confronted, how hard it is to settle into a new space,"[10] in other words a lesson for a society in disarray. Lopakhin (Andrey Tolubeev) was very much a businessman of the era of free markets and privatization, whose projects met with considerable sympathy from the audience. His moment of truth came not at the end of Act III, as usual, but in Act IV, when he embraced Varya and laid her head on his breast, but still could not utter a marriage proposal. Dwarfed by the set, most of the characters seemed to be variations on Charlotta, playing comic bits to while away the tedium. As her letter indicated, Kryukova's Ranevskaya was the only one out of synch, coming across as unloving and unloved.[11]

Many of the proliferating Chekhov productions (there were five new *Uncle Vanya*s in the 1992/3 Moscow season alone) sought to find new forms by stripping away all the appurtenances of the past, and thereby producing *ostranenie*, the Formalist literary device of "making it strange." A student production of *Uncle Vanya* at the Shchukin school in 1993 was directed by Nikolay Volkov, a former Éfros actor whose muffled vocal intonations and inhibited passions had in his time transformed the image of the stage hero. His young actors wore no makeup, glued-on beards or frockcoats, and made no effort to project age; in the absence of "undesirable and crudely naturalistic pseudo-verisimilitude"[12] a purity and freshness returned to the text, and the relationship between a puerile Vanya and a keenly perceptive Sonya was sharply delineated.

More often, in the first blush of creative license there was a desperate search for novelty. Of the establishment directors, the most controversial was Moscow's Sergey Solovev, who staked out Chekhov's plays as his particular preserve. On Staraya Basmannaya (late Karl Marx street but where the Prozorov sisters once lived), his students presented a *Three Sisters* in close physical proximity with the audience. The initial effect was irritating, "as if thieves have broken into a museum."[13] Vershinin wore a black eyepatch, and Soleny was barefoot.

But Solovev's experimentation was wholly superficial; his heart was with the Art Theatre tradition or rather a perversion of it. The languor and poignancy of his all-star *Uncle Vanya* (1992) at the Maly was an attenuation of naturalistic staging. It was noteworthy for the grotesquely cynical performance of V. Solomin as an alcoholic Astrov; exiting on his knees in Act I, drawling his speech about conservation in self-mockery, he was an extreme comic turn in an otherwise conventional setting. His brother Yury Solomin presented a Vanya devoted to his deceased sister to the point of obsession; this was a thin-skinned individual deeply hurt when Astrov calls a spade a spade (and a vulgarian a vulgarian).[14]

Solovev had taken part in the bitter tug-of-war with his former boss Yury Lyubimov for the management of the Taganka, both the space itself and its company. In 1994, he announced his intention to stage the entire Chekhov canon there, beginning with *The Seagull*. In an interview, Solovev renounced "director's theatre" and declared his eclecticism:

> I consider that any treatment of Chekhov "in one's own way" is idiotic and came at a time when people went to the theatre not for the text or for the performance but specifically for the interpretation . . . In my production there are details both academic and from other genres [. . .] Before me every treatment of Chekhov was done with "gloves on." I'm not interested in any kind of teagulls [*sic*: *chaek*], or concepts or subtexts. I am like the audience, which is awfully annoyed by everything going on in the modern theatre. And it is as a representative of this audience, which doesn't like anything, that I do my production, which it ought to like.[15]

Two hundred and sixty million rubles (misreported on the TV news as dollars) were spent to cater to the general public's taste. The ensuing *Seagull* out-Stanislavskied Stanislavsky in its lavish, cinematic setting and noisy sound effects. The designer V. Arefeev filled his sound stage with a tropical jungle: downstage was a malarial swamp of real water, with all kinds of flora luxuriating in it; far upstage was the house, a three-storey brick fortress. The space was littered with a rowboat, velocipedes, both kerosene and electric lamps, and in Act II a monsoon-like rain beat down. The depth was so great that characters upstage at the house were nearly invisible, one might say out of camera range.

The vulgarity of the stage business was pure Hollywood. The crippled Sorin leapt into Shamraev's arms at one point, and Nina's debut at acting were shown on a film strip. But the water indulged the worst excesses. In Act I two naked men swam in it, and yet failed to shock any of the *fin de siècle* women. A shirtless Trigorin fished up a pair of boots. At the end, Treplev rowed out to the middle of the lake to shoot himself in public; not wishing to get wet, he simply lay back dead in the boat. Like a doubting Thomas, Dorn then dipped his fingers in the wound, while Arkadina watched from a window. This immersion in liquid had none of the poetical allusiveness of the Japanese *Seagulls*: it more closely resembled Vincent Crummles' attachment to his practicable pump.

The critics dismissed the acting as either coarse or wasted; only Elena Korikova as Nina came off well, chiefly because she had a soliloquy and didn't suffer so much from lack of dramatic reciprocity. Those whose memories hearkened back fifteen years to when Lyubimov and Vysotsky reigned at the Taganka grieved; the general public oohed and aahed over the set and was struck by the topicality of Masha's speech about the way women drink and Sorin's about wasting money on agriculture. The latter conjured up a senate full of incompetent windbags incapable of restoring the Russian economy. But in general Solovev's real discovery was that Chekhov could be made to sound like the Mexican soap operas so popular on Russian television.

Those who were serious about applying new forms to Chekhov and whose liberties had strong artistic rationales behind them could more easily be found in the proliferating co-operatives and theatre studios. These were based on Western commercial practice with private subsidies and actors contracted for short durations, often featuring young performers in non-realistic or denuded settings. A Moscow "Co-op" staging by Leonid Trushkin of *The Cherry Orchard* (1990) was dominated by an enormous bookcase, which opened like a peepshow to reveal the locales of the play. It began with a clown marionette suspended over the bookcase, playing an infernal violin, and announcing the play's title and subtitle, "A Comedy." The puppet motif was carried through in all the characters except Lopakhin, who were whisked in and out of the action on turn-tables and slamming doors, like so many clock cuckoos. Ranevskaya was incarnated in Tatyana Vasileva, a gravel-voiced actress who exuded the aura of "a woman with a past"; her disinterest in the orchard and eagerness to get back to Paris implied in this context that Russia itself was keen to move on to other things.[16]

Another young actor, Igor Larin, reduced the play to a one-man show, originally entitled *Sounds of Death* (*Zvuki smerti*); he settled instead for *A Dream about the Cherry Orchard* (*Son o vishnevom sade*) (Osnobyak, St. Petersburg, 1993). It was a Treplevian soliloquy about a world soul, a "figment of the imagination" of Lopakhin, portrayed by curly-headed Larin as a *preux chevalier* come with a trumpet to wake the sleeping beauty from her castle in the autumn garden. (The latter was represented by a kind of glass bell or vitrine protecting decorative ruins.) When Ranevskaya, depicted as a somnambulist, and Gaev, in nightshirt and periwig as a remnant of the past, failed to respond, Prince Charming turned into a crude businessman with a briefcase, whose recurrent phrase was "the advancement of trade." Foreseeing, or perhaps hoping for, angry reaction to this deconstruction, Larin planted a decoy lady in the audience, who stalked out in outrage every night.[17]

The less-frequented of Chekhov's plays also provided opportunities for revisionist readings. Sergey Zhenovach turned to *The Wood Demon* (1993), not only because it was relatively neglected but because it was Chekhov's only "wide-open" play, whose denouement could not be guessed in advance; even the happiness of its ending was dubious. In his staging, he tried to achieve a sense of what theatre was like before the MAT existed. The critics, already bemused by Zhenovach's attraction to minor works and obsolete genres such as vaudeville and melodrama, were not amused by this broadly played comic operetta and its sunny optimism. For them, it came off as parody.[18]

A troika of young directors, Mikhail Mokeev and Klim and Vladimir Berzin, mounted a four-hour *Platonov* without an intermission (1993), which was so uninterested in the characters' individual psychologies that it subdivided them (Nikolay Triletsky was split in two), merged them (Glagolin Sr. and Ivan Triletsky were combined, as were Bagrov, Vengerovich Sr. and Petrin), or multiplied them (anonymous proscenium servants, messengers). Platonov himself was played by Yury Ekimov as a scrawny, pasty-faced youth. The play began at the end with the gunshot, and then divided the action into a series of acting-class exercises – "chess game," "sur la plage," "confessions" and the like, during which any pretence at characterization was totally abandoned. Observers *au courant* of fashionable literary theory cited this as an example of the absence of the author and the permissible dismantling of what was never an authoritative text to begin with.[19]

The most chronic deconstructor of Chekhov was Yury Pogrebnichko, another former collaborator of Lyubimov and artistic director of Moscow's Teatr na Krasnoy Presne: in his hands, *The Seagull* became *Why Did Konstantin Shoot Himself?* In a characteristically postmodern fashion, it self-consciously referred to all its predecessors, featuring a tiny portrait of Chekhov hung on a vertical pole centre stage along with the stuffed gull and displaying in the lobby photos of actors dressed to imitate famous portraits of Stanislavsky and Komissarzhevskaya.

Pogrebnichko's *Three Sisters* (1990) also ironized tradition by not so much playing the drama as playing with it. The audience entered a small, uncomfortable hall to see a shallow, ten-foot deep stage filled with rubbish and a long table with three oddly dressed young women at it. A rope cordoned off the stage to suggest that it was a museum display. Designer Yury Kononenko assembled a still life out of such found objects as an iron bedstead, a rusty washstand, plaster busts of "great men," including Lenin, and a log hanging in chains from the ceiling. The

45 *Three Sisters* deconstructed by Yury Pogrebnichko, Krasnaya Presnaya Theatre, Moscow, 1990.

costumes appeared to come from storage or garbage dumps, or hastily altered from modern clothing.

Copying a device Lyubimov had used at the start of his *Three Sisters*, taped voices of virtuosi from the MAT were played, a medley of the recent past (the Revolution, the Civil War, emigration, Soviet militarism) and the present; phrases existed in their direct and sometimes literal meaning, isolated from context or subtext. When Vershinin referred to those "humble birch trees dear to my heart," Olga pointed out, with the studied pose of a salesman in an auto showroom, the desiccated log chained aloft like an oversized swing. When he remarked, "How many flowers you have and how hospitable the house is," the spectators' gaze was then directed to the funeral wreaths placed near a mound of earth incongruously located in a corner of the room. His pronouncements about the future were met with audience laughter, provoked in part by a parade of actors with numbers on their backs, mounting up to ever higher figures. Wigs suggestive of clowns, a wooden leg for Anfisa and a false belly for Andrey proclaimed that this was a puppet show or Meyerhold's theatre of the "social mask."[20]

Although the first impression was of an aggressively iconoclastic parody, Pogrebnichko was making a serious attempt to crystallize a current state of mind, a sense that the paternal home had been destroyed so long ago no one can remember it. The spirit of the play was not betrayed, because the characters still clung to their unfulfilled dreams, waiting a lifetime, as Beckett might say, for it to add up to a life. The message to Russian audiences was, we need a living language of today, no matter how vulgar and impoverished. A precise correspondence was established between a contemporary collective consciousness and the cultural paradigm within which it operated.[21]

Pogrebnichko expanded his earlier experiment into *There's a Theatre for You . . . and Beyond That Empty Space (based on A. P. Chekhov's comedy "The Seagull") (Vot tebe i teatr . . . i dalshe pustoe prostranstvo [po komedii A. P. Chekhova "Chaika"])*, a fantasia on the theatricality of the piece. One American observer has characterized it as "a sort of Joseph Cornell box construction with movable pieces and a weird sense of humor."[22] Taking figures of speech *au pied de la lettre*, Pogrebnichko created a Harpo-Marxist world: when Nina referred to the shades of Shakespeare, Napoleon and Caesar, they materialized and haunted the rest of the play as uncanny eavesdroppers. The *Hamlet* and "Mousetrap" analogies, so portentously explicated by generations of critics, were reduced to absurdity as hordes of tiny plush mice popped out of pockets and waistcoats when Treplev demanded a new form of art, when Sorin wished he had been at least a minor man of letters and when Trigorin jotted down the smell of heliotrope. There was nothing sacred about the attribution of speeches either: in her desperate attempt to retain her lover, Arkadina confiscated Charlotta's description of her youth from *The Cherry Orchard*.

Such intertextuality was very much in evidence when Genrietta Yanovskaya and Kama Ginkas entered the lists with *Ivanov and Others* (*Ivanov i drugie*, Moscow Theatre of the Young Spectator, 1993). For years the couple had been a prickly thorn in the theatrical establishment's side; they were not fully approved of by the government, which grudgingly apportioned them a former children's theatre for their use. Their powerful adaptations of Bulgakov (*Heart of a Dog*) and Dostoevsky (*Notes from Underground*) had enhanced their reputations for exciting stagecraft and a deep strain of misanthropy. Much was expected of this venture into Chekhov, directed by Yanovskaya and lit by Ginkas. Her own general concept was laconic: "End of the century. Times are changing. They are breaking everyone, and me as well. Bonds are severed and human bonds too."[23]

The title was reminiscent of Gorky's late plays (*Egor Bulychev and Others*, *Dostigaev and Others*), but more pungently of the line from Sartre's *Huis-clos*, "L'enfer, c'est les autres." Ivanov and all the rest were "superfluous men," not Turgenev's stranded idealists but Strindbergian vampires battening on one another, yet unable to dispense with one another's company. To confine this irritating interaction, Sergey Barkhin designed a rusty iron box whose walls rumbled like thunder-sheets, and whose rusty metal poles stood in for trees with cutouts that cast leafy outlines on the floor, beneath a filigreed metallic roof. Two huge, thick poles lying on a diagonal across the stage served as tree trunks or a laden table. Three oversized rockers and a samovar completed the picture. Barkin intended to conjure up "an image of stinking gas tanks that people still pretend is paradise,"[24] but his design was sufficiently evocative to remind observers of a burnt-out forest, rotting armaments, a junk yard, a world left smouldering after a pogrom or a bomb attack.

For all the bleakness of the space, a joyous sense of improvisation was conveyed to the audience over three and a half hours of frantic activity. Everything was new and strange and constantly in motion, as one *lazzo* followed another. Serious moments were regularly undercut or interrupted. Act I was not the usual nocturne, but an explosive row. Act II glittered with fireflies. The drinking scene ended with the three topers uptilted in their rockers. Viktoria Verberg as Anna was no wilting orchid, but a woman bursting with sexual appetite and raw energy, who straddled Ivanov in her lust. Borkin's promised fireworks were made manifest with torches, sparklers and catherine wheels, a whole pyrotechnic display erupting at the play's end.

Ivanov himself refuted all performance traditions, particularly the star complex; unlike any earlier avatars, he felt no responsibility or guilt. As played by Sergey Shakurov, he was not Manfred, Hamlet or Tartuffe, but simply a real human being exuding health and strength. He first entered from a swim with a wet towel on his head, and his subsequent pauses, silences, glances, and subtext were highly original. In the Act III monologue he peeled a potato, packing the slightest movements with emotion. He and Sasha frantically devoured apples to the rhythm of their inner fever during their final discussion. As Yanovskaya remarked in an interview, Ivanov, not wishing to be married, "skates around people as in a rink."[25] So Ivanov dressed for his wedding with one skate on.

Perhaps the most striking element of this production were the "others," homunculi from the Chekhovian crucible. Allusions to other plays, such as young ladies on tiptoe *à la* Arkadina and a lotto game, were

46 S. Shakurov as Ivanov and A. Salimonenko as Waffles amid the rusty pipes of *Ivanov and Others*, directed by Genrietta Yanovskaya, Theatre of the Young Spectator, Moscow, 1993.

constantly on offer to the knowing; lines from one drama rebounded off speeches from another. Epikhodov interrupted Ivanov's first-act solilo-quy to offer his pistol; when the harried landowner thought of his debts, Simeonov-Pishchik appeared, feeling his pockets in a panic. Wearing on his head the kerchief that Nemirovich had vetoed in the original *Vanya*, Waffles turned up; so did the Passerby from Act II of *Cherry Orchard*. The two Mashas were combined into one, now quoting from *The Seagull*, now from *Three Sisters*. On the other hand, Charlotta was doubled, and the twin governesses hopped like bunnies, repeating "Alone, alone, all, all alone." Surrounded by these literary hallucinations, Ivanov could not help but look like a crank.[26]

Such disingenuous intertextuality and hilarious sendups of former Soviet interpretations are best appreciated by sophisticated professionals or accidental spectators who come without preconceptions. As the mil-lennium approaches, they view Chekhov through the prism of a way of life that has been shattered to the core. These productions encode the

common destiny of the Russian people; the aching, piercing sadness of
the ridiculous Chekhovian rituals is achieved by a precise combination of
familiar signs. Drawing on metatext, social commentary, theatrical and
national history, a shared legacy of winks and nudges, their message may
be opaque to non-Russians, but it comes across loud and clear to a
generation of Russians grappling with their cultural heritage in the face
of an obscure future.[27]

Notes

EMKT Ezhegodnik Moskovskogo Khudozhestvennogo Teatra (Moscow).

IP1 Vl. I. Nemirovich-Danchenko, *Izbrannye pisma* (Moscow: Iskusstvo, 1954).

IP2 Vl. I. Nemirovich-Danchenko, *Izbrannye pisma v 2-kh tomakh* (Moscow: Iskusstvo, 1974).

PSS A. P. Chekhov, *Polnoe sobranie sochineniya i pisem v 30-ti tomakh* (Moscow: 1974–84).

PSSP the letter volumes in that edition.

StanRE Rezhisserskie éksemplyary K. S. Stanislavskogo 1898–1939. Vols. 2–3. Ed. I. N. Vinogradskaya and I. N. Soloveva (Moscow: Iskusstvo, 1981–3).

StanSS K. S. Stanislavsky, *Sobranie sochineny v 8-mi tomakh* (Moscow: Iskusstvo, 1954–6).

VCT Les voies de la création théâtrale (Paris: Centre national de la recherche scientifique).

Surkov E. D. Surkov, ed., *Chekhov i teatr: pisma, feletony, sovremenniki o Chekhove- dramaturge* (Moscow: Iskusstvo, 1961).

INTRODUCTION

1 Quoted in Maciej Karpinski, *The theatre of Andrzej Wajda*, trans. Christina Paul (Cambridge: Cambridge University Press, 1989), p. 124.

2 Karel Kraus in *Otomar Krejca et le Théâtre Za Branou de Prague* (Lausanne: La Cité, 1972), p. 31.

3 Nikolay Éfros, *Novosti dnya* (31 Oct. 1899).

4 For those who wish to pursue these subjects: South Africa is dealt with in Estelle Botha, "Anton Chekhov: reception of a Russian dramatist in South Africa," in *The waking sphinx: South African essays on Russian culture*, ed. Henrietta Mondry (Johannesburg: University of the Witwatersrand, 1989), pp. 168–78. J. Douglas Clayton covers "Chekhov in Canada" in a forthcoming collection of conference papers from the University of Ottawa (1997). A brief overview of Scandinavian Chekhov appears in Ralf Långbacka, *Möten med Tjechov* (Stockholm: Söderström, 1986), pp. 50–1. The Chekhov craze did not hit Australia until the 1930s, when the Russian émigré Dolia Ribush took seven months to rehearse *The Cherry Orchard* in Melbourne (1938).

I COMPROMISING WITH THE THEATRE (RUSSIA, 1880–1896)

1 Vl. I. Nemirovich-Danchenko, *Iz proshlogo* (Moscow: Academia, 1936), p. 153.
2 M. P. Chekhov, "Vokrug Chekhova. Vstrechi i vpechatleniya," in *Vokrug Chekhova*, ed. E. M. Sakharova (Moscow: Kniga,1990), p. 176.
3 A. Drossi, "Yunosheskie gody A. P. Chekhova," *Priazovskaya rech* 11 (16 Jan. 1910), quoted in A. Ya. Altshuller, "Chekhov v akterskom krugu (V. N. Davydov, P. M. Svobodin, A. P. Lensky)" in *Chekhov i teatralnoe iskusstvo: sbornik nauchnykh trudov* (Leningrad: Ministerstvo Kultury RSFSR, 1985), p. 19.
4 V. S. Tretyakov, ed., *Ocherki istorii Taganrogskogo teatra s 1827–po 1927 god* (Taganrog: Izd. Khudozhestvennoy sektsii Taganrogskogo okrolitrosveta, 1928), pp. 36–8, 59–61.
5 A. P. Chekhov, "Oskolki moskovskoy zhizni," *Oskolki* (22 Oct. 1883, 18 Feb. 1884) in *PSS* XVI, 60, 81. See Ya. Grinvald, *Tri veka moskovskoy stseny* (Moscow: Moskovsky Rabochy, 1949), pp. 159–63. The best book on Lentovsky is Yu. A. Dmitriev, *Mikhail Lentovsky* (Moscow: Iskusstvo, 1978).
6 For Korsh, see T. Pavlova, "'Davydovskie sézony' v teatre Korsha" (1886–8 gody) in *Voprosy teatra* 72 (Moscow: VTO, 1973) and "Teatr Korsha i zritel" in *Problemy sotsiologii teatra* (Moscow: no pub., 1974).
7 A. P. Chekhov, "Oskolki moskovskoy zhizni" (19 Nov. 1883) in *PSS* XVI, 65.
8 B. M. Markiewicz, *Chad zhizni, drama v pyati deistveiakh* (St. Petersburg: no pub., 1884), III, 9.
9 Chekhov to A. N. Pleshcheev (9 Oct. 1888), *PSSP* III, 20.
10 Chekhov to N. A. Leikin (4 Dec. 1887), *PSSP* II, 142; to A. S. Suvorin (17 Dec. 1888), *PSSP* III, 87.
11 Chekhov to A. S. Suvorin (25 Nov. 1889), *PSSP* III, 291.
12 M. P. Chekhov, "Vokrug Chekhova," pp. 269–71.
13 A. R. Kugel, quoted in Altshuller, "Chekhov v akterskom krugu," p. 41; A. Ya. Altshuller, "'Tip vo vsyakom sluchae lyubopytny' (A. P. Chekhov i L. B. Yavorskaya)," in *Chekhoviana: stati, publikatsii, essé*, ed. V. Ya. Lakshin (Moscow: Nauka, 1990), pp. 140–51.
14 Chekhov to A. S. Suvorin (3 Nov. 1888); to I. L. Leontev (16 and 17 Nov. 1888), *PSSP* III, 56, 73.
15 *StanSS* v, 344. Chekhov's love-hate relationship is discussed in M. P. Chekhov, *Anton Chekhov, teatr, aktery i "Tatyana Repina"* (Petrograd: Izd. avtora, 1924), pp. 23 *et seq.*; Em. Beskin, "Lyubil-li Chekhov teatr?," *Teatr i iskusstvo* 26 (1910): 503–4; and A. Kuzicheva, "Lyubil li Chekhov teatr?," *Voprosy teatra* 13 (1993): 116–37.
16 Chekhov to I. L. Leontev (11 Nov. and 20 Dec. 1888), *PSSP* III, 65–6, 94.
17 Chekhov to A. S. Suvorin (20 June 1896), *PSSP* VI, 157.
18 Chekhov to N. A. Leikin (15 Nov. 1887), *PSSP* II, 149.
19 F. Mukhtorov, "'Ivanov' i 'Medved' u Korsha," in *Chekhovsky yubileiny sbornik* (Moscow: I. D. Sytin, 1910), p. 428.

20 I. L. Leontev-Shcheglov, "Iz vospominany ob Antone Chekhove," *Niva* 6/7 (1906), quoted in Surkov, p. 215.

21 Vl. I. Nemirovich-Danchenko, *Retsentsii, ocherki, stati, intervyu, zametki 1877–1942* (Moscow: Iskusstvo, 1980), p. 127. For critical reaction to Chekhov's farces, see V. N. Neverdinova, "Odnoaktnye komedii A. P. Chekhova," in *Chekhovskie chteniya v Yalte. Chekhov i russkaya klassika* (Gos. biblioteka SSSR, V. I. Lenina, 1978), pp. 115–22.

22 Quoted in G. A. Timé, "A. P. Chekhov i komicheskii 'maly zhanr' v dramaturgii 1880-kh-nachala 1890-kh godov," *Russkaya Literatura* 1 (1980), p. 155.

23 "Chelovek (Nemnozhko filosofii)," *PSS* v, 461.

24 Leontev-Shcheglov, in Surkov, p. 216.

25 Chekhov to Aleksandr Chekhov (10 or 12 Oct. 1887), *PSSP* II, 128.

26 A. Ya. Altshuller, "Chekhov v akterskom krugu (V. N. Davydov, P. M. Svobodin, A. P. Lensky)" in *Chekhov i teatralnoe iskusstvo* (Leningrad: Ministerstvo Kultury RSFSR, 1985), p. 23.

27 M. P. Chekhov, "Vokrug Chekhova," pp. 254–5.

28 Mukhtorov, "'Ivanov' i 'Medved,'" p. 429.

29 Chekhov to Aleksandr Chekhov (20 Nov. 1887), *PSSP* II, 150.

30 Petr Kircheev, "Novosti dnya," quoted in I. Yu. Tverdokhlebov, "K tvorcheskoy istorii pesy 'Ivanov', in *V tvorcheskoy laboratorii Chekhova* (Moscow: Nauka, 1974), pp. 99–100; T. K. Shakh-Azizova, "Russky Gamlet ('Ivanov' i ego vremya)," in *Chekhov i ego vremya* (Moscow: Nauka, 1977), pp. 232–46.

31 A. M. Fedorov, *Pamyat A. P. Chekhova* (Moscow: no pub., 1909), in Surkov, p. 367.

32 Chekhov to Al. P. Chekhov and A. S. Kiselev (24 Nov. 1887), *PSSP* II, 153.

33 *Sochineniya G. Uspenskago* (Moscow: Iu. N. Erlikh, 1891), III, 433–6.

34 Altshuller, "Chekhov v akterskom krugu," pp. 24–5.

35 "V Moskve" (1891), *PSS* VII, 500.

36 Chekhov to Al. P. Chekhov (20 Nov. 1887), *PSSP* II, 152.

37 D. Gorodetsky, in *Ogonek* 24 (1904), quoted in Surkov, p. 208.

38 Chekhov to A. S.Suvorin (2 Oct. 1888), *PSSP* II, 9.

39 M. P. Chekhov, "Vokrug Chekhova," p. 255. Trigorin's pleas for a renewed life in Act III of *The Seagull* somewhat echo those of the father in *Second Youth*.

40 A. R. Kugel, *Russkie dramaturgi* (Moscow: Mir, 1934), p. 33.

41 Tverdokhlebov, "K tvorcheskoy istorii," p. 97.

42 The actress M. A. Krestovskaya wrote to Chekhov (3 Oct. 1896) complaining that the character of Ivanov seemed too full of gaps, and she requested the "Korsh" version for her touring company. Quoted in *Teatralnaya zhizn* 23 (1959): 19.

43 Quoted in A. Ya. Altshuller, "Chekhov i Aleksandrinsky Teatr ego vremeni," *Russkaya literatura* 3 (1968): 164.

44 *PSS* XVII, 156. After he got to know her personally, he was to write "Savina

has an insufferable character" (to Suvorin, 23 Dec. 1888), *PSSP* III, 100; and after he saw Eleonora Duse as Cleopatra, he deplored the fact that Savina should be taken as the supreme example of acting in Russia.

45 Chekhov to A. S. Suvorin (7 Jan. 1889), *PSSP* III, 132.
46 Quoted in Altshuller, "Chekhov i Aleksandrinsky Teatr," p. 167.
47 Davydov to Chekhov (15 Jan. 1889) in Surkov, p. 204.
48 Davydov to Chekhov (22 Jan. 1889) in Surkov, pp. 204–5.
49 Chekhov to A. S. Suvorin (7 Jan. 1889), *PSSP* III, 132.
50 *Ibid.*
51 M. G. Savina, "Pochemu ya otkazalas igrat v 'Chaike'," in *Chekhovsky yubileiny sbornik*, p. 430.
52 N. A. Leikin to Chekhov (23 Feb. 1889), in *PSSP* XII, 343.
53 Leontev-Shcheglov in Surkov, pp. 217–18.
54 Spectator quoted in Vl. Prokofev, "Legenda o pervoy postanovke 'Chaiki,'" *Teatr* 11 (1946): 44–5; N. M. Ezhov quoted in A. Kuzicheva, "Lyubil li Chekhov teatr?," p. 126.
55 Quoted in S. Balukhaty, *Chekhov – dramaturg* (Leningrad: Goslitizdat, 1934), p. 90.
56 I. Grek, *Oskolki* (1889), pp. 4–5.
57 A. P. Chudakov, *Chekhov's Poetics*, tr. F. J. Cruise and D. Dragt (Ann Arbor: Ardis, 1983), pp. 149–52.
58 D. Gorodetsky in Surkov, p. 209.
59 P. Svobodin to Chekhov (10 Aug. 1889) in Surkov, p. 210.
60 Ars. Gurlyand, "Iz vospominany ob A. P. Chekhove," *Teatr i iskusstvo* 28 (1904, quoted in Surkov, p. 206.
61 Chekhov to A. S. Suvorin (14 Aug. 1888), *PSSP* II, 313.
62 Gurlyand, "Iz vospaminany ob A. P. Chekhove," p. 207.
63 P. M. Svobodin to Chekhov (2 Oct. 1889), p. 211.
64 *Ibid.*
65 *Ibid.*, p. 212. The reference is to the Parisian director André Antoine whose naturalistic Théâtre Libre was at the cutting-edge of the *avant-garde*.
66 Chekhov's correspondence to Svobodin has not survived. See letter to A. N. Pleshcheev (21 Oct. 1889), *PSSP* III, 268–9.
67 Chekhov to A. P. Lensky (6 Oct. 1889), *PSSP* III, 258.
68 A. P. Lensky to Chekhov (Nov. 1889) in Surkov, p. 214.
69 Vl. I. Nemirovich-Danchenko to Chekhov (6 Nov. 1889) in *IP1*, p. 54.
70 Chekhov to A. S. Suvorin (12 Nov. 1889), *PSSP* III, 285.
71 M. P. Chekhov, "Vokrug Chekhova," p. 261.
72 Ivan Ivanov, *Artist* (1890): 124–5.

2 A BRACE OF GULLS (RUSSIA, 1896–1898)

1 Quoted in Z. S. Paperny, "'Chaika' na stsene i na ékrane," in *Chekhovskie chteniya v Yalte* (Moscow: Kniga, 1976), p. 85.
2 T. L. Shchepkina-Kupernik, *Dni moey zhizni* (Moscow: Federatsiya, 1928),

pp. 325–6 and *Teatr v moey zhizni* (Moscow-Leningrad: Iskusstvo, 1948), p. 307.

3 Another reflection of a real actress was in Nina's line about an artist being above the crowd and drawn in a chariot. In the 1890s, Mariya Ermolova had played Grillparzer's Sapho at the Maly and entered in a golden chariot drawn by the people, as an apotheosis of the artist. A. Ya. Altshuller, "Chekhov v akterskom krugu (V. N. Davydov, P. M. Svobodin, A. P. Lensky)," in *Chekhov i teatralnoe isskustvo* (Leningrad: Ministerstvo Kultury RSFSR, 1985), p. 41.

4 E. Karpov, "Istoriya pervogo predstavleniya 'Chaiki' na stsene Aleksandrinskogo teatra 17 okt. 1896) in *O Chekhove* (Moscow: Sovremennoe tvorchestvo, 1910), pp. 61–74.

5 E. Karpov in *Chekhovsky yubileiny sbornik* (Moscow: I. D. Sytin, 1910), p. 431.

6 Quoted in Paperny, "'Chaika' na stsene i na ékrane."

7 Vl. I. Nemirovich-Danchenko to Chekhov, in *EMKT* 1944 (Moscow: Izd. muz. moskovskogo ordena Lenina i Trudovogo klasnogo znanem khudo. akad. teatra, 1945), I, 104.

8 Leontev-Shcheglov, "Iz vospominaniya" in Surkov, p. 219.

9 I. I. Shneiderman, *Mariya Gavrilovna Savina* (Moscow-Leningrad: Iskusstvo, 1956), p. 330. Shneiderman gives the lie to Savina's claim (M. G. Savina, "Pochumu ya otkazalas igrat v 'Chaike,'" in *Chekhovsky yubileiny sbornik*, p. 430) that she attended two rehearsals, but thought the part better suited to Komissarzhevskaya and generously gave it up despite the wishes of Suvorin and Levkeeva.

10 M. G. Savina to A. S. Suvorin, quoted in Surkov, p. 243. Yurev's stories about her rehearsing Nina at the first rehearsals and then becoming jealous of Komissarzhevskaya are made up from whole cloth. Yu. M. Yurev, *Zapiski*, ed. E. M. Kuznetsova (Leningrad-Moscow: Iskusstvo, 1963), II, 42–3.

11 Karpov, "Istoriya"; Kugel quoted in Vl. Prokofev, "Legenda o pervoy postanovke 'Chaiki,'" *Teatr* 11 (1946): 52. Also see M. M. Chitau, "Premera 'Chaiki,'" in *A. P. Chekhov v vospominaniyakh sovremennikov* (Moscow Khudozhestvennaya literatura, 1986), pp. 350–5.

12 Leontev-Shcheglov in Surkov, p. 49.

13 Prokofev, "Legenda," p. 50; S. D. Balukhaty, *"Chaika" v postanovke MKhATa. Rezhisserskaya partitura K. S. Stanislavskogo* (Leningrad-Moscow: Nauka, 1938); I. N. Potapenko, *Niva* 26–7 (1914), quoted in Surkov, p. 222. Komissarzhevskaya claims to have wept all night on reading the play. Yu. P. Rybakova, *V. F. Komissarzhevskaya, letopis zhizni i tvorchestva* (St. Petersburg: Rossysky Institut Istorii Iskusstv, 1994), p. 81.

14 P. P. Gnedich, quoted in Prokofev, "Legenda," p. 53.

15 *Ibid.*, p. 54. Also see P. Gaideburov, "Polveka s Chekhovym," *Teatralny almanakh* (Moscow: 1948), p. 303.

16 The Kievan poet Sergey Berdyaev quoted in V. Ya. Zvinyatskovsky, "'Dekadent' (V. I. Bibikov – korrespondent A. P. Chekhova)," in

Chekhoviana: stati, publikatsii, essé, ed. V. Ya. Lakshin (Moscow: Nauka, 1990), p. 134.

17 *Novosti i birzhevye vedomosti* (1904): 232–4, quoted in Prokofev, "Legenda," p. 48.

18 Prokofev, "Legenda," p. 53.

19 Karpov, "Istoriya."

20 *Ibid.*

21 Prokofev, "Legenda," p. 52.

22 Al. Lugovy, "Sud tolpy. Iz teatralnykh vospominany," *Ezhegodnik imperatorskikh teatrov* 7 (1911), prilozhenie 1911–13, p. 11.

23 A. I. Suvorina in *A. P. Chekhov* (Leningrad, 1925), quoted in Surkov, pp. 231–3. At the first dress rehearsal Karpov, wary of Komissarzhevskaya's inexperience, tried to make her play the last scene far upstage behind a table. Davydov and Sazonov dissuaded him from this "talking head" effect. Rybakova, *Vera Kommissarzhevskaya*, p. 82.

24 Karpov "Istoriya."

25 *Ibid.*

26 Lugovy, "Sud tolpy," pp. 10–13.

27 Leontev-Shcheglov in Surkov, p. 219.

28 *Ibid.*, p. 220; Yurev, *Zapiski*, II, 219–20; Karpov, "Istoriya," p. 239; Vl. Brender, "Yubiley provala 'Chaiki,'" *Teatralnaya gazeta* 16 (1916): 9.

29 *Realist* 1896; see also nos. 288, 293 (1896). For a list of contemporary Russian ephemera about Chekhov's plays, see L. F. Masanov, *Chekhoviana. Vypusk I. Sistematichesky ukazatel literatury o Chekhove i ego tvorchestve* (Moscow: Gos. Tsentr. Knizhnaia palata RSFSR, 1929).

30 Bedny Ionafan, *Peterburgsky listok* (1896).

31 Rylov, *Peterburgskaya gazeta* (1896).

32 Quoted in Prokofev, "Legenda," p. 46.

33 A. S. Suvorin, *Dnevnik* (17 Oct., 21 Oct. 1896) (Moscow-Petrograd: L. D. Frenkel, 1923), pp. 125–6, 128.

34 Quoted in Al. Gladkov, *Meierkhold* (Moscow: Soyuz teatralnykh deyateley, 1990),I, 155.

35 A. I. Urusov, *Stati o teatre, literature i ob iskusstve* (Moscow: I. N. Kolchev, 1907), II–III, 34–5. Also see T. Shakh-Azizova, "Predvozvestnik," *Teatralnaya zhizn* 4 (1994): 6–9.

36 Quoted in Prokofev, "Legenda," p. 47.

37 P. P. Gaideburov, *Literaturnoe nasledie. Vospominaniya, stati, rezhisserskie eksplikatsii* (Moscow: VTO, 1977), p. 135.

38 Urusov, *Stati o teatre.*

39 Gaideburov, *Literaturnoe nasledie.*

40 Quoted in Prokofev, "Legenda," p. 54. Also see "Vera Fedorovna Kommissarzhevskaya na stsene imp. Aleksandrinskogo teatra 1896–1902," in *Sbornik pamyati V. F. Kommissarzhevskoy* (St. Petersburg: Gos. izd-vo khudozh. literatury, 1911): 61–73.

41 Yury Belyaev, quoted in D. Talnikov, "Problema rezhissury i russkaya klassika," in *Teatralny almanakh* (Moscow: VTO, 1947), p. 183.

42 Gaideburov, *Literaturnoe nasledie*, p. 130.
43 Suvorin, *Dnevnik* (18 Oct. 1896), p. 126. Chekhov's hypersensitive reaction and his refusal to write another play "if I live another 700 years" might be compared with Henry James's at the failure of *Guy Domville*; but Chekhov himself later admitted he had overreacted.
44 V. F. Komissarzhevskaya to Chekhov (21 Oct. 1896) in Surkov, p. 246.
45 Yurev, *Zapiski*, 1, 222.
46 Karpov in *Chekhovsky yubileiny sbornik*, p. 432.
47 *Moskovsky Khudozhestvenny teatr* (Moscow: Gos. izd-vo izobrazitelnogo iskusstva, 1938), p. 698; in English in L. Senelick, ed. and trans., *National theatre in northern and eastern Europe, 1746–1900* (Cambridge: Cambridge University Press, 1991), pp. 414–16.
48 Prokofev, "Legenda," p. 55.
49 "A. P. Chekhov v Khudozhestvennom teatre," in *StanSS* v, 329.
50 "Iz proshlago," *StanSS* v, 13.
51 Stanislavsky to Vl. I. Nemirovich-Danchenko (29 Jan. 1899), quoted in Paperny, "'Chaika na stsene," p. 85. In *My Life in Art*, Stanislavsky emphasizes his boredom with the play when he sat down to write the staging.
52 V. I. Nemirovich-Danchenko to Chekhov (31 May 1898), *IP1*, 117.
53 On this subject, see M. Murzina, "Teatr A. P. Chekhova v russkoy kritike," in *Teatralnaya kritika: istoriya i teoriya*, ed. B. N. Lyubimov (Moscow: Ministerstvo Kultury RSFSR, 1989), pp. 96–7.
54 D. S. Mirsky, *A history of Russian literature* (New York: Alfred A. Knopf, 1964), p. 334.
55 V. I. Nemirovich-Danchenko in *Novosti dnya* (26 Feb. 1901).
56 V. I. Nemirovich-Danchenko to Chekhov (before 9 Sept. 1898), *IP2* (Moscow Iskusstvo, 1979), 1, 151–2.
57 S. Balukhaty, *"Chaika" v postanovke MkhATa*, pp. 47–8.
58 V. I. Nemirovich-Danchenko to Stanislavsky (2 Sept. 1898), *IP2* I, 145.
59 "Chaika," *StanRE*,II, 117.
60 A. Gladkov, *Meierkhold* (Moscow: Soyuz teatralnykh deyateley, 1990), 1, 149; V. E. Meyerhold, *Stati, rechi, pisma, besedi* (Moscow: Iskusstvo, 1960), 1, 116.
61 M. Stroeva, "Chekhov i Khudozhestvenny teatr (K voprosu o strukture rannikh spektakley MKhTa)," in *Chekhovskie chteniya v Yalte. Chekhov i teatr* (Moscow: Kniga, 1976), p. 14.
62 Chekhov attended two rehearsals in September, seemed pleased with the look of things, and only corrected a couple of details concerning Treplev.
63 Books which reproduce photographs purporting to be stage shots of the "first" Art Theatre production of *Seagull* are in error. Until 1902, production shots were taken in a photographer's studio. Only after 1902, when the company had moved to its new building in Kammerherr Lane with its larger stage were stage shots taken at special rehearsals. The photographs of the "first" MAT *Seagull* are actually of the first revival.
64 O. Nekrasova, *Viktor Andreevich Simov* (Moscow: Iskusstvo, 1952), p. 110. Also see V. Berezkin, *Khudozhnik v teatre Chekhove* (Moscow: Izobrazitelnoe iskusstvo, 1987), pp. 186–7.

65 K. Rudnitsky, "'Chaika' – 1898," in *Chekhovskie chteniya v Yalte. Chekhov i teatr* (Moscow: Kniga, 1976), p. 65.

66 Urusov, *Stati o teatre*, II, 34–8.

67 Rudnitsky, "'Chaika' – 1898," p. 72.

68 Quoted in Léon Dominique, *Le Théâtre russe et la scène française*, tr. Nina Nidermiller and Michèle Wiernik (Paris: Olivier Perrin, 1969), p. 251.

69 I. Kirillova, "Pesa Konstantina Trepleva v poéticheskoy strukture 'Chaiki,'" in *Chekhov i teatralnoe iskusstvo* (Leningrad: Ministerstvo Kultury RSFSR, 1985), p. 100.

70 *StanRE* II, 69.

71 Stanislavsky to Nemirovich-Danchenko (10 Sept. 1898), *StanSS* VII, 143. The *locus classicus* for Chekhov's complaints about sound effects and other naturalistic devices is his remark, "The stage is art. Kramskoy has a certain genre painting, on which faces are superbly depicted. What if the painted nose was cut out of one of the faces and replaced with a living one? The nose is 'realistic' but the picture is spoiled. The stage demands a *certain conventionality*. – You have no fourth wall. Nevertheless, the stage is art, the stage reflects a quintessence of life, nothing superfluous should be brought on stage." (*Literaturnoe nasledstvo*, 68 [Moscow: Nauka, 1960], pp. 418–19.) But this would appear to come from a later period.

72 Sergey Glagol, *Kurer* (19 Dec. 1898); Urusov, *Stati o teatre*.

73 Vl. I. Nemirovich-Danchenko, *Iz proshlogo* (Moscow: Academia, 1936), pp. 168–9.

74 L. N. Andreev, *Pisma o teatre* (1911–14), in *Russian dramatic theory from Pushkin to the symbolists*, ed. and trans. Laurence Senelick (Austin: University of Texas Press, 1981), p. 238.

75 Gladkov, *Meierkhold*, I, 149–50.

76 *StanRE* II, 55.

77 *Ibid.*, II, 117.

78 *Ibid.*, II, 163.

79 Quoted in Rudnitsky, "'Chaika' – 1898," p. 78.

80 *Moskovsky listok* (20 Dec. 1898), quoted in I. Vinogradskaya, *Zhizn i tvorchestvo K. S. Stanislavskogo: letopis* (Moscow: Iskusstvo, 1971), I, 257.

81 *Kurer* (19 Dec. 1898).

82 *EMKT 1944*, p. 290.

83 *StanRE* II, 159, 163.

84 *Meierkhold*, I, 151.

85 T. Shchepkina-Kupernik, *Dni moei zhizni*, quoted in Surkov, p. 244.

86 Quoted in E. M. Sakharova, "Pervye zriteli (po materialam chekhovskogo rukopisnogo arkhiva Gosudarstvennoy biblioteki SSSR imeni V. I. Lenina), in *Chekhovskie chteniya v Yalte. Chekhov i teatr*, p. 38.

87 Letter of A. S. Lazarev-Gruzinsky to Chekhov (19 Jan. 1899), quoted in Vinogradskaya, *Zhizn i tvorchestvo*, I, 235.

88 A. L. Vishnevsky, "Iz vospominany o Chekhove," in *Chekhovsky yubileiny sbornik*, p. 434.

89 Vl. I. Nemirovich-Danchenko to Chekhov (18–21 Dec. 1898), *IP2*, I, 160–1.

90 *Slovo*, sbornik 2 (Moscow: 1914), p. 287.

91 Vl. I. Nemirovich-Danchenko to Chekhov. Meyerhold often spoke of the abundance of tears he shed in the role.

92 *Moskovsky listok* (20 Dec. 1898).

93 P. A. Sergeenko to Chekhov (25 Dec. 1898), quoted in Sakharova, "Pervye zriteli," p. 39.

94 Vl. I. Nemirovich-Danchenko to Chekhov (before 9 Sept. 1898), *IP2*, I, 152.

95 Sergeenko to Chekhov; also Ya. E. Feigin, "Pismo o sovremennom iskusstve," *Russkaya mysl* 10 (1899): 191.

96 Glagol, *Kurer.*

97 Chekhov to A. M. Gorky (9 May 1899), *PSSP* VIII, 170.

98 O. L. Knipper-Chekhova, "Ob A. P. Chekhove," *Vospominaniya i stati. Perepiska* (Moscow: Iskusstvo, 1972), I, 49.

99 I. Levitan to Chekhov (8 Jan. 1899), quoted in Surkov, p. 355.

100 Gladkov, *Meierkhold*, I, 153.

101 *Vl. I. Nemirovich-Danchenko vedet repetitsiyu* (Moscow: Iskusstvo, 1965), pp. 147–8.

102 Shchepkina-Kupernik in Surkov, p. 245.

103 Chekhov to Olga Knipper (28 Sept. 1900), *PSSP* IX, 125.

104 A. L. Vishnevsky, *Klochki vospominany*, ed. Al. Slonimsky (Leningrad: Academia, 1928), p. 61.

105 V. Volkenshtein, *Stanislavsky* (Moscow: Shipovnik, 1922), p. 442.

106 P. P. Gnedich, *Novoe vremya* (18 Jan. 1899), quoted in Vinogradskaya, *Zhizn i tvorchestvo*, I, 256.

3 MOSCOW NIGHTS (THE MOSCOW ART THEATRE, 1898–1905)

1 P. P. Gaideburov, *Literaturnoe nasledie. Vospominaniya, stati, rezhisserskie éksplikatsi* (Moscow: VTO, 1977), p. 336. The Art Theatre productions have been exhaustively dealt with by Russian scholars: M. Stroeva's *Chekhov i Khudozhestvenny Teatr* (Moscow: Iskusstvo, 1955) is the most thorough, but riddled with the usual Marxist-Leninist gobbledegook of its period. Part of her chapter on *Three Sisters* was published in *The Tulane Drama Review* (Fall 1964) as "*The Three Sisters* at the MAT." Nikolay Éfros' monographs on *Three Sisters* and *Cherry Orchard* (1919) are full of rich detail and sharp observation. Stanislavsky's directorial scores for *Three Sisters* and *Cherry Orchard* have been published in *StanRE*, Vol. 3: 1901–4; that for *Uncle Vanya*, edited by I. N. Soloveva, was privately published in 1994. Also see N. Gourfinkel, "Tchékhov au Théâtre artistique de Moscou," *Revue de la société d'histoire du théâtre* 4 (1954): 251–86; Michael Heim, "Chekhov and the Moscow Art Theatre," in *Chekhov's Great Plays*, ed. J.-P. Barricelli (New York: New York University Press, 1981); and Bogdanovich, "'Dyadya Vanya' i 'Tri sestry' na stsene Khudozhestvennogo teatra," in *Anton Pavlovich Chekhov. Ego zhizn i sochineniya*, ed. V. I. Pokrovsky (Moscow: V. Spiridonov and A. Mikhailov, 1907).

2 V. Maslikh, "Chekhov i Maly teatr," *Teatralnaya zhizn* 2 (1960): 12–20.

3 N. G. Zograf, *Maly Teatr v kontse XIX-nachale XX veka* (Moscow: Nauka, 1966), p. 138.

4 V. A. Nelidov, *Teatralnaya Moskva (sorok let moskovskikh teatrov)* (Berlin-Riga: S. Kretschetow, 1931), pp. 239–40.

5 V. F. Komissarzhevskaya to Chekhov (9 Apr. 1900), quoted in Surkov, ed., p. 246.

6 Chekhov to E. P. Karpov (4 Oct. 1899) *PSSP* VIII, 277.

7 Quoted in A. Ya. Altshuller, "Chekhov i Aleksandrinsky teatr ego vremeni," *Russkaya Literatura* 3 (1968), p. 171.

8 Vl. I. Nemirovich-Danchenko to Chekhov (27 Oct. 1899), *IP2*, I, 201–4. Nemirovich had first solicited the play in the very letter in which he reported on the successful opening night of *The Seagull* (28 Feb. 1898).

9 Butova, quoted in Surkov, p. 46

10 P. Gromov, "Chekhov, Stanislavsky, Meierkhold. U istokov teatralnikh iskany nachala veka," in *Chekhov i teatralnoe iskusstvo* (Leningrad: Ministerstvo Kultury RSFSR, 1985), p. 53; O. Mandelshtam, "O pese A. Chekhova 'Dyadya Vanya,'" (1936), *Sobranie sochineny*, ed. G. Struve *et al.* (Paris: YMCA Press, 1981), IV, 107–9.

11 V. E. Meyerhold to Chekhov (4 Sept. 1900), in *Literaturnoe nasledstvo. Chekhov.* 68 (Moscow: Nauka, 1960), p. 439.

12 Chekhov to V. E. Meyerhold (early Oct. 1899), *PSSP* VIII, 274–5.

13 V. Volkenshtein, *Stanislavsky* (Moscow: 1922), p. 67. Later he was to profess surprise at his success in the role, "I do nothing in it, but the audience praises me." L. Ya. Gurevich, ed. *O Stanislavskom* (Moscow: VTO, 1948), p. 266.

14 P. I. Kurkin to Chekhov (27 Oct. 1899), quoted in E. M. Sakharova, "Pervye zriteli po materialam chekhovskogo rukopisnogo arkhiva Gosudarstvennoy biblioteki SSSR imeni V. I. Lenina," in *Chekhovskie chteniya v Yalte. Chekhov i teatr* (Moscow: Kniga, 1976), p. 43.

15 N. I. Korobov to Chekhov (17 Jan. 1900), quoted in Sakharova, "Pervye zriteli," p. 46.

16 A. M. Gorky to Chekhov (20 Oct.–6 Nov. 1898), quoted in Surkov, pp. 359–60.

17 A. M. Gorky to Chekhov (21 or 22 Jan. 1900), quoted in Surkov, p. 365.

18 *Moya zhizn v iskusstve*, in *StanSS* I, 234.

19 Chekhov to Olga Knipper (28 Sept. 1900), *PSSP* IX, 125.

20 Chekhov to Olga Knipper (15 Sept. 1900), *PSSP* IX, 117.

21 Stanislavsky, *Moya zhizn v iskusstve*.

22 *Ibid.*, p. 235.

23 K. Rudnitsky, *Rezhisser Meierhold* (Moscow: Iskusstvo, 1969), p. 16.

24 Stanislavsky to Baron Drizen (3 Nov. 1909), *StanSS* VII, 251.

25 Stanislavsky to Chekhov (Jan. 1901), *StanSS* VII, 205.

26 M. Stroeva, "Chekhov i Khudozhestvenny teatr (k voprosu o strukture rannikh spektakley MKhATa)," in *Chekhovskie chteniya v Yalte. Chekhov i teatr* (Moscow: Kniga, 1976), p. 16.

27 Quoted in I. N. Solovova, "'Tri sestry' – 1901," in *Chekhovskie chteniya v Yalte. Chekhov i teatr*, p. 108.
28 Stroeva, "Chekhov i Khudozhestvenny teatr," p. 17.
29 Yu. Sobolev, *V. I. Nemirovich-Danchenko* (St. Petersburg: Soltntse Rossii, 1918), p. 100.
30 Olga Knipper to Chekhov (27 Oct. 1899) in O. L. Knipper, *Vospominaniya i stati. Perepiska* (Moscow: Iskusstvo, 1972), I, 99.
31 *IP1*, p. 207.
32 Gorky (21–8 Mar. 1901) in Surkov, p. 362.
33 A. Gladkov, *Meierkhold* (Moscow: Soyuz teatralnykh deiateley, 1990), I, 200; V. Vilenkin, *Vasily Ivanovich Kachalov* (Moscow: Iskusstvo, 1954), p. 142.
34 Volkonsky, *Stanislavsky*, p. 68; Gurevich, *O Stanislavskom*, pp. 266–7. A detailed account in English of the original production is given in Nick Worrall, "Stanislavsky's production of Chekhov's *Three Sisters*," in *Russian Theatre in the Age of Modernism*, ed. R. Russell and A. Barratt (London: Macmillan, 1990), pp. 1–32.
35 *Moskovskie vedomosti* 7, 11 (25 Feb. 1901).
36 *Russkoe slovo* 4, 17 (Feb. 1901).
37 Olga Knipper to Chekhov, *Vospominaniya*, I, 306, 309, 320.
38 N. Éfros, *'Tri sestry': pesa A. P. Chekhova v postanovke Moskovskogo Khudozhestvennogo teatra* (Petrograd: Svetozar, 1919), pp. 17, 22, 24.
39 A. S. Suvorin, *Dnevnik* (Moscow-Petrograd: I. D. Frenkel, 1923), p. 284.
40 S. Karlinsky, "Russian anti-Chekhovians," *Russian Literature* 15 (1984), pp. 191–2.
41 V. N. Sementkovsky, "Po povodu dramy g. Chekhova. O publike. Personazhi dramy A. P. Chekhova 'Tri sestry,'" *Moskovskie vedomosti* 7, 11 (23 Feb. 1901).
42 I. Ignatov, "'Tri sestry,'" *Russkie vedomosti* (1 Feb. 1901).
43 V. G., "Novaya drama Chekhova," *Moskovskie vedomosti* (3 Feb. 1901).
44 V. P. Burenin, "Kriticheskie ocherki," *Novoe vremya* 9280 (4 Jan. 1902); 9301 (25 Jan. 1902); 10079 (26 Mar. 1904).
45 V. P. Burenin, *Sochineniya. Tom V: Dramaticheskie karikatury* (Petrograd: A. S. Suvorin, 1917); see L. Senelick, "Stuffed seagulls. Parodies of Chekhov as signs of cultural reception," *Poetics Today* 8, 2 (1987): 287–8.
46 James Lynch, "Moskva. Melochi zhizni" and "*Tri sestry*," *Kurer* (4 Feb. 1901; 21 Oct. 1901), in L. N. Andreev, *Polnoe sobranie sochineny* (Moscow: no pub., 1913), VI, 321–5.
47 Andreev, *Polnoe sobranie sochineny*, VI, 323.
48 A. K. Lyadov the composer wrote in a letter, "I liked *Three Sisters* a lot; the play is intelligent, talented, life-like, despite being 'depressive' [*upadochnaya*] – a great deal is 'wound' on a single bobbin." "To da se," *Teatralnaya gazeta* 16 (1916): 15.
49 *Chekhov v vospominaniyakh sovremennikov* (Moscow: Iskusstvo, 1952), p. 481.
50 A. Blok, *Sobranie sochineny v 8 tomakh* (Moscow-Leningrad: Iskusstvo, 1963), VIII, 281.

51 T. Shchepkina-Kupernik, quoted in Surkov, p. 245.

52 Stanislavsky to Z. S. Sokolova (7 Sept. 1901), *StanSS* VII, 218.

53 Chekhov to M. P. Lilina (15 Sept 1903), *PSSP* XI, 248.

54 Stanislavsky to Chekhov, (20 Oct. 1903), *StanSS* VII, 265. See Victor Borovsky, "Discord in the cherry orchard. Chekhov and Stanislavsky," *Encounter* (Jan.–Feb. 1990): 65–72.

55 *IP2*, I, 344. The Soviet director Nikolay Petrov later noted another significant development. In Chekhov's earlier plays, a "pause" (with a lower case p) was purely psychological, relating to a character's inner life, whereas the Pauses (with an upper case P) in *Cherry Orchard* relate to a general problematic. N. Petrov, *50 i 500* (Moscow: VTO, 1960), pp. 427–36.

56 Chekhov to L. A. Avilova (May–Sept. 1901), *PSSP* x, 99.

57 Chekhov to Vl. I. Nemirovich-Danchenko (2 Nov. 1903), *PSSP* XI, 294.

58 *Ibid.*

59 Chekhov to Olga Knipper (24 Mar. 1904), *PSSP* XII, 69. This letter dates from after the opening, when cast changes were mooted. Chekhov detested Khalyutina's performance as Dunyasha and Alexandrov's as Yasha, because they didn't do what the stage directions called for.

60 Chekhov to Olga Knipper (30 Oct. 1903), *PSSP* XI, 290.

61 Nelidov, *Teatralnaya Moskva*, pp. 282–3.

62 Stanislavsky to Chekhov (31 Oct. 1903), *StanSS* VII, 267.

63 I. A. Bunin, *O Chekhove* (New York: Chekhov Press, 1955), p. 216.

64 V. O. Toporkov, *Chetyre ocherki o K. S. Stanislavskom* (Moscow: Sovetskaya Rossiya, 1963), p. 9.

65 N. Éfros, '*Vyshnevy Sad*' *v postanovke Moskovskom khudozhestvennom teatre* (Petrograd: Svetozar, 1919), pp. 87–8; Nikolaev called it "primitive and forced." N. I. Nikolaev, *Éfemeridy* (Kiev: Izd. Kievskago Obshchestva Iskusstva i Literatury, 1912), p. 145.

66 Chekhov to Stanislavsky (10 Nov. 1903), *PSSP* XI, 302.

67 Chekhov to Olga Knipper (14 Oct. 1903), *PSSP* XI, 272–3.

68 Stanislavsky, "Mysli o teatre. Iz zapisnykh knizhek: 1898–1936," *Teatr* I (1983): 78.

69 V. I. Rostotsky, "O. L. Knipper-Chekhova," in *Mastera MKhAT* (Moscow-Leningrad: Iskusstvo, 1939): 250–1.

70 B. Zingerman, *Teatr Chekhova i ego mirovoe zachenie*, ed. A. A. Anikst (Moscow: Nauka, 1988), p. 361.

71 Chekhov to Olga Knipper (27 Feb. 1904), *PSSP* XII, 19.

72 Knipper-Chekhova, *Vospominaniya*, I, 59.

73 M. Stroeva, *Rezhisserskie iskaniya Stanislavskogo 1898–1917* (Moscow: Iskusstvo, 1973), 122.

74 Nikolaev, *Éfemeridy*, p. 145.

75 Chekhov to Stanislavsky (23 Nov. 1903), *PSSP* XI, 312.

76 Chekhov to Olga Knipper (23 Nov. 1903), *PSSP* XI, 313.

77 Chekhov to Vl. I. Nemirovich-Danchenko (22 Aug. 1903), *PSSP* XI, 242. Amiard-Chevrel has noted that although Chekhov went into great detail in his letters about casting, scenery and staging, he never questioned the basic

interpretation of the play. C. Amiard-Chevrel, *Le Théâtre artistique de Moscou (1898–1917)* (Paris: Centre National de la Recherche Scientifique, 1979), p. 130.

78 *StanRE* III,369.

79 *Ibid.*, pp. 357, 397, 427.

80 *Ibid.*, p. 439. Stanislavsky is not the only culprit in this over-elaboration; after the second dress rehearsal, Nemirovich had the last act set repainted so that the bare patches left by removed portraits could be seen on the walls. Yu. Sobolev, *Vl. I. Nemirovich-Danchenko* (St. Petersburg: Solntse Rossii, 1918), p. 101.

81 V. E. Meyerhold, *Stati, rechi, pisma, besedy* (Moscow: Iskusstvo, 1968), I, 122.

82 Vilenkin, *Kachalov*, p. 123.

83 Hugh Walpole, "Epikhodov: a note on a Russian character," in *The Soul of Russia*, ed. Winifred Stephens (London: Macmillan, 1916), p. 35; his essay gives a blow-by-blow account of Moskvin's performance.

84 S. Yablonovsky, "Gorkovoy ili Chekhovskoy?," *Illyustrirovannaya Rossiya* (Paris) (14 Aug. 1937).

85 Stanislavsky to the Petersburg actress V. Pushkareva (26 Dec. 1903).

86 S. Lyubosh, "'Vyshnevy sad,'" in *Chekhovskie yubileiny sbornik* (Moscow: I. D. Sytin, 1910), p. 448.

87 Chekhov to Vl. I. Nemirovich-Danchenko, Mar. 1904, *PSSP* XII, 74.

88 Chekhov to Olga Knipper (10 Apr. 1904), *PSSP* XII, 81.

89 Yu. Aikhenvald, "Sovremennoe iskusstvo," *Russkaya mysl* (1904): 262.

90 The grassy knolls were made of sheepskins dyed green and the haycocks were wicker baskets overlaid with a blanket of hay. Soviet revivals would project clouds against the painted backcloth. John Mitchell, *Staging Chekhov: Cherry Orchard* (New York: Institute for Advanced Studies in the Theatre Arts, 1991), p. 128. Chekhov specifically objected to this "horrible" set because it did not conform with his stage directions.

91 Nikolaev, *Éfemeridy*, pp. 139–40, 145–6. Stanislavsky made the audience wait a full minute before the entrance of the family in Act I, according to Yury Zavadsky, J. D. in Mitchell, *Staging Chekhov: Cherry Orchard*, p. 20.

92 Nikolaev, *Éfemeridy*, p. 160.

93 *Sochineny V. P. Burenina* v, 201–2; *Teatr i iskusstvo* (21 and 28 Mar. 1904). See Senelick, "Stuffed Seagulls," pp. 289–90.

94 Vl. I. Nemirovich-Danchenko to N. Éfros (before 21 Dec. 1908), *IP2*, I, 470–1.

95 *Russky sovetsky teatr 1926–1932. Chast pervaya*, ed. A. Ya. Trabsky (Leningrad: Iskusstvo, 1982), p. 173.

96 V. E. Meyerhold to Chekhov 8 May 1904, in Meyerhold, *Perepiska 1896–1939* (Moscow: Iskusstvo, 1976), p. 42; "K istorii tekhnika teatra" in *Stati*, I, 119.

97 A. Bely, "On modern drama," in Laurence Senelick, ed., *Russian Dramatic Theory from Pushkin to the Symbolists* (Austin: University of Texas Press, 1981), p. 92.

98 Maurice Baring, *The Puppet Show of Memory* (Boston: Little, Brown, 1923),

p. 268. Baring's own play about Russian life, *The Double Game*, is more like a standard melodrama than a Chekhovian mood-piece. See M. Baring, *The grey stocking and other plays* (London: Constable, 1912).

99 Vilenkin, *Kachalov*, p. 147.

100 Vl. I. Nemirovich-Danchenko, "Iz rezhisserskogo eksemplyari 'Ivanova,'" *Teatr* 1 (1960): 150.

101 Yu. Aikhenvald, "Sovremennoe iskusstvo," *Russkaya mysl* 11 (Nov. 1904): 237–8; A. Bely, "'Ivanov' na stsene Khudozhestvennogo teatra," *Arabeski* (Moscow: Musaget, 1911), pp. 405–8.

102 Altshuller, "Chekhov i Aleksandrinsky teatr," p. 169.

103 Gaideburov, *Literaturnoe nasledie*, p. 137.

104 L. Leonidov, *Proshloe i nastoyashchee* (Moscow: Iskusstvo, 1948), pp. 102–3.

105 E. T. Karpov, "Dve posledniya vstrechi s Ant. Pav. Chekhovym," *Ezhegodnik imperatorskikh teatrov* 5 (1909): 7–8. Ivan Bunin considered all of Karpov's memoirs of Chekhov to be lies. I. Bunin, *O Chekhove* (New York: Chekhov Publishing House, 1955), pp. 379, 410.

106 *Teatr i muzyka* 36 (6 Nov. 1923), quoted in Osip Mandelstam, *The complete critical prose and letters*, ed. J. G. Harris (Ann Arbor: Ardis, 1979), pp. 188–90.

107 A. A. Mgebrov, *Zhizn v teatre*, ed. E. Kuznetsov (Leningrad: Academia, 1929), I, 244–5.

108 Volkenshtein, *Stanislavsky*, pp. 41–4.

109 *Ibid.*, p. 69.

110 *Ibid.*, p. 85.

4 COMPETITORS AND IMITATORS (RUSSIAN EMPIRE, 1898–1917)

1 I. A. Rostovstev to A. P. Chekhov (5 Dec. 1900), quoted in *PSS* XIII, 405.

2 V. A. Nelidov, *Teatralnaya Moskva (sorok let moskovskikh teatrov)* (Berlin-Riga: S. Kreschetov, 1931), p. 204

3 N. G. Zograf, *Maly Teatr v kontse XIX-nachala XX veka* (Moscow: Iskusstvo, 1966), p. 26.

4 V. Maslikh, "Chekhov i Maly Teatr," *Teatralnaya zhizn* 2 (1960): 19. This statement contradicts Nemirovich's that Yuzhin thought strong directing unnecessary for Chekhov's plays.

5 Zograf, *Maly Teatr*, p. 91; Nelidov, *Teatralnaya Moskva*, pp. 250–1, 258.

6 V. O. Toporkov, *Chetyre ocherki o K. S. Stanislavskom* (Moscow: Sovetskaya Rossiya, 1963), pp. 5–6.

7 *Ibid.*, p. 8

8 Quoted in A. Ya. Altshuller, "Chekhov i Aleksandrinsky Teatr ego vremeni," *Russkaya Literatura* 3 (1968), p. 174.

9 Quoted in Vl. Prokofev, "Legenda o pervoy postanovke 'Chaiki,'" *Teatr* 11 (1946), p. 59

10 S. I. Smirnova-Sazonova, quoted in Altshuller, "Chekhov i Aleksandrinsky Teatr," p. 174.

11 Prokofev, "Legenda," p. 60.

12 M. G. Svetaeva, *Mariya Gavrilovna Savina* (Moscow: Iskusstvo, 1988), p. 278.

13 Prokofev, "Legenda."

14 *Ibid.*

15 Potapenko in Surkov, p. 230.

16 Diary entry 16 Nov. 1902, quoted in *Literaturnoe nasledstvo. Chekhov.* 63 (Moscow: Nauka, 1960): 516–17.

17 P. P. Gnedich in Surkov, p. 363; see also "Homo Novus," *Teatr i iskusstvo* 19 (1903): 390.

18 Letter to Molchanov, in Svetaeva, *Savina*, p. 278.

19 Svetaeva, *Savina*, p. 279.

20 *Ibid.*

21 E. Ya. Dubnova, "'Dyadya Vanya' na stsene peterburgskogo Dramaticheskogo teatra V. F. Komissarzhevskoy," in Rossiiskaya akademiya nauk, *Chekhoviana. Chekhov v kulture XX veka* (Moscow: Nauka, 1993), pp. 117–29; Yu. P. Rybakova, *V. F. Komissarzhevskaya, letopis zhizni i tvorchestva* (St. Petersburg: Rossysky Institut Istorii Iskusstv, 1994), pp. 270–1.

22 Svetaeva, *Savina*, p. 279.

23 N. N. Khodotov, *Blizkoe-dalekoe* (Leningrad-Moscow: Iskusstvo, 1962), p. 172.

24 V. F. Komissarzhevskaya to Chekhov (Sept. 1900) in Surkov, pp. 246–7; Chekhov to V. F. Komissarzhevskaya (13 Nov. 1900), *PSSP* IX, 139.

25 Yu. M. Yurev, *Zapiski*, ed. E. M. Kuznetsova (Leningrad-Moscow: Iskusstvo, 1953), II, 135.

26 See L. Petrovskaya, *Teatr i zritel provintsialnoy Rossii vtoraya polovina XIX veka* (Leningrad: Iskusstvo, 1979), pp. 165–6.

27 A. G. Golovacheva, "'Zavtra edu v Elets' ('Epilog' chekhovskoy 'Chaiki')," in *Chekhoviana: stati, publikatsii, essé*, ed. V. Ya. Lakshin (Moscow: Nauka, 1990), pp. 155–6

28 Olga Knipper, *Vospominaniya i stati. Perepiska* (Moscow: Iskusstvo, 1972), II, 371.

29 Al. Gladkov, "Vospominanye i zametki, zapisi o Vs. E. Meierkholde," *Tarusskie stranitsy* (1961): 302; about Kherson, I. N. Pevtsov, "Beseda ob aktera," *Illarion Nikolaevich Pevtsov (1879–1943)* (Leningrad: Gosud. Akademichesky teatr dramy, 1935), p. 36.

30 *Teatr i iskusstvo* 41 (1902): 750.

31 *Yug* (Kherson, 28 Sept. 1902), quoted in K. Rudnitsky, *Rezhisser Meierkhold* (Moscow: Iskusstvo, 1969), p. 30.

32 De-Lin, "Teatralny razezd posle predstavleniya," *Yug* (28 Sept. 1902), quoted in Rudnitsky, *Rezhisser Meierkhold.*

33 Lazarevsky to Chekhov (13 and 17 April 1903), quoted in Rudnitsky, *Rezhisser Meierkhold*, p. 31.

34 O. A. Lordkipanidze, *A. P. Chekhov v dorevolyutsionnom gruzinskom teatre* (Tbilisi: Metsniereba, 1978), pp. 48–51.

35 *Kavkaz* 114 (2 May 1899), quoted in *ibid.*, p. 19.

36 *Drozba* 17 (21 Jan. 1904) in Lordkipanidze, *A. P. Chekhov*, p. 79.
37 Quoted in N. Volkov, *Meierkhold* (Moscow-Leningrad: Academia, 1929), I, 185.
38 V. F. Komissarzhevskaya to Chekhov (29 Dec. 1904), in Surkov, pp. 274–8
39 I. N. Pevtsov, "Beseda ob aktera," p. 35. After seeing the MAT staging, Meyerhold wrote to Chekhov (8 May 1904) that he had no reason to feel ashamed of his own production, and penned the famous passage (quoted in chapter 3) about the abstract nature of the play and the Maeterlinckian quality of the third act. V. E. Meyerhold, *Perepiska 1896–1939* (Moscow: Iskusstvo, 1976), pp. 45–6.
40 E. Karpov, "Dve poslednie vstrechi s Ant. Pav. Chekhovym," *Ezhegodnik imperatorskikh teatrov* 5 (1909): 1–9.
41 Rostovtsev, letter to Chekhov (5 Dec. 1900).
42 V. Vilenkin, *Vasily Ivanovich Kachalov* (Moscow: Iskusstvo, 1954), p. 146.
43 19 Mar. 1904 in E. M. Sakharova, "Pervye zriteli po materialam chekhovskogo rukopisnogo Gosudarstvennoy biblioteki SSSR imeni V. I. Lenina," in *Chekhovskie chteniya v Yalte. Chekhov i teatr* (Moscow: Kniga, 1976), p. 52.
44 (20 Mar. 1904) in *ibid.*
45 P. P. Gaideburov, *Literaturnoe nasledie*, ed. Sim. Dreyden (Moscow: VTO, 1977), p. 5.
46 *Ibid.*, pp. 138–9; P. Gaideburov, "Polveka s Chekhovym," *Teatralny almanakh* (Moscow: VTO, 1948), pp. 304–8.
47 *Yuzhnoe obozrenie* of Odessa, quoted in *ibid.*, p. 12.
48 Gaideburov, *Literaturnoe nasledie*, pp. 143–4.
49 *Ibid.*, pp. 101–2.
50 *Den* (7 Feb. 1913), quoted in *ibid.*, p. 26. Gaideburov himself was an outstanding actor in the Chekhov repertory: in *Three Sisters* he played Andrey, Tusenbach and even Chebutykin, in *Uncle Vanya*, Astrov and Vanya, in *Ivanov*, Ivanov and Shabelsky; in *Seagull*, Treplev (his first role) and Sorin (his last). But his special success was as Petya Trofimov, which he played over three hundred times.
51 "Ariel" [L. M. Vasilevsky], "Teatr Gaideburova. 'Vishnevy sad,'" *Novaya zhizn* (Petersburg, 10 May 1918).

5 CHEKHOV GOES WEST (EUROPE, 1888–1938)

1 Chekhov to O. L. Knipper (4 Mar. 1904), *PSS* XII, 55.
2 *Warsaw Journal* (11 May 1906), quoted in N. B. Shik, "O dramaturgii Chekhova (otkliki zarubezhnykh sovremennikov)," in *Chekhovskie chteniya v Yalte. Chekhov i teatr* (Moscow: Kniga, 1976), p. 175; Juliusz Tyszka, "Stanislavsky in Poland: ethics and politics of the Method," *New Theatre Quarterly* 5, 20 (Nov. 1989), p. 361. Also see R. Sliwowski, "Vospriyatie tvorchestva Chekhova v Polshe (konets XIX–seredina XX veka)," in Rossiiskaya akademiya nauk, *Chekhoviana. Chekhov v kulture XX veka. Stati, publikatsii, essé* (Moscow: Nauka, 1993), pp. 173–80.

3 A. Hyvönen, *Eino Kalima. Tšehov-ohjaajana* (Helsinki: Suomalaisen Krijallisuuden Seura, 1986), pp. 153–5. After World War II, Kalima's Chekhov productions emphasized faith in a better future and a sense of victory over circumstances.

4 Sh. Sh. Bogatyrev, "Chekhov v Chekhoslovakii," *Literaturnoe nasledstvo* 68 (Moscow: Nauka, 1960), p. 753. See also Otakar Fencl, "A. P. Čechov a Národni divadlo," *Národni divadlo* 5 (1954): 3–18; Ilja Svatoňová, "A. P. Čechov na českych scenách 1889–1914," in *Čtvero setkáni s ruskym realismen* (Prague: Nakl. Českoslovanske akademie věd, 1958), pp. 293–345; and *Dějiny českého divadlo III Činohra 1848–1918* (Prague: Academia nakladatelstvi československe Akademie věd, 1977): 317–18.

5 (16 June 1897), quoted in Bogatyrev, "Chekhov v Chekhoslovakii," p. 754.

6 *Thalie* 27 (1898): 172, quoted in Bogatyrev, "Chekhov v Chekhoslovakii," p. 755.

7 Bogatyrev, "Chekhov v Chekhoslovakii," pp. 760–2. Similarly, in 1907, when Jaroslav Kamper opened the Vinohrady Theatre he appealed to Stanislavsky for help on *Cherry Orchard*. This time the Russian director turned him over to his assistants.

8 I. Vodak, *Čas* (4 May 1921), quoted in Bogatyrev, "Chekhov v Chekhoslovakii," p. 765. The progressive writer Maria Majerová pointed out that Anya's "nebulous future" was becoming a "beautiful reality" (*Rudé právo*, 4 May 1921).

9 František Špicer, *Rudé právo* (12 Jan. 1932), in Bogatyrev, "Chekhov v Chekhoslovakii," p. 768.

10 R.-D. Kluge, "Die frühe Rezeption A. P. Čechovs in Deutschland (1890–1914)," *Zeitschrift für slavische Philologie* 48 (1988), p. 132; S. Melchinger, *Anton Chekhov*, trans. Edith Tarcov (New York: Ungar, 1972), pp. 163–4.

11 Kluge, "Die frühe Rezeption," p. 133.

12 M. Szenessy, "Tschechow deutsch und doch nicht rühselig," *Frankfurter Allgemeine Zeitung* (27 Apr. 1974), quoted in Christa M. Christa, *The German versions of Chekhov's Three Sisters* (New York: Peter Lang, 1988), p. 2.

13 Christa, *The German versions*, pp. 366–7, 372.

14 Heinrich Stümcke, "Tschechow als Dramatiker," *Bühne und Welt* 6 (1903/4): 955–7, quoted in Birgit Kirschstein-Gamber, *Die Čechov-Szene. Untersuchungen Text und Realisierung der Regieanweisung im Drama Anton Pavlovič Čechovs* (Altendorf: Albert-Ludwigs- Universität, 1979), p. 109.

15 Erich Freund, *Literarischen Echo* 5 (1902/3): 347.

16 *Bühne und Welt* 5 (1902/3): 712, quoted in Kirschstein-Gamber, *Die Čechov-Szene*, p. 108.

17 Shik, "O dramaturgii Chekhova," pp. 172–3; P. P., "'Dyadya Vanya' na Berlinskoy stsene," in *Anton Pavlovich Chekhov. Ego zhizn i sochineniya*, ed. V. I. Pokrovsky (Moscow: V. Spiridonov and A. Mikhailov 1907).

18 *Bühne und Welt* 2 (1904/5): 79, quoted in Kirschstein-Gamber, *Die Čechov-Szene*, p. 108.

19 *Zhizn i svoboda* (22 Feb. and 1 Mar. 1906), quoted in Shik, "O dramaturgii Chekhova," p. 174.

20 Klaus Bednarz, *Theatralische Aspekte der Dramenübersetzung dargestellt am Beispiel der deutschen Übertragenungen und Bühnenarbeitungen der Dramen Anton Čechovs* (Vienna: Notring, 1969), p. 112.

21 Alfred Kerr, *Mimenreich (Die Welt im Drama)* (Berlin, 1917), quoted in Kluge, "Die frühe Rezeption," p. 136.

22 Quoted in Shik, "O dramaturgi Chekhova."

23 S. Jacobson, "Die Möwe," *Die Schaubühne* 5, 16 (1909): 464.

24 Ludwig Klinenberger, *Bühne und Welt* 11 (1908/9): 874.

25 *Bühne und Welt* 14 (1911/12): 119, quoted in Kirschstein-Gamber, *Die Čechov-Szene*, p. 109.

26 *Neues Wiener Tageblatt* (13 Oct. 1916), quoted in Bednarz, *Theatralische Aspekte*, p. 120.

27 Paul Fechter, *Deutsche Allgemeine Zeitung* (22 Dec. 1926), quoted in Bednarz, *Theatralische Aspekte*, p. 114.

28 Heinrich Huesmann, *Welt Theater Reinhardt: Bauten, Spielstätten, Inszenierungen* (Munich: Prestel Verlag, 1983); Charles Castle, *Oliver Messel a biography* (London: Thames and Hudson, 1986), pp. 84–5.

29 P. A. Otte, "Tschehoff Uraufführung in Gera. Der unnützige Mensch Platonoff," *Das Theater* 17 (Apr. 1928): 182.

30 Quoted in Joseph Wulf, *Theater und Film im Dritten Reich* (Gütersloh: S. Mohn, 1964), pp. 227, 229.

31 *Tonfilm, Theater, Tanz* (Nov. 1940), quoted in Bednarz, *Theatralische Aspekte*, p. 119.

32 K. Waleszewski, *La littérature russe* (Paris: A. Colin and Cie, 1900), p. 426.

33 E.-M. de Voguë, "Anton Tchékoff," *Revue des deux mondes* 7 (1 Jan. 1900): 203; Yu. Felichkin, "Rol teatra v vospriyaty tvorchestva Chekhova vo Frantsii," in Lituraturny Muzey A. P. Chekhova, *Sbornik statey i materialov vypusk V* (Rostov: Rostovskoe knizhnoe izd., 1969), p. 155.

34 This went unmentioned in the press, and is known only from his memoirs. L. I. Gitelman, *Russkaya klassika na frantsuzkom stsene* (Leningrad: Iskusstvo, 1978), p. 97.

35 E. Halpérine-Kaminsky, "Madame Lydie Yavorskaïa. Princesse Bariatinsky," *Le Théâtre* 89 (Sept. 1902): 20.

36 "A. P. Chekhov v Parizhe," *Teatr* 371 (6 Jan. 1909): 8.

37 Felichkin, "Rol teatra v vospriyaty," p. 156.

38 Quoted in Raul Radice, "Come i nostri registri e attori hanno presentato in Italia l'opera di Čechov," in *Goldoni nel teatro russo. Čechov nel teatro italiano* (Rome: Accademia nazionale dei lincei, 1976), p. 152.

39 Ettore Albini, *Corriere della sera* (17 May 1924), quoted in Radice, "Come i nostri registri," p. 154.

6 COMES THE REVOLUTION (RUSSIA, 1917–1935)

1 O. L. Knipper-Chekhova, "Iz moikh vospominany o Khudozhestvennom teatre i ob A. P. Chekhove," in *Artisty MKhATa za rubezhom* (Prague: Nasha rech, 1922), p. 29.

2 Boris Geier, "Évolyutsiya teatra," in *Russkaya teatralnaya parodiya XIX nachala XX veka*, ed. M. Ya. Polyakova (Moscow: Iskusstvo, 1976), pp. 579–83.

3 "V Peterburge," *Chekhovsky yubileiny sbornik* (Moscow: I. D. Sytin, 1910), p. 530.

4 K. Fay, "Chekhovsky spektakl," *Teatralnaya gazeta* 13 (1916): 8

5 Vl. I. Nemirovich-Danchenko, *Retsentsi, ocherki, stati, intervyu, zametki 1877–1942* (Moscow: Iskusstvo, 1980), pp. 151–2; *EMKT 1945* (Moscow: 1946), I, 348.

6 *IP1*, p. 335.

7 Sim. Dreiden, *V zritelnom zale - Vladimir Ilich* (Moscow: Iskusstvo, 1986), II, 164.

8 Knipper-Chekhova, "Iz moikh vospominany . . ."

9 V. Ashmarin, "Ivanov," *Izvestiya VTsIK* (15 Nov. 1918). Stanislavsky later explained the failure by pointing out that "the inner leitmotiv" was overshadowed by the externals of life. The tragedy should have been about the need for reform of intolerable conditions of life, not the hero's malaise. But this was hindsight through red-tinted glasses. A. Ninov, "Vremya Chekhova i ego teatr (vvedenie)," in *Chekhov i teatralnoe iskusstvo* (Leningrad: Ministerstvo Kultury RSFSR, 1985), pp. 9–10.

10 A. M. Gorky, "Nesvoevremmenye mysli," *Novaya zhizn* (mosk. izd.) (5 June 1918).

11 K. S. Stanislavsky to V. V. Luzhsky (Dec. 1918), quoted in Dreiden, *V zritelnom zale*, pp. 247–9.

12 "Vospominaniya L. Ya. Gurevich" in *O Stanislavskom*, ed. L. Ya. Gurevich (Moscow: VTO, 1948), pp. 158–9.

13 "Zapiski," *Teatr i iskusstvo* 16–17 (1918): 179.

14 V. A. Nelidov, *Teatralnaya Moskva (sorok let moskovskikh teatrov)* (Berlin-Riga: S. Kretschetow, 1931), p. 429.

15 Dreiden, *V zritelnom zale*, p. 241.

16 Arthur Ransome, *Six weeks in Russia in 1919* (London: George Allen and Unwin, 1919), pp. 92–3.

17 V. V. Luzhsky, "Prezhny i novy zritel na spektaklyakh Moskovskogo Khudozhestvennogo teatra," *Zhizn i iskusstvo* 22 (1927): 4–5.

18 O. Litovsky, "Teatr nuzhdaetsya v revolyutsii," *Sovetskaya strana* (15 Mar. 1919).

19 Vl. Mayakovsky, *Misteriya Buff* in *Pesy* (Moscow: Detskaya literatura, 1971), p. 104.

20 P. M. Kerzhentsev, "Teatralny muzey," *Vestnik teatra* 48 (1920): 4. L. Trotsky, *Literature and Revolution* tr. R. Strumsky (New York: International Pub., 1924) p. 32.

21 Quoted in Yu. Smirnov-Nesvitsky, *Vakhtangov* (Leningrad: Iskusstvo, 1987), p. 176.

22 N. K. Krupskaya, *O Lenine*, p. 95, quoted in *Moskovsky Khudozhestvenny teatr v sovetskuyu épokhu. Materialy i dokumenty*, ed. M. L. Rogachevsky and G. P. Mironova, 2nd edn., enlarged (Moscow: Iskusstvo, 1974), p. 28.

23 N. Podgorny, "Neizgladimye vpechatleniya," *Gorkovets* (21 Jan. 1941).

24 Nelidov, *Teatralnaya Moskva*, p. 426.
25 Boris Zakhava, *Sovremenniki* (Moscow: Iskusstvo, 1969), p. 236.
26 *Ibid.*, pp. 270–2.
27 Smirnov-Nesvitsky, *Vakhtangov*, p. 333.
28 E. B. Vakhtangov, *Materialy i stati* (Moscow: Iskusstvo, 1959), p. 187.
29 E. B. Vakhtangov, "Iz zapisnoy tetrady," in *Teatralny stranitsy* (Moscow: Iskusstvo, 1969), p. 356.
30 Smirnov-Nesvitsky, *Vakhtangov*, pp. 177–8.
31 *Ibid.*, p. 178.
32 N. Smirnova, "V chertakh groteska i russkoy satiry," in *Vosprosy teatra* 10 (Moscow: 1986): 181–2.
33 Smirnov-Nesvitsky, *Vakhtangov*, p. 179.
34 Vl. I. Nemirovich-Danchenko to O. S. Bokshanskaya (9 Mar. 1924), *IP2*, II, 303–4.
35 Huntly Carter, *The new theatre and cinema of Soviet Russia* (New York: International Publishers, 1925), pp. 201–2.
36 P. P. Gaideburov, "Polveka o Chekhovym. Iz bloknota aktera," *Teatralny Almanakh* (Moscow: 1948), p. 320.
37 *StanSS* I, 276
38 V. Ya. Vilenkin, *Vasily Ivanovich Kachalov* (Moscow: Iskusstvo, 1954), p. 221.
39 Yu. Sobolev, "'Vishnevy sad' sgorel – zemlya ostalas . . . ," *Novy Zritel* (22 Apr. 1925): 14–15, and "Vishnevy sad na 'novoy pochve,'" *Novy Zritel* (19 May 1925): 13–14; I. N. Bersenev's report (20 Jan. 1932) in *Russky sovetsky teatr 1926–1932. Chast pervaya*, ed. A. Ya. Trabsky (Leningrad: Iskusstvo, 1982), p. 221.
40 I. Bachelis, "'Smeshnaya pesa' 'Vishnevy sad' v teatre p/r Simonova," *Teatralnaya dekada* 24 (1934): 6.
41 Quoted in Berezkin, *Khudozhnik v teatre Chekhova*, p. 178. Khokhlov redirected it in 1946 at the Ivan Franko Theatre in Kiev.
42 L. A. Malyugin, "Chekhov na Leningradskoy stsene" *Teatralny almanakh* (Moscow: VTO, 1947), p. 102.
43 *Andrey Mikhailovich Lobanov. Dokumenty, stati, vospominaniya* (Moscow: Iskusstvo, 1980), p. 208.
44 Quoted in Berezkin, *Khudozhnik v teatre Chekhova*, p. 35; *Andrey Mikhailovich Lobanov*, pp. 23–6.
45 A. M. Gorky, in Surkov, p. 358.
46 Quoted in Konstantin Rudnitsky, *Rezhisser Meierkhold* (Moscow: Iskusstvo, 1969), p. 474. The rehearsal transcripts are published in *Meierkhold repertiruet. Spektakli 30-kh godov*, ed. M. M. Sitkovetskaya and O. M. Feldman (Moscow: Artist Rezhisser Teatr, 1993), pp. 145–210.
47 P. Gromov, "33 obmoroka," in *Vstrechi s Meierkholdom*, ed. M. A. Valentey *et al.* (Moscow: Iskusstvo, 1967), pp. 480–1.
48 Shestakov, quoted in Berezkin, *Khudozhnik v teatre Chekhova*, p. 34; Chopin and Chaikovsky were used in the rehearsals.
49 Norris Houghton, *Moscow Rehearsals* (New York: Harcourt, Brace, 1936), p. 100.

50 Rudnitsky, *Rezhisser Meierhold*, p. 475; V. E. Meyerhold, *Stati, rechi, pisma, besedy* (Moscow: Iskusstvo, 1968), II, 310.
51 Gromov, "33 obmoroka," p. 482.
52 Houghton, *Moscow Rehearsals*, p. 111; T. Esenina, "O V. E. Meierkholde i Z. N. Raikhe. Pisma K. L. Rudnitskomu," *Teatr* (1993): 108; I. I. Yuzovsky, *Razgovor zatyanulsya za polnoch* (Moscow: Iskusstvo, 1966), pp. 245–62.
53 Igor Ilinsky, *Sam o sebe* (Moscow: Iskusstvo, 1973), pp. 301–2.
54 A. Gladkov, "Meierkhold govorit," *Novy mir* 8 (1961): 228.

7 CHEKHOV LEARNS ENGLISH (UNITED KINGDOM AND IRELAND, 1900–1940)

1 Margaret Webster, "A letter to Chekhov," New York *Times* (23 Jan. 1949). The subject of Chekhov's introduction to the British stage has been dealt with thoroughly in Victor Emeljanow, ed., *Chekhov: the critical heritage* (London: Routledge and Kegan Paul, 1981); Patrick Miles, *Chekhov on the British stage 1909–1987* (Cambridge: SAM and SAM, 1987); Patrick Miles, ed., *Chekhov on the British stage* (Cambridge: Cambridge University Press, 1993) and Robert Tracy, *The flight of the seagull: Chekhov on the English stage* (unpub. Ph.D. dissertation, Harvard University, 1959). See also M. A. Shereshevskaya, "Chekhov v Anglii," *Literaturnoe nasledstvo* 68 (1960).
2 Leo Wiener, *Anthology of Russian literature* (New York: G. P. Putnam's sons, 1903), II, 459.
3 Alfred N. Bates, *The drama: its history, literature and influence on civilization* (London: Athenian Society, 1903), p. 73.
4 Percy Lubbock, *George Calderon. A sketch from memory* (London: Grant Richards, 1921), pp. 40, 42. For Calderon's article, see *Quarterly Review* (July 1912); for Meyerhold's "Russian dramatists," see Laurence Senelick, ed., *Russian dramatic theory from Pushkin to the Symbolists* (Austin: University of Texas Press, 1984), pp. 200–9.
5 Percy Lubbock, "George Calderon," in *Dictionary of national biography 1912–1921* (Oxford: Oxford University Press, 1927), p. 105; *George Calderon*, p. 85. Calderon's *The little stone house* (London: Sidgwick and Jackson, 1913) is a *grand guignol* piece which takes place in Russia. The only Chekhovian notes are the stage direction "There is an atmosphere of silence, solitude, and Russian monotony" (p. 9), and a game of patience is played throughout.
6 Michael Coveney, *The Citz: 21 years of the Glasgow Citizens Theatre* (London: Nick Hern, 1990), p. 18.
7 G. B. Shaw to Laurence Irving (25 Oct. 1905), *Collected letters 1898–1910*, ed. Dan H. Laurence (London: Max Reinhardt, 1972), p. 569. Irving had dramatized Dostoevsky's *Crime and punishment*; hence Shaw's assumption that he was *au courant* of the Russian literary scene.
8 George Calderon, *Two plays of Tchekhof* (London: Mitchell Kennerly , 1912), p. 28.

9 *Glasgow University Magazine* (10 Nov. 1909) and *Glasgow Herald* (3 Nov. 1909), quoted in Jan McDonald, "Production of Chekhov's plays in Britain before 1914," *Theatre Notebook* 34, 1 (1980): 25–6. Calderon's lecture later appeared as the preface to his translations, an essay which is one of the most perceptive on Chekhovian drama in English.

10 *The World* (6 June 1911).

11 Frank Swinnerton, *The Georgian literary scene* (London: William Heinemann, 1935), p. 295; Giles Playfair, *The story of the Lyric Theatre, Hammersmith* (London: Chatto and Windus, 1925), p. 215; Giles Playfair, *Hammersmith hoy* (London: Faber and Faber, 1930).

12 Hugh Walpole, "Epikhodov: a note on Russian character," in *The soul of Russia*, ed. Winifred Stephens (London: Macmillan, 1916), p. 36.

13 *Times* (30 May 1911): 13; *Daily Telegraph* (30 May 1911).

14 "Jacob Tonson," *New Age* (8 June 1911): 132.

15 See Stephen Le Fleming, "Coping with the outlandish," in Patrick Miles, ed., *Chekhov on the British Stage*, pp. 53–64.

16 Edward Morgan, "Lydia Yavorska," *Theatrephile* 3, 9 (1990): 6.

17 Desmond MacCarthy, *New Statesman* (16 May 1914): 180.

18 Quoted in Benedict Nightingale, "A true master receives his due," *Times* (London) (22 Feb. 1992): 1.

19 Gilbert Phelps, *The Russian novel in English fiction* (London: Hutchinson's University Library, 1956), p. 188.

20 G. B. Shaw, *Heartbreak House, Great Catherine and plays of the war* (London: Constable, 1926), p. vii; Phelps, *The Russian novel*, p. 151.

21 Stark Young, *Immortal shadows* (New York: Charles Scribner's Sons, 1948), pp. 208–9.

22 Graham Sutton, "Tchekov," *The Bookman* (Apr. 1926): 66.

23 Andrew E. Malone, *The Irish drama* (London: Constable, 1929), p. 244.

24 Ernest Boyd, *The contemporary drama of Ireland* (Boston: Little, Brown, 1917), p. 40; William J. Feeney, *Drama in Hardwicke Street. A history of the Irish Theatre Company* (Rutherford: Farleigh Dickinson University Press, 1984), p. 30. Much of this section is indebted to Feeney's detailed account of the Irish Theatre seasons.

25 *The Independent* (29 June 1915).

26 Quoted in Feeney, *Drama*, pp. 102–3.

27 Feeney, *Drama*, pp. 104–5. Eimar O'Duffy's novel of this time *Printer's Error* has its hero plunge into fads of the day; since Russian literature is in vogue, he buys a copy of plays "of someone whose name is variously spelled and pronounced as Tchekoff, Tchaykoff, Chehoff, Tshayhoff, and Checkoff," and attends a yawn-inducing *Vanya* at the "Eclectic Theatre."

28 Feeney, *Drama*, pp. 243–4.

29 Holloway, quoted in Feeney, *Drama*, pp. 248, 246.

30 Feeney, *Drama*, p. 248.

31 Holloway, quoted in Feeney, *Drama*, p. 262.

32 Malone, *Irish drama*, p. 90.

33 Patrick Kavanagh, *The story of the Abbey Theatre from its origins in 1899 to the present* (New York: Davin-Adair, 1950), p. 148; R. M. Fox, "Irish drama knocks at the door," *Life and letters and the London Mercury* (Apr. 1949): 18; Peter Luke, ed. *Enter certain players. Edwards, MacLiammóir and the Gate 1928–1978* (Dublin: Dolmen Press, 1978). A Gaelic translation of *The Cherry Orchard* by Muiris Ó Catháin, *Cúrsaí Cleamhnais*, was staged at the Abbey on 16 Sept. 1947. Brinsley McNamara, *Abbey plays 1899–1948 including the productions of the Irish literary theatre* (Dublin: Colm O Lochlainn, 1948), p. 75.

34 Lennox Robinson, *Killycreggs at twilight and other plays* (London: Macmillan, 1939), pp. 119, 123, 140.

35 Sydney Carroll, *Sunday Times* (8 June 1919): 4.

36 *New Statesman* (7 June 1919): 238–9.

37 *New Statesman* (31 June 1920): 496.

38 Constantine Nabokoff, *Contemporary Review* (Jan.–June 1926): 345–6.

39 D. W. Martin, "On translation from the Russian: Chekhov in English," *Durham University Journal* 76, 2 (June 1984): 236–7. Unlike the Russian novels and short stories for which she had been paid a flat fee, the Chekhov plays earned Garnett royalties until her death in 1946, when the rights passed to her son. Carolyn G. Heilbrun, *The Garnett family* (New York: Macmillan, 1961), p. 182.

40 Emeljanow, *Chekhov: the critical heritage*, p. 27.

41 Lillah McCarthy, Barker's erstwhile wife, reported of one actor who "had played, and played well, in one of Chekhov's plays. I went round to congratulate him. Admiring Chekhov as I do, I asked him what he thought of Chekhov's way of writing. 'Who?' he asked. 'Chekhov,' I replied. 'I have heard of him,' said he." Lillah McCarthy, *Myself and friends* (New York: E. P. Dutton, 1933), p. 55.

42 Margaret Webster, *The same, only different. Five generations of a great theatre family* (New York: Alfred A. Knopf, 1969), p. 317.

43 Hal Burton, ed., *Great acting* (New York: Hill and Wang, 1967), p. 136.

44 [Joseph Thorp], "At the play," *Punch* (3 June 1924), in *Punch at the theatre*, ed. Sheridan Morley (London: Robson Books, 1980), pp. 144–5.

45 Entry for 2 June 1925, *The journals of Arnold Bennett* (Garden City, NY Garden City Publishing Co., 1933), p. 828.

46 *The Spectator*, quoted in Patrick Miles, *Chekhov on the British stage*, p. 15; Webster, *The same*, p. 316.

47 Playfair, *The story*, pp. 216–17.

48 Doris Arthur Jones, *The life and letters of Henry Arthur Jones* (London: Victor Gollancz, 1930), pp. 350–2.

49 Bennett, *The journals of Arnold Bennett*.

50 Sutton, "Tchekov," p. 66.

51 Ernest Short, *Sixty years of theatre* (London: Eyre & Spottiswoode, 1951), pp. 368–9.

52 A. E. Wilson, *Theatre guyed. The Baedeker of Thespia* (London: Methuen, 1935), pp. 144–5.

53 Ivor Brown, *Observer* (17 Nov. 1935): 17.

54 Quoted in James Forsyth, *Tyrone Guthrie, a biography* (London: Hamish Hamilton, 1976), p. 120.

55 Tyrone Guthrie, *A life in the theatre* (New York: McGraw-Hill, 1959), p. 127.

56 *Ibid.*, p. 126. Alec Guinness considered it one of the three best productions Guthrie ever directed in his long career.

57 Forsyth, *Tyrone Guthrie*, p. 131; Simon Callow, *Charles Laughton, a difficult actor* (London: Methuen, 1987), pp. 64–5; Janet Dunbar, *Flora Robson* (London: George G. Harrap, 1960), pp. 162–3. Laughton later played Gaev in a student production he directed in Los Angeles.

58 Jane Mederos Baldwin, *A paradoxical career: Michel Saint-Denis' life in the theatre* (unpub. Ph.D. dissertation, Tufts University, 1991), p. 143. Gielgud attempted to reassure Komisjarevsky that his defection was not disloyal: "I know [Saint-Denis] will not give anything like such beauty to the production you did – and I shall always think with love and admiration of that Barnes performance – but he is an interesting producer and very good to work with – I believe he might do something quite different and stimulating in a different way." Letter of 8 July 1938 quoted in *The stage art of Komisarjevsky* (Cambridge, Mass.: Harvard Theatre Collection, 1991).

59 Michael Redgrave, *In my mind's I* (London: Weidenfeld and Nicholson, 1983), p. 113; Burton, *Great acting*, pp. 107–8.

60 Quoted in Rosamund Gilder, "Chekhov international," *Theatre Arts Monthly* (May 1938): 373.

61 Ivor Brown, *Observer* (30 Jan. 1938); also see A. V. Cookman, "The theatre," *London Mercury & Bookman* (Mar. 1938): 533–4.

62 Richard Huggett, *Binkie Beaumont: eminence grise of the West End theatre 1933–1973* (London: Hodder and Stoughton, 1989), pp. 240–2.

63 Nightingale, "A true master," p. 1; J. C. Trewin, "At the play," in *Punch at the theatre*, p. 80.

64 Ariadne Nicolaeff, "Standards in translating Chekhov's plays," in Patrick Miles, ed., *Chekhov on the British Stage*, p. 214.

8 AT HOME ABROAD (EUROPE AND ENGLAND, 1917–1938)

1 Edmond Sée, *L'Oeuvre* (16 Apr. 1921), quoted in Sophie Laffitte, "Chekhov vo Frantsii," in *Literaturnoe nasledstvo* 68 (Moscow, 1960): 711.

2 *Ertova* 85 (17 April 1920), quoted in O. A. Lordkipanidze, *A. P. Chekhov v dorevolyutsionnom gruzinskom teatre* (Tbilisi: Metsniereba, 1978), p. 26.

3 *Sakhalko sakhme* 831 (22 May 1920), quoted in *ibid.*, pp. 31–2.

4 Sergei Ostrovsky, "Maria Germanova and the Moscow Theatre Prague Group," in Laurence Senelick, ed., *Wandering stars: Russian émigré theatre 1905–1940* (Iowa City: University of Iowa Press, 1993), pp. 84–101; Michèle Beyssac, *La vie culturelle de l'emigration russe en France: chronique (1910–1930)* (Paris: Presses universitaires, 1971).

5 Quoted in Aldo Rendini and Andrea Camilleri, "Pietro Sharoff," in

Enciclopedia dello spettacolo, ed. Silvio d'Amico (Rome: Le Maschere, 1961), VIII, 1917.

6 *Ibid.*; also see Pietro Scharoff, "Confessioni d'un regista russo in Italia," *Scenario* 1 (1933) and C. M. Pensa, "Il 'libro' di Scharoff," *Scenario* 7 (1952): 15–16.

7 Vl. I. Nemirovich-Danchenko to S. L. Bertonson (6 Feb. 1933) in K. Arensky, *Pisma k Khollivud. Po materialam arkhiva S. L. Bertonsona* (Monterey, Cal.: K. Arensburger, 1968), pp. 189–90.

8 Theodore Komisarjevsky, *Myself and theatre* (London: Heinemann, 1929), pp. 155–6.

9 Gielgud interviewed in *Radio Times* (7 Nov. 1986), quoted in David Allen, "David Jones directs Chekhov's 'Ivanov,'" *New Theatre Quarterly* 15 (Aug. 1988): 246.

10 J. T. Grein, "The world of theatre," *Illustrated London News* (16 Jan. 1926): 104.

11 *Times* (8 Dec. 1925); *New Statesman* (19 Dec. 1925): 301.

12 Omicron, *Nation and Athenæum* (12 Dec. 1925): 402.

13 Ilya Érenburg, *Sobranie sochineny* (Moscow: Iskusstvo, 1967), VII, 459.

14 *The journal of Arnold Bennett* (Garden City, NY: Garden City Publishing Co., 1933), pp. 907–8.

15 Aleksey Bartoshevich, "Theodore Komisarjevsky, Chekhov and Shakespeare," in Senelick, *Wandering stars*, p. 106.

16 Bartoshevich, "Theodore Komisarjevsky," p. 107. See "On producing Tchehov, an interview with Theodore Komisarjevsky," *Drama* (Feb. 1926), repr. in *Drama* (1989): 17.

17 Victor Emeljanow, "Komisarjevsky directs Chekhov in London," *Theatre Notebook* 37, 2 (1983): 69–70.

18 Komisarjevsky, *Myself and the theatre*, p. 157.

19 Irving Wardle quoted in Gordon McVay, "Peggy Ashcroft and Chekhov," in Patrick Miles, ed., *Chekhov on the British stage* (Cambridge: Cambridge University Press, 1993), p. 85.

20 Komisarjevsky, *Myself and the theatre*, p. 172.

21 James Agate, *Sunday Times* (30 Jan. 1938). See Robert Tracy, "Komisarjevsky's 1926 *Three Sisters*" and McVay, "Peggy Ashcroft" in Miles, ed., *Chekhov on the British stage*, pp. 65–100.

22 John Gielgud, *Stage directions* (New York: Capricorn books, 1966), p. 87.

23 Hal Burton, ed., *Great acting* (New York: Hill and Wang, 1967), p. 142.

24 R. J., *Spectator* (27 Feb. 1926): 363.

25 Gielgud, *Stage directions*, p. 95.

26 Victor Emeljanow, "Komisarjevsky's *Three Sisters*: the prompt book," *Theatre Notebook* 41, 3 (1987): 56–66. The production inspired a "Chekhovian dinner" with each course and dish based on a line of the play, *e.g.*, Melon Bobik ("Bobik is cold") and Smelts aux mains de Soleny ("My hands smell like a corpse.") *The greedy book*, ed. Brian Hill (London: Rupert Hart-Davis, 1966), pp. 188–9.

27 Emeljanow, "*Three Sisters*," p. 60.

28 *Ibid.*, p. 63.
29 *Ibid.*, p. 65.
30 Hannen Swaffer, *Sunday Express* (29 Sept. 1929): 5.
31 Ashley Dukes, "The scene in Europe. Russia in England," *Theatre Arts Monthly* (Sept. 1936): 667.
32 Christopher Hassall, *The timeless quest. Stephen Haggard* (London: Arthur Barker, 1948), p. 95. The most insightful review was Desmond MacCarthy's in *New Statesman* (30 May 1936): 858–60.
33 "P.T.," *New English Weekly* (18 June 1936): 194–5.
34 Margaret Webster, *The same, only different* (New York: Alfred A. Knopf, 1969), p. 317.
35 Hassall, *The timeless quest.*
36 Aniouta Pitoëff, "Tchékhov et les Pitoëff," *Europe* (Aug.–Sept. 1954): 138.
37 Georges Pitoëff, *Nôtre théâtre* , ed. Jean de Rigault (Paris: Messages, 1949), p. 21.
38 T. Shakh-Azizova, "Pitoevy, ili russko-frantsuzky Chekhov," in *Chekhoviana. Chekhov i Frantsiya* (Moscow: Nauka, 1992), p. 191.
39 M. Bataillon, "Quand la France découvre Anton Tchékhov," *Silex* 16 (1980), p. 57. Bataillon provides cast lists for all of Pitoëff's Chekhov productions.
40 *Ibid.*
41 *La Tribune à Génève*, 1921, quoted in Jacqueline Jomaron, *Georges Pitoëff metteur en scène* (Lausanne: L'Age d'homme, 1979), p. 129.
42 *Le Peuple* (22 Apr. 1921).
43 *Nouvelle revue française* (1 June 1921).
44 Descaves quoted in Clément Borgal, *Metteurs en scène* (Paris: Fernore, 1963), p. 176; Claude Roger Marx, *Comœdia illustré* (17 Apr. 1921) quoted in Laffitte, "Chekhov vo Frantsii," pp. 711–12.
45 Quoted in Jomaron, *Georges Pitoëff*, p. 130. Komisarjevsky believed that inexperienced actors were the best exponents of an unusual dramatic style in France "for the experienced French actor has mastered a set of conventions which have mastered him in turn." "On producing Tchehov," p. 17.
46 Pitoëff to Copeau (19 July 1921); Copeau to Pitoëff (9 Aug. 1921), in Bataillon, "Quand la France," p. 59.
47 Quoted in Jomaron, *Georges Pitoëff*, p. 129.
48 Achard, *Le Peuple* (22 Apr. 1921).
49 Pitoëff, *Notre théâtre*, pp. 52–3.
50 Jomaron, *Georges Pitoëff*, p. 122.
51 *Bonsoir* (28 Apr. 1922); *Le Temps*, quoted in Lafitte, "Chekhov v Frantsii," p. 712.
52 Alfred Savoir quoted in Laffitte, "Chekhov vo Frantsii."
53 Pitoëff, *Nôtre théâtre*, p. 48.
54 Pierre Brisson in *Les Annales politiques et littéraires* (8 May 1921).
55 *Paris-Journal* (21 Dec. 1922). Michel Simon left a performance gasping, "Why, they were acting in Russian! I didn't even notice." Véra Volmane, "Tchékhov et le Théâtre d'art de Moscou," *Europe* (Aug.–Sept. 1954): 131.

56 Pitoëff, *Nôtre théâtre*, p. 14.
57 Jean Hort, *La vie héroïque des Pitoëff* (Genève, 1966), p. 296.
58 Aniouta Pitoëff, *Ludmilla, ma mère. Vie de Ludmilla et de George Pitoëff* (Paris: René Julliard, 1955), p. 178.
59 Hort, quoted in Bataillon, "Quand la France," p. 63; Lenormand also noted that it was the "apogee of the Pitoëffs in the way of ensemble quality."
60 A. Pitoëff, *Ludmilla, ma mère*, p. 179.
61 Quoted in Jomaron, *Georges Pitoëff*, p. 133. Excerpts from the critics appear in Frédéric de Towarnicki, "Quand Paris découvre Tchékhov," *Spectacles* 1 (1960).
62 H.-R. Lenormand, *Les Pitoëffs. Souvenirs* (Paris: Odette Lieutier, 1943), p. 171.
63 Mme. Gérard d'Houville, quoted in *ibid.*, p. 173.
64 Jean Nepveu-Degas, "Message de Tchékhov," *Cahiers de la Compagnie Jean-Louis Barrault-Madeline Renaud* 6 (July 1954): 76–7.
65 *Ibid.*
66 Dubec, *Candide* (31 Jan. 1939). In Aniouta Pitoëff's memory, however, it was an immense success, the audiences filled with ordinary people.
67 Shakh-Azizova, "Pitoevy, ili russko-frantsuzky Chekhov."
68 Finkelshtein, quoted in L. I. Gitelman, *Russkaya klassika na frantsuzkom stsene* (Leningrad: Iskusstvo, 1955), p. 110.
69 "Une mouette nous revient," *Le Journal* (16 Jan. 1939).
70 Quoted in A. Pitoëff, "Tchékhov et les Pitoëff," p. 137.
71 B. Crémieux, *La Lumière* (20 Jan. 1939) and J. R. Bloch, *Ce Soir* (11 Feb. 1939).
72 Quoted in Bataillon, "Quand la France," p. 66; A. Frank, *Les Pitoëff*, p. 11.
73 Borgal, *Metteurs en scène*, p. 196; Robert Kemp, *Le Temps* (30 Jan. 1939), quoted in Bataillon, "Quand la France."
74 J. R. Bloch, quoted in A. Pitoëff, *Ludmilla, ma mère*, p. 232.
75 Giorgio Strehler, *Un théâtre pour la vie. Réflexions, entretiens, notes de travail*, ed. S. Kessler, trans. E. Genevois (Paris: Fayard, 1980), p. 303
76 See in Lafitte, "Chekhov v Frantsii," p. 711.
77 Towarnicki, "Quand Paris," p. 17.

9 AMERICA DISCOVERS CHEKHOV (USA, 1900–1944)

1 Quoted in *Theatre Magazine* (New York, Apr. 1938): 44. Reviews of the major productions discussed in this chapter can be found in Victor Emeljanow, *Chekhov: the critical tradition* (London: Routledge and Kegan Paul, 1981). A useful survey is Thomas Winner, "Chekhov v SShA," *Literaturnoe nasledstvo* 68 (1960). I have been unable to consult Zev Raviv, *The production of Chekhov's plays on the American professional stage* (unpub. dissertation, Yale University, 1964).
2 "Plays," *The Nation* (21 Nov. 1912): 175.
3 *The Dramatist* 6 (July 1915): 590–1.
4 Lawrence Langner, *The magic curtain* (New York: E. P. Dutton, 1951), p. 45. In Chicago c.1916 a friend proposed to Sherwood Anderson that a theatre

be opened for the "Chicago Intelligentsia" devoted to Synge and Chekhov. *Sherwood Anderson's memoirs*, ed. R. L. White (Chapel Hill: University of North Carolina Press, 1969), p. 358.

5 Langer, *The magic curtain*, p. 100.

6 New York *Tribune* (24 May 1916): 11.

7 See his *The art of theatre* (New York, 1925) for Cheney's distinctions between the commercial theatre and the art theatre.

8 Lucy France Pierce, "The Seagull Theatre of Moscow," *The Drama* 9 (Feb. 1913): 168–9, 177.

9 N. Ostrovsky, "The Moscow Art Theatre: a model," *Theatre Arts* 1, 4 (Aug. 1917): 180–2.

10 *StanSS* VI, 124. See the essays by Elena Polyakova, Anatoly M. Smeliansky and Inna Soloviova in Laurence Senelick, ed., *Wandering stars: Russian émigré theatre, 1905–1940* (Iowa City: University of Iowa Press, 1993), pp. 32–83.

11 L. A. Leonidov, *Rampa i zhizn. Vospominaniya i vstrechi* (Paris: Russkoe teatralnoe izd. za-grantisey, 1955): 184–5.

12 New York *Herald* (31 Jan. 1923): 10.

13 Edmund Wilson, *The Twenties from notebooks and diaries of the period*, ed. Leon Edel (New York: Farrar, Straus and Giroux, 1975), p. 322. *The Cherry Orchard* had already been performed, rather genteelly, by the Amateurs of Brookline, Mass., in Feb. 1922. See J. Brooks Atkinson, "The Cherry Orchard," *Boston Evening Transcript* (18 Feb. 1922).

14 Burton Rascoe, New York *World Telegram* (22 Dec. 1942); Rose Caylor, "A 'word' on Anton Chekhov," in *Uncle Vanya*, tr. and adapt. R. Caylor (New York: Covici-Friede, 1930), p. 14.

15 Langer, *The magic curtain*, p. 168.

16 Stark Young (8 Jan. 1923), in *Immortal shadows* (New York: Charles Scribner's Sons, 1948). *Cf.* H. T. Parker, "Now to Chekhov," *Boston Evening Transcript* (17 May 1923).

17 Young (10 Jan. 1929) in *ibid.*, p. 108.

18 On émigrés, see Senelick, "Introduction," *Wandering Stars*, pp. ix–xx.

19 Eva Le Gallienne, *At 33* (New York, 1934), p. 224.

20 Letter of Irwin Shaw to the author.

21 "Great world theatre," *Theatre Arts Monthly* (1926): 804. W. Dorr Legg, "Exploring frontiers: an American tradition," *New York Folklore* XIX, 1–2 (1993): 222.

22 Jack Poggi, *Theater in America. The impact of economic forces 1870–1967* (Ithaca, NY: Cornell University Press, 1968), p. 139. Lists of casts and reviews of Le Gallienne's Chekhov productions can be found in Robert A. Schanke, *Eva Le Gallienne. A bio-bibliography* (New York: Greenwood Press, 1989), pp. 42ff.

23 Hallie Flanagan, "Experiment at Vassar," *Theatre Arts Monthly* (Jan. 1928). She quotes extensively from the reviews in *Dynamo* (New York: Duell, Sloan and Pearce, 1943), pp. 25–30.

24 J. Brooks Atkinson, "Enshrining Chekhov," New York *Times* (2 June 1929), 8, x.

25 J. Brooks Atkinson, "Concerning Chekhov," New York *Times* (4 May 1930).

26 John Hutchens, "Brighter nights. Broadway in review," *Theatre Arts Monthly* (June 1930): 461.
27 Stark Young, *New Republic* (28 Dec. 1942): 858.
28 Lillian Gish with Ann Pinchot, *Lillian Gish. The movies, Mr. Griffith and me* (Englewood Cliffs: Prentice-Hall, 1969), p. 309.
29 George Jean Nathan, *Since Ibsen* (New York: Alfred A. Knopf, 1939), p. 92.
30 Caylor, *Uncle Vanya*, pp. 92–3.
31 Caylor, "A 'word,'" pp. xviii–xxi; John Gassner, "Introduction" to *Twenty best European plays on the American stage* (New York: Crown, 1957), p. 15; Atkinson, "Concerning Chekhov." Also see Robert Littell, "The Russians are coming," and "The editor goes to the play," *Theatre Magazine* (June 1930): 18–20, 42–3.
32 Atkinson, "Enshrining Chekhov," p. x.
33 Atkinson, "Concerning Chekhov"; also see "The great world theatre," *Theatre Arts Monthly* (June 1930): 454–8.
34 Harold Clurman, *The fervent years. The story of the Group Theatre and the thirties* (New York: Harcourt Brace Jovanovich, 1975), p. 37. Odets quoted in Wendy Smith, *Real life drama. The Group Theatre and America, 1931–1940* (New York: Alfred A. Knopf, 1990), p. 242.
35 Smith, *Real life drama*, pp. 382–3, 387–8; Poggi, *Theater in America*, pp. 154, 156; Gerald Weales, "The Group theatre and its plays," in *Stratford-upon-Avon studies 10: American theatre* (New York: St. Martin's Press, 1967), p. 73. The original cast included Stella Adler as Masha, Frances Farmer as Olga, Phoebe Brand as Irina, Luther Adler as Andrey, Ruth Nelson as Natasha, Morris Carnovsky as Vershinin, Philip Loeb as Kulygin, Sanford Meisner as Tusenbach, and Elia Kazan as Soleny.
36 Jared Brown, *The fabulous Lunts* (New York: Athenaeum, 1986), pp. 250–5.
37 *Ibid.*, pp. 258–9
38 Stark Young, "Gulls and Chekhov," *Theatre Arts Monthly* (Oct. 1938): 737. Young's translation was published with copious notes by Samuel French in 1939; without the notes, it was republished with his translations of the three later plays in the Random House Modern Library format in 1956.
39 Gassner, "Introduction," p. 40.
40 *Stage* (May 1938): 11; Ruth Woodbury Sedgwick, "Stage awards the palm," *Stage* (June 1938): 5; Tad Mosel with Gertrude Macy, *Leading lady. The world and theatre of Katherine Cornell* (Boston: Little, Brown, 1978), p. 447–8.
41 *Ibid.*, p. 448; Guthrie McClintic, *Me and Kit* (New York: Little, Brown, 1933), p. 269.
42 Mosel, *Leading lady*, p. 452.
43 New York *Times* (26 Jan. 1944): 22, 1–3.
44 McClintic, *Me and Kit*, p. 270.
45 *Life* (14 Dec. 1942): 33–5.
46 Rosamund Gilder, "Today and yesterday. Broadway in review," *Theatre Arts Monthly* (Apr. 1944): 200.
47 Eva Le Gallienne, "Director's note," *The Cherry Orchard* (1968 program).

10 UNDER DURESS (RUSSIA, 1938–1945)

1 "O vklyuchenii v repertuar MkhAT 'Trekh sester' A. P. Chekhova. Vystuplenie na zasedanie v MkhAT 3 dek. 1938 goda," in P. A. Markov, *V Khudozhestvennom teatre. Kniga zavlita* (Moscow: VTO, 1976), p. 411. Basic sources of information about the 1940 MAT *Three Sisters* are *Vl. I. Nemirovich-Danchenko vedet repetitsiyu. "Tri sestry" A. P. Chekhova v postanovke MkhAT 1940 goda* (Moscow: Iskusstvo, 1965); Vl. I. Nemirovich-Danchenko, *Rozhdenie teatra: vospiminaniya stati, zametki, pisma* (Moscow: Pravda, 1989); Gremislavsky in V. Berezkin, *Khudozhnik v teatre Chekhova* (Moscow: Izobrazitelnoe iskusstvo, 1987), pp. 197–201; A. Roskin, *<Tri Sestry>* na stsene Khudozhestvennogo teatra (Leningrad: VTO, 1946); M. Stroeva, "Rabota V. I. Nemirovicha-Danchenko nad spektaklem 'Tri sestry,'" *Teatr* 7 (1954); and V. Ya. Vilenkin, *Vospominaniya s kommentariyami*, 2nd edn. (Moscow: Iskusstvo, 1991).

2 Vilenkin, *Vospominaniya*, pp. 62–3.

3 Nemirovich-Danchenko, *Stati*, p. 317

4 "James Lynch," "Tri Sestry," *Kurer* (21 Oct. 1901) in L. N. Andreev, *Polnoe sobranie sochineny* (Moscow: no pub., 1913), VI, 323–5.

5 *Nemirovich-Danchenko vedet repetitsiyu*, pp. 149, 154, 189; G. A. Khaichenko, *Stranitsy istorii sovetskogo teatra* (Moscow: Iskusstvo, 1983), p. 96.

6 *Nemirovich-Danchenko vedet repetitsiyu*, p. 150.

7 *Ibid.*, p. 170.

8 Anatoly Éfros, "Fragments sur la Mouette," *Théâtre en Europe* 2 (Apr. 1984): 15–16.

9 Vilenkin, *Vospominaniya*, p. 68.

10 See Berezkin, *Khudozhnik v teatre Chekhova*, for information about the design.

11 Vilenkin, *Vospominaniya*.

12 Anatoly Smelyansky, "Oktyabrskie vechera," *Russkaya mysl* (27 Nov. 1992), p. 14; "Danchenko directs. Notes on *The Three Sisters*," *Theatre Arts Monthly* (Oct. 1943): 605.

13 Roskin, *<Tri Sestry>*, pp. 122–3; Khaichenko, *Stranitsy*, pp. 97–8; Vilenkin, *Vospominaniya*, p. 69.

14 Vilenkin, *Vospominaniya*, pp. 69–70.

15 Michel Saint-Denis, *Theatre, the rediscovery of style* (New York: Theatre Arts Books, 1960), p. 53.

16 Michel Saint-Denis, "Reflections on the Russian theatre," *Theatre Arts* (June 1958), p. 12.

17 N. Nabokov, "The Moscow Art Theatre: old and new," *Listener* (5 June 1958): 68–72; and William Gerhardie, *Times* (London, June 1958), quoted in Cynthia Marsh, "The Moscow Art Theatre in Britain" in Patrick Miles, ed., *Chekhov on the British Stage* (Cambridge: Cambridge University Press, 1993), pp. 116–17.

18 A. Ya. Tairov, *O teatre* (Moscow: Iskusstvo, 1970), pp. 394–9.

19 D. Talnikov, "Problema rezhissury i russkaya klassika," in *Teatralny Almanakh* (Moscow: VTO, 1947), p. 178.

20 Quoted in Alisa Koonen, *Stranitsy zhizni* (Moscow: Iskusstvo, 1975), p. 412.
21 Talnikov, "Problema."
22 Quoted in *ibid.*, p. 180
23 Koonen, *Stranitsy zhizni*, p. 413.
24 P. P. Gaideburov, *Literaturnoe nasledie*, ed. Sim. Dreiden (Moscow: VTO, 1977), p. 158.
25 N. Krymova, "Andante kantabile," *Moskovsky nablyudatel* 11–12 (1993): 34–5.

II BREAKING WITH TRADITION (RUSSIA, 1950–1970)

1 Anatoly Éfros, *Prodolzhenie teatralnogo rasskaza* (Moscow: Iskusstvo, 1985), pp. 33–4. The basic sources for this chapter and the next are K. Rudnitsky, *Spektakli raznykh let* (Moscow: Iskusstvo, 1974); A. M. Smeliansky, *Nashi sobesedniki, Russkaya klassicheskaya dramaturgiya na stsene sovetskogo teatra 70-kh godov* (Moscow: Iskusstvo, 1981); V. Berezkin, *Khudozhnik v teatre Chekhova* (Moscow: Izobrazitelnoe iskusstvo, 1987); T. K. Shakh-Azizova, "Sovremennoe prochtenie chekhovskikh pes (60–70–e gody)," in *V tvorcheskoy laboratorii Chekhova* (Moscow: 1974), pp. 336–53; and E. Kalmanovsky, "'Dyadya Vanya' i teatralnaya sovremennost," in *Chekhov i teatralnoe iskusstvo. Sbornik nauchnykh trudov* (Leningrad: Ministerstvo Kultury RSFSR, 1985), pp. 133–53.
2 Quoted in G. Brodskaya, "Chekhov v Khudozhestvennom teatre 1970-kh godov," in *Chekhov i teatralnoe iskusstvo*, p. 176.
3 P. Gromov, "Chekhov, Stanislavsky, Meierkhold," in *Chekhov i teatralnoe iskusstvo*, p. 69.
4 A. Fadeev, *Za tridtsat let* (Moscow: 1957), p. 848; the text dates from 1944. N. Virta, "'Dyadya Vanya' na stsene Tambova," *Tambovskaya pravda* (23 July 1952), quoted in Rudnitsky, *Spektakli*, p. 102.
5 Pavel Markov, "New trends in the interpretation of Chekhov," *World Theatre* 9, 2 (Summer 1960): 107.
6 *Ibid.*, p. 106.
7 *Andrey Mikhailovich Lobanov. Dokumenty, stati, vospominaniya* (Moscow: Iskusstvo, 1980), pp. 99–112.
8 See "Mechta o cheloveke" in M. Iofev, *Profili iskusstv* (Moscow: Iskusstvo, 1956), pp. 25–37.
9 1959; John D. Mitchell, *Staging Chekhov: Cherry Orchard* (New York: Institute for Advanced Studies in the Theatre Arts , 1991), p. 232.
10 M. Zlobina, "Pechalny prioritet," *Teatr* 5 (1957): 113; M. Stroeva, "Chekhov étogo goda," *Teatr* 8 (1960): 135–6.
11 T. Zabolaeva, "'Promezhutochny' geroy ('Ivanov')" in *Chekhov i teatralnoe iskusstvo*, p. 124; K. Rudnitsky, "Vremya i mesto" in *Klassika i sovremennost. Problemy sovetskoy rezhissury 60–70-kh godov*, ed. A. M. Smeliansky (Moscow: Nauka, 1987), p. 192.
12 T. Shakh-Azizova, "Dolgaya zhizn traditsy" in *Chekhovskie chteniya v Yalte. Chekhov i teatr* (Moscow: Kniga, 1976), p. 25.
13 Rudnitsky, "Vremya i mesto."

14 T. Shakh-Azizova, "S tochki zreniya teatra . . . (Chekhov v kontekste russkoy klassiki)," in *Chekhovskie chteniya v Yalte. Chekhov i russkaya literatura* (Moscow: Gos. Ord. Lenina Biblioteka SSR, 1978), pp. 147–9.

15 Brodskaya, "Chekhov v Khudozhestvennom teatre," pp. 177–9.

16 Georgy Tovstonogov, *Krug mysley. Stati, rezhisserskie kommentarii, zapisi reptitsy* (Moscow: Iskusstvo, 1972), p. 157. Also see G. A. Tovstonogov and A. P. Kuzicheva, "'Moy lyubimy dramaturg . . .' (Neopublikovannoe intervyu)" and V. Ya. Lakshin, "G. A. Tovstonogov," in Rossiiskaya akademiya nauk, *Chekhoviana. Chekhov v kulture XX veka* (Moscow: Nauka, 1993), pp. 136–44.

17 Shakh-Azizova, "Dolgaya zhizn traditsy," p. 28; K. Rudnitsky, *Teatr* 5 (1965): 35. Tovstonogov's commentary on his production appeared in English as "Chekhov's *Three Sisters* at the Gorky Theatre," tr. J. C. Vining, *The Drama Review* 13, 2 (Winter 1968): 146–55.

18 Tovstonogov, *Krug mysley*, p. 155.

19 *Ibid.*, p. 129.

20 Shakh-Azizova, "Dolgaya zhizn traditsy," p. 27.

21 Tovstonogov, *Krug mysley*, p. 191.

22 *Ibid.*, p. 156.

23 Smeliansky, *Nashi sobesedniki*, p. 268.

24 Yu. Rybakov, *G. A. Tovstonogov. Problemy rezhissury* (Leningrad: Iskusstvo, 1977), pp. 96–8.

25 Rudnitsky, "Vremya i mesto," pp. 215–16.

26 Rybakov, *G. A. Tovstonogov*, pp. 98–9.

27 Rudnitsky, "Vremya i mesto."

28 Leonid Zorin, "'Tri sestry' – 1965,'" in *Chekhovskie chteniya v Yalte. Chekhov i teatr* (Moscow: Kniga, 1976), p. 130.

29 T. Shakh-Azizova, "Sovremennye prochtenie chekhovskikh pes [60–70–e gody]," in *V tvorcheskoy laboratorii Chekhova* (Moscow: Nauka, 1974): 344–5.

30 *Ibid.*, p. 345. Also see V. Maksimova, *Zhizn akter obraz (iskusstvo sovetskogo aktera 60–8okh godov)* (Moscow: Znanie, 1984), pp. 84–7.

31 Zabolaeva, "'Promezhutochny' geroy," pp. 123–5.

32 Rudnitsky, "Vremya i mesto," pp. 192–9.

33 O. N. Efremov, "Subda naslediya," in *Chekhovskie chteniya v Yalte. Chekhov i teatr* (Moscow: Kniga, 1976), p. 10. Also see Efremov interviewed by V. Maksimova, quoted in Shakh-Azizova, "Sovremennoe," p. 346; T. K. Shakh-Azizova, "Russky Gamlet ('Ivanov' i ego vremya)" in *Chekhov i ego vremya* (Moscow: Nauka, 1977): 232–46.

34 Quoted in Zabolaeva, "'Promezhutochny' geroy," p. 127. Years later, Efremov confessed he had hoped to get Ivanov more out of his depression, but Smoktunovsky couldn't do it. Efremov, "A path to Chekhov," in Patrick Miles, *Chekhov on the British Stage* (Cambridge: Cambridge University Press, 1993), p. 128.

35 M. Turovskaya, "Kino-Chekhov-77–Teatr," *Iskusstvo kino* 1 (1978): 95.

36 Rudnitsky, "Vremya i mesto," pp. 201–4.

37 Turovskaya, "Kino-Chekhov-77–Teatr," p. 89.

38 Marianna Stroeva, "Chekhov i Khudozhestvenny teatr (K voprosu o strukture rannikh spektakley MKhTa," in *Chekhovskie chteniya v Yalte. Chekhov i teatr* (Moscow: Kniga, 1976), p. 12.

39 Quoted in Shakh-Azizova, "Sovremennoe prochtenie," p. 348.

40 Anatoly Éfros, "Raznye est uslovnosti," *Teatralnaya zhizn* 17 (1960): 10, Éfros analyzes *The Seagull* in *Repetitsiya - lyubov moya* (Moscow:Iskusstvo , 1975), pp. 12–18, 112–14, 118–21, 114–26, 161–8 and 196–9.

41 Shakh-Azizova, "Dolgaya zhizn traditsii," p. 30.

42 A. Éfros, "Fragments sur la Mouette," pp. 30–3.

43 P. Selem, "Efros ou l'exil," *Théâtre en Europe* 2 (Apr. 1984): 37–8.

44 Éfros discusses aspects of *Three Sisters* in *Repetitsiya - lyubov moya*, pp. 20–1, 25–32, 41–6, 65–8, 96–7, 183–4, 187–93, 216–18, 242, 255–7, 278–83, 316–9.

45 Selem, "Efros ou l'exil."

46 V. Gaevsky, *Fleita Gamleta. Obrazy sovremennogo teatra* (Moscow: Soyuzteatr, 1990), pp. 55–65.

47 Éfros, *Repetitsiya - lyubov moya*, pp. 31–2, 216–18. Twenty years later Éfros said he would take a different tack, and play the whole thing quietly. Soleny and Tusenbach would not quarrel but be reconciled. He would take as his starting point Stanislavsky's "It would seem that they can't stand their grief, but, on the contrary, they look for merriment, laughter, boisterousness; they want to live, and not vegetate." Éfros, *Prodolzhenie*, pp. 12–13, 31.

48 V. B. Shklovsky, "Chaika-1969," *Teatr* 5 (1969).

49 Efremov interviewed by V. Maksimova, quoted in Shakh-Azizova, "Sovremennoe," p. 346.

50 K. Shcherbatov, "'Chaika' étogo goda," *Komsomolskaya Pravda* (5 July 1970), quoted in *Teatr "Sovremennik"* (Moscow: Iskusstvo, 1973), p. 112.

12 FERMENT IN AN AGE OF STAGNATION (RUSSIA, 1970–1990)

1 A. Minkin, "Mokroe delo," *Moskovsky nablyudatel* 3–4 (1994): 57. *Novy Mir* (*New World*) was the journal which first carried such literary evidence of the Thaw as Solzhenitsyn's *One Day in the Life of Ivan Denisovich*.

2 John D. Mitchell, *Staging Chekhov: Cherry Orchard* (New York: Institute for Advanced Studies in the Theatre Arts, 1991), p. 130.

3 Mariya Knebel, *Vsya zhizn*, 2nd edn. (Moscow: Iskusstvo, 1993), p. 570.

4 T. K. Shakh-Azizova, "Dolgaya zhizn traditsy," in *Chekhovskie chteniya v Yalte. Chekhov i teatr* (Moscow: Kniga, 1976), pp. 29–30. In 1968, the Abbey Theatre invited Mariya Knebel to Dublin to direct *The Cherry Orchard*, with Siobhan McKenna as Ranevskaya and Cyril Cusack as Gaev. Rehearsing on the set of *Playboy of the Western World*, Knebel drew on the notion of Ireland the classic land of emigration, rife with impractical landowners. As Ranevskaya, McKenna differed from Knipper and Dobrzhanskaya: she possessed a mysterious, transcendant quality, a yearning for something impossible. The actors were surprised that Knebel did not require a samovar on the set; she was startled in turn when they suggested that

Lopakhin wouldn't marry Varya because he was a pederast. Mariya Knebel, "'Vishnevy sad' v Irlandii," *Teatr* 5 (1969): 158–66.

5 E. Taranova, "'Nachalos s nedorazumeny . . . '" in *Chekhov i teatralnoe iskusstvo* (Leningrad: Ministerstvo Kultury RSFSR, 1985), pp. 166–7. Astute Western interpretations of this production were offered by Spencer Golub and Maria Szewcow, "The theatre of Anatolij Efros," *Theatre Quarterly* 7, 26 (Summer 1977): 18–47.

6 Interview with Alla Demidova, *Literaturnaya gazeta* (25 Aug. 1976).

7 Konstantin Rudnitsky, "Vremya i mesto," in *Klassika i sovremennost. Problemy sovetskoy rezhissury 60–70-kh godov*, ed. A. Smeliansky (Moscow: Nauka, 1987), pp. 205–7.

8 Smeliansky, *Nashi sobesedniki*, p. 299.

9 *Ibid.*, p. 300.

10 M. Turovskaya, "Kino-Chekhov-77–Teatr," *Iskusstvo kino* 1 (1978): 91.

11 Rudnitsky, "Vremya i mesto," 207–9; Laurence Senelick, "The Moscow Scene," *Educational Theatre Journal* (May 1977): 253.

12 Grigory Kozintsev, *Literaturnoe obozrenie* 4 (1979): 104, quoted in Rudnitsky, "Vremya i mesto," p. 219.

13 Aleksandr Gershkovich, *Teatr na Taganke (1964–1984)* (Benson, Vt: Chalidze Publications, 1986), p. 139.

14 Smeliansky, *Nashi sobesedniki*, pp. 220–1; Marie-Luise Bott, "'Drei Schwestern' in Moskau – eine Groteske," *Theater Heute* 3 (1984): 20.

15 Rudnitsky, "Vremya i mesto," pp. 216–18. Gershkovich interprets it more lyrically, seeing it as the "real, non-theatrical and yet legendary Moscow we had never noticed in life. It was bathed in the golden rays of the setting sun, and the cupola of the white-stone church on a distant hill endowed it with an almost irreal vista." He wondered if the theatre's miracle-working would give the sisters their wish (*Teatr na Taganke*, p. 138).

16 Gershkovich, *Teatr na Taganke*, p. 136; T. Knyazevskaya, "Providcheskoe u Chekhove," *Teatralnaya zhizn* 4 (1994): 12–13.

17 N. G. Lordkipanidze, *Rezhisser stavit spektakl* (Moscow: Iskusstvo, 1990), p. 31; Alma Law, "An 'actor's director' debuts in the West," *American Theatre* (June 1987): 18.

18 Lordkipanidze, *Rezhisser stavit spektakl*, p. 47.

19 *Ibid.*, pp. 24–5.

20 P. M. Benyash, "Neyasnoe novatorstvo," *Teatr* 5 (1983): 62. Also see A. Zverev, "Yavlenie i chelovek; 'Dyadya Vanya' A. P. Chekhova na segod-nyashney stene," *Literaturnoe obozrenie* 3 (Mar. 1984): 95–7; and Konstantin Shcherbakov, "Svet fonarya v tumane. Uroki chekhovskoy dramaturgii," *Literaturnoe obozrenie* 1 (Jan. 1985); 86–8.

21 Rudnitsky, "Vremya i mesto," p. 223.

22 T. Brodskaya, "Chekhov v Khudozhestvennom teatre 1970-kh godov," in *Chekhov i teatralnoe iskusstvo* (Leningrad: Ministerstvo Kultury RSFSR, 1985), p. 186.

23 V. Gaevsky, *Fleita Gamleta* (Moscow: Soyuzteatr, 1990), pp. 23–6.

24 Rudnitsky, "Vremya i mesto," pp. 209–12.

25 It reminded one American observer of the last scene in *Silkwood*, when Meryl Streep sings "Amazing Grace" over a freezeframe of Karen Silkwood gazing at a pair of headlights in her rearview mirror. James Curtis, "The triumph of *Hamlet*: some thoughts on the Moscow Art Theatre's current production of *The Seagull*," *Soviet and East-European Drama, Theatre and Film* 8, 2–3 (Dec. 1988): 30. Also see Shcherbakov, "Svet fonarya," pp. 83–6.

26 O. N. Efremov, "A path to Chekhov," in Patrick Miles, ed., *Chekhov on the British Stage* (Cambridge: Cambridge University Press, 1993), p. 130.

27 Brodskaya, "Chekhov v Khudozhestvennom teatre," p. 193.

28 Anatoly Éfros, *Prodolzhenie teatralnogo rasskaza* (Moscow: Iskusstvo, 1985), pp. 33–4.

29 Z. Abdullaeva, "Doktor Astrov i drugie," *Literaturnoe obozrenie* (Nov. 1985): 87–90.

30 Information from A. M. Smeliansky.

13 OUT OF THE RUBBLE (CENTRAL AND EASTERN EUROPE, 1945–1985)

1 Otomar Krejča interviewed by Karel Kraus and Josef Topol, "Tschechow-Inszenierung heute," *Neue Zürcher Zeitung* 321 (2 May 1967): 41–2.

2 *Theater in der Zeitenwende* (Berlin: Henschelverlag, 1972), I, 158.

3 Quoted in Gerard Dick, "Die deutsche Čechov – Interpretation der Gegenwart," *Zeitschrift für Slawistik* (Berlin: Akademie, 1959).

4 Christa M. Christa, *The German versions of Chekhov's Three Sisters* (New York: Peter Lang, 1988), pp. 372–8, 404–10.

5 "Iwan spielt Regisseur," *Sauerländisches Volksblatt* (21 Mar. 1952); "Eine Komödie in der Komödie," *Frankfurt Abendpost* (1 Nov. 1952); "Tschechow war schliesslich eine Russe," *Schwäbische Landeszeitung* (29 Aug. 1953); Birgit Kirschstein-Gamber, *Die Čechov-Szene. Untersuchungen Text und Realisierung der Regieanweisung im Drama Anton Pavlovič Čechovs* (Altendorf: Albert-Ludwigs-Universität, 1979), p. 112.

6 Juliusz Tyszka, "Stanislavsky in Poland: ethics and politics of the Method," *New Theatre Quarterly* 5, 20 (Nov. 1989): 363–4.

7 B. Dąbrowski, "Słowo aktora," *Przyjaźń* (5 Sept. 1954), quoted in S. V. Bukchin, "Na polskoy stsene," in *Chekhovskie chteniya v Yalte. Chekhov segodnya* (Moscow: Ministerstvo Kultury SSSR, 1987), p. 29.

8 N. Modzelewska, "Rycerze wiecznej rozterki," *Przegląd Kulturalny* 45 (1958); Karl Hartmann, *Das polnische Theater nach dem zweiten Weltkrieg* (Marburg: N. G. Elwert, 1964), pp. 24–31, 111, 188ff.

9 A. Tarn, "Konfrontacje. Czechow i MChat," *Dialog* 8 (1958): 148.

10 *World Theatre* (1960): 142.

11 Edward Csato, *The Polish Theatre*, tr. C. Censkalska (Warsaw: Polonia, 1963), p. 70.

12 Andrzej Wirth, "Donzuanizm jakó, krytyka epoki," *Nowa kultura* 37 (1962): 4; Roman Szydłowski, "Konfrontacje. Angry young man of 1880," *Dialog* 10 (1962): 117.

13 Roman Szydłowski, "Teatr poetycki Adama Hanuszkiewicza," *Trybuna Ludu* 22 (1977).

14 M. Smetana in *Divadlo* 9 (1954): 802; Sh. Sh. Bogatyrev, "Chekhov v Chekoslovakii," *Literaturnoe nasledstvo* 68 (Moscow: Nauka, 1960): 770–2.

15 Rolf-H. Klefer, "Szenographie und modernes Theater. Zum Werk des Prager Architekten und Bühnenbilder Josef Svoboda," *Neue Zürcher Zeitung* (28 Feb. 1974); *World Theatre* (1960): 144. Svoboda describes his method in *The secret of theatrical space. The memoirs of Josef Svoboda*, ed. and trans. J. M. Burian (New York: Applause Books, 1993), pp. 58–9.

16 Otomar Krejča, "L'infini tchékhovien est impitoyable," *Théâtre en Europe* 2 (Apr. 1984): 65–7.

17 Krejča in "Tschechow-Inszenierung heute," p. 42.

18 Krejča, "L'infini tchékhovien," p. 68.

19 Quoted in Karel Kraus, "Sur la prétendue passivité des personnages tchékhoviens," *Théâtre en Europe* 2 (Apr. 1984): 70.

20 Krejča in "Tschechow-Inszenierung heute."

21 Jindrich Honzl, "La mobilité du signe théâtral," *Travail théâtral* 26 (1978). Honzl launched one of the more thoughtful critiques of Stanislavsky in *Zaklady a praxe moderneho divadla* (Prague, 1963).

22 Kraus, "Sur la prétendue passivité," pp. 74–5.

23 Siegfried Melchinger, "Das Prager Experiment," *Theater Heute* 10 (1969): 40–1; Denis Bablet, *Josef Svoboda* (Paris: La Cité, 1970), pp. 154–8.

24 Melchinger, "Das Prager Experiment." Jarka Burian, *The scenography of Josef Svoboda* (Middleton, Conn.: Wesleyan University Press, 1971), p. 38.

25 J.-P. Léonardini in *Otomar Krejca et le Théâtre za Branou de Prague* (Lausanne: La Cité, 1972), pp. 61–2.

26 Emile Copfermann in *ibid.*, pp. 63–8; Claude Olivier in *ibid.*, p. 72.

27 For a scene-by-scene diagram see Denis Bablet in *ibid.*, pp. 82–3.

28 van, "Otomar Krejča und sein *Platonow*," *Neue Zürcher Zeitung* 58 (28 Feb. 1974); b.b.r., "Otomar Krejča inszenierte in Prag: Kontinuität einer Theaterarbeit," *Arbeiter Zeitung* (Zürich, 28 Feb. 1974).

29 Georges Banu, "Strehler et l'antépurgatoire tchékhovien," *Travail théâtral* 26 (1978).

30 Otomar Krejča, "Les pièces de Tchékhov," *Travail théâtral* 26 (1978).

31 Banu, "Strehler"; Marie-Louise Bablet, "Otomar Krejca et 'La Cerisaie' de Chékhov," *Travail théâtral* 26 (1978).

32 See Béatrice Picon-Vallin, "*Les Trois Soeurs*," in *VCT* 10 (1982), p. 94.

33 Carolina de Maegd-Soëp, "Anton Tsjechov in België," *Ons Erfdeel* 25, 1 (1982): 71; Dirk De Corte, "*De Kersentuin* in De K.V.S.," *Dokumenta* 4 (1986): 143.

34 T. Nicolesco, *Tchékhov en Roumanie 1895–1960. Bibliographie littéraire sélective* (Bucharest: Editions de l'Académie de la République populaire roumaine, 1960), pp. 17–18.

35 Lucien Pintilié, "A la recherche du sens d'une étrange comédie," *Travail théâtral* 26 (1978).

36 R. Michaelis, *Theater Heute* 1 (1969).

37 Maria Shevtsova, "Chekhov in France, 1976–9: productions by Strehler, Miquel and Pintilié," in *Transformations in modern European drama*, ed. Ian Donaldson (Atlantic Highlands, N.J.: Humanities Press, 1983), pp. 83–5.

38 *World Theatre* (1960), p. 140.

39 László Gerold, "Four out of eleven productions. Hungarian language theatre in 1977–8," *Scena* 2 (1979), p. 94.

40 Dieter Hadamczik, Jochen Schmidt and Werner Schulze-Reipell, *Was spielten die Theater?* (Cologne: Deutscher Bühnenverein, 1978), pp. 32, 34, 43.

41 Peter Szöndi, *Theory of the modern drama. A critical edition*, ed. and trans. M. Hays (Minneapolis: University of Minneapolis Press, 1987), pp. 20–1.

42 Christa, *The German versions*, pp. 392, 436–7; R. Tietze, "Russisch-Protokoll," in H. Braem, ed. *Übersetzen-Werkstatt* (Munich: Taschenbuch Verlag, 1979), p. 97. Also see Karla Hielscher, "Die Rezeption A. P. Čehov im deutschen Sprachraum seit 1945," in *Aspekte der Slavistik*, ed. Wolfgang Gicke and Helmut Jachnow (Munich: Otto Sagner, 1984), pp. 73–161; and Herta Schmid, "Čechov-Inszenierungen auf deutschen Bühnen: 1964–1984," *Forum Modernes Theater* 1, 1 (1986): 81–4.

43 *General-Anzeiger der Stadt Wupperthal* (23 Nov. 1954).

44 Henning Rischbieter, "Die Wahrheit, leise und unerträglich," *Theater Heute* 6 (1965): 24ff. See also Eric Bentley, *What is theatre? incorporating The dramatic event and other reviews 1944–1967* (New York: Athenaeum, 1968), pp. 431–4.

45 Willi Schmidt, *Theater Heute* 7 (1966).

46 Siegfried Melchinger, "Apologie der leisen Wahrheit. Über den Fall Tschechow in München," *Theater Heute* 7 (1966): 20; he reiterated these opinions in his 1968 monograph on Chekhov and in another important article in *Theater Heute* 12 (1968). Melchinger believed that it was Ingmar Bergman's 1961 production of *The Seagull* which established Chekhov's classic status.

47 Henning Rischbieter, "Tschechow-Forderungen," *Theater Heute* 9 (1968): 3. Also see Schmid, "Čechov-Inszenierungen," and Kirschstein-Gamber, *Die Čechov-Szene* (Altendorf: no pub., 1979), pp. 122–69.

48 Volker Canaris, *Peter Zadek der Theatermann und Filmemacher* (Munich: Carl Hanser, 1979); S. Melchinger, *Theater Heute* 1 (1969).

49 H. Rischbieter, "Theater Forderungen," p. 44.

50 Canaris, *Peter Zadek*.

51 Rischbieter, *Theater Heute* 11 (1973).

52 H. Rischbieter, "Kommt uns nur noch die Farce bei?," *Theater Heute* 8 (1981); 22–31. When Langhoff restaged *The Cherry Orchard* in French for the Comédie de Genève at the Avignon Festival in 1983, he omitted some of the blasphemies. Everything continued to revolve around Ranevskaya (Christiane Coheny), but her vulgarity was refined and her motivation clarified (she can't stand the orchard, it's too importunate). See Colette Godard, "Histoire de théâtre, d'orphelines, d'amour de mur," *Théâtre en*

Europe 2 (Apr. 1984): 90–1; Georges Banu, "'Les cerisaies étrangères,'" in *Chekhoviana. Chekhov vo Frantsii* (Moscow: Nauka, 1992), pp. 238–40.

53 Quoted in Rischbieter, "Kommt uns nur," p. 16.

54 Henning Rischbieter, "Alptraum Alltag. Tschechows 'Möwe' in Mülheim und München," *Theater Heute* 5 (1984): 22–3.

55 Henning Rischbieter, "Museum der Sentimentalität. Peter Stein inszeniert 'Drei Schwestern' an der Schaubühne," *Theater Heute* 3 (1984): 12–15; T. Knyazevskaya, "Providcheskoe u Chekhove," *Teatralnaya zhizn* 4 (1994): 13. Stein's interpretation might be contrasted with that of Ingmar Bergman (1978), which also pointed up vocally and physically the increasing disintegration of the sisters as a unit and their gradual solipsism. See Arthur Holmberg, "*The Three Sisters*," *Theatre Journal* (Dec. 1979): 541–2.

56 Erika Fischer-Lichte, "Die Inszenierung der Übersetzung als kulturelle Transformation," in *Soziale und theatralische Konventionen als Problem der Dramenübersetzung*, ed. E. Fischer-Lichte, B. Schultze and H. Turk (Tübingen: Gunter Narr, 1988), pp. 144, 135. Stein himself insisted that "the essential quality of Chekhovian drama is the presence of contradictions in the slightest detail." Olivier Ortolani, "Le père du théâtre du vingtième siècle. Tchékhov et *Les trois soeurs*. Entretien avec Peter Stein," *Théâtre/Public* 84 (nov.-déc. 1988): 66–25. Stein's production may have influenced Volker Braun's 1982 play *Übergangsgesellschaft* (*Society in Transition*), which merged the three sisters with the GDR; one character remarks, "It was fine once, everything was fine. We rolled out pictures of the rising sun and stayed living in the dark."

57 Godard, "Histoire de théâtre," p. 89; Peter von Becker, "Einmal in einer Gewitternacht," *Theater Heute* 3 (1984): 17.

14 *UT PICTURA POESIS* (ITALY AND FRANCE, 1945–1985)

1 François Mauriac, "Tragic quotidien," *Express* 101 (26 Apr. 1955).

2 *World Theatre* 9. 2 (1960), p. 140.

3 Orazio Costa Giovangigli, "Esperienze di regia čechoviana," in *Goldoni nel teatro russo. Čechov nel teatro italiano* (Rome: Accademi nazionale dei lincei, 1976), p. 159.

4 Director's notes in *ibid.*, pp. 161–2.

5 *World Theatre* (1960), p. 124.

6 Giovangigli, "Esperienze," p. 171.

7 *Zeffirelli. The Autobiography of Franco Zeffirelli* (New York: Weidenfeld & Nicholson, 1986), pp. 115–16.

8 Eberhard Fechner, *Strehler inszeniert* (Berlin: Friedrich Verlag, 1963), p. 81; David L. Hirst, *Giorgio Strehler* (Cambridge: Cambridge University Press, 1983), pp. 26–7.

9 Giorgio Strehler, *Un théâtre pour la vie. Réflexions, entretiens, notes de travail*, ed. S. Kessler, trans. E. Genevois (Paris: Fayard, 1980), pp. 305–6. Originally *Per un teatro umano. Pensieri scritti, parlati ed attuati* (Milan: Giangiacomo Feltrinelli, 1974).

10 Hirst, *Giorgio Strehler*, p. 25.

11 Ettore Gaipa, *Giorgio Strehler* (Berlin: Henschelverlag, 1963), pp. 36–7.

12 Roberto Rebora and Franco Vogli in *Sipario* (June 1959); Gaipa, *Giorgio Strehler* (1963), pp. 37, 67.

13 Giorgio Strehler, "La Cerisaie: une enquête sur le temps," *Théâtre en Europe* 2 (Apr. 1984): 41–2, 49; Strehler, *Un théâtre pour la vie*, p. 311. The production has been analyzed by Georges Banu, "'La Cerisaie' ou une façon de disparaître," in *Strehler. VCT* 16 (1989), pp. 257–79.

14 Strehler, *Un théâtre pour la vie*, p. 314.

15 Massimo Gallerani, quoted in Hirst, *Giorgio Strehler*, p. 29.

16 Strehler, *Un théâtre pour la vie*, p. 326. It took a generation for Strehler's design solution to penetrate traditions in North America and the former Soviet Union, but when it did, it did so with a vengeance. Ingrid Agur canopied the stage for Kaarin Raid's production in Tallinn (1993) with a tulle curtain filled with petals, which dropped on Firs and the furniture at the end to give an impression of funeral mounds (E. Alekseeva, "Na poroge schastya," *Moskovsky nablyudatel* 11–12 [1993]: 53). In 1994, the Russian designer Simon Pastukh reversed this tissue in his setting for the Indiana Repertory Theatre's *Orchard*, strewing the stage floor with thousands of pink petals "that whisper and lift and fly whenever people move" (Stephen Haff, "The sensuous Chekhov," *American Theatre* [Apr. 1994]: 20). Louise Campeau's set for the Quebec *Platonov*, *Comédie russe*, in 1993 literally carpeted the floor in dead leaves (Stéphane Lépine, "La saule ne pleure pas," *Jeu* 67 [1993]: 37).

17 Strehler, "La Cerisaie," p. 40.

18 Maria Shevtsova, "Chekhov in France, 1976–9," in *Transformations in Modern European Drama*, ed. Ian Donaldson (Atlantic Highlands, N.J.: Humanities Press, 1983), pp. 85–91.

19 Strehler, *Un théâtre pour la vie*, p. 324.

20 Vadim Gaevsky, *Fleita Gamleta* (Moscow: Soyuzteatr, 1990), pp. 314–15.

21 Strehler, "La Cerisaie," p. 42.

22 Maurizio Porro, "Lioubov et Valentina Cortese," *Théâtre en Europe* 2 (Apr. 1984): 80; Georges Banu, "Ce dont on se souvient . . . ," *Théâtre en Europe* 2 (Apr. 1984), pp. 56–7.

23 Georges Banu, "Strehler et l'antépurgatoire tchékhovien," *Travail théâtral* 26 (1978).

24 Banu, "Ce dont on se souvient . . . ," p. 56.

25 Banu, "Strehler et l'antépurgatoire."

26 Gaevsky, *Fleita Gamleta*, pp. 329–30.

27 R. Guyot, *Cahiers du communisme* (Jan. 1960), quoted in Yu. Felichkin, "Rol teatra v vospriyaty tvorchestva Chekhova vo Frantsii," in Literaturny Muzey A. P. Chekhova, *Sbornik statey i materialov vypusk V* (Rostov: Rostovskoe knizhnoe izd., 1969), pp. 157–8, 161.

28 Georges Banu, "Entretien avec Antoine Vitez," *Silex* 16 (Grenoble, 1980), p. 75.

29 *Ibid.*, p. 74.

30 Sophie Laffitte, "Chekhov vo Frantsii," *Literaturnoe nasledstvo* 68 (Moscow, 1960): 730.

31 Jean-Louis Barrault, "Pourquoi *La Cerisaie?*," *Cahiers de la Compagnie Jean-Louis Barrault-Madeleine Renaud* 6 (Paris: Julliard, 1964).

32 *World Theatre* 9, 2 (1960), p. 117.

33 Christine Hamon, "De la traduction au jeu," in *Brook. VCT* xiii (1985), pp. 261–2. The translation was published in *L'Avant-scène* 218 (1960).

34 Barrault, "Pourquoi *La Cerisaie?*," p. 91. For some the fundamental difference between French and Russian cultures was too great a gulf to straddle. "The French language, French diction are at odds with such playwriting as Chekhov's," opined Gabriel Marcel. "It even seems that the words must be pronounced with a different stress. We felt this even during the unforgettable productions realized by the Pitoëffs. The question, whether a decent treatment of such a play as *Cherry Orchard* is possible in French, remains extremely dubious." He concluded that the production was mediocre but necessary to be shown (*Nouvelles littéraires*, 28 Oct. 1954).

35 Kenneth Tynan, *Curtains* (New York: Athenaeum, 1961), p. 385.

36 Guy Dumur, "Lioubov et Madeleine Renaud," *Théâtre en Europe* 2 (Apr. 1984): 78. Also see Jean-Louis Barrault, *Souvenirs pour demain* (Paris: Seuil, 1972), pp. 242–4.

37 Quoted in L. I. Gitelman, *Russkaya klassika na frantsuzkom stsene* (Leningrad: Iskusstvo, 1978), p. 124.

38 Marcel Capron, *Combat*, quoted in *L'Avant-scène* 218 (1960): 31; Léon Dominique, *Le théâtre russe et la scène française*, tr. Nina Nidermiller and Michèletan Wiernik (Paris: Olivier Perrin, 1969), p. 145.

39 J.-J. Gautier in *Figaro* (27 Apr. 1955).

40 *Progrès de Lyon* (6 May 1955).

41 Interview with Jean Vilar, *World Theatre* 9, 2 (1960), p. 147. In the process, he combined the two Vengerovichs to produce a hybrid: a visionary Shylock crossed with a poet's consciousness. Stanisław Siekierko, "Premiera zaginionej sztuki Czechowa w TNP," *Teatr* 17 (1956): 10–11.

42 *Jean Vilar par lui-même* (Avignon: Maison Jean Vilar, 1991), p. 182.

43 *World Theatre* 9, 2 (1960), p. 146.

44 *Ibid.*, p. 116; Jean-Claude Bardot, *Jean Vilar* (Paris: Armand Colin, 1991), p. 352.

45 In brochure of *Ivanov* (Paris, 1956); Laffitte, "Chekhov vo Frantsii," p. 738; *World Theatre* 9, 2 (1960), p. 113.

46 Robert Abirached, "Anton Tchékhov. Les Trois Soeurs," *Nouvelle revue française* 169 (1 Jan. 1967): 155–6.

47 M. Bataillon, "Quand la France découvre Anton Chékhov," *Silex* 16 (1980), p. 69.

48 Eugène Ionesco, *Notes et contre-notes* (Paris: Gallimard, 1966), p. 97.

49 Banu, "Entretien avec Antoine Vitez," p. 75.

50 *Ibid.*, p. 82. Vitez's translation of *Ivanov* was published by De Noël in 1958, and his *Seagull* by Gallimard in 1984.

51 Antoine Vitez and Émile Copferman, *De Chaillot à Chaillot* (Paris, 1981), p. 45.

52 André Helbo *et al.*, eds., *Approaching theatre* (Bloomington: Indiana University Press, 1987), pp. 196–208.

53 Banu, "Entretien avec Antoine Vitez," p. 76.

54 Colette Godard, "Histoire du théâtre, d'orphelines, d'amour de mur," *Théâtre en Europe* 2 (Apr. 1984), p. 82.

55 *Ibid.*, p. 83.

15 ALL-AMERICAN CHEKHOV (USA, 1950–1995)

1 Spencer Golub, *Newsnotes on Soviet & East European Drama and Theater*, 3, 3 (Nov. 1983): 2–3 (originally a program note for a Trinity Square Theatre production of *Cherry Orchard*, Providence, R.I.).

2 Margaret Webster, "A letter to Chekhov," *New York Times* (23 Jan.) 1949.

3 Joshua Logan, *The wisteria trees. An American play based on Anton Chekhov's The Cherry Orchard* (New York: Random House, 1950). As early as 1930, commenting on audience resistance to things Russian, Robert Littell suggested disguising *The Cherry Orchard* as an American product: "Change the names, hire a soft-spoken negro for the old servant . . . , switch the cherry orchard to a magnolia grove, make . . . Lopakhin over into a self-made poor white, bring in a few references to the Wa'h, hire actors who spoke pure Charleston, S.C., and you have a grand, heart-breaking old play about the ruined South." "The Russians are coming," *Theatre Magazine* (June 1930): 19.

4 Irwin Shaw, Arthur Miller, Paddy Chayefsky and Robert Anderson: letters to the author. Tennessee Williams, *Memoirs* (Garden City, NY: Doubleday, 1975), p. 41; *Five o'clock angel: letters of Tennessee Williams to Maria St. Just 1948–1982* (New York: Deutsch, 1990), p. 385. John van Druten's *Playwright at work* (1953) specifically named Chekhov as the father of the new drama.

5 John Gassner, "Introduction" to *Twenty best European plays on the American stage* (New York: Crown, 1957), p. 15.

6 Norris Houghton, *World Theatre* (1960): 131.

7 Olympia Dukakis quoted in Jean Hackett, *The actor's Chekhov. Nikos Psacharopoulos and the company of the Williamstown Theatre Festival on the plays of Anton Chekhov* (Newbury, Vt.: Smith and Kraus, 1992), pp. 44, 32. See Norris Houghton, *Exits & entrances. A life in and out of the theatre* (New York: Limelight Editions, 1991), pp. 237–43. An informed audience member recorded in his diary, "The underlying tensions of the script were utterly unrevealed. Montgomery Clift, in a terribly uneven performance, did have visceral moments but used no intellect in the part at all to give it style. His posture and his speech vied with each other for sloppiness. His delivery of his lines after Nina exits got a most out-of-place laugh because of their absurd casualness and then he went out and shot himself. I haven't seen such a bad starring performance since De Havilland did Juliet." Donald Vining, *A gay diary Volume Three 1954–1967* (New York: Pepys Press, 1981), pp. 4–5.

8 *Time* (13 Feb. 1956). See Eric Bentley, *What is theatre?* (New York: Athenaeum, 1968), pp. 221–4, 251–7, 286–90.

9 Quoted in Julia S. Price, *The off-Broadway theater* (New York: Scarecrow Press, 1962), p. 182.

10 "Critical box score and summary," *Theatre Arts* 7 (1960): 59; Brooks Atkinson, "'A Country Scandal' at Greenwich Mews," New York *Times* (6 May 1960), p. 21; Brooks Atkinson, "Chekhov premiere," New York *Times* (15 May 1960): 1; B. Bohle, "The openings," *Theatre Arts* 44, 7 (1960): 58; Walter Kerr, "New York theatre letter. Early Chekhov comedy," New York *Herald Tribune* (22 May 1960).

11 Walter Kerr, *ibid.*; see also Brooks Atkinson, "Early Chekhov," New York *Times* (7 May 1960); "Chekhov premiere," New York *Times* (15 May 1960). A later New York revival, *A Country Scandal* (1975), directed by Stuart Vaughan at the CSC Rep, turned Chekhov into the Molière of *Scapin*, with tumbles and falls, hiding in a chest, etc. Mel Gussow, "'Country Scandal' by CSC Company," New York *Times* (8 Oct. 1975), p. 24.

12 Walter Kerr, New York *Herald Tribune* (23 Mar. 1962); Howard Taubman, New York *Times* (23 Mar. 1962); John Simon, "Play reviews," *Theatre Arts* (June 1962): 63, 73.

13 Alma Law, "An 'actor's director' debuts in the West," *American Theatre* (June 1987): 45.

14 Jack Poggi, *Theater in America. The impact of economic forces 1870–1967* (Ithaca, NY: Cornell University Press, 1968), p. 224. None of the productions made any money.

15 Gordon Rogoff, "Fire and ice: Lee Strasberg," *Tulane Drama Review* (Winter 1964): 152–3.

16 Quoted in Elia Kazan, *A life* (New York: Doubleday, 1988), p. 707.

17 Paul Gray, "Stanislavski and America: a critical chronology," *Tulane Drama Review* (Winter 1964): 56–7; "The bottomless cup: an interview with Geraldine Page," in *ibid.*, pp. 114–30.

18 F. W. Dupee, "To Moscow again," *New York Review of Books* (30 July 1964): 4.

19 Kazan, *A life*, p. 708; *Randall Jarrell's letters*, ed. M. Jarrell (Boston: Houghton Mifflin, 1985), p. 490. Jarrell's translation was published with his commentary by Macmillan in 1969. Production photographs were captioned with the characters', not the actors', names as if they had been taken from the Prozorov family album.

20 Quoted in *ibid.*, pp. 711–12.

21 Robert A. Schanke, *Shattered applause. The lives of Eva Le Gallienne* (Carbondale and Edwardsville: Southern Illinois University Press, 1992), p. 229.

22 James Forsyth, *Tyrone Guthrie, a biography* (London: Hamish Hamilton, 1976), pp. 278, 281, 286; Alan Pryce-Jones, "Openings. Minneapolis. *The Three Sisters*," *Theatre Arts* (Aug.–Sept. 1963): 13–14.

23 Poggi, writing in 1967, *Theater in America*, pp. 239–40.

24 Tom Brennan, quoted in Hackett, *The actor's Chekhov*, p. 35.

25 Louis Zorich and John Glover, quoted in *ibid.*, pp. 60, 141.

26 *Ibid.*, p. 1.

27 *Ibid.*, pp. 2, 15, 57, 75, 153, 156, 178.

28 M. Terry, letter to author. Adrienne Kennedy, an African-American playwright of a later generation, also imbibed Chekhov as inspiration; see her *People who led to my plays* (New York, 1987).

29 John Gruen, "The avant-garde discovers Chekhov," New York *Times* (5 Jan. 1975).

30 *Ibid.*

31 *Ibid.*

32 *Ibid.*

33 Jean-Claude Van Itallie, "'Chekhov's characters seem to be ourselves,'" *New York Times* (2 Feb. 1977): 1, 7; letter to author.

34 "Should black actors play Chekhov? Yes – Maya Angelou. Yes – Ed Bullins," New York *Times* (4 Feb. 1973): 1, 16.

35 The text is in *The Collected Plays of Neil Simon*, vol. 2 (NY: Avon Books, 1979). Reviews include Richard Watts, "Neil Simon looks at Chekhov," New York *Post* (28 Nov. 1973); J. Beaufort, "'Good Doc' – Neil Simon-ized Chekhov," *Christian Science Monitor* (30 Nov. 1973); Walter Kerr, "Chekhov meets Neil Simon, both lose," New York *Times* (9 Dec. 1973); Jack Kroll, "What's up, Doc?," *Newsweek* (10 Dec. 1973); Brendan Gill, *New Yorker* (10 Dec. 1973).

36 Mel Gussow, "'Vanya' stars tie success to Nichols," New York *Times* (18 June 1973).

37 Walter Kerr, "A too tearful Vanya," New York *Times* (10 June 1973). See also Jack Kroll, "Life with Uncle," *Newsweek* (10 June 1973); Kevin Kelly, "Nichols 'Vanya' falls short," *Boston Globe* (15 July 1973). Nicol Williamson was more in control when he repeated *Uncle Vanya* (RSC, Other Place, 1974), in a metal cage with 150 spectators in the centre of the action. Michael Billington, "Tchékhov en Angleterre," *Théâtre en Europe* 2 (Apr. 1984), p. 63.

38 Richard Gilman, "Broadway critics meet 'Uncle Vanya,'" *Theatre Quarterly* (Feb.–Apr. 1974): 67–72.

39 Leo Hecht, "*The Three Sisters* at the Arena," *Newsnotes on Soviet and East European Drama and Theater* 4, 1 (Mar. 1984): 6.

40 "Serban defends his *Cherry Orchard*," New York *Times* (13 March 1977).

41 Richard Eder, "The life of plays," New York *Times* (1 July 1977).

42 J. Beaufort, "An 'opened-up' *Cherry Orchard*: less light," *Christian Science Monitor* (23 Feb. 1977); Walter Kerr, "A daring, perverse and deeply original 'Cherry Orchard,'" New York *Times* (27 Feb. 1977); C. P., *Time* (28 Feb. 1977); Brendan Gill, *New Yorker* (17 June 1977).

43 Laurence Shyer, "Andrei Serban directs Chekhov: *The Seagull* in New York and Japan," *Theater* (Fall/Winter 1981); Jerrold A. Phillips, "Serban's Three Sisters," *Newsnotes on Soviet and East European Drama and Theater* 3, 2 (June 1983): 10–13.

44 Susan Letzler Cole, *Directors in rehearsal. A hidden world* (New York: Routledge, 1992), pp. 11, 15, 20, 27.

45 Alvin Klein, "Wilson's view of Chekhov," New York *Times* 23, 12 (25 Mar. 1984): 6; Philip Middleton Williams, *A Comfortable House. Lanford Wilson, Marshall W. Mason and the Circle Repertory Theatre* (Jefferson, N.C.: McFarland., 1993), pp. 21, 34, 70, 97, 11–12. Wilson's *Three Sisters* is published by Dramatists Play Service (1984).

46 David Mamet, *Writing in restaurants* (New York: Viking, 1986), p. 121.

47 Richard Christiansen, "New Theatre's 'Orchard' needs more ripening," Chicago *Tribune* 1 (16 Mar. 1985): 13.

48 Michael Billington, "Made-for-TV Chekhov from Mamet and Mosher," New York *Times* 2, 29 (13 Feb. 1991): 1. For the Goodman Theatre production of *Uncle Vanya*, see Richard Christiansen, "'Uncle Vanya' is fascinating, but frustrating," Chicago *Tribune* 1 (1 May 1990). Mamet's adaptations were published by Grove Press: *The Cherry Orchard* in 1985, *Uncle Vanya* in 1989. Professor Donald Fanger has suggested to me that the awkward translatorese of all these versions may be a conscious choice to provide stumbling-blocks for actors to overcome.

49 Mel Gussow, "Speaking in Mamet's words, to the subconscious," New York *Times* C, 14 (18 Apr. 1991): 3.

50 Performance pieces and plays drawn from Chekhov's life include *Anton Chekhov's Garden Party* by William Shust (1972), a one-man show portraying the author reading his early works in Yalta to the touring actors of the MAT; a revised version, *Chekhov on the Lawn* by Elihu Winer (Theatre East, NY 1984); *Chekhov in Yalta* by John Driver and Jeffrey Haddow (Mark Taper Forum, Los Angeles, 1981), an historically inaccurate, Ortonesque farce about the Art Theatre visiting Chekhov and seducing one another; *Chekhov* by sculptor and film-maker Stuart Sherman (Performing Garage, NY, 1985), a twelve-minute vignette repeated twice, the first part of a trilogy meant to deal also with Strindberg and Brecht; *Anton, himself* by Karen Sunde (Actors Theatre of Louisville, 1989), another one-man meander through his past; and *Talking Things over with Chekhov* by John Ford Noonan (Actors' Playhouse, 1990), whose author chats with an offstage Chekhov, while a playwright and actress meet and talk in six brief scenes. Of *Chekhov and Maria* by Jovanka Bank (1993), a two-hander about the writer's "possessive and incestuous sister," the L. A. *Times* remarked that it "explodes in a way that Chekhov's characters never could." Which says it all. See Jerome Katsell, "Review of Chekhov on the Lawn," *Newsnotes on Soviet and East European Drama and Theatre* 2, 1 (Mar. 1982): 10–11; *Theatre Journal* (May 1982): 266; Christoph Edwards, "Chekhov year?," *Drama* (Winter 1984): 34–5; Mel Gussow, "The stage: 'Chekhov,' a miniaturist's view," New York *Times* (28 July 1985); Karen Sunde, *Anton, himself* in *Moscow Art Theatre past, present and future* (Louisville: Actors Theatre of Louisville, 1989), pp. 31–47; Mel Gussow, "Two characters in search of an offstage author," New York *Times* (13 May 1990); Jeremy Kingston, "One sister more trouble than three," New York *Times* (18 Jan. 1993): 30.

51 Sid Smith, *Chicago Tribune* (21 Sept. 1985) quoted in *Orchards Orchards*

Orchards (New York: Broadway Play Publishing, 1987). See Louis Lappin, "Chekhov and the American imagination," *Theater* 18, 1 (Fall/Winter 1986): 97–9.

52 Felicia Londré, "The way they were," *American Theatre* (Dec. 1991): 22; Florence A. Falk, "Dangling conversation," *American Theatre* (Dec. 1991): 21.

53 Brendan Lemon, "Vanya's uncles," *New Yorker* (9 May 1994): 79. Preserving the rehearsal format, Louis Malle filmed this successfully as *Vanya on 42nd Street* (1994). Among the welter of reviews, see Philip Strick's in *Sight and Sound* (Dec. 1994): 61/1, and Richard Combs, "Chekhov in New York," *Times Literary Supplement* (13 Jan. 1995): 18.

16 CHEKHOV WITHOUT TEARS (UNITED KINGDOM, 1950–1993)

1 Kenneth Tynan, *Curtains* (New York: Athenaeum, 1961), pp. 433–4. In addition to the works of Patrick Miles cited above, useful surveys of Chekhov in England in the late forties and early fifties can be found in Audrey Williamson, *Theatre of two decades* (New York: Macmillan, 1951) and *Contemporary theatre 1953–1956* (New York: Macmillan, 1956).

2 W. J. Turner, *English ballet* (London: Collins, 1946), pp. 47–8. In the mid-1980s, although the emphasis had moved to the comic, Chekhov's moderation was still seen as the source of his popularity, which Ian McKellen attributed to "the British sense of the ridiculous, our love for the eccentric and, above all, an ingrained fascination with the middle classes." Ian McKellen, "Wild flowers, wild bees, wild honey," *Drama* (Winter 1984): 5–7.

3 Zinovy Zinik, "Russian dreams and nightmares," *Times Literary Supplement* (3 Aug. 1984), p. 871.

4 Michael Billington, "Tchékhov en Angleterre," *Théâtre en Europe* 2 (Apr. 1984): 61; Caryl Brahms, "Chekhov the dramatist of farewells," *Times* (23 May 1966).

5 Vera Gottleib, "Chekhov in limbo: British productions of the plays of Chekhov," in *The play out of context: transferring plays from culture to culture*, ed. Hanna Scolnicov and Peter Holland (Cambridge: Cambridge University Press, 1988), pp. 164–5.

6 Hal Burton, ed., *Great acting* (New York: Hill and Wang, 1967), p. 92.

7 Billington, "Tchékhov en Angleterre," p. 62; Benedict Nightingale, "A true master receives his due," *Times* (22 Feb. 1992): 1; Kenneth Tynan, *Tynan Right and Left* (New York: Atheneum, 1967), pp. 110–11. The weak link was Joan Greenwood as Elena, soon replaced by Rosemary Harris.

8 Penelope Gilliatt, "The current cinema," *New Yorker* (18 Apr. 1977): 132.

9 *World Theatre*, Chekhov Centenary Issue (Summer 1960): 126–7. This calls to mind Jouvet's response to an irate spectator who protested that Molière would not approve of Jouvet's *Tartuffe*: "Do you have his phone number?" Also see J. W. Lambert, "Plays in performance," *Drama* (Aut. 1958): 16–18. When the Art Theatre returned in 1964, it was dismissed as boring and irrelevant.

10 Leo Baker, "Hints from the Moscow Art Theatre," *Drama* (Winter 1958): 33–5.
11 Michel Saint-Denis, "Chekhov and the modern stage," *Drama Survey* 3 (Spring-Summer 1963): 80.
12 Jane Mederos Baldwin, *A paradoxical career: Michel Saint-Denis' life in the theatre* (unpub. Ph.D. diss., Tufts University, 1991), p. 298.
13 Tynan, *Curtains*, p. 40.
14 J. W. Lambert, "Plays in performance," *Drama* (Winter 1960): 24; Tynan, *Tynan Right and Left*, pp. 39–40; Irving Wardle, *The Theatres of George Devine* (London: Cape, 1978), pp. 218–24. For a minority, unfavorable report, see *The Kenneth Williams diaries*, ed. Russell Davies (London: Harper Collins, 1993), pp. 775–6; Williams thought Harrison lacking in comic technique.
15 Roman Szydłowski, "Konfrontacje. Angry Young Man of 1880," *Dialog* 10 (1962): 113–18.
16 Billington, "Tchékhov en Angleterre," p. 65. Olivier brought in Josef Svoboda as scenographer of his *Three Sisters* at the National Theatre (1967); Svoboda provided a brilliant setting of stretched rods in layers, with a special emphasis on the window apertures; but the English technicians were incapable of maintaining the freshness of the lighting effects beyond the first performances. Jarka Burian, *The scenography of Josef Svoboda* (Middleton, Conn.: Wesleyan University Press, 1971): 48–51. Svoboda was also distressed by Olivier's request for a vision of Moscow to appear in the last act. *The secret of theatrical space. The memoirs of Josef Svoboda*, ed. and trans. J. M. Burian (New York: Applause Books, 1993), pp. 98–9.
17 Quoted in David Allen, "Jonathan Miller directs Chekhov," *New Theatre Quarterly* 5, 17 (Feb. 1989): 60.
18 Ross Wetzsteon, "The director in spite of himself: an interview with Jonathan Miller," *American Theatre* (Nov. 1985): 8–9.
19 Jonathan Miller, *Subsequent Performances* (London: Faber and Faber, 1986)
20 Rodney Ackland, "From Komisarjevsky to Jonathan Miller," *Spectator* (18 Sept. 1976).
21 Allen, "Jonathan Miller"; John Elsom, *Listener* (1 July 1976).
22 Michael Coveney, *The Citz: 21 years of the Glasgow Citizens Theatre* (London: Nick Hern, 1990), p. 146.
23 Vera Gottleib, "The politics of British Chekhov" in Patrick Miles, ed., *Chekhov on the British stage* (Cambridge: Cambridge University Press, 1993), p. 148.
24 *The Observer* (3 Oct. 1965), quoted in David Allen, "David Jones directs Chekhov's 'Ivanov,'" *New Theatre Quarterly* 4, 15 (Aug. 1988), p. 239.
25 Representative reviews include Ned Chaillet, *Times* (8 Sept. 1976): 11; J. W. Lambert, *Sunday Times* (12 Sept. 1976): 39; Clive Barnes, "Chekhov sweeps London with three plays going," *NY Times* (18 Sept. 1976): 25; Virginia Llewellyn Smith, "Bouncing Chekhov," *Times Literary Supplement* (24 Sept. 1976): 1208; Benedict Nightingale, "Would Chekhov accept this Anglo-Saxon 'Ivanov'?," *NY Times* (26 Sept. 1976), II, 5; and W. Stephen Gilbert, "Enough of Ivanov," *Plays and Players* (Nov. 1976): 26–7.

26 *The Cherry Orchard: A new English version* (London: Pluto Press, 1978), p. v. The published script is larded with innumerable stage directions, which reproduce the light and sound cues and actions of Eyre's production to some degree. The proliferation of such stage directions at every line is almost as oppressive as in Barrie or O'Neill but without the justification of being the author's inventions.

27 Billington, "Tchékhov en Angleterre," p. 63.

28 See David Allen, "'The Cherry Orchard': a new English version," and Valentina Ryapolova, "English translations of Chekhov's plays; a Russian view," in Miles, ed. *Chekhov on the British stage*, pp. 156–8, 226, 232–3.

29 John Goodwin, ed., *Peter Hall's diaries. The story of a dramatic battle* (New York: Harper and Row, 1983), pp. 321–7, and Peter Hall, *Making an exhibition* (London: Sinclair-Stevenson, 1993), p. 85. See Harold Hobson, "Hobson's choice," *Drama* (Spring 1978): 34–5.

30 Billington, "Tchékhov en Angleterre," p. 64.

31 *Ibid.*, p. 63. Also see reviews by Ned Chaillet, *Times* (30 Aug. 1978):8, and Irving Wardle, *Times* (9 Apr. 1980): 8; J. W. Lambert, "Trevor Nunn does it again," *Sunday Times* (3 Sept. 1978): 36; Heather Neill, "Royal Progress," *Times Educational Supplement* (6 Oct. 1978): 22–3; James Fenton, "Chekhov in full splendour," *Sunday Times* (13 Apr. 1980): 41; review by Robert Zarkin, *Plays & Players* (May 1980): 26–7; and Lynne Truss, "Positive re-actions hold key to sisters' interplay," *Times Higher Education Supplement* (25 Oct. 1980): 10.

32 Thomas Kilroy's version of *The Seagull* was published in 1993 with an informative introduction by the author (Loughcrew: Gallery Press). For Alfreds, see Stuart Young, "Changes of direction: Mike Alfreds' methods with Chekhov," in Miles, ed., *Chekhov on the British stage*, pp. 168–84.

33 Quoted in David Allen, "Exploring the timeless depths: Mike Alfreds directs Chekhov," *New Theatre Quarterly* 2, 8 (Nov. 1986): 323.

34 *Listener* (Oct. 1981), quoted in *ibid.*, p. 321.

35 David Allen, "Exploring the timeless depth," p. 335.

36 Michael Ratcliffe, "Cherry on top," *Drama* 2 (1986): 23.

37 Gottleib, "Chekhov in limbo," p. 168; Martin Hoyle, "The Cherry Orchard," *Plays and Players* (Feb. 1986): 19.

38 Gottleib, "Chekhov in limbo," p. 170.

39 Coveney, *The Citz*, p. 260.

40 Ratcliffe, "Cherry on top," p. 34.

41 Allen, "Exploring the timeless depths," p. 332.

42 Michael Frayne, "Introduction," *Wild Honey* (London: 198–), pp. xiii–xiv.

43 Vera Gottlieb, "Why this farce?," *New Theatre Quarterly* 7, 27 (Aug. 1991): 223.

44 Michael Frayne, "Introduction," *The Sneeze* (London: Heinemann, 1989), pp. xii–xiii. Frayne's translations of the four major plays and four vaudevilles were published in one volume by Methuen in 1988.

45 A similar attempt to turn *Platonov* into Feydeau was *Comédie russe* by Pierre-Yves Lemieux, directed by Serge Denoncourt at the Théâtre de l'Opsis,

Québec, 1993. The result was reported to be "époustouflant". Stéphane Lépine, "Le saule ne pleure pas," *Jeu* 67 (1993): 36.

46 Zinik, "Russian dreams and nightmares," p. 871; *London Theatre Record* (2–29 July 1984): 615; Christopher Edwards, "London: Chekhov Year?," *Drama* 154 (1984): 34; Sheridan Morley, "Wild Honey," *Plays and Players* 372 (Sept. 1984): 28.

47 *Neue Zürcher Zeitung* (13 Nov. 1985).

48 The collected newspaper reviews for *Piano* can be found in *London Theatre Record* 10, 16 (1990): 1040–5; and 17 (1990): 1110–12. Also see John Peter in *Sunday Times* (12 Aug. 1990); Peter Sherwood in *Times Literary Supplement* (17 Aug. 1990): 874; 5, 3.Carole Woodis in *Plays and Players* (Oct. 1990): 35.

49 Zinovy Zinik, "Mother Russia's nanny," *Times Literary Supplement* (3 Aug. 1991): 17.

50 Michael Billington, "Missing the magic," *Guardian Weekly* (1 Sept. 1991): 26.

51 Irving Wardle, "Problems of playing Chekhov for laughs," *Times* (29 Apr. 1985); T. J. Binyon, "Baring the Slav soul," *Times Literary Supplement* (28 Dec.–3 Jan. 1991).

52 The collected newspaper reviews for *Mrs Vershinin* appear in *London Theatre Record* 8, 21 (1988): 1450–2. The British stage also saw its share of biographical works about Chekhov himself. Both John Gielgud and Michael Pennington portrayed the author in one-man shows, and in 1992 the Chekhov Players of Brighton offered *Fresh Oysters* by Sidney Malin, "the true love story" of "the beautiful actress Olga Knipper and the stricken Anton Chekhov." In November 1994 Stuart Fortey's comedy *A House by the Sea* recreated the St. Petersburg rehearsals for the 1896 performance of *The Seagull* (BAC, London).

53 Benedict Nightingale, "A true master receives his due," *Times* (22 Feb. 1992): 1.

54 *Ibid.*

17 CHEKHOV *SANS FRONTIÈRES* (THE WORLD, 1900–1995)

1 Antoine Vitez, *Le Matin* (21 Nov. 1984), quoted in Patrice Pavis' preface to *Oncle Vania*, tr. Tonia Galievsky and Bruno Sermonne (Paris: Gallimard, 1986), p. 139.

2 Peter Brook, *The Empty Space* (New York: Avon Books, 1969), p. 72.

3 Peter Brook, "La Cerisaie: une immense vitalité," *Théâtre en Europe* 2 (Apr. 1984): 50–3.

4 Paris: Centre international de créations théâtrales, 1981; the production is thoroughly analyzed in *P. Brook et la coexistence des contraires. Sources et modèles. VCT* XIII (1985).

5 Vadim Gaevsky, *Fleita Gamleta* (Moscow: Soyuzteatr, 1990), pp. 314, 317–18; Georges Banu, "Les cerisaies étrangères," in *Chekhoviana. Chekhov vo Frantsii* (Moscow: Nauka, 1992), pp. 234–5; Eric Shorter, "Chekhov through English eyes in French," *Drama* (Autumn 1981): 6–8.

6 Mel Gussow, "Peter Brook returns to Chekhov's vision," New York *Times* (19 Aug. 1981).

7 Georges Banu, "Ce dont on se souvient . . . ," *Théâtre en Europe* 2 (Apr. 1984): 48–9, 53–7; Jonathan Lieberson, "Chopping up 'The Cherry Orchard,'" *New York Review of Books* (3 Mar. 1988): 27–8

8 Gaevsky, *Fleita Gamleta*, pp. 320–1.

9 *Ibid.*, pp. 312–16.

10 Béatrice Picon-Vallin, "L'espace et le temps," in *Brook. VCT* XIII, pp. 291–2.

11 Information from Anatoly Smeliansky.

12 Lieberson, "Chopping up," p. 28.

13 *Ibid.*

14 Akiba Tarō, *Nihon shingeki shi* (Tokyo: Shishōsha, 1955), pp. 160, 203, 220, 235; translation provided by J. L. Anderson. For an overview of Japanese criticism of Chekhov, see Kim Rekho, "Nash sovremennik Chekhov: obzor rabot yaponskikh literaturovedov," *Literaturnoe obozrenie* 10 (1983): 20–8.

15 Oozasa Yoshio, *Nihon gendai engekishi: Meiji taisho hen* (Tokyo: Hakusuisha, 1985), pp. 114–15; information from Aya Mihara.

16 Laurence Shyer, "Andrei Serban directs Chekhov: *The Seagull* in New York and Japan," *Theater* (Autumn/Winter 1981): 60–3.

17 Ninel Sorokina, "Chistaya voda, gretskie orekhi i Chekhov," *Dramaturg* 2 (1993): 179–81; Yu. Rybakov, "'Chaika' po-yaponsky," *Moskovsky nablyudatel* 11–12 (1993): 52; L. Garon, "Uvidim li my Ninu Zarechnuyu v kimono?," *Teatr* 3 (1993): 34–9; program for production.

18 Erika Fischer-Lichte, "Die Inszenierung der Übersetzung als kulturelle Transformation," in *Soziale und theatralische Konventionen als Problem der Dramenübersetzung*, ed. E. Fischer-Lichte, B. Schultze and H. Turk (Tübingen: Gunter Narr, 1988), pp. 129–44. My description is based on the earliest version at the Toga Festival, for which Aya Mihara kindly provided me with a videotape. Suzuki kept on developing the work, and eventually turned it over to the Lithuanian director Jonas Jurasik. Fischer-Lichte's accounts are of one of these later versions, performed outside Japan.

19 Erika Fischer-Lichte, "Intercultural aspects in post-modern theatre: a Japanese version of Chekhov's *Three Sisters*," in *The play out of context: transferring plays from culture to culture*, ed. Hanna Scolnikov and Peter Holland (Cambridge: Cambridge University Press, 1988), pp. 173–84; Marie Myerscough, "East meets west in the art of Tadashi Suzuki," *American Theatre* (Jan. 1986): 10. A *Three Sisters* directed by Yukio Ninagawa at the Ginza Saison Theatre Tokyo in 1993 was set in a rehearsal studio.

20 Georges Banu, *L'acteur qui ne revient pas* (Paris: Aubier, 1986), pp. 48–9; Anatoly Éfros, "O Chekhove i o nashey profesii," *Moskovsky nablyudatel* 11–12 (1993): 4.

21 Kirsikka Siikkala, "*La Cerisaie* d'Efros: le carrousel des âmes perdues," *Théâtre en Europe* 2 (Apr. 1984): 33–4.

22 Alma Law, "An 'actor's director' debuts in the West," *American Theatre* 4, 3

(June 1987): 17–19; Benjamin Henrichs, "Friede den Menschenfressern," *Die Zeit* 25 (1990): 59.

23 Feng Jing, "Beijing debut of Chekhov," *Beijing Review* 34, 41 (July–Oct. 1991): 45–6.

24 Kristen Johnson-Neshati, "To go through life is not the same as to walk across a field: Oleg Yefremov rehearses *Ivanov*," *Theater Three* 10/11 (1992): 128–35.

25 Pierre Lavoie, "L'idiot de la famille . . . 'Oncle Vania'/trois productions," *Jeu* 3 (1993): 76–88.

26 New York *Times* (10 May 1993): 89.

27 Robert Erenstein, *Theatre in the Netherlands* (Rijswijk: Dutch Ministry of Culture, 1992), pp. 48–9.

28 Lavoie, "L'idiot."

29 Michael S. Cain and James Niesen, "Scenes from a collaboration: a Soviet-American theatrical experiment," *Theater Three* 10/11 (1992): 136–44; Marvin Carlson, "The St. Petersburg/Irondale collaboration," *Soviet and East European Performance* 10, 3 (Winter 1990): 43–7.

30 "Charging up Chekhov," *American Theatre* (July/Aug. 1986): 6.

31 William Shebar, "To work and be proud of it," *Harvard Magazine* (May–June 1990): 33–4, 36–7.

32 Jim O'Quinn, "Squat's *The Three Sisters*," *The Drama Review* (Dec. 1980): 111–12.

33 Alfred Nordmann, "The actors' brief: experiences of Chekhov," *Theatre Research International* (Summer 1994): 139–40.

34 Eridice Arratia, "Island hopping rehearsing the Wooster Group's *Brace Up!*," *The Drama Review* 36, 4 (Winter 1992): 121.

35 Paul Schmidt, "The sounds of *Brace Up!* Translating the music of Chekhov," *The Drama Review* 36, 4 (Winter 1992): 154. Schmidt's translation was published by the Theater Communications Group in 1992.

36 Susie Mee, "Chekhov's *Three Sisters* and the Wooster Group's *Brace Up!*" *The Drama Review* 36, 4 (Winter 1992): 146.

37 Schmidt, "The sounds of *Brace Up!*" p. 155.

38 Arratia, "Island hopping," p. 129.

39 Schmidt, "The sounds of *Brace Up!*" p. 156.

40 Mee, "Chekhov's *Three Sisters*," p. 147.

41 "Saved by the bells," *New Statesman and Society* 6, 260 (9 July 1993): 30.

42 Nordmann, "The actors' brief," p. 141.

43 Mee, "Chekhov's *Three Sisters*," p. 152.

44 A. M. Smeliansky, "'Vishnevy sad' Petera Shtaina," *Moskovsky nablyudatel* 11–12 (1992): 14–15.

45 John Freedman, "The first Chekhov International Theatre Festival," *Slavic and East European Performance* 13, 1 (Spring 1993): 3; M. and V. Ivanov, "Iskusstvo byt," *Teatr* 3 (1993): 2–11.

46 N. Krymova and A. Svobodin, "'Vishnevy sad' Petera Shtaina," *Moskovsky nablyudatel* 11–22 (1992): 9, 11–12.

47 A. M. Smeliansky, "'Zhivesh v takom klimate . . .' Fiziologiya nyneshney rossiiskoy zhizni," *Russkaya mysl* 3953 (6 Nov. 1992): 16; N. Krymova and A. Svobodin, "'Vishnevy sad' Petera Shtaina," pp. 11–13.

48 A. M. Smeliansky, "Oktyabrskie vechera. Teatralnye vpechatleniya odnogo mesyatsa," *Russkaya mysl* 3956 (27 Nov. 1992): 14.

49 Freedman, "The first Chekhov," pp. 36–7.

50 A. Zaslavskaya, "'Vishnevy sad' Andreya Sherbana," *Moskovsky nablyudatel* 11–12 (1992): 51–3; I. Myakova, "Vzglyad Ranevskoy," *Teatr* 3 (1992): 111–15.

51 Freedman, "The first Chekhov."

52 G. Kovalenko, "'Vishnevy sad' Otomara Kreichi," *Moskovsky nablyudatel* 11–12 (1992): 42–4.

53 T. Shakh-Azizova, "'Vishnevy sad' Otomara Kreichi," *Moskovsky nablyuda-tel* 11–12 (1992): 46, 48.

54 Gaevsky, *Fleita Gamleta*, p. 317.

18 THE *PERESTROIKA* OF CHEKHOV (EASTERN EUROPE AND RUSSIAN FEDERATION, 1989–1995)

1 Sergey Zhenovach, "Tsepochka sluchaev," *Moskovsky nablyudatel* 11–12 (1993): 29.

2 A. Minkin, "Mokroe delo," *Moskovsky nablyudatel* 3–4 (1994): 57.

3 Istvan Horvai, "Moy Chekhov," in *Chekhovskie chteniya v Yalte. Chekhov segod-nya* (Moscow: 1987), pp. 38–9.

4 René Solis, "Tamás Ascher: Une accumulation de chutes," *La Libération* (23 May 1990); László Bérczes, "Platonov. Én Balkay Géza – szerepeiröl," *Film, Színház, Muzsika* (4 Aug. 1990): 6; Judit Szántó, "Gyilkosság – orosz módra," *Világszínház* (July 1990): 30; René Solis, "Le Katona avec éclat," *La Libération* (22 May 1990).

5 Rafal Węgrzyniak, "Grzegorzewski's Chekhov," *Theatre in Poland* 1 (1994): 24–6; Elizabeth Swain, "*Ivanov and others*," *Slavic and East European Performance* 13, 3 (Fall 1993): 44–8; also see Małgorzata Sugiera, "Poetyka Grzegorzewskiego," *Dialog* 2 (1990): 144–54 and 3 (1990): 108–19; Elżbieta Morawiec, *Powidoki Teatru* (Cracow, 1991).

6 Tadeusz Burzyński, "A cruel comedy," *Theatre in Poland* 1 (1994): 30–2.

7 Susan Jonas, "Less mattering and more art: Chekhov's comic dramaturgy and Sturua's *Three sisters*," *Theater Three* 10/11 (1992): 202–10; T. J. Binyon, "Baring the Slav soul," *Times Literary Supplement* (28 Dec.–3 Jan. 1991): 15. A round table on this production was held in the *Scottish Slavonic Review* 16 (Spring 1991): 103–15, from which come the quotations from McVay (p. 105) and Sturua (p. 112).

8 M. A. Vasileva, "Chekhov i grotesk ('Dyadya Vanya' v postanovke Eimuntasa Nekroshyusa)" in *Chekhovskie chteniya v Yalte. Chekhov: vzgljad iz 1980-kh* (Moscow: Ministerstvo Kultury SSSR, 1990): 146–35; Elinor Fuchs, "Splendid transgressions," *American Theatre* (Dec. 1991): 24–5; Joel

Berkowitz, "The State Theatre of Lithuania's *Uncle Vanya*," *Soviet and East European Performance* 11, 3 (Winter 1991): 54–7. In 1995 Nekrošius pursued his revisionism in a *Three Sisters* whose women were temptresses and whose officers were boorish sots. See Andrzej Wirth, *Teatr* (Warsaw) 7/8 (1995).

9 Alyona Solntseva, "Russian theater at the time of late perestroika," *Theater Three* 10/11 (1992): 90–100.

10 A. Shapiro, "Bylo," *Moskovsky nablyudatel* 11–12 (1993): 16.

11 A. Svobodin, "Ogonennye vetvi" and "Neobkhodimy postscriptum," *Moskovsky nablyudatel* 11–12 (1993): 17–21.

12 Vadim Gaevsky, "Neozhidanny Chekhov. 'Dyadya Vanya' v Shchukinskom uchilishche," *Moskovsky nablyudatel* (Apr. 1993): 27.

13 Anatoly Smelyansky, "Oktyabrskie vechera. Teatralnye vpechatleniya odnogo mesyatsa," *Russkaya mysl* 3956 (27 Nov. 1992): 14.

14 Inna Soloveva, "Milaya sestra," *Moskovsky nablyudatel* 11–12 (1993): 47–9.

15 *Novaya gazeta* (4 Feb. 1994), quoted in Minkin, "Mokroe delo," pp. 59–60; also see V. Begunov, "Igra na chuzhom pole," *Teatr* 3 (1993): 53–9.

16 Elise Thoron, "Two productions of Chekhov," *North American Chekhov Society Bulletin* 1 (Apr. 1992).

17 E. Gorfunkel, "Son Lopakhina," *Moskovsky nablyudatel* 11–12 (1993): 37.

18 Sergey Zhenovach, "Tsepochka sluchaev," *Moskovsky nablyudatel* 11–12 (1993): 29; A. Karas, "Leshy, koldun, obmanshchik i svat," *Moskovsky nablyudatel* 11–12 (1993): 31–2.

19 M. Smolyanitsky, "Personazh mërtv," *Moskovsky nablyudatel* 11–12 (1993): 40. *Platonov* had received a starker, more casual reinterpretation at the Sibilev Studio in 1991 under Chekhov's title *Without Patrimony (Bezottsovshchina)*; see John Freedman, "Renewing a tradition: Moscow's Sibilyov Studio," *Slavic and East European Performance* 12, 3 (Spring 1992): 24 6.

20 Jane House, "Chekhov at the Festival des Antiques, Montréal May/June 1993," *Slavic and East European Performance* 13, 3 (Autumn 1993): 54–7; also see M. Gaevskaya, *Teatr* 3 (1993): 11–19..

21 Solntseva, "Russian theater at the time of late perestroika," pp. 93–6.

22 Richard Borden, "Chekhov on the Moscow stage 1993–4," *North American Chekhov Society Bulletin* (Apr.1994): 1–2; also see B. Tukh, "Chego khochet zhenshchina, togo kochet Bog," *Teatr* 3 (1993): 97–100.

23 T. K. Shakh-Azizova, "Rezhisser chitaet Chekhova. 'Ivanov i drugie' v Moskovskom Tyuze," *Ékran i stsene* 39–40 (7–14 Oct. 1993): 5.

24 Swain, "*Ivanov and others*," pp. 44–8.

25 Shakh-Azizova, "Rezhisser chitaet Chekhova."

26 I. N. Soloveva, "'Vy menya ispugali,' *Ivanov i drugie*," *Moskovsky nablyudatel* 11–12 (1993): 22–6.

27 Solntseva, "Russian theater"; Stéphane Lépine, "Le saule ne pleure pas," *Jeu* 67 (1993): 40–3. The intertextual approach has been used outside of Russia. In the highly charged battle of the sexes made out of *The Bear* and *The Marriage Proposal* by Vladimir Mirzoev and the Horizontal Eight of Toronto (1992), passages from *Uncle Vanya* and *Three Sisters* were inter-

polated; the female characters were portrayed simultaneously by two actresses and the male characters switched their roles every so often. See J. Adam, "The dance of images: Vladimir Mirzoev and Toronto's Horizontal Eight," *New Theatre Quarterly* 39 (Aug. 1994): 284. In 1994 the Polish playwright Slawomir Mrożek premiered a new play, *Love in the Crimea*, which continually interleaves Chekhovian themes, characters and clichés with high and popular culture. See Daniel Gerould, "Mrożek's Chekhovian tragicomedy stirs mixed emotions," *Slavic and East European Performance* (Summer 1994): 13–15.

Index of Chekhov productions

Index of titles and characters

(CO=*The Cherry Orchard*; IV=*Ivanov*; SG=*The Seagull*; TS=*Three Sisters*; UP=*Untitled Play*; UV=*Uncle Vanya*)

Index of proper names

Richter-Forgach, Theodor. 245
Ridgeway, Philip 142–3, 155, 162
Rilke, Rainer Maria 102–3
Rilla, Paul 235
Rischbieter, Henning 252–3, 255, 261
Riverside Studio, London 314
Rix, Brian 319
Roberts, Leona 187
Robertson, Toby 311
Robinson, Lennox 138–9
Robson, Flora 146
Roggisch, Peter 253
Roksanova, M. L. 49–50, 52
Rolland, Romain 162, 169
Römer, Anneliese 256
Roninson, G. 223
Roos, Volker 257
Rosenberg, Marvin 4
Roshchin-Insarov, Nikolay 26
Ross, David 286
Rossetti, Christina 157
Rostand, Edmond 11, 112
Rossini, Giaocchino 8
Rostova, Mira 285
Rostovstev, I. A. 83, 93
Roth, Beatrice 339
Rousseau, J.-J. 264
Royal Court Theatre, London 140, 308, 314, 321–2
Royal Shakespeare Company 307, 311–12
Rozov, Viktor 208, 213
RSC Warehouse, London 314
Rudic, Laurance 317
Rudnitsky, Konstantin 213
Rusanov, Nikolay 64

Sacher-Masoch, Leopold 319
Sadovskaya, Olga 68
Sagalchik, A. 211
Saiko, N. 227–8
Saint-Denis, Michel 146, 157, 162, 194–5, 273, 305, 307–8, 310, 322, 384 n.58
St. Martin's Theatre, London 141, 159–60
St. Petersburg Theatre Salon 336–7
Saltykov-Shchedrin, Mikhail 121
Samoilov, P. V. 53
Sanin, Aleksandr 152
Sardou, Victorien 9, 99
Sartre, Jean-Paul 358
Savina, Mariya 20–2, 29–30, 86–9, 363 n.44, 365 n.9, 10
Savitskaya, Margarita 61–2
Sazonov, N. F. 19–20, 25, 30, 32, 53, 85, 203, 366 n.23
Scales, Prunella 309

Schaubühne an Lehniner Platz, Berlin 259–63
Schechner, Richard 341–2
Schildkraut, Joseph 187
Schiller, Friedrich 116
Schillertheater, Berlin 105
Schlumberger, Jean 163
Schmidt, Paul 288, 339–40
Schmidt, Willi 252
Schopenhauer, Arthur 15
Schubiger, Christophe 343
Schultz, Michael 295
Scnitzer, Werner 246
Scofield, Paul 323
Scott, George C. 296
Scribe, Eugène 132
Second Moscow Art Theatre 123
Sée, Edmond 150, 171
Selivanova, L. V. 86
Selyutina, L. 226
Sendak, Maurice 260
Senelick, Laurence 293
Serban, Andrei 248, 297–9, 324, 328, 331, 342, 344–5
Serban, Milenko 249
Sermonne, Bruno 282
Seyler, Athene 146, 306
Shakespeare, William 1, 25, 75, 82, 108, 112, 116, 134, 146–7, 150, 176, 195–6, 238, 275, 277, 291, 312, 324, 348, 357
Shakh-Azizova, Tatyana 207.
Shakurov, Sergey 358
Shapir, Olga A. 111
Shapiro, Adolf 208, 220, 351
Shared Experience Company 316–18
Sharko, Zinaida 205
Sharoff, Peter 152–3, 237, 264
Shaw, George Bernard 108, 132, 134–5, 155, 170, 173, 195, 238, 253, 275, 381 n.7
Shaw, Irwin 177, 284
Shawn, Wallace 304
Shchepkin, Mikhail 20
Shchepkina-Kupernik, Tatyana 48, 50
Shchukin, Boris 117
Shchukin School, Moscow 352
Sher, Anthony 322–3
Sherman, Stuart 404 n.50
Shestakov, V. A. 127
Shestov, Lev 107
Shiki Theatre Co., Tokyo 331
Shiraishi, Kayoko 333
Shirvindt, Aleksandr 214
Sholem Aleichem 295
Shostakovich, Dmitry 126
Shtein, M. 208
Shust, William 404 n.50